The Late Byzantine Army

حضرت اسكندر داراى موش الله حنلاه الماروكى يقول ددى

The Late Byzantine Army

Arms and Society, 1204–1453

Mark C. Bartusis

PENN

University of Pennsylvania Press

Philadelphia

THE MIDDLE AGES SERIES
Ruth Mazo Karras, General Editor
Edward Peters, Founding Editor

A complete list of books in the series is available from the publisher.

Publication of this book was supported by a grant from Northern State University

Copyright © 1992 University of Pennsylvania Press
All rights reserved
Printed in the United States of America on acid-free paper
First paperback printing 1997

10 9 8 7 6 5 4 3 2 1

Published by
University of Pennsylvania Press
Philadelphia, Pennsylvania 19104-6097

Library of Congress Cataloging-in-Publication Data

Bartusis, Mark C.
    The late Byzantine army : arms and society, 1204–1453 / Mark C. Bartusis.
        p.   cm. — (Middle Ages series)
    Includes bibliographical references and index.
    ISBN 0-8122-1620-2 (alk. paper)
    1. Byzantine Empire—Army.   I. Title.   II. Series.
U43.B9B37   1992
355′.009495—dc 20   92-14823
                                                     CIP

Frontispiece. Battle between Alexander the Great and the Persian shah Darius. In large measure the attire and weapons of the ancient combatants reflect late Byzantine fashion. Miniature painting from the *Alexander Romance*, early or mid-fourteenth century. Library of S. Giorgio di Greci, Venice, fol. 61v (photo: Istituto Ellenico di Studi Bizantini e Postbizantini di Venezia).

To my parents

Contents

viii   Contents

List of Illustrations and Tables

Acknowledgments

The research and writing of this book were conducted over a ten-year period, during which time I was the recipient of material support from several institutions and organizations, and of advice and assistance from numerous individuals, to whom I wish to express my gratitude. A Gennadeion Fellowship in Post-Classical Studies at the American School of Classical Studies at Athens, an International Research and Exchanges Board Fellowship to the Philosophy Faculty of the University of Belgrade, and Dumbarton Oaks Junior and Summer Fellowships afforded me the opportunity to utilize research facilities, which otherwise would have been impossible. The hospitality of the American Research Institute in Turkey and release time from Northern State University were appreciated. In addition, the librarians of Dumbarton Oaks, the Gennadeion Library in Athens and Northern State University were most helpful in facilitating my work.

A number of individuals have read parts of the book while it was in draft and/or provided valuable advice during the course of my work: Professors Alexander Kazhdan, Božidar Ferjančić, Stephen Reinert, and Khalifa Bennasser. To these I offer my thanks. Dr. Mirjana Živojinović of the Byzantine Institute of the Serbian Academy of Sciences and Arts deserves special mention for introducing me to the Slavic sources and for providing counsel generously and enthusiastically during my stay in Belgrade.

A Note on Transliteration, Pronunciation, and Dates

Byzantine Greek is a nightmare to transliterate. In the interest of standardization, I have transliterated almost all Greek (as well as Slavic and Turkish) technical terms and names of people and places according to the form in which they appear in the *Oxford Dictionary of Byzantium* (1991), the editors of which have adopted a system for Greek that uses a modified letter-for-letter approach ("a" for alpha, "b" for beta) but employs common English forms wherever they are well established ("Constantine" rather than "Konstantinos"). Nevertheless, there are a few cases in which I depart from their schema. For example, I use *kavallarios* (as it was pronounced) instead of the *ODB*'s *kaballarios*.

Even though Byzantine Greek sounded much like modern Greek, scholars sometimes pronounce it as if it were ancient Greek or some mixture of ancient and modern. The *ODB* system of transliteration, while it has the virtue of simplicity and is rather faithful to the spelling of Greek, is quite misleading in regard to pronunciation. Consequently, and with no claim to be doing justice to the complexities of the medieval Greek language, I provide a few general rules here to help the reader approximate the late Byzantine pronunciations of the strange names and terms that appear in this book.

i, *oi*, and the final *e* are all pronounced as *ee* in *tree*
-es at the end of words (Metochites, Maroules) is pronounced as *eece* in
    Greece, except in plural forms (tzangratores, posotetes), where it is
    pronounced as *ess* in *less*
au and *eu* are respectively pronounced "af" and "ef"
b is pronounced "v" except in the names Berilas and Syrbanos, and in
    foreign words such as bey and Bayezid
ch is pronounced as in the Scottish *loch* or German *nach*
d is pronounced as *th* in *then*
g between two vowels is pronounced as the *y* in *mayor*

h at the beginning of a word is silent
rh is pronounced as *r*

Finally, in Slavic words, *c* is pronounced "ts," *č* and *ć* are pronounced "ch," *dj* is pronounced as the *j* in *judge*, *j* is pronounced as the *y* in *yellow*, *š* is pronounced "sh," and *ž* is pronounced "zh" as in *measure* and *vision*.

Dates

The Byzantine year began on September 1. A few dates are cited in the form "1267/8," which signifies the period from September 1, 1267, to August 31, 1268.

Abbreviations

Akropolites	*Georgii Acropolitae Opera*, ed. A. Heisenberg, vol. 1. Leipzig, 1903.
Angold, *Byzantine Government*	M. Angold. *A Byzantine Government in Exile: Government and Society Under the Laskarids of Nicaea (1204–1261)*. London, 1975.
Byz	*Byzantion: revue internationale des études byzantines.* Brussels, 1924ff.
BZ	*Byzantinische Zeitschrift.* Leipzig, Munich, 1892ff.
CFHB	Corpus Fontium Historiae Byzantinae.
CSHB	Corpus Scriptorum Historiae Byzantinae, 50 vols. Bonn, 1828–97.
DOP	*Dumbarton Oaks Papers.* Washington, D.C., 1941ff.
Doukas	*Ducas. Istoria Turco-Bizantina (1341–1462)*, ed. V. Grecu. Bucharest, 1958.
Geanakoplos, *Emperor Michael*	D. Geanakoplos. *The Emperor Michael Palaeologus and the West, 1258–1282: A Study in Byzantino-Latin Relations.* Cambridge, Mass., 1959.
Gregoras	*Nicephori Gregorae Byzantina Historia*, ed. L. Schopen, 3 vols., CSHB. Bonn, 1829, 1830, 1855.
JÖB(G)	*Jahrbuch der Österreichischen Byzantinistik (byzantinischen Gesellschaft).* Vienna, 1961ff.
Kantakouzenos	*Ioannis Cantacuzeni eximperatoris historiarum libri IV*, 3 vols.: vol. 1, ed. L. Schopen; vols. 2–3, ed. B. Niehbuhr, CSHB. Bonn, 1828, 1831, 1832.
Laiou, *Constantinople*	A. Laiou. *Constantinople and the Latins: The Foreign Policy of Andronicus II, 1282–1328.* Cambridge, Mass., 1972.
Migne, *PG*	J.-P. Migne. *Patrologiae cursus completus. Series graeca*, 161 vols. Paris, 1857–66.
MM	F. Miklosich and J. Müller. *Acta et diplomata Graeca medii aevi sacra et profana*, 6 vols. Vienna, 1860–90.

Mutafčiev,   P. Mutafčiev. "Vojniški zemi i vojnici v Vizantija prez
"Vojniški zemi"   XIII—XIV v.," *Spisanie na Bŭlgarskata Akademija na
                   naukite*, Kniga 27, Klon istoriko-filologičen i
                   filosofsko obščestven 15 (Sofia, 1923), 1—113; repr. in P.
                   Mutafčiev, *Izbrani proizvedenija*, I (Sofia, 1973), 518—
                   652.

Nicol, *Epiros II*   D.M. Nicol. *The Despotate of Epiros, 1267—1479: A
                      Contribution to the History of Greece in the Middle Ages.*
                      Cambridge, Eng., 1984.

Nicol, *Last*   D.M. Nicol. *The Last Centuries of Byzantium, 1261—
Centuries*   1453*. London, 1972.

ODB   *The Oxford Dictionary of Byzantium*, ed. A.P.
                   Kazhdan et al., 3 vols. New York, 1971.

Oikonomidès,   N. Oikonomidès. "A propos des armées des premiers
"A propos des   Paléologues et des compagnies de soldats," *TM* 8
armées"   (1981), 353—71.

Ostrogorsky,   G. Ostrogorskij. *Pour l'histoire de la féodalité
Féodalité*   byzantine*. Brussels, 1954.

Ostrogorsky,   G. Ostrogorsky. *History of the Byzantine State*, rev.
History*   ed., trans. J. Hussey. New Brunswick, N.J., 1969.

Pachymeres,   *Georges Pachymérès. Relations historiques*, ed. A. Failler,
ed. Failler   French trans. V. Laurent, vol. 1, 2 pts. Paris, 1984.

Pachymeres,   *Georgii Pachymeris de Michaele et Andronico
Bonn ed.   Palaeologis*, ed. I. Bekker, 2 vols., CSHB. Bonn, 1835.

PLP   E. Trapp, R. Walther, H.-V. Beyer. *Prosopographisches
                   Lexikon der Palaiologenzeit*. Vienna, 1976ff.

Pseudo-Kodinos   *Pseudo-Kodinos. Traité des offices*, ed. J. Verpeaux.
                   Paris, 1966.

REB   *Revue des Études Byzantines*. Paris, 1949ff.

Regesten   F. Dölger. *Regesten der Kaiserurkunden des
                   oströmischen Reiches*, 5 pts. Munich, 1924—65. Part 3:
                   Regesten von 1204—1282, rev. ed. by Peter Wirth.
                   Munich, 1977.

SAN(U)   Srpska Akademija Nauka (i Umetnosti).

TM   *Travaux et Mémoires du Centre de Recherche d'Histoire
                   et Civilisation de Byzance*. Paris, 1965ff.

VizVrem   *Vizantijskij Vremennik*. St. Petersburg, 1894—1927.
                   New series, Moscow—Leningrad, 1947ff.

Zakythinos,   D. Zakythinos. *Le despotat grec de Morée*, 2 vols. Paris,

Despotat	1932; Athens, 1953. Rev. ed. by Chryssa Maltezou. London: Variorum Reprints, 1975.
ZRVI	*Zbornik radova Vizantološkog instituta.* Belgrade, 1952ff.

Introduction: The Setting, the Questions, and the Sources

In the year 330, acknowledging that the Roman Empire's center of gravity had long since shifted eastward, that the frontiers of the western half of the Empire were shaky and its economy even shakier, the emperor Constantine founded a new capital on the site of the ancient Greek town of Byzantion, a city that would be named after him, the City of Constantine, or Constantinople. For over a thousand years it would be a Christian city, the capital of the Byzantine Empire, the Christian Roman Empire. That a Roman emperor established a Christian capital in the Greek-speaking part of the Empire meant that the civilization of Byzantium would be heir to the three great cultural traditions of the ancient world: Christian religion and morality, Greek language and culture, and Roman law and administration. The synthesis of these traditions led to a dynamism and creativity that goes far to explain both the survival of the Roman imperial idea and the flowering of a new civilization. At the crossroads of East and West, Byzantium became the bulwark of Christendom against the Arabs, the Christianizer of the Slavs, the preserver of ancient Greek culture, and up through the eleventh century the only European state worthy of the name.

The expression "Byzantine Empire" is a modern creation. The Byzantines called their polity the "Empire of the Romans" and themselves "Romans," in Greek *Rhomaioi*. Roman influence was so great that there are scholars today who eschew the word "Byzantine" entirely and speak merely of the "East Roman Empire." Indeed the centuries immediately following

The most accessible and readable introduction to all aspects of the Byzantine army from the seventh to early eleventh century is found in A. Toynbee, *Constantine Porphyrogenitus and His World* (London, 1973). Also, see W. Kaegi, *Byzantine Military Unrest 471–843: An Interpretation* (Amsterdam, 1981); the chapter on the army in S. Runciman, *Byzantine Civilization* (New York, 1956); J. Haldon, *Recruitment and Conscription in the Byzantine Army c. 550–950. A Study of the Origins of the Stratiotika Ktemata* (Vienna, 1979), which is written for the specialist; and H. Kuhn, *Die byzantinische Armee im 10. und 11. Jahrhundert* (Vienna, 1991). The army during the era of the Komnenoi is discussed in detail by A. Hohlweg, *Beiträge zur Verwaltungsgeschichte des oströmischen Reiches unter den Komnenen* (Munich, 1965), and in passing by M. Angold, *The Byzantine Empire 1025–1204: A Political History* (London, 1984).

Constantine's reign justifiably are called both "late Roman" and "early Byzantine," for it took several centuries, as the Christian Empire centered at Constantinople adapted to and overcame a series of internal and external crises, to acquire a character distinct from that of its ancient Roman predecessor.

The great Roman Empire of Augustus and his successors was an unwieldy political unit, difficult to administer and even harder to defend. As early as the end of the third century the emperor Diocletian (284–305) saw the utility of establishing regional administrative centers under Augusti and Caesars, each with a share of the imperial power. By the end of the fourth century the partition of the Empire into western and eastern halves had become permanent, and the loss of the western half to the Goths, Vandals, and other Germanic invaders in the course of the fifth century left the eastern half alone and weakened, but nevertheless intact. Although later emperors, for centuries, would feel it their duty to restore the lost western provinces to Roman authority, the dazzling but costly successes of Justinian I (527–65) in recovering a large fraction of the West would not be repeated. Renewed pressure from the great Persian Empire, along with the appearance of new enemies threatening the eastern provinces, the Slavs, the Avars, and in the seventh century the Arabs, focused attention toward saving the East, and plans for restoration, though never entirely abandoned, were put on the back burner.

In order to respond to these threats the army underwent first a retrenchment and later a major reorganization during the seventh and eighth centuries which fundamentally altered its composition. By the fourth century the legions and auxiliaries of the early Roman Empire had been supplanted by frontier troops (*limitanei*) who were given property in return for hereditary military service. Through the reforms of Diocletian and Constantine the mobile cavalry called *comitatenses*, originally a bodyguard, eventually became the heart of the army. The later Roman Empire was characterized by the increasing use of foreign troops, especially Germans. In the fourth century Goths were employed as allied troops called *foederati* who served under their own officers. They were autonomous, their pay was exempt from taxation, and overall they grew in political influence. Later Germans were recruited individually as mercenaries, and these long remained the most important part of the army.

The reorganization of the army that began in the seventh century divided the Empire into a number of large military districts called "themes," first in Asia Minor and later throughout the Empire, each commanded by a governor (*strategos*, literally "general") who combined civil and military functions. The system of themes furnished a native army that drew its livelihood from the land where it was stationed. These military reforms have often been attributed to the emperor Herakleios (610–41), though according to many scholars elements of these reforms existed before his reign, and indeed their ultimate fruition did not occur until the tenth century.

Whereas a great deal is known about the tactics, equipment, and field organization of the army through the tenth century, the issue of how soldiers were recruited remains hotly contested. Although we know that during a mobilization the army administration called up the men it wanted from a list of soldiers who bore a military obligation, it is still unclear who exactly bore such an obligation. One school contends that the majority of soldiers in the eighth through tenth centuries held relatively small landholdings located in the themes of the armies in which they served in time of war. According to this view, these soldiers were both farmers and soldiers, and though their legal and fiscal status, reflecting their obligation of military service, was slightly different from the rest of the population, in standard of living and ordinary pursuits they were indistinguishable from simple peasants. This view, evoking the romantic notion of a peasant army as the backbone of the Byzantine army, has proved very seductive because of its simplicity, if not its logic. Critics have argued, for example, that an effectively functioning army of part-time farmers, part-time soldiers is inconceivable and could scarcely have been responsible for the army's dazzling successes against the Arabs in the tenth century. Nevertheless, this view has been difficult to disprove.

Another school of thought maintains that the situation was much more complicated than this, that those who performed the military service and those who worked the land that provided the soldiers' livelihood were two distinct groups of men. Since there are no records of outlining the mechanisms whereby the soldiers were maintained by the peasant farmers, the arrangements between the two groups of men would have to have been either customary or private. Given that the available source material has been subjected to some of the most intensive examination of any Byzantine sources, it is becoming increasingly doubtful, barring the discovery of new material, that these questions will ever be resolved to the satisfaction of most researchers.

In any event this new system successfully held back the Arabs, dealt with a new threat from the Bulgars, and eventually restored the Balkans to Byzantine control. The southern Mediterranean and Palestine, however, were lost. Internally, the crises of the seventh and eighth centuries transformed the rural economy of the Empire. The large estates of the late Roman period cultivated by the dependent peasants known as *coloni* broke up, and this led to the emergence of an agrarian system characterized by the village community composed of free, tax-paying peasants. The restoration of central authority to Greece in the ninth century and the strengthening of central government in the tenth century were accompanied by a full attack on the village community by large landowners. By the eleventh century it seemed a foregone conclusion that the bulk of the peasantry could no longer be considered free taxpayers but *paroikoi*, peasants in one way or another dependent on a large landowner, lay or religious, or on the state itself as the largest landowner of all.

By the end of the ninth century, the army was divided into the provincial thematic troops headed by the strategoi and the Tagmata commanded by *domestikoi*. The Tagmata were created by Constantine V (741–75) as a reorganized central army stationed around Constantinople to serve as garrison, rapid response, and bodyguard troops. In the tenth century various measures were taken to ensure the economic basis of the thematic armies whose existence, no less than that of the peasant community, was threatened by the acquisition of property by large landowners. Around 967 an emperor ordered that the minimum value of a military holding be tripled, a measure probably connected with the innovation of heavy cavalry. By the end of the century the state increasingly found itself unable to prevent military holdings, technically inalienable, from passing into the hands of monasteries and other large landowners. Nevertheless, the tenth century was an age of expansion. The victories of the army under Nikephoros II Phokas (963–69) and John I Tzimiskes (969–76) can be attributed to the support given to these campaigns by the land-hungry aristocracy. Basil II (976–1025) secured the conquests of his predecessors in Syria, and during his reign the Russians were converted, the Bulgars were defeated, and the Empire was at its largest expanse since the reign of Justinian.

The eleventh century was characterized by a decline of the army. The imperial government, under the control of the civil aristocracy of the capital, emasculated the military out of fear of the provincial magnates who dominated the officer corps. Further, the government assumed that cuts in the military budget were one of the dividends earned through the triumphs of the previous era. But the appearance of new enemies, the Normans in Sicily threatening the western frontiers, the Seljuk Turks replacing the

Arabs to the east, and the Pechenegs invading from the north, proved them wrong.

The central government distrusted the provinces, and its desire to curb the power of provincial magnates was assisted by a gradual process whereby the holders of the old military estates no longer were required to maintain local troops or serve themselves but instead paid a direct tax to the fisc. With the decline of the armies of the themes, the new tax receipts were used to hire foreign mercenaries. But the inadequacy of foreign mercenaries was demonstrated in 1071 at Mantzikert near Lake Van in eastern Anatolia when an undisciplined and heterogeneous army, though numerically superior, was annihilated by the Seljuk Turks. In the same year at the other end of the Empire the Byzantines lost the last of their Italian possessions to the Normans.

The central government's hostility toward the military led to a series of military revolts culminating in the coup of Alexios I Komnenos (1081–1118). Although Alexios attempted to renovate provincial military organization, the old thematic organization was dead. During his reign and probably during the first half of that of his son and successor, John II, the process was brought to completion whereby the obligations burdening the old military estates were transformed into simple taxes. Alexios responded in a make-shift fashion to new threats from the Normans to the west and from the Pechenegs to the north. He hired foreign mercenaries of every ethnic stripe but instituted no real reform of the army. His army was made up of an imperial guard and elite troops, who were often foreigners; smallholding foreign peoples settled within the Empire and with an obligation to per-form military service; permanent and temporary mercenaries, usually for-eigners; troops of allied or client states; and finally some ethnically Byzan-tine troops organized into troop divisions bearing the name of their place of origin (Thracians, Thessalians). The numerous appeals he made to the West for military aid were a small element in the origin of the First Crusade (1096–99). The extreme reliance on foreign troops before and after the First Crusade had the effect of introducing both Turkish and Western European military practices, equipment, and tactics into the army.

It was John II Komnenos (1118–43) who probably was responsible for emphasizing once again the link between military recruitment, military financing, and land. Defeated Pechenegs and Serbs were settled in Asia Minor as soldiers. He and his son Manuel I (1143–80) may have tried to rebuild a national army, on a certain scale at least, by supplementing the army of mercenaries and settled foreign prisoners with new troops attached to the land through the new institution of the military pronoia. A *pronoia* (literally, "providence" or "solicitude") was a kind of grant of a source of revenue by the emperor to an individual or group of individuals. Some scholars claim that the popularity of the army as an occupation increased through Manuel I Komnenos' widespread utilization of pronoia.[1] Others question this view. In many parts of the Empire, such as the area around Smyrna in Asia Minor, in Epiros and even perhaps in the Morea, the real expansion of pronoia as a military institution seems to have started only after 1204, when it also became an important social and economic institution.

The military reforms of Manuel Komnenos were adequate for neither his ambitions nor his needs. An ill-fated expedition to Italy drained the Empire financially, and the thorough defeat of his army at the hands of the Seljuks at Myriokephalon in 1176 underscored the fundamental weakness of his policies. The last decades of the twelfth century constituted an era of court intrigue in the capital and disaffection if not open rebellion in the provinces. The Bulgarian brothers Peter and Asen launched a revolt against Byzantine rule, an independent Bulgaria was organized under Kalojan, and an independent Serbia emerged under Stefan Nemanja. On the military front, the late twelfth-century Jewish traveler Benjamin of Tudela commented on the Byzantine use of mercenaries: "They hire from amongst all nations warriors called Loazim [barbarians] to fight with the Sultan Masud, King of the Togarmim [Seljuks], who are called Turks; for their natures are not warlike, but are as women who have no strength to fight."[2]

The Fourth Crusade (1199–1204), culminating in the sack of Constantinople and the conquest of most of the territory of the Empire, is a textbook example of a noble plan gone awry. Initiated by Pope Innocent III, the original intention of the crusade was to attack the Turkish Ayyubid dynasty in Egypt, but along the way financial and other considerations diverted the French and Venetian crusaders to Constantinople, where they restored the deposed emperor Isaac II Angelos (1185–95, 1203–04) to power.

According to an earlier agreement, Isaac was to provide the crusaders with military and financial aid to continue the crusade, but since fiscal problems within the Empire made this impossible, the crusaders had no

1. Ostrogorsky, *Féodalité*, 28–31, 48–53.
2. *The Itinerary of Benjamin of Tudela*, ed. and trans. M. Adler (London, 1907), 13.

choice but to camp outside the city and wait. As time passed anti-Latin sentiment within the city grew and resulted in a palace coup which overthrew Isaac and his son Alexios. The crusaders then seized the city and the Empire itself, dividing Thrace, Macedonia, Thessaly, the Morea, Attica, and Thebes among themselves. In the sense that the Fourth Crusade and the subsequent Latin Conquest intensified the anarchy that already existed within the provinces, it was merely the grace blow to an Empire which because of the enormous financial and political problems of the later twelfth century had become increasingly fragmented to the point of disintegration.

The history of late Byzantium, from 1204 to 1453, is in many ways a rather gloomy story. The Fourth Crusade had killed the spirit of the medieval Roman Empire. In time the Byzantine successor states in Asia Minor and in the mountains of western Greece, around which resistance to the Latin occupation centered, did manage to recover a large measure of Byzantine territory, and eventually Michael VIII Palaiologos (1259–82) was able to recover Constantinople. But the restored Empire of the Palaiologan dynasty was a second-rate state surrounded by hostile neighbors as strong or stronger than it was. A modest recovery during the thirteenth century was overshadowed by the rise of medieval Serbia to a position of prominence within the Balkans and, to an even greater extent, by the rise of the Ottoman Turks, both developments leading to a steady diminution of the Empire's size. It would be no great exaggeration to say that by the middle of the fourteenth century, most informed Byzantines knew their world was coming to an end, that recovery was impossible. By the fifteenth century the end was expected at any moment.

Internally the last centuries were as paradoxical as any age can be. Despite the gravity of external threats, unity eluded the Byzantines. The government was racked by civil wars, palace coups, and religious controversies. The smaller the stakes, the more earnest were the quarrels. With government control over the provinces continuing its progressive decentralization and fragmentation, this was the age of the great landowner. As early as the twelfth century the great estate had replaced the village as the basis of rural social organization. This process, interposing a new layer of authority between the state and the subject, has been termed the "feudalization" of Byzantium. By the fourteenth century the village community had disappeared as a barrier separating the peasant family from the state and the large landowner, and almost all peasants paid their taxes to a landlord rather than to the state. Nevertheless, while the society was in its death throes, desperately trying to adapt to change without sacrificing its traditions, this was also the golden age of Byzantine monasticism, and the art and literature of the period were among the finest the Byzantine world produced.

It has been said that the history of Rome is the history of its army. If true for Rome, then in no small measure it must also be true for its heir Byzantium. The successes and failures of the Byzantine army determined the size, longevity, and even the tone of life within the Empire. And as an institution it reflected the problems and possibilities inherent within Byzantine society. This book examines these twin aspects of the army during Byzantium's final centuries. On the one hand, it deals with the army's organization and administration, the kinds of soldiers who were in it, how many there were, and how they were paid. On the other hand, it considers the effects of imperial policies on soldiers, the relationship between military, provincial, and imperial administration, the institutions, events, and policies that affected soldiers, and the impact of the army on the economy, finances, and agrarian relations of the Empire.

To explore these issues, two approaches are employed. Part One focuses on the army's development over time as an instrument of imperial policy. It offers a chronological treatment stressing change and adaptation, and describes the modification and restructuring of the army over the years as it accommodated varying political goals, opportunities, and circumstances. Yet, while change was certainly a characteristic of the late Byzantine army, too great an emphasis on its dynamic aspects can misrepresent its nature and the nature of late Byzantine society. There were indeed many aspects of military organization—the means of paying soldiers, of launching campaigns, of guarding territory—that were subject to much less change over time. Part Two, therefore, is a topical treatment of the army and of the social and economic foundations of soldiers, emphasizing the element of continuity within the military. Because the sources reveal so little about the mundane processes that underpinned the army's structure, this approach, in contrast to that of Part One, adopts the small fiction, common in institutional histories, that the army can be studied as a static institution and that information gathered from almost any sub-period within the late Byzantine era can be collated to produce generalizations more or less universally applicable. Although neither of these approaches is satisfactory in itself, together they provide some sense of the general character and complexity of the army and society of late Byzantium.

The expression "late Byzantium" implies chronological, geographical, and political bounds. Following the convention in Byzantine studies, the termini for starting and ending the investigation are the traditional dates 1204 and 1453, the year of the fall of Constantinople to the Latins of the Fourth Crusade and the year of the fall of the city to the Ottoman Turks. In terms of dramatic institutional or social changes the earlier date is the less defensible. Certainly the loss of Constantinople, the dispersion of the imperial court, and the formation of Byzantine rump states in western Asia Minor, in Epiros, and in Trebizond on the Pontus were traumatic developments, but the events of 1204 caused less disruption in the institutions of Byzantine life than one might think. Socially, culturally, and economically, the numerically inferior Latins left little imprint on most of the areas they conquered. It was for the most part a colonial occupation. Trade in the Aegean remained in the hands of Venice and other Italian cities, but the political position of the Latins was always tenuous. While fiefs were parceled out and the conquerors tried to blanket Byzantium with their feudal legal and social institutions, the native peasant remained a paroikos, the Greek landlord came to terms with his new foreign overlord and kept his property, and the population remained Orthodox. Nevertheless, the events of 1204 profoundly altered the orientation of political history, and to the extent that the army was an instrument of politics, this is a good date to begin.

On occasion it is useful to refer to the periods before 1204 and after 1453, particularly in order to trace the development of an institution that arose before 1204 or continued after 1453, or when, for purposes of illustration, material is available from an earlier or later age. Moreover, due to the nature of the sources, there is no way to avoid placing the greatest emphasis on the century from around 1260 to around 1350, the age of the early Palaiologoi, from the restoration of the Empire under Michael VIII Palaiologos (1259–82) through the last phases of the civil wars involving John VI Kantakouzenos (1347–54).

Geographically, the scope of inquiry is limited to the areas of western Asia Minor, Thrace, Macedonia, central Greece, including Thessaly and Epiros, the Morea, and the Aegean, in other words, to the areas where Byzantine soldiers fought. The Empire of Trebizond, the separatist state on the Pontus, though arguably Byzantine, as well as Crete and Cyprus, both in Latin hands, are generally excluded from discussion due to their relative isolation and independent development throughout the period. Further, within this time period and geographical area, I am concerned only with the soldiers and armies of Byzantium. Since I have chosen to focus my attention on internal history, the tiny navy, intimately connected as it was to the policies of the Italian city-states, will only be mentioned in passing. Moreover, "Byzantium" is defined rather broadly to include not only the restored Empire centered in Constantinople from 1261 but also the Byzantine states of the Nicaean era—the Empire of Nicaea and the so-called Despotate of Epiros—as well as the Despotate of the Morea which came to prominence during the fourteenth century. In addition, evidence relating to the soldiers who fought for the smaller, semi-autonomous Greek-speaking political units that existed within the defined geographical area is also useful. These smaller principalities, products of the Latin Conquest, of the Serbian invasion of the mid-fourteenth century and of general political fragmentation, were firmly within the sphere of traditional Byzantine institutional and administrative practices.

Finally, since this is intended to be a social and administrative history, and not a military history, matters relating to tactics, strategy, and the course of individual campaigns have been virtually ignored except when they can provide information about the type, quality, or size of troop contingents. Although a major investigation of late Byzantine military tactics is possible and doubtless would prove fruitful, it is a subject that must remain outside the scope of this book.

Nearly all the sources for late Byzantine history provide information about soldiers. These include Greek narrative histories, documents, letters, saints' *lives*, inscriptions, lead seals, and treatises on politics and even theology. In addition, there are a variety of Serbian, Bulgarian, Western European, and Turkish chronicles, documents, and legal sources. The information contained in these sources can be divided into two categories: general data about the structure and deeds of the army as an institution and about the policies and developments affecting the soldiers as a social class (the Macrocosm), and specific data about the deeds and characteristics of smaller groups of soldiers and individual soldiers (the Microcosm).

The most valuable sources for the study of the army up through the eleventh century are the military manuals, or *taktika*. There is evidence that these were written during the late period (the poet Manuel Philes once notes that the general Michael Doukas Glabas Tarchaneiotes wrote a book "on various military topics"), but unfortunately none are extant. A single idiosyncratic exception is a treatise written in 1326 on the art of governing and military affairs by the marquis of Montferrat Theodore Palaiologos (1291–1338) entitled *Instructions and Prescriptions for a Lord Who Has Wars to Wage and Governing to Do*. Theodore was Emperor Andronikos II's second son by Yolande-Irene of Montferrat. When Irene's brother died in 1305, she inherited the marquisate of Montferrat, located to the west and southwest of Turin. Not wishing to return to Montferrat herself, she arranged that it be conferred upon Theodore, who in 1306, at the age of fifteen, headed west to govern his domain. The original work, written in Greek during one of his two return visits to Byzantium (totaling less than five years), is lost, as is a Latin translation of the work Theodore himself made. We know the treatise only through a fourteenth-century French translation based on Theodore's Latin translation. Since he lived almost all of his adult life in the West, where he acquired all of his firsthand military experience, his *Instructions* are much more a product of the Western European than the Byzantine cultural sphere. And while we might regard Theodore as a man at home in both East and West, and whose writing should display a cosmopolitan familiarity with the entire southern Mediterranean scene, I have thought it unwise to use the *Instructions* as evidence of Byzantine military practices, except where Theodore makes specific reference to eastern affairs and to armor and weapons.[3]

Without contemporary military manuals, a large part of our knowledge of the army must be deduced from the narrative histories. While these are primarily concerned with military affairs in terms of battles, sieges, and troop movements, events which in themselves are of little interest to this study, the information I have sought in them is more the occasional indication of the composition of an army, the parenthetical note on practical military administration, the digression on military policy, or the rare comment on the difference between traditional and contemporary military practices. For the study of the army, the most important of these are the memoirs of John VI Kantakouzenos (ca.1295–1383) who, as a general and an emperor, probably had the best knowledge of military affairs of any late Byzantine writer. His work, which covers the period from 1320 to 1356, is a detailed account of the era of the civil wars, and while he tends to present his own actions during this turbulent period in the best possible light, his comments on the organization and administration of the army and on fiscal policies have made it possible to write the present study.

After Kantakouzenos, the historian I have used the most is George

3. Manuel Philes in E. Martini, ed., "A proposito d'una poesia inedita di Manuel File," *Reale Istituto Lombardo di Scienze e Lettere, Rendiconti*, serie II, 29 (Milan, 1896), 470, and cf. *Manuelis Philae Carmina Inedita*, ed. E. Martini (Naples, 1900), no. 96. Theodore Palaiologos, *Les Enseignements de Théodore Paléologue*, ed. C. Knowles (London, 1983). Regrettably, by failing to provide a modern translation the editor has ensured that only specialists will ever look at this very interesting work.

Pachymeres (1242–ca.1310), a scholar and close friend of Andronikos II, whose history spans the period from 1255 to 1308. Pachymeres is our chief source for the reign of Michael VIII and the early part of Andronikos II's reign. Since his theme is the fortunes of the Empire as a whole, and since he is quite critical of the policies of Michael VIII, he provides much valuable information regarding the institutions and evolution of the military. Supplementing the works of Pachymeres and Kantakouzenos is the history of the polymath Nikephoros Gregoras (1290/1–1360), which deals with the years from 1204 to 1359 but is most useful for the fourteenth century. While Gregoras, like Pachymeres, had no firsthand experience of military matters, and while his history prefers to focus on the Empire's religious quarrels in which he was a leading participant, his antipathy toward Kantakouzenos provides a valuable counter to the biases of the latter.[4]

On a second tier is the history of George Akropolites (1217–82), covering the period from the fall of Constantinople during the Fourth Crusade to its reconquest by Michael VIII (1203–61). Although Akropolites is a reliable historian who had experience as a diplomat, an associate of Theodore II Laskaris, and a military commander, albeit an unsuccessful one, his history lacks the details and digressions that make the works of Kantakouzenos and Pachymeres so important. For the army of the thirteenth century mention must also be made of the Greek version of the *Chronicle of the Morea*, a long narrative in verse concerned primarily with the crusader states of Greece in the period from 1204 to 1292. A product of the fourteenth century, it also exists in French, Italian, and Aragonese versions. The Greek version was written by a Hellenized Frank in the second half of the fourteenth century and was based on either a Greek or a French prototype from the early fourteenth century. While the work is often inaccurate and certainly tends to exaggerate troop strengths, it is nevertheless quite valuable for military terminology and for the course of Byzantine campaigns in the Morea and elsewhere in Greece.[5]

After the middle of the fourteenth century the usefulness of the narrative historians declines markedly. No Byzantine who lived through the

4. For a description and discussion of the works of Kantakouzenos, Pachymeres, and Gregoras as literature and as history, see H. Hunger, *Die hochsprachliche profane Literatur der Byzantiner* (Munich, 1978), I, 447, 476, with bibliography, and also, Laiou, *Constantinople*, 345–50.

5. M. Jeffreys, "The Chronicle of the Morea: Priority of the Greek Version," *BZ* 68 (1975), 304–50. D. Jacoby, "Quelques considérations sur les versions de la 'Chronique de Morée,'" in Jacoby, *Société et démographie à Byzance et en Romanie latine* (London, 1975), no. VII, 133–89; and "Les états latins en Romanie: phénomènes sociaux et économiques (1204–1350 environ)," in Jacoby, *Recherches sur la Méditerranée orientale du XIIe au XVe siècle* (London, 1979), no. I, 8.

second half of the fourteenth century wrote a contemporary history. Those historians who do deal with this period all wrote their histories after 1453, and though their histories provide occasionally valuable information on the army as an institution, they are generally not very useful. George Sphrantzes (1401–78), a high official and close associate of the last emperors, wrote a partially autobiographical account of the years from 1413 to 1477. While he displays a great familiarity with court life and diplomatic relations between Byzantium and the Ottomans, and even though he fought in the Morea by the side of the future emperor Constantine Palaiologos and was present at the fall of Constantinople, he says relatively little of military affairs. For the purposes of the present study the utility of the extended version of Sphrantzes' history, fabricated by Makarios Melissourgos in the sixteenth century, is restricted almost entirely to the (not always reliable) information it provides on the fall of Constantinople.

The other fifteenth-century historians focus on the rise of the Ottomans and speak of little but troop movements and conquests, ignoring or ignorant of Byzantine internal and institutional history. Doukas (ca.1400–70), a Greek from Asia Minor, wrote a history of the years from 1341 to 1462, with real detail beginning only with the accession of Sultan Bayezid in 1389. The history of the Ottomans written by the Athenian Laonikos Chalkokondyles (1423–90) spans the period from 1298 to 1464. Even though he spent years at the Byzantine court at Mistra in the Morea, his account of events there is of little use to this study. Kritoboulos of Imbros (b.ca.1405), an aristocratic Greek who wrote a history of the conquests of the Turkish sultan Mehmet II from 1451 to 1467, is an important source for the fall of Constantinople with details on Mehmet's conquest of the Morea.[6]

In addition to the accounts of the fall of Constantinople provided by Sphrantzes (the only eyewitness of this group), Doukas, Chalkokondyles, and Kritoboulos, there are a number of Western accounts of the events of 1453. The most important of these include the firsthand reports of the archbishop of Mytilene Leonard of Chios (d.1459), the Venetian Nicolò Barbaro, and the Florentine Giacomo Tedaldi.[7]

To round out this survey of Greek literary sources, mention may be

6. See the Bibliography for full citations and available translations of the works of these authors. For more on their lives and works, see the introduction to Philippides' translation of Sphrantzes; the introduction to Magoulias' translation of Doukas; A. Wifstrand, *Laonikos Chalkokondyles, der letzte Athener* (Lund, 1972); and the introduction to Reinsch's edition of Kritoboulos.

7. On these works, see the introduction to the translations of Leonard and Tedaldi in *The Siege of Constantinople 1453: Seven Contemporary Accounts*, trans. J. Melville Jones (Amsterdam, 1972), and of N. Barbaro in *Diary of the Siege of Constantinople, 1453*, trans. J. Jones (New York, 1969).

made of collections of correspondence, a rich source of information for the late Byzantine period, as well as of saints' *lives* which occasionally furnish useful details.

The one Byzantine source most nearly resembling certain aspects of a military treatise or *taktikon* is the treatise by the so-called Pseudo-Kodinos, an anonymous unofficial discourse on court ceremonies written around 1355 that offers priceless information about the palace guard divisions, the military officers who belonged to the court hierarchy, and military administration. There has been a tendency in the scholarship to accept Pseudo-Kodinos' testimony at face value, but in fact he is not always reliable. One example will suffice to demonstrate the caution with which we need to approach the treatise. At one point, he writes of an official called the megas hetaireiarches who, he says, was responsible for receiving visitors at the imperial court. Whatever function may have been attached to this title in the fourteenth century, we know from earlier sources that by origin the hetaireiarchai were connected to the division of palace guards called the Hetaireiai. Yet Pseudo-Kodinos explains that the megas hetaireiarches was so named "because he receives companions [*hetairoi*], that is, friends."[8] This kind of error has serious implications because it suggests that Pseudo-Kodinos was not adverse to reporting unsubstantiated or erroneous material or, worse, to fabricating information. This does not mean that we must dismiss Pseudo-Kodinos as a source, but we do need to seek corroborating evidence before accepting his testimony. This I have sought to do. When no corroborating evidence is forthcoming, I will note that the sole source is the Pseudo-Kodinos treatise, and this may be regarded as an appropriate caveat.

Information about individual soldiers and small groups of soldiers has been drawn for the most part from late Byzantine documents, most of which are found in monastic archives. Providing the most fertile ground for social and economic research, documents were issued by emperors, patriarchs, lay and religious officials, and private individuals.[9] They include imperial grants of privileges for monasteries, towns, and individuals, land sales, wills, inventories of the landholdings of monasteries and of a few

8. Pseudo-Kodinos, 178. On the work itself and the author, see the introduction to Verpeaux's edition, pp. 23–40. For another similar example, see M. Bartusis, "The Megala Allagia and the Tzaousios," *REB* 47 (1989), 189–90.

9. On the uses of documentary sources in Byzantine historical research, see, for example, G. Vernadsky, "Zametki o vizantijskih kupčih gramatah XIII veka," in *Sbornik v čest' na Vasil N. Zlatarski* (Sofia, 1925); Colloque international sur la paléographie grecque et byzantine, *La Paléographie grecque et byzantine* (Paris, 1977), articles beginning on p. 383, esp. those of N. Svoronos and J. Lefort; and P. Karlin-Hayter, "Preparing the Data from Mount Athos for Use with Modern Demographic Techniques," *Byz* 48 (1978), 501–18.

laymen, rulings involving disputes over land, land surveys, and various other types of acts. As the list indicates, most documents deal with land, so if it is possible to determine anything at all about the economic status of a particular soldier mentioned in the documents, it is because the soldier had some economic attachment to land, either as a landowner or as a landlord. Conversely, if the documents ever do mention soldiers who were mercenaries, we cannot identify them as such because, by definition, mercenaries per se have no economic attachment to land.

However, the documentary sources do provide nearly all the evidence about the poorer types of soldiers and the paramilitary guards. Further, through careful analysis of the exemption formulas found in imperial grants and other documents, which exempt monasteries, towns, or individuals from various fiscal burdens, it is often possible to trace the evolution of the taxes and obligations that were used for military purposes and to reconstruct the military practices they reflected. In this regard, contemporary Serbian documents complement the data of the Byzantine sources. Particular mention should be made of the Law Code (*Zakonik*) of Stefan Dušan (1331–55), king and, from 1345, emperor of Serbia, which was compiled in the late 1340s after his conquest of Byzantine territory in Thessaly, Epiros, and almost all of Macedonia. Since his Empire was strongly influenced by Byzantine institutions and since there are no late Byzantine legal compilations accurately reflecting current legal practices, the information Dušan's Law Code provides about the law and the soldier helps fill an important gap.

Among other non-Greek sources, the accounts of Western travelers and documentary materials issued by the Italian city-states, particularly Venice, occasionally provide useful, if superficial, information. Finally, with few exceptions, Turkish sources, which in any event are not very abundant, have little to contribute to the study of Byzantine internal history.

Only one major work has ever been written on the late Byzantine army. This is Petur Mutafčiev's richly documented study of the economic basis of late Byzantine soldiers, which successfully distinguishes the three basic types—pronoia soldiers, smallholding soldiers, and mercenaries—and provides an outline of military administration and policies that is still useful today.[10] The present study has been influenced greatly by Mutafčiev's work. Some of my most fundamental conclusions, though drawn from a fresh and thorough reexamination of the sources (many of which Mutafčiev had no

---

10. Mutafčiev, "Vojniški zemi." There is also F. Dölger's review (in German) of this work in *BZ* 26 (1926), 102–13, which, however, dwells extensively on points not germane to the history of late Byzantium.

access to), can do little more than amplify those he himself reached. Nevertheless, there are some serious problems with Mutafčiev's work. Conceptually, Mutafčiev saw a great deal of continuity between the military practices of the middle and late Byzantine periods. This led him to associate, incorrectly, the middle Byzantine "peasant soldier" who held "military lands" (*stratiotika ktemata*) with the late Byzantine soldier (*stratiotes*) who held a grant of pronoia. Such misinterpretations arose because of Mutafčiev's methodology, which relied excessively on middle Byzantine legal texts and terminology.

For example, when analyzing the alienation, bequeathal, and legal status of "military lands," Mutafčiev turned to Constantine Harmenopoulos' *Hexabiblos*, an unofficial fourteenth-century compilation of laws.[11] To elucidate Harmenopoulos, Mutafčiev referred to the laws of the emperors Constantine Porphyrogennetos (913–59) and Nikephoros Phokas (963–69), as well as other middle Byzantine legal texts, while overlooking the fact that Harmenopoulos' work, the only one of its kind from the late period, does not contain a single law issued after the tenth century. The *Hexabiblos* is an unofficial work of an antiquarian and is based entirely on the very middle Byzantine texts that Mutafčiev cited for corroborating evidence. Since the *Hexabiblos*' testimony cannot be confirmed by other late Byzantine sources, its value for the study of late Byzantine legal practices becomes very questionable and, consequently, it is necessary to challenge all of Mutafčiev's conclusions that are based on the *Hexabiblos* and middle Byzantine legal texts.

Aside from Mutafčiev, all other works either focus on particular aspects of the army or deal with the army and soldiers in passing. The foremost work of the former type is George Ostrogorsky's landmark study of the institution of pronoia which, because it has been translated into a Western European language, has had an impact on Western scholarship far beyond that of Mutafčiev's "Vojniški zemi."[12] This is significant because Ostrogorsky viewed pronoia as an essentially military institution and the key feature of a "feudalized" late Byzantine army, whereas Mutafčiev thought that the institution of pronoia had a strong nonmilitary component as well and that pronoia was just one of many ways by which soldiers

---

11. Mutafčiev, "Vojniški zemi," 532, 539–45. The most recent edition of Harmenopoulos' work is by K. Pitsakis, Πρόχειρον Νόμων ἢ Ἑξάβιβλος (Athens, 1971).

12. *Pronija, Prilog istoriju feudalizma u Vizantiji i u južnoslovenskim zemljama* (Belgrade, 1951). French trans.: Ostrogorsky, *Féodalité*.

were financed.[13] As research on pronoia continues, it has become increasingly clear that some revision of Ostrogorsky's thesis is necessary, not always in the direction of Mutafčiev's conceptualization and methodology, but in the direction of his conclusions. The most important contribution along these lines, in relation to a study of the army, is a relatively recent article by Nicolas Oikonomidès which suggests that pronoia, as one of several ways to remunerate soldiers, was more a fiscal tool that could be adapted to accommodate soldiers of various social and economic levels than a grant, as Ostrogorsky wrote, that always made a man a "feudal" aristocrat.[14] Finally, among the works that deal with soldiers in passing are studies of late Byzantine administration, works that examine the social and economic foundations of late Byzantine society and thereby illuminate the status of soldiers, and more general historical surveys that provide background material on the military policies of the emperors.

13. A good comparison of the two theses is found in I. Ševčenko's review of Ostrogorsky's *Pronija*, "An Important Contribution to the Social History of Late Byzantium," *Annals of the Ukrainian Academy of Arts and Sciences in the U.S.* 2 (1952), 448–59.
14. Oikonomidès, "A propos des armées."

SERBIA

BULGA

Niš

Sofia

Kosovo ✕

Prizren

Velbužd ✕

Strymon R.

Marica R.

Tzepaina Philippopolis
Stenimachos

Klokotnica ✕

Skopje

Vardar R.

Prosek

Rhodope Mtns.

Nestos R.

Melnik

Prilep

Strumica

MACEDONIA

Ohrid

Pelagonia

Siderokastron
Serres Drama

Xanthi Gratianoupolis
Peritheorion

Berat

Devol

Prespa Vodena

Gynaikokastron

Zichna Philippi
Kavalla

Kastoria

Thessaloniki

Chrysopolis

Anaktoropolis

Dyrrachion

Avlon
Kanina

EPIROS

THESSALY

Verria

Chortaites
Chalkidike
Hierissos

Rhentina

THASOS

Komitissa

Potidaia

Mt. Athos

Servia

Kassandreia

Longos

LEMNOS

Butrinto

Ioannina

Larissa

Trikkala

Acheloos R.

Phanarion

Demetrias

Pharsala

AEGEAN

Arta

Vonitza

Neopatras

Oreos

Naupaktos

Kephissos ✕

Boeotia

NEGROPONTE

KEPHALENIA

Patras

Thebes

Attica

Chlemoutsi

Achaia

Kalavryta

Andravida
Sergiana

Corinthe

Athens

Prinitza

IONIAN

M O R E A

Argos

Nauplia

Nikli

TINOS

Leontari

SPETSAI

SEA

Makry Piagi

Androusa

Sparta

Mistra

Methone

Korone

Lakonia

Monemvasia

KERKYRA

Mt. Taïgetos

Chandax

RIA

Varna

Mesembria

Sliven

Anchialos

Sozopolis

BLACK SEA

Haimos Mtns.

Klokotnica

Černomen

Skopelos

Adrianople

Herakleia

DAPHNOUSIA

Paphlagonia

T H R A C E

Vizye

Didymoteichon

Pythion

Arkadiopolis

Therapeia

Riva

Tzouroullos

Selymbria

Optimaton

Gratianoupolis

Pamphilon

Rhaidestos

Epibatai

Constantinople

Pelekanos

Nikomedeia

Peritheorion

Apros

Herakleia

PRINKIPO

Nicaea

Trikokkia

Rhousion

Ainos

SEA OF
MARMARA

Tzympe

Kyzikos

Bithynia

Sangarios R.

Gallipoli

Lopadion

Prousa

Belikome

Poimanenon

A S I A

TENEDOS

Skammandros

Achyraous

M I N O R

Mytilene

Pergamon

LESBOS

Neokastra

Magedon

Hermos R.

Nea Phokaia

Phokaia

Magnesia

Meander R.

Smyrna

Sardis

CHIOS

Nymphaion

Philadelphia

Klazomenai

Kaistros R.

Thrakesion

S E A

Ephesus

Tralles

Antioch

Anaia

Miletos

Melanoudion

PATMOS

Mylasa

NAXOS

KOS

ANAPHI

RHODES

CRETE

Chandax

0   100 miles

THE LATE BYZANTINE WORLD

SERBIA

Danube R.

BULGARIA

LATIN
EMPIRE

DESPOTATE

KINGDOM
OF
THESSALONIKI

OF

EPIROS

EMPIRE OF

NICAEA

SULTANATE

DUCHY OF ATHENS

OF RUM

• Ikonion

PRINCIPALITY
OF
ACHAIA

VENETIAN

POSSESSIONS

The Aegean ca. 1214

SERBIA

Danube R.

BULGARIA

LATIN
EMPIRE

DESPOTATE
OF
EPIROS

DUCHY OF ATHENS

SULTANATE

OF RUM

Ikonion

PRINCIPALITY
OF
ACHAIA

VENETIAN

POSSESSIONS

■ The Empire of Nicaea ca. 1250

WALLACHIA

Danube R.

SERBIA   BULGARIA

Dobrudja

Herakleia

THESSALY   EMIRATE OF
KARASI

OTTOMAN
EMIRATE

EPIROS

DUCHY OF ATHENS

EMIRATE OF
SARUHAN

EMIRATE
OF AYDIN   Philadelphia

PRINCIPALITY
OF
ACHAIA

VENETIAN

EMIRATE OF
MENTESHE

POSSESSIONS

HOSPITALLERS

■ Byzantine territory   ca. 1328

WALLACHIA

Danube R.

Dobrudja

S E R B I A

BULGARIA

OTTOMAN EMIRATE

EMIRATE OF
SARUHAN

Phokaia

DUCHY OF ATHENS

EMIRATE
OF AYDIN   Philadelphia

PRINCIPALITY

OF

ACHAIA

V E N E T I A N

EMIRATE OF
MENTESHE

P O S S E S S I O N S

HOSPITALLERS

■ Byzantine territory   ca. 1350

SERBIA

WALLACHIA

Danube R.

ALBANIA

OTTOMAN EMPIRE

Ankara •

VARIOUS

LATIN

POSSESSIONS

VARIOUS

LATIN

POSSESSIONS

■ Byzantine territory ca. 1402   ■ ▨ ca. 1403

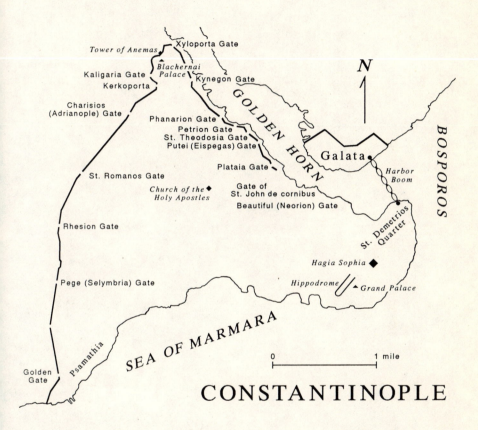

CONSTANTINOPLE

Tower of Anemas — Xyloporta Gate
Kaligaria Gate
Blachernai Palace
Kerkoporta
Kynegon Gate
Charisios (Adrianople) Gate
Phanarion Gate
Petrion Gate
St. Theodosia Gate
Putei (Eispegas) Gate
St. Romanos Gate
Plataia Gate
Church of the Holy Apostles
Gate of St. John de cornibus
Beautiful (Neorion) Gate
Rhesion Gate
Pege (Selymbria) Gate
Psamathia
Golden Gate

GOLDEN HORN

Galata
Harbor Boom
BOSPOROS
St. Demetrios Quarter

Hagia Sophia
Hippodrome — Grand Palace

SEA OF MARMARA

N

0   1 mile

Part I

The Army as Instrument of Policy

1. The Nicaean Period (1204–61)

After the Fourth Crusade Constantinople became the capital of a Latin Empire with Baldwin of Flanders as emperor and feudal overlord of all. As its share of the spoils, Venice received three-eighths of the city plus such valuable commercial properties as Negroponte, Gallipoli, the Aegean islands, and later Crete. In Macedonia Boniface of Montferrat carved out the Latin kingdom of Thessaloniki. In the south what became known as the Duchy of Athens and Thebes was granted by Boniface as a fief to the Burgundian Otto de la Roche. Venice had originally been assigned the Peloponnesos, but when it declined to take possession of it, William of Champlitte and Geoffrey Villehardouin with the support of Boniface conquered the area and established the French Principality of Achaia or of the Morea.

At first the attitude of the Byzantine population toward the Latin Conquest was universal shock and despair. Subsequently, some simply accepted it as divine retribution for their sins. Others resisted the invaders, but most either were defeated or surrendered when the Latins agreed not to dispossess them of their property. These people learned to tolerate and even collaborate with their new masters. But a few, in isolated areas, were able to survive and continued the armed struggle against the Latins.

On the Black Sea coast, the so-called Empire of Trebizond which had been founded by members of the Komnenos family shortly before 1204 struggled on independently with only marginal contact with the rest of Byzantine civilization. Around Arta in western Greece and modern Albania, Michael Doukas (1204–15) organized the separatist state that modern historians call the Despotate of Epiros, which soon extended from Naupaktos in the south to Dyrrachion in the north. Since Epiros produced no historians of its own, what is known of its internal history is provided by other Byzantine and Latin sources. Little can be said of Michael I's army or

For the general history of the Nicaean era, with bibliography, see Angold, *Byzantine Government*; D. Nicol, *The Despotate of Epiros* (Oxford, 1957); and Ostrogorsky, *History*, 418–50.

even his campaigns. Apparently he hired Latin mercenaries.[1] Last but hardly least was the state organized in western Asia Minor by the despot Theodore Laskaris (1204–22), a son-in-law of Emperor Alexios III Angelos (1195–1203) who had fled to Asia Minor and organized local resistance from his base at Prousa.

The conquests of the Latins in the area of Constantinople progressed quickly. During 1204 Thrace and most of Macedonia, including Thessaloniki, were seized by the crusaders, and after Theodore Laskaris was defeated at Poimanenon, most of the towns of Bithynia fell into Latin hands. But the fortunes of the Latins quickly reversed as the tsar of Bulgaria became involved in affairs to his south. In early 1205 the Greek population of Thrace rebelled against Latin authority, encouraging Tsar Kalojan's military intervention. In April at the battle of Adrianople the Latin army was annihilated. Emperor Baldwin was captured and never seen again. To counter the Bulgarians, the Latins were forced to withdraw from Asia Minor, allowing Theodore Laskaris to bring under control various independent Byzantine leaders, often by force. The next year the new Latin emperor Henry of Flanders invaded Asia Minor but again Bulgarian incursions forced him to return to Thrace. In 1207 Boniface of Montferrat was killed while battling the Bulgarians, and that same year Emperor Henry concluded a two-year peace with Theodore Laskaris. By 1206 Theodore was styling himself Emperor of the Romans and, to make the title official, he assembled a synod of bishops at Nicaea in 1208 and chose a patriarch whose first act was to crown him emperor.

In 1211, allied with the Seljuk sultan Kaj-Khusrau I and the emperor of Trebizond, the Latin emperor began a new offensive against Theodore. He managed to advance into Nicaean territory as far as Nymphaion, but once Theodore defeated the Seljuks at the battle of Antioch on the Meander, it was clear that the Latin Empire was not strong enough to destroy the Nicaean state. After another series of victories and defeats a new treaty was concluded in 1214 defining the frontiers between Nicaea and the Latin Empire. This freed Theodore to campaign in Paphlagonia against the Greeks of Trebizond who had been allied with the Latin emperor. He seized all the territory of Trebizond west of the town of Sinope. The Seljuks then took Sinope, and the Greeks of Trebizond became isolated vassals of the Turks.[2]

1. Nicol, *Despotate*, 33.
2. Angold, *Byzantine Government*, 240.

Meanwhile, Michael Doukas was consolidating his power base and establishing the principality of Epiros. Taking advantage of the decade of disorder in Bulgaria following the death of Kalojan in 1207, he moved into Macedonia and with the help of a few independent Bulgarian rulers laid siege to Thessaloniki several times. But it was through the efforts of his brother Theodore Doukas (1215–30) that the Epirote state made its bid as the true successor of the old Byzantine Empire. Beginning in 1215 this remarkable general seized most of Macedonia, then Serres in 1221, and finally Thessaloniki in 1224. The Latin kingdom of Thessaloniki founded by Boniface of Montferrat ceased to exist. Shortly afterward Theodore was proclaimed emperor and later crowned. His possessions extended from the Adriatic to the Aegean, and included Epiros, Thessaly, and most of Macedonia. Constantinople itself was within his reach. His armies in fact approached the city, but in 1230 at the height of his power he was defeated and captured by the Bulgarians at the battle of Klokotnica on the Marica between Philippopolis and Adrianople. His Empire of Thessaloniki now broke into three parts: Epiros, Thessaly, and Thessaloniki, with Thrace and Macedonia snatched up by Bulgaria.

Theodore Doukas' defeat opened the door for the Nicaean rulers. Theodore I Laskaris died in 1222 and was succeeded by his son-in-law John Vatatzes, the greatest of the Nicaean emperors. In 1224 Vatatzes defeated the Latins at Poimanenon, the scene of Theodore I's defeat twenty years earlier, and the next year concluded a treaty with the Latins in which the latter abandoned almost all of their possessions in Asia Minor. That same year he responded to the news that the people of Adrianople wished to deliver their city to him by making his first excursion into Europe, conquering much of Thrace without significant opposition. Twenty years after the Latin Conquest, over half of the territory captured by the crusaders was lost. The Latin possessions in the Aegean area were now more or less limited to Constantinople, southern Greece, and a number of islands.

The goal of the foreign policies of both Epiros and Nicaea was the reconquest of Constantinople, since whichever state held the old capital would be indisputably legitimized as the successor of the old Empire. By 1234, after concluding an alliance with John Asen of Bulgaria, Vatatzes was in a position to make his own attempt at retaking the city. Strange bedfellows he and Asen were, since the tsar also desired Constantinople as the capital of a Byzantino-Bulgarian empire, an old Bulgarian dream. But for the moment Asen regarded the Nicaean state as less of a threat than Epiros and the alliance as an avenue toward acquiring Constantinople himself.

According to the agreement Vatatzes was allowed to occupy the Gallipoli peninsula and southern Thrace up to the Marica River.[3] During the next two years the two leaders made a couple of unsuccessful joint assaults upon Constantinople, but the alliance broke down when Bulgaria realized it was fundamentally antithetical to its interests to help the Nicaean state, and soon the two states were again embroiled in hostilities.

One of the reasons for the failure of the Nicaean-Bulgarian assaults on Constantinople was that Vatatzes' fleet was inadequate to prevent the Venetians from resupplying the city. Nicaean blockades were either penetrated or driven off. The mixed results of Vatatzes' various naval expeditions contrast dramatically with his remarkable successes on land. In 1230 he provided aid to some Greeks who rebelled against the Venetians in Crete, but in 1233 thirty galleys were wrecked while on expedition there and the next year another attempt to conquer the island failed. In 1233 he unsuccessfully tried to retake Rhodes, and in 1241 a Nicaean fleet was defeated on the Sea of Marmara by a smaller Latin force. Acquiring an effective fleet was a top priority, but this was one area where Vatatzes' efforts were unfruitful.[4]

In contrast, throughout the 1240s Vatatzes was able to profit from the misfortunes of his neighbors with a series of major conquests in Europe. Exploiting the internal quarrels between the members of Theodore Doukas' family, Vatatzes led an expedition to Thessaloniki in 1242. Although he was not able to take the city, he secured his hold over the Aegean coast as far as the Strymon River.[5] On hearing the news that the Mongols had invaded Seljuk territory he returned to Asia, and after a major Seljuk defeat in 1243 at the hands of the Mongols, a treaty was concluded between Nicaea and the enervated Seljuk state. Later, in 1246, after the death of Tsar Koloman, Vatatzes seized Bulgarian territories in Macedonia, in the course of which he captured Thessaloniki from Theodore Doukas' son, the despot Demetrios. For the first time the states of Epiros and of Nicaea now had a common border. The final struggle to decide which of the two states in exile was the true heir to the Byzantine imperial tradition would soon begin.

Vatatzes is known for a number of successful military policies aimed at creating an effective campaign army and, just as importantly, at securing the Nicaean frontier in Asia Minor so that this army would be free to campaign in Europe. Vatatzes and his immediate successors enjoyed a remarkably

3. Ibid., 278.
4. Ibid., 198.
5. Nicol, *Despotate*, 138–39. Angold, *Byzantine Government*, 279.

stable Anatolian frontier, a crescent-shaped swath of land from the Black Sea to the southern Aegean, formed in the east by the upper branches of the Sangarios River and in the south by the Meander valley. Its stability was due to the amiable relations Vatatzes established between Nicaea and the Seljuks of Ikonion, a product of skillful diplomacy as well as military preparedness exemplified by the chain of fortifications he built along the Meander valley.[6]

Further, to minimize the depredations of marauding Turkoman and splinter Seljuk bands over which the Seljuk sultans had little control, the Nicaean emperors endeavored to keep the civilian population inhabiting the mountainous frontiers at the fringes of the Nicaean state from abandoning their homes. These highlanders performed a vital and quite hazardous function for the Nicaean state by acting as a buffer between the Turkish marauders and the valleys of the Nicaean Empire. The historian Pachymeres writes that the emperors, in order to maintain the eastern frontier, "turned to the mountains, securing [them] with many strong settlers from all over." Somewhat later, faced with increasing Turkish pressure, they "did not leave those living on the mountains [*pros tois oresin*] uncared for, who, not having an incentive to remain, were prepared to emigrate if anywhere enemies should attack somehow. . . . But they granted tax exemptions to all, pronoiai to the more illustrious among them, and imperial letters to those with an enterprising spirit." The policy of granting these men various benefits, including tax exemption, and to a special few, grants of pronoia, was designed to foster continued occupation of the border areas because the Nicaean emperors knew that continued occupation would include localized defense of their own lands and occasional sorties into Turkish territory for booty.

In the sense that these duties were performed by the highlanders as a matter of personal survival even before they received special privileges, they did not technically become "soldiers," which is why the historian Pachymeres, our only source for these developments, does not in fact call them such. He simply says that Nicaean policy affected "all" of those inhabiting the border areas, not a certain subset of the population who became "soldiers." After receiving their tax exemption and other benefits they performed no additional service and their only obligation to the state was to remain on their lands. The Nicaean highlanders were essentially a localized militia composed of the able inhabitants of the frontier zones who,

6. See C. Foss, "Late Byzantine Fortifications in Lydia," *JOB* 28 (1979), 297–320.

without much organization or discipline, defended their lands and harassed their opposite numbers in Turkish territory as best they saw fit. In this they performed a function well worth the exempted tax revenue, gifts, and pronoiai given them. As a result their economic condition improved and they were persuaded to remain, and their activities allowed Nicaean commanders to direct their military resources elsewhere.[7]

John Vatatzes was also quite skillful at adapting to unforeseen circumstances. Around 1239 a large group of Cumans—a Turkic people of the steppes—fleeing before the Mongols, crossed the Danube and invaded Thrace. There they pillaged and attacked the towns that had only recently come under Nicaean control until around 1242 when Vatatzes, responding to the situation, "with gifts and diplomacy made them over from a very savage to an obedient people" and succeeded in settling most of them in Anatolia throughout the Meander valley and the region east of Philadelphia. In an encomium to his father, Theodore II Laskaris refers to this episode: "Having removed the Scyth [sc., Cuman] from the west and the western lands, you led his race to the east as a subject people and, substituting [them] for the sons of Persians [sc., the Turks], you have securely fettered their assaults toward the west." Most were enrolled in the army and soon afterward received baptism. Vatatzes' policy toward the Cumans was distinguished not by its novelty—Cumans had served in the army since the reign of Alexios I Komnenos (1081–1118)—but by its enormous scale and relatively successful outcome.[8]

The Cumans served the Empire in two capacities, as reserve light cavalry and as standing troops. The Cuman reserve light cavalry were settled in Asia Minor. Some perhaps lived on the fringes of the Empire and led the more dangerous life of the highlander, probably practicing the same mixture of agriculture and transhumance in the hills of Anatolia as did the indigenous population and similarly serving as a buffer between Nicaean farmers and Turkish nomads. These Cumans were frequently mustered for campaigns in Europe. In 1242 they crossed from Asia with Vatatzes to participate in his abortive siege of Thessaloniki; in 1256 Vatatzes' successor, Theodore II Laskaris, left a force of 300 Cumans and Paphlagonians (inhabitants of the area of Anatolia west of Sinope) with the Nicaean governor

<hr>

7. Pachymeres, ed. Failler, I, 29–31 (Bonn ed., I, 16–17). M. Bartusis, "On the Problem of Smallholding Soldiers in Late Byzantium," *DOP* 44 (1990), 2–3.

8. Akropolites, 53–54, 65. F. Uspenskij, in *Žurnal Ministerstva narodnogo prosveščenija* 225 (1883), 339. Bartusis, "On the Problem," 12. On the earlier Cumans, see C. Asdracha, *La région des Rhodopes aux XIIIe et XIVe siècles* (Athens, 1976), 80–82; G. Ostrogorski, "Još jednom o proniarima Kumanima," *Zbornik Vladimira Mošina* (Belgrade, 1977), 63–74; and the references in G. Moravcsik, *Byzantinoturcica*, 2nd ed. (Berlin, 1958), II, 167–68.

of Thessaloniki; 2,000 Cuman light cavalry fought at the battle of Pelagonia in 1259; the majority of Alexios Strategopoulos' 800 troops which retook Constantinople in 1261 were Cuman; and Michael VIII Palaiologos' European campaigns of 1263–64, 1270–72, and 1275 included large Cuman contingents. In all of these campaigns it is most likely that the Cumans were mustered out of their settlements and afterwards returned to them. Their usefulness lay in the fact that, as inhabitants of the Empire, they were available for service on demand, and since they were an unsophisticated, war-loving people, holding their settlements on condition of military service, they willingly participated in campaigns and at little cost to the treasury. The descendants of the Cumans settled by Vatatzes are last encountered in 1292 during Andronikos II Palaiologos' unsuccessful campaign against Epiros. The army was an undisciplined mix of Turks and Cumans who terminated the campaign by an unauthorized retreat. They probably returned to Asia, but were not heard from again.[9]

The other group of Cumans were those who served as standing troops. These appear as a distinct group only once, but very significantly, at the time of Michael VIII's election to the regency in 1258. After the Latin mercenaries were consulted in the matter, the Cumans present at court offered in turn their opinion in good Greek, which implies that they spent considerable time in the company of Greek speakers. Their presence at court suggests that they were permanent standing troops who were either imperial guards or simply a mounted division that could respond more quickly to emergencies than their compatriots in the countryside from which they were drawn. One assumes their numbers were modest, perhaps a hundred or two. The real importance of the group laid in its tendency to foster the Hellenization, assimilation, and eventually the social advancement of its members. One such Cuman was Sytzigan, the son of a Cuman tribal leader, who was renamed Syrgiannes after baptism. Later he wedded a member of the Palaiologos family and before 1290 was granted the very high title of megas domestikos by Andronikos II. His son was the pinkernes (a court title literally meaning "cupbearer") Syrgiannes Palaiologos, friend of Andronikos III Palaiologos and John Kantakouzenos. It would seem that a large percentage of the Cumans who remained in the Empire after the 1290s were assimilated and lost their distinct ethnic identity. In this sense Vatatzes' expedient for dealing with the Cumans was quite successful.[10]

Like the Cumans, Latins were another foreign group that figured

9. Bartusis, "On the Problem," 12–13.

10. Ibid., 13 note 62. D. Nicol, *The Byzantine Family of Kantakouzenos (Cantacuzenus) ca.1100–1460* (Washington, D.C., 1968), 24–25.

prominently in the Nicaean armies. The Crusades had attracted large numbers of Latin warriors to the Aegean. During the thirteenth century, throughout the period of the Latin Empire, they provided the Laskarides of Nicaea with a steady supply of mercenaries, and the emperors relied upon them heavily. At the battle of Antioch on the Meander in 1211, for example, the Nicaean forces consisted of 2,000 cavalry, of which 800 were Latin mercenaries, the rest being Byzantine. They fought well but fell almost to a man, an excellent advertisement for their reliability in an age when foreign troops were usually only too eager to flee the field. The increasing importance of Latin mercenaries during the reign of John Vatatzes was symbolized by the creation of the office of megas konostaulos ("grand constable"), the "chief of the Frankish mercenaries." The fact that the first megas konostaulos, Michael Palaiologos, became emperor is not without a certain significance.[11]

During the reign of John Vatatzes we see the first Latin pronoiars, called *kavallarioi*, living in the area of Smyrna. *Kavallarios* (from the medieval Latin *caballarius*) was employed in late Byzantine demotic and semi-demotic written sources, and probably in the spoken Greek of the time, to denote the horse soldier in general. The literary sources usually speak of the cavalry soldier by using the formal *hippeus* ("horseman") and reserve *kavallarios*, if they employ it at all, to mean important Latin cavalrymen ("knights") or a specific title held by Latins in Byzantine service. In the documentary sources of the Nicaean and early Palaiologan periods, *kavallarios* was the usual title for a Latin horse soldier holding a typical military pronoia. As a group the kavallarioi probably paralleled the *stratiotai* (literally, "soldiers") of the documentary sources. In this usage *kavallarios* does not so much mean "horse soldier" as "knight," less the military function of a soldier (cavalryman) than his rank in society. All thirteenth-century kavallarioi had the title "sir" (*syr*) attached to or accompanying their names, most were or probably were pronoiars, and since most had names of Western European origin, they were probably Latins or recent descendants of Latins.[12]

The granting of pronoiai to thirteenth-century Latins in the service of Byzantium can be viewed as both a means of honoring and rewarding outstanding Latin soldiers and a means of reducing the burdensome outlay of gold pressing the fisc. Yet the transformation of Latin soldiers from

11. M. Bartusis, "The *Kavallarioi* of Byzantium," *Speculum* 63 (1988), 343 note 1.
12. Ibid., 343–47. About thirteen late Byzantine kavallarioi are known by name; see the Appendix.

mercenaries to pronoiars also changed the basic nature of their military service. A pronoia soldier dwelling in the provinces was a reserve soldier who neither served year round nor was available for service at a moment's notice. Therefore, the Latin soldiers who were permanent residents of the Empire found themselves divided into two groups, standing mercenaries and reserve pronoiars.

During Vatatzes' reign we begin to see the manner in which provincial administration was restored in the decades following the Fourth Crusade. On the whole the Empire of Nicaea tended to rely on the provincial administrative structures current in Byzantium prior to the Latin Conquest. Since the Nicaean state was occupying areas that once had been Byzantine provinces, it was eminently practical to restore, at least formally, the provincial organization of the pre-conquest period, particularly when a return to or continuation of the old constitutional forms could only bolster the legitimacy of the Nicaean regime. In light of this, it is not surprising that we detect during the Nicaean period the kind of loose structural division of military forces into central and provincial armies that had existed during the late twelfth century.

On one side there was the central army composed of the military corps called the Tagmata. These included the soldiers of the imperial court and household, as well as the field army, the heart of any campaign force. During the age of the Komnenian emperors (1081–1185) and continuing throughout the Nicaean era, these troops were in large measure foreigners and mercenaries. Also, at times during both periods there were foreign peoples settled in the provinces who performed campaign service, and these formed part of the same central army. Yet despite the heavy reliance of both the Komnenoi and Laskarides on foreign troops and mercenaries, provincial soldiers continued to exist. Since the seventh century these provincial armies and the territory within which they were based were called "themes" (*themata*), but the sense of the word "theme" as the provincial army itself had disappeared in the eleventh century. From the twelfth century a provincial army was an army "of a theme," the term then and until the end of Byzantium restricted to designating merely administrative and geographic units. In the early twelfth century the provincial, or "thematic," armies were small, insignificant, and useless for holding out invaders or in providing reserve troops for campaigns, the primary functions of the earlier thematic system. One might be tempted to think there was no longer anything like a "provincial army" at this time, but this is very unlikely since only rarely did any Byzantine institution ever vanish completely.

The Komnenoi undertook a restoration of their enfeebled provincial military apparatus, culminating with the efforts of Manuel I in western Asia Minor. In order to counter the Seljuk threat Manuel created a number of new, smaller themes by carving up and redefining the areas of older traditional themes. This restored thematic system had little in common with the thematic system as it had developed during the seventh and later centuries. The integrated military and administrative system present during the ninth and tenth centuries under the early Macedonian dynasty and characterized by the military governors called *strategoi* ("generals") and by the military estates (*stratiotika ktemata*) that provided the livelihood for provincial soldiers had not survived the eleventh-century crisis. Although the sources do not say what kind of soldiers were assigned to these new themes, they should probably be regarded as troops who were permanently settled in the theme and who garrisoned the frontier fortresses built or restored by the Komnenoi. Only by positing that these soldiers felt a strong affinity to local soil—a characteristic of the old thematic troops—can one explain the success of Manuel's new themes.[13]

The Nicaean Empire was heir to these developments and nothing demonstrates their successfulness so dramatically as the relative stability of the eastern borders of the Byzantine and Nicaean states from around 1180 to around 1260. Even though the thematic structure was always evolving and certain temporary adaptations were dictated by necessity, the list of Nicaean themes is nearly identical to that of the themes of western Asia Minor before the Latin Conquest. Around the year 1240, counterclockwise from the Black Sea area there were the themes of Paphlagonia, of the Optimaton, of Bithynia, of Skammandros or the Troad, of Neokastra, of the Thrakesion, and of Mylasa and Melanoudion. Each theme had its governor, an imperial appointee called a *doux*, or "duke" (following twelfth-century practice), usually holding office for only one year, who commanded the army of the particular theme.[14] As for the provincial armies themselves during the Nicaean period we have but a single reference. The historian Akropolites writes of a certain Constantine Margarites (Appendix, no. 6)

13. H. Ahrweiler, "Recherches sur l'administration de l'empire byzantin aux IXe–XIe s.," in Ahrweiler, *Études sur les structures administratives et sociales de Byzance* (London, 1971), no. VIII, 1–36. H. Ahrweiler, "L'histoire et la géographie de la région de Smyrne entre les deux occupations turques," in Ahrweiler, *Byzance: les pays et les territoires* (London, 1976), no. IV, 124–30. On the refortification of Asia Minor under the Komnenoi, see H. Ahrweiler, "Les fortresses construites en Asie Mineure face à l'invasion seldjoucide," in *Études sur les structures*, no. XVII, 182–89.

14. Angold, *Byzantine Government*, 193, 244–50. Ahrweiler, "Smyrne," 123–30, 133–37, 163–64.

who "hailed from Neokastra and achieved top rank in the army of this theme," evidently sometime during the reign of John Vatatzes. This evidence, while singular, accords with the testimony of the documentary sources which often speak of this theme. Moreover, if there was an army of the theme of Neokastra, we may assume the other Nicaean themes had their own armies as well.[15]

The function of the Nicaean thematic armies is not directly evident. Presumably they garrisoned the fortresses and towns of their respective themes and defended the eastern frontier on a localized basis. The sources do not provide much information about the activities of the Nicaean thematic armies until the reign of Theodore II Laskaris. At that time provincial troops were campaigning with Nicaean forces in Europe. Earlier, campaign forces were composed exclusively of divisions of the field army and were in large measure foreign, particularly Latin, mercenaries, but toward the end of the Nicaean period the distinction between field and thematic armies gradually blurred. This resulted from three developments. First, during the 1250s Theodore II Laskaris and then, to an even greater extent, Michael VIII began using Anatolian thematic troops for European campaigns. Second, from the beginning of the reconquest of Thrace and Macedonia, campaign troops were used to garrison and occupy the fortresses of Europe. A third development was the increasing tendency to make grants of pronoiai to field army troops.[16]

The first development resulted from a need for large numbers of trained soldiers with which to wage European campaigns and from a lack of money with which to hire mercenaries. These two factors, plus Theodore II's general xenophobia, led him to turn to thematic troops for his campaigns. The first attested provincial troops used in Europe were the cavalry from Paphlagonia who accompanied Theodore II in the mid-1250s. Under Michael VIII this practice accelerated. The historian Pachymeres provides a list of the troop contingents (*allagia*) comprising the army of Michael VIII's brother, the despot John Palaiologos, during the 1260s. Aside from the Cumans and the Latins—both standard elements in the Nicaean campaign army—and troops from Thrace and Macedonia, there were numerous contingents from Asia Minor: Paphlagonians, Mesothinians, Phrygians, Mysians, Carians, and troops from Magedon. The rough correspondence between the Nicaean themes and these troop divisions (Paphlagonia = Paphlagonians, Optimaton = Mesothinians, Skammandros = Mysians,

15. Angold, *Byzantine Government*, 193.
16. Ibid., 189–91, 193–94.

Neokastra = Magedonians, Thrakesion = Phrygians, Mylasa and Melanou-dion = Carians) confirms what other sources tell us as well, that Michael VIII was drawing campaign troops from all the eastern provinces.[17]

The second development, the garrisoning of conquered European fortresses with campaign troops, began as early as 1237 and continued through the end of the Nicaean era.[18] It is a usual step in the process of military conquest that, if successful, part of the campaign army must become an army of occupation, if only temporarily. The occupying forces remain in the area until reliable local forces can be recruited and until the military front is established at some point beyond the region recently won. In the Nicaean reconquest of Thrace and Macedonia the ratio of occupation forces to territory conquered was rather high primarily because of geography. The direction of the reconquest was essentially linear following the old Roman road called the Via Egnatia from Thrace into Macedonia. This meant, for example, that after the southern Thracian plain had been retaken and Nicaean armies moved westward into Macedonia, Thrace had to be strongly garrisoned because it was still subject to attack from the Bulgarians to the north and the Latins in Constantinople.

Once John Vatatzes had succeeded in reconquering nearly all of Thrace and most of Macedonia, the Nicaean European possessions formed a swath of land no more than 150 miles wide that cut the Balkans in half, with the unhumbled Bulgarian Empire to the northeast, the Serbian kingdom with its growing pretensions to the northwest, the troublesome Epirote and Thessalian rulers to the south, and to the east, though in decline, Latin Constantinople. Historically, this area has proved itself the easiest part of the Balkans to conquer but the most difficult to hold. Consequently, Vatatzes and his successors were forced to maintain a strong military presence in most of this territory by manning the strategically important fortresses of Thrace and Macedonia with the campaign troops that had conquered them. But since many fortresses needed strong garrisons long after they had been conquered, how did the Nicaean emperors compensate for the loss of manpower that the front-line campaign army would suffer? One solution was to recruit new troops from the conquered territories. However, the quality of these troops was often less than satisfactory.[19] Another solution,

17. Akropolites, 139. Pachymeres, ed. Failler, I, 403 (Bonn ed., I, 310). See also Pachy-meres, ed. Failler, I, 173, 273, 291 (Bonn ed., I, 122, 205, 220). *Chronicle of the Morea*, ed. J. Schmitt (London, 1904), vv. 4555, 6487–90. Geanakoplos, *Emperor Michael*, 77–78, 157–58, 229. Zakythinos, *Despotat*, II, 133.

18. Angold, *Byzantine Government*, 189–90, provides a number of examples.

19. See Angold, *Byzantine Government*, 185, 191.

as we have seen, was to send thematic troops from Asia on the European campaigns. This freed more campaign troops for garrison service.

The administration of Thrace and Macedonia continued to have the character of a military occupation well into the reign of Michael VIII. Although there are no actual accounts of Anatolian soldiers or field troops being settled in Europe, it is reasonable to think then that one of the later Nicaean emperors saw the expedience of settling divisions of the campaign armies, including the thematic troops drafted for the campaigns, in Europe permanently so that they could respond more rapidly to external threats. In the thirteenth century, as in the seventh century during Emperor Herakleios' recovery of Asia Minor from the Persians, reconquest meant that land was available to soldiers for rewards and incentives. Growing Turkish pressure and Michael VIII's own Anatolian military policies made life in the east increasingly unattractive, and certainly by Michael VIII's reign soldiers, pronoiars and otherwise, were being settled in Europe. There is no reason to think that all of these were indigenous to Thrace and Macedonia.

In order to establish effective control and to defend the reconquered territories, these developments led to a reorganization, or perhaps more accurately, an evolutionary change in provincial administration. During the twelfth century a theme was administered by a doux who enjoyed both civil and military authority. Within the theme towns were administered by a new civil official called the *prokathemenos*. Perhaps most towns also had a *kastrophylax* (literally, "fortress guard"), an official first appearing in the eleventh century and charged with maintaining the fortifications and security of the town. In the early Nicaean period, this arrangement was formalized: the doux governed the theme, assisted in the cities by the prokathemenoi and the kastrophylakes who respectively had civil and military responsibilities. No doubt in times of crisis their responsibilities would tend to overlap, but in times of peace, the prokathemenoi handled civil matters, and the kastrophylakes kept up the fortifications and organized the watch.

Toward the end of the thirteenth century the office of doux gave way to that of the *kephale* (literally, "head"), so that by the fourteenth century the kephale was both the civil and military administrator of the primary provincial unit, no longer the theme but a much smaller territory sometimes called a *katepanikion* composed of a more or less major fortified town (*kastron*) and the countryside surrounding it.[20] Within the katepanikion,

20. On the katepanikion, see Lj. Maksimović, *The Byzantine Provincial Administration Under the Palaiologoi* (Amsterdam, 1988), 70–83.

the kephale governed day-to-day affairs. Since almost every town had a kephale, the office of prokathemenos lost its importance in civil administration and by the fourteenth century became, if not simply an honorary position, then a subordinate in the civil sphere to the kephale. In addition to more mundane duties such as settling civil disputes in towns and in the neighboring countryside and tending to the fortification and watch of his town, the kephale was the supreme military commander and was obliged, in the words of a fourteenth-century appointment formula, "to excite, to ready, and to rouse the soldiers found there that they should lack nothing in regard to their horses and arms, and be found eager in the imminent service of my majesty."[21] While most kephalai were governors of kastra, their jurisdictions varied, sometimes encompassing larger provincial units, even whole provinces. On the other hand, lesser kephalai governed individual towns and the lands surrounding them, islands, or even groups of villages.

Although kephalai had far-ranging powers and in most affairs were answerable to no one save the emperor, there were nevertheless two important governmental functions in which the kephalai generally did not play much of a role. These were the creation of fiscal surveys and the administration of certain soldiers who lived in the provinces. For practical reasons, fiscal surveys and some aspects of provincial military administration were still conducted on a thematic basis. For example, the fiscal assessors (*apographeis*) encountered in the documentary sources had a wide jurisdiction, usually embracing a theme, sometimes two or more themes. The reason for this is that many landowners and almost every monastery had possessions in more than one katepanikion, and sometimes in more than one theme. Thus, for fiscal surveys the thematic provincial unit was still useful, and so it continued to exist.

The third development which led to the blurring of the distinction between the field army and the thematic armies in the Nicaean period was the increasing tendency to grant pronoiai to troops in the field army. This practice was begun under the Komnenoi, and the Nicaean emperors continued it, and although their armies were much smaller than those of the Komnenoi, the percentage of pronoiars in the army, while still and ever to be a minority, was now higher than ever before. There does not seem to have been any attempt under the Komnenoi or Laskarides to incorporate

---

21. K. Sathas, *Μεσαιωνικὴ Βιβλιοθήκη* (Venice and Paris, 1872–94), VI, 642. On the office of kephale, see Maksimović, *Byzantine Provincial Administration*, 117–66.

the institution of pronoia within the thematic system. Although the military pronoiar generally lived in the provinces, he was not a provincial soldier, but no less than those foreign troops frequently encountered in the sources who were given land in return for service, he belonged to the Tagmata, the central imperial army. As long as only a very small minority of imperial troops were pronoiars—with most remaining mercenaries—it was still possible to view the military pronoiar as a special type of soldier within the central army. However, the manpower needs of Vatatzes brought about a change in this relationship as he further extended the military pronoia system. We have no figures, but by the end of the thirteenth century, it was possibly more common for a soldier in the central army to have been a pronoiar than a mercenary.

During John Vatatzes' reign, the struggle with Epiros reached its crescendo. His last campaign was a major offensive against Epiros in 1252, a response to the capture of a few Macedonian towns by Michael II Doukas (ca.1230–67/8). Not only did Vatatzes expel Michael's army, but he conquered western Macedonia and northern Epiros, including the major towns of Kastoria, Pelagonia, Ohrid, Prilep, and Vodena. The resulting peace treaty gave Nicaea the towns of Servia and Dyrrachion and wedded Michael II's son Nikephoros to one of Vatatzes' granddaughters. Vatatzes' plans to advance on Constantinople were brought to an end with his death in 1254, and his son and successor Theodore II, a sickly vacillating scholar whose epilepsy made him subject to great mood swings, could do nothing to revive them. The Bulgarians immediately launched an invasion into Thrace which Theodore spent over a year repelling until a peace treaty restored the status quo ante. During this war Theodore experienced some difficulty raising troops. In one instance he recruited soldiers as he marched toward the enemy, and in another we find him drafting hunters into his army.[22]

Meanwhile, Michael II of Epiros responded to Vatatzes' death by invading Nicaean territory in Macedonia. The megas logothetes (and historian) George Akropolites whom Vatatzes had left behind in Macedonia as military governor found himself outmaneuvered while several Nicaean commanders defected to Michael's side. In 1257 Theodore II sent Michael Palaiologos, the future emperor, to face Michael II with a body of inferior troops. In a battle outside Vodena, Palaiologos led some 500 Paphlagonians and Turks against Theodore, one of Michael's sons. Theodore's forces were

22. Akropolites, III, 124–25. Angold, *Byzantine Government*, 185.

defeated and he himself was slain. Such minor successes established Michael Palaiologos' reputation as a capable soldier, but they could not prevent the loss of most of western Macedonia.[23]

The Nicaean era concludes with three major events: the accession—or rather, the usurpation—of Michael VIII Palaiologos, the battle of Pelagonia, and the reconquest of Constantinople. At the death of the thirty-six-year-old Theodore II in 1258, Patriarch Arsenios and the protovestiarios George Mouzalon became the regents for Theodore's son, John IV Laskaris, who was about eight years old. The aristocracy and the army had little love for Mouzalon. As a man of low birth, he reflected Theodore's anti-aristocratic policy aimed at curbing the power of the Anatolian magnates. Further, Mouzalon's lack of military experience lowered him in the eyes of the army. But even more important, as a creature of Theodore, he reminded the soldiery of Theodore's policies regarding the army.

Even though the Latin pronoia soldiers in the provinces may have enjoyed more overall prestige and material wealth, the Latin mercenaries permanently attached to the emperor's court had a much greater opportunity to play a political role during the Nicaean era. It is this, more than their satisfactory performance in the field, that led Theodore II Laskaris to alienate them by fantasizing about an army composed entirely of "Greeks," and by allowing, quite foolishly, the pay of his own Latin mercenaries to fall in arrears. Michael Palaiologos and the Latin mercenaries held Mouzalon responsible for their treatment under Theodore. Indeed without the support and active participation of the Latin mercenaries, Michael Palaiologos' usurpation would not have succeeded.[24]

During a memorial service for Theodore held shortly after his death and attended by representatives of the aristocracy and the army, a mob outside the church, including many soldiers, demanded that John IV show himself. A riot ensued and a group of soldiers broke into the church and murdered George Mouzalon and his brothers. It is interesting that Mouzalon's assassin, a certain Charles, evidently a Latin mercenary, was not punished for the act.[25] Soon afterward, Michael Palaiologos was chosen as regent, and on January 1, 1259, in response to his claim that he could not protect the interests of John IV without sufficient authority, he was pro-

23. Nicol, *Despotate*, 160–65. V. Kravari, *Villes et villages de Macédoine orientale* (Paris, 1989), 47. Angold, *Byzantine Government*, 282.

24. Pachymeres, ed. Failler, I, 79–81. Angold, *Byzantine Government*, 81, 185–87. Geanakoplos, *Emperor Michael*, 35–36, 38–46.

25. Pachymeres, ed. Failler, I, 87, 371. Geanakoplos, *Emperor Michael*, 39–41.

claimed co-emperor and, with the patriarch's assent, he and John IV Laskaris were jointly crowned shortly afterward.

Meanwhile an anti-Nicaean coalition of powers was conspiring in western Greece. In Epiros Michael II Doukas had been busy making alliances with King Manfred of Sicily, William II Villehardouin, prince of Achaia and overlord of the lords of Negroponte and of the French Duchy of Athens, and King Stefan Uroš I of Serbia. Vatatzes had been allied with Manfred's father, the German emperor Frederick II Hohenstaufen (d.1250), and Vatatzes had even provided Frederick some soldiers who fought for him in Italy in 1238.[26] But the Normans of Sicily were traditional enemies of Byzantium and for centuries had been seeking a permanent foothold in Greece.

After the failure of diplomatic efforts to thwart the coalition, Michael VIII decided to crush Michael Doukas as quickly as possible. He ordered his brother the sevastokrator John Palaiologos, the megas domestikos Alexios Strategopoulos, and John Raoul to take their armies, then wintering in Macedonia, to attack Michael. The army was supplemented with men from Thrace and Macedonia who joined John Palaiologos in Thessaloniki, from which point the combined Nicaean forces marched to Ohrid and Devol, surprising Michael II and his army at Kastoria. Hastily Michael withdrew to Avlon, at that time in Manfred's possession.[27]

At Michael II's request, Manfred quickly sent aid: 400 German cavalry.[28] William II also arrived on the scene with a feudal levy including Greek archons from the Morea. Present with Michael II were his sons Nikephoros and the bastard John, who commanded a contingent of Vlachs from Thessaly. These armies converged on the plain of Pelagonia (modern Bitola) in western Macedonia. According to the incredible figures of the *Chronicle of the Morea*, William commanded 8,000 heavily armed and 12,000 light-armed troops, and Michael 8,000 and 18,000. According to the Greek and French versions of the chronicle, the Nicaean forces included 1,500 Hungarian and 300 German mercenaries from the West, 600 Serb and an unstated number of Bulgarian cavalry, 1,500 Turkish and 2,000 Cuman cavalry, and many Greek archers.[29]

26. Geanakoplos, *Emperor Michael*, 48.
27. Nicol, *Despotate*, 176.
28. Akropolites, 168, and M. Sanudo, *Istoria del regno di Romania*, ed. C. Hopf in *Chroniques gréco-romanes* (Berlin, 1873), 107, though Pachymeres, ed. Failler, I, 117, gives the figure 3,000.
29. Nicol, *Despotate*, 176, 179. See D. Geanakoplos, "Greco-Latin Relations on the Eve of the Byzantine Restoration: The Battle of Pelagonia, 1259," *DOP* 7 (1953), 124–25.

Michael VIII advised his brother to exploit the disunity of the enemy. He assigned his heavily armed troops to the surrounding hills and ordered the light-armed Turks, Cumans, and Greek archers to harass the enemy on the plain by attacking their idle horses and plundering their supplies. At this point the army of Michael II lost its morale and fled to Prilep, while John the Bastard defected to the Nicaean side. The historian Gregoras and the *Chronicle* explain Michael II's flight as the result of the disinformation spread by a "deserter" whom the sevastokrator John had sent to Michael's camp. He claimed either that Michael's allies had agreed to betray Michael for money provided by the sevastokrator or that the Nicaean forces were so superior that opposition was pointless. On the other hand, the historians Pachymeres and the Venetian Sanudo explain John the Bastard's defection in terms of discord among the allies. Pachymeres reports that some of William's knights had made improper glances at John's beautiful wife. John was so enraged by William's refusal to chasten his knights that he offered the sevastokrator help in defeating William. In sum, the mutual suspicion of the allies along with some deception led to the desertion of Michael II and the defection of John the Bastard.[30]

The next day, a battle was fought somewhere between Pelagonia and Kastoria. Discovering the flight of Michael II, the Latins of Manfred and William also sought to depart but the Nicaeans fell upon them. As the Nicaean forces attacked William, John attacked from the rear, and many of those who attempted to flee were cut down by the Cumans and Turks. In the end most of the Latins were killed and many others were captured, including William himself and thirty Frankish barons. Following up their victory, the Nicaean army split into two parts. The sevastokrator John with John the Bastard marched into Thessaly and sacked Latin Thebes, while Stratego-poulos and John Raoul invaded Epiros and briefly captured Arta.[31]

Although Michael II Doukas was soon able to recover, regroup, and again make trouble for Michael VIII, the battle of Pelagonia was of great significance. An allied victory would have strengthened the Latin Empire and weakened Nicaea. Instead, the ambitions of Manfred of Sicily and of Michael Doukas were foiled, the Principality of Achaia was weakened dramatically, and the stage was set for Michael VIII's conquests in Greece.

With the pressure from the west lifted, Michael set about planning the reconquest of Constantinople. Achieving this objective would provide him

---

30. Varying accounts: Geanakoplos, *Emperor Michael*, 67–73, and his "Greco-Latin Relations," 99–141. The battle as a whole: Nicol, *Despotate*, 174–82.

31. Kravari, *Villes et villages*, 48. Angold, *Byzantine Government*, 282.

with the legitimacy he needed to obscure the unpleasant facts of his usurpation. His basic strategy was to isolate the city politically by forming alliances with its neighbors as previous emperors had done. The Latin Empire had been steadily declining in strength, and despite trips to the West to appeal personally for aid, the Latin emperor Baldwin II of Courtenay (1228–61) had received little tangible help.

In 1260 Michael put two plans in motion. The first was to lay siege to the settlement at Galata across the Golden Horn from the main part of the city. The second was to win entry into the city through the treachery of a certain Latin nobleman whom we know from Akropolites' history simply as "Asel," that is, Ansel. Akropolites writes that this Ansel promised to open the gates of the city in return for his own safe conduct. In January 1260 Michael invaded Thrace, seized a number of towns including Selymbria, and then began his siege of Galata. However, the inhabitants of Galata put up a strong defense reinforced by men and arms from the city itself, and since the help of Ansel never materialized, Michael was forced to abandon the siege in April.[32]

Although this siege prompted the doge of Venice to authorize the Venetian bailli of Negroponte to make agreements with the Latin rulers in the Aegean to provide a permanent garrison for Constantinople of one thousand men, their own interests precluded them from funding even this modest number of soldiers. Michael meanwhile firmed up relations with Bulgaria, the Seljuks, and even the Mongols. Realizing he could not take Constantinople without a fleet to counter that of the Venetians, he negotiated a treaty with Venice's great rival, Genoa. According to the terms of the treaty of Nymphaion of March 1261, Genoa, in return for trade concessions, was to provide up to fifty ships for the emperor's use, though he himself would pay the salaries of their crews. Among the other military clauses of the treaty, Genoa was to allow the exportation of horses and armor to Byzantium and to allow Genoese to enter Byzantine military service, for which Genoa would supply the arms and horses and the emperor, again, the pay. Sixteen galleys were dispatched immediately to Michael, but as it turned out they would not be needed to retake Constantinople.[33]

In early 1261 Michael II of Epiros had recovered sufficiently from his humiliation at Pelagonia to resume encroaching upon Nicaean territory in Macedonia, and so once again Michael VIII sent an army there under the

32. Geanakoplos, *Emperor Michael*, 75–79.
33. Ibid., 80–90. Text of the treaty (only the Latin version survives): J. Zepos and P. Zepos, *Jus graecoromanum* (Athens, 1931), I, 488–95.

command of his brother John. At the same time the emperor ordered the caesar Alexios Strategopoulos to lead a force of about 800 Greek and Cuman troops to the Bulgarian frontier to curb preemptively any agitation from those parts. Since Strategopoulos would march by Constantinople on the way, he was further ordered, in the words of Pachymeres, "to approach the city in passing and in a threatening manner to brandish the sword against the Italians, but not to do anything else, for he did not have sufficient forces."[34]

When Alexios arrived near the city, he found that the Venetian fleet was away besieging the Nicaean island of Daphnousia, about seventy miles from the mouth of the Bosporos in the Black Sea, stripping the city of almost all its soldiers. Since no reliable source satisfactorily explains why the Venetians decided at that moment to besiege Daphnousia, there has always been speculation that Michael had provoked this siege as part of a grand plan to retake Constantinople. However, two facts militate against this. First, Strategopoulos' force was extremely small for such a feat and, further, Michael himself was not present at the reconquest. It is this second point that is the most persuasive evidence for the accidental nature of the reconquest. Michael personally had conducted the abortive siege the year earlier. The political value of being present when the city was retaken was so great that if he thought there was a reasonable chance of taking the city he would have been on the scene. Nevertheless, there is abundant evidence that the Nicaean Greeks were in contact with the Greek inhabitants of the city and its environs. No doubt contingency plans had been made should the opportunity for retaking the city present itself.[35]

According to Pachymeres, Strategopoulos approached the city and made contact with certain people called Thelematarioi. These were free native farmers who lived around Constantinople and who had maintained their independence during the period of the Latin Empire by serving as middlemen in the economic activity between the Nicaean and Latin territories. Pachymeres writes about them:

> There were some inhabitants from Chryseia and vicinity who, having loose convictions, were able to lean toward the Romans or toward the Italians, since the Romans put stock in their being Roman, while the Italians believed themselves safe from them because of their familiarity with them. They [the Italians] had no one else in whom to trust. To banish these inhabitants might

34. Pachymeres, ed. Failler, I, 191. Gregoras, I, 83, supplies the figure 800. Cf. Akropolites, 181. Geanakoplos, *Emperor Michael*, 92–93.
35. Geanakoplos, *Emperor Michael*, 97–104.

have brought on danger from [the area's] desolation. Hence they were between the Romans and the Italians, and because of this they were called
Thelematarioi, cultivating the land outside the City, living there and remaining free from both sides since both needed their affection so they would not be
harmed.

The name "Thelematarios" by which they were known even prior to the
reconquest of 1261 meant "free-willed" in the sense that they did as they
pleased, declaring no allegiance and having no master. Indeed their position as independent middlemen in the economic activity between the
Nicaean and Latin territories could only be maintained insofar as they
abstained from taking sides.[36]

Yet at least some of the Thelematarioi remained Byzantine at heart.
Led by a certain Koutritzakes they informed Strategopoulos about the
absence of the Latin fleet, about the weakness of the city's defenses, and
how entry into the city might be achieved. At first Alexios hesitated. He was
not the kind of general accustomed to exceeding his orders. Moreover, his
force was rather small and he felt the Latin fleet might return unexpectedly.
But in the end he could not deny that this was a chance worth taking. On
the agreed night, July 25, 1261, Strategopoulos hid his troops at a monastery
located outside the walls across from the Pege Gate. Meanwhile some 500
Thelematarioi surmounted the city's walls from the inside and killed the
sleeping guards. They moved to the Pege Gate and broke it open, allowing
Strategopoulos' troops to race from cover and enter the city. They met very
little opposition. Emperor Baldwin was so startled by the turn of events
that he fled to safety with neither sword nor crown. But suddenly the
Venetian fleet appeared, and fearing an encounter with the Latin army,
Alexios took the advice of a Greek who had been in Baldwin's service and
set fire to a Latin residential neighborhood. Rushing to save their wives and
children, the Latins took no further thought of defense and evacuated the
city. After fifty-seven years the city on the Bosporos was once again under
Byzantine control.[37]

Encamped at Meteorion, south of Poimanenon, Michael VIII was
asleep in his tent when the news arrived. His sister Eulogia, according to
Pachymeres, tickled his toes with a feather to awaken him and tell her
disbelieving brother of the capture of the city. Michael entered Constanti-

---

36. Pachymeres, ed. Failler, I, 157 (Bonn ed., I, 110). The location of this "Chryseia" is
uncertain. Bartusis, "On the Problem," 13–14.

37. Pachymeres, ed. Failler, I, 191–203 (Bonn ed., I, 138–48). Geanakoplos, *Emperor
Michael*, 104–15.

nople three weeks later, on August 15, the feast of the Dormition of the Virgin, a special day for the Byzantines and chosen for that very reason. The next month he was crowned a second time in the great church of Hagia Sophia, this time without John IV. On Christmas Day, 1261, he had the young John Laskaris blinded and imprisoned. Michael Palaiologos was now the sole emperor of the restored Byzantine Empire.[38]

38. Akropolites, 183. Pachymeres, ed. Failler, I, 205–207 (Bonn ed., I, 150–51). Geanakoplos, *Emperor Michael*, 119–22, 145. Nicol, *Last Centuries*, 40–41.

2. The Reign of Michael VIII Palaiologos (1259–82)

Upon assuming the throne Michael VIII directed most of his energies toward countering the threats from the West and toward extending his authority over the Despotate of Epiros and the remaining Latin states in the Morea. Careful diplomacy was the means for attaining the first goal and force of arms the second. The reconquest of Constantinople in 1261, relocating the center of gravity of the Byzantine world from the sheltered confines of Asia Minor to a more strategic and symbolic position in Mediterranean affairs, necessitated a military buildup and at the same time furthered the Laskarides' dream of restoring the Empire as constituted before the events of the early thirteenth century. Consequently, Michael's military policies centered around protecting Constantinople, amassing armies large enough to tackle the Latins in the Morea and the Greeks in Thessaly, and ensuring the continued Byzantine control over the European provinces of Thrace and Macedonia.[1]

After the reconquest of Constantinople in 1261, Michael VIII created four new military divisions: the Thelematarioi, the Gasmouloi, the marine Tzakones, and the Prosalentai. At least three of the four continued to exist as military bodies for generations. Since the best testimony to the success of a new troop division is its endurance, there is no better evidence of Michael VIII's brilliance in military organization.

Once the city was retaken Michael set about repopulating it. He allotted agricultural land inside and outside of Constantinople to his palace officials, and "because of their zeal and goodwill, good land for producing fruit and excellent for everything sown on it was delivered in hereditary title to the Thelematarioi." These Thelematarioi, who lived in the vicinity of Constantinople and had helped Alexios Strategopoulos in its recapture,

For the general history of Michael VIII's reign, with bibliography, see Geanakoplos, *Emperor Michael*; Nicol, *Last Centuries*, 43–96; and Ostrogorsky, *History*, 450–65.

1. On Michael's rebuilding of the walls and harbors of Constantinople, see Geanakoplos, *Emperor Michael*, 129–30.

were formed into a special military group. Very little is known of their military activities. They are specifically mentioned as fighting troops for the first and only time at the battle of Apros in 1305, where they formed the rearguard. Evidently, having been rewarded with lands, they became hereditary imperial servants, and most likely it was their sons and grandsons who fought at Apros. A brief reference from 1318 to "some of the Thelematarioi" who were called as witnesses in a case involving an accusation of heresy suggests that the Thelematarioi remained a group with very modest status. On the other hand, a document from 1349 notes that a certain "Katakalon from the Thelematarioi soldiers" had been receiving eight hyperpyra yearly, evidently as part of a pronoia grant, ever since the reign of Andronikos II. If Katakalon was in fact a pronoiar, this would mean that the status of some Thelematarioi had risen greatly since Michael VIII's day. Thus, while the Thelematarioi continued to exist as soldiers through the middle of the fourteenth century, their terms of service and socioeconomic position may have undergone some evolution.[2]

Michael VIII also set out to rebuild a Byzantine navy.[3] For this he sought and obtained the services of Gasmouloi living in and around the city. The Gasmouloi (or Vasmouloi), like the Thelematarioi, were a product of the interrelations of Byzantines and Latins. But unlike the Thelematarioi, the Gasmouloi were a product not of economic but of conjugal relations and fraternization that had begun long before the Latin Conquest and continued long afterward. The origin of the word *gasmoulos* is uncertain, though some derivation based on the Latin *mulus*, "mule," is quite possible. They are described in the *Advice for an Overseas Passage*, a treatise written around 1330 by a Latin self-described "friar preacher" for the purpose of urging the king of France Philip VI of Valois (1328–50) to undertake a crusade. The anonymous author, who had little love for anything eastern, but who claims to have spent more than twenty-four years abroad, cautions his reader about the various foreign peoples one would encounter:

> And they are called Gasmouloi who were begotten on their father's side by a
> Greek and on their mother's side by a Latin or on their father's side by a Latin

2. Pachymeres, ed. Failler, I, 221 (Bonn ed., I, 164); Bonn ed., II, 549. MM, I, 135, line 32. Arkadios Vatopedinos, «Γράμματα τῆς ἐν Κωνσταντινουπόλει μονῆς τῆς Θεοτόκου τῆς Ψυχοσωστρίας», *Byzantinisch-Neugriechische Jahrbücher* 13 (1937), 308, no. 3, lines 125–27 and 138–39. M. Bartusis, "On the Problem of Smallholding Soldiers in Late Byzantium," *DOP* 44 (1990), 13–15.

3. On the renewal of the fleet, see Geanakoplos, *Emperor Michael*, 125ff., and H. Ahrweiler, *Byzance et la mer* (Paris, 1966), 336ff.

and mother's side by a Greek. In faith they are fickle, in promise deceitful, in word mendacious, adroit in evil, ignorant of good, impudent to their betters, prone to discord, accustomed to plundering, inclined to savagery, adverse to piety, hungry for carnage and death, restless in everything, given to drink, incontinent without restraint, slaves to greed, gluttony and intemperance, loving no one beside themselves and what belongs to them. They present themselves as Greeks to Greeks and as Latins to Latins, being all things to everyone, not to make a profit . . . but to destroy.[4]

The Gasmouloi were assigned to the fleet as mercenary soldiers, but apparently the need for soldiers to fortify and repopulate the capital and man the navy was such that Michael soon had to look elsewhere. Consequently, he transplanted families from the Morea and possibly elsewhere to Constantinople and enrolled the men as soldiers in his new fleet. Pachymeres writes that Michael "had great need to settle the city with light-armed soldiers, and so he had many Lakones, arriving from the Morea, settled as natives, distributing places near the city. Bestowing the yearly pay, he also supplied them with many other liberalities, and used them for many [things] inside and outside [Constantinople], for they displayed worthy behavior in the wars." These Lakones-Tzakones came to Constantinople in late 1261 or early 1262 and supplemented the Gasmouloi who had formed the first military contingents of Michael's new fleet. Like the Gasmouloi, they were light-armed soldiers. And while their presence is specifically noted only during the course of two naval campaigns (in 1262 and 1273), it seems that throughout the 1260s and 1270s these Tzakones, together with the Gasmouloi, formed the basic Byzantine marine force.[5]

In the passage quoted above Pachymeres calls them "Lakones" or Lakonians, people from the southeastern Morea, around Mistra. He felt their name had been corrupted into "Tzakones." When describing the composition of the naval expedition to Thessaly in 1273, Pachymeres writes, "many others [were] from the Lakones whom they called Tzakones, corrupting [their name], whom the ruler transplanted with their wives and children to Constantinople from the Morea and the western parts, and who were numerous and warlike." Gregoras, too, paraphrasing Pachymeres,

4. *Directorium ad faciendum passagium transmarinum*, ed. C. Beazley, in *American Historical Review* 13 (1907–1908), 100–101; also in *Recueil des historiens des croisades. Documents arméniens*, II (Paris, 1906), 490–91, with a fifteenth-century French trans. On the possible authors, see K. Setton, *A History of the Crusades*, vol. 3: *The Fourteenth and Fifteenth Centuries*, ed. H. Hazard (Madison, Wisc., 1975), 52 note 84, 543.

5. Pachymeres, ed. Failler, I, 253, 277, 539 (Bonn ed., I, 188, 209, 423). Gregoras, I, 133ff.

points out the peculiar name of these soldiers: "Joining the [Gasmouloi were] the Lakones, a sea army in arms, coming to the emperor from the Peloponnesos, whom the common spoken language called Tzakones."[6]

The word *tzakon*, the origin of which is still uncertain, was used during the Byzantine era in a number of distinct ways. Of interest to us here are two of these: first, it denoted a wide variety of military or paramilitary professions including light-armed soldiers, fortress guards, palace guards, and paramilitary police; and second, it was used as an ethnic designation for an indigenous inhabitant of Lakonia in the Peloponnesos. In the cited passages from Pachymeres and Gregoras, it is used in both of these senses. Michael VIII's Tzakones, or Lakones, as Pachymeres and Gregoras thought they should properly be called, were those men whom he transplanted from the Morea, at first perhaps only from Monemvasia, later from other parts of the Morea (these being *ethnic* Tzakones), and probably from elsewhere as well to serve as marines, light-armed troops to guard the walls of the city, and, as we learn from other sources, even as a division of palace guards. Although there is no need to think that Michael's Tzakones were exclusively recruited from the population of Lakonia, or even the Morea, Pachymeres clearly thought that the majority of these men had come from the eastern Peloponnesos. Thus, Michael's Tzakones were Tzakones by occupation and, at least to some extent, Tzakones by ethnicity.[7]

The single word denoting two distinct groups of imperial servants has understandably caused some confusion in modern scholarship, and perhaps not a little among the Byzantines themselves. In a letter from the 1280s Patriarch Gregory of Cyprus notes specifically that a group of men were Tzakones by "race" (*genos*). By so qualifying the word Gregory was indicating that he did not mean the occupation of light-armed soldier, but an ethnic label. And yet, if we ask why Peloponnesians should have been in Constantinople in the 1280s, the most likely reason is that they (or their fathers) were among the men recruited by Michael VIII to perform the function implied by the word "Tzakon."[8]

The profession of Tzakon was, at least occasionally, hereditary. The

6. Pachymeres, ed. Failler, I, 401–403 (Bonn ed., I, 309). Gregoras, I, 98. M. Bartusis, "On the Problem," 15–17.

7. S. Caratzas, *Les Tzacones* (Berlin, 1976), 128, 156, who derives the word from *diakon*, "deacon."

8. Gregory II, of Cyprus, in S. Eustratiades, ed., «Τοῦ σοφωτάτου καὶ λογιωτάτου καὶ οἰκουμενικοῦ πατριάρχου κύρου Γρηγορίου τοῦ Κυπρίου Ἐπιστολαί», Ἐκκλησιαστικὸς Φάρος 4 (1909), 128, no. 166. M. Bartusis, "Brigandage in the Late Byzantine Empire," Byz 51 (1981), 396–97.

Tzakones by "race" whom Gregory of Cyprus mentions were probably descendants of the original transplanted Tzakones. This is not surprising since the original Tzakones had received not only pay, but "places [*topoi*] near the City," which were probably rather small and inadequate for substantial farming (since Pachymeres does not employ a word like "land"), but nevertheless provided a home that the emperor could easily have treated as a conditional grant in order to ensure the continued service of the original Tzakones' heirs. Such an imperial policy would ensure a constant supply of resident mercenaries and, further, since conditional possession of however modest a property would deter many mercenaries from leaving their jobs to seek employment elsewhere, it would have put the emperor in an advantageous position when negotiating pay raises.

With the Gasmouloi and the Tzakones providing an adequate supply of marines for his new fleet, Michael now sought rowers. Pachymeres writes that "he outfitted and built a fleet and [as] rowers [*proselontes*] he assigned more than a thousand from the lands." "From the lands" (*ek ton choron*) is Pachymeres' way of saying that the rowers did not come from depopulated Constantinople; indeed much of Michael's efforts were directed toward luring people back into the city. The origin of these new rowers is not difficult to imagine. With the collapse of the Latin Empire, large numbers of peasants found themselves temporarily without a master as their Latin lords fled. Michael certainly had no problem raising an unskilled labor force, especially because of what he was offering in regard to pay: land. "In the order of servants to them [the marines], as if one might say to row ships forward, were the Proselontes ['rowers']; to the good and greatest part [of these] the ruler assigned lands near the shore everywhere."[9] Thus, we should view the word *Prosalentai*—"Proselontes," according to the literary form of the word that Pachymeres preferred—as the formal designation of imperial rowers during the reign of Michael VIII.

A survey of the references to the Prosalentai in the documentary sources shows they were indeed assigned lands near the sea: on Lemnos, where a group of Prosalentai held land for at least some eighty years, from before 1284 to after 1361, indicating that the institution itself was remarkably stable and probably hereditary; on the Kassandreia peninsula of the Chalkidike during the 1330s, where the Prosalentai were clearly not dependent peasants but free landowners, and where their landholdings seem to have been considerable, at least several hundred acres; on the Longos peninsula

9. Pachymeres, ed. Failler, I, 223, 403 (Bonn ed., I, 164, 309).

adjacent to Kassandreia; and in the area east of the mouth of the Strymon. The Prosalentai were given lands near the shores so that they could live near their work and were settled in groups to facilitate their rapid mustering. Some of their settlements were large enough to encompass more than an entire village. They lived on their landholdings and were a legal category of landowners with "rights" comparable to those of churches, monasteries, pronoiars, and other lay landlords. Nevertheless they were rowers, an occupation that was never the source of much status or material reward in the medieval centuries, and their position was not so secure that some of their members could not on occasion descend into the class of dependent peasants.[10]

As free peasants who lived on relatively modest landholdings in specifically designated settlements near the sea, the Prosalentai held their lands on condition of continued service as rowers for the fleet. No doubt regulations developed regarding the frequency with which service could be demanded and the status of holdings that did not provide a man fit to row. But we know nothing of these matters, nor whether such service was organized on a communal or an individual basis, though it is likely that some kind of system was established whereby settlements were obliged jointly to provide a fixed number of rowers.

With the rehabilitation of Constantinople attended to, Michael was ready to undertake his broader goal of restoring the pre-1204 borders of Byzantium. In 1262 he launched a series of major simultaneous expeditions against his enemies toward the west: Michael II Doukas of Epiros, the Latins of the Morea, and the Venetians of the Aegean. In response to the renewed transgressions of Michael Doukas upon Byzantine territory, Michael VIII had sent an army to Macedonia under the general Alexios Strategopoulos, the hero of the hour, fresh from his triumph in retaking Constantinople. However, Strategopoulos returned to lackluster form, his army was defeated, and he himself captured. And so in 1262 and again in 1263 the emperor sent another army there under his brother the despot John. Although the second of these campaigns concluded quite successfully, as soon as John departed Michael II resumed hostilities. Finally, Michael VIII decided to lead an army there himself. In the summer of 1264 he began the march westward at the head of a huge force, but before he had even reached Macedonia the ruler of Epiros evidently sued for peace. With

10. Bartusis, "On the Problem," 17–19.

Michael II suitably chastened, a treaty was concluded and for the next ten years the border with Epiros was secure.[11]

Also in 1262 the protostrator Alexios Philanthropenos took the new Genoese-Byzantine fleet and attacked numerous islands held by the Venetians. Manning this fleet were Michael's new naval troops: "For the Gasmouloi were bold for battle, and while these were assigned for battle, those called Proselontes [that is, Prosalentai] were assigned to the rowing only. In addition, there were the Lakonians whom the ruler had transplanted from the Peloponnesos." It seems that this same year Michael also sent an expedition to Crete to support the local Greeks in their struggle against Venetian rule.[12]

While these campaigns were underway, Michael VIII planned the reconquest of the Morea which had been in Latin hands for over half a century. William II of Achaia, who had been a prisoner ever since the battle of Pelagonia in 1259, finally agreed to cede to Michael a number of towns in the southwestern Morea, including Monemvasia and Mistra, in return for his freedom. Early in 1262, after swearing an oath of loyalty to Michael, William returned to the Morea and, as promised, delivered a few of these towns to the Byzantines. However, he quickly broke his oath (the pope officially released him from it) and began negotiating alliances with Venice and other Western powers. According to the *Chronicle of the Morea*, when the new Byzantine governor of Mistra noted suspicious movements of William's troops around Lakonia, he requested help from the capital. Quickly Michael organized an expedition under his brother the sevastokrator Constantine and the subordinate commanders the parakoimomenos Makrenos and the megas domestikos Alexios Philes.[13]

Transported by Genoese ships, this army, composed of all the Turkish mercenaries and of Greek troops from Magedon in Asia Minor, sailed to Monemvasia. The sevastokrator Constantine conquered the Slavic population of Mount Taigetos, built fortresses, and briefly besieged Sparta. Abandoning this siege he marched to Andravida, the Latin capital. According to the *Chronicle*, Constantine's 15,000 men were surprised along the way by a mere 300 Franks under the bailli of Andravida. The ensuing battle, fought

11. Nicol, *Epiros II*, 8. A. Failler, "Chronologie et composition dans l'histoire de Georges Pachymère," *REB* 39 (1981), 149, 154.

12. Pachymeres, ed. Failler, I, 277, and cf. 271 (Bonn ed., I, 209, 205). Geanakoplos, *Emperor Michael*, 158, 184.

13. Pachymeres, ed. Failler, I, 123–25 (Bonn ed., I, 87–88). Failler, "Chronologie," *REB* 38 (1980), 92.

near Prinitza, was a rout as the Byzantines broke into disorganized flight. Those who escaped the massacre fled to Mistra where the sevastokrator regrouped his forces.[14]

Later, perhaps in the spring of 1263, Constantine renewed hostilities in the Morea, again attempting to take Andravida. He marched to a place called Sergiana and, after a skirmish with William II's forces, withdrew to lay siege to the fortress of Nikli. There the Turks among his forces, complaining that they had not been paid for six months, deserted to William at Andravida. Constantine abandoned the siege and returned to Constantinople, leaving Makrenos and Philes in command. William now took the offensive, and probably in 1263 at a place called Makry Plagi the Byzantine forces suffered a major defeat. The commanders Makrenos and Philes were among the many captured. The Franks pillaged the area of Mistra and Monemvasia and withdrew. After this the war bogged down into a series of indecisive skirmishes.[15]

The presence of these mercenary Turks, who seem to have played a pivotal role in this campaign, and the absence of Latin troops reflected a significant shift in the nature of the foreign troop contingents within the army. Although Michael's reputed love for the soldiery certainly extended to the Latin mercenaries who had helped him to the throne, their importance as a campaign force actually declined during his reign. At the battle of Pelagonia in 1259 it is quite possible that there were no Latins among the Nicaean forces. Latins were sent neither on this Morean campaign nor on a later one in 1276 because, in the words of Pachymeres, it was "agreed the Italikon [that is, the Western Europeans in the army] was not suitable for battle with Italians [that is, any Western Europeans]."[16] The western orientation of Michael's policies made the military services of Cumans and Turks much more useful in these and other campaigns. One wonders too whether the reconquest of Constantinople could have affected the supply of Westerners to the Aegean, and in turn to Byzantium, or whether the Latin mercenaries in Byzantine employ tended to be restricted to imperial guard service with the result that they generally remained in the presence of the emperor. Whatever the reason, the use of Latin soldiers declined considerably during Michael's reign and set a precedent for later emperors. Michael

14. *Chronicle of the Morea*, ed. J. Schmitt (London, 1904), vv. 4706–855. Geanakoplos, *Emperor Michael*, 159.

15. Geanakoplos, *Emperor Michael*, 171–75. Date: Pachymeres, ed. Failler, I, 274 note 2.

16. D. Geanakoplos, "Greco-Latin Relations on the Eve of the Byzantine Restoration: The Battle of Pelagonia, 1259," *DOP* 7 (1953), 124–25 and notes. Pachymeres, ed. Failler, I, 273 (Bonn ed., I, 205).

VIII's successor, Andronikos II, for his part, also preferred Turks and
Cumans for his one major European expedition in 1292, and his later
recruitment of the Western Catalan Company indicates that there might
not have been sufficient Latins on the scene available for mercenary service.

In the period following the Latin Conquest, Turks became a significant element in the Byzantine military only after the accession of Michael
VIII. Without doubt the ranks of the Nicaean armies included some Turks,
but their numbers must have been small because the sources barely even
allude to their existence. Rather it was Michael VIII, probably due to his
experiences while in exile at the Seljuk court at Ikonion (Konya), who
greatly increased the number of Turks participating in Byzantine campaigns. In 1256, fearing persecution for reasons not entirely clear, Michael
fled to the court of Izz al-Din Kayka'us II, the Seljuk sultan of Rum. Until
his return to Nicaea early in 1257, he fought the Mongols for several months
in the sultan's service. It is uncertain whom he commanded. According to
Gregoras, he led Greek subjects of the sultan: "Since there were of old
under him [the sultan] many subject [*dedoulomenoi*] Romans, he ordered
that they be assigned under the general Palaiologos in a division of the
army, clad in their native equipment and arms whether Roman or foreign,
in order to cause the Mongols consternation, who would figure an allied
force from the Romans had just arrived." Pachymeres, however, says Michael came to Ikonion with numerous close associates and he "made battle
with those under imperial standards." Michael himself, in an autobiographical passage from a charter for a monastery he later founded, claims he
commanded "Persians," that is, Turks.[17]

In any event, Greek troops were not strangers to the service of the
Seljuk sultans of Asia Minor. Some were mercenaries, others were allied
troops sent by neighboring sovereigns; some may even have been slaves.
The chronicler Ibn Bibi reports that Greeks of unknown origin as well as
Frankish mercenaries fought at the battle of Köse Dag against the Mongols
in 1243. According to a Western traveler, John Vatatzes in the 1240s kept at

17. Geanakoplos, *Emperor Michael*, 29. Gregoras, I, 58–59. S. Vryonis, *The Decline of Medieval Hellenism in Asia Minor and the Process of Islamization from the Eleventh Through the Fifteenth Century* (Berkeley, Calif., 1971), 234, 468. On the other hand, A. Bombaci, "The Army of the Saljuqs of Rūm," *Istituto orientale di Napoli, Annali*, n.s. 38 (1978), 353–54, 364–65, puts forth the unlikely suggestion that Gregoras' "subject Romans" were actually just Greek slaves dressed up as Byzantine soldiers. Pachymeres, ed. Failler, I, 45. A. Dmitrievskij, *Opisanie liturgičeskih rukopisej . . . Tom I*. Τυπικά (Kiev, 1895), 791. Date: Failler, "Chronologie," *REB* 38 (1980), 17–18. For evidence of Turks, Cumans, and Vlachs in Vatatzes' army, see J. Langdon, "John III Ducas Vatatzes' Byzantine Imperium in Anatolian Exile," diss., Univ. of California (Ann Arbor, Mich.: University Microfilms, 1979), 203 and note 461.

the disposal of the sultan 400 cavalry "lances" (a Western European term with no parallel in Byzantium, designating a cavalry unit composed at this time of a man-at-arms and the one or two squires who accompanied and served him). And Akropolites says that Izz al-Din acquired 400 Byzantine soldiers in 1256 when he visited Sardis and that they helped him retake Ikonion and regain possession of the throne which his brother had usurped.[18]

The identity of the Turks who participated in the Morean expedition of 1262–63 is difficult to discern. According to the *Chronicle of the Morea*, Michael VIII "went to Turkey and hired Turks," 2,000 in number. Yet Pachymeres notes that, along with the other forces, Michael sent "the entire Persikon," that is, all the Turkish troops in the army, which rather implies that there already was an existing Turkish contingent within the army. One would be tempted to dismiss the *Chronicle*'s account but for the passages describing the desertion of the Turks, an event that the Venetian chronicler Sanudo also refers to. The *Chronicle* specifically states that they crossed to the Latin side because they had not been paid for six months and, further, that their original term of service had only been for a year. A fixed employment period would mean that at least some of the Turks on the Morea campaign were supplemental mercenaries hired for this campaign.[19]

The situation is further complicated by the fact that the Seljuk sultan Izz al-Din, his family and retainers were at the Nicaean court in 1260 or early 1261, just prior to Michael's reconquest of Constantinople, having sought refuge from the Mongols. Izz al-Din spent the next few years more or less in semi-captivity while serving as a pawn in Michael's diplomatic maneuvering with the Anatolian Mongols, who strongly desired Izz al-Din's permanent retirement.[20] The sources say very little about any troops the sultan may have had with him. Neither Pachymeres nor Gregoras was impressed by the size of Izz al-Din's retinue, nor do they give any indication that any of the sultan's troops performed any military activities during the

18. Bombaci, "The Army of the Saljuqs," 357, 361, 367. Simon de Saint-Quentin, *Histoire des Tartares*, ed. J. Richard (Paris, 1965), 70. Akropolites, 143–45. Vryonis, *Decline of Medieval Hellenism*, 234 and note 550. Failler, "Chronologie," *REB* 38 (1980), 17.

19. *Chronicle of the Morea*, vv. 4549–55, 5099f., 5722–29. Zakythinos, *Despotat*, II, 133. Geanakoplos, *Emperor Michael*, 157–58, 173. Pachymeres, ed. Failler, I, 273 (Bonn ed., I, 205). V. Laurent, "Une famille turque au service de Byzance: les Mélikès," *BZ* 49 (1956), 361.

20. P. Wittek, "Yazijioghlu 'Ali on the Christian Turks of the Dobruja," *Bulletin of the School of Oriental and African Studies* (London University) 14 (1952), 648. Geanakoplos, *Emperor Michael*, 81, 181. Laurent, "Mélikès," 361. C. Cahen, *Pre-Ottoman Turkey* (New York, 1968), 279. P. Mutafčiev, *Dobrudža, sbornik ot studii* (Sofia, 1947), 189–95. *The Encyclopaedia of Islam*, new ed. (Leiden, 1960ff.), s.v. "Kayka'us." Vryonis, *Decline of Medieval Hellenism*, 466–67.

years he was residing in the Empire.[21] Yet later, after the sultan's flight to the Crimea late in 1264, Gregoras clearly states that Izz al-Din's Turks remained in the Empire, became Christians, and enrolled in the army.[22]

The Turkish chronicle of Yazidjioglu offers a little more information. According to this account, only after Izz al-Din was already in Constantinople did his army arrive. The chronicle states that these troops were used against the enemies of Michael VIII in the West, which could be a reference to the Morean campaign of 1262–63. The chronicle further claims that Michael gave Izz al-Din's Turks the Dobrudja region at the mouth of the Danube and that his Turkish troops settled there, calling to their families still in Asia to join them and in time creating two or three towns of thirty to forty Turkish clans. Though the details differ from Gregoras' account, the chronicle reports that there indeed was widespread conversion among Izz al-Din's Turks. Even if Michael did not cede the Dobrudja to them, he at least directed them there. Certainly it was necessary to settle Izz al-Din's Turks somewhere and to minimize the possibility of internal disturbances by separating them from their leader Izz al-Din. Since they had to be removed from the area of Constantinople, yet could not be expected to return to Asia, it seems reasonable to suppose Michael sent them northward, hoping they would act as a buffer against the Bulgars and the Mongols.[23]

This arrangement, however, was only temporary. Izz al-Din had spent his time in Byzantium plotting with Constantine Tich of Bulgaria and the Crimean Mongols. In 1262 (a busy year for the Byzantine army) Tsar Constantine had invaded Byzantine Thrace and paid for it with the Byzantine occupation of Philippopolis, Stenimachos, and the Black Sea towns of Mesembria and Anchialos. In order to recover these Constantine schemed with Izz al-Din and with Mangu Khan of the Tartars of southern Russia. In the late fall of 1264 Mangu sent a force to Bulgaria. A joint Bulgar-Mongol expedition invaded Thrace up to the vicinity of Constantinople and, after the usual pillaging, freed Izz al-Din from his confinement at the town of Ainos and returned northward.[24]

21. Gregoras, I, 82. Pachymeres, ed. Failler, I, 185 (Bonn ed., I, 132).

22. Gregoras, I, 101, 229, 248. Cf. Pachymeres, ed. Failler, I, 313 (Bonn ed., I, 240). Failler, "Chronologie," *REB* 39 (1981), 173.

23. G. Balaščev, Ὁ αὐτοκράτωρ Μιχαὴλ Η´ ὁ Παλαιολόγος καὶ τὸ ἱδρυθὲν τῇ συνδρομῇ αὐτοῦ κράτος τῶν Ὀγούζων παρὰ τὴν δυτικὴν ἀκτὴν τοῦ Εὐξείνου (Sofia, 1930), 25–26. See *Encyclopaedia of Islam*, s.v. "Gagauz," and Wittek, "Yazijioghlu," 640, 648.

24. Geanakoplos, *Emperor Michael*, 181–82. Wittek, "Yazijioghlu," 656 and note 3. Date: Failler, "Chronologie," *REB* 39 (1981), 153–54.

In the aftermath of this invasion, those Turks who were already or were willing to become Christians remained in the Empire and, as Gregoras reports, entered (or remained in) the army, though subsequent events indicate these were probably a minority. The rest followed Izz al-Din to the Crimea or perhaps remained in the Dobrudja, outside of imperial control. All this means that by 1265, at the latest, there were Christian Turks living inside the Empire who were soldiers. Some of these were imperial guards making up the ranks of the Mourtatoi and possibly the Vardariotai (see Chapter 12), and there is evidence that by the 1280s there were Turks serving as reserve soldiers as well (Appendix, nos. 37–38).

It is testimony to Michael's abilities that he could be warring on three fronts and still deal with unforeseen developments. Aside from the various campaigns in Epiros, the Aegean, and the Morea, the Bulgarian invasion of 1262 was only one of two unexpected crises faced by Michael VIII that year demanding military action. According to Pachymeres, shortly after and as a result of the blinding of John IV Laskaris in December 1261, a popular revolt erupted in the mountainous area called Trikokkia, the frontier region to the west of Nicaea. The peasants inhabiting the area produced a boy who they claimed was John IV and whom they proclaimed as emperor. Michael sent an army against them, but the peasants of Trikokkia were renowned as archers and they succeeded in occupying at least one fortified position, forcing the army to begin a siege. After quite some time, the episode ended through negotiations which divided the rebels. Most, through various threats and promises, were eventually persuaded to lay down their arms; others fled to the Turks.[25]

The inhabitants of Trikokkia, who lived in a mountainous frontier region of the Empire, were among the Anatolian highlanders whom the Nicaean emperors had treated with such solicitude. The position of these highlanders, which had remained relatively stable during the reigns of John III Vatatzes and Theodore II Laskaris and for the first few years of Michael VIII's reign, underwent a radical transformation during the 1260s as they were converted from localized frontier militiamen to campaign troops. At some point after or in the midst of the Trikokkia revolt, Michael sent an official named Chadenos to Asia Minor to initiate a new agrarian program.

25. Pachymeres, ed. Failler, I, 259–67 (Bonn ed., I, 193–201). Migne, *PG*, 140, cols. 948f. H. Ahrweiler, "L'histoire et la géographie de la région de Smyrne entre les deux occupations turques," in Ahrweiler, *Byzance: les pays et les territoires* (London, 1976), no. IV, 9. P. Wittek, *Das Fürstentum Mentesche* (Istanbul, 1934), 16. G. Georgiadis-Arnakis, Οἱ πρῶτοι Ὀθωμανοί (Athens, 1947), 39.

Chadenos' mission represented one aspect of the emperor's attempt to gain firm control over the population of Anatolia whose loyalties laid with the Laskarides. "And as quickly as possible," Pachymeres writes, Chadenos "stopped at the places and found exceedingly rich men, heavy with property and animals, and he imposed military service on them from the things by which the livelihood of each of them was composed. And reckoning out 40 nomismata per one [man], and most of them from the property of each man, he [Chadenos] ordered the rest of the fixed tax, being not a little, to be sent to the imperial treasury."[26]

Despite the tortuous syntax of the text, it seems that Chadenos was actually conducting a fiscal reassessment (an *exisosis*) and that the 40 hyperpyra represented the yearly value (*posotes*) of the standard pronoia assigned to each man. According to this scenario, after a cadastral survey of the tax-exempt holdings of the highlanders, Chadenos redistributed to each land in pronoia with a posotes of 40 hyperpyra, and their tax-exempt status was withdrawn and their military duties were enlarged. In compensation they received a yearly salary (*rogai*) to supplement their pronoiai. The result of Chadenos requiring the highlanders to pay taxes was that, after half a century, they again became part of the monetary economy of the Empire. In effect the intention was to reestablish state control over the frontier regions, particularly important in light of the usurper Michael's lack of popularity in Anatolia. Further, the transformation of the highlanders from patrimonial landowners to pronoiars, together with their receipt of salary, weakened their economic and psychological bond to their local soil and allowed them greater mobility, enabling Michael VIII to use them in his European campaigns.[27]

Of course, there is no real need for pronoia to have been involved here at all. The highlanders had been patrimonial landowners (with tax exemption and some pronoia); after a redistribution and diminution of their property to 40-hyperpyra parcels, they could just as well have remained patrimonial (or allodial) landowners over these reduced, or at least regularized, landholdings (though, perhaps, without tax exemption). The important point is that they henceforth derived their livelihoods not only from any possible pronoiai (or from their adjusted patrimonial holdings), but from imperial cash payments as well. It was this salary, or more accu-

26. Pachymeres, ed. Failler, I, 31–33 (Bonn ed., I, 18).

27. Pachymeres, ed. Failler, I, 317, 403, and esp. 35 (Bonn ed., I, 243–44, 310, 20). Oikonomidès, "A propos des armées," 359–60. H. Glykatzi-Ahrweiler, "La concession des droits incorporels," in Ahrweiler, *Études sur les structures*, no. I, III note 48.

rately, this salary plus a continuing *attachment* to land, that was the key to Michael's policy. The salary the highlanders received became more than the mere supplement it had been; it was now an essential component of their existence.[28] Moreover, a continuing attachment to the land not only maintained the highlanders' stake in the fortunes of the eastern frontier, but more important, it relieved the fisc of the unnecessary expense of financing permanent standing troops, which would have been the case had the highlanders become simple mercenaries. Michael's goal of humbling Asia and creating more soldiers was better served by allowing the highlander some landholding (either original patrimony or pronoia) of sufficiently modest size and burdened with sufficient taxes that it could not adequately support him, thus forcing his dependence on the salary supplied by the state, which in turn burdened him with military duties comprising at least campaign service. In this way, the highlander was still a farmer or landlord, but also a part-time, or reserve, soldier.

The Palaiologan highlander was therefore fundamentally different from his Nicaean predecessor, who was more an independently operating, paramilitary border guard. Under the Laskarides, if a highlander were asked his occupation, he might have answered "farmer" or "herdsmen," but never "soldier." The mercenaries at the emperor's court were soldiers, as were the military pronoiars. But unlike them, the Nicaean highlanders did not regularly—if ever—participate in military enterprises commanded by imperial officers. Although they received tax exemption, stipends, and occasionally pronoiai, they apparently performed no organized military activities directed by Byzantine officials, which is why it is difficult to consider them Byzantine imperial soldiers. Through the changes wrought by Michael VIII, however, they were transformed into soldiers.

According to Pachymeres, the effects of Chadenos' reforms were disastrous. The men's morale was crushed. In the face of Turkish and Mongol attacks, some fled to mountain lairs where they turned to brigandage, forming bands that terrorized the remaining Byzantine population. Others "became sword's work," surrendered to or made separate peace with the Turks. Others retreated to the shrinking Anatolian frontier where they continued to receive a salary, albeit with increasing irregularity, into the 1290s. Indeed one of the reasons for the defections was the chronic lateness of their pay about which "the archons were stingy" and which was "too

---

28. Pachymeres, ed. Failler, I, 33–35 (Bonn ed., I, 19), and Gregoras, I, 138.

little, too late" after "the leaders of the armies took their own share by theft." As a result more and more land fell out of Byzantine control.[29]

Chadenos' program was undertaken for two reasons, one political and one military: to consolidate Michael VIII's personal control over Asia Minor and to raise troops for his western campaigns. Although Pachymeres, writing some forty years after the event, correctly saw the long-term failure of the program, this is perhaps unfair to Michael who, despite territorial losses in Asia Minor, did successfully pacify the Anatolian population and enjoyed remarkable advances in Europe. Reading Pachymeres, one is made to feel that Michael, blinded by infelicitous partisan motives, consciously traded Asia for Europe.[30] This oversimplification explains why Pachymeres' history practically begins with the story of the highlanders. Michael VIII's highlander policy was a brilliant piece of statecraft, but at the same time it possessed the same weakness of all state policies that attempt to solve domestic and military problems simultaneously. Such programs can rarely be optimal solutions to more than one problem, but are only compromises or lowest common denominators.

While Chadenos was enacting his agrarian reform in Asia Minor, the despot John Palaiologos was dispatched there in 1263, immediately after his successful campaign against Michael Doukas in Epiros. While we do not know whether Chadenos' activities were restricted to any one particular area or embraced all of the remaining possessions in Asia Minor, the despot John led his army southward where during 1264 he reconquered the Meander valley, including the city of Tralles (modern Aydin), the Kaistros valley, and the town of Magedon. He remained in the area until 1267 or so, when the emperor recalled him for further military operations in Europe. As long as he was on the scene, the Anatolian frontier was stabilized, but following his departure the southern and southeastern frontier collapsed. The Meander valley was depopulated, the area of Caria to the south was completely lost, and Tralles was destroyed. Once again Pachymeres blames this on Michael VIII's preference for western over eastern affairs.[31]

29. Pachymeres, ed. Failler, I, 31–35, 293 (Bonn ed., I, 18–20, 222–23); Bonn ed., II, 208. Cf. Gregoras, I, 138. Georgiadis-Arnakis, Οἱ πρῶτοι Ὀθωμανοί, 41–42. G. Arnakis, "Byzantium's Anatolian Provinces During the Reign of Michael Palaeologus," *Actes du XIIe Congrès international d'études byzantines* (Belgrade, 1964), II, 40–41. Mutafčiev, "Vojniški zemi," 595. Wittek, *Das Fürstentum Mentesche*, 17 note 1. Nicol, *Last Centuries*, 89.

30. Cf. Georgiadis-Arnakis, Οἱ πρῶτοι Ὀθωμανοί, 40–41.

31. Pachymeres, ed. Failler, I, 289–93, 404 note 1. Nicol, *Last Centuries*, 90–91. Failler, "Chronologie," *REB* 38 (1980), 92.

From Michael's point of view, matters involving the western frontier deserved the most attention. In 1266 Charles of Anjou (1266–85) acquired Sicily after defeating King Manfred at the battle of Benevento. The next year he negotiated the treaty of Viterbo with the pope, William II of Achaia, and the titular Latin emperor of Constantinople Baldwin. One of the purposes of the alliance was to regain Constantinople, and for almost all the remainder of Michael VIII's reign the threat of invasion from the West hung over his head. During the 1270s almost all of Michael's actions were directed toward ensuring that Charles not establish a foothold in the Balkan peninsula.

In 1270 the emperor sent an army composed of Asiatic Greeks, Cumans, and Turks to Monemvasia under a new commander, possibly the protostrator Alexios Philanthropenos. There they faced William II of Achaia. For almost two years the armies of both sides devastated the Morea but no major battles were fought despite, according to the *Chronicle of the Morea*, the superior size of the Byzantine forces. In 1272 Charles of Anjou supplied William with reinforcements, 700 horse and foot, but these had little effect. Neither side risked an encounter because, if we are to believe the *Chronicle*, William was outmanned, and Michael VIII chose not to squander men on defeating William. His aim was merely to weaken William and demonstrate to Charles that the Morea was not the route to the conquest of Byzantium.[32]

When William II died in 1278, the Principality of Achaia fell under the direct control of Charles of Anjou. But since Charles had his hands full elsewhere and in any event already had decided against an invasion via southern Greece, this actually benefited Byzantine plans for expansion in the Morea. Imperial troops waged almost constant warfare against the baillis of Achaia and gradually drew more and more territory under Byzantine control. Even though the major part of the Peloponnesos was still in Latin hands at Michael VIII's death, the momentum was clearly with the Greeks.[33]

The fleet that had brought the Byzantine army to Monemvasia was no longer a joint Genoese-Byzantine product. Michael VIII's alliance with this Italian city-state had proved to be a disappointment. Since the Genoese captains were naturally reticent to commit their ships and crews to combat, Michael from the start felt he was not getting his money's worth (since he

32. *Chronicle of the Morea*, vv. 6487–90. Geanakoplos, *Emperor Michael*, 229–30.
33. Geanakoplos, *Emperor Michael*, 325–26.

was paying their salaries). Matters came to a head in 1263, when at the battle of Settepozzi (Spetsai), off the coast of the Peloponnesos, a smaller Venetian fleet defeated the allied Genoese fleet. Toward the end of that year Michael decided to dismiss the Genoese because he felt that his own reconstituted Byzantine fleet and other less expensive ways of acquiring naval power were adequate for the matters at hand. However, the treaty of Viterbo convinced him that even if he did not need the Genoese fleet, he needed their friendship. In 1267 a new agreement was reached with the Genoese settling them in Galata across the Golden Horn from Constantinople. The next year, covering all his bases, he concluded a treaty with the Venetians who had been no less disquieted by the treaty of Viterbo.

In 1270 the first occasion arose to demonstrate that the Empire did not need the material support of Italian city-states to wage sea battles. A purely Byzantine fleet proved its worth by laying siege to the town of Oreos on Negroponte. Twenty-four galleys succeeded in defeating the Latin fleet of twenty galleys and capturing some 500 troops.[34]

Events such as this made Michael begin to think and act like a real imperial power. Pachymeres illustrates this with two examples, both involving soldiers as well as the Genoese. In one instance a member of the Prosalentai struck a Genoese of Galata after the latter taunted him with the declaration that Constantinople would soon be Latin again. The Genoese drew his sword and slew the man. Incensed that one of his rowers should be so treated, the emperor called on the army from inside and outside the city to expel the Genoese from Constantinople. The Genoese authorities pleaded with the emperor who relented only after they agreed to pay a hefty indemnity. In another incident, around the spring of 1276, some Genoese from Genoa (not Galata), evidently pirates, sailed their two galleys past the Blachernai palace without making the proper salute mandated by the treaty of Nymphaion. Then in the Black Sea they seized a Genoese ship from Phokaia laden with alum, another affront because the emperor had granted the Zaccaria brothers of Phokaia exclusive right to export alum from the Black Sea. On their return they repeated the insult of refusing the salute. Michael sent a fleet in pursuit manned by Gasmouloi and led by the vestiarios Alexios Alyattes. They overtook these Genoese and blinded them according to custom.[35]

---

34. Failler, "Chronologie," *REB* 39 (1981), 195–99. Geanakoplos, *Emperor Michael*, 235–36.

35. Pachymeres, ed. Failler, I, 535–43. Geanakoplos, *Emperor Michael*, 250–52.

On the whole, however, Michael had nothing against pirates if they could serve his ends. The Aegean was teeming with Latin corsairs during the thirteenth century, and Michael often employed them against the Venetians and other Latin rulers in the area. This, no less than his own navy, gave him his sense of independence on the seas. For example, around 1278, the Genoese privateer Giovanni de lo Cavo received dominion over the islands of Rhodes and Anaphi for services rendered to Byzantium, the Venetian chronicler Sanudo even speaking of him as Michael VIII's "admiral."[36]

Particularly noteworthy were the exploits of the adventurer Licario, a Veronese of humble origin, who undertook a personal rebellion against the Latin lords of Negroponte (Euboea). After seizing a castle on the island around 1273 or perhaps earlier, he requested entry into imperial service, met Michael VIII, and was promised aid in defending his fortress. In return Licario became a Western-style vassal of the emperor, an application of an appropriated Western feudal concept. Such a bond, foreign to the Byzantine tradition, was nevertheless understandable to a man like Licario.

The chronology of Licario's career is still uncertain, but during the 1270s, with his own Latin troops and infantry supplied by Michael, he conquered most of Negroponte except for its capital, as well as a swarm of Aegean islands. As a reward the emperor granted him Negroponte as a fief, the titles megas konostaulos and later megas doux, plus a Byzantine wife and a handsome dowry. In return he agreed to provide the emperor with 200 men. Licario's conquests were ephemeral—most of the islands were retaken by the Latins within twenty years—but such dazzling exploits could not help but increase the prestige of Licario's patron, Michael VIII.[37]

During the 1270s the Byzantines seemed to have had more success at sea than on land. The governor of Adrianople, the megas konostaulos Andronikos Tarchaneiotes, in the wake of a Mongol invasion that he himself had provoked, fled to the court of John I Doukas (the Bastard) of Thessaly, where he goaded the latter into opening hostilities with Byzantium. In 1273 Michael sent an army to Thessaly under the joint command of the despot John Palaiologos and Alexios Kavallarios consisting, according to the Venetian Sanudo, of 30,000 cavalry. Of all the campaigns from the

36. Geanakoplos, *Emperor Michael*, 211. Also, see P. Charanis, "Piracy in the Aegean During the Reign of Michael VIII Palaeologus," in Charanis, *Social, Economic and Political Life in the Byzantine Empire* (London, 1973), no. XII, 127–36; and I. Katele, "Piracy and the Venetian State: The Dilemma of Maritime Defense in the Fourteenth Century," *Speculum* 63 (1988), 865–89.

37. Pachymeres, ed. Failler, I, 525. Geanakoplos, *Emperor Michael*, 235–37, 295–99. *PLP*, no. 8154.

1270s through the 1290s, for this one alone do any of the Byzantine historians provide details regarding the composition of the expeditionary forces. Gregoras writes that Despot John "gathered whatever forces happened to be present, mustered from the Paphlagonian and Bithynian cavalries, including the tagmata of the Cumans and the Tourkopouloi, and departed enlisting the infantry forces from Thrace and Macedonia." Further, a fleet of some seventy-three ships manned at least in part by Tzakones and Gasmouloi and under the command of the protostrator Alexios Philanthropenos was ordered to attack Latin shipping off Greece.[38]

The army marched into southern Thessaly and besieged John I in his capital fortress of Neopatras. Somehow he engineered his escape and made a quick alliance with John de la Roche, ruler of Athens and Thebes, from whom he was lent 300 knights.[39] That this small contingent made a big difference in the outcome of events calls into question all the figures the sources provide for this campaign. John I returned to Neopatras and launched a surprise attack against the Byzantine troops. Disobeying their commanders, the besieging army dispersed, and then the Latin lords of the Aegean sent a naval force to attack the Byzantine fleet anchored off Demetrias. While the Latins had perhaps only half as many ships, they put up a strong fight and might have won had the despot John not ridden the forty miles from Neopatras in one night and appeared with reinforcements. In the end all but two of the Latin ships were either destroyed or captured.[40]

Gregoras' designation of the Turks who fought in this campaign as "Tourkopouloi" is interesting. The Tourkopouloi were Christianized Turks or, more narrowly, the Christian offspring of a Christian mother and a Turkish father. A byproduct of Christian-Turkish contacts, they almost always appear in a military context. Although there were many people who could be defined as Tourkopouloi from the eleventh century on, the term itself is rather uncommon.[41] Tourkopouloi served as light cavalry in various Latin crusader states from the twelfth through the fifteenth century, and

38. Gregoras, I, 111, 117. Geanakoplos, *Emperor Michael*, 279–80, 282–85. Pachymeres, ed. Failler, I, 421 (Bonn ed., I, 324): 40,000 troops including the naval forces. Failler, "Chronologie," *REB* 39 (1981), 192, 202. Nicol, *Epiros II*, 19.

39. Pachymeres, ed. Failler, I, 423–25. Gregoras, I, 114: 500 cavalry.

40. Pachymeres, ed. Failler, I, 421 (Bonn ed., I, 324): 73 ships vs. 30 Latin ships. Sanudo, *Istoria del regno di Romania*, ed. C. Hopf in *Chroniques gréco-romanes* (Berlin, 1873), 121: 80 galleys vs. 12 Latin galleys and 50 lesser ships. Gregoras, I, 117: 50 ships vs. 30 Latin ships. Geanakoplos, *Emperor Michael*, 283–85.

41. A. Hohlweg, *Beiträge zur Verwaltungsgeschichte des oströmischen Reiches unter den Komnenen* (Munich, 1965), 67–69. Vryonis, *Decline of Medieval Hellenism*, 229 note 510. Raymond d'Aguilers, *Historia Francorum qui ceperunt Iherusalem*, ed. and trans. J. Hill (Philadelphia, 1968), 37. On the word itself, see K. Amantos in Έλληνικά 6 (1933), 325–26.

some Tourkopouloi cavalry were fighting for Geoffrey de Villehardouin in 1206 in Thrace and Macedonia. In Byzantine sources Pachymeres and Gregoras are the only major historians from any period to use the word.[42]

Since Gregoras claims that at least some of Izz al-Din's Turks remained in Byzantium after the sultan's flight in 1264 and became Christians, it would seem that he uses the word *Tourkopoulos* to distinguish these and their descendants from non-Christian Turks. The Turks found within the army in the various other campaigns during this period (1270–72 in the Morea, 1281 in Albania, and 1292 in Epiros) can probably be identified similarly. Given the context of Gregoras' passage, and since neither Pachymeres nor Gregoras, nor any other source, mentions the enlistment of foreign Turks at the time, the "Tourkopouloi" of the Thessalian campaign, who Pachymeres reports were lead by Nikephoros Rimpsas, a Christianized Turk who probably had led the Turkish troops under John Palaiologos at Pelagonia, were unquestionably inhabitants of the Empire, and probably cavalry, though it is not clear whether they were reserve troops (such as pronoiars) or standing mercenaries. In the early fourteenth century, as we shall see, Tourkopouloi played a major role during the Catalan episode. The few that remained in Byzantine service afterward were either assimilated or else completely overshadowed by the Turkish forces called in from Asia Minor to fight in the Byzantine civil wars.[43]

Having dealt with Charles of Anjou's ally in the Morea as well as with an unexpected disturbance in Thessaly, Michael now directed his attention to Charles himself. After gaining a foothold in the Balkans by seizing Dyrrachion, Charles initiated a course of territorial expansion in Albania, and the local Albanian population declared him their king in 1272. Naturally regarding this as a most serious threat, Michael VIII ordered his forces in 1274 to occupy Butrinto and Berat, and the defending Angevin forces were thrown back to Dyrrachion and Avlon. Byzantine troops now joined by

---

42. R. Smail, *Crusading Warfare (1097–1193)* (Cambridge, Eng., 1956; repr. 1967), 111–12, 179–80, 184. H. Mayer, *The Crusades* (Oxford, 1972), 164. J. Riley-Smith, *The Feudal Nobility and the Kingdom of Jerusalem, 1174–1277* (London, 1973), 5, 243. The *Chronicle* of Leontios Makhairas: passages cited in G. Moravcsik, *Byzantinoturcica*, 2nd ed. (Berlin, 1958), II, 327–28, with other references. Villehardouin, *La conquête de Constantinople*, ed. E. Faral (Paris, 1938–39), ch. 316, 322; English trans. M. Shaw in *Joinville and Villehardouin, Chronicles of the Crusades* (Baltimore, 1963), 143.

43. Pachymeres, ed. Failler, I, 425 (Bonn ed., I, 329). Angold, *Byzantine Government*, 189. Akropolites, 170–71. Wittek, "Yazijioghlu," 650, 661–62, but cf. Laurent, "Mélikès," 366 note 5. A "George Tourkopoulos" witnessed an act in 1365: G. Ferrari dalle Spade, "Registro Vaticano di atti bizantini di diritto privato," *Studi Bizantini e Neoellenici* 4 (1935), 265, no. XI; and a fifteenth-century paroikos may have borne this name: P. Lemerle et al., *Actes de Lavra* (Paris, 1970–82), III, no. 161, lines 29–30.

sympathetic Albanians laid siege to Dyrrachion. Hostilities continued for the next couple of years, but for the moment Charles' advance had been checked.[44]

By 1276 Nikephoros I of Epiros (1267/8–96), Michael II Doukas' son and successor, and John Doukas of Thessaly had entered into diplomatic relations with Charles of Anjou. After wrapping up a brief war with Bulgaria, Michael VIII sent another army to Thessaly under the megas stratopedarches John Synadenos and the megas konostaulos Michael Kavallarios. On the plain of Pharsala, perhaps in 1277, the imperial army was defeated, Synadenos captured, and Kavallarios mortally wounded. Nikephoros I and John Doukas now intensified their opposition to the Union of Lyons which in 1274 formally united the Byzantine and Western Churches. In early 1278 Michael sent another army to Thessaly to quiet them, but some of Michael's generals, hostile to the Union themselves, defected to the enemy. Nevertheless the imperial forces prevailed and the deserters were returned to Constantinople in chains.[45]

Throughout these years Charles of Anjou had not been idle. By 1280 he had prepared a large army for a campaign in Albania. Some 2,000 Angevin knights and Saracen archers with 6,000 infantry, under the command of the Burgundian knight Hugo le Rousseau de Sully, moved across Albania seizing Kanina and besieging Berat. The Byzantine governor called for help and Michael responded with an army, including Turks, under the megas domestikos Michael Tarchaneiotes with, as subordinates, the emperor's son-in-law Demetrios-Michael Angelos (brother of Nikephoros I), the megas stratopedarches John Synadenos, and the tatas of the court the eunuch Andronikos Eonopolites. The army approached Berat probably in March 1281. Its orders were to avoid open battle and to focus on ambushes and raids. But after a few minor skirmishes the Latin commander Sully was captured while out surveying the field. The Angevin troops took flight and most of them, their supplies and their generals fell into Byzantine hands, as did Kanina and Dyrrachion.[46]

The failure of this expedition convinced Charles of Anjou that an invasion of Byzantium by land was not feasible. He assembled a huge new army and quickly arranged a new alliance with the Venetians. In March 1282, just as this army was about to depart for Constantinople on a Venetian fleet, a rebellion broke out in Palermo known as the Sicilian Vespers. The

---

44. Geanakoplos, *Emperor Michael*, 279–80.

45. Pachymeres, ed. Failler, I, 526 note 2. Geanakoplos, *Emperor Michael*, 309.

46. Sanudo, *Istoria*, 129. Geanakoplos, *Emperor Michael*, 329–34. Nicol, *Epiros II*, 25–26.

Angevin governors were expelled from Sicily and the population declared for Peter of Aragon. Through his financial and diplomatic support of the dissidents, Michael played a significant role in shaping the nature and course of the rebellion, the crowning achievement in the long career of a master diplomat. Now forced to concentrate on domestic affairs, Charles abandoned the eastern expedition and the threat to Byzantium dissolved.[47]

Meanwhile in Asia Minor the situation had deteriorated to such an extent that Michael VIII was compelled to undertake personally a number of expeditions there. In 1280 he visited northern Asia Minor to secure the Sangarios front, while his son Andronikos II headed to the Meander valley where he rebuilt the city of Tralles. This did much to raise the spirits of the local population, but nevertheless it fell to the Turks, permanently, almost as soon as he left. The next year Michael returned to Asia. Without fighting any pitched battles, he built and restored several forts along the Sangarios River and planted forests to impede enemy advances. Finally, he briefly returned to the same area in 1282. Since most of his military forces were engaged elsewhere, the purpose of these expeditions was more to show the flag and strengthen the remaining Byzantine positions than to attempt a reconquest.[48]

In 1282 John I Doukas of Thessaly formally joined the Angevin camp and attacked Macedonia. Michael sought help from his son-in-law Nogai, khan of the Golden Horde, who controlled the area north of Bulgaria. In November 1282 Michael organized an army and planned to lead a campaign himself against Thessaly, but he died in December after receiving Nogai's 4,000 troops in Constantinople. Andronikos II sent these allied Mongols to Serbia under the command of the general Michael Glabas in order to fight King Milutin, who at the time was directing a guerrilla war against Byzantine Macedonia. There they did little but collect booty before departing the Empire.[49]

During the reign of Michael VIII a degree of stability had come to the military and administrative organization of the European provinces. When discussing the provincial armies there, Byzantine historians of the Palaiologan period rarely make any distinction more specific than "Thrace" and "Macedonia." Thus, we read of the "Thracians" and "Macedonians," the "Thracian and Macedonian armies," the "army" or "forces from Thrace and Macedonia," or in one interesting passage, "the military settled in the

47. S. Runciman, *The Sicilian Vespers* (Cambridge, 1958). Geanakoplos, *Emperor Michael*, 335–67.

48. Failler, "Chronologie," *REB* 39 (1981), 242–48. Laiou, *Constantinople*, 23–25.

49. Laiou, *Constantinople*, 28, 30.

Thracian villages." For these historians, the border between the two areas was the Nestos River or Kavalla (Christoupolis). To the west was Macedonia, to the east was Thrace.[50]

The documentary sources, however, show that for administrative and fiscal purposes the western provinces were divided into smaller administrative units based on geography which, following traditional practice, were still called "themes." For the Palaiologan period, documents note the existence of the themes of Thessaloniki, of Serres and the Strymon, of Boleron and Mosynopolis (the coastal area between the Nestos and Marica rivers), and at least for a time, of Verria (Berroia).[51] Other provincial administrative units existed that were on the scale of these themes, but since there is little documentation for these areas, we do not know their official names. Nevertheless, narrative and other sources allow us to locate them. There was what Kantakouzenos calls the "*eparchia* of the Rhodope," which comprised the towns of the upper Marica between and including the fortresses of Stenimachos and Tzepaina. Adjacent to this region and further down the Marica was a string of fortresses called Achridos or the Morrha. Continuing along the Marica one encountered the region of Adrianople and Didymoteichon, two towns naturally drawn together by geography but, as a result of the Palaiologan civil wars, were usually two distinct provincial units. To the east, between the regions of Adrianople, Didymoteichon, and the suburbs of Constantinople, was the Thracian plain, another provincial unit extending northward to the Black Sea cities. Lastly, aside from the Constantinopolitan administrative unit, there may have been another provincial unit embracing the southern Thracian littoral.[52]

Of course, from the mid-thirteenth through the mid-fifteenth century none of these territories was under continuous Byzantine rule. Moreover, the needs of the moment frequently led to the merging of one provincial unit with one adjacent to it or the temporary redefinition of the vague borders delimiting a particular unit. And even the term "theme" most likely was not applied to every one of the provincial units noted.[53] In the late Byzantine period there was a tendency to extemporize, and this must always be borne in mind as we seek the structural norms for institutions.

During the Nicaean period the army in Asia Minor underwent a

50. Pachymeres, ed. Failler, I, 403 (Bonn ed., I, 310); Bonn ed., II, 549. Gregoras, I, 111, 229–30, 353–54. Kantakouzenos, I, 101, 326; II, 253–54.
51. See Lj. Maksimović, *The Byzantine Provincial Administration Under the Palaiologoi* (Amsterdam, 1988), 43–61, 88–102.
52. Ibid., 38–70. Kantakouzenos, I, 135, 146; II, 161, 406. C. Asdracha, *La région des Rhodopes aux XIIIe et XIVe siècles* (Athens, 1976), 244–45, 257–60.
53. See Maksimović, *Byzantine Provincial Administration*, 43–61, 88–102.

significant transformation. At first the central army was primarily still a mercenary army, though certainly with a significant pronoiar presence. It functioned as a highly mobile force and formed the basis of any expeditionary army. The provincial armies, in their themes, handled localized defensive responsibilities. Perhaps these local armies were small, but through their attachment to the land they were more highly motivated than mere mercenaries. Through the efforts of John Vatatzes, Theodore II, and Michael VIII, all this changed. By the 1250s and 1260s the troops of the central army were a more even mix of mercenaries and pronoiars. Some still formed the heart of the expeditionary forces, but others were permanently assigned to garrison duty on the European frontiers. Provincial Anatolian troops were increasingly ordered on European campaigns and the indications are, at least in the case of the highlanders, that Michael VIII was trying to lessen their ties to the land by forcing them to rely on a remuneration in gold. When these developments are coupled with the fact that as the European reconquest was being consolidated, the Anatolian provinces began their disintegration, soon to be followed by a migration of population to Europe, it is not surprising that Palaiologan military administration differed substantially from that of the Nicaean period.

After the reign of Michael VIII the sources say very little of troops drawn from Anatolia, except that both highlanders and pronoiars were fleeing to the west. Many of these were resettled in Europe. Nevertheless, Anatolian troops are occasionally encountered in later years. For two of Andronikos II's campaigns in 1302, the forces were drawn from both native Anatolian troops and troops from Europe, and even as late as 1328 Kantakouzenos speaks of some troops mustered for a European campaign who were "of the cities subject to the Romans in the east," although here he is referring merely to the few remaining possessions in Bithynia.[54]

---

54. Pachymeres, Bonn ed., II, 310–11, 333. Kantakouzenos, I, 326.

3. The Reign of Andronikos II Palaiologos (1282–1328)

At his father's death Andronikos II inherited not only the Empire but Michael VIII's military policies, and to the best of his ability he tried to continue them. However, the day of reckoning had come for Michael VIII's grand ambitions that had drained the Empire of its resources, and Andronikos, at the head of an Empire surrounded on all sides by hostile neighbors, found he lacked the means to do much more than tread water. The financial situation was very grave. In 1285 Andronikos was forced to accept his advisors' counsel to reduce the size of Michael's fleet. To finance his varied military enterprises special taxes were levied and the coinage was debased. In the battlefield, Turkish advances in Asia could not be checked. Attempts to improve the situation through administrative reforms and improving morale failed. While it is true that during his reign the affairs on the Empire's western frontiers were stabilized, and in northern Greece and in the Morea there were even some small advances, this was thoroughly overshadowed by the loss of Asia Minor, where Andronikos applied so much effort to no avail, and by the disastrous experience with the Catalan mercenaries. It was as clear to contemporaries as it is to us today that under Andronikos II the Empire, which had been on the offensive since the reign of John Vatatzes, had entered a period of retrenchment, a period from which it would never really emerge.

For the first decade of his reign Andronikos played out his father's hand in Thessaly, the Aegean, Epiros, and the Morea. In 1283 he launched an expedition against Thessaly which had been planned by Michael VIII. The army was financed through a ten-percent tax on the revenues of pronoiars, and it would be levied frequently thereafter. In theory the receipts were to come from the landlords, but in practice it was yet another burden on their paroikoi. The large army so raised, under the command of Andronikos' first

---

For the general history of Andronikos II's reign, with bibliography, see Laiou, *Constantinople*; Nicol, *Last Centuries*, 97–156; and Ostrogorsky, *History*, 466–98.

cousin, the protovestiarios Michael Tarchaneiotes, marched to the town of Demetrias, then held by Michael, the son of John I Doukas. There it was met by a fleet of eighty ships under Tarchaneiotes' brother-in-law Alexios Raoul and the megas stratopedarches Synadenos. While the town fell, an epidemic which broke out during the siege precluded further operations and forced a Byzantine retreat. The first campaign of Andronikos' rule ended ominously in failure.[1]

In 1285 Andronikos brought to a close a war with the Venetians that had begun under Michael VIII in 1281. The new peaceful relations with the city-state were cited by those in the imperial government who maintained that since the imperial budget had to be cut, the truce with the Venetians obviated the need for so many ships and so many sailors, marines, and rowers. Faced with increasing financial burdens, Andronikos decided to take the advice of his counselors and reduce the size of his father's fleet. The effect of this new policy on the Gasmouloi, the Tzakones, and the Prosalentai varied. Least affected by the decision were the Prosalentai since they did not rely on cash payments, but were compensated for their rowing services through the lands they held from the emperor. As late as 1296 they were still carrying out their duties in Constantinople, and the documentary sources show that the Prosalentai existed as an institution well into the second half of the fourteenth century. Even though Kantakouzenos and Gregoras do not mention the Prosalentai by name, this probably means little except that these fourteenth-century historians were showing their usual disdain for the technical nomenclature of the day. Where rowers are encountered in later sources, we are most likely still dealing with the heirs of the Prosalentai created by Michael VIII.[2]

With the exception of Pseudo-Kodinos' brief discussion of the Tzakones in their role as a palace guard (see Chapter 12), all mention of Tzakones in the area of Constantinople ends after the 1280s. Even though, like the Prosalentai, they received at least some land for their services, the fact that they also received a cash salary meant that they were undoubtedly among those discharged following the reduction in the fleet. A letter of the patriarch of Constantinople Gregory of Cyprus from around 1285–86 speaks of the impoverishment of "Dorians and Peloponnesians" settled at

1. Laiou, *Constantinople*, 38–39. Nicol, *Epiros II*, 31.
2. Pachymeres, Bonn ed., II, 237–38, 240. See also the comments of K.-P. Matschke, "Johannes Kantakouzenos, Alexios Apokaukos und die byzantinische Flotte in der Burger-kriegsperiode, 1340–1355," *Actes du XIVe Congrès international des études byzantines*, II (Bucharest, 1975), 204 note 52.

Herakleia in Thrace. Whatever number of marine Tzakones survived in their occupation after 1285, their absence from the sources suggests that they probably lost their distinctive ethnic character with the passage of time and were consequently incorporated within the Gasmouloi.[3]

Of all the naval forces, those most seriously affected were the Gasmouloi. Since there is no evidence that the Gasmouloi received any land as part of the remuneration for their services, Andronikos II's decision in 1285 decimated their ranks. Out of work, many went over to the Turks and "some deserted to the employ of the Latins." By 1300 some Gasmouloi were found in Venetian service on Crete. "Others became hirelings to those renowned Romans distinguished by wealth, others gave up their arms and turned to farming."[4] Yet not all of the Gasmouloi were disbanded in 1285. Some continued to serve in the fleet. In a letter of Marco Minoto, the Venetian bailli of Constantinople, from March 1320, we read that "in Constantinople, Venetians, both Christians and Jews, are being despoiled by Gasmouloi, Greeks, and officials of the emperor." These Gasmouloi seem to have played a significant political role during the civil wars of the 1340s. Later one finds the "Gasmouloi of Gallipoli" in the service of the Ottoman sultans.[5]

In the fifteenth century there is evidence of peasants (*paroikoi*) performing Gasmouloi service and of a change in the remuneration of this service. Although thirteenth-century Gasmouloi were mercenaries, at least one fifteenth-century paroikos and family received a mitigation of his taxes for what is called "service as a Gasmoulos" (*gasmoulike douleia*). On the other hand, another fifteenth-century document speaks of a tax called the "finding of Gasmouloi" (*euresis basmoulon*), which might indicate that Gasmouloi were still hired soldiers. It seems that, perhaps as early as the fourteenth century, service as a Gasmoulos lost its distinctive ethnic basis

3. Gregory II, in S. Eustratiades, ed., «Τοῦ σοφωτάτου καὶ λογιωτάτου καὶ οἰκουμενικοῦ πατριάρχου κύρου Γρηγορίου τοῦ Κυπρίου Ἐπιστολαί», Ἐκκλησιαστικὸς Φάρος 4 (1909), 105–106, no. 149. M. Bartusis, "On the Problem of Smallholding Soldiers in Late Byzantium," *DOP* 44 (1990), 17.

4. Pachymeres, Bonn ed., II, 70–71. Gregoras, I, 175. Laiou, *Constantinople*, 64, 75–76. S. Carbone, ed., *Pietro Pizolo, notario in Candia*, vol. 1: *1300* (Venice, 1978), 8, no. 4.

5. G. Thomas, *Diplomatarium Veneto-Levantinum* (Venice, 1880–99), I, 165, cited and trans. by S. Bowman, *The Jews of Byzantium, 1204–1453* (University, Ala., 1985), 247–48, doc. no. 41. Matschke, "Johannes Kantakuzenos, Alexios Apokaukos und die byzantinische Flotte," 193–205. H. Ahrweiler, *Byzance et la mer* (Paris, 1966), 384, 405. Gregoras, II, 736–40. Kantakuzenos, II, 575. Doukas, 181, 225, and also 233. H. Antoniadis-Bibicou, *Études d'histoire maritime de Byzance* (Paris, 1966), 35. Cf. D. Jacoby, "Les Vénitiens naturalisés dans l'empire byzantin," in Jacoby, *Studies on the Crusader States and on Venetian Expansion* (London, 1989), no. IX, 223.

and was no longer restricted to marine duties, but included service as light-armed soldiers in the army as well. In the fifteenth and sixteenth centuries on the Venetian-held isle of Naxos, service as a Gasmoulos (*servitio et tenimento vasmulia*) was considered hereditary and included duties on land as well as at sea (*in mare come in terra*).[6]

The reduction in the size of the fleet forced Byzantium once again to depend on the Genoese for naval support. A Genoese fleet participated in Andronikos' next major campaign, an expedition against Epiros in 1292. Nikephoros I Doukas had been silent since the Sicilian Vespers incident had quashed Angevin plans to conquer the Empire, but in 1291 Charles of Anjou's son, Charles II, concluded an alliance between his kingdom of Naples and the Despotate of Epiros, reawakening Byzantine fears. According to the *Chronicle of the Morea*, the only source for the campaign, a Byzantine force of 30,000 infantry and 14,000 cavalry (figures very difficult to believe), mainly Turks and Cumans, laid siege to Ioannina in 1292. Meanwhile, a fleet of some forty or sixty Genoese ships with Byzantine soldiers anchored near Arta, the capital of the Despotate. After some initial successes, the army withdrew at news of the approach of Florent of Hainault, prince of Achaia, who had come north to help Nikephoros with some 400 or 500 men. The retreat was disorganized, and Florent pursued the Byzantines to southern Macedonia. The fleet at Arta retreated as well after some inconsequential plundering. And so this campaign also ended with its objectives unfulfilled.[7]

But it was in the Morea that the Byzantines were able not only to maintain the status quo but to continue Michael VIII's policy of reconquest. We know very little about the course of military events in the Morea during Andronikos' reign. The area was isolated from the capital and from the major historians of the period, who lived in Constantinople. The central government seems to have had little dealings with the Morea other than appointing its governors (kephalai). The meager information provided by Western sources, including the *Chronicle of the Morea*, speaks of truces alternating with periods of war between the Byzantines and the Latins and implies that over the decades Byzantine territorial holdings were gradually enlarged. Evidently, there was a major offensive under Androni-

6. N. Oikonomidès, *Actes de Docheiariou* (Paris, 1984), no. 60, lines 77–78. Arkadios Vatopedinos, «Ἁγιορειτικὰ ἀνάλεκτα ἐκ τοῦ ἀρχείου τῆς μονῆς Βατοπεδίου», *Γρηγόριος ὁ Παλαμᾶς* 3 (1919), 335, no. 34. P. Zerlentis in *BZ* 13 (1904), 144 (1433), 154 (1524), 156 (1534), and commentary, 139–41.

7. *Chronicle of the Morea*, ed. J. Schmitt (London, 1904), vv. 8791–93, 9086. Nicol, *Epiros II*, 38–43. Laiou, *Constantinople*, 40–41. Nicol, *Last Centuries*, 123.

kos II's nephew Andronikos Palaiologos Asen. Asen was the son of John Asen III of Bulgaria and he held the post of governor of the Byzantine Morea from 1316 or perhaps a bit earlier, until 1321 when he was recalled to Constantinople at the beginning of the civil war between Andronikos II and his grandson. A chronicle entry from 1320 speaks of one of his victories and claims that "the Morean army" (*to Moraïtikon phousato*) was composed of 36,000 men, an impossibly high figure. Although Asen seems to have been a rather successful military leader, since Byzantine possessions in the Morea increased during his tenure of office, we know next to nothing about the army he or any other governor commanded. Since there is no mention of the transport of troops to the Morea after the protostrator Alexios Philanthropenos' last naval expedition in 1276, an indigenous army must have been organized, at least partially composed of the Melingoi and Tzakonians inhabiting the mountains around Mistra and recruited by Michael in 1262 in return for special privileges. But what other soldiers were in this army and how they were raised and organized is unknown.[8]

Numerous scholars have asserted that Andronikos II introduced an administrative reform in 1308 by abolishing the one-year limit on the term of the Byzantine governor of the Morea, which had been in effect since the 1260s. It has been argued that this policy was motivated originally by the need to keep close rein on the Morean governors but, as time passed, the need for continuity of policy and greater independence of action induced Andronikos to adopt this reform. Such a change of policy would underscore the increasing administrative isolation of the Morea which might well have led to an evolution of military organization different from that of the rest of the Empire. The evidence for this reform is quite indirect and consists of two brief passages. The first is from the *Chronicle of the Morea*, and it is the sole evidence that there ever was a one-year-term policy. We read that in September 1289, when Florent of Hainault became prince of Achaia, he immediately sent messengers to the Byzantine governor of the Morea to sue for peace. The governor at the time explained to his envoys, however, that "his captaincy and his office would not last longer than a year since the emperor did not let any of his captains go a year without changing them." Consequently, if the prince "wanted to make the peace for as long as he [the governor] was in office, he [the governor] would make it as strong and as good as he could devise. But if he [Florent] wanted to make it for a

---

8. Laiou, *Constantinople*, 39–40, 253–56. *PLP*, no. 1489. P. Schreiner, *Die byzantinischen Kleinchroniken* (Vienna, 1975–79), I, 242. Zakythinos, *Despotat*, II, 134. *Chronicle of the Morea*, v. 4567. *Regesten*, no. 1907.

longer period, he should arrange to make it with the emperor." In the end Florent opted for the latter course and received a chrysobull directly from Andronikos II.[9]

The second piece of evidence is a remark found in John Kantakouzenos' memoirs. Recounting a conversation between the author and Andronikos II, Kantakouzenos pointed out to the emperor that his father had been appointed governor of the Morea at the age of twenty-one and that he had died in office eight years later. Since Kantakouzenos was born around 1295, this passage would suggest that his father's tenure in office was as early as ca.1286 to ca.1294 (if his son was born after his death, which may well have been the case) or as late as from ca.1298 to ca.1306 (if the older Kantakouzenos fathered his son at the age of 18). The *Chronicle* claims that the one-year policy was still in effect in 1289, however, so Kantakouzenos the elder could not have been appointed governor any earlier than 1288. This date is based on the possibility that the reform of the one-year policy was motivated precisely by the events of 1289 and, further, that the kephale who dealt with Florent's envoys in 1289 was Kantakouzenos the elder himself, hypothetically appointed governor late in 1288 and working under the impression that his term was about to expire.

Thus, if we take the evidence of Kantakouzenos and the *Chronicle* at face value, we might conclude that the one-year policy was in effect in 1289 and that it changed sometime between late 1289 and around 1306. Yet it must be admitted that the evidence for a one-year limit for the terms of Morean governors is rather weak, and it is not at all inconceivable that the *Chronicle*'s report is erroneous, that the governor in 1289 may have hesitated negotiating a peace for some other reason, and that the excuse "the end of my term is drawing near" may have simply been a convenient diplomatic ploy. In any event, if there ever had been a one-year limit, this policy ended no later than ca.1298 and probably years earlier, and thus the isolation of the Morea, to the extent to which the abandonment of this policy had any effect upon it, began earlier than is usually thought.[10]

Elsewhere in the west, Serbia's guerrilla war with Byzantium, which

9. *Livre de la Conqueste de la princée de l'Amorée. Chronique de Morée (1204–1305)*, ed. J. Longnon (Paris, 1911), p. 240. The Greek version of the *Chronicle* (ed. Schmitt, vv. 8689ff.) is similar.

10. Kantakouzenos, I, 85. D. Nicol, *The Byzantine Family of Kantakouzenos (Cantacuzenus)* (Washington, D.C., 1968), 27–30, 35-36. Zakythinos' opinion (*Despotat*, I, 68–70; II, 63–65), adopted with reservation by Laiou, *Constantinople*, 255–56, and by others, that Kantakouzenos was governor from 1308 to 1316, is untenable because Kantakouzenos the elder could not have been 21 years of age in 1308 if his son was an adult, as he certainly was, in 1320.

had begun in 1282, continued on and off for well over a decade. In 1298 Andronikos sent an army to Macedonia under the megas konostaulos Michael Tarchaneiotes Glabas, but the general soon advised Andronikos that inasmuch as his army was incapable of fighting a guerrilla war, the emperor should make peace. After diplomatic negotiations the Serbian king Milutin was presented in 1299 with a Byzantine bride, Andronikos' five-year-old granddaughter Simonis. Sometime thereafter Andronikos II sent an "allied force" (*symmachikon*) to Serbia to help crush the revolt of Stephen Dragutin. Although it was in Andronikos' interest to help Milutin maintain his throne, this was undoubtedly a mere token force, probably mounted, and composed not of pronoiars but of something on the order of Latin mercenaries or Tourkopouloi. We do not know whether it ever returned.[11]

As a result of his reliance on the Genoese for sea transportation, Andronikos II was drawn into a pointless war with Venice from 1296 to 1302. It started as a conflict between Venice and Genoa over their trading operations in the East. Hostilities began in 1293, and after Galata was attacked by the Venetians in 1296, Andronikos II rather unwisely thought it essential to come to the aid of his Genoese allies. When the Genoese and Venetians settled their differences in 1299, Andronikos felt the Empire could press for better terms before ending its role in the conflict. Venice chose to continue the war against Byzantium, and so it dragged on until 1302, when a new treaty was signed basically renewing the truce of 1285. Neither side gained or lost much from this war. There were few casualties, Byzantium surrendered a few Aegean islands to Venice, and both sides lost many ships and suffered the destruction of much property. For Byzantium, the war drained economic resources that were needed much more urgently elsewhere.[12]

Indeed, matters in Asia Minor demanded immediate action. Beginning with a long sojourn there from 1290 to 1293, Andronikos increasingly turned his attention from the western provinces toward the deteriorating situation in Anatolia where the Turks had been making steady inroads since the 1260s. He attempted to strengthen the morale of the population by his presence and by rebuilding fortifications, but despite the best of intentions, this could do little to stem the stream of refugees into the European provinces.[13]

11. Laiou, *Constantinople*, 28, 93–99. Pachymeres, Bonn ed., II, 286. L. Mavromatis, *La fondation de l'empire serbe: le kralj Milutin* (Thessaloniki, 1978), 51–52.

12. Laiou, *Constantinople*, 101–14.

13. Ibid., 76–79.

It is not that Andronikos did not have ideas to bolster the defenses of the Empire. He tried to appoint good generals and he began to employ pre-organized bodies of soldiers. Before his return to Constantinople in 1293, he appointed the pinkernes Alexios Philanthropenos to govern and command the army of all of Asia Minor except for the Ionian coast. Philanthropenos proved to be a fine general and a wise governor. In 1294 and 1295 he scored a series of dazzling victories against the Turks of the Meander valley. It was said that so many prisoners were taken that the price of a Turkish slave fell below that of a sheep. Some Turks surrendered and formed part of Philanthropenos' army. Another important part of his army was composed of cavalry divisions of Cretan mercenaries. These Cretans, refugees from the Venetian occupation of their island, came to Byzantium with their wives and children, and Andronikos II settled them at Anaia and Ephesus and provided them with appropriate salaries financed through the ten-percent tax on pronoiai.[14]

As Philanthropenos' victories piled up, discontent over high taxation and the ineffectiveness of the central government in handling the Turkish threat prompted many to regard Philanthropenos, the first real leader in years, as the savior of Asia Minor. The Cretan soldiers advanced him as their sole ruler, and amid a large measure of popular support Philanthropenos reluctantly accepted the challenge toward the end of 1295. A frightened Andronikos II offered him the title of caesar in return for his obedience. But Philanthropenos moved too slowly and soon, with the initial fervor spent, Libadarios, the governor of Neokastra, who had remained loyal to Constantinople, succeeded in either persuading or bribing the Cretans to capture and blind their rebellious commander. After this these Cretans disappear from the sources and do not figure in the campaigns of Andronikos II's son Michael IX and the Catalans during the early years of the fourteenth century, although Kantakouzenos once makes a mysterious reference to a village near Thessaloniki that had been settled, evidently before he arrived on the political scene, that is, before 1320, by an "army" from Crete.[15]

14. A. Laiou, "Some Observations on Alexios Philanthropenos and Maximos Planoudes," *Byzantine and Modern Greek Studies* 4 (1978), 89–99. Pachymeres, Bonn ed., II, 209, 227. Gregoras, I, 197. E. Zachariadou, «Cortazzi καὶ ὄχι Corsari», Θησαυρίσματα 15 (1978), 64.

15. Laiou, *Constantinople*, 80–83. Nicol, *Last Centuries*, 132. H. Ahrweiler, "L'histoire et la géographie de la région de Smyrne entre les deux occupations turques," in Ahrweiler, *Byzance: les pays et les territoires* (London, 1976), no. IV, 26, 164–65. Kantakouzenos, I, 455. D. Papachryssanthou, *Actes de Xénophon* (Paris, 1986), 176.

The Cretan cavalry bears a certain resemblance to highlanders as refashioned by Michael VIII. The Cretans likewise received a salary as part of their remuneration, and since they were "settled" in Asia, they too probably held land, though it is unknown whether their tenure was allodial or conditional. Yet it is doubtful that Andronikos was attempting to reconstitute a declining system of border defenses because the inhabitants of the frontier highlands by their nature lived a life best suited to a pastoral people, and it is very unlikely that refugees from Crete, especially if they were political refugees, would have become shepherds in Asia.[16]

After Alexios Philanthropenos, the next man sent to Asia Minor was Andronikos II's first cousin John Tarchaneiotes, a general. He arrived in 1298, and his mission was not to win quick victories but to reform the region's fiscal and military administration. It seems that many soldiers had lost the properties they had been holding in pronoia, while others had increased their holdings through bribes to their superiors and were no longer serving as soldiers. Tarchaneiotes sought to end corruption and carried out a fiscal reassessment (*exisosis*) of property holdings, evidently around the Meander valley.

Although his reforms successfully revitalized the army and even led to the construction of a small fleet, he faced opposition from the large landowners who had nothing to gain and much to lose from his fiscal policies. He was also opposed by the Church, which adds an interesting wrinkle to the social situation in Asia Minor. Tarchaneiotes was an Arsenite, a supporter of Patriarch Arsenios whom Michael VIII had deposed. Arsenios had excommunicated Michael for having blinded the young John Laskaris in 1261. Since support for the house of Laskaris and enmity toward Michael VIII were still strong in Asia Minor, Andronikos, in choosing Tarchaneiotes for this command, probably had to weigh the attraction the bulk of the population of Asia Minor would feel toward an Arsenite governor against the possibility that he was sending to Asia another Philanthropenos. The patriarch at the time (an anti-Arsenite) resisted the appointment, but Tarchaneiotes swore to be loyal to the house of Palaiologos. Despite his successes, matters came to a boil when some pronoia-holding soldiers who had been harmed because of Tarchaneiotes' fiscal policies laid an accusation of rebellion against him before the anti-Arsenite bishop of Philadelphia. With charges of treason pending, Tarchaneiotes fled to Thessaloniki to join Andronikos II, probably around mid-1300, and due to the

16. Cf. Mutafčiev, "Vojniški zemi," 527, and Nicol, *Last Centuries*, 131.

convergence of economic and religious interests the social reform was abandoned. The higher clergy had found more in common with the large landowners, including pronoia soldiers, than with the central government and the less wealthy soldiers of Asia Minor.[17]

At a moment when prospects for internal reform in Asia Minor must have seemed quite dim to Andronikos, fortune intervened and raised hopes for a purely military solution. Late in 1301 a group of some 10,000 (Gregoras) to 16,000 (Pachymeres) Alans, half of whom were warriors, suddenly appeared on the northern frontier. Having fled southward from the Mongols, they petitioned the emperor for permission to enter the Empire and become soldiers. Andronikos seized the opportunity and enrolled them as supplemental mercenaries for two campaigns he had been planning. The Alans, generally considered a Christian Turkic people, had last fought for Byzantium during the late eleventh and twelfth centuries as mercenaries.[18]

In the spring of 1302, supplied with money, provisions, and horses, the Alans were divided into three groups: one was led by the megas hetaireiarches Mouzalon to fight the Turks around Nikomedeia; another, led by Andronikos II's son Michael IX, marched south toward Magnesia. Their wives and children remained in Thrace. The Alans assigned to Mouzalon began to desert as soon as they had crossed into Asia. Bands of them indiscriminately plundered Byzantine territory, and by July 1302, Mouzalon's army consisted of barely 2,000 men, of which perhaps something more than half were Alans. While Mouzalon was defending Nikomedeia, an army composed of some 5,000 light cavalry drawn from nomadic tribes appeared between Nikomedeia and Nicaea. It was commanded by Osman, the Turkish emir of Bithynia. There on the plain of Bapheus Mouzalon's army was defeated. This first major victory for the founder of the Ottoman state, followed as it was by the pillage of the northwest corner of Asia Minor, hastened the flight of the Byzantine population westward.

Meanwhile, in April 1302 Michael IX departed for Asia with an army of Alans and other troops. His forces remained intact until they reached Magnesia on the Hermos River. Without fighting a pitched battle, the

---

17. Laiou, *Constantinople*, 87–89. Nicol, *Last Centuries*, 132–33.

18. Laiou, *Constantinople*, 89–90. Gregoras, I, 205. Pachymeres, Bonn ed., II, 307–308. Date by Pachymeres, II, 304, 307. Gregoras (I, 204) indicates 1300. Nicol, *Last Centuries*, 133, and *Regesten*, no. 2241, say 1302. J. Kinnamos, *Ioannis Cinnami epitome*, ed. A. Meineke (Bonn, 1836), 148, where they are called "Massagetoi." Ostrogorsky, *History*, 370. The *Chronicle of the Morea*, vv. 1213–15, says Theodore II Laskaris hired Alans along with other foreign peoples, but this information is not very reliable. On the Alans in general, see G. Moravcsik, *Byzantinoturcica*, 2nd ed. (Berlin, 1958), II, 183–84; and *Encyclopaedia of Islam*, new ed. (Leiden, 1960ff.), s.v. "Alan."

native Byzantine divisions eventually deserted and the Alan mercenaries likewise requested permission to abandon the expedition. Michael persuaded the Alans to remain with him another three months and wrote to Constantinople for additional money. At the end of the three months, the Alans refused to stay any longer and returned to Gallipoli. In a fortress in hostile territory with only a fragment of his army, Michael found himself in a very difficult position. Secretly he fled to Pergamon, but as soon as those in Magnesia heard this news, the remainder of his army and many of the city's inhabitants followed him in a desperate scramble for safety. As for the Alans, after a period of negotiation, they returned their borrowed horses and arms to Andronikos and apparently departed from the Empire.[19]

In 1303, faced with increasing Turkish advances in Anatolia, Andronikos contemplated one last reform in Asia Minor. The situation required drastic action: "Because of these things it appeared necessary to take the one measure still remaining: to release from the overlords however much was given in pronoia to the monasteries, the churches, and the imperial entourage, and to assign everything—including even the lands attached to single monks' cells—to soldiers, so that they would stay and defend their own." Andronikos was either thinking of distributing all these properties as land grants to soldiers or planning a transfer of pronoiai from one set of landlords to another, in this case, from religious or civilian pronoiars to pronoia soldiers. Either scenario might have created more soldiers with a better reason to stay and fight, and even though the patriarch did not oppose the plan, Pachymeres notes that due to the breakdown of the administration in Anatolia and the flight of the population, it was never realized.[20]

As the situation in the east worsened and the inhabitants of Asia Minor increasingly felt themselves abandoned by the central government, an occasional individual decided to take matters into his own hands. Around 1303, amid the flight of imperial soldiers westward, an officer named Kotertzes tried to establish an emergency defense. He drew a following around him who were "as enemies of his enemies and friends of his friends," a phrase encountered now and again in Byzantium during the final centuries, perhaps borrowed from the terminology of Western feudalism, and which shows that with the disintegration of central authority power acquired more and more a personal aspect. There was little Andronikos II could do to

19. Laiou, *Constantinople*, 90–91. Nicol, *Last Centuries*, 133–35.
20. Pachymeres, Bonn ed., II, 390. Trans. adapted from Laiou, *Constantinople*, 119, and E. Fisher, "A Note on Pachymeres' 'De Andronico Palaeologo,'" *Byz* 40 (1970), 233.

help or halt Kotertzes or another imperial officer, a certain Attaleiates, who in 1304, with the support of its inhabitants, seized control of Magnesia.[21]

Around the same time, a strange figure named John Choiroboskos (the "Pigherd") appeared on the scene. Around 1304 he gathered about 300 peasants in Thrace with the intention of launching an expedition against the Turks in Asia Minor but, since the government feared this might lead to a general insurrection, he was imprisoned. After nine months he escaped and with refugees from Asia Minor he went eastward and campaigned against the Turks. Captured in battle, he escaped and fled back to Thrace where he was commissioned by Michael IX to lead a thousand peasants against the Catalans and their Turkish allies who were now in Europe. This makeshift army accomplished little more than the pillaging of the area around Thessaloniki.[22]

Following the defeats at Bapheus and Magnesia, when affairs looked as if they had reached their lowest ebb, Andronikos received news that boosted his hopes and held promise for the salvation of Asia Minor. In 1302, fresh from warring for the Aragonese king of Sicily Frederick II, the Catalan Grand Company was seeking new employment. Its colorful leader Roger de Flor, erstwhile member of the crusading Knights Templar, from which he was expelled, and sometime pirate, contacted Andronikos II and offered the services of his army of adventurers. After negotiations Andronikos eagerly agreed to provide them with four months' pay in advance at twice the normal mercenary rate and to provide Roger himself with the title of megas doux and a niece of the emperor as a wife. In September 1303 the Company arrived at Constantinople, an army of assorted Catalans, Aragonese, Calabrians, and Sicilians, some 6,500 strong, we are told, not including the Company's sailors and the soldiers' wives, mistresses, and children.[23]

The Catalans were a violent lot. Bloody confrontations erupted within days between the Catalans and the Genoese of Galata who had helped transport them to the city, and so Andronikos urged them to cross the Sea of Marmara and billet outside the city of Kyzikos. There they spent the

21. Pachymeres, Bonn ed., II, 407–408. *PLP*, no. 1656. Nicol, *Last Centuries*, 135.

22. Laiou, *Constantinople*, 191–92.

23. Nicol, *Last Centuries*, 136. Laiou, *Constantinople*, 131–34. Laiou devotes a major portion of her book (pp. 131–233) on the Catalan campaign and the diplomatic maneuverings surrounding it. Also, see C. Carrère, "Aux origines des compagnies: la compagnie catalane de 1302," in *Recruitement, mentalités, sociétés: colloque international d'histoire militaire* (Montpellier, 1974), 1–7.

winter of 1303–1304 and were joined by the Alans still in Byzantine service who had survived the battle of Bapheus, something less than 1,800 men, whose fates now intertwined with the Catalans. From the start the Alans and the Catalans had little love for one other, and it galled the Alans to learn how little they were being paid in relation to the enormous salaries of the Catalans. An altercation in April 1304 in Kyzikos left 300 Alans dead, including the son of their leader, George. Five hundred then deserted, so that by May 1304 only a thousand Alans remained with the Catalans, and by the summer of 1304, most of these were gone as well.

Meanwhile the Catalan campaign began in the spring of 1304. It was a dazzling blitzkrieg that took the Turks entirely by surprise, covering the area from the Sea of Marmara, down to Philadelphia where they broke a Turkish blockade of the city, west to Magnesia, south to Ephesus, and then, if we are to believe Ramon Muntaner, the Catalan chronicler of the expedition, eastward across Asia Minor all the way to the famous Iron Gates of the Taurus mountains in Armenia and back to Magnesia to reclaim the booty they had previously amassed, all in a span of less than five months. On the negative side, the Byzantines derived no permanent benefit from these conquests. The relatively small size of the Catalans army did not permit them to leave garrisons behind in the towns they conquered; in many cases, the Turks reclaimed them as soon as the Catalans left. Further, the Catalan expedition was accompanied by the extortion, looting and murder of the Greek population they had liberated, bickering among their leaders, and hostilities between them and the Alan troops accompanying them who after deserting began plundering on their own. Tensions between the Catalans and the native Greek population of Asia Minor reached their climax when the Company laid siege to the city of Magnesia which had refused to allow them inside to collect their booty. The siege ended only after Andronikos recalled them to Europe in August 1304.[24]

In 1304 Roger de Flor demanded more money for his troops. Andronikos II imposed a new tax on crops called the *sitokrithon*, demanded one-third of the revenues of the pronoiai in the European provinces, ceased paying the salaries of the palace staff, and even tried to fool the Catalans with debased coins. In 1305 there was a revolt in Bithynia triggered by the impositions of tax collectors who had come to collect the usual land taxes

24. Pachymeres, Bonn ed., II, 420, 422–24. Nicol, *Last Centuries*, 136–38. Laiou, *Constantinople*, 135–37, 146.

for the salaries of the soldiers there. The feeling was that much of the tax revenues of Asia Minor were being usurped by local magnates.[25]

The Company spent the winter of 1304–1305 at Gallipoli, virtually occupying the peninsula, and in the spring of 1305 they refused to move until their back pay was supplied. New negotiations with the emperor eased tensions, but then events took a significant turn for the worse. For reasons not entirely clear, Roger de Flor decided to visit Michael IX's camp in Adrianople in April 1305. Relations between the Catalans and the imperial army had been strained from the beginning, and in late 1304 Michael had to promise his troops that the Catalans would not join their ranks. Indeed Michael's army now included the Alans who had abandoned the Catalans and who just now had been recalled from the Bulgarian frontier where they had been campaigning with "the Persians of old, whom they called Tourkopouloi," both under the command of the Bulgarian Vojisil and "their own commanders." The Alans were present in Adrianople at the moment Roger de Flor made his fateful visit there. In Michael's camp the Alan leader George avenged the death of his son by murdering Roger, and a riot broke out in which, according to some accounts, all of Roger's 300-man escort was similarly dispatched.[26]

When this news reached Gallipoli the Catalans vowed revenge. They attacked and plundered everything within their reach. Finally, in July 1305 the Catalans inflicted a crushing defeat on Michael IX's vastly superior forces near the town of Apros in Thrace. According to the anonymous Western author of the *Advice for an Overseas Passage*, "the Catalans . . . did not have even 2,500 cavalry, of which there were not 200 of military blood, while Michael was with 14,000 [cavalry] and a multitude of infantry." The Alan light cavalry, forming the left flank along with the Tourkopouloi, both still under the command of Vojisil, withdrew after the first encounter, contributing decisively to the defeat. The Tourkopouloi then deserted to the Catalans and their Turkish allies. Gregoras adds that "these were the one thousand Tourkopouloi who followed Sultan Izz al-Din when he fled to the Romans, [and] received holy baptism," and whose numbers were augmented by subsequent children. Since the Alans did not have the option of joining the Catalans, they merely pillaged the area around Apros. After this battle the situation in Thrace became hopeless. Evidently the Alans spent the rest of 1305 and early 1306 plundering from winter quarters

25. Laiou, *Constantinople*, 141, 187–88.
26. Ibid., 141–46. Nicol, *Last Centuries*, 138–39. Pachymeres, Bonn ed., II, 483, 523–24.

somewhere in Thrace. About the summer of 1306, with Thrace devastated by the Catalans, the Alans began a migration into Bulgaria, apparently seeking employment with the ruler there. At the foot of the Haimos range a Catalan force caught up with them, and there the remainder of the Alan warriors who had entered Byzantium in 1301 were annihilated and their wives and children enslaved.[27]

The Alan episode was a major disaster, but since it occurred amid the Catalan crisis, contemporaries as well as modern historians have naturally tended to assign it only secondary importance. Andronikos' error in dealing with the Alans is clear. Every time the Alans deserted the Byzantine forces—either those of Mouzalon, Michael IX, or the Catalans—they returned to Thrace, to their wives and children. With hindsight it is apparent that Andronikos should have been counseled to follow John Vatatzes' example with the Cumans and to expend the effort, time and money to transport all the Alans as a group to Asia. Perhaps they still would have proved to be inadequate soldiers, but if their families were in Asia, they would have had much more difficulty and much less reason to return to Thrace.

As for the Tourkopouloi, since this was the first time they had been called upon to fight fellow Turks—those allied with the Catalans—it is not difficult to explain their defection at Apros. But there may have been another reason. Pachymeres writes that the Tourkopouloi who had defected were "Christians of late, who not much earlier roamed to the emperor from the northern regions." One scholar, using this and some Turkish evidence, suggested that while some of Sultan Izz al-Din's Turks stayed in Byzantium after his flight, others went to the Crimea, remained there some thirty-five years, and then returned to Byzantium where they were received as prodigal children, so to speak. If so, although it is impossible to know for sure, we may imagine a group of Turks migrating with their families, mixing with resident Tourkopouloi, and spurring their disaffection.[28]

Meanwhile, after the battle of Apros, the victorious Catalans and the Turks and Tourkopouloi with them moved from the Gallipoli peninsula and took the town of Rhaidestos, making it their headquarters from which for over two years they pillaged and terrorized Thrace. By the summer of

27. *Directorium ad faciendum passagium transmarinum*, ed. C. Beazley in *American Historical Review* 13 (1907–1908), 80. Gregoras, I, 229–30. Pachymeres, Bonn ed., II, 524–25, 545, 549. Laiou, *Constantinople*, 147, 162, 170. Nicol, *Last Centuries*, 137, 139.

28. P. Wittek, "Yazijioghlu 'Ali on the Christian Turks of the Dobruja," *Bulletin of the School of Oriental and African Studies* 14 (1952), 657. Pachymeres, Bonn ed., II, 574.

1307, beset by squabbling among their leaders, and now consisting of some 6,000 Spaniards and 3,000 Turks, the Company decided to head westward in search of new lands to conquer. Marching into Macedonia, they spent the winter of 1308 on the Kassandreia peninsula, plundering Mount Athos and the area around Thessaloniki. But once they realized they could not hope to take Thessaloniki, that their position on Kassandreia was untenable, and that their retreat to Thrace was now blocked by an imperial army, the Company decided in the spring of 1309 to march into Thessaly.

A very worried ruler of Thessaly, the young John II Doukas (ca.1303–18), sought Andronikos II's help, and the emperor responded by dispatching the general Chandrenos from Thessaloniki. Forced to move on, the Catalans entered Boeotia in 1310 and contacted Walter of Brienne, the ruler of the French Duchy of Athens and Thebes, one of the remnants of the Latin conquests of the Fourth Crusade. Walter took the Catalans into his employ and they overran Thessaly with great success. Ultimately, however, they turned on Walter, and in 1311 at the battle of Kephissos in Boeotia the numerically inferior Grand Company decisively defeated the flower of French chivalry in Greece, killing Walter and most of his knights and seizing the Duchy of Athens for themselves. At last the Catalans settled down, and the Catalan Duchy of Athens remained in existence until 1388.[29]

When the Catalan army had moved southward into Thessaly in 1309, some of the Turks accompanying them broke away and split into two groups. One, about 1,500 strong, probably including most of the Tourkopouloi, went to Serbia and were engaged by King Milutin, who immediately used them for a brief unsuccessful incursion into the Empire which was beaten back by the general Chandrenos. Afterwards they were settled in Serbia and a couple of years later they revolted and were crushed. The other group, mostly Muslim Turks, 1,300 horse and 800 foot under their leader Halil, decided to return to Asia and requested safe passage from Andronikos. In 1310 the emperor agreed to arrange transportation for Halil and his Turks, but trouble broke out when an imperial official tried to prevent the Turks from departing with their booty. Halil sent for reinforcements from Asia and began pillaging Thrace. Michael IX led an army against him. "Barely 2,000 Turks surrounded Emperor Michael . . . who was in camp with more than 10,000 soldiers. . . . They were easily conquered and shamefully fled. And his tents and imperial throne and crown

29. Laiou, *Constantinople*, 143–47, 161–69, 182–83, 220–27. Nicol, *Last Centuries*, 139–43. Wittek, "Yazijioghlu," 663–66.

and many other spoils were had in booty."[30] For the next two years Halil's army held much of Thrace, roaming and pillaging at will. In 1312 or shortly thereafter, Milutin sent a force of 2,000 cavalry to fight Halil. With this help the Byzantines were able to confine the Turks to the Gallipoli peninsula where they suffered massive losses, only a handful ever returning home. A few of the Tourkopouloi seem to have rejoined Byzantine service, but little is heard from them after this.[31]

Milutin's aid was the first instance in which a Serbian leader provided any military assistance to Byzantium. The Serbian archbishop Danilo in his history of the kings of Serbia speaks of these troops as relatives and friends of Milutin, giving the enterprise the nationalistic feel of a minor crusade, ideally serving the purposes of Danilo's work.[32] On the other hand, it is possible that these 2,000 troops were actually a group of 2,000 Cumans whom Milutin, at an unknown date, had once lent to Michael IX.[33] After Michael IX's death in 1320, Milutin requested the return of these allied auxiliary troops, but in light of the imminent civil war between Andronikos II and his grandson, this request was ignored. In the meantime the 2,000 Cumans were settled in Thrace, where no doubt their primary function was to serve as a defensive buffer between Byzantine Thrace and the Bulgarians and Mongols to the north. In 1327 Andronikos II, fearing that they were plotting with the Mongols, ordered them transplanted from Thrace to Lemnos, Thasos, and Lesbos. What became of them is not known. In the event, though these 2,000 Cumans had come to Byzantium as allied troops, they were transformed, through settlement, into reserve troops with a military obligation.[34]

The years after the Catalan disaster, from 1313 to 1320, were a period of retrenchment and stabilization. Byzantium was in no position to expand its

---

30. *Directorium ad faciendum passagium transmarinum*, 80.

31. M. Živojinović, "Žitije arhiepiskopa Danila II kao izvor za ratovanja Katalanske Kompanije," *ZRVI* 19 (1980), 266–72. Cf. Laiou, *Constantinople*, 166, 232–33, and Wittek, "Yazijioghlu," 663. Nicol, *Last Centuries*, 146. Pachymeres, Bonn ed., II, 632–33.

32. Laiou, *Constantinople*, 233 and note 137. The *Chronicle of the Morea*, ed. Schmitt, vv. 3577–79, 3598–99, 3708, claims that Michael VIII requested aid from Stefan Uroš prior to the battle of Pelagonia and that the Serbian king responded by sending 600 cavalry. Since Michael and Uroš were enemies at this time, however, and since no other source mentions the aid, this evidence may be disregarded. See D. Geanakoplos, "Greco-Latin Relations on the Eve of the Byzantine Restoration: The Battle of Pelagonia," *DOP* 7 (1953), 124 and note 116.

33. Gregoras, I, 268. Mavromatis, *Milutin*, 70 and note 212. Kantakouzenos, I, 259.

34. Bartusis, "On the Problem," 13. There is some question whether Milutin assisted the Byzantines not once but twice during this decade, the second campaign occurring shortly after the first. See Laiou, *Constantinople*, 233 note 138; Živojinović, "Žitije arhiepiskopa Danila," 270–72; and Mavromatis, *Milutin*, 70 note 213.

territory, but neither were its neighbors on the offensive. Consequently, the period saw very little military activity. The borders with Bulgaria and Serbia were quiet. In Greece, Epiros and Thessaly were still recovering from the Catalans as well. In Asia Minor, for reasons that are still poorly understood, there was a lull in Turkish expansion. The Empire was graced with a brief moment for recovery before the next crisis, civil war.

Even though the guiding principles of Andronikos II's military policy remained more or less constant—to preserve whatever could be preserved in Asia Minor while keeping pressure on Epiros and holding Serbia, Bulgaria, and any other enemy at bay through diplomatic means—the actions he took to implement this policy were little more than extemporaneous reactions to threatening situations. This can be seen in his attempts to defend the Empire by utilizing the refugees from Crete, the Catalan Company, and the large migration of Alans. The results of these experiments were either mixed or disastrous.

The most significant development during Andronikos' reign, the gradual loss of Asia Minor, was a consequence of the long-term policies toward the area initiated by Michael VIII and the internal reaction against these policies. Certainly one can blame the wealthy landowners of Asia Minor for their selfishness, their lack of unity, and their opposition to the central government headed by a dynasty which they regarded as illegitimate. On the other hand, Michael VIII bears his share of blame as well. He moved the armies of Asia Minor westward, militarized the highlanders, and discontinued their pay. When, in the later years of the thirteenth century, corrupt provincial officials reduced the salaries of the frontier soldiers and pocketed the difference, this was to a great extent a result of the atmosphere Michael VIII had created.[35] Although Andronikos II did the best he could under the circumstances, we can discern a pattern in his approach to the military in general that involved, probably out of necessity, makeshift efforts and low budgets.

---

35. Laiou, *Constantinople*, 116.

4. The Era of the Civil Wars (1321–57)

By around 1320 Andronikos II saw the possibility of a positive change in the Empire's fortunes. Granted Asia Minor was all but lost, but the northern and western borders of the Empire were holding, and Thrace and Macedonia were recovering from the Catalan devastation. In Greece, Thomas Doukas of Epiros (1296–1318), harassed by the Angevins, had sought aid from Byzantium, and his assassination allowed Andronikos to extend imperial authority over the region. Meanwhile, John II Doukas of Thessaly had died in 1318 without children, and his domain was divided between Andronikos and the Catalan Duchy of Athens, with another part remaining independent. Despite the political fragmentation brought on by the Fourth Crusade and the natural inaccessibility of the area, despite the great autonomy enjoyed by the lords and towns in this, the most "feudalized" area of Byzantium, much of Thessaly and Epiros was now nominally under imperial control. In 1320 Andronikos II and Michael IX were planning an expedition to restore Byzantine rule to the entire area.[1]

Further, by 1321, through increased taxation and the greater diligence of tax collectors, the fisc had raised the impressive sum of nearly one million hyperpyra. "It was the old emperor's intention to establish twenty permanent triremes against sea and coastal enemies, and a land army in Bithynia of one thousand permanent cavalry and in Thrace and Macedonia, 2,000 of the same," the rest of the revenues to be used for embassies and other imperial needs. Modest aspirations perhaps, but a sign of renewed optimism.[2]

Yet, in the words of Gregoras (I, 318), "as if by the throw of a die," all of

---

For the general history of this period, with bibliography: Nicol, *Last Centuries*, 157–261; Ostrogorsky, *History*, 499–533; Laiou, *Constantinople*, 284–300; U. Bosch, *Kaiser Andronikos III. Palaiologos* (Amsterdam, 1965); D. Nicol, *The Byzantine Family of Kantakouzenos (Cantacuzenus)* (Washington, D.C., 1968), 44–103; G. Soulis, *The Serbs and Byzantium during the Reign of Tsar Stephen Dušan (1331–1355) and His Successors* (Washington, 1984), 1–90; and G. Weiss, *Joannes Kantakuzenos—Aristokrat, Staatsmann, Kaiser und Mönch—in der Gesellschaftsentwicklung von Byzanz im 14. Jahrhundert* (Wiesbaden, 1969).

1. Nicol, *Epiros II*, 75–94. Laiou, *Constantinople*, 257–59.
2. Gregoras, I, 317–18. Laiou, *Constantinople*, 121, 246–47.

Andronikos' plans for restoring the Empire were shattered by a series of suicidal civil wars that ravaged Byzantium intermittently for more than thirty years and that drained the Empire of its last measure of strength and vitality. The first of these, between Andronikos and his grandson Andronikos III, occurred from 1321 to 1322 and from 1327 to 1328, with an uneasy peace during the intervening years. In a sense this civil war was a referendum on the reign and policies of the aged Andronikos, and it ended with his abdication. Ironically, it was less the military failures of Andronikos that his grandson exploited than Andronikos' tax policies which at the very least could have been considered a solid option for restoring the Empire. The second civil war, between the usurper John VI Kantakouzenos and the regency for Andronikos III's son John V Palaiologos, began soon after the death of Andronikos III in 1341 when Kantakouzenos, his closest friend and advisor, declared himself Emperor and ended in 1347 when the regency for John V formally acknowledged Kantakouzenos as co-emperor. The final civil war of this era lasted from 1352 to 1357 and began as a response to Kantakouzenos' efforts to work his son Matthew into the picture. Naturally John V viewed this as an attempt to overthrow the Palaiologan dynasty. Sporadic fighting ensued and before it was brought to an end, Matthew was declared Emperor (1353) and John Kantakouzenos resigned (1354). The feud between the Palaiologoi and the Kantakouzenoi finally concluded in 1357 when Matthew renounced his claim to the imperial purple and John V at last became sole emperor.

The era of the civil wars seems to have produced no innovations in military organization and administration. Rather, the rival factions during the civil wars and the emperors during the periods between the civil wars appear to have relied on the same types of troops, particularly pronoiars and companies of soldiers (such as the Catalans), that had been employed earlier in Andronikos II's reign. However, changes did occur in the composition of the army. During the civil wars, Latins again appeared as mercenaries in Byzantium, though this may be due to the fact that the forces involved were so small that the Byzantine historians, principally Kantakouzenos, were more apt to notice and report the presence of small groups of Latins.[3] Much more significant was the increasing tendency to utilize the services of Serbs, Bulgarians, and especially Turks to wage both civil and foreign war.

3. Kantakouzenos, I, 98, 140, 141, 173, 300–301, 317–18, 378–79; II, 166. Gregoras, I, 317–18.

The first of the civil wars was a referendum on the government's policies of the previous forty years coupled with an underlying clash of temperaments. Superficially there was a tired, moralistic, domineering old man in his sixties hard-pressed by a handsome, frivolous, bellicose, and a bit dissolute grandson whom he loved dearly, but who felt and acted like a child living under the wing of his aged grandfather. Beyond this there were the failed policies, the loss of Asia Minor, the flood of refugees, the Catalan debacle, and the high taxes to buy off the Empire's enemies. Not that Andronikos III had any new answers, or that there were deep ideological issues involved. Rather there was more a perception that it was time for the government to be placed in younger hands.

What precipitated the break between the two Andronikoi was a family tragedy. Andronikos III's companions murdered a man who they thought was one of their friend's romantic rivals but who turned out to be Andronikos' younger brother Manuel. Michael IX, their father, who was already quite ill, died soon afterward in 1320, and Andronikos II, with some justification, held his grandson responsible for both deaths. Concluding that his grandson was not fit to be emperor, Andronikos II disinherited and removed him from the imperial line of succession. Andronikos III was urged to rebellion by his coterie. Foremost among them were the wealthy and aristocratic John Kantakouzenos, his best friend; the unprincipled and ambitious Syrgiannes, friend of the younger Andronikos, half-Mongol but related to both the Palaiologos and Kantakouzenos families; Theodore Synadenos, then governor of Prilep, who had been a close friend of Michael IX; and the parvenu Alexios Apokaukos, a man of humble origin whose rise to prominence was due to his friendship with Kantakouzenos as well as to the instability of the times. In April 1321, from a base in Adrianople, Andronikos declared war on his grandfather. In order to raise an army and win some popular support, he proclaimed freedom from taxation for the towns of Thrace. When Syrgiannes led the assembled army to Constantinople, Andronikos II capitulated. In June 1321 an agreement was reached whereby the Empire was partitioned: Andronikos II would rule from Constantinople, his grandson from Adrianople.[4]

In December 1321, Syrgiannes changed sides and urged Andronikos II to attack his grandson. For six months there was scattered fighting in Thrace, which involved the participation of the tsar of Bulgaria. At the end of 1321 Theodore Svetoslav sent 300 heavily armed cavalrymen to Byzan-

---

4. Laiou, *Constantinople*, 284–89. Nicol, *Last Centuries*, 160–65.

tium, ostensibly to help Andronikos III, but really, Kantakouzenos suggests, to imprison him on behalf of Andronikos II, Svetoslav's grandfather-in-law. These troops accomplished nothing and returned home.[5]

Foreign powers were to play a major role in the civil wars, and it is not surprising that Byzantium's long-time foe to the north became involved first. Gone were the days when each state tried to destroy the other—they were now both far too weak—but each state looked for opportunities to seize a few border towns or add to the internal disorders of their neighbor. Such was the aid provided by Svetoslav. During the entire Nicaean and early Palaiologan periods there is no reliable evidence of any exchange of allied troops between Byzantium and Bulgaria at all, and the only times the states cooperated militarily were for two joint Byzantino-Bulgarian sieges of Constantinople in the 1230s, although the respective rulers each commanded his own troops. Perhaps Bulgarians were present at the battle of Pelagonia, but this evidence, from the *Chronicle of the Morea*, is highly dubious and is confirmed by no other source.[6]

By the late spring of 1322, just as Andronikos III was nearly out of money, Thessaloniki joined his side, and Andronikos II decided to sue for peace. In July 1322 a second settlement was concluded known as the treaty of Epibatai. Andronikos III was recognized as the colleague of Andronikos II and restored as heir to throne. He was to receive a stipend for his personal expenses and his army was to be paid by the state. Five years of uneasy peace followed, characterized by mutual distrust, with the grandfather in the capital and the grandson in Didymoteichon.

The reason the civil wars were so disastrous was that foreign policy fell to pieces as so much of the Empire's military resources and energies were channeled into internecine combat. Only in the periods between civil wars do we see efforts to improve the external situation of the Empire. In this sense these first periods of civil war were the most unfortunate because this was when Byzantium lost its final chance to bring about a satisfactory *modus vivendi* with the Ottoman Turks in Asia Minor. In the mid-1320s, after the first phases of civil war, Andronikos II made a few halfhearted attempts to turn attention back to Asia. In 1324 he called the blind old general Alexios Philanthropenos out of retirement and sent him to Asia. Though he was entrusted with no army, his reputation was still powerful enough to induce the Turks besieging Philadelphia to withdraw. About a year later John

5. Kantakouzenos, I, 108. Bosch, *Andronikos*, 23.
6. Akropolites, 50–52. Nicol, *Last Centuries*, 26. *Chronicle of the Morea*, ed. J. Schmitt (London, 1904), v. 3708.

Kantakouzenos, fresh from assisting Andronikos III deal with a border war with the Bulgarians from 1322 to 1324 and a major Mongol pillaging expedition into Thrace in 1324, led an army into Bithynia, evidently with some success. Nevertheless, in 1326, with no help from Constantinople, the important city of Prousa (Bursa) fell to Osman, and his son Orhan made the city his capital. This left only the areas around Nicaea and Nikomedeia, the area directly across from Constantinople, and isolated outposts like the cities of Philadelphia and Herakleia, still among the Byzantine holdings in Asia Minor.[7]

Writing in 1326, Andronikos II's son, Theodore Palaiologos, the marquis of Montferrat, emphasizes military unpreparedness and the cupidity of imperial officials as the cause of the Empire's woes, and seems to address implicitly the loss of Asia Minor:

> I would like to consider the condition of the land of the Empire of Greece and of the previously mentioned lordship, and how and in what manner it exists: first, oppressed and burdened by war with its large and powerful neighbors, Christians as well as pagans, and badly disposed in the use of weapons and natural ability, the inhabitants of the said land are not at all accustomed to arms or the things necessary for war nor show any honor at all to those who desire to occupy themselves with these or with the distress of the government in the said lordship, but they act more for the love of money and for those in the said lordship who concern themselves with acquiring money and who have themselves named tax collectors and officials and pluck the rights and the incomes of the said lordship. . . .
>
> It seems that the inhabitants of the land do not have any fortresses for defending and guarding themselves against their enemies, but completely lack them. When an enemy attack comes, all flee and leave their land and their homes along with their wives and children until they find a castle or fortress where they can be safe. The fortresses found in this country are small, and they are badly furnished and badly equipped for defense. For the castellans and the officers assigned to the defense and to the guard of the said places seek profit in taking money only for themselves, not for the defense or guard of the said lands, but they take money from the inhabitants because they are hired men and do not care for their sheep.[8]

A few years later, the anonymous Western author of the *Advice for an Overseas Passage* similarly pondered the ills of the Empire and how easily it could be conquered. He first illustrates the military weakness of the Empire by referring to two Byzantine defeats at the hands of numerically inferior

7. Laiou, *Constantinople*, 281, 290–92. Nicol, *Last Centuries*, 154–55, 166.

8. Theodore Palaiologos, *Les Enseignements de Théodore Paléologue*, ed. C. Knowles (London, 1983), 107–108.

foes: the battle of Apros in 1305, in which Michael IX was trounced by the Catalan Company, and an encounter in the suburbs of Constantinople in 1311 between Michael IX and the Turks under Halil who had earlier broken from the Catalans. He then points out the external threats to the Empire, and the theme of population flight is not neglected: "The Mongols surround and trample them. The Turk, the Slav, the Bulgar and whatever other enemy invades, exterminates and annihilates. They have no hope except in the common cry 'Phyge! Phyge!' which in our Latin means 'Flee! Flee!'" He speaks of the desolation and depopulation of the Empire, the incompetence of its rulers, and the corruption of the Byzantine Church.[9]

Certainly both authors had reason to exaggerate the plight of the Empire. The author of *Advice* wanted the king of France to undertake a crusade against Byzantium in order to use it as a base of operations against the Turks. Theodore Palaiologos was bitter because his father had not granted him a military command on either of his brief return visits to Byzantium and because his requests for financial aid had gone unanswered. In his mind, such insults to his dignity confirmed that neither defenses nor finances were managed efficiently. And yet, since neither author mentions civil war as a reason for the Empire's difficulties, it would appear that their deleterious effects were not yet evident. If one adds the squandering of men and resources in internecine strife to the picture they paint of the Empire, it would be difficult not to conclude that by the second quarter of the fourteenth century the combination of external enemies intent on conquest and civil war had rendered the Byzantine cause hopeless.

The final stage of the civil war between the Andronikoi began in the fall of 1327. Andronikos III aligned himself with Michael Šišman of Bulgaria who was promised aid against Serbia if he helped Andronikos against the grandfather. Meanwhile Andronikos II entered into negotiations with the Serbian king Stefan Dečanski. The previous year Dečanski had supported the revolt of Andronikos II's nephew John, governor of Thessaloniki, but now as an ally of Andronikos II he sent "twelve tagmata" under the general Hrelja to join the forces in Macedonia in their struggle against Andronikos III. Although the aid provided by Dečanski's predecessor Milutin at the tail end of the Catalan catastrophe was rather altruistic, at least as much as military aid to a neighboring state can ever be, future aid from the kings of Serbia was much more self-serving and designed to weaken the Byzantine

---

9. *Directorium ad faciendum passagium transmarinum*, ed. C. Beazley, in *American Historical Review* 13 (1907–1908), 79–91, esp. 80–81 (English summary, 73–75).

state. In this particular case, Dečanski's aid was purely formal. Hrelja and his troops remained in Byzantium only a few months, took part in no major battles, and on the whole provided very little assistance to the older Andronikos.[10]

In early 1328 several cities declared for Andronikos III. The aid promised from Michael Šišman never materialized. Instead in 1328 Šišman sent a force of around 3,000 cavalry composed of Bulgars and Mongols into Thrace, ostensibly to help Andronikos II, but in reality to plunder. Arriving before the walls of Constantinople, he changed his mind again and returned home. With his grandfather lacking allies, Andronikos III slipped into Constantinople on a May night in 1328 with 800 of his supporters, and Andronikos II was forced to abdicate.[11]

Once Andronikos III emerged as sole emperor, he quickly dealt with another feeble invasion into Thrace by Michael Šišman and then directed his attention toward Asia Minor. In June 1329 he and Kantakouzenos led a major expedition into Asia with 2,000 soldiers from Constantinople and something less than this number from Thrace. At Pelekanos their army encountered the forces of Orhan, Osman's son and successor, encamped with about 8,000 men. Although the Byzantine army was able to hold its own for several days, a decision to withdraw prompted a Turkish counterattack that wounded Andronikos and utterly routed his army. At nightfall news of the emperor's injury spread panic among the troops. As they reached the coast and their ships, a battle was fought in which the Byzantines were decisively defeated.[12]

Afterward the collapse of Byzantine authority in Asia Minor accelerated rapidly. The battle of Pelekanos was the first and only major battle ever fought between the Byzantines and the Ottomans. Nicaea surrendered in 1331, Nikomedeia in 1337, and Andronikos agreed to pay a yearly tribute to Orhan in 1333. Except for Philadelphia and a few coastal cities, the East was lost. Without the military strength to reconquer Asia, Andronikos' policy gradually changed from direct confrontation to mere containment. Late in 1329 Byzantine authority was once again asserted over the Genoese of Chios and in 1336 a plan by some Genoese to control Lesbos was forcibly thwarted. The strategy was to control the Aegean islands adjacent to Asia and thereby

10. Laiou, *Constantinople*, 294–96. Nicol, *Last Centuries*, 167. Kantakouzenos, I, 261. M. Bartusis, "Chrelja and Momčilo," *Byzantinoslavica* 41 (1980), 202.

11. Kantakouzenos, I, 294–95. Gregoras, I, 418. Nicol, *Last Centuries*, 167–69. Laiou, *Constantinople*, 295, 297.

12. Nicol, *Last Centuries*, 173–75.

prevent Turkish expansion. Meanwhile, Andronikos began to cultivate the other emirs of Asia Minor, most notably Umur Pasha of Aydin, in hopes that these would cause problems for Orhan and the Ottomans and relieve the pressure on Byzantium. Unlike his grandfather, Andronikos was a general at heart, and since circumstances prevented further campaigns against the Turks, he decided in the early 1330s to direct his energies along the western frontier.

In 1330 at the battle of Velbužd, Stefan Dečanski of Serbia defeated Michael Šišman of Bulgaria. The Bulgarian army was destroyed and Šišman himself mortally wounded. Afterwards there were palace coups in both countries. John Alexander came to the throne in Bulgaria, and in 1331 the nobles of Serbia murdered Dečanski and placed his son Stefan Dušan on the throne. Dušan married a sister of John Alexander and united Serbian and Bulgarian interests, leaving him a free hand to attempt the age-old dream of the south Slavic states, the conquest of Byzantium.

Stefan Dušan's policy was much more artful than Stefan Dečanski's, though its aim was similar, to maintain disorder in Byzantium wherever possible. He began, like Dečanski, by offering aid to a rebel. Syrgiannes, who had been governor of Thessaloniki since the end of the civil war, had fled to Serbia to escape charges of treason. Supplied with troops by Dušan he invaded Macedonia and seized several towns in 1334. Andronikos III marched to Thessaloniki, and in the end Syrgiannes was murdered by an imperial officer. Andronikos III and Dušan then concluded a peace treaty that basically brought a return to the status quo ante, and shortly afterward Dušan received aid from Byzantium during a Hungarian invasion. When the king of Hungary heard that Andronikos had sent "a large and brave army," he withdrew from Serbia, and the Byzantine allied army returned home after receiving Dušan's thanks. Even though this episode turned out happily for all involved, Dušan's willingness to involve himself in Byzantine internal affairs was a prelude to what the future held in store.[13]

The greatest military triumph of Andronikos III's reign was the restoration of Byzantine authority in Thessaly. Although Thessaly had come under nominal imperial rule in 1318, effective control remained in the hands of the area's semi-autonomous lords. Taking advantage of the chaos in the area, the despot of Epiros John Orsini invaded Thessaly in 1333. Andronikos sent an army there under Michael Monomachos and he himself followed.

13. Kantakouzenos, I, 450, 453, 458. Soulis, *Serbs and Byzantium*, 6–7. Nicol, *Last Centuries*, 181. Bosch, *Andronikos*, 95.

In a matter of weeks all of Thessaly up to the borders of the Catalan Duchy of Athens were restored to direct Byzantine rule, and Monomachos was appointed governor of the region. Next on the agenda was Epiros, the northern part of which had been held by Byzantium since 1318, though like Thessaly its inhabitants were quite unruly. In 1336 or 1337 John Orsini was poisoned by his Greek wife Anna, destabilizing the situation in southern Epiros. In 1338 Andronikos and Kantakouzenos responded to a rebellion among the Albanians in northern Epiros by marching there with an army that included some 2,000 foot troops, "light-armed and archers," provided by the Seljuk emir of Aydin Umur. After a brief campaign in the mountains of Albania followed by a battle in which the Albanians were crushed and many enslaved by Umur's Turks, this allied force returned home to Asia.

The moment was now propitious to effect the incorporation of southern Epiros into the Empire. Fearing an invasion, Anna decided to submit to Byzantium, and Theodore Synadenos was appointed governor. In 1339 and 1340 there was a revolt centering around Nikephoros Orsini, Anna's son. One army led by Michael Monomachos and Kantakouzenos' cousin John Angelos and another led by the emperor and Kantakouzenos himself restored order, partly through siege warfare, partly through Kantakouzenos' remarkable powers of persuasion. In the end Andronikos III had achieved rather cheaply what Michael VIII and Andronikos II had failed to accomplish with much greater effort—the restoration of Thessaly and Epiros to imperial rule.[14]

The appearance of Umur's Turks in the Albanian campaign was the first use of Turkish allied troops since Andronikos II once called them into Thrace during the civil war in 1321. After a single battle, this "Persian army" had returned to Asia.[15] But because of Kantakouzenos' close relationship with Umur this gingerly use of Turks soon came to an end. Despite the unpleasant memories of the Tourkopouloi, the Byzantines once again began to rely on Turks to fight their wars. After all, it seemed that there was an endless supply of new groups of Turks willing at a moment's notice to come to Europe and, just as important, to return to Asia when no longer needed.

Emperors typically requested aid from one of the Turkish emirs in Asia, and thus the Turks who fought for Byzantium from the 1320s through the 1350s ought to be classified as supplemental allied troops, or auxiliaries. The

---

14. Nicol, *Epiros II*, 102–22. Nicol, *Last Centuries*, 182–87. On the Albanian campaign: Kantakouzenos, I, 496–99; Gregoras, I, 544–45; Bosch, *Andronikos*, 136; P. Lemerle, *L'émirat d'Aydin, Byzance et l'Occident* (Paris, 1957), 111, 115.

15. Kantakouzenos, I, 151–52. Laiou, *Constantinople*, 291–92. Bosch, *Andronikos*, 32.

campaign of 1337 presaged the significant role these allied Turkish forces would play during the next twenty years. Kantakouzenos calls Umur's Turks "auxiliary infantry" (*symmachia peze*); to Gregoras they were simply mercenaries (*misthophoroi*). In fact Kantakouzenos consistently refers to Umur, as well as the emir of Bithynia Orhan, and their troops, as allies (*symmachoi*). Granting that this kind of terminology suited Kantakouzenos' purposes as he wrote his memoirs, there is a certain appropriateness in such a characterization. The Turks came in a body, fought in a body, and departed in a body, and though they may be thought of loosely as mercenaries, nothing indicates that the Turkish troops in any of the campaigns sponsored by Umur, or later Orhan, were formally paid by any Byzantine leader. Rather, as in the Albanian campaign, they fought for booty, slaves, and movable property.

After the successful conclusion of these campaigns, Andronikos III unexpectedly died in June 1341 at the age of forty-five. The question of who should now direct the government led to the second civil war. On one side there was John Kantakouzenos and his party and on the other a Constantinopolitan party headed by the megas doux Alexios Apokaukos, Andronikos III's widow Anne of Savoy, and Patriarch John Kalekas, who claimed to represent the interests of the heir-presumptive, Andronikos' son John who was only nine when his father died. For five and a half years the Byzantines, aided by various allied armies of Turks, Serbs, and Bulgarians, waged war among themselves, and once again any plans for a coherent defense of the Empire had to be set aside. The most tangible consequence of this civil war was the conquest of Macedonia by the Serbs under Stefan Dušan. Kantakouzenos successfully defended his right to lead Byzantium, but at the cost of a great diminution of the Empire's territory.

Byzantium's neighbors took advantage of the death of Andronikos III. Stefan Dušan attacked Macedonia, the emir of Saruhan raided the coast of Thrace, and Tsar John Alexander of Bulgaria threatened to invade. Kantakouzenos campaigned and persuaded Dušan to withdraw, he drove off the raiding Turks, and with the help of Umur, who sent ships to the mouth of the Danube, he forced the Bulgarians to renew their peace treaty with Byzantium. Afterward he learned that the Principality of Achaia was interested in surrendering to the Empire. He prepared another army to head to the Morea, but no sooner had he left Constantinople than Alexios Apokaukos led a rebellion in the name of the young John V. Kantakouzenos' family and supporters were rounded up, and the patriarch John Kalekas declared himself regent.

Kantakouzenos responded by having himself proclaimed emperor in October 1341 at Didymoteichon, all the while maintaining that he too was ruling only in the name of the legitimate heir to the throne John V Palaiologos. Generally the aristocracy sided with Kantakouzenos, and the urban common people sided with Apokaukos. In town after town the wealthy and powerful were expelled and popular governments installed. At the end of 1341 John V was officially crowned emperor and Kantakouzenos was officially outlawed. In March 1342 Kantakouzenos departed from Didymoteichon with most of his army in order to receive the submission of Thessaloniki, promised to him by Theodore Synadenos, then governor of the Empire's second city. But before he arrived Synadenos was driven out of the city by a rebellion known as the Zealot revolt. The Zealots were a group of anti-aristocratic reformers who established a regime in Thessaloniki which lasted for seven years with only nominal control from Constantinople.[16]

With desertions reducing his troop strength to only 2,000 men and his fortunes at their lowest ebb, Kantakouzenos now made for Serbia to seek aid from Stefan Dušan. Always ready to fuel internal divisions within Byzantium, Dušan provided Kantakouzenos with soldiers on each of the three separate occasions the usurper fled to Serbia during 1342–43. On Kantakouzenos' first return to Byzantium, Dušan lent him an army commanded by twenty of his best officers. Kantakouzenos headed east but was stopped short at Serres, where the inhabitants refused to join his side. Encamped outside the town for almost two weeks, his troops fell to an epidemic which Kantakouzenos attributed to food poisoning. Most of his forces either died or deserted, and with only 500 men left he returned to Serbia.[17]

On his second departure from Serbia, the allied forces, according to John, were a "useless mob" since Dušan was using his best troops to garrison towns, and the remaining troops were exhausted from continuous campaigning. Soon after setting out, the dreadful state of the Serbs' morale became apparent when they began sending their horses and arms homeward out of fear that they would never return. Desertions followed and Kantakouzenos again made his way back to Serbia. For John's final departure, Dušan provided him with a "small and third-rate" force which was supplemented, however, with a contingent of Dušan's Latin mercenaries

16. Nicol, *Last Centuries*, 191–201.
17. Kantakouzenos, II, 276, 292–96. Soulis, *Serbs and Byzantium*, 14–19.

for the express purpose of capturing the town of Verria (Berroia). These Latins, ethnically Aragonese or Catalan, later entered Kantakouzenos' employ and probably can be identified as those found in Kantakouzenos' service in Constantinople during the 1350s.[18]

By the time of Kantakouzenos' third departure from Serbia, in early 1343, his fortunes were improving. A number of towns and leaders in northern Thessaly had come over to his side, and he appointed his cousin John Angelos to govern the area. Shortly thereafter Angelos annexed Epiros to Thessaly on his own initiative, and he remained governor of both areas until they were conquered by the Serbs around 1346. Meanwhile, to relieve his wife and the forces defending Didymoteichon, Kantakouzenos again had called in Umur Pasha who pillaged Thrace, he claims, with "31,000" horse and foot troops during the winter of 1342–43. Kantakouzenos reports similarly enormous numbers for two other occasions in which Umur helped out his Byzantine friend. In the fall of 1343 after losing Dušan's support when several Macedonian towns joined his side, and facing the arrival at Thessaloniki of a fleet from Constantinople, the Turkish emir returned with 200 ships and "30,000" troops, nearly all infantry, and together he and Kantakouzenos unsuccessfully attempted to take Thessaloniki. Also, from late spring through September 1345 Umur campaigned with Kantakouzenos in Thrace with "20,000" horse.[19]

During 1345 the momentum shifted in Kantakouzenos' favor as a number of Thracian towns moved to his side. In mid-1345 Alexios Apokaukos was murdered while visiting a prison in Constantinople. The prisoners, who hacked off his head and stuck it on a pole, made no attempt to escape for they thought they would be honored for delivering the Empire from a tyrant. Nevertheless, Empress Anne allowed Apokaukos' supporters and the Gasmouloi of the capital to massacre all of the prisoners, some 200, whether or not they had participated in the deed.[20]

Empress Anne continued to look for outside help to defeat Kantakouzenos. In 1346 the independent Bulgarian ruler of the Dobrudja Balik sent her one thousand "picked" troops under the command of his brothers, Feodor and Dobrotič. This force was soundly defeated by Kantakouzenos' partisan, the protostrator George Phakrases. While Anne was just as willing as Kantakouzenos to employ Turks, she was unable to establish the kind of

18. Kantakouzenos, II, 331–32, 349, 354–57. Nicol, *Byzantine Family*, 52–54.
19. Nicol, *Epiros II*, 126–29. Kantakouzenos, II, 344–46, 530. Lemerle, *Émirat*, 144–79, 204–17.
20. Nicol, *Last Centuries*, 206–207.

affable relations he had with Umur and, to a lesser extent, with Osman's son Orhan, emir in Bithynia.[21] For example, in the summer of 1346 she requested a force from the emir of Saruhan. No sooner had the 6,000 troops arrived in Thrace than they began to plunder indiscriminately, eventually moving to the side of Kantakouzenos whose forces they had been summoned to fight.[22]

In February 1347 pro-Kantakouzenos conspirators in Constantinople admitted John into the city. Soon afterward Empress Anne submitted to his authority and this civil war came to an end. With John VI Kantakouzenos now in charge of a nominally united though seriously weakened Empire there was no further talk of recovering Asia Minor, or even of further advances in the Morea. Rather, all attention was focused on the Serbian occupation of Macedonia, and later of Thessaly and Epiros, and on the continued safety of Constantinople. In 1348 and 1350 campaigns into Macedonia met with only minor success. Dušan controlled all of Macedonia except for Thessaloniki, still in the hands of the Zealots. Serres had fallen to him in 1345, and the next year he was formally crowned "Emperor of the Serbs and Greeks" there. In 1348, the year of Umur's death, Kantakouzenos began to take advantage of his alliance with Orhan, a relationship cemented two years earlier through Orhan's marriage to one of John's daughters. In the spring Orhan sent "more than 10,000" troops under the command of his son Sulayman to campaign with Kantakouzenos' son Matthew against Serbia. But before encountering any Serbian forces the Turks—who for the first time were not Seljuk but Ottoman—began to plunder and enslave.[23]

Later that year the Serbs conquered all of northern Greece. The Serbian Empire, now larger than Byzantium, extended from the Danube to the Gulf of Corinth, and from the Adriatic Sea to the Nestos River in eastern Macedonia. The successes of Andronikos III had been erased and only Thessaloniki remained outside Dušan's grasp. In 1350, amid the dissension of its Zealot leaders who had grown more and more radical, Kantakouzenos recovered Thessaloniki. For this operation and a new offensive against the Serbs John VI had again called to Orhan, who sent "20,000 cavalry" led by his son Sulayman, but this force was recalled to Asia Minor before playing any role in the hostilities.

21. Kantakouzenos, I, 584–85. Nicol, *Last Centuries*, 208–209.

22. Lemerle, *Émirat*, 220–23.

23. Nicol, *Last Centuries*, 210, 212–13, 225–26. Soulis, *Serbs and Byzantium*, 24–31. On Orhan's aid: Kantakouzenos, III, 32; and John VI Kantakouzenos, "The History of John Cantacuzenus (book 4): Text, Translation and Commentary," ed. T. Miller, diss., Catholic Univ. 1975, 281–83.

Overall John's attempts to deal with the Serbs met with little success. Late in 1350 he retook Verria with the help of Turkish pirate ships, and later, for a short time, Vodena. But except for distant Philadelphia and the Morea, Byzantium was reduced to Constantinople, Thrace, a few Aegean islands, a few coastal towns in Asia Minor, and Thessaloniki. There was no money in the treasury, trade had come to a standstill, and Thrace was devastated. Only in the Morea was the situation stable during this period. In 1349 John VI sent his second son the despot Manuel there as governor, a post he held until his death in 1380. Evidently his rule was characterized less by further conquests than by the stabilization of the Byzantine position. Nothing is known of administrative and institutional developments. Isolated from the capital, the Byzantine Morea seems to have experienced an independent internal development. Scholars have tended to assume there was a high degree of decentralization that allowed the local Greek aristocracy much autonomy.[24]

John Kantakouzenos realized that the only way to maintain any control over these disparate areas was through the rebuilding of a Byzantine fleet. A fleet would also free the Empire from its dependence on the Genoese for the capital's food supply and trade. But by taking to the sea the Byzantines again landed themselves at the center of the disputes between the Venetians and Genoese over control of trade in the Black Sea and Aegean areas. The waters around Constantinople were the arena for numerous confrontations between these Italian rivals, and the Byzantines, now reduced to pawns in a much larger international power struggle, were frequently drawn into their quarrels.

The Genoese viewed Kantakouzenos' plans for a fleet as a threat to their position relative to the Venetians. Fearing a loss of their trade privileges in Constantinople, they opened hostilities in 1348. In a rare show of civic solidarity the inhabitants of the capital rose to the occasion, contributing their manpower to defend the walls and their money to quickly build ships. By the spring of 1349, nine warships and one hundred smaller vessels were ready to face the Genoese. The outcome of the first and only encounter of the two fleets was quite curious. The Byzantines had long been away from the sea and it showed. As their fleet rounded the eastern side of the city, a sudden gale spread panic among the unskilled, newly recruited crews

---

24. Nicol, *Last Centuries*, 234–37. Soulis, *Serbs and Byzantium*, 35–38, 43–47. On Orhan's troops: Kantakouzenos, III, 111. On Manuel Kantakouzenos: Nicol, *Byzantine Family*, 122–29. Zakythinos, *Despotat*, II, 134, suggests without evidence that Manuel's appointment "without doubt" led to the organization of the army on a regional plan.

who thought their ships were sinking. To the astonishment of the Genoese, who at first thought this had to be some clever stratagem, the crews abandoned ship. The Genoese captured the empty ships and the Byzantines sued for peace.

After this humiliating defeat, Kantakouzenos raised taxes for another fleet. The money came slowly but the ships were built and were used in 1350 for the recovery of Thessaloniki. The following year the Byzantines were drawn into yet another conflict between the Venetians and Genoese when a Venetian fleet attacked Galata. Both sides sought Byzantine support but Kantakouzenos declined to join the fray until the Genoese made a perfunctory attack on Constantinople. The Byzantines readied for war, but the Venetian commanders, judging they were outnumbered, withdrew, leaving the Byzantine fleet to be defeated in July 1351. In the end, again abandoned by his supposed ally, John VI concluded a treaty with Genoa in May 1352.[25]

The final civil war, a pointless affair arising from petty suspicions and bruised egos, was skillfully orchestrated by the Venetians in hopes of bringing a more compliant John V Palaiologos to full power in Constantinople. It was less a war between Byzantine factions—John V against Matthew Kantakouzenos and, reluctantly, his father—than another episode in the Veneto-Genoese struggle. The war involved few Byzantine troops but a great many Turks, who were allied with the Genoese and on the side of the Kantakouzenoi, and Serbs and Bulgarians, who were allied with Venice and on the side of Palaiologos.

As the years passed the rivalry between Matthew and John V had grown. The settlement of 1347, recognizing John VI Kantakouzenos as senior emperor, nevertheless had affirmed the precedence and legitimacy of the Palaiologos family's claim to the throne. This compromise had put Matthew Kantakouzenos, John VI's oldest son, in a difficult position and weakened his claim to succeed his father. The supporters of all three men, John V, John VI, and Matthew, urged their masters toward a decisive resolution of the matter. During the war between Venice and Genoa that began in 1351, the Venetians offered to help John V, then living in Thessaloniki, to make war against John VI, and contact was made even with Stefan Dušan who seems to have supported the plan. Civil war was temporarily averted through negotiations, but in the summer of 1352 John V invaded Matthew's territory and laid siege to Adrianople. John VI was forced to relieve his son with a body of Turkish troops. In October 1352 with

25. Nicol, *Last Centuries*, 227–34, 243–44.

financial backing from Venice, John V called on the Serbs and Bulgarians for assistance. Tsar John Alexander sent a contingent of cavalry and Dušan sent 4,000 troops. John Kantakouzenos' urgent request to Orhan brought "not less than 10,000 cavalry" to Thrace to face a Serbian force allied with John V. Late that year a battle was fought on the Marica River in which Orhan's Turks fighting on Kantakouzenos' behalf decisively defeated the Serbs fighting on John V's behalf, the allied Bulgarian cavalry choosing to withdraw without engaging the Turks.[26]

Except for the assistance the Serbian prince Marko Kraljevic would provide Andronikos IV in 1376 at the insistence of Sultan Murad I, this was the last aid either of the Slavic states gave Byzantium.[27] It is interesting to compare the military aid furnished to Byzantium by the Serbian and Bulgarian rulers. Alliances and intentions notwithstanding, the Bulgarians sent military aid three times during the last two and a half centuries of Byzantium: in 1321, 1328, and 1352. In every case, its purpose was to help one side or the other during civil war, but only in 1352 was there actually combat. The Serbs, during the same long period, sent troops in 1312 or shortly after, in 1327, in 1342–43, and in 1352. Only in 1312 did the aid, against Halil's Turks, have any positive effect. Otherwise, as with the Bulgarians, the aid was consumed in civil war with real combat taking place only in 1352.

The reason why the Serbs and the Bulgars, with only one exception, furnished allied troops to Byzantium solely during periods of civil war is not difficult to discern. The Slavic states and Byzantium were never on good terms; at best they were at peace. Byzantium, for its part, sent aid to the Slavs only on two occasions, shortly after 1299 and in 1334, both times to display good will after the signing of a peace treaty. Otherwise they were willing to take advantage of disorders in Bulgaria and Serbia whenever the opportunity arose. For example, at Theodore Svetoslav's death in 1323 Byzantium provided military support for his brother Vojisil, who had long served Byzantium as a general, in his unsuccessful attempt to accede to the Bulgarian throne.[28]

The Slav rulers reciprocated by attempting to destabilize Byzantium whenever possible. Viewing matters in a broad context, whether or not it was in the long-term interests of the Slavs to help the Empire in its struggles

26. Nicol, *Last Centuries*, 244–46, 248. Soulis, *Serbs and Byzantium*, 47–50. On the allied troops: Nicol, *Byzantine Family*, 80 and note 113; Gregoras, III, 180–81; Kantakouzenos, III, 246 (claiming Dušan sent 7,000 cavalry), 248.

27. J. Barker, *Manuel II Palaeologus (1391–1425): A Study in Late Byzantine Statesmanship* (New Brunswick, N.J., 1969), 28 note 65.

28. Laiou, *Constantinople*, 290.

in Asia, such a policy held no immediate benefit for either Serbia or Bulgaria. On the one hand, the Slavs could feel only threatened by Byzantine successes in Asia, since these would free troops for European campaigns. On the other hand, once a Byzantine rebel, usurper, or fearful emperor facing domestic disturbances turned to the Slavs, assistance made much sense. No matter which element prevailed, the Empire was weakened by the conflict, and the Slav ruler, regardless of which side he had supported, could demand a generous reward for his aid or generous terms of peace lest he be tempted to support future rebels (a situation Machiavelli knowledgeably addresses in Chapters 3 and 13 of *The Prince*). Relations between Serbia and Bulgaria also made intervention in Byzantine internal affairs attractive. Since both rival states had their eyes on the Empire, neither could afford to abstain from aiding one or the other Byzantine side once the other Slavic state had become involved. A state that remained neutral gained nothing and risked having no say in its Slavic neighbor's aggrandizement.

Much more serious than the threats posed by Byzantium's Slavic neighbors was a new development involving the Ottoman Turks. In 1352 the town of Tzympe on the Thracian coast near Gallipoli suffered a minor earthquake. Abandoned by its inhabitants, it was quickly occupied by a group of Turks. While Kantakouzenos was desperately trying to convince them to leave, another, more serious earthquake shook the coast of Thrace in 1354. Orhan's son Sulayman sent a large number of Turks to occupy the towns and villages which had been deserted by the native population. Special attention was paid to the refortification of Gallipoli. The era had ended in which the Byzantines could rely on the rapid appearance and rapid departure of Turkish allied troops. The Turks were now coming to stay.[29]

After his defeat at the Marica in 1352 John V Palaiologos was taken into custody, and he and his family were sent to the island of Tenedos where he passed the time plotting a return to Constantinople. In 1353 Matthew Kantakouzenos officially replaced John V in the order of imperial succession, and the next year he was crowned emperor. Nevertheless, although John V had been defeated militarily, popular opinion had now shifted in his favor. In November 1354 he crept back into Constantinople and, amid a large measure of popular support for Palaiologos, Kantakouzenos was forced to capitulate. The resulting settlement divided political power between Matthew Kantakouzenos and John V, for the weary John VI had

29. Nicol, *Last Centuries*, 248–50.

decided it was time to abdicate. But again such a compromise solution proved unworkable, and the spring of 1355 saw renewed fighting between Matthew and John V. After another period of peace, Matthew with the help of some 5,000 Turks sent by Orhan marched on the capital during the summer of 1356. While en route he was captured by the Serb governor of Drama and offered to John V for ransom. Matthew now had no choice but to surrender all claims to the throne. In December 1357 he formally renounced his title and John V Palaiologos became undisputed ruler of an Empire in ruins.[30]

30. Ibid., 246–48, 250–57. On Orhan's troops: Kantakouzenos, III, 324, and cf. Gregoras, III, 564.

5. The Last Century (1357–1448)

> With God's help, the enemy will not now, nay never, conquer us while
> we are capable of bearing arms and fighting for the honor with which
> we prefer to die.
>
> —Manuel II Palaiologos[1]

From the late 1350s the Ottoman Turks began their conquest of the Balkan
peninsula. By around 1365 Byzantium as a political unit was reduced to
Constantinople and its suburbs for some twenty or thirty miles; Thessaloniki and its environs, now isolated and in tenuous contact with the
capital; the Byzantine Morea, entirely on its own; a number of Aegean
islands such as Lemnos, Thasos, and Tenedos; a few coastal cities on the Sea
of Marmara and the Black Sea such as Selymbria, Rhaidestos, and Anchialos; and a few odds and ends such as distant Philadelphia in Asia Minor
which had long since lost all contact with the capital. The once proud
Empire was now but a minor state dependent on the Ottoman Empire.
That it lasted past the turn of the fifteenth century was only due to civil war
and the other crises that racked the Ottoman state. In the end Byzantium
was merely Constantinople and part of the Morea, owing its pathetic
existence solely to the sultan's pleasure.

Very little can be said about the army during this final century because
the number and quality of both narrative and documentary sources decline
dramatically. The historians who dealt with the era, primarily Doukas and
Chalkokondyles, wrote their works after the fall of Byzantium and placed
their emphasis on the rise of the Ottoman Empire. Consequently, they had
little interest in the details of the paltry Byzantine military forces of the
period. Likewise, the rapid shrinking of the territory controlled by Byzantium led to a corresponding diminution in the production of documents

---

For the history of this period, with bibliography, see Nicol, *Last Centuries*, 263–389;
Ostrogorsky, *History*, 533–67; and J. Barker, *Manuel II Palaeologus (1391–1425): A Study in Late
Byzantine Statesmanship* (New Brunswick, N.J., 1969).

1. B. Laourdas, ed., Ὁ «Συμβουλευτικὸς πρὸς τοὺς θεσσαλονίκεις» τοῦ Μανουὴλ
Παλαιολόγου, in Μακεδονικά 3 (1955), 288–99, cited by A. Vacalopoulos, *Origins of the Greek
Nation* (New Brunswick, N.J., 1970), 120.

and in the ability and inclination to preserve them. Nevertheless, it is safe to assume that the general military practices of the earlier Palaiologan period continued, though certainly in a very enfeebled form. Soldier companies, Gasmouloi, Prosalentai, Varangians, and Cretan mercenaries still appear in the sources. Latins, individually and in small groups, continued to seek military employment at the Byzantine court, though in diminishing numbers.

The chronology of the Turkish advance into Europe during the 1360s and 1370s has still not been firmly established. First, various Turkish groups were involved aside from the Ottomans. There were those in the service of the emirs of Aydin, of Saruhan, and of Karasi, as well as independent groups of marauders. Further, for every conquest of a major town noted by some chronicler, many villages were overrun and numerous small towns were sacked or captured. Often the territory surrounding a town fell long before the town itself. Nevertheless, even a brief listing of the major towns captured during these years provides a sense of the rapid pace of the conquest. In 1361 Didymoteichon fell, though whether the conquerors were Ottomans is unknown. In 1363 Philippopolis (Plovdiv), then in Bulgarian hands, was taken, followed by the fall of Adrianople probably in 1369, whose conquerors were non-Ottoman Turks. In 1377 Adrianople became the first European Turkish capital when Murad I formally entered the town. Three years later Ohrid and Prilep fell.

The efforts of the emperors and their allies to counter the Turkish advance were tentative at best. In 1366 a cousin of the emperor, Count Amadeo VI of Savoy, with some 1,500 soldiers conducted a private crusade, seizing Gallipoli with the help of the Genoese ruler of Lesbos and some Greeks. He also took Mesembria and Sozopolis, besieged Varna, and threatened Bulgaria which, thinking the Turkish invasion was none of its concern, had been involved in a low-key border war with Byzantium since around 1363.[2]

In 1367, following the expedition of Amadeo of Savoy and John V's own journey the previous year to Hungary in an abortive attempt to secure military aid, the emperor proposed a plan to raise more soldiers from within the remains of the Empire itself. He wanted "to establish soldiers in the villages outside of Constantinople up to Selymbria and to give them the fields in them and all the land in them." John seems to have been planning to install smallholding soldiers in the villages between Constantinople and Selymbria, or perhaps some soldiers with modest pronoia grants. Since two

2. Nicol, *Last Centuries*, 274–77.

of the villages involved were held by the Church, the patriarch and an assembled synod refused to consent to the plan. There is no evidence that any aspect of the scheme was ever implemented. Seventeen years later one of the villages in question was still in the possession of the Church, although it was nearly deserted.[3]

No matter how depressing and demoralizing their plight may have been, the later Palaiologan emperors never abandoned the hope that a way could be found to restore the Empire's defenses. Yet attempts at internal reform were unsuccessful and the Byzantines could not count on aid from their Balkan neighbors. Consequently, most of their efforts involved diplomatic pleas to Western powers for military aid. Beginning in 1369, when John V journeyed to the West, these requests frequently included personal pleas from the emperor, despite how unprecedented and ideologically humiliating it was for the Emperor of the Romans, hat in hand, to court barbarians. Some of these travels took the emperor as far afield as England, but ultimately all such requests, either in person or through ambassadors, produced very little tangible results, though they continued until the very end. The rulers of the West had their own problems and were ambivalent toward Byzantium. Some wished to conquer it themselves; others, the pope in particular, felt that submission to the Church of Rome must precede Western aid. As Michael VIII had found out, any emperor who toyed with the notion of the union of the Churches was playing with political dynamite. Even so, the Byzantines knew well that a union of the Churches did not guarantee aid. Yet by playing the union card, they could always at least get the ear of the West, and so negotiations continued throughout the last century culminating, in the twelfth hour and to no avail, in the proclamation of union at the Council of Florence in 1439.

In September 1371, while John V was still in the West, the despot John Uglješa and his brother King Vukašin were killed battling the Turks at Černomen on the Marica River in Thrace. Ever since the fragmentation of Stefan Dušan's empire after his death in 1355, Vukašin had been ruling the district between Prilep and Ohrid, while Uglješa held Serres. Their deaths marked the end of Serbian power in the Middle Ages and of everything Dušan had worked for. One may ask why there were no Byzantine soldiers at the battle on the Marica (or at the later battle of Kosovo in 1389). After all, at least a few soldiers were always available for civil wars or, later, to serve

3. MM, I, 507–508. A. Laiou-Thomadakis, *Peasant Society in the Late Byzantine Empire* (Princeton, N.J., 1977), 218. M. Bartusis, "On the Problem of Smallholding Soldiers in Late Byzantium," *DOP* 44 (1990), 9.

the sultan as a symbol of the Empire's subservience. The specific reason is that John V had left his eldest son, Andronikos, in charge while he traveled west. Andronikos, who had his own designs on the throne, may have felt that passive acquiescence to the triumphs of the Ottomans could make his own position more secure. Yet there were larger issues involved. D.M. Nicol has attributed the hesitancy of the Byzantines to support the Serbs to a failure of leadership and lays the blame at the feet of John V: "it was the senior Emperor [John V] who lacked the initiative and the courage to inspire a spirit of resistance in his people; nor had he the vision to apply his moral authority as the one true Orthodox Emperor to the task of organizing a collective will to survive among the Christians of the Balkans."[4]

In the short run the Byzantines took advantage of the Serbian defeat by recapturing Serres. This was the work of Manuel II, then governing Thessaloniki, who at the same time instituted a new plan to revive the army. He decided to deprive the monastic dependencies in the area of Thessaloniki of half the tax exemption they had been enjoying on their properties and to use these revenues to finance pronoia grants to soldiers. While the monks of Mount Athos were outraged at this policy, which remained in effect at least until the early fifteenth century, it is not known what real impact it had on the defenses of the Empire.[5] What is most significant about the plan and its implementation is that even at this late date the leaders of Byzantium were still capable of fresh ideas and, specifically, that the leadership still had faith in pronoia grants as a means of financing soldiers, or, more likely, that no other means were available.

Although the battle of Marica showed the futility of a purely regional military solution to the Turkish problem, pleas for aid from the West went unanswered. So from around 1373 and until his death John V adopted a policy of cooperation with the Turks, becoming in essence a vassal of the sultan. Here "vassal" is used in a nontechnical sense, implying only that John was acknowledging his dependence on the sultan's will. Early in 1373, as the customary sign of subordination to the Turkish ruler, John V joined Murad I's camp in Asia Minor and fought alongside him.

While John V was away from the capital his eldest son Andronikos IV and Murad's son Savci Beg staged a rebellion against their fathers, and for the next twelve years Byzantium was involved in a series of coups and civil wars. In many ways this was a replay of the civil wars of the 1340s and 1350s in that disorders in Byzantium were simply the outward symptoms of the

4. Barker, *Manuel*, 16. Nicol, *Last Centuries*, 304.
5. P. Lemerle et al., *Actes de Lavra* (Paris, 1970–82), IV, 52–53, and see herein, p. 169.

foreign policy maneuvering of the Turks, the Genoese, and the Venetians, in whose interest it was that Byzantium be divided by internal discord. Andronikos' resentment at his father's growing attachment to his younger brother Manuel and his fear that he would be excluded from the succession were cultivated by the Genoese and the Turks, whereas the Venetians stood on John V's side. The revolt of the two sons was put down militarily by their fathers. Savci was blinded at Murad's order; the sultan ordered that John V do the same. Dutifully John V had his son Andronikos and his grandson the future John VII blinded, though evidently they later regained their sight. Both were imprisoned and Andronikos was officially removed from the imperial order of succession.

In 1376 Andronikos escaped from his confinement in Constantinople, and with Genoese support and Turkish approval he laid siege to the city. John V and his other sons Manuel and Theodore finally capitulated and were imprisoned in the Tower of Anemas in the northwest corner of the city. Andronikos was obliged to turn Gallipoli over to the Turks to repay them for supporting his coup, and when the so-called Chioggia war between Genoa and Venice began that year, Andronikos provided aid to the Genoese.[6]

In 1379 John V and his sons made their escape. With the support of Murad I, they reentered Constantinople with a Turkish army and some Venetian help and reestablished John V's government. It is typical of this period that the only opposition we hear of was from a garrison of Genoese soldiers. John and Manuel agreed to pay tribute to the Turks, to provide military forces for regular and annual service, and apparently to hand over Philadelphia, the last Byzantine possession in Asia Minor.[7] Andronikos IV fled to Galata, which Manuel then besieged for more than a year. A settlement was reached in 1381 and confirmed by formal treaty the next year which recognized Andronikos as heir to the throne and allowed him to rule some territory on the coast of the Sea of Marmara with Selymbria as his capital.

The rebellion of Andronikos IV illustrates one of the chief characteris-

6. Barker, *Manuel*, 24–29. While Pseudo-Phrantzes (Makarios Melissourgos, in V. Grecu, ed., *Georgios Sphrantzes, Memorii 1401–1477* [Bucharest, 1966], 196) claims that in return for subservience and tribute, Murad promised Andronikos 6,000 horse and 4,000 foot, the more reliable Doukas, 73, mentions only Genoese aid. Barker, *Manuel*, 28 note 65, suggests that the real fighting was by the Genoese with the Turks simply observing.

7. Barker, *Manuel*, 35. Chalkokondyles (*Laonici Chalcocondylae Atheniensis Historiarum libri decem*, ed. I. Bekker [Bonn, 1843], 63) says Manuel promised a tribute of 3,000 gold pieces and annual military service. Pseudo-Phrantzes, ed. Grecu, 196, cited by Barker, *Manuel*, 34 note 89, claims that Manuel agreed to continue the tribute Andronikos promised and also to serve Murad with 12,000 foot and horse, an absurd figure.

tics of Byzantine military activities during the last century. As a state subject to the Turkish sultan, Byzantium was sometimes the obedient vassal, sometimes the rebel, making the most of opportunities to assert a measure of independence, but always its military affairs were intimately tied to Ottoman policies. The sultans took an equally active interest in Byzantine internal affairs. Their conscientious efforts to maintain dissension within the Empire, a game the Serbian and Bulgarian rulers had played during the early part of the century, contrasts well with the motives behind the aid provided earlier by Umur Pasha and even Orhan. The military assistance Andronikos IV received in 1376 and John V received in 1379 were only the first of several occasions in which the Ottoman sultans sent allied troops to the aid of a claimant to the Byzantine throne.

In 1382 Manuel II, eliminated from the line of succession, assumed the governorship of Thessaloniki, where he initiated an independent resistance against the Turks. After several small victories which discomfited his father's policy of accommodation, Murad launched a counter-offensive, retaking Serres and laying siege to Thessaloniki. Manuel's troops were defeated in mid-1384 at the battle of Chortaites near Thessaloniki. Outside of the Morea, this was probably the last pitched battle the Byzantines fought with the Turks.[8]

Even though by the end of the fourteenth century there was hardly an army at all, this did little to hinder the endemic petty squabbling of the Byzantine leadership. In 1385 Andronikos IV violated the treaty of 1382 by attacking a fort held by his father. According to a chronicle, a battle was fought between Constantinople and Selymbria. "Then departing for Selymbria, he [Andronikos IV] continued hostilities with his father. He marched out against his father along with the *politikon* army to a place located near the town called Melitias. Defeated, he returned to Selymbria," where he died soon afterward.[9]

I have not encountered the phrase "the *politikon* army" elsewhere. Here it refers to the army John V commanded and could mean either "the state army" or "the army of the city," that is, the army of Constantinople. Since this particular chronicle often speaks of Constantinople as "the Polis" ("the City"), I think the chronicler wanted to indicate the "army of the City" more than "the army of the state." In fact other sources occasionally

8. G. Dennis, *The Reign of Manuel II Palaeologus in Thessalonica, 1382–1387* (Rome, 1960), 57–76.

9. P. Schreiner, *Die byzantinischen Kleinchroniken* (Vienna, 1975–79), I, 68. R.-J. Loenertz, "Fragment d'une lettre de Jean V Paléologue à la commune de Gênes, 1387–1391," *BZ* 51 (1958), 37–40. Barker, *Manuel*, 51.

use the suffix -*tikon* to designate regional armies (for example, *Moraïtikon phossaton*, "Morean"; *Serriotikon mega allagion*, "of Serres"; *Vizyeteikon mega allagion*, "of Vizye"; and the tortuous *Melenikiotikon strateuma*, "of Melnik"). Later the same chronicler employs the adjective *Christopolitikon* to modify "galley" (see note 12 below), which shows that he was not unfamiliar with the linguistic construction. On the other hand, the best example I can find of a clear use of the word *politikon* in the sense of "of the city" is found in a document from Chios from 1259 that mentions a church called *to Politikon*.[10] Nevertheless, there is no need to strain for distinctions where none may have existed. Around 1400, when the chronicle entry was copied, if we discount the independent Morea, the State was indeed more or less the City. When the army of the City, which also happened to be the State army, met Andronikos, it is unlikely that there were a hundred men on each side.

Meanwhile, Murad continued his advance through the Balkans. In 1385 he took Sofia, in 1386 Niš, in 1387 Verria, and that same year Thessaloniki finally surrendered after a three-year siege. In 1389 at the battle of Kosovo Polje (the Field of Blackbirds) Murad along with his Christian vassals defeated the allied forces of Prince Lazar of Serbia, Tvrtko I of Bosnia, and the Serb Vuk Branković. During the battle Murad was assassinated, but the accession of his son Bayezid brought little respite to Byzantium.

After Andronikos IV's death in 1385, his son John VII succeeded to his appanage and pretensions. In 1390 with Turkish and Genoese troops he besieged Constantinople and won entry into the city. According to the Russian traveler Ignatius of Smolensk,

> There was a din all over the city, and soldiers lit the whole city with lanterns as they raced around the city on foot and on horseback among the crowds [of people] in their nightclothes. They [the soldiers] carried weapons in their hands and had arrows ready in their bows as they cried, "Long live Andronikos!" All the people, men, women, and even little children answered, with all the citizens shouting, "Long live Andronikos!," inasmuch as [the soldiers] turned their arms violently on those who did not cry out this way immediately. . . . There were no slain to be seen anywhere, such was the fear inspired by the brandished weapons.[11]

10. Schreiner, *Kleinchroniken*, I, 242; M. Bartusis, "The Megala Allagia and the Tzaousios," *REB* 47 (1989), 188, 190; and Akropolites, 114. *Regesten*, no. 1870. In the eleventh century Michael Psellos described the civil aristocracy in Constantinople with the phrase "the *politikon* race," which implies both senses of "political" and "Constantinopolitan": P. Lemerle, *Cinq études sur le XIe siècle byzantin* (Paris, 1977), 258.

11. G. Majeska, *Russian Travelers to Constantinople in the Fourteenth and Fifteenth Centuries* (Washington, D.C., 1984), 102–103, 411–12. Barker, *Manuel*, 71 and note 192.

Ignatius' report of this forced acclamation (which evidently referred to the deceased Andronikos IV, perhaps to John VII himself, or perhaps Ignatius confused the names) indicates that support for John VII was not quite unanimous.

In any event, John V continued to resist from the Golden Gate fortress in the southwestern corner of the city, while Manuel escaped to seek help. According to the same chronicler who spoke of the battle of Melitias, he acquired ships from the Knights Hospitaller of Rhodes, Kavalla (Christoupolis), and other places, and in August 1390 "the emperor kyr Manuel returned with two Rhodian galleys and a Lemnian [galley] and a Christopolitikon [galley] and his own *politikon* [galley] and other small ships," and succeeded in freeing his father and driving John VII out of Constantinople. Peter Schreiner's opinion that *phossaton* ("army") was the implied noun modified by "Lemnian," "Christopolitikon," and *politikon* is a needlessly intricate interpretation since the passage provides two perfectly serviceable nouns ("galley" and "ships") to be modified by all three adjectives. In this context, Manuel's "own *politikon* galley" was "his own ship of the City," the one on which he had fled Constantinople.[12]

Following John VII's abortive coup in 1390, Doukas reports that Bayezid required John V to provide a son for the sultan's campaigns as well as a hundred Byzantine soldiers. So low a figure is eloquent testimony to the pitiful size of the "army." During 1390 and, after John V's death, during 1391–92 Manuel II campaigned with his nephew John VII in Bayezid's army, assisting in the Turkish capture of Philadelphia. There was of course nothing voluntary about such service; it was a humiliating sign of the emperor's vassalage to the Ottoman sultan. In Manuel's own words, "It is especially unbearable to have to fight along with those and on behalf of those whose every increase in strength lessens our own strength." In a letter to a friend, written while on one of these campaigns, Manuel laments "the scarcity of supplies, the severity of winter, and the sickness which has struck down many of our men, which, as you can understand, has greatly depressed me."[13]

In 1393 after a revolt in Bulgaria resulting in the country's direct subjection to the sultan, Bayezid decided it was time to take Constantinople. From the spring of 1394 and for the next eight years he laid siege to the

12. Schreiner, *Kleinchroniken*, I, 69; II, 342. Cf. Barker, *Manuel*, 76–77; Majeska, *Russian Travelers*, 412; and G. Kolias, «Ἡ ἀνταρσία Ἰωάννου Ζ΄ Παλαιολόγου ἐναντίον Ἰωάννου Ε΄ Παλαιολόγου (1390)», Ἑλληνικά 12 (1952), 50.

13. Doukas, 75. Manuel II Palaiologos, *The Letters of Manuel II Palaeologus*, ed. G. Dennis (Washington, D.C., 1977), no. 19, lines 8–10; no. 16, lines 64–66. Barker, *Manuel*, 79, 87–99.

city. A more or less constant blockade was accompanied by intermittent assaults of varying intensity involving, according to Doukas, up to 10,000 Turkish troops at a time.[14] The long siege was interrupted only by the indecisive battle of Rovine in Wallachia, fought in May 1395 between Bayezid and Mircea of Wallachia, during which the petty Serbian princes Marko Kraljević and Constantine Dragaš, vassals no less than John V and Manuel II, were killed while fighting for the sultan, and by the battle of Nikopolis (September 1396) in which as many as 100,000 crusaders— French, Germans, Wallachians, Hungarians, and others—under John Stracimir of Vidin, Mircea of Wallachia, and Sigismund of Hungary were crushed by Bayezid and his vassal Stefan Lazarević of Serbia.

With the blockade still in place Manuel II received some good news. Jean le Meingre, more commonly known as Marshall Boucicaut, a nobleman who had fought at Nikopolis, was authorized by the French king Charles VI to lead an army to Constantinople. At the end of June 1399 he departed from the south of France with a force of some 1,200 troops, including 400 men-at-arms, 400 armed attendants, and many archers. Others joined his army along the way, and he arrived in Constantinople with 600 men-at-arms, 600 armed grooms, and one thousand archers.[15]

At summer's end Boucicaut and Manuel II launched a joint expedition against the Black Sea fortress of Riva, built by the Venetians but now held by Turks, located near the mouth of the Bosporos. According to the account given by the Western chronicler of Boucicaut's exploits (whose figures seem somewhat high), the allies arrived by sea and found a Turkish force of 6,000 or 7,000 men waiting for them in front of the fortress. Since, we are told, the Christian army was larger than this, the Turks shifted most of their troops from Riva to augment the army outside the walls, hoping to attack the allies as they assaulted the fortress. However, Boucicaut and Manuel II divided their army. Manuel and his guard, along with an allied force of Hospitallers and a large number of men-at-arms and crossbowmen, moved against the Turkish army outside the walls, while Boucicaut himself attacked the fortress and seized it without much difficulty. The Turkish force outside withdrew without engaging Manuel.[16]

After this morale-building episode Boucicaut carried out a number of

---

14. Doukas, 79.

15. *Le livre des faicts du bon messire Jean le Maingre, dit Boucicaut, Maréschal de France et Gouverneur de Jennes*, in J. de Froissart, *Les Chroniques*, ed. J. Buchon, vol. 3 (Paris, 1838), XXX–XXXII, 601–603. D. Hadjopoulos, "Le premier siège de Constantinople par les Ottomans (1394–1402)," diss., Université de Montréal 1980, 166. Barker, *Manuel*, 162.

16. *Livre des faicts*, XXXIII, 605–606. Hadjopoulos, "Le premier siège," 168–70.

other raids in the vicinity of Constantinople, but he himself realized that he was adding but a footnote to the story of the Turkish conquest of the Balkans. He suggested Manuel head west and plead his case for massive aid in person. At the end of 1399 Manuel and Boucicaut departed the city, leaving John VII in charge. According to Boucicaut's chronicler, one hundred men-at-arms and one hundred armed attendants, as well as some archers, were left behind, along with provisions and their monthly pay. They remained in Constantinople under one of Boucicaut's lieutenants at least until the end of the siege, busying themselves with some small-scale raiding and plundering.[17]

Years had passed and the city still had not fallen. The walls and the resolve of the defenders held, and with ships and food provided by the Venetians and to a lesser extent the Genoese, the inhabitants were able to outlast Bayezid. The Turks still did not control the sea, and as long as Christian ships could run the blockade, Bayezid's plans were frustrated. What finally ended the siege was the rise of the Mongols under Timur (Timur-lenk, or Tamburlaine), who in 1401 captured Baghdad and forced Bayezid to direct his energies eastward. In July 1402 at the battle of Ankara Bayezid's forces were crushed, and he himself was captured and died the next year. The Ottoman Empire disintegrated as Timur swept through Asia Minor, and rival Turkish emirs, whose lands had been forcibly assimilated into the Ottoman state, now reasserted their independence. In the ensuing chaos, the siege and blockade of Constantinople were abandoned.

After Timur's death in 1405, his hastily constructed empire fragmented, and a number of Bayezid's sons sought to restore Ottoman authority. According to an Ottoman custom designed to avoid civil war, the son who managed to succeed his father usually had all the other sons murdered. In this case none of the sons was able to overpower and eliminate the others immediately, and so from 1402 until 1413 they fought a prolonged civil war. With a respite from the Ottoman peril, the Byzantines contributed actively to the Turkish time of troubles by providing whatever aid and comfort they could to the various claimants.[18]

Immediately following the battle of Ankara, Bayezid's son Sulayman established himself as ruler of the European provinces. He concluded treaties in 1403 with John VII and other Christian leaders which, among other things, returned Thessaloniki to Byzantium. Meanwhile in Asia

17. *Livre des faicts*, XXXIII–XXXIV, 607. Barker, *Manuel*, 200, 207, 219 note 28, 238 note 69.

18. On fifteenth-century Byzantine-Ottoman relations, see E. Werner, *Die Geburt einer Grossmacht—Die Osmanen* (Weimar, 1985).

Minor, Mehmet, another of Bayezid's sons, attacked his brother and rival Isa who at first took refuge in Constantinople but later returned to Asia, where Mehmet killed him. From 1407 through 1411 Mehmet and his brother Musa were allied against Sulayman, whom the Byzantines supported. When Sulayman was defeated and executed by Musa in 1411, the latter invested Constantinople by land and sea. The Turkish naval attack was driven off by some ships Manuel II was able to assemble, and the Turks had no luck surmounting the city's walls.[19] Manuel now courted Mehmet. New hostilities between Mehmet and Musa concluded with Musa's defeat and execution in 1413. In a very weakened condition, Mehmet made peace with Byzantium and restored its territory in accordance with the 1403 treaty. Finally, as a kind of postscript, in 1415 a pretender to the Ottoman throne named Mustafa appeared who claimed to be Bayezid's eldest son (the real Mustafa having disappeared after the battle of Ankara). In 1416 after an abortive attack upon Mehmet he took refuge in Thessaloniki, and shortly afterward the Byzantines imprisoned him on Lemnos. It was always good to have an Ottoman pretender available if needed.

The Ottoman civil war and its aftermath granted Manuel II the opportunity to attend to matters he had put off far too long. First on his list was a visit in 1415 to the Byzantine Morea, a distant, increasingly isolated province which he felt demanded his personal attention. When Manuel Kantakouzenos had died childless in 1380, Theodore Palaiologos, John V's fourth son, was appointed despot of the Morea. In 1382 he arrived with no army and no sure means of acquiring one. A funeral oration composed by Manuel II for his brother reveals that Theodore had faced opposition from some members of the Kantakouzenos family, who after Manuel Kantakouzenos' thirty-one-year rule had come to regard the Morea as an appanage of their family. Manuel II says that a son of Matthew, Manuel Kantakouzenos' brother,

> attacked my brother [Theodore] by various means, allying himself with Turks and Latins. Suddenly he spread confusion everywhere, springing like a hurricane out of calm seas. . . . His threats were terrifying but his actions no less so, inasmuch as he had a mercenary army and was supported by a considerable number of local people. He also possessed fortresses which had been given to him by his father.

Even though this Kantakouzenos died only a year or so after Theodore's arrival, Theodore still had to deal with the rebellious lords of the Morea

---

19. Barker, *Manuel*, 285–86.

who had become accustomed to autonomy, as well as with the Latins neighboring the Byzantine Morea. A Western source reports that in 1384 Manuel, although he himself was under siege in Thessaloniki, managed to send Theodore one hundred cavalry "lances" to fight the Navarrese Company (called the "White Company"), an army of adventurers who had taken over the enfeebled Principality of Achaia in 1381.[20]

During the early years of his rule in the Morea, Theodore I remained an obedient vassal of the sultan. In 1387–88, at Theodore's request, Murad I sent his general Evrenos to attack the Latin lords of the Morea.[21] The accession of Bayezid had changed relations, however, as he tightened the ties of dependency between himself and his Christian Balkan vassals. Early in 1394 he required Theodore to accompany him when he attacked Thessaly, but Theodore escaped and this ended his previously cordial relations with the Ottomans. Late in 1394 or early in 1395 Bayezid sent Evrenos to ravage the Morea at the request of Carlo Tocco, count of Kephalenia, who in 1394 had acquired Athens and Corinth, part of the fragmented Principality of Achaia, at the death of his father-in-law the Florentine Nerio Acciajuoli. Theodore, also a son-in-law of Nerio, seized the occasion to attack Corinth with a force, according to an Italian source, of 20,000 men. Although Evrenos defeated Theodore at Corinth, a chronicle reports that Demetrios Palaiologos Raoul, one of Theodore's generals, "with his own army, Albanians and Romans," scored some successes against the Navarrese of Achaia in mid-1395.[22]

The Albanians in Demetrios Raoul's army and those no doubt constituting some or most of Theodore's forces at Corinth were new troops who had recently been settled in the Morea and enrolled as soldiers. In the later decades of the fourteenth century, there was a steady migration of Albanians into the Morea. After Theodore arrived on the scene he began to

20. Manuel II Palaiologos, *Manuel II Palaeologus, Funeral Oration on His Brother Theodore*, ed. and trans. J. Chrysostomides (Thessaloniki, 1985), 113–19, quote: 116–17, trans. by ed. R.-J. Loenertz, "Pour l'histoire du Péloponèse au XIVe siècle (1382–1404)," *Études byzantines* 1 (1943), 163, 166. D. Nicol, *The Byzantine Family of Kantakouzenos (Cantacuzenus)* (Washington, 1968), 157–59. Zakythinos, *Despotat*, II, 135; I, 148. G. Dennis, "The Capture of Thebes by the Navarrese (6 March 1378) and Other Chronological Notes in Two Paris Manuscripts," in Dennis, *Byzantium and the Franks, 1350–1420* (London, 1982), no. XV, 43–47.

21. Schreiner, *Kleinchroniken*, II, 335. Loenertz, "Pour l'histoire," 168.

22. Zakythinos, *Despotat*, I, 155; II, 136, citing L. LeGrand, "Relation du Pèlerinage à Jérusalem de Nicolas de Martonia, notaire Italien (1394–1395)," *Revue de l'Orient latin* 3 (1895), 657. Loenertz, "Pour l'histoire," 185–86. Schreiner, *Kleinchroniken*, I, 244–45, which also includes another version of the same chronicle which says that Demetrios Raoul led "the army of Leontari [a town in the Morea] and of the Albanians." Zakythinos, *Despotat*, II, 135, speaks of an "army corps of Leontarion.".

encourage actively this immigration. In Manuel II's funeral oration for his brother, he speaks of Theodore's settlement of 10,000 Albanians, adding that these soldiers supplemented "the forces of the Peloponnesos which in themselves were not small."[23]

The Albanians became one of the elements central to the defense of the Byzantine Morea; another was the Hexamilion, a line of fortifications across the Isthmus of Corinth separating the Peloponnesos from the rest of Greece. With the weakening of Latin power in the Morea, Byzantine strategy was redirected toward the Turks. Since the Ottomans still had no adequate navy, they could invade the Morea in force only via land, and therefore the key to protecting the Morea from the Ottomans was the defense of the Isthmus. In 1397, following up their victory over Theodore I two years earlier, a Turkish force reportedly consisting of 50,000 or 60,000 men under Evrenos and Iakoub Pasha destroyed the existing fortification at the Hexamilion. Eleven years later, while visiting the Morea to install his young son Theodore II as despot following the death of Theodore I, Manuel II made initial plans to rebuild it. He may have been influenced by John VII's restoration of a wall across the peninsula of Kassandreia at Potidaia in 1407 during John's last year as governor of Thessaloniki. Such walls had indeed proved their utility. Gregoras reports that around 1307 Andronikos II had built a wall from Kavalla to the ridge of the neighboring mountain so that the Catalan Company, then based on the Kassandreia peninsula, could not return to Thrace.[24]

The new fortification at the Isthmus was erected upon the remains of an existing fortified wall built by Justinian in the sixth century, though the earliest barrier there dates as far back as 480 B.C. when the Greeks were trying to hold back Xerxes during the Persian Wars. Most of the wall was rapidly constructed in 1415 over a period of twenty-five days, and it included some 150 towers with forts at either end.[25] The construction was financed by a new tax called the *phloriatikon*, which aroused the ire of the inhabitants of the Morea and led to a rebellion later the same year. In the end Manuel reestablished his authority over the lords of the region, but the lack of local

23. *Manuel II Palaeologus, Funeral Oration*, 118–21, and cf. Gemistos Plethon's "preface" to the oration, 67–68. C. Woodhouse, *George Gemistos Plethon, The Last of the Hellenes* (Oxford, 1986), 90–91. Cf. Nicol, *Last Centuries*, 358.

24. J. Bompaire, *Actes de Xéropotamou* (Paris, 1964), no. 28. Gregoras, I, 246. Though Gregoras claims that Andronikos built a wall, it is more likely that he actually fortified the antique aqueduct running northward from the town, part of which exists in fine condition today.

25. Barker, *Manuel*, 311, with bibliography; 312 note 20.

support for a unified defense did not bode well for the future. And the future of the Hexamilion was remarkably bleak. At the first testing of the restored fortification in 1423, an invading Turkish army of 25,000 men (according to an Italian source) under the general Turahan found it unmanned. Turahan promptly destroyed it and followed up his effortless victory by ravaging the Morea.[26]

Indeed, though the Hexamilion seems to have been a fine fortification, the government did not have the resources and the population was too rent by factionalism to garrison it properly. In the years immediately following its building the humanist George Gemistos Plethon twice wrote to Manuel II suggesting ways to ensure that the fortification would have a proper complement of troops, he himself offering to recruit and organize the soldiers. His advice, which involved some radical reforms for the army that will be discussed later, went unheeded, but Gemistos' enthusiasm for the Hexamilion and his understanding of its weaknesses illustrate the state of Morean affairs in which short-term projects were feasible but long-term cooperation impossible.[27]

Evidently the fortification was repaired after its destruction in 1423, for when Turahan again invaded the Morea in 1431, he demolished it once again. In 1443 the despot of the Morea Constantine Palaiologos, the future Constantine XI, rebuilt the wall which had been lying in ruin for twelve years. In a letter from around 1444, George Bessarion, one of Gemistos Plethon's former students, repeated the idea that the Isthmus was the key to defending the Morea. He urged the despot to build a city at the Isthmus and live there himself, advice Constantine evidently ignored.[28] In 1446 the Hexamilion again fell quickly to Turahan's army and was again destroyed. According to Doukas, the fortification had been defended by 60,000 (!) Albanians and Greeks, and he attributes its fall to the perfidy of the former. Finally, the despots Thomas and Demetrios Palaiologos attempted to restore the Hexamilion in the early 1450s, but the ill-fated fortification did nothing to stop another Turkish invasion by Turahan in 1452. If rulers were graded by their intentions, Manuel would have scored high with the Hexamilion. But the dreadful record of this fortification, which the Turks

26. *Letters of Manuel II Palaeologus*, ed. Dennis, no. 68. Barker, *Manuel*, 310–17, 371.

27. S. Lampros, Παλαιολόγεια καὶ Πελοποννησιακά (Athens, 1912–30), III, 251–53, 261, 310–11. Woodhouse, *George Gemistos Plethon*, 100–101, 103, 105.

28. Lampros, Παλαιολόγεια, IV, 33–34. There is a summary of the letter in Vacalopoulos, *Origins*, 172–78.

seem to have breached whenever they pleased, lends a certain pathetic irony to Dionysios Zakythinos' claim that the Hexamilion was "one of the more brilliant successes of Manuel's Morean policy."[29]

After Manuel's return from the Morea, he and his son John VIII continued their attempts to obtain Western aid and to exploit the weakness of the Ottoman regime. When Mehmet died in 1421 the emperors put forth the pretender Mustafa as the Byzantine candidate in the tussle for the Ottoman throne. The next year, after Mustafa was defeated and executed by Mehmet's son Murad II, it was necessary to teach Byzantium a lesson. From June until August 1422 Murad laid siege to Constantinople with some 10,000 men. For the first time in their struggles with Byzantium the Turks employed cannon. Although these evidently had little effect on the course of the siege, thirty years later the results would be much different.

According to the chronicler John Kananos, the siege of 1422 brought out the best within the Byzantine spirit. He recounts how people from all walks of life bravely contributed to the defense effort: "Not only the soldiers and those skilled in war did these things, but the archons of the government and those skilled of the countryside and all of the common people, the whole of the priests and monks and the braver of the archpriests and the holiest of spiritual holies." After the failure of a Turkish general assault, Murad was forced to abandon the siege because civil war had broken out again in Anatolia. In another triumph of Byzantine diplomacy Manuel II had successfully prompted Murad's younger brother Mustafa to make his bid for control of the Ottoman state. Even though Murad was soon able to defeat and, as usual, execute his brother, Constantinople had withstood its second major Ottoman siege. According to Kananos, while more than a thousand Turks fell, only about thirty Byzantines were killed and fewer than a hundred wounded.[30]

In 1424 a humiliating peace treaty granted the sultan further territorial concessions as well as the promise of yearly tribute. The Empire was now reduced almost to Constantinople, its suburbs, and the distant, factionalized Morea. Meanwhile the Turks had been besieging Thessaloniki. In 1423, faced with starvation and a dwindling population, its governor, another of Manuel II's sons, the despot Andronikos, decided his only option

29. Nicol, *Last Centuries*, 379, 381–82, 401. Schreiner, *Kleinchroniken*, II, 444. Chalkokondyles, Bonn ed., 381. Doukas, 279. Zakythinos, *Despotat*, II, 141–42; I, 169.

30. Giovanni Cananos, *L'assedio di Costantinopoli*, ed. and Italian trans. E. Pinto (Messina, 1977), lines 29, 462–68, 558–61 (see under Kananos in Bibliography).

was to offer the city to the Venetians in hopes that the Turks would abandon their siege. Even this desperate act did not save the city, which fell in 1430.

The fires of civil strife were fanned once again by the sultan in 1442. John VIII's brother Demetrios, despot at Mesembria, took advantage of the anti-union fervor that had swept the city following the proclamation of the union of the Eastern and Western Churches at the Council of Florence (1438–39) by laying siege to Constantinople. Murad II provided military support in the abortive effort. During the remainder of the 1440s Constantinople enjoyed a respite from Ottoman expansion as the Turks spent their time dealing with opposition elsewhere in the Balkans in which the Byzantines played no military role. Indeed, aside from the few troops garrisoning Constantinople, perhaps a few hundred, many of whom were foreign, the emperor had no army. The conquest of Constantinople awaited merely the next determined Turkish effort.

The situation in southern Greece was quite different. The 1430s and 1440s marked the highpoint for the Byzantine Morea. In order to minimize the endemic feuding characteristic of Morean affairs (which seems to have infected all who came to the area) each of John VIII's three youngest brothers were given a portion of the Byzantine territory there to rule as despots. From 1432 Theodore II was based in Mistra, Constantine (the later emperor) held the area around Kalavryta, and Thomas ruled the region around Chlemoutsi. Constantine, whose appanage was in the northeastern part of the Peloponnesos, was responsible for most of the military advances during this period. In 1430 he took Patras after a long siege, and in 1432 the Latin Principality of Achaia came to a long-expected end. Except for Korone, Methone, Nauplia, and Argos, all held by Venice, the Peloponnesos was now in Greek hands. In 1444 Despot Constantine seized Athens, Thebes, and Boeotia, and he received the allegiance of the Vlachs of the Pindos mountains, whom he provided with a military commander to battle the Turkish settlers in Thessaly. Meanwhile the Albanians in the mountains north of Naupaktos came over to the Greek side.[31]

If we are to believe the few sources that give figures for the size of the Morean army, it is easy to account for these successes. An anonymous memoir of the council of Basel in 1437 reports that the army of the Morea consisted of "50,000 cavalrymen without infantry," while in 1439 Jean Torzelo in his *Advis* to Philip the Fair of Burgundy offers the figure of

31. Chalkokondyles, Bonn ed., 319, 341.

15,000 men.[32] As already noted, Doukas estimated the Albanian and Greek forces at the Isthmus in 1446 at 60,000. The great disparity of these figures casts doubt on all of them, especially when we learn that Constantine's frequent diplomatic appeals for Western aid paid off in 1445 when he received a detachment of a mere 300 Burgundians.[33] Further, if there truly were tens of thousands of warriors in the Morea, we might ask why they never lent aid to the government in Constantinople. The Byzantine successes in the Morea at this time can better be attributed to the fact that they were the last to survive the battle royal of petty Morean states.

In 1448 John VIII died and his brother Despot Constantine was chosen as his successor. The next year Constantine XI arrived in Constantinople to assume the imperial throne and his role at the fall of Byzantium.

32. S. Lampros, ed., «Ὑπόμνημα περὶ τῶν ἑλληνικῶν χωρῶν καὶ ἐκκλησιῶν», Νέος Ἑλληνομνήμων 7 (1910), 364, and Baron de Reiffenberg, *Monuments pour servir à l'histoire des provinces de Namur, de Hainaut et du Luxembourg*, V (Brussels, 1848), 542 (inaccessible to me), both cited by Zakythinos, *Despotat*, II, 136.

33. K. Hopf, *Chroniques gréco-romanes* (Berlin, 1873), 195, cited by Vacalopoulos, *Origins*, 179.

6. The Fall (1451–53)

Early in 1451 Sultan Murad II died and was succeeded by his son Mehmet II. The Byzantines once again tried to profit from the customary uncertainties that followed the accession of a new sultan by informing the Ottoman government that the allowance for Prince Orhan was in arrears. Orhan, a shadowy figure said to have been a grandson of Sulayman, had been living in exile in Constantinople. Constantine XI demanded that Orhan's allowance be doubled and even threatened to release him as a rival to Mehmet. Playing the pretender card had paid off under Manuel II, but this time Sultan Mehmet, his position secure, his attitude bellicose, and his dream the conquest of Constantinople, decided it was time to erase the irritating little state on the Bosporos. In May 1453, amid the din of cannon heralding a new age, Byzantium met the ultimate destiny of all empires.

In the winter of 1451–52 the sultan ordered the encirclement of the city to begin. He sent his general Turahan to invade the Morea in order to ensure that the despots Demetrios and Thomas could not help their brother the emperor. During the spring and summer of 1452 a fortress, known today as Rumeli Hisar, was built not far from Constantinople on the western shore of the Bosporos to control the Black Sea passage. By August 1452 preliminary investing of the city by sea had begun.

The Byzantines did what they could to prepare for the contest. Walls were repaired, moats cleared, and arms gathered. Toward the end of 1452, according to Doukas, the emperor sent officials to Chios for supplies. They returned with four ships, plus a ship from the Morea which held "a great number of stout fighting men and plenty of armor."[1] Simultaneously, Constantine made a series of futile diplomatic appeals to Western and Balkan leaders. Meanwhile, Mehmet II prepared a fleet and ordered the seizure of all the towns in the vicinity of Constantinople still held by the

---

For the siege and fall, see Nicol, *Last Centuries*, 390–417; Ostrogorsky, *History*, 567–72; S. Runciman, *The Fall of Constantinople, 1453* (Cambridge, Eng., 1965); A. Vacalopoulos, *Origins of the Greek Nation* (New Brunswick, N.J., 1970), 187–233; and C. Mijatovich, *Constantine Palaeologus, The Last Emperor of the Greeks* (1892; repr. Chicago, 1968).

1. Doukas, 321.

Byzantines. By the early spring of 1453 Mesembria, Anchialos, Vizye, Herakleia on the Marmara, and other towns were in Turkish hands. On April 2 Mehmet's troops assembled before the walls of Constantinople and began the fifty-five-day siege.

The sources for the siege and fall of the city fall into several categories. Most important are the eyewitness accounts, nearly all of which were composed by Latins who for one reason or another happened to be present in Constantinople at this fateful moment. Of these the most notable are a day-by-day diary of the siege written by the Venetian ship's doctor Nicolò Barbaro and a long letter, written to Pope Nicholas V only eleven weeks after the fall, by Leonard of Chios, the Genoese archbishop of Mytilene. Shorter accounts were written by the Florentine Giacomo Tedaldi and Benvenuto, the consul of the Anconitan colony of Constantinople. The only firsthand account written in Greek is a brief section in the memoirs of George Sphrantzes. It consists almost entirely of a report of Constantine XI's diplomatic appeals at the beginning of the siege, but does provide some interesting data on the number of defenders. The Turkish account of the siege by Tursun Beg, found within a more or less personal history of the reign of Mehmet II written by a man who became a high official in the Ottoman state, also provides some useful details.

Aside from the eyewitness accounts, there are numerous other contemporary descriptions of the siege by men who were not present but presumably had spoken to eyewitnesses. The most important of these are the Greek histories of Kritoboulos, Doukas, and Chalkokondyles, followed by the Latin account of Zorzi Dolfin, and, lastly, the Slavic account of Konstantin Mihailović, who in fact claims, though probably falsely, to have been an eyewitness. Surprisingly, fifteenth-century Ottoman writers had little to say about the siege that is not known from other sources.

Many sixteenth-century authors wrote accounts of the siege but these are among the least reliable sources and I have elected not to make much use of them. Nevertheless, a few words need to be said about one of the longest narratives of the siege, that of Makarios Melissenos (Melissourgos). Writing in the third quarter of the sixteenth century, Makarios used the relatively brief autobiographical history of George Sphrantzes as the basis of a long, elaborate history of the Palaiologan dynasty up to 1477. Two facts cast doubt upon the good faith of Makarios' work. First, Makarios maintained the fiction that George Sphrantzes was the actual author of his own history, and second, Makarios was a skilled counterfeiter who is known, for example, to have forged Byzantine imperial documents while metropolitan of

Monemvasia. Generations of scholars accepted Makarios' history as a genuine Byzantine source, and since it contains one of the most detailed and certainly the most colorful account of the events of 1453, his words have had a great influence on most modern narratives of the siege and fall. Only for the past twenty-five years or so has it been generally acknowledged that Makarios wrote the long history he attributes to George Sphrantzes.

Much of Makarios' account of the siege is a paraphrase of Leonard of Chios' letter to the pope; many other details are found nowhere else. No doubt some details may be based on eyewitness testimony no longer extant, but there is no way to distinguish these from simple fabrications. Indeed it is necessary to question the veracity and motives of all of the sixteenth-century accounts of the siege and fall because in subsequent years the events of 1453 acquired a mythical stature. To have been present at the fall, to have fought bravely at the fall, to be related to someone who had fought bravely at the fall were marks of distinction that could be supplied by an obliging chronicler. Consequently, while references in all of the accounts, even those of eyewitnesses, to the presence and military duties of particular individuals must be viewed critically, this is especially necessary with regard to the later accounts.

On Easter Monday, April 2, when the advance contingent of Mehmet's army pitched camp on the landward side of city, the emperor ordered the boom—a great chain of iron and wood on wooden floats—placed across the entrance to the harbor of the Golden Horn from the tower of Eugenios to the walls of Galata. Among the troops that assembled before the walls was an allied force sent by Despot George Branković of Serbia, a dutiful vassal of the sultan. No doubt these troops did not have their hearts in the enterprise. In the words of Mihailović, the Serb who claims to have been among them, "We had to ride forward to Stambol and help the Turks conquer it; but the city would never have been conquered by our help."[2]

On April 5 the sultan arrived and camped midway along the land walls across from the Gate of St. Romanos. The Turks had several large cannon and many culverins, smaller bombards, and arquebuses, as well as more conventional weapons such as large frame-mounted crossbows, common crossbows, slings, and bows. The Florentine chronicler Tedaldi calculated that they used a thousand pounds of gunpowder each day of the siege. The largest of the cannon was a monster some twenty-nine feet long which

---

2. Konstantin Mihailović, *Memoirs of a Janissary*, ed. and trans. B. Stolz (Ann Arbor, Mich., 1975), 90–91.

hurled stones weighing 1,200 pounds. It was cast at Adrianople and brought to Constantinople on a carriage drawn by sixty oxen and manned by 200 soldiers. Because of the pressures and heat generated, it could be fired only seven times a day. In one of history's great ironies, the man who designed it was a Christian. During the summer of 1451 a Hungarian engineer named Urban had approached Constantine XI and was hired for a small sum. But either because his salary was insufficient to live on or because even this modest amount was not forthcoming, he entered the employ of the sultan.[3]

Within a week the cannon were fully deployed and the constant bombardment began. By then the defenders had taken up their positions on the walls of the city. Roughly triangular in shape, Constantinople was protected by fourteen miles of walls. The sea walls were about five and a half miles long, rising almost from the shore. The swift currents along this section made it an unlikely location for any assault. Along the three and a half miles of the short river called the Golden Horn, the walls rose behind the waterfront docks and warehouses used by the Italian ships that harbored there. Since this was where the Latins of the Fourth Crusade had breached the walls of the city, great care was taken with the harbor boom to ensure that the Turkish fleet could not enter the Golden Horn. On the land side was a triple line of defenses extending the four miles from the Sea of Marmara in the south to the Golden Horn in the north. Built a thousand years earlier and repaired continuously, it consisted of a moat and two lines of walls. The moat was some sixty feet wide and on its scarp was a low, crenelated breastwork. The outer wall had towers about forty-five feet high, and the inner line of walls were some fourteen feet thick and about forty feet high with massive towers about sixty feet in height. The land walls, the mightiest fortifications known to the medieval world, had never been breached. Lacking men, the defenders decided they would man only their outer section.[4]

3. Leonard of Chios, in Migne, *PG*, vol. 159, cols. 928–29, 932. Kritoboulos, *Critobuli Imbriotae historiae*, ed. D. Reinsch (Berlin and New York, 1983), 64, 66–68. Tursun Beg, *The History of Mehmed the Conqueror by Tursun Beg*, ed. with summary trans. H. Inalcik and R. Murphey (Minneapolis and Chicago, 1978), 34. A. Pertusi, "The Anconitan Colony in Constantinople and the Report of Its Consul, Benvenuto, on the Fall of the City," in *Charanis Studies*, ed. A. Laiou-Thomadakis (New Brunswick, N.J., 1980), 207. G. Tedaldi, trans. J. Melville Jones, *The Siege of Constantinople 1453: Seven Contemporary Accounts* (Amsterdam, 1972), 3. Runciman, *Fall*, 78. Nicolò Barbaro, *Diary of the Siege of Constantinople, 1453*, trans. J. Jones (New York, 1969), 30. Chalkokondyles, *Laonici Chalcocondylae Atheniensis Historiarum libri decem*, ed. I. Bekker (Bonn, 1843), 385–86. Doukas, 307–309.

4. On the fortifications of Constantinople, see B. Tsangadas, *The Fortifications and Defense of Constantinople* (Boulder, Col., and New York, 1980).

Every modern account of the siege provides slightly different details regarding the personnel present and how they were deployed. The reason for this is that contemporary sources themselves disagree on these matters, and modern historians have had to make choices about which sources to give the most credibility. The disagreement, even among eyewitnesses, regarding topography, numbers, and lists of personnel is understandable. Numbers are a subjective matter. Someone stationed at one point in the city might have had only the vaguest knowledge of who was manning another section. Details may have become blurred when an account was written weeks, months, or even years later. These are honest mistakes but the myth of the fall could lead to deliberate fabrication as well. This should be borne in mind as we recount the disposition of the defenders' forces during the siege.

Catarin Contarini, a Venetian, was put in charge of the Golden Gate and its adjacent towers down to the Sea of Marmara. According to Makarios Melissourgos, one "Jacob" Contarini was "at the outer harbor as far as the vicinity of Hypsimathia," by which he evidently meant the area of the sea walls south of the Golden Gate more commonly referred to as Psamathia. Although Nicolò Barbaro, in his detailed lists of the Venetians present at the siege, confirms that a Catarin Contarini was in the city, he does not mention a Jacob among all of the other Contarinis present.[5]

The defense of the mile-long stretch of walls between the Golden Gate and the Pege (Selymbria) Gate was assigned to Maurizio Cataneo, a Genoese, with 200 crossbowmen including a few Greeks. Makarios Melissourgos' reworking of Leonard of Chios' account places a "Manuel from Genoa" with 200 archers and crossbowmen at the Golden Gate.[6]

Leonard of Chios says that the Genoese Giovanni Giustiniani Longo was positioned at the Gate of St. Romanos, whereas Zorzi Dolfin places John and Andronikos Kantakouzenos there. Dolfin, writing some twenty-five years after the siege, was not an eyewitness. Further, his references to particular individuals defending specific parts of the city are usually confirmed by no other source. I prefer not to dismiss his testimony in these matters out of hand, but a caveat is called for. In any event Sphrantzes does speak of a John Kantakouzenos present at the fall who was evidently a close

5. Leonard of Chios, col. 934. Dolfin, trans. Jones, *The Siege of Constantinople*, 128–29, provides his first name, and also adds that a certain Andronikos Kantakouzenos was there: for a possible identification, see D. Nicol, *The Byzantine Family of Kantakouzenos (Cantacuzenus)* (Washington, D.C., 1968), 179–81. Barbaro, *Diary*, 73. Pseudo-Phrantzes (Makarios Melissourgos), in *Georgios Sphrantzes, Memorii 1401–1477*, ed. V. Grecu (Bucharest, 1966), 396.

6. Leonard of Chios, col. 934. Pseudo-Phrantzes, 396.

associate of the emperor, and Andronikos was probably the megas domestikos and ambassador known from other sources. However, earlier in his
account Dolfin already had positioned an Andronikos Kantakouzenos at
the Golden Gate.[7] As for Giustiniani, he had arrived toward the end of
January 1453 with two ships and 400 (Leonard of Chios, Kritoboulos) or
700 (Barbaro) men recruited from Genoa, Chios, and Rhodes (Kritoboulos). With him came the German engineer John Grant, who applied himself
to the mining and counter-mining operations.[8]

Since Barbaro states that Giustiniani was assigned to the land walls as
captain of the land forces, it is possible that he and some other unnamed
commander were present at the Gate of St. Romanos, the latter assigned
specifically to that stretch of the wall. Leonard of Chios reports that Giustiniani commanded 300 Genoese soldiers plus picked Greek troops. On the
other hand, Barbaro describes the 300 men at the Gate of St. Romanos as
"all foreigners with not a Greek among them, because the Greeks were
cowards." Perhaps these were the same men.[9]

Barbaro says that the emperor himself was at the Charisios (Adrianople) Gate, which accords with Leonard who reports that Constantine took
up position near Giustiniani.[10] On the emperor's right side the Venetian
brothers Paolo, Troilo, and Antonio Bochiardi fought at the Miliandron,
the stretch of walls to the north of the Charisios Gate.[11]

Theodore Karystenos, "an aged but vigorous Greek, most skilled with
the bow," and Theophilos Palaiologos, "of noble lineage and deep scholarship, both Catholics, along with the German engineer John" Grant saw to
the repairs and defense of the area of the Kaligaria Gate, to the south of the
Blachernai Palace.[12] The Venetian colony of the city was led by the bailli
Girolamo Minotto, who defended the walls at the Blachernai Palace.[13] And

7. Leonard of Chios, col. 934. Dolfin, trans. Jones, *Siege*, 129. Sphrantzes, 102. On the
possible identities of John and Andronikos Kantakouzenos, see Nicol, *Byzantine Family*, 179–
81, 196–98.

8. Leonard of Chios, col. 928. Kritoboulos, 40–41. Barbaro, *Diary*, 22. On Giustiniani,
see *PLP*, no. 8227. Chalkokondyles, 394, says he arrived with 300 soldiers. On John Grant,
Pseudo-Phrantzes, 388.

9. Barbaro, *Diary*, 22, 50. Leonard of Chios, col. 934. Pseudo-Phrantzes, 386, gives the
figure 300, while elsewhere, 396–98, he offers 400. Doukas, 355, claims that the emperor and
Giustiniani were at the walls with 3,000 Greeks and Latins.

10. Barbaro, *Diary*, 28. Leonard of Chios, col. 934. Cf. Chalkokondyles, 394.

11. Leonard of Chios, col. 934. Pseudo-Phrantzes, 396, calls it the "Myriandrion."

12. Leonard of Chios, col. 934; trans. Jones, *Siege*, 27. Cf. Pseudo-Phrantzes, 398 and 396,
where Theophilos Palaiologos is placed instead in command of the forces around the Pege
Gate. Dolfin, trans. Jones, *Siege*, 129, places one Emanuel Guideli at the Kaligaria Gate as well.

13. Barbaro, *Diary*, 28. Leonard of Chios, col. 935. Dolfin, trans. Jones, *Siege*, 129. Pseudo-
Phrantzes, 396.

at the northeastern tip of the city a certain Girolamo Italiano and the Genoese Leonard di Langasco were manning the Xyloporta Gate.[14]

According to Leonard of Chios, the Venetian Gabriel Trevisano, captain of the two galleys, defended the area from the Kynegon Gate to the tower of Phanarion with 400 Venetians, including the crews from his ships.[15] Next to him, according to one manuscript of Leonard of Chios, were the Venetian Bembo brothers, Alvise and Antonio, defending the area southeast of the Phanarion Gate with 150 Venetian soldiers.[16]

Along the middle of the Golden Horn walls Dolfin places Alexios Disypates at what he calls the "Pharos" Gate, by which he probably meant the Phanarion Gate; Zuan Blacho at the Gate of St. Theodosia; Metochites Palaiologos at the "Plutei" Gate (probably the Putei or Eispegas Gate); and someone he calls "Philanthropo" (probably a Philanthropenos) at the Plataia Gate. No other contemporary source specifies who was guarding these areas or mentions any of these men. This is understandable in that at least three of the men were Byzantines, and the contemporary sources are most interested in the activities of their fellow Latins.[17]

Barbaro and Leonard of Chios both say that the megas doux Loukas Notaras was stationed on the shore of the Golden Horn with reserve troops who could be sent wherever they were needed, and Barbaro adds that these troops consisted of one hundred cavalry. Doukas says that Notaras had a roving group of 500 men, and later that he had these men at the Imperial Gate. Dolfin confirms that Notaras was at the Imperial Gate. This was probably the Gate of St. John *de cornibus*, which was known by both names.[18]

Pseudo-Phrantzes (Melissourgos) claims that the sailors, officers, and

---

14. Leonard of Chios, col. 935; Pseudo-Phrantzes, 398. On Girolamo: *PLP*, no. 8139. Without good reason, some scholars identify Leonard di Langasco as Leonard of Chios. Dolfin, trans. Jones, *Siege*, 129, places one Manuel Palaiologos there.

15. Leonard of Chios, col. 935. Cf. Barbaro, *Diary*, 47. Dolfin, trans. Jones, *Siege*, 129, also places him at the Kynegon Gate. On the other hand, Pseudo-Phrantzes, 398, says that Trevisano with fifty soldiers guarded the tower in the middle of the harbor which protected the harbor entrance. This would have put him at the eastern end of the Golden Horn near the boom.

16. Leonard of Chios, trans. Jones, *Siege*, 27–28. Leonard says they were in the area from Phanarion to what he calls the "Imperial" Gate. There were at least three gates with that name (see G. Majeska, *Russian Travelers to Constantinople in the Fourteenth and Fifteenth Centuries* [Washington, D.C., 1984], 353 and note 115) but none fit Leonard's topography. Barbaro, *Diary*, 73, confirms the presence of these two men at the siege.

17. Dolfin, trans. Jones, *Siege*, 129.

18. Barbaro, *Diary*, 28. Leonard of Chios, col. 935. Doukas, 345, 355. Dolfin, trans. Jones, *Siege*, 129. On this gate, see Majeska, *Russian Travelers*, 353. Pseudo-Phrantzes, 398, claims Notaras guarded the Petrion Gate area up to the Gate of St. Theodosia.

captains of a ship from Crete who, as many others, had arrived more or less accidentally in time for this momentous occasion, manned the "towers of Basil, Leo and Alexios" in the area of the Beautiful Gate (the Neorion Gate toward the eastern end of the Golden Horn), and that after the fall they surrendered only when certain terms were granted. Although Pseudo-Phrantzes is not the most reliable source, there is in fact a brief account of the return of these Cretans to their island after the fall.[19] The harbor of the Golden Horn itself was guarded by Alvise Diedo, a Venetian captain of two or more merchant galleys, who retained command of his vessels.[20]

At the easternmost point of the city Cardinal Isidore, archbishop of Kiev, defended the quarter of St. Demetrios up to the sea walls. He had arrived in the city late in 1452 to serve as papal legate and was accompanied by our chronicler Leonard of Chios and a contingent of 200 men.[21] The Ottoman prince Orhan guarded another quarter on the seaward side "with the Turks in his pay,"[22] while the consul of the Catalan community of the city was guarding the walls to the south of the old Hippodrome. In various places "the priests and monks were spread along the walls, keeping watch for the sake of their country's safety."[23]

Finally, Leonard of Chios writes that "Demetrios Palaiologos, the father-in-law, and Nicolo Gudelli, the son-in-law, assigned to traverse the city, were kept in reserve with a lot of soldiers." Makarios Melissourgos changed this passage to "Demetrios Kantakouzenos and his son-in-law Nikephoros Palaiologos took up position in the Church of the Holy Apostles and in other places with 700 men to serve as a reserve where needed." Even though Makarios was writing a hundred years after the event, scholars usually ignore the eyewitness Leonard and speak of a Demetrios Kantakouzenos and a Nikephoros Palaiologos at the fall, but in fact no contemporary source records the presence of either of these men.[24]

19. Pseudo-Phrantzes, 398, 430. R. Browning, "A Note on the Capture of Constantinople in 1453," *Byz* 22 (1952), 379–87.

20. Barbaro, *Diary*, 73. Leonard of Chios, col. 935, calls him Andrea, and Pseudo-Phrantzes, 398, Antonio.

21. Leonard of Chios, col. 935; Pseudo-Phrantzes, 398. Barbaro, *Diary*, 11. Doukas, 315: fifty Italians and others hired on Chios.

22. Barbaro, *Diary*, 28. Runciman, *Fall*, 141 and note on page 224.

23. Leonard of Chios, col. 935; trans. Jones, *Siege*, 27. Cf. Pseudo-Phrantzes, 396, 368.

24. Leonard of Chios, col. 935; Pseudo-Phrantzes, 398. Nicol, *Byzantine Family*, 192–95, identifies Makarios' "Demetrios Kantakouzenos" as Demetrios Palaiologos Kantakouzenos, a high official under John VIII. In fairness to Makarios, Nikephoros Palaiologos had already slipped into an early Italian translation of Leonard of Chios' letter. Although I have not been able to check this version, there seems to be no other way to explain how Jones, *Siege*, 28, renders this passage in his translation of Leonard: "Demetrios Palaiologos Kantakouzenos the

This survey of the approximate positions of the defenders is heavily weighted toward Latins, Venetians, and Genoese. Where were the Byzantines? The only eyewitnesses who mention the disposition of Byzantines at all are Barbaro and Leonard. The latter alone places some Greeks at the Pege, St. Romanos, and Kaligaria gates; he also notes the reserve force under Demetrios Palaiologos. Barbaro and Leonard mention the emperor and the megas doux Notaras, Barbaro also noting the latter's hundred cavalry. There certainly had to be other positions manned by Byzantines, and we should expect these to have been the areas not specified by the eyewitnesses. In particular, no source tells us who was in the area of the Rhesion Gate, a relatively large section of the land walls between the St. Romanos and Pege gates, nor do we know who was manning the harbor walls from the Xyloporta to the Kynegon gates (somewhat less than half a mile in length). Also, the defense of at least two miles of the southern sea walls is unaccounted for, though this area was evidently lightly defended for no one expected an attack from that direction.

Aside from large frame-mounted and handheld crossbows and assorted small arms, the defenders had some small cannon and arquebuses, some of which were mounted shipboard. There were limitations to the firearms of the defenders. According to Leonard of Chios, the cannon "could not be fired very often, because of the shortage of powder and shot." Further, "the largest cannon had to remain silent, for fear of damage to our own walls by vibration." And Chalkokondyles: "At first the Greeks also set their cannon on the walls, and fired shot weighing a talent and a half [about 75 pounds] at the sultan's cannon. But this shook the walls, and did more damage to them than to the enemy. Also, their largest cannon burst when it was first fired."[25]

Most of the Turkish army was positioned along the land walls. In the northern section were the sultan's European troops and at the south the Anatolian troops. Most of these were *sipahis*, the main force of the Ottoman army since the second half of the fourteenth century. Primarily native Turkish horsemen, but including some Christians from conquered areas, the sipahis held grants of revenues from the sultan called *ziamets* and *timars*.

---

father-in-law and Nicolo Gudelli the son-in-law of Nikephoros Palaiologos were kept with him in reserve." Dolfin, trans. Jones, *Siege*, 129, says that Nicolo "Guideli," along with Battista Gritti, guarded the Pege Gate. Barbaro, *Diary*, 73, confirms the presence of a Battista Gritti at the siege. Mijatovich, *Constantine Palaeologus*, 179, drawing on a Slavic chronicle of the siege, speaks of a "Nikola Goudeli" as "Prefect of the city."

25. Barbaro, *Diary*, 11, 32, 50–51, 63. Leonard of Chios, cols. 934, 928; trans. Jones, *Siege*, 16. Doukas, 335. Chalkokondyles, 389; trans. Jones, *Siege*, 46.

Depending on the size of their grants they were obligated to present additional warriors for campaign service as well. The sipahis provided gunners, armorers, smiths, and marines in addition to cavalry.

Accompanying the sultan at the middle of the land walls were the famous Janissaries, Christian or ex-Christian slaves who served for life as infantry and who were recruited by forced levy (*devşirme*) from Christian families. After the sipahis they were the most important part of the army. Contemporary reports of up to 15,000 Janissaries present at the siege are certainly exaggerated. Early in Mehmet II's reign they were increased to 5,000 men from no more than 3,000 under Murad II. Behind all of these, throughout the length of the land walls were the irregular troops, less disciplined but numerous. These consisted of the irregular light cavalry including the *akincis*, or "raiders," who fought from booty and the *azaps*, an irregular militia, exempt from taxes in wartime, who served as infantry, builders, and rowers. On the northern side of the Golden Horn and Galata other troops were stationed to protect the passage of supplies from the Bosporos, which the Turkish fleet patrolled.[26]

We will never know how many Turkish troops besieged Constantinople, though not for lack of figures. Eyewitnesses provide estimates ranging from 60,000 to more than 300,000. Other contemporary sources report figures as high as 400,000. As all medieval estimates of troop sizes, these numbers are unreliable, and the high figures were certainly the product of exaggeration. Moreover, all of the eyewitness data are supplied by defenders; there are no contemporary Turkish figures. Further complicating matters is the fact that not all the besiegers were combatants. As Tedaldi reports, while there were 200,000 men present on the Turkish side, only 60,000 were soldiers (and of these, 30,000 or 40,000 were cavalry): "A quarter of them were equipped with coats of mail or leather jackets. Of the others, many were armed after the fashion of France, some after the fashion of Hungary and others again had helmets of iron, and Turkish bows and crossbows. The rest of the soldiers were without equipment, except that they had shields and scimitars, which are a kind of Turkish sword. The rest of the 200,000 were thieves and plunderers, hawkers, workmen and others who followed the army."[27]

26. F. Babinger, *Mehmed the Conqueror and His Time* (Princeton, N.J., 1978), 444–49. Runciman, *Fall*, 35–36. Leonard of Chios, col. 927.

27. Tedaldi, trans. Jones, *Siege*, 3. Barbaro, *Diary*, 27, 62: 150,000 to 160,000. Sphrantzes, 96: 200,000. Pertusi, "Anconitan Colony," 207: 300,000. Leonard of Chios, col. 927: more than 300,000. Kritoboulos, 40: more than 300,000 not counting camp followers. Chalkokondyles, 383, and Doukas, 333: 400,000. Cf. Babinger, *Mehmed the Conqueror*, 84, who estimates

There were very few defenders. Leonard of Chios writes that

> our numbers were small indeed, and the greater part of the Greeks were men of
> peace, using their shields and spears, their bows and swords, according to the
> light of nature rather than with any skill. The majority had helmets, and body
> armor of metal or leather, and fought with swords and spears. Those who were
> skilled in the use of bow or cross-bow were not enough to man all the
> ramparts.

The most accurate estimate of the number of defenders seems to be that of
the high official and eyewitness George Sphrantzes. He writes that "in spite
of the great size of our City, our defenders amounted to 4,773 Greeks, as
well as just about 200 foreigners." He then explains the source of his data:

> I was in a position to know this for the following reason: the emperor
> ordered the tribunes [*demarchoi*] to take a census of their neighborhoods and
> to record the exact number of laity and clergy able to defend the walls, and
> what weapons each man had for defense. Each of the tribunes completed this
> task and brought the list of his neighborhood to the emperor.
>
> The emperor said to me: "This task is for you and no one else, as you are
> skilled in arithmetic and also know how to guard and keep secrets. Take these
> lists and compute, in the privacy of your home, the exact figure of available
> defenders, weapons, spears, shields, and arrows." I completed my task and
> presented the master list to my lord and emperor in the greatest possible
> sadness and depression. The true figure remained a secret known only to the
> emperor and to myself.

The numeral "4,773" has a certain air of authority, but "200 foreigners"
seems impossibly low for the total number of non-Greek defenders at the
fall, and the combined total is the lowest provided by any source. According to Tedaldi there were six to seven thousand fighting men; the Anconitan consul says 7,000 defenders; Doukas reports 8,000 or less; and
Leonard of Chios writes that "the Greeks numbered at the most 6,000
fighting men. The rest, Genoese, Venetians and those who had come
secretly to help from Pera [Galata], were hardly as many as 3,000."[28]

---

that there were no more than 80,000 soldiers. Runciman, *Fall*, 76, follows Babinger by
suggesting there were probably 80,000 regular troops (including 12,000 Janissaries) and some
20,000 irregulars, plus camp followers.

28. Leonard of Chios, col. 933; trans. Jones, *Siege*, 25. *Georgios Sphrantzes*, ed. Grecu, 96.
Trans. adapted from M. Philippides, *The Fall of the Byzantine Empire: A Chronicle by George
Sphrantzes, 1401–1477* (Amherst, Mass., 1980), 69–70 (see under Sphrantzes in Bibliography).
Tedaldi, trans. Jones, *Siege*, 4, makes the curious statement that "in the city there were
altogether 30,000 to 35,000 men under arms, and six to seven thousand fighting men, making
42,000 at the most." The higher figure seems to correspond more to the population of the city

What about the figure "4,773"? If Sphrantzes did collect information on the number of defenders in the manner he describes, it seems likely that his final tally was either accurate or an undercount. What of his "200" foreigners? Here I do not think we ought to dismiss this figure out of hand. It is quite possible, based on his orders as he reports them and his sources of information (neighborhood officials), that he was charged only with tallying the number of defenders who were under *imperial* command, that is, excluding the foreigners who fought under their own commanders and were not subject to the neighborhood officials. His 200 foreigners might have been simply an estimate of the number of foreigners scattered around the city fighting under the authority of Byzantine officials. Overall, a reasonable estimate of the number of defenders in Constantinople at the time of the fall is 7,000 or 8,000: some 5,000 Byzantines and 2,000 or 3,000 foreigners. Obviously the defenders were seriously outmanned. Even using the highest figure for the number of defenders (9,000) and the lowest for the number of besiegers (60,000), the contest was quite one-sided.

Of these 5,000 Byzantines it is impossible to say what percentage were soldiers, that is, men who before the siege knew war as their primary pursuit. Most of Loukas Notaras' one hundred cavalry were probably soldiers. Certainly there would have been soldiers by the emperor's side, but we simply have no information regarding them. The sources, here and there, speak of "soldiers" but never an "army." A reasonable guess, merely a guess, is that there were a hundred or so soldiers under Byzantine command during the siege. Many of these were probably Latin mercenaries. Thus most of the defenders were civilians: aristocrats with military training and others who learned while doing.

The number of ships in the Turkish fleet should have been easier to count than the number of troops, but even here there is much variation, from a low of more than ninety-two (Tedaldi) to a high of 400 (Sphrantzes). But inasmuch as ships varied in size and usefulness from low-lying, triple-oared triremes to fishing boats, total fleet size is meaningless. Of the major craft, we have Tedaldi's report that the Turks had sixteen to eighteen galleys, sixty to eighty galliots, and sixteen to twenty smaller vessels for carrying horses (aside from other small craft), and Leonard of Chios' testimony that there were six triremes, ten biremes, and seventy

at the time of the siege. Pertusi, "Anconitan Colony," 207. Doukas, 361. Leonard of Chios, cols. 933–34; trans. Jones, *Siege*, 25. Pseudo-Phrantzes, 386, evidently unhappy with Sphrantzes' figures, altered them to 4,973 Byzantines and 2,000 foreigners.

galleys. On the whole, the Turkish fleet was rather small compared with the size of their army. This was because the Turks lacked sailors. Being an inland people, they, like the Arabs in the seventh century, needed time to learn the ways of the sea.[29]

The size of the defenders' fleet patrolling the Golden Horn fluctuated somewhat. In at least one episode some of the Western defenders fled, and in the course of the siege four new ships arrived. The sizes the sources provide for the total fleet of the defenders range from ten (Leonard of Chios) to thirty-nine (Tedaldi). Within this fleet, almost entirely Venetian and Genoese craft, there do not seem to have been many more than about nine large armed ships. Only three of these were Byzantine. Thus, though these figures are even more difficult to compare than the number of troops, the largest figure cited for the defenders' fleet is thirty-nine ships, while the smallest figures cited for the besiegers' fleet exceed ninety-two.[30]

On April 20 minor reinforcements for the defenders arrived: three Genoese ships commissioned by the pope and a Byzantine cargo ship laden with wheat supplied by King Alfonso of Aragon. As the sultan watched in frustration they managed to break through the Turkish blockade, momentarily restoring the spirits of the besieged population by confirming that Mehmet II still did not control the seas. To deal with this situation he decided to shut down the Golden Horn harbor. Since several attempts to destroy the harbor boom had failed, a new stratagem was devised. On April 22 the inhabitants of the city were amazed to see the Turks wheeling their ships overland north of Galata from the Bosporos to the Golden Horn. The journey of nearly a mile put them in a position to harass continuously the ships in the harbor. Quickly a plan was concocted to burn the Turkish craft in the Golden Horn, but dissension between the Venetians and Genoese delayed its execution until April 29, and then the attack failed.

29. Tedaldi, trans. Jones, *Siege*, 3. Leonard of Chios, col. 930: 250 ships total; immediately afterward he speaks of "70 biremes." Barbaro, *Diary*, 31: 145 ships. Chalkokondyles, 384: 30 triremes and 200 smaller vessels. Pertusi, "Anconitan Colony," 207, and Doukas, 333: 300. Sphrantzes, 96. Cf. Runciman, *Fall*, 75–76, who estimates six triremes, ten biremes, about fifteen galleys, about seventy-five *fustae* (single-oared long boats) and twenty *parandaria* (heavy sailing-barges for transport), plus other smaller ships and boats. Babinger, *Mehmed the Conqueror*, 449–50.

30. Leonard of Chios, col. 930: seven Genoese and three Cretan ships. Doukas, 337: eight large ships and twenty smaller ones, with many small craft. Barbaro, *Diary*, 29–30: thirty-seven ships of which five were unarmed. Tedaldi, trans. Jones, *Siege*, 4: thirty nefs and nine galleys (two light galleys, three Venetian merchant galleys, three belonging to the emperor and one to Giustiniani). Cf. Runciman, *Fall*, 84–85, who estimates that when the siege began there were in the harbor twenty-six ships (ten Byzantine, the others Western) aside from small craft and Genoese merchant ships.

It was not easy to ensure the smooth cooperation of the motley assemblage of Venetians, Genoese, Anconitans, Catalans, sailors from Crete, and Greeks within the city. The emperor spent much of his time soothing bruised egos and softening age-old animosities. The eyewitnesses, being almost all Latins, make occasional disparaging comments about the Byzantines. Leonard of Chios, who had a very low opinion of Greeks, reports that the emperor melted down church treasure "that from them coins should be struck and given to the soldiers, the sappers and the builders, who selfishly cared so little for the public welfare that they were refusing to go to their work unless they were first paid."[31] On the other hand, a few Italian ships fled the city on May 18, one of the few instances of desertion reported during the siege. Generally, however, most of the defenders were able to put aside petty differences and cooperate in the common cause.

In order to cope with the daily Turkish bombardment, Kritoboulos writes, the defenders "extended great beams from above the walls, and let down bales of wool on ropes, and placed with them similar things so as to break the force of the stone balls as much as possible and lighten the effect." To the extent that there was time and manpower to rebuild damaged sections of the walls with wood, stones, earth, brush, and hides, the defenses against the enemy artillery actually became more effective. Thus "the stone ball, hurled with great force, fell and was buried in the soft and yielding earth, and did not make a breach by striking against hard and unyielding materials." On May 18 the Turks filled in part of the moat and tried to wheel a wooden turret up to the walls, but the defenders were able to burn it down. From May 16 to May 25 the Turks engaged in extensive mining operations, all successfully foiled by the defenders.[32]

Finally, with the land walls sufficiently weakened, the sultan decided on a general assault. May 28 was to be a day of rest with the attack to follow the next day. In the hours before the final assault Emperor Constantine addressed his troops. According to Leonard of Chios the long exhortation ended with the words, "Finally, my fellow soldiers, show obedience to your superiors in all things, and know that this is the day of your glory; if but a drop of your blood is shed, you will earn for yourselves a martyr's crown and glory everlasting."[33]

31. Leonard of Chios, col. 934; trans. Jones, *Siege*, 26. Cf. Pseudo-Phrantzes, 400.
32. Kritoboulos, 49; trans. C. Riggs, *History of Mehmed the Conqueror by Kritovoulos* (Princeton, N.J., 1954), 48–49. Barbaro, *Diary*, 50–51.
33. Leonard of Chios, col. 939; trans. Jones, *Siege*, 35.

The assault began hours before dawn and was planned in three waves, each concentrating on the weakest section of the land walls, around the gates of St. Romanos and Charisios, where Giustiniani and the emperor were positioned. After a massive artillery barrage to soften the defenses, the sultan's irregulars charged. Disorganized and undisciplined, their two-hour attack was repelled but it managed to weary the defenders. Next the Anatolian Turks were ordered to the walls but they too were repelled. Finally, about an hour before dawn the Janissaries were sent against the city's defenses. After an hour of fierce fighting they succeeded in battling to the inner walls. Some of them, about fifty, found their way into the city through the small gate called Kerkoporta, just south of the Kaligaria Gate. They mounted the tower above the gate and flew the Ottoman standard. At the same time, around dawn, Giustiniani was wounded and carried off. Their leader now missing, the defenders panicked, and the Janissaries broke through his position and poured into the city.

By noon the city was the sultan's. The Turkish army spent the rest of the day plundering, enslaving, and raping, the barbarity of which was comparable only to that of the Latins of the Fourth Crusade during their sack of the city nearly two and a half centuries earlier. According to Kritoboulos about 4,000 people had been killed and at least 50,000 were taken prisoner.[34] One or two thousand Byzantines and foreigners made a rapid escape on Venetian, Genoese, and Cretan ships, among whom was Giustiniani, who later died of his wounds on the way to Chios. Others were captured but arranged ransom. Such was the good fortune of Leonard of Chios and Cardinal Isidore, unrecognized by their captors and ransomed by Genoese merchants of Galata. Others were less lucky. Girolamo Minotto, bailli of the Venetians, was killed in battle. The megas doux Loukas Notaras was taken prisoner and later executed. The Ottoman prince Orhan was captured and beheaded. As for Constantine XI, though many legends sprang up about the last emperor, no eyewitness reports his fate. His body was never found. It would not be an overestimation of his character to accept the general opinion that he died, sword in hand, fighting as a simple soldier upon the walls of the city he had ruled. Around mid-afternoon Mehmet II made his formal entrance. Within days the Queen of Cities, the New Rome, the capital of the Christian Byzantine Empire, became the capital city of the Empire of the Great Turk.

The story of Byzantium and its military deeds ends with a kind of

34. Kritoboulos, 75. Leonard of Chios, col. 942: 60,000.

postscript. Although the capital was lost, the Byzantine states of the Morea and of separatist Trebizond survived for several more years. In 1453, after a certain Manuel Kantakouzenos became the leader of an uprising of the Albanians in the Morea against the despots Thomas and Demetrios Palaiologos, the sultan sent Umur Pasha, the general Turahan's son, to restore order. The following year, when Turahan himself arrived at the request of Thomas and Demetrios, Manuel Kantakouzenos was forced to flee the Morea.[35] After the Turks had dealt with the rebellion, Thomas and Demetrios returned to bickering among themselves and plotting with Western powers. In May 1458 the sultan decided to teach the brothers a lesson. He crossed the Isthmus and captured Corinth after a long siege. By the end of the year he had conquered one-third of the Morea. Having learned nothing, Demetrios and Thomas continued to quarrel. In 1460, resolving to transform the entire Morea into an Ottoman province, Mehmet II again invaded, brutally crushing all resistance with a truly remarkable savagery. Thomas Palaiologos escaped westward, Demetrios surrendered Mistra without a struggle and later dwelt within the Ottoman Empire on a princely pension. The Despotate of the Morea had come to an end. The next year, with the capitulation of distant Trebizond, the last remaining vestige of the medieval Graeco-Roman political tradition, Byzantium was no more.

35. Nicol, *Byzantine Family*, 201–202.

Part II

The Army as Institution

7. Mercenaries and Their Financing

The late Byzantine state employed several methods to compensate or reward soldiers for their services. Soldiers were remunerated through grants of cash, land, and the rights to state revenues, all of which were conditional on continued military service. Rewards took similar form and also included grants of movable property and valuables, all of which, by definition, were not conditional on further service. It is important to emphasize two points. First, none of these methods of financing the services of soldiers—money, property, revenues—was restricted to soldiers alone. Civil servants and the aristocracy, including the emperor's relatives, received the same kinds of pay or rewards for their nonmilitary services. If the sources place greater emphasis on the pay of soldiers, it is because soldiers formed the overwhelming bulk of imperial employees and their activities in general were more visible and noteworthy than the daily deeds of clerks. Second, while most soldiers may be categorized according to their primary type of remuneration—mercenary, smallholding soldier, pronoia soldier—there nevertheless is evidence that combinations of pay methods were often employed, creating personalized pay "packages" for individual soldiers or groups of soldiers which varied with the kind and quality of troops in question. If we add to this the likelihood that soldiers did at times move from one category to another, the distinction between mercenary, smallholding soldier, and military pronoiar, though never immaterial, could become a bit blurred.

In 1350 during a meeting with the Serbian emperor Stefan Dušan, John Kantakouzenos claims to have said the following: "To us, it is not only ignoble, slavish and a great dishonor to serve for pay instead of for the love of honor and friendship, but to me it is one of the most impossible things, that Romans would ask something for my and my partisans' safety if ungrateful people made war against me."[1] Throughout history we encoun-

---

1. Kantakouzenos, III, 143. Pachymeres, Bonn ed., II, 482, also disapproved of mercenaries, but for more practical reasons.

ter this notion that the citizens or subjects of a state would or at least should never ask a cent for the defense of their ruler or country. It is a noble sentiment, but as Kantakouzenos was well aware, as an emperor and a general, it cannot satisfy the military needs of a state. For prolonged campaigns and for standing forces the state must remunerate its soldiers. In most Western societies of the past, states generally either paid foreigners to perform these duties or provided native soldiers with some other form of remuneration other than direct cash payments (such as land or tax revenues).

Since soldiers serving for pay historically have tended to be foreigners, the word *mercenary* has received the added sense of a man having no "patriotic allegiance" to the state for which he is fighting. This sense is necessary today when all national armies, except during the rarest of crises, are financed with cash, and it would make us somewhat uncomfortable to speak of the soldiers of such armies as "mercenaries." In Byzantium as well, there was a hesitancy to acknowledge the existence of nonforeign, "Byzantine" mercenaries. Our sources give the impression that there were only "foreign" mercenaries: Latins, including Italians, Frenchmen, Germans, Englishmen, and Catalans, as well as Alans and Turks. Phrases such as "the Byzantine mercenaries" (*hoi Rhomaion misthophoroi*) are very rare, even though they need not have had an ethnic connotation.[2] Even when the sources mention mercenaries who had been obtained from within the Empire, such as Michael VIII's Gasmouloi and Andronikos II's Cretans, the sources explain their ethnicity as if to demonstrate that they were not really "Byzantine" (*Rhomaioi*, literally "Romans").

Were there actually ethnically Byzantine mercenaries? The members of the palace guard called *Paramonai* (see Chapter 12) seem to have been, and no doubt some native mercenaries existed within campaign armies. But the ease with which our historians have omitted them from their writings ought to suggest that they formed only a minority of the mercenary forces of the Empire. Nevertheless, I prefer to divorce the word *mercenary* from any inherent ethnic connotation. The mercenary is a hired soldier whose remuneration takes the form of direct and regular cash stipends. Once he is identified we can then ask whether he was native or foreign, or, as the Byzantines would say, *Rhomaios* or *xenos*.

During the early medieval centuries the decline or even the absence of a monetary economy in Western Europe forced rulers to turn to feudal

2. E.g., Kantakouzenos, I, 488.

levies, communal militias, and other means of raising troops. The economic revival of Western Europe which began in the eleventh century gradually changed all this, so that by the thirteenth century mercenaries frequently achieved a position of parity and at times even predominance in the armies of Western Europe. In southern Italy foreign mercenaries were a principal component, supplementing the feudal contingents of papal, imperial, and Angevin armies throughout the thirteenth century. For example, at the battle of Benevento in 1266, almost two-thirds of King Manfred of Sicily's cavalry were German and Italian mercenaries, while his infantry was almost entirely composed of Saracen archers who had been settled in Sicily by the Normans. On the other side, though Charles of Anjou's cavalry was French, many of the horsemen were mercenaries and not feudal vassals. Both sides also employed the famed Genoese and Pisan crossbowmen who were beginning to make an impact on the battlefield.[3]

In the towns of northern Italy the tradition of militia service had slowed the shift toward mercenaries but their utility was driven home as a result of a few major military encounters. The lesson learned was that cavalry was superior to infantry, and professional cavalry was superior to communal cavalry. At the battle of Montaperti in 1260 the Florentine army, composed of communal cavalry, communal infantry, infantry levied from the rural areas of the Florentine state, and a very small mercenary cavalry contingent, was defeated by a numerically inferior force of Ghibelline nobles and German cavalry hired by Siena. In 1289 the battle of Campaldino was another victory of trained cavalry over infantry militia. The Tuscan Guelf League led by Florence fielded 1,600 cavalry and about 10,000 infantry; of the one thousand cavalry Florence provided, nearly half were French mercenaries. They defeated the Ghibelline army composed of 800 cavalry and 8,000 infantry led by Arezzo.

In northern Europe as well, although the accelerated use of mercenaries had to await the region's somewhat slower economic growth, mercenaries had been part of feudal armies from an early date. By the thirteenth century, due to the return of the cash economy, mercenary cavalries, usually organized under their sovereign and composed of native nobles who had hired themselves out, sometimes exceeded the feudal levies.[4] The increased

---

3. M. Mallett, *Mercenaries and Their Masters* (London, 1974), 13–15.

4. C. Bayley, *War and Society in Renaissance Florence* (Toronto, 1961), 3. Mallett, *Mercenaries*, 12, 14, 21. C. Gaier, "Analysis of Military Forces in the Principality of Liège and the County of Looz from the Twelfth to the Fifteenth Century," *Studies in Medieval and Renaissance History* 2 (1965), 215, 229–31.

use of mercenaries in the West is one of the reasons for the great similarity between Western—especially Italian—and Byzantine armies during the thirteenth and fourteenth centuries.

Since Byzantium, despite occasional serious economic and fiscal crises, had never lost its monetary economy, there was a significant mercenary presence in the armies of all eras. Certainly from the eleventh century the majority of the army was composed of mercenaries, but even before then, during the great age of the themes when the armies of the provinces were financed through military lands, mercenaries made up the ranks of the Tagmata stationed around Constantinople. In the late period mercenaries were an indispensable part of the army, and nothing better illustrates John Kantakouzenos' awareness of this fact than the scene during his acclamation as emperor in Didymoteichon in 1341. Assisting the new emperor with ceremonially donning his dark red boots were his nearest blood relatives and the most distinguished of his Latin mercenaries.[5]

The utility of mercenaries was twofold. They could remain under arms almost constantly, even in the winter, and they could be hired as need arose and dismissed afterward.[6] Gregoras (I, 485) reports that Andronikos III once told his soldiers while campaigning in Bulgaria, "You know, men, that we are cut off far from the fatherland. And neither do we have allied cities that can aid us today in this unexpected war, nor can we summon a mercenary army from somewhere." The inference is that mercenary armies were often summoned as needed. In a broader perspective this means that, since the resources available to the emperors were always meager at best, only some of the mercenaries we encounter in the sources were permanent employees of the emperor. The rest were hired only when necessity or opportunity presented itself. For example, upon his arrival in the Morea in 1349, Manuel Kantakouzenos hired men from the area south of Vonitza to deal with the Morea's rebellious inhabitants, and we recall that just before Andronikos II engaged the services of the Catalan Company he hired the several thousand Alans who offered themselves to imperial officials with the intention of enlisting for pay.[7] There is rarely any indication that the bulk of such troops was ever intended to remain part of a standing army once the immediate circumstances prompting their employment had changed.

Those mercenaries who did enter permanent imperial service per-

5. Kantakouzenos, II, 165.

6. Kantakouzenos, II, 354: "Since they served for pay, they were always ready for campaigns"; I, 488, 493.

7. Gregoras, I, 205. Kantakouzenos, III, 88; II, 425–26.

formed several specific tasks aside from general campaign duty. According to Kantakouzenos (I, 42) the palace guard contained a large number of mercenaries. Likewise garrison troops in Constantinople were often mercenaries, as in 1354 when the Golden Gate fortress is noted as having a Latin (Catalan) mercenary garrison.[8] What little evidence there is for the economic foundation of the garrisons of other towns suggests that they too had at least a significant mercenary contingent. For example, in 1321 Kantakouzenos delayed his departure from Constantinople by claiming that he could not proceed "before the money was given to him which he could use for the mercenaries of the army and for the garrisons of the towns in Thessaly."[9]

Aside from the palace guards and garrison troops, mercenaries were employed as marines in the fleet (the Gasmouloi), and the highlanders of Asia Minor during the reign of Michael VIII received pay as part of their incomes, as did the Cretan cavalry settled in Asia Minor by Andronikos II. Although mercenaries were often found in the feudal armies of northern Europe, permanent mercenary forces were quite rare. For example, in the principality of Liège, aside from the guilds of bowmen which were funded by towns for their defense and which first appeared in the thirteenth century, there were no standing mercenary forces until the late fifteenth century. In northern Italy as well, while it had long been practice to hire foreign mercenaries for specific campaigns, it was only the Italian towns' obligations toward the joint army of the Tuscan League (formed in the 1260s) that led to the maintenance of permanent mercenary forces.[10]

Late Byzantine narrative sources depict a central government without sufficient resources to finance an adequate army. From campaign to campaign we read of emperors requesting aid from abroad, appropriating church property, utilizing their personal fortunes, or even simply ordering their tax collectors to be more zealous about their task. The flight of the population before the Turks, Serbs, and other invaders certainly made tax levying difficult, and the partisan politics of the civil wars in combination with the general "feudalization" of the late Empire diminished the tax base as privileges and exemptions were granted with increasing frequency to the great monastic and lay landowners. Yet, however irregularly they were

---

8. Kantakouzenos, III, 292, 301, 303. D. Nicol, *The Byzantine Family of Kantakouzenos (Cantacuzenus)* (Washington, D.C., 1968), 84–85. John VI Kantakouzenos, "The History of John Cantacuzenus (book 4)," ed. T. Miller, diss., Catholic Univ. 1975, 275. Oikonomidès, "A propos des armées," 357 note 40.

9. Kantakouzenos, I, 87. Also, II, 578; and MM, V, 261, lines 2–4.

10. Gaier, "Analysis of Military Forces," 251f. Mallett, *Mercenaries*, 13–14.

collected, and from however dwindling a population, taxes were the main source of revenue for financing mercenaries.

There was in fact a fundamental relation between taxation and mercenaries. The reason Andronikos II's advisors in 1285 argued against the expense of a fleet was that the mercenaries on the ships "were paid taxes from the public treasury." In the early fourteenth century Pachymeres writes that Andronikos II had tried to be more diligent about "collecting the usual taxes from property so that these might be used as pay for the army." In this regard one may also mention the financial terms of the agreement of 1354 ending hostilities between John V and John Kantakouzenos: "Concerning the money collected yearly from the public taxes, whatever should be needed for the mercenaries of the army and the preparation of the triremes and the other needs of the public administration, is to be spent by the government as usual." Anything left over was to be shared equally by the two emperors. Thus we see that the public taxes (*demosia*) were the normal means of financing mercenaries, and that mercenaries represented one of the principal governmental expenses.[11]

There were several types of tax revenues collected by the state. The most important were the taxes on agricultural production but there were also commercial taxes and duties, fines imposed by private contracts and criminal proceedings, state claims to treasure caches and to the estates of those dying without issue, as well as bequeathals to the state and the proceeds of confiscated estates. Public works corvées (*angareiai*) and the defunct military levies, both of which had been transformed more or less into simple taxes prior to the late period, also provided some state revenue. The tax income produced by these taxes and charges was at best only marginally adequate for the salaries of mercenaries and other military expenses such as supplies and ships.[12]

Since it is very likely that most state revenues were directed toward defense, any sudden increase in military pay outlays threatened imperial finances and required new efforts to raise money. There were several ways to do this. One, a traditional technique that did not require raising new taxes, was to debase the coinage. This was done by Andronikos II to acquire the sums necessary to pay the Catalans. In this instance, as always,

11. Pachymeres, Bonn ed., II, 70, 618, and also, II, 307. Laiou, *Constantinople*, 75–76. Mutafčiev, "Vojniški zemi," 643. Kantakouzenos, III, 291, and also, I, 136–37.

12. On the taxes, see F. Dölger, *Beiträge zur Geschichte des byzantinischen Finanzverwaltung* (Leipzig and Berlin, 1927; repr. Hildesheim, 1960), 59ff.; and D. Zakythinos, "Crise monétaire et crise économique à Byzance du XIIIe au XVe siècle," in Zakythinos, *Byzance: état—société—économie* (London, 1973), no. XI, 68.

the ploy did not fool the recipients for long. Another method was to divert tax revenues from one recipient to another by altering the path of tax revenues once they left the hands of the peasant. Andronikos tried this twice when he needed money to pay the Catalans. First he held back the pay of the palace employees, and later he "fastened onto the pronoiai in the west and took away a third from these."[13] Twenty years earlier the same method had been used to finance both a campaign in Thessaly and the Cretan cavalry settled in Anatolia. At that time "one-tenth of the pronoiai of those holding pronoiai" was redirected toward the treasury, and naturally, "while it was collected from the lords, the paroikoi of the powerful paid everything."[14]

An obvious means of raising extra money was to increase taxes. When the Alans came to enlist in the army in 1301, "it was necessary to give them money and horses and arms." Some money came from the treasury, but this was not sufficient. According to Gregoras,

> Thereupon those levying taxes in the countryside were sent out in a mass and one after another. The tax collectors raised the taxes. Every weapon and every horse were collected. Villages, cities, the homes of the great, the homes of those enrolled in military service, hermitages, the common people, theaters, markets, all were searched and surrendered horses and money, involuntarily and with lamentation.[15]

Although Gregoras exaggerates, it is significant that he does not speak of this as a massive confiscation, but as an episode in tax collecting. Much of the wealth raised was in kind because, we may assume, specie was unavailable, Andronikos' decision having caught the taxpayer unprepared, or because the needs of the Alans could not be fulfilled by cash alone.

In the late period very few taxes were ever specially earmarked for military purposes. This had not always been the case. In documents from the later eleventh and twelfth centuries a number of burdens appear that were created for military purposes. They were called variously the *exelaseis*, "drawing out" (or *ekbolai*), of *kontaratoi* (spearmen), *pezoi* (infantry), *ploïmoi* (sailors), *toxotai* (bowmen), and so on. Even though there is still disagreement regarding whether these, in origin, were taxes to furnish or hire such troops or were levies on the peasant population for the actual

13. Pachymeres, Bonn ed., II, 397, 493. Gregoras, I, 222–23. Laiou, *Constantinople*, 133, 141, 188.

14. Pachymeres, Bonn ed., II, 69, 209. Laiou, *Constantinople*, 38–39, 116–17. Cf. Nicol, *Last Centuries*, 116.

15. Gregoras, I, 205. Laiou, *Constantinople*, 89. Also, Gregoras, I, 317.

recruitment of such troops, it is clear that by the late twelfth century these burdens were satisfied by money payments. By the thirteenth century there is no evidence that the few *exelaseis* that still existed were used for any specifically military purpose.[16] These burdens disappear after the early Palaiologan period, last appearing only in documents granting monastic or church properties exemption from these burdens. Seven documents grant exemption of the *exelasis* (or *ekbole*) of *kontaratoi*; two, that of *pezoi*; and seven, that of *ploïmoi*.[17] Since these documents tend simply to be confirmations of the privileged status of monasteries with long histories of tax exemptions, and since the total number of documents containing these exemptions is small (sixteen total exemptions in only ten documents), it seems that the Palaiologan appearance of these burdens was merely an archaistic transmission from the Nicaean and earlier periods, and that they were probably moribund during the Palaiologan period.

With few exceptions, there were no "military taxes" in late Byzantium. Rather, taxes from various sources were collected and disbursed as mercenary pay, civil servant salaries, or whatever. The exceptions involved cases either where a tax was created to deal with a specific exigency or where the effects could be seen on a local level, discouraging its diversion into other enterprises. For example, in 1304 Andronikos II levied a new tax on grain called the *sitokrithon* (from *sitos*, "wheat," and *krithe*, "barley") in order to finance the Catalans. This tax was collected in kind and then the grain was sold for cash.[18] In another instance, Manuel II in 1405 ordered that an Athonite monastery's property on Lemnos be freed of the *kapeliatikon*

16. See E. Branouse, Βυζαντινὰ ἔγγραφα τῆς μονῆς Πάτμου, I (Athens, 1980), no. 10 (1186), and the eulogy to Alexios III Angelos (1195–1203), in G. Stadtmüller, *Michael Choniates, Metropolit von Athen* (Rome, 1934), 284, 291 = S. Lampros, Μιχαὴλ ᾿Ακομινάτου τοῦ Χωνιάτου τὰ σωζόμενα (Athens, 1879–80), I, 308, 310, as well as the various opinions of D. Xanalatos, *Beiträge zur Wirtschafts- und Sozialgeschichte Makedoniens im Mittelalter* (Speyer, 1937), 45; Mutafčiev, "Vojniški zemi," 578–79; A. Solovjev and V. Mošin, *Grčke povelje srpskih vladara* (Belgrade, 1936; repr. London, 1974), 428, 457–58; F. Dölger, *Aus den Schatzkammern des Heiligen Berges* (Munich, 1948), 109; P. Lemerle, "Un chrysobulle d'Andronic II Paléologue pour le monastère de Karakala," in Lemerle, *Le monde de Byzance* (London, 1978), no. XVII, 443–44; H. Ahrweiler, *Byzance et la mer* (Paris, 1966), index; and Oikonomidès, "A propos des armées," 357 and note 34. Angold, *Byzantine Government*, 225, considered the *exelasis ploïmon* to be one of the main sources of tax revenue for the Nicaean state.

17. MM, IV, 288, for Lemviotissa (1255–60); J. Lefort, *Actes d'Esphigménou* (Paris, 1973), no. 6 (1258–59), and app. A (1259); P. Lemerle et al., *Actes de Lavra* (Paris, 1970–82), II, no. 71 (1259); MM, V, 13, for Nea Mone on Chios (1259); J. and P. Zepos, *Jus graecoromanum* (Athens, 1931), I, 663, for Hagia Sophia (1267–71); W. Regel et al., *Actes de Philothée*, *VizVrem* 20 (1913), suppl. 1, no. 3 (1287) and its falsification no. 4; Dölger, *Schatzkammer*, no. 38, for Karakala (1294); Lemerle et al., *Lavra*, II, no. 89 (1298); and *Schatzkammer*, no. 37, for Iviron (1310).

18. Laiou, *Constantinople*, 141, 187–88.

which a tax collector had "imposed due to the necessity of warfare there."
The *kapeliatikon*, a sales tax on wine (from *kapeleion*, "wine-shop"), was not
inherently connected with military needs. It had been imposed (or reim-
posed) on the monasteries of Athos soon after the Christian defeat on the
Marica in 1371.[19] Moreover, it is likely that the tax for financing guard
service called the *vigliatikon* (from *vigla*, "watch") remained closely tied to
military (or paramilitary) purposes (see Chapter 13).

Once tax money was collected in the provinces, it first passed through
the imperial treasury in Constantinople before being disbursed to local
troops.[20] Though data are meager, it is possible to calculate roughly the
percentage of state revenues entering the treasury that were directed toward military ends, that is, toward mercenaries and the fleet. The treaty of
Epibatai in 1322 stipulated that Andronikos III was to receive a personal
pension of 36,000 hyperpyra yearly. Four years and four months later
Kantakouzenos reports that this money had not been delivered to Andronikos and that by Kantakouzenos' own calculation the money Andronikos II owed his grandson for the pension and for mercenary pay
amounted to 350,000 hyperpyra. Dividing 350,000 by 4⅓, we get an annual
income for Andronikos III of around 81,000 hyperpyra. Subtracting the
pension of 36,000 hyperpyra, we are left with about 45,000 hyperpyra for
the expenses of mercenaries. Since Andronikos II would have spent at least
this amount on mercenaries, and probably a bit more on the small fleet, the
total military outlay from the treasury in the 1320s was something on the
order of 100,000 to 150,000 hyperpyra. The magnitude of this figure is
reasonable when we compare it to Kantakouzenos' figures for the sum
necessary for the mercenaries of the army and the garrisons of Thessaly in
1321 at the time John was appointed governor of that region (50,000
hyperpyra), and for the sum Alexios Apokaukos was given in 1340 to
refurbish the fleet and hire mercenaries (100,000 hyperpyra). Both of these
represented extraordinary expenses resulting from special circumstances.
Moreover, it must be emphasized that this yearly outlay of 100,000 to
150,000 hyperpyra did not represent the true military budget because a

19. Lemerle et al., *Lavra*, III, no. 157, lines 9ff. N. Oikonomidès, "Le haradj dans l'empire
byzantin du XVe siècle," in Oikonomidès, *Documents et études sur les institutions de Byzance
(VIIe–XVe s.)* (London, 1976), no. XIX, 684. V. Mošin, "Akti iz svetogorskih arhiva," *Spomenik
Srpske kraljevske akademije nauka* 91 (1939), 166 and note 10. P. Charanis, "The Monastic
Properties and the State in the Byzantine Empire," in Charanis, *Social, Economic and Political
Life in the Byzantine Empire* (London, 1973), no. I, 116–17.

20. Kantakouzenos, I, 87. Gregoras, I, 138.

large fraction of the revenues received by soldiers, in the form of pronoiai and tax exemption, never found its way into the central treasury. These revenues could have easily doubled the figure.[21]

There is only one figure available for the Empire's annual state revenues. Gregoras states that around 1320, through tax increases and great diligence, Andronikos II raised state revenues to the unprecedented level of one million hyperpyra. Given that ordinary state income was probably considerably less than this, the figure of 100,000 to 150,000 hyperpyra represents something like one-third or even one-half of the money normally available to the treasury. The figure of one million hyperpyra also illustrates the difficulties the treasury faced in financing the Catalans who received, according to one calculation, nearly one million hyperpyra over a two-year period, a sum far exceeding the normal revenues directed toward the military and necessitating the extraordinary measures undertaken by Andronikos II to pay them.[22]

Tax revenue, while the usual source of money, was not the only avenue utilized to finance mercenaries. During the civil wars and even during his period of joint rule with John V, Kantakouzenos frequently paid military expenses out of his own family's fortune, supplementing it with voluntary contributions from other wealthy citizens. In one instance, Kantakouzenos called an assembly of citizens to obtain money for an army. Represented were merchants, soldiers, craftsmen, some common people, and monastic and ecclesiastical officials. Similarly, in 1305 Andronikos II sought voluntary contributions from the citizenry in order to wage war against the Catalans, and although much money was raised, apparently it was not enough for an adequate army.[23]

---

21. Kantakouzenos, I, 167, 237. M. Bartusis, "The Cost of Late Byzantine Warfare and Defense," *Byzantinische Forschungen* 16 (1990), 81–83. Cf. M. Hendy, *Studies in the Byzantine Monetary Economy c.300–1450* (Cambridge, 1985), 205. Kantakouzenos, I, 87, 540.

22. Gregoras, I, 317. Laiou, *Constantinople*, 186 note 108: in 1303, 498,220 or 372,665 hyperpyra, and in 1304, probably 498,220 hyperpyra. Cf. Hendy's calculations (*Studies in the Byzantine Monetary Economy*, 222–23), which nearly double these figures. There is insufficient data to make any but the wildest estimate of the percentage of the Empire's economic resources consumed by the military. See Bartusis, "Cost," 84–86, where, using the available fiscal data, I attempted such an estimate and concluded, with countless reservations, that the military in the first half of the fourteenth century consumed something like 5 percent of the total resources of the Empire. In a society in which nearly all of the inhabitants lived at or only marginally above the level of subsistence, 5 percent of total production would have been a very high percentage of disposable production (production beyond the minimum subsistence requirements of the population).

23. Kantakouzenos, I, 137; II, 68, 350; III, 33–34; and cf. III, 10. Pachymeres, Bonn ed., II, 576. Laiou, *Constantinople*, 167.

Finally, two other sources of money may be noted. Gregoras reports with disapproval that in 1352 Kantakouzenos had used church treasures to finance his Turkish troops against John V, and in 1383 the metropolitan of Thessaloniki complained that church property was being appropriated for the defense of the city. An even more traditional means of raising irregular funds for mercenaries than by the confiscation of church property was through the acquisition of plunder. Usually booty consisted of movable property, that is, war materials and food, but occasionally money was involved as well. For example, in 1328 after Andronikos III and company seized Vodena from the partisans of his grandfather and captured the personal treasures of a number of wealthy aristocrats, Andronikos ordered that 12,000 pieces of gold found among the jewelry and other wealth be distributed to the army.[24]

The regular salary of mercenaries was called *misthos* or *misthophora*, very rarely *siteresia* or *lemmata*, or more colloquially, *roga*, all of which simply meant "pay."[25] The three major Palaiologan historians, Pachymeres, Gregoras, and Kantakouzenos, all occasionally use the expression "yearly pay" in reference to mercenaries. Since they never specify an actual rate of pay when doing so, one might think that this meant mercenaries were paid yearly as opposed to, say, monthly. However, on the single occasion a *rate* of pay is mentioned—Pachymeres' account of the causes of animosity between the Alans and the Catalans—the rate of pay is expressed as a monthly sum. Furthermore, Western sources, such as the chronicles of the Catalan campaigns by Muntaner and Moncada, and the records of the Venetian senate concerning the defense of Thessaloniki, all similarly treat rates of mercenary pay as monthly sums.[26]

If the expression "yearly" of the Greek historians actually had some meaning and was not merely a kind of decorative epithet for the word "pay," then "yearly pay" must have referred to one of two things: either the

24. Gregoras, III, 179. G. Dennis, *The Reign of Manuel II Palaeologus in Thessalonica, 1382–1387* (Rome, 1960), 89–91. Kantakouzenos, I, 279, and cf. II, 425–26.

25. Pseudo-Kodinos, 187. D. Kydones, *Démétrius Cydonès correspondance*, ed. R. Loenertz (Vatican, 1956, 1960), I, no. 10, line 1. Pachymeres, Bonn ed., II, 416, 424. Gregoras, I, 138, 220. N. Choniates, *Nicetae Choniatae Historia*, ed. J. van Dieten (Berlin, 1975), 208. *Chronicle of the Morea*, ed. J. Schmitt (London, 1904), vv. 4634, 5100. G. Schirò, ed., *Cronaca dei Tocco di Cefalonia di Anonimo* (Rome, 1975), *glossario*, 570.

26. Pachymeres, Bonn ed., II, 420. Muntaner, *Cronicà*, ed. E.B., 9 vols. in 2 (Barcelona, 1927–52), ch. 199; English trans. by Lady Goodenough, *The Chronicle of Muntaner*, 2 vols. (London, 1920–21), II, 482–83. *The Catalan Chronicle of Francisco de Moncada*, trans. F. Hernández (El Paso, Tex., 1975), 21, ch. 6. K. Mertzios, Μνημεῖα Μακεδονικῆς Ἱστορίας (Thessaloniki, 1947), 49–53. K. Sathas, Μνημεῖα Ἑλληνικῆς Ἱστορίας. *Documents inédits relatifs à l'histoire de la Grèce au moyen âge* (Paris, 1880–90), I, 146, lines 28–31.

mercenary's base pay per year devoid of daily stipends, in cash or kind, for food and lodging while on campaign, or the pay of a permanently enrolled mercenary in a standing army or garrison force. Evidence for the second possibility is stronger and is derived from the context of the Greek references to "yearly pay." Those who received such pay were the highlanders of Anatolia, the Tzakones settled in Constantinople by Michael VIII, the Cretans settled in Anatolia by Andronikos II, the soldiers (mainly infantry) who surrendered Apros to Andronikos III in 1322 and then became the younger emperor's "servants" (*oiketai*), and Andronikos III's troops in 1327 who had to stay home because they had not been paid.[27] The connection between all these groups of soldiers is that they were all permanent residents within the Empire and they had not been hired for any particular campaign. Thus, these mercenaries were part of the standing army, and as such their pay could be calculated on a yearly basis. Otherwise, mercenaries hired for specific enterprises, such as the Alans and Catalans, simply received "pay."

In addition, it seems reasonable to think that the pay of temporary campaign mercenaries would not be considered "yearly," because such fighters were usually hired for periods of time shorter than a year, in other words, for all or part of a single campaign season. The Catalans were to be paid four months' pay in advance and every four months thereafter, plus two months' pay when they decided to return home. Some mercenaries John V requested from the pope in 1355 were to be hired for an initial six-month period. The one hundred Vlachs or other noncitizen soldiers whom the senate of Venice authorized the governors of Thessaloniki to hire in 1423 were to be held for either four or six months. And finally, while in Anatolia during the spring of 1302, Michael IX contracted the Alan mercenaries to remain on campaign another three months, at the end of which period they began to desert. In the West practices were similar. Thirteenth-century Italy mercenaries normally served under three-month contracts. Official Venetian regulations from 1372 for hiring mercenaries specify four-month contracts with an additional two months at the discretion of the employer. The contract period for condottieri during the fourteenth century was usually two or three months, with six months as the maximum; by the early fifteenth century it had increased to usually six months or more, and the contracts included extension clauses.[28]

---

27. Gregoras, I, 138. Pachymeres, ed. Failler, I, 253 (Bonn ed., I, 188), and Bonn ed., II, 209. Kantakouzenos, I, 142, 238.

28. Muntaner, *Cronicà*, ch. 199 (trans. by Goodenough, II, 482–83). *The Catalan Chronicle of Francisco de Moncada*, 21, ch. 6. A. Theiner and F. Miklosich, *Monumenta spectantia ad*

Information concerning the actual rate of pay for mercenaries fighting for Byzantium in the late period is extremely scanty. For the last two and a half centuries we have only three sets of figures for the pay of mercenaries in Byzantine service: (1) The 1261 treaty of Nymphaion gives the pay rate for the soldiers (*supersalientes*) on the Genoese galleys in the service of Byzantium as 2.5 hyperpyra per month, in addition to ration allotments of bread and wine.[29] (2) Ramon Muntaner reports that the Catalans received 4 gold ounces per month for cavalry and 1 for infantry, with similar amounts for the small contingent of sailors and marines among them. Later when the duke of Athens hired them, the Catalans, again according to Muntaner, received 4 ounces per month for heavy cavalry, 2 for light cavalry, and 1 for infantry. Pachymeres offers the figures of 2 and 3 gold ounces per month for the initial period of employment for the Catalans, which one assumes would correspond to the pay of infantry and cavalry, respectively. Since the gold ounce received by the Catalans was equal to around 8.5 hyperpyra, the pay of the Catalans, using Muntaner's figures, was equivalent to about 34 and 8.5 hyperpyra per month for horse and foot. (3) In the same passage where he cites the pay of the Catalans, Pachymeres notes that the Alans at that moment were being paid "only three nomismata per month in addition to the horses given to them."[30]

Since there are so few Byzantine figures, and since the Catalan rates of pay seem rather high, it is useful to compare these figures to what the Venetians were paying their own mercenaries in the Aegean area during the fourteenth and fifteenth centuries (Table A). In order to produce figures that are at least nominally comparable, we use the Venetian gold ducat as the standard which, compared with the hyperpyron, was a relatively stable currency during this period. From the table, the range of mercenary pay as calculated was 1.9 to 5.2 ducats per month, though this would usually have been supplemented with a rations allotment and housing. As one would expect, crossbowmen tended to command the higher end of the range, and sergeants and archers the lower. These figures are in accord with the typical pay rate of infantry in fourteenth-century Italy: 3 florins (a coin roughly

unionem (Vienna, 1872), 30, no. VIII. *Regesten*, no. 3052. Sathas, Μνημεία Ελληνικῆς Ἱστορίας, I, 146, lines 28–31. Nicol, *Last Centuries*, 133–34. Mallett, *Mercenaries*, 14, 80–88. M. Mallett and J. Hale, *The Military Organization of a Renaissance State* (Cambridge, Eng., 1984), 17. Bayley, *War and Society*, 9ff.

29. Zepos, *Jus graecoromanum*, I, 493. H. Antoniadis-Bibicou, *Études d'histoire maritime de Byzance* (Paris, 1966), 144. *Regesten*, no. 1890.

30. Muntaner, *Cronicà*, ch. 199, 204, 240 (trans. by Goodenough, II, 482–83, 495, 575). *The Catalan Chronicle of Francisco de Moncada*, 21, ch. 6, gives similar figures but in silver ounces. Pachymeres, Bonn ed., II, 420. Laiou, *Constantinople*, 187 note 108.

TABLE A.   Sample salaries for mercenaries in the service of Venice in the Aegean area

		Salary[a] as cited	Equivalent in ducats per month
1360s	sergeants of the Venetian bailli in Constantinople[b]	2 ducats/mo.	2.0
1387	crossbowmen on Corfu[c]	4 ducats/mo.	4.0
1394	crossbowmen at Argos	14 hyp./mo.	5.2
	sergeants at Argos[d]	8 hyp./mo.	3.0
1403	marines at Chandax[e]	9 (Cretan) hyp./mo.	1.9
1404	crossbowmen on Crete	12 (Cretan) hyp./mo.	2.5
	archers on Crete[f]	9 (Cretan) hyp./mo.	1.9
1423	*stratioti* in Thessaloniki[g]	2 ducats/mo.	2.0
1424	marines sent to Thessaloniki	4–5 ducats/mo.	4.0–5.0
	crossbowmen sent to Thessaloniki[h]	4 ducats/mo.	4.0

[a]hyp. = hyperpyra; mo. = month.
[b]C. Diehl, *Études byzantines* (Paris, 1905), 251 note 2. G. Ostrogorsky, "Löhne und Preise in Byzanz," *BZ* 32 (1932), 303 note 1.
[c]F. Thiriet, *Régestes des délibérations du Senat de Venice concernant la Romanie* (Paris, 1958–61), I, no. 730.
[d]Ibid., no. 861. In 1394, 1 ducat = 2 hyperpyra 17 karatia: T. Bertelé, "Moneta veneziana e moneta bizantina," *Venezi e il Levante fino ad secolo XV* (Florence, 1973), I, pt. 1, p. 50.
[e]Thiriet, *Régestes*, II, no. 1093, and I, p. 277: 83 ducats = 397 Cretan hyperpyra.
[f]Ibid., no. 1166. Equivalence as in note above.
[g]K. Sathas, Μνημεῖα Ἑλληνικῆς Ἱστορίας. *Documents inédits relatifs à l'histoire de la Grèce au moyen âge* (Paris, 1880–90), I, 146, lines 28–31. Thiriet, *Régestes*, II, no. 1898.
[h]F. Thiriet, *Délibérations des assemblées vénitiennes concernant la Romanie* (Paris, 1966–71), II, no. 1277.

equivalent to the ducat) per month.[31] They are also comparable to the pay rate of Turkish Janissaries in the first half of the fifteenth century (bearing in mind the inaccuracies produced by converting currencies across time and country). At this time the approximate daily wage of a Turkish Janissary, including allowances received for clothing and arms, was about 4.5 Ottoman silver *akçe* (aspers). Since in 1465 the gold florin (approximately equal to the ducat) was worth 40 *akçe*, the equivalent monthly pay of the Janissaries would have been something like 3.4 ducats, in order of magnitude comparable to the other figures cited for infantry.[32]

31. Mallett, *Mercenaries*, 137.
32. The calculation: (4.5 × 30 =) 135/40 ≈ 3.4 florins. The pay rate: F. Babinger, *Mehmed the Conqueror and His Time* (Princeton, N.J., 1978), 73 note 9, 448–49. The equivalency: H. Lowry, "Changes in Fifteenth Century Ottoman Peasant Taxation," *Continuity and Change in Late Byzantine and Early Ottoman Society*, ed. A. Bryer and H. Lowry (Birmingham, Eng., and Washington, D.C., 1986), 37.

We now return to the few Byzantine figures we have and convert them into ducats: (1) The 2.5 hyperpyra of the Genoese marines were equivalent to around 1.7 ducats per month, or perhaps a bit more.[33] (2) The 34 and 8.5 hyperpyra monthly for the Catalans, since the hyperpyron in 1304 still equalled about two-thirds of a ducat, were about 23 ducats for cavalry and 5.7 for infantry, calculated on a monthly basis.[34] (3) The Alans' 3 hyperpyra per month, using the same equivalencies, were equal to around 2 ducats per month.[35] The pay of the Genoese marines and the Alans is in accord with the 1.9 to 5.2 ducat range, though at the lower end of the scale. Even the pay of the Catalan infantry, at 5.7 ducats, was not out of line by contemporary standards. It was the Catalan cavalry whose pay was extremely high when compared with the other figures. Although indeed they were cavalry, and the Venetian figures cited in the table all refer to infantry of various sorts, contemporary mercenary cavalry in Italy do not seem to have received anything nearing the magnitude of the Catalans' pay. During the second half of the fourteenth century in Italy the typical monthly pay for the three-man "lance" (two men-at-arms and a page) was in the 18 to 20 ducat range, from which we may assume the men-at-arms each received about 7 to 8 ducats per month of this pay.[36] The Catalan cavalry seems to have been receiving three times the standard rate, and by the same token the Alan cavalry, albeit a light cavalry, was probably underpaid as they had in fact claimed.

There is no evidence that increases in mercenary pay were carried out on any kind of schedule. Instead the sources note only that the pay of individual or groups of mercenaries was increased when they had performed particularly well and faithfully.[37] Further, in at least one case a general increase in pay followed a victory, that of Andronikos III's general Synadenos over a force from Constantinople in 1328. Although it was a rather minor victory, the young emperor increased the pay of his mercenaries and the revenues assigned to his pronoiars, thereby "making them

---

33. The ducat was not struck until 1284. In 1281 there were about 12 *grossi* to the hyperpyron, and starting in 1284, 18 *grossi* to the ducat. Zakythinos, "Crise monétaire," 25. F. Thiriet, *Régestes des délibérations du Senat de Venise concernant la Romanie* (Paris, 1958–61), 225.

34. Dölger, *Schatzkammer*, 169: 12 Venetian silver *grossi* = 1 hyperpyron, with 18 *grossi* to the ducat.

35. There is a tradition reported in Moncada's chronicle (p. 21, ch. 6) and repeated by J. Pascot, *Les Almugavares* (Brussels, 1971), 43, that the Alans and Tourkopouloi received one-half the pay of the Catalans. I can only suggest that Moncada, who was fully acquainted with Pachymeres' history, calculated the pay of the Alans as if it were 3 pure gold hyperpyra (i.e., 23 to 24 carats fine; originally 72 to the pound, or 6 to the ounce). Three pure gold hyperpyra at one time equaled one-half of a gold ounce, or half the pay of the Catalan infantry.

36. Mallett, *Mercenaries*, 37, 136. Mallett and Hale, *Military Organization*, 17.

37. E.g., Kantakouzenos, II, 361.

more eager for war." When the continued loyalty of soldiers was most necessary, as during the civil wars, a pay increase or the promise of a pay increase was not uncommon. During the negotiations before the treaty of Epibatai, Andronikos III defended increasing his mercenaries' pay to his grandfather with the words, "Concerning the increase in pay, you yourself know it had to be done," and in 1327 Andronikos III, at that time possessing little more than his word, promised pronoiars and mercenaries, respectively, further grants of revenues and pay raises.[38]

There are very few figures available for the size of mercenary pay increases. In 1425 seventy *stratioti* in Thessaloniki had their salaries increased by 10 *aspra* per month, or 1/6 ducat at the prevailing rate of equivalence.[39] In 1403 the marines at Chandax received a raise from 8½ to 9 Cretan hyperpyra per month, or about 1/10 ducat (about 6%).[40]

Gifts supplemented regular pay and increases of pay. Prior to combat distributions of gold and other gratuities, along with the promise of further largess, served as an incentive for zeal on the battlefield, and after successful battles bravery was rewarded on both an individual and a group basis.[41] There is no distinction in the sources regarding the kinds of soldiers, including pronoiars, that might receive rewards, nor is there any preferred type of reward. Probably depending on what was available at the moment, the most common gifts seem to have been, naturally enough, gold, horses, and arms. One interesting example of a money reward as an incentive occurred in 1350 during Kantakouzenos' preparations for his assault upon Vodena, which was held at the time by some Serbs. "The emperor announced that a reward of four pounds of gold would go to the first man who removed a flag from the walls," with correspondingly lesser amounts to those who followed him. Four pounds of gold or, more accurately, four pounds of hyperpyra or 288 hyperpyra, were equivalent at this time to 144 ducats. According to the calculations above, this figure represented about twenty-five times the Catalan infantry's monthly wage, a sum for which one indeed might have shown some daring.[42]

38. Kantakouzenos, I, 287, 164. Gregoras, I, 397.

39. Mertzios, Μνημεῖα Μακεδονικῆς Ἱστορίας, 52–53, and pl. 4a, line 2. On the equivalency, see the figures in T. Bertelé, "Lineamenti principali della numismatica bizantina," *Rivista Italiana di Numismatica* 12 (1964), 94, and Dölger, *Schatzkammer*, 169.

40. Thiriet, *Régestes*, II, no. 1093; I, p. 227.

41. Kantakouzenos, I, 346. Pachymeres, Bonn ed., II, 211. Gregoras, I, 265.

42. Kantakouzenos, III, 129. Equivalence: T. Bertelé, "Moneta veneziana e moneta bizantina," *Venezi e il Levante fino ad secolo XV* (Florence, 1973), I, pt. 1, 43–44. There were always 72 hyperpyra to the pound.

Mercenaries also received distributions of money on special state occasions. Gold was distributed to the army during the coronation of Andronikos III in Constantinople in 1325 and after Kantakouzenos' acclamation as emperor in Didymoteichon in 1341. During the course of the latter event, Kantakouzenos notes that not only were his mercenaries paid any back pay that was owed plus further gifts of gold, but "to the others that held incomes from land [i.e., pronoiars], he distributed a goodly amount of gold to them and sent them home." Beyond incentives and rewards before and after battles, it seems that these ceremonial occasions were the only time nonmercenary soldiers, such as pronoia soldiers, received gold directly. Otherwise, the terms for "pay" are never used in connection with nonmercenary soldiers, nor is there any clear evidence that such soldiers received any money pay, not even for maintenance during campaigns.[43]

The process of administering money pay to soldiers is practically indiscernible from the sources. The fragmentary evidence simply confirms what we know of the rudimentary nature of the late Byzantine system of administration. When the Catalan Company and other assorted foreign and native contingents campaigned in Anatolia in 1304, "the army numbered in the thousands; those of the Italikon [the Catalans] were 6,000; the rest were one thousand Alans. The rest of the Rhomaïkon [the Byzantine force proper] was under the megas archon Maroules. The megas doux [Roger de Flor] was leader of all, arranging and granting the pay, and in the manner of an emperor or general, carrying off the spoils as he pleased."[44] Pay seems to have been the direct responsibility of the army commander. One assumes the actual distribution was handled by trusted subordinates, though this competence is attributed to no particular official.

We know somewhat more about the efficiency—or the inefficiency— of disbursals of mercenary pay. For various reasons, most commonly a lack of funds, official corruption, or perhaps simply the parsimony of rulers, mercenaries do not seem to have been paid promptly. Examples of this are numerous. The Turks fighting for Michael VIII in the Morea during the 1262–63 campaign left his employ because their pay was six months late. Around 1275 many of the highlanders of Asia Minor abandoned their posts due to arrears in pay, and later, under Andronikos II, two officials were found guilty of absconding with the pay destined for the highlanders. According to Kantakouzenos, the mercenaries of Andronikos III were

43. Kantakouzenos, I, 203; II, 175. Mutafčiev, "Vojniški zemi," 598.
44. Pachymeres, Bonn ed., II, 424.

unpaid for some five years, and since farmers and merchants refused to advance them credit, they could not serve.[45] Around 1381 Demetrios Kydones wrote of the misfortunes of a French mercenary from Picardy whom he had in good faith recommended to Manuel II for employment:

I am discontented seeing this soldier again, having thought he was helped by my letter. Now he has sold his horse and is seeking a moneylender for his arms. And indeed he has been inscribed among the poor. . . . There is no end to the daily delays but one must await tomorrow eternally. This is easy for those paying the wages, since they continue to dine splendidly at home. . . . Along with those who similarly toil in arms with him, it is possible to come in a group to the emperor's door to petition, to number the months, to complain about hunger and to speak against those in authority . . . and by shouting to demand the pay. . . . For narrating one's misfortunes affords some consolation for those suffering, as I believe lamentation consoles sorrow. But this man was robbed of this consolation . . . being a stranger and neither understanding the language of each of them nor being able to set forth to them the things in his heart. . . . Nor did it occur to him to expect his need to be consoled through begging, because he is ignorant of the language of the poor by which they move us to pity.[46]

45. *Chronicle of the Morea*, ed. Schmitt, v. 5100. Gregoras, I, 138. Pachymeres, Bonn ed., II, 208. Mutafčiev, "Vojniški zemi," 595. Kantakouzenos, I, 238. Other examples: Kantakouzenos, II, 175; Pachymeres, ed. Failler, I, 79 (Bonn ed., I, 54).
46. *Démétrius Cydonès correspondance*, ed. Loenertz, no. 238. For the initial letter of recommendation, see herein, pp. 209–10.

8. Smallholding and Pronoia Soldiers and Their Financing

The smallholding soldier is usually viewed as someone who held a more or less direct grant of land as compensation for or on condition of military service. Known also in modern scholarship as the settled soldier or the peasant soldier, he is essentially distinct from the pronoia soldier, who generally had a much higher social position and only an indirect connection to the land from which his income was derived, and from the mercenary, who had no inherent connection to land.[1]

The concept of a "small holding" can be defined in any number of ways. For Byzantium the only definition that provides a clear dividing line between "small" and "large" landholding is a fiscal one. Accordingly, I define the small holding as a property whose owner was not the recipient of fiscal privileges, such as a grant of paroikoi or tax exemption, that were granted on an individual basis by the emperor. Thus, landowners who received any kind of personal grant, gift, or privilege from the emperor were large landowners, and those who did not were small holders. Since one could say that such privileges by their nature made a man an aristocrat, there was a correlation and interrelation between social and fiscal status, even though there may have been large landowners who held no fiscal exemptions, as well as some smaller landowners who held paroikoi. Consequently, I regard the smallholding soldier as a soldier whose remuneration was based on his relationship to a specific property, but whose claim to this remuneration did not proceed from an individual benefaction bestowed by the emperor.

The smallholding soldier need not have been the actual cultivator of the land involved; he may have leased it to others to work. Nor is it necessary for him to have inhabited personally the property from which his livelihood derived, or to have owned or even possessed the property in

---

1. For further discussion of the smallholding soldier, see M. Bartusis, "On the Problem of Smallholding Soldiers in Late Byzantium," *DOP* 44 (1990), 1–26.

question. It is easy to imagine a situation whereby a property burdened with a military obligation could not produce an actual soldier from among the members of the household who held the property. The property holder might have then found a proxy, perhaps a relative not associated with the household or simply an acquaintance, to perform the required military service. Although this scenario is unattested in the late period, it parallels the distinction often made between the middle Byzantine *stratiotes* and *strateuomenos*, respectively, the man who bore (or whose landholding bore) the military burden, and the man who actually performed the required service.

This definition of the smallholding soldier is adequate to exclude those who were strictly mercenaries, because the salary of these was not derived from any *particular* property. It also excludes the majority of pronoia soldiers. There is no need to be concerned with the actual annual, economic value of pronoiai, or to place them within the late Byzantine economic spectrum. It really does not matter how large or small the annual income of a pronoia was, as long as it was granted through an individual, personal act of the emperor. It is self-evident that any man, regardless of his social or economic status, whose livelihood was established by the direct, individual, and personal intervention of the emperor was neither a peasant nor a "small holder." Rather, he was a special, privileged individual.

The practice of granting arable land to soldiers was an institution which existed continuously throughout Byzantine history with precedents in the Roman past. In the late Byzantine period we have seen how John Vatatzes settled the Cumans in Anatolia and enrolled them in the army, "distributing quantities of land to them for habitation." We have seen the various groups of smallholding soldiers created by Michael VIII after the reconquest of Constantinople: the Thelematarioi, who "because of their zeal and goodwill" received "good land for producing fruit and excellent for everything sown on it" in hereditary title on the condition of further military service; the rowers called Prosalentai to whom Michael assigned "lands everywhere near the shore," settling them in groups at various locations throughout the northern Aegean; and similarly, the Tzakones-Lakones from the Morea and elsewhere, brought to Constantinople to serve as marines and light-armed troops, whom Michael VIII "settled as natives, distributing places near the city."

Present in all of these examples are a number of common characteristics. All of these soldiers tended to form the lower end of the social spectrum of professional soldiers: light cavalry (Cumans), guards and marines (Tzakones), infantry (Thelematarioi), and rowers (Prosalentai). From this we may conclude that the lands with which they were associated were relatively modest. They cultivated their own land (the Cumans and Prosalentai certainly, the Tzakones and Thelematarioi probably). Further, either they were a large group of transplanted foreigners (the Cumans and the Tzakones) or the emperor had a particular area in which he wanted soldiers to be settled for direct defense (the Thelematarioi) or for convenience of mustering (the Prosalentai and the Tzakones). In at least two of the examples (the Prosalentai and the Cumans) the soldiers were certainly settled in colonies. Finally, all four of these groups of soldiers seem to have had hereditary military obligations that persisted through generations.

The settling of soldiers in colonies is an interesting phenomenon not without precedent in the Roman and Byzantine worlds. It offered numerous advantages to both the state and the soldiers themselves. First, the practice accommodated the social needs of less civilized peoples or recent immigrant groups. The Cumans and, to a lesser extent, the Tzakones could maintain their social organization within their communities, and their leaders similarly could maintain their prerogatives over their people once they were settled within the Empire. Also, the grouping of smallholding soldiers into communities or colonies facilitated their administration by the state. Mustering the troops could be accomplished without great effort, and the eternal problem of individual soldiers becoming too impoverished to serve could have been alleviated through a communal obligation of military service. Finally, settling soldiers in groups allowed a greater specialization among smallholding, settled peoples. Since there was no need for all of them to share equally the roles of farmer and soldier, some could spend more time away from the land soldiering while others concentrated on agriculture.

Above all, the institution of smallholding soldiers was useful to the state for two reasons. First, smallholding soldiers were less of a drain on the fisc than mercenaries. After the initial land grant, the only expenses incurred by the treasury were for rations, at least for those associated with the navy. Of the groups cited only the marine Tzakones, as far as we know, received regular pay in addition to their land grants. Second, of the three primary types of soldiers, pronoiar, mercenary, and smallholding, the latter had the strongest attachment to the land. This made them good defensive troops who at least in theory could have been planted on whatever ground needed to be defended.

Nevertheless, smallholding soldiers were not the warriors of choice among late Byzantine emperors. Only two emperors, as far as we can tell for certain, created smallholding soldiers, John Vatatzes and Michael Palaiologos, and both created such soldiers for reasons that were not based entirely on military requirements. Vatatzes' decision to make the Cumans smallholding soldiers was partially an attempt to avert a potential disaster by finding something to do with thousands of newly subjected semi-civilized peoples. Michael VIII's creation of the Thelematarioi was a means of rewarding the men who had helped him retake Constantinople and, just as important, of maintaining the political support of the inhabitants in the area around the city. His transplantation of the Tzakones was partly undertaken to repopulate the capital. Only the creation of the Prosalentai seems to have had little but military need at heart.

Significantly, the Prosalentai, as rowers, required less training and equipment than the other groups of smallholding soldiers, and this points to some of the problems inherent within the institution. It is no accident that all of the examples of smallholding soldiers fall into the light-armed category of warrior. Giving a soldier land and asking him or his family or even his friends to work it will not yield sufficient income to produce the kind of soldier the state most wanted, heavily armed cavalry. As in the medieval West, evidence derived from the tax records of pronoia soldiers (discussed later in this chapter) shows that it required at least several households of paroikoi and hundreds of acres of arable land to produce one such soldier.

Further, it seems that it would have been difficult to dismiss a smallholding soldier. A mercenary could be denied his salary and, with a bit more effort, a pronoia soldier could be denied his revenues. Both were essentially fiscal acts. But to fire a smallholding soldier and refuse him his remuneration meant taking away his land, at best an awkward affair. Even more troublesome is the matter of how the state dealt with smallholding households that could not produce a fit soldier, an issue with which students of middle Byzantine military lands have had to wrestle.

Many questions involving smallholding soldiers cannot yet be answered. For example, we do not know whether it was the rule for at least the families of the smallholding soldier to work such land themselves or whether it was common or even permissible to lease it for a rent. Nor do we know whether the land from which the smallholding soldier derived his livelihood generally was encumbered with a tax burden or received a tax exemption (*exkousseia*). While it is logical to think that there were some soldiers (as well as guards) who received tax exemption on their land on condition of service, this notion remains in the realm of mere conjecture. With the important exception, of course, of certain pronoiars, I know of no instance from the late Byzantine period in which it is certain that someone received tax exemption in return for personal military or paramilitary services.

One of the most puzzling issues is whether *individual* smallholding soldiers existed during the late Byzantine period, men whose plots of arable land from which they derived their livelihoods were not associated with one of the artificial colonies of soldiers created by late Byzantine emperors. While it is not impossible, or even unlikely, that such soldiers existed, I have found no trace of them. Moreover, scholars have occasionally speculated that a few families of smallholding, thematic soldiers may have survived into the late period. As far as I can tell, there is no evidence in the late period for such an "organic" arrangement of smallholding soldiers. Thus, I see no obligation of military service which, through men or through property, had its origin prior to 1204. If individual smallholding soldiers existed, their numbers must have been so small and their effect upon policy so minimal, that neither the documentary nor narrative sources thought them worthy of mention.

In light of all this it is necessary to conclude that smallholding soldiers were not very common in late Byzantium and that those men who were smallholding soldiers tended to be foreigners settled in groups. This would explain why Gregoras and Kantakouzenos, when speaking of the economic basis of the soldiers within the army, distinguish only two kinds of soldiers: pronoiars and mercenaries. Certainly, some of the smallholding groups of soldiers created by Michael VIII continued to exist into the fourteenth century, such as the Prosalentai and Thelematarioi, and even new groups may have been created, such as the 2,000 Cumans lent by Milutin and then settled in Thrace toward 1320 (see Chapter 3). However, it seems that they were always special elements within the military. Indeed what is known of military policies during the fourteenth century suggests that the institution of collective pronoia was supplanting that of the smallholding soldier and that collective pronoia soldiers had certain characteristics in common with smallholding soldiers. For the moment, collective pronoia does not fit my definition of a small holding, because in every known example of the phenomenon the recipients derived their remuneration from property held jointly, that is, each member of the group did not derive his income from a specific property. Yet the similarities are noteworthy as will be seen once we turn to revenues as a means of remunerating soldiers.

In the late Byzantine period a pronoia (literally, "providence," "care," "solicitude") was a grant by the emperor of the state's fiscal and usufructuary rights over a defined set of revenue sources to an individual or group of individuals. The fiscal rights bestowed in pronoia were generally the claim on the taxes and state charges burdening dependent peasants (paroikoi) and the taxes burdening immovable property, usually land, but including mills, mines, fisheries, docks, and so forth. What I am calling the usufructuary rights permitted the holder of a pronoia to demand the rents and other charges on state property and the labor services of specified paroikoi. Characteristically, the pronoiar appropriated the state's fiscal and usufructuary rights over revenue sources only to the extent that the state itself held these rights. In other words the state could grant the pronoiar usufructuary rights only over properties which the state itself owned. Since the state's rights over particular revenue sources varied and since there were different kinds of revenue sources, the rights granted and the forms of particular grants varied widely.[2]

Although pronoiai were granted to a variety of recipients, the majority of pronoiars were probably soldiers. Military pronoiars were a fundamental part of late Byzantine armies. In fact from reading the historians, the sense is strongly conveyed that the only two common ways to remunerate soldiers were with money and with pronoia. Smallholding soldiers are usually ignored. Consider George Pachymeres' description of the state of the army in Anatolia in the early years of the fourteenth century: "Not only were the Roman forces weakened, but having lost their pronoiai, they fled hastily from the east to the west, keeping only their lives; it was impossible to install others with fixed salaries." Kantakouzenos makes this same twofold

---

2. For other definitions of pronoia, and military pronoia in particular, see P. Lemerle, *The Agrarian History of Byzantium from the Origins to the Twelfth Century* (Galway, 1979), 222; N. Oikonomidès, "Contribution à l'étude de la pronoia au XIIIe siècle," in Oikonomidès, *Documents et études sur les institutions de Byzance* (London, 1976), no. VI, 168–69; idem, "A propos des armées," 353–54; H. Glykatzi-Ahrweiler, "La concession des droits incorporels," in Ahrweiler, *Études sur les structures administratives et sociales de Byzance* (London, 1971), no. I, 110–11; idem, "La 'pronoia' à Byzance," in *Structures féodales et féodalisme dans l'occident méditerranéen* (Rome, 1980), 681–89; and *ODB*, s.v. "pronoia." Also, compare the definitions and comments of Mutafčiev, "Vojniški zemi," 561ff.; A. Hohlweg, "Zur Frage der Pronoia in Byzanz," *BZ* 60 (1967), 288–308; K. Hvostova, *Osobennosti agrarnopravovyh ostnošenij v pozdnej Vizantii XIV–XV vv.* (Moscow, 1968), 205–24; P. Charanis, "On the Social Structure and Economic Organization of the Byzantine Empire in the Thirteenth Century and Later," in Charanis, *Social, Economic and Political Life in the Byzantine Empire* (London, 1973), no. IV, 132; Ostrogorsky, *Féodalité*, passim; I. Ševčenko, "An Important Contribution to the Social History of Late Byzantium," *Annals of the Ukrainian Academy of Arts and Sciences in the U.S.* 2 (1952), 458; and M. Sjuzjumov, "Suverenitet, nalog i zemel'naja renta v Vizantii," *Antičnaja drevnost' i srednie veka* 9 (1973), 60–63.

distinction between mercenaries and pronoiars, referring to the latter as those soldiers who received "income from villages" (*prosodoi ek chorion*). For example, he writes regarding his plans for a military campaign in 1341 that he had intended to "take the mercenaries of the army and the strongest of those having incomes from villages." Gregoras also speaks of two basic types of remuneration. In 1327 Andronikos III, in a bid to secure the allegiance of his troops, promised "to those serving as soldiers resources of incomes and increases of salary."[3]

One passage from Kantakouzenos makes the relation between pronoia and "incomes" clear. As he recounts the measures he took to refurbish the army in 1341, he writes that he "ascertained the amount of pronoia assigned by the emperor to each" man. If a pronoiar lacked part of his pronoia, this part was restored, and "to those that held incomes from the emperor that were not deficient, he similarly ordered that other incomes be added to what they were holding."[4] This connection between pronoia and "incomes" is important because it establishes the social position of the military pronoiar. Since his direct relation was to the income produced by revenue sources and not to the revenue sources themselves, he was at least one step distant from the source of his income. The Byzantines conceived of the military pronoiar not as a soldier-farmer but as a soldier-landlord.

In the documentary sources a pronoia is most often called an *oikonomia* ("arrangement, dispensation"), sometimes a *posotes* ("quantity or value"), and rather infrequently a *pronoia*. The equivalence of these terms is illustrated by a series of documents that refer to a certain village named Choudena by all three words.[5] While each of these words had its own meaning, each in its own way could be used to refer to Choudena as an object held in pronoia. Choudena was a village (*chorion*), but when held in pronoia, it represented a quantity of income (*posotes*) that comprised the imperial grant (*oikonomia*) to the pronoiar. In this way, while *pronoia*, *posotes*, and *oikonomia* all had distinct meanings, they could all be applied to a pronoia. On the other hand, the appearance of *posotes*, *oikonomia*, or even *pronoia*, by itself, did not necessarily mean a pronoia was involved. For example, a document from 1280/1 speaks of a posotes of 830 hyperpyra

---

3. Pachymeres, Bonn ed., II, 389. Kantakouzenos, II, 81. Gregoras, I, 397. Also, Kantakouzenos, I, 287; II, 175. Mutafčiev, "Vojniški zemi," 525–26, 530, 547.

4. Kantakouzenos, II, 63. Other passages speaking of pronoia as "incomes": Kantakouzenos, I, 119, 169, 443, 457; II, 367, 476; and Gregoras, I, 300, 438. Oikonomidès, "A propos des armées," 353.

5. L. Petit and B. Korablev, *Actes de Chilandar, I. Actes grecs*, *VizVrem* 17 (1911), suppl. 1, no. 45 (1334), no. 47 (1334), no. 126 (1335).

given to a certain Demetrios Mourinos not as a pronoia, but as a gift (*dorea*) which became Mourinos' "personal property" (*prosopika ktemata*), terminology never used with pronoiai.[6]

Similarly, only rarely were holders of pronoiai referred to by the term *pronoiarios*, from which we derive the term "pronoiar" employed today.[7] In the thirteenth century the expression frequently used to denote pronoiars was simply "those holding pronoiai" or a similar phrase,[8] while in the fourteenth century the word for pronoiar was exclusively *stratiotes* ("soldier"). All of these expressions and words can be found within the exemption clauses of documents granting or confirming the possession of land by monasteries. Time and again emperors decreed that this or that parcel of land was not to be bothered by "those holding pronoiai," by "those stratiotai holding pronoiai in this place," by "those serving militarily," by "stratiotai," or by "pronoiars." A parallel usage is seen in the exemption clauses of a couple of Serbian documents which employ the Slavic form *pronijar* (and not merely *vojnik*, "soldier") in acts for monasteries in areas where Byzantine terminology was able to influence Serbian practices.[9] Indeed, from the late thirteenth through the fourteenth century there was a strong correlation in the documentary sources between the word *stratiotes* and "pronoiar." Nevertheless, while we can usually translate *stratiotes* as "pronoia soldier," there are times when the word simply meant "soldier" with no connection to pronoia. This is the case when the word appears in the prefaces (*prooimia*) of documents which, for example, speak of the virtues of brave stratiotai. It is always necessary to consider the context in which the word *stratiotes* appears.

Sometimes the meaning is easy to discern. In Andronikos II's 1319 chrysobull for the town of Ioannina we read of "stratiotai reckoned in the

6. N. Oikonomidès, *Actes de Docheiariou* (Paris, 1984), no. 9.

7. E.g., A. Papadopoulos-Kerameus, «Ἰωάννης Ἀπόκαυκος καὶ Νικήτας Χωνιάτης», in Τεσσαρακονταετηρὶς τῆς καθηγεσίας Κ.Σ. Κόντου (Athens, 1909), 380 (from 1228); P. Lemerle et al., *Actes de Lavra* (Paris, 1970–82), III, no. 161, lines 4–5 (1409); no. 165, line 13 (1420); Arkadios Vatopedinos, «Ἁγιορειτικὰ ἀνάλεκτα ἐκ τοῦ ἀρχείου τῆς μονῆς Βατοπεδίου», Γρηγόριος ὁ Παλαμᾶς 3 (1919), 336, no. 35, lines 12–13 (1415); 337, no. 36, lines 19–21 (1406).

8. E. Branouse, Βυζαντινὰ ἔγγραφα τῆς μονῆς Πάτμου, I (Athens, 1980), no. 23, line 7 (1214); no. 25, lines 17–18 (1258); and M. Nystazopoulou-Pelekidou, Βυζαντινὰ ἔγγραφα τῆς μονῆς Πάτμου, II (Athens, 1980), no. 67, lines 5–8 (1262) (hereafter, Nystazopoulou, *Patmos*). Cf. MM, VI, 197, lines 13–16 (1258); MM, IV, 138, line 31 (1232); Branouse, Βυζαντινὰ ἔγγραφα, no. 30, lines 2–3 (1262); Petit and Korablev, *Chilandar*, no. 41, lines 80–81 (1319), and no. 139, line 6 (1326).

9. S. Novaković, *Zakonski spomenici srpskih država srednjega veka* (Belgrade, 1912), 673 xvi (1342–45), 751 ii (1369).

ranks of the *allagia* ['units'] and holding an oikonomia," which clearly implies pronoia soldiers.[10] To cite another example, a property description from 1321 speaks of one particular property as bordering "the rights of the stratiotes Neokastrites which were taken away from the monastery of Docheiariou."[11] Without doubt Neokastrites (Appendix, no. 55) was a pronoiar, but was he a soldier? This question is fundamental, yet the answer is not as obvious as it may seem. The identification of the word *stratiotes* with "pronoiar" may have been so strong that *stratiotes* may have been employed in the documents even in those cases when the subject was simply "pronoiar" and not "pronoia soldier." This is most likely to have happened in cases where a document speaks of property that had been "given to stratiotai." Since there was no word used in the fourteenth century other than *stratiotes* with which to designate a pronoiar, *stratiotai* in the phrase "land given to stratiotai" could conceivably have meant either military or nonmilitary pronoiars. Therefore, one must approach anonymous references to "stratiotai" with some caution and look for evidence of military activity before concluding that such individuals were pronoia soldiers.

The case of the stratiotes Neokastrites, however, is not an anonymous use of the word *stratiotes*. From the context of the passage it is clear that Neokastrites was a pronoiar, and further, since the epithet *stratiotes* is attached directly to his name (in the form "stratiotes N."), I think we can also assume he was a soldier. Two considerations lead to this conclusion. First, it is observable that of the approximately three dozen "stratiotai NN." from the late Byzantine period, none can be shown, from either the literary or documentary sources, to have held a courtly hierarchical rank either prior to or during the period in which he was termed a *stratiotes* (for a list, see the Appendix). Although such stratiotai NN. occupied a distinguished position in society, enjoying other contemporary marks of distinction such as the title *kyr* and the designation *doulos/oikeios* ("servant/familiar") of the emperor, their epithet of function *stratiotes* gave them no status in the titular hierarchy reflected in the lists of precedence. Therefore, since social and economic statuses among laymen were closely related, it is necessary to think that the stratiotai NN. formed a group that consisted in large part or perhaps entirely of pronoiars who held grants of pronoia inferior to the pronoia grants of men who possessed courtly ranks. This means that it is

10. MM, V, 81, lines 19–20.
11. Lemerle et al., *Lavra*, II, no. 108, lines 349–50. Appendix, no. 55.

unlikely that any "great men" were found among the stratiotai NN. of late Byzantium.[12]

The possibility remains that there were lesser nonmilitary imperial servants among the stratiotai NN. Here we must consider (1) that there is very little evidence of lesser nonmilitary imperial officials holding pronoiai and none that any was ever called a *stratiotes*, (2) that soldiers were the most numerous of all imperial servants, and (3) that *stratiotes*, after all, meant "soldier." Therefore, while the possibility certainly exists that an occasional "stratiotes N." in the documentary sources may not have been a soldier, such cases are negligible. With due caution for possible exceptions, we proceed from the supposition that most, if not all pronoiars in the documentary sources who are called *stratiotai* were military pronoiars and, more specifically, pronoia soldiers.

The granting of a pronoia was a complicated process. The prospective pronoiar first received an imperial writ (called a *prostagma*) assigning him a "quantity" (*posotes*) of pronoia in a stated area. On the basis of this act local officials, with the help of local records including earlier surveys, assembled a collection of paroikoi, land and rights adding up to the assigned posotes. The procedure was an involved one, probably occurring in stages as each successive element of the grant was added until the final posotes was attained.[13] The pronoia grant was created by exploiting many sources of revenues, and it is important to emphasize that each new pronoia was not necessarily created out of whole cloth. Most pronoiai were rich mixtures of diverse income-producing elements (properties, paroikoi, and rights), many of which had at one time been held by other pronoiars. The imperial government seems to have been engaged constantly in bestowing, transferring, exchanging, and expropriating pronoiai and their component elements. The emphasis was always on the fiscal value (posotes) of the grant, not the actual properties involved, which themselves were fungible. For example, a series of documents speaks of the soldier Nikephoros Martinos (see Appendix, no. 48), who held, as part of his pronoia, a small village with a posotes of 24 hyperpyra. In 1317 the village was donated to the Prodromos monastery near Serres by Andronikos II, who ordered that Martinos receive an equivalent posotes.

Michael VIII's 1272 prostagma for his son Andronikos, a document that defined Andronikos' position and rights as co-emperor, lists a few

12. On this, see M. Bartusis, "On the Status of Stratiotai During the Late Byzantine Period," *ZRVI* 21 (1982), 53–59.

13. On this process, see Oikonomidès, "Contribution," 159–60, 173.

sources for pronoia revenues. Although the document was specifically referring to additional grants of pronoia to worthy soldiers, the emperor's directives could equally be applied to new grants. Michael explains that grants were to be made

> neither from a pronoia vacant by accident lest when [his] pronoia is diminished some deficiency comes to a soldier in the *allagion* ["unit"], nor from some of the imperial taxes because these must be guarded for distributions and salaries on behalf of Romania [Byzantium], but from some things that may perhaps be found from a *perisseia* of the fiscal assessors [*apographeis*] or from the seizure of things that someone holds by theft.

Later in the document, Michael adds yet another indirect source: "If a soldier is not found conducting himself well in his duty, you should chasten him suitably and substitute another soldier who is deserving of the oikonomia of the one who erred."[14]

These are unequivocal official statements of Michael VIII's pronoia policy. First, Andronikos was cautioned against granting property in pronoia that was already held by another soldier. Next, he was directed not to make use of imperial taxes in his grants because these were needed for other purposes. This reference to tax revenues should probably be interpreted as tax revenues *not yet* granted to pronoiars. In other words, Michael wished to protect the remaining tax revenues the state was still collecting by forbidding any new redirection of state tax revenues to pronoiars. This also implies that Michael did not want property and paroikoi still held by the state itself and under direct state exploitation to be used for pronoia grants. Thus it is quite likely that in 1272, when this document was issued, most of the properties, paroikoi, and fiscal charges being granted in pronoia had been held previously by some other pronoiar. Soldiers and other pronoiars died or were stripped of their pronoiai for misconduct or other reasons, and their pronoiai, with their component elements reshuffled, were redealt to other soldiers.

Michael's emphasis on "recycling" pronoia grants is seen in the three sources of revenues Andronikos was given explicit permission to exploit. Two of these resulted from fiscal surveys. Someone could be found holding land in *perisseia*, that is, holding more land than allowed by his praktikon

14. A. Heisenberg, *Aus der Geschichte und Literatur der Palaiologenzeit*, in Heisenberg, *Quellen und Studien zur spätbyzantinischen Geschichte* (London, 1973), no. I, 40–41. See M. Bartusis, "A Note on Michael VIII's 1272 Prostagma for His Son Andronikos," *BZ* 81 (1988), 268–71.

(official property list) or failing to utilize his assigned land properly. Hence, "by reason of perisseia" this land could be transferred to someone else, perhaps a pronoiar. This was a common occurrence. Pachymeres complains that one of the problems with the army in Anatolia at the end of the thirteenth century was that "many of the soldiers, seizing frequent opportunities, increased their own pronoiai."[15] Another source, also resulting from a fiscal survey, was property that someone was found to be holding illegally, and this involved a more general range of circumstances than perisseia. Finally, Andronikos could deprive an unsatisfactory soldier of his pronoia and assign it to another.

One other source of revenue for pronoia grants which Michael's 1272 prostagma does not mention was escheated peasant properties (called *exaleimmata*). Most commonly these were the homesteads of paroikoi which had reverted to the state or to the property owner's lord through the owner's flight or death without legal heir. Although there was a strong tendency in the fourteenth century for a paroikos' escheat to revert not to the state but to his lord, this type of property always remained a source of revenues for pronoia grants and other fiscal procedures when the original owner of the escheated property was a paroikos of the state itself.[16]

As a rule the state granted only those revenue sources in pronoia to which it had a right. This included state taxes and charges, state lands, and paroikoi not held by a private landowner. Further, the state's claim on perisseia and escheat was an extension of its traditional prerogatives over illicitly or improperly utilized properties. Even the confiscation of monastic property for the benefit of pronoiars could be viewed as an application of this principle, since most monastic holdings originally had been granted through imperial gift. The absence of serious protest against this practice suggests that the emperor was within his rights to rescind such gifts, especially for the defense of the Empire. Sometimes monasteries managed to get their properties back. In 1355 a village and 1,000 modioi of land were returned to the monastery of Docheiariou, which had been taken from the monastery years earlier and granted, respectively, to a certain Michael Pitzikopoulos and the soldier Theodore Mouzalon, both of whom were dead in 1355 (see Appendix, no. 72). Reference was made earlier to the

15. Pachymeres, Bonn ed., II, 258. Cf. J. Bompaire, *Actes de Xéropotamou* (Paris, 1964), no. 19.

16. Nystazopoulou, *Patmos*, no. 66. See M. Bartusis, "Exaleimma: Escheat in Byzantium," *DOP* 40 (1986), 55–81, esp. 63.

soldier Neokastrites who in 1321 held 600 modioi of land that had been "taken from the monastery of Docheiariou." In 1337 this land, as well as 900 modioi which were taken from Docheiariou around 1327 and given to the Varvarenoi soldiers, was restored to the monastery.[17]

Aside from properties themselves, fiscal revenues earlier granted to monasteries sometimes were assigned to pronoiars. The best known example of this took place shortly after the battle of Marica in 1371 when, in the face of the Ottoman advance, the imperial government decided "to pronoiarize half of the Athonite and Thessalonian *metochia*." It seems that the monastic (and perhaps ecclesiastical) landowners of the area of Thessaloniki simply lost the base taxes on half of their properties (*metochia*). Put another way, they lost half of the tax exemption they had enjoyed on their properties. The measure was hardly Draconian, and it certainly was within the state's prerogatives to award and withdraw tax exemption as it saw fit, but after a generation during which these properties had enjoyed tax-free status, thanks to Stefan Dušan's blanket tax exemptions for the monasteries of (at least) Mount Athos, it was difficult for the churchmen involved to accept the new policy.[18]

Once the proper posotes of revenues was assembled it was officially transmitted to the pronoiar by means of a praktikon of conferral (*praktikon paradoseos*). Praktika were legal, official inventories of an individual's or corporate entity's landholdings. The praktika of pronoiars, sometimes called *stratiotika praktika*, were a particular category of praktika distinguishable from those held by normal landowners only by some combination of references to pronoia, an oikonomia, a posotes, the military occupation of the recipient, the fact that some kind of service burdened the landholding, or some other expression denoting that the properties were in fact held in pronoia. We have three such stratiotika praktika, all from the 1320s and all for pronoia soldiers who were members of the military division called the

17. Oikonomidès, *Docheiariou*, nos. 18, 21, 23, 41, and p. 16. Cf. A. Solovjev and V. Mošin, *Grčke povelje srpskih vladara* (Belgrade, 1936; repr. London, 1974), no. 11, lines 34–38. See also G. Dennis, *The Reign of Manuel II Palaeologus in Thessalonica, 1382–1387* (Rome, 1960), 89–91.

18. V. Mošin, "Akti iz svetogorskih arhiva," *Spomenik Srpske kraljevske akademije nauka* 91 (1939), 165. Lemerle et al., *Lavra*, IV, 52–53, 124; and cf. Ostrogorsky, *Féodalité*, 161–73; P. Charanis, "The Monastic Properties and the State in the Byzantine Empire," in Charanis, *Social, Economic and Political Life*, no. I, 116–17; and I. Ševčenko, "Nicolas Cabasilas' 'Anti-Zealot' Discourse: A Reinterpretation," in Ševčenko, *Society and Intellectual Life in Late Byzantium* (London, 1981), no. IV, 159. Other examples: D. Papachryssanthou, *Actes de Xénophon* (Paris, 1986), no. 25, lines 109–10; Solovjev and Mošin, *Grčke povelje*, no. 21, lines 5–9; and cf. Lemerle et al., *Lavra*, II, no. 97.

Thessalonian Mega Allagion: Basil Berilas, Michael Sabentzes, and Nicholas Maroules.[19]

Like the praktika of monasteries and of lay nonpronoiars, these praktika provide a list of paroikoi, by village and by household, naming the members of each household, their movable property (pigs, cows, asses, oxen, sheep, goats, beehives), and immovable property (arable land, vineyards, gardens, fruit trees, mills, fish ponds, threshing floors, buildings), sometimes indicating the legal status of the property (hereditary possession, from a dowry), and conclude with the *telos* or tax on each paroikos household and its property. This is followed by a list of lands, their general location or name, usually their size, and a figure for each in hyperpyra representing the official property tax on the land. Interspersed are other fiscal assets (such as fishing rights or the rights to a mill or a boat landing) and various fiscal charges, all with their yearly value in hyperpyra. After this the official posotes of the pronoia is given. Finally, the praktika mention how and when the payments were to be made to the pronoiar.

The telos, or tax, of the paroikos households was the quintessential element of a grant of pronoia. The pronoiar's praktikon list each paroikos along with his family and his property, and provide the telos the paroikos would pay to the pronoiar. The soldier Michael Sabentzes held eight paroikos households with twenty-nine persons, spread over four villages. Their total telos amounted to 12 hyperpyra of Sabentzes' total posotes of 70 hyperpyra. Arable farmland (called *ge*) was a basic part of pronoia grants, and in the praktika it appears in the form of both small parcels and large tracts. It seems that this land was state-owned and formed what we might call a "pronoiastic reserve." Evidently it was leased to the pronoiar's paroikoi or other peasants in return for a rent amounting to a percentage of the produce.[20]

Most of the other items included within the posotes of a praktikon were specific fiscal charges that the emperor now granted to the pronoiar.

19. P. Schreiner, "Zwei unedierte Praktika aus der zweiten Hälfte des 14. Jahrhunderts," *JÖB* 19 (1970), 33–49, with additional commentary and revised readings by N. Oikonomidès, "Notes sur un praktikon de pronoiaire (juin 1323)," in Oikonomidès, *Documents et études*, no. XXIII, 335–46. Papachryssanthou, *Xénophon*, nos. 15, 16. Two other praktika for laymen are extant: P. Lemerle, "Un praktikon inédit des archives de Karakala (janvier 1342) et la situation en Macédoine orientale au moment de l'usurpation de Cantacuzène," in Lemerle, *Le monde de Byzance: histoire et institutions* (London, 1978), no. XVIII, 281–86; and W. Regel et al., *Actes de Zographou, I. Actes grecs, VizVrem* 13 (1907), suppl. 1, no. 29 (from 1333). On the megala allagia, see herein, Chapter 9.

20. A. Laiou-Thomadakis, *Peasant Society in the Late Byzantine Empire* (Princeton, N.J., 1977), 47–48, 145, 148, 217–20. Oikonomidès, "A propos des armées," 354.

There were a great number of these and every praktikon had a slightly different combination. Most of these supplemental charges had originated before the late Byzantine period as charges that fluctuated from year to year. For example, the *choirodekateia* (literally, "pig tithe") and *melissoenno-mion* (literally, "bee pasturage charge"), two common taxes often mentioned together in the documents, apparently had once been charges that peasants paid the fisc depending upon the number of pigs and beehives they owned. Yet, by the late period, the choirodekateia and melissoennomion for a village were stated as fixed sums with no relation to the number of pigs or beehives held by the pronoiar's paroikoi. In effect, these charges had become simply another kind of tax with little or no relation to their original meaning or purpose.

This was the case with most of these supplemental charges: the *enno-mion*, originally a charge for the use of state land as pasturage or a pasture charge on animals; the *opheleia*, an obscure charge based on a percentage (generally 10 percent) of the telos of the paroikos households; the *linobro-cheion*, the charge for the use of the place where flax was processed.[21] Sometimes the pronoiar who received such charges also held the paroikoi that paid them, but frequently state revenues were directed toward pronoiars who had no hold on the properties that produced the revenues. For example, John V once exempted a village held by the monastery of the Great Lavra from the choirodekateia, which we are told had been assigned previously to soldiers.[22] In this instance the monastery and not the pronoia soldiers held the paroikoi who paid the charge.

The praktika specify a few additional demands on the pronoiars' paroikoi. They were required to perform corvées (*angareiai*) on the pronoiar's lands for a certain number of days each year. This generally amounted to either twelve or twenty-four days per year. Further, the praktikon usually noted the frequency of the *kaniskia* (literally, "little baskets"), a traditional obligation by which each paroikos household gave his lord a small gift in kind, generally three times a year. Such in-kind burdens could also include the *oikomodion* and the *oinometrion*. The former gave the pronoiar the right to demand a modios (by volume) of wheat and barley for every 3 hyperpyra of telos paid by his paroikoi. Analogously, the oinome-

---

21. See the *ODB*, s.v. "ennomion," "opheleia," and, for the *linobrocheion*, see Bompaire, *Xéropotamou*, 146, and F. Dölger, *Sechs byzantinische Praktika des 14. Jahrhunderts für das Athoskloster Iberon* (Munich, 1949), 123.
22. Lemerle et al., *Lavra*, III, no. 131, line 5.

trion provided the pronoiar with one measure of local wine for every 1 hyperpyron of telos.[23]

The sum of the revenues produced by the constituent elements of the praktikon was the posotes or total yearly value of the pronoia. The posotetes of the pronoiai of Sabentzes, Maroules, and Berilas were 70, 72, and 80 hyperpyra, placing these pronoia soldiers toward the lower end of the scale of pronoiars. The official posotes, however, differed substantially from the actual value of the oikonomia. The reason for this is that all three of these pronoia grants contained a substantial quantity of arable land that the pronoiar leased out. The tenants, whether the pronoiar's own paroikoi or other peasants, paid a rent which in the late period was generally one-third of the harvest, or 1 hyperpyron for every 10 modioi of arable land.[24] If we make a conservative estimate of the rent the pronoiar might have realized (half the possible rent) from leasing the large tracts of arable land (i.e., excluding escheated parcels) and add to it the stated minimum income he received from the other revenue sources within his praktikon, we see that the true economic value of a pronoia grant exceeded its official posotes by a factor of at least two or three (Table B).

Moreover, adding the value of the kaniskia, the oikomodion and the oinometrion, plus possible rents obtained from any of the other properties in the praktika (mills, docks, escheat), made the difference between the official posotetes and the true value of the pronoia even more dramatic. Thus the true yearly value of a soldier's pronoia was at least in the 150 to 220 hyperpyra range and probably higher. This is not to say that every pronoiar actually collected two or three times the official posotes of his oikonomia, but it does represent the income he *could* attain if diligent. The goal was, after all, a rate of return on one's holdings equivalent to that of a private landlord.

In Chapter 7 the testimony of the Venetian sources was collected to establish a mercenary pay scale of 1.9 to 5.2 ducats per month for the crossbowmen, archers, marines, and sergeants in Venice's employ. We saw that the few Byzantine figures for rates of mercenary pay tended to fall within this range, except for that of the Catalan cavalry which, at the equivalent of 23 ducats per month, far exceeded the upper limit of the scale. On a yearly basis, the Catalan cavalry's 23 ducats per month was equal to 276 ducats per year. The minimum 150 to 220 hyperpyra range of pronoia values

23. For these terms, see the *ODB*, s.v. "corvée," "kaniskion," "oikomodion," "oinometrion."

24. *ODB*, s.v. "rent."

TABLE B.   Estimated minimum economic values of three pronoia grants from 1321–25

	Sabentzes	Maroules	Berilas
official posotes	70 hyp.[a]	72 hyp.	80 hyp.
area of arable land (*ge*)	2,100 mod.[a]	2,050 mod.	4,500 mod.
possible rent on this arable land (1 hyp. per 10 mod.)	210 hyp.	205 hyp.	385 hyp.[b]
estimated rent on this arable land (possible rent/2)	105 hyp.	102.5 hyp.	192.5 hyp.
minimum other charges	39 1/3 hyp.	37 7/12 hyp.	23.5 hyp.
estimated rent plus minimum other charges	144 1/3 hyp.	140 1/12 hyp.	216 hyp.

[a]hyp. = hyperpyra; mod. = modioi.
[b]Berilas' *ge* was composed of 2,000 mod. of average land, assessed at the normal rate (1 hyp. per 50 mod.), and 2,500 modioi of land of second and third quality, assessed at a lower rate (by calculation, 1 hyp. per 67.6 mod.). Since the latter logically would have been rented at a correspondingly lower rate, the figures have been adjusted accordingly (200 hyp. + 185 hyp. = 385 hyp.).

calculated above corresponds to about 100 to 150 ducats per year.[25] Thus, when compared to the estimated pronoia values of other horsemen, the Catalan cavalry's rate of pay, while certainly still high, is no longer quite so outrageous.

In fact, the calculated incomes of these pronoiars may well have been preferable to the pay of the Catalan cavalry. Most mercenaries, certainly the Catalans, could not expect to be employed year round. If the campaign season was only six months, the mercenary might have seen only half of the "yearly" calculated pay, and that only in the rare event that it was paid as promised. It is quite likely that a man would rather have faced the vagaries of agricultural production and the inconvenience of collecting taxes from peasants than accept a nominally higher sum but place himself at the mercy of imperial officials for his monthly sustenance. Further, we know from practices in Italy that "monthly" mercenary pay was not always distributed

25. T. Bertelé, "Moneta veneziana e moneta bizantina," *Venezi e il Levante fino ad secolo XV* (Florence, 1973), I, pt. 1, 41–42.

according to the calendar month. In the fifteenth century, for example, the "month" was usually about forty-five days, so there might be only eight pay periods per year.[26] Figured on such a basis, the Catalan cavalry's pay would be reduced to 184 ducats per year, comfortably within the minimum range of pronoia values.

Overall, despite the dozens of figures preserved in the documents, we know the total official posotetes of very few pronoiai. This is because pronoiai were fragmented things, and there was little necessity for most documents to mention the *total* size of a pronoia. There are only about ten cases where we can say with certainty that the figure given represented the entire official posotes of a particular pronoia. At the lower end of the scale were the three soldiers Sabentzes, Maroules, and Berilas with their official posotetes of 70 to 80 hyperpyra, and the Palaiologan highlanders on the eastern frontier with 40 hyperpyra each. The last case is problematic because, as explained in Chapter 2, it is not absolutely certain that these men became pronoiars. But even if Michael VIII did transform them into pronoia soldiers, the devaluation of the hyperpyron from the mid-thirteenth to the early fourteenth century may make it necessary (as Michael Hendy has suggested) to as much as double the value of their nominal 40 hyperpyra in order to compare it with fourteenth-century figures.[27]

Yet there do seem to have been pronoia soldiers who held posotetes lower than the 70 to 80 hyperpyra of Sabentzes, Maroules, and Berilas. These were the pronoia soldiers who received their pronoiai through grants that were not individualized, personal acts of an emperor, but through group grants. We speak of such soldiers as the recipients of "collective pronoia," a phrase coined by Nicolas Oikonomidès. One example are the Klazomenitai soldiers of Serres, who in 1342 received a chrysobull granting each of them hereditary title to a posotes of either 10 or 12 hyperpyra from the pronoia that the group shared.[28] Even though the privileges they were granted in 1342 were issued through a chrysobull and thus formally constituted a personal act of the emperor, the grant was bestowed impersonally and to anonymous soldiers (the Klazomenitai are not named, nor are individual names found in the documents relating to the other two groups of collective pronoia soldiers: the Varvarenoi soldiers and the soldiers from

26. J. Hale, *War and Society in Renaissance Europe, 1450–1620* (Baltimore, Md., 1985), 109–10.

27. Oikonomidès, "A propos des armées," 359–60. M. Hendy, *Studies in the Byzantine Monetary Economy c.300–1450* (Cambridge, Eng., 1985), 163.

28. P. Lemerle, *Actes de Kutlumus*, rev. ed. (Paris, 1988), no. 20.

the company of judge of the army Sgouros). In other words, its recipients had a social status not noticeably higher than, say, a group of peasant villagers who received an imperial writ lowering their taxes.

The manner in which these 10 and 12 hyperpyra were to be allotted is not specified by the document. Most likely their initial request for this imperial favor noted who was to get what, probably based on rank. In any event, 10 or 12 hyperpyra is certainly a modest sum, but did it represent the total posotes of each soldier's share of the pronoia? At this time 12 hyperpyra were approximately equal to 6 ducats. Even allowing that the true value of a pronoia grant could be at least twice its face value once all the fringe benefits were taken into consideration, the value of each Klazomenites' posotes was still less than the salary of the lowest paid mercenary in the late period, whether employed by Byzantium or Venice (the equivalent of 1.9 ducats per month, calculated on a yearly basis of eight "monthly" pay periods, would amount to at least 15 ducats).

It is possible that pronoia constituted only part of the Klazomenitai soldiers' remuneration, the remainder consisting of regular mercenary pay.[29] It is equally possible that in 1342 only *part* of the Klazomenitai's pronoia was transformed into a hereditary possession, the rest remaining only a lifetime grant. The document states that some Klazomenitai should receive, in hereditary tenure, 12 hyperpyra, others 10, "from the posotes they hold," and it would be difficult to prove that this did not mean a *partial* transformation. Indeed, in another praktikon, for a man named Michael Monomachos, 50 hyperpyra "from his oikonomia" were granted in hereditary tenure out of a total posotes (by calculation) of 102.5 hyperpyra. Thus, we really do not know whether the Klazomenitai were receiving a full or partial transformation of their oikonomiai into hereditary possession. Since a partial transformation as low as one-quarter of an oikonomia is attested, it is possible that the total individual oikonomiai of the Klazomenitai were in the range of 40 to 48 hyperpyra, and, perhaps, even higher.[30] Thus, their oikonomiai could easily have been at least half that of Sabentzes, Maroules, and Berilas.

After receiving his complete praktikon the new pronoia soldier presumably visited his pronoia, made his presence known to his paroikoi and

29. As Oikonomidès, "A propos des armées," 369, argues.
30. Regel et al., *Zographou*, no. 29, line 4. Oikonomidès, *Docheiariou*, no. 26, and cf. the case of the kavallarios Syrmanuel Mesopotamites (Appendix, no. 69) who similarly received 20 hyperpyra "from his oikonomia" in hereditary tenure.

the others who worked his lands, and cleared up any confusion about financial arrangements. After this, unless his military services were immediately needed, he set up house somewhere. Was this near his pronoia? This straightforward question is one of the most difficult to answer. Its importance lies in the fact that the geographic proximity of a man to the sources of income that provide his livelihood is relevant for defining the nature of his control over this income and, in turn, his social status in an agrarian society. At the very least we can say that the pronoia soldier holding pronoia in the theme, say, of Thessaloniki, probably lived in that theme, if for no other reason than that he or his agent needed to collect his income periodically, in cash or in kind, from his pronoia.

Beyond this, in favor of the notion that pronoia soldiers lived on estates and, in the words of George Ostrogorsky, "were masters of the paroikoi who tilled their lands," a thesis grounded in the Western European feudal model, there is little evidence.[31] On the contrary, the Byzantine tradition of civic life militated against the idea of the pronoia soldier isolating himself out in the countryside. Rather than turning for comparison to the Western (French or German) feudal model, it might be better to consider medieval northern Italy, where civic life endured the early medieval crises. No less than his ancient Roman counterpart, the Italian seigneur lived an urban life, the life of an absentee landlord. We should expect the pronoia soldier, fundamentally a landlord as well, to have preferred the community of population centers. Further, it is quite clear that pronoiars, or at least pronoia soldiers, were generally not "masters" of their paroikoi. The handful of paroikoi held by some pronoia soldiers was scattered over several villages, making this very difficult. Aside from the traditional corvées and kaniskia, paroikoi were essentially income-producing units for the support of the pronoiar.

The praktika only detail the property soldiers held in pronoia. Some pronoia soldiers owned allodial or patrimonial property which was not recorded in their military praktika. Add to this the element of hereditary pronoia, and the actual possessions and holdings of a soldier become a diverse mix of rights and properties, including those he inherited and could bequeath, partly pronoia, partly patrimony, as well as those he acquired during his lifetime, such as further grants of pronoia, part of which he might have the right to bequeath, and properties he purchased or received

---

31. G. Ostrogorsky, "Observations on the Aristocracy in Byzantium," *DOP* 25 (1971), 11. For the strongest evidence supporting Ostrogorsky's view, see Ostrogorsky, *Féodalité*, 90.

as gifts. Moreover, the ownership or possession of such properties might be shared with other individuals or monasteries and be subject to complicated fiscal processes.

Periodically there were fiscal reassessments (*exisoseis*, literally "equalizings") of pronoiai and other landholdings to ensure that everyone was holding his property lawfully and, like modern property tax assessments, to increase state revenues. A fiscal assessor (*apographeus*) traveled through a particular region reevaluating the fiscal values (posotetes) of properties, rights, and paroikos households, and then issuing new, revised praktika. These periodic reassessments were a basic feature of late Byzantine fiscal policy. In fact, the praktika of the soldiers Sabentzes, Maroules, and Berilas are actually revised praktika reflecting the results of a particular reassessment conducted in the region of Thessaloniki.

From the end of the thirteenth through the middle of the fourteenth century there were at least four reassessments carried out specifically to strengthen the army. For example, in 1298 when Andronikos II sent John Tarchaneiotes to Anatolia with money and troops to make one last effort to set the fiscal affairs of the region in order, Pachymeres explains that "many of the soldiers, seizing frequent opportunities, increased their own pronoiai and lived idly through bribes to their leaders; others often more worthy fell into poverty when they abandoned their own oikonomiai, deliberately choosing an impediment to military service. Both of these were a loss to the state, and this inequality required a reassessment [*exisosis*]."[32]

The most detailed account of a reassessment appears in connection with affairs following the death of Andronikos III in 1341. After describing the deplorable state of the army, Kantakouzenos writes that it had come to his attention that a certain Patrikiotes, a fiscal assessor, had enriched himself through the abuse of his position. Kantakouzenos decided not to lay charges against him since, he claims, Patrikiotes came forward without being summoned and was willing "to re-equalize the means of living of the soldiers" from the wealth he had obtained illicitly. This was not a typical reassessment because Kantakouzenos himself was directly involved in the process:

> After this the megas domestikos [Kantakouzenos] summoned one by one those of the senate, those otherwise distinguished by birth, and then the soldiers, and he ascertained the amount of pronoia given by the emperor to

32. Pachymeres, Bonn ed., II, 258. Mutafčiev, "Vojniški zemi," 526, 530, 632–33. Laiou, *Constantinople*, 87–89. And for other reassessments, Kantakouzenos, I, 169, 287–88.

each and whether he now held more or less than that which was assigned. According to the answers of each in regard to what he held, he ordered Patrikiotes to restore the necessary amounts for those deprived, and to add over and above as much as seemed good to him, proportionately adding to each the benefaction. To those holding incomes from the emperor that were not deficient, he ordered similarly that other incomes be added to what they were holding.

And indeed in sixty days the redistribution took place: for those holding less he added that which was lacking along with a [further] addition, and for those lacking nothing the addition was added. And everyone considered that he was in command of sufficient revenues and professed great gratitude toward the megas domestikos, and they were eager to fight the enemies of the Romans of whatever land. And cleansing their arms, they re-equipped themselves, and they procured horses, more and better ones than before. And in short they appeared vexed that they were not led right away for defense against enemies.[33]

Although this reassessment arose from a desire to strengthen the army, it affected not only pronoia soldiers but "those of the senate" and "others distinguished by birth" as well.

Fiscal reassessments were particularly necessary to safeguard any legitimate alterations in the pronoiar's oikonomia because a pronoia was technically inalienable. Thus, any sale or donation of any part of a pronoia needed to be approved by the emperor. For example, in 1299/1300 the soldier Demetrios Harmenopoulos (Appendix, no. 40) leased seven escheated peasant properties that he held in pronoia to the Great Lavra. However, after some friction between the monks of Lavra and those of the monastery of Xenophon, Harmenopoulos canceled the agreement and in 1303 leased the properties to Xenophon for 3 hyperpyra per year. This sum is not called a rent, but an *epiteleia* (literally, "for the tax"), indicating that the monastery technically was not leasing the land but merely had assumed its tax burden, which it furnished to Harmenopoulos. If this transaction was approved by the state, his next praktikon would most likely have noted that part of his pronoia included this annual epiteleia from Xenophon. The conditional and revocable nature of the pronoia grant was acknowledged by Harmenopoulos when he added the legal phrase that the agreement would remain in effect only for "as long as I hold the mercy of our mighty and holy lord and emperor."[34]

Additions to an oikonomia and the granting of hereditary rights over

33. Kantakouzenos, II, 58–63. Ostrogorsky, *Féodalité*, 101–103. Heisenberg, *Palaiologenzeit*, 74–75.

34. Papachryssanthou, *Xénophon*, no. 6. On the *epiteleia*, see the *ODB*, s.v. "epiteleia."

portions of an oikonomia were the two most common ways to reward a pronoia soldier for meritorious service. Additional pronoia brought an immediate benefit to the pronoiar and required administrative effort and possibly some expense on the part of the state, while a grant of hereditary rights cost the state nothing in the short run but had more serious long-term effects. Only one source, the 1272 prostagma Michael VIII issued for his son Andronikos, provides any figures for an increase added to a pronoia. Among his many other responsibilities, Michael explains to Andronikos that when on campaign, "If a soldier should appear useful in his military service, he may be made a benefaction by you or may receive an addition to his oikonomia, up to 24 or 36 hyperpyra." In other words, pronoia soldiers could be rewarded for admirable service either by a single, lump-sum "benefaction" or by an increase in their annual posotes.[35]

Michael VIII was the first emperor to make military pronoiai hereditary on a large scale, granting this right to those soldiers who gave their lives for the state or otherwise served well. For example, in 1232 the *vestiarites* Constantine Kalegopoulos (who may not have been a soldier) held certain fishing rights near Smyrna in pronoia. In 1259, apparently after his death, the same pronoia was held by the soldier Michael Angelos (Appendix, no. 18). Eight years later, after Angelos' death, the pronoia was transferred not to a new pronoiar but to Angelos' wife and children.[36] Pachymeres speaks of this development: "Loving the soldiery exceedingly, [Michael VIII] established their pronoiai, if they should fall in war and die, as hereditary to the children, even if the mothers should have the fetus in their wombs." But Michael did not stop there: "He provided for those of the senate magnificently, increasing and adding to their pronoiai," and "for the soldiery . . . he increased the daily kindnesses, and fulfilled the things promised to them by chrysobulls, and he ordered toward the better disposed that they have forever the pronoiai of life and the bestowed *siteresia* for their children."[37]

The meaning of the word *siteresion* is troublesome. Both Pachymeres and Gregoras refer to the Catalan Company's pay as siteresia, though Patriarch Athanasios once uses the word, perhaps, to mean pronoia.[38]

35. Heisenberg, *Palaiologenzeit*, 40–41. See Bartusis, "A Note on Michael VIII's 1272 Prostagma," 271.

36. Ostrogorsky, *Féodalité*, 83–84.

37. Pachymeres, ed. Failler, I, 131, 139 (Bonn ed., I, 92, 97–98). Ostrogorsky, *Féodalité*, 93–94. Mutafčiev, "Vojniški zemi," 570–71, 598, 639.

38. Pachymeres, Bonn ed., II, 416. Gregoras, I, 220. Athanasios I, *The Correspondence of Athanasius I Patriarch of Constantinople*, ed. A.-M. Talbot (Washington, D.C., 1975), no. 83, lines 52–55, and p. 409.

Should siteresion not mean pronoia in this passage, then Pachymeres is indicating either that military pronoiars received pay in addition to pronoia or that Michael made the pay of some mercenaries hereditary. Both possibilities are rather interesting but there is little corroborative evidence for either. In any event, although Michael VIII may not have been the first emperor to make pronoia grants hereditary, it is clear that he was the first emperor to make military pronoiai hereditary on a large scale. Nevertheless it must be emphasized that not every military pronoiar received hereditary rights over his pronoia; rather, it was only those soldiers who gave their lives for the state and had otherwise served well.

When pronoia acquired a hereditary component, military service tended to become a family tradition. For example, the fourteenth-century Deblitzenos family, with the tzaousios Manuel, his son the soldier Demetrios, and the grandson the military man Manuel, represent three generations of warriors, all pronoiars.[39] Another example of a service tradition, as well as a very early case involving the inheriting of a pronoia, appears in a letter from the patriarch of Constantinople Gregory of Cyprus (1283–89) to the megas logothetes Theodore Mouzalon about a soldier named Chrysokompas.

Chrysokompas lived in the area of Skammandros in northwestern Asia Minor with a wife, and a son by his deceased first wife. "Since the son was already sufficiently of age to take up arms and to be reckoned in the military ranks, [Chrysokompas] sent him to camp." According to the patriarch, Chrysokompas stayed home either because of old age or because he wished to cultivate the civilian life (*koinos bios*). Meanwhile the relatives of the first wife did not fancy the idea of the young man serving in the army while his father and stepmother remained at home, "since pronoia, house and whatever else came from him who owed military service, they passed from the mother to the child." In other words, both the estate and a military obligation encumbering the estate had come from the first wife's side of the family. Were it not for the mention of pronoia, one might think the subject was a middle Byzantine military estate.

At this point in the story things got ugly. While on leave the son was advised by his mother's relatives to throw his stepmother out of the house. He deferred out of regard for his father and the rules of hospitality. Then the rumor was circulated that the son and his stepmother were paramours.

---

39. N. Oikonomidès, "The Properties of the Deblitzenoi in the Fourteenth and Fifteenth Centuries," in *Charanis Studies*, ed. A. Laiou-Thomadakis (New Brunswick, N.J., 1980), 176–98. Appendix, nos. 44, 77.

An anonymous state fiscal official heard the gossip, rushed to the "home of the soldiers," and inflicted some unnamed injury, "doing what barbarians might do." The patriarch asked Mouzalon to interview the principals personally. "If not, torture and the gallows shall rob them of home and property."[40]

As usual there is more to the incident than we are told. A fiscal official would have had little reason to involve himself in allegations of immorality. Since the patriarch notes that the official had been "entrusted with the management of the state taxes in Skammandros," a much more likely reason for his involvement was that taxes had not been paid or military service had not been rendered. As a catalyst there was a quarrel over the possession of property between Chrysokompas and his deceased wife's family.

In fourteenth-century documents there are numerous examples of pronoiai becoming hereditary and, just as important, occasional examples of the denial of this privilege. In 1307 one thousand modioi from the oikonomia of the judge of the army Diplovatatzes became a hereditary holding. Similarly, the hetaireiarches John Panaretos and George Troulenos were granted hereditary rights over 30 hyperpyra and 1,600 modioi from their respective oikonomiai in 1310 and 1318.[41] On the other hand, in 1325 the widow of a certain Sarakenos was not granted her deceased husband's 80-hyperpyra oikonomia.[42] Many of those who received such hereditary rights were titled aristocrats (judge of the army, megas adnoumiastes, hetaireiarches, eparch), men who would have been military leaders if they had any military competence at all. Very few are called "soldiers." It is not surprising that any list of men who received special privileges from the emperor would be biased toward the higher social levels. Nevertheless, since some soldiers received hereditary rights over rather small posotetes (such as the Klazomenitai soldiers of Serres), we may assume that it was not uncommon for soldiers to hold hereditary pronoia.

40. Gregory II, of Cyprus, in S. Eustratiades, ed., «Τοῦ σοφωτάτου καὶ λογιωτάτου καὶ οἰκουμενικοῦ πατριάρχου κύρου Γρηγορίου τοῦ Κυπρίου Ἐπιστολαί», Ἐκκλησιαστικὸς Φάρος 3 (1909), 295–96, no. 129. M. Bibikov, "Svedenija o pronii v pis'mah Grigorija Kiprskogo i 'Istorii' Georgija Pahimera," ZRVI 17 (1976), 94–96.

41. A. Guillou, Les archives de Saint-Jean-Prodrome (Paris, 1955), nos. 2, 6, 8. A. Laiou, "The Byzantine Aristocracy in the Palaeologan Period," Viator 4 (1973), 145. Other examples: Petit and Korablev, Chilandar, no. 132; F. Dölger, Aus den Schatzkammern des Heiligen Berges (Munich, 1948), no. 16; W. Regel, Χρυσόβουλλα καὶ γράμματα τῆς ἐν τῷ Ἁγίῳ Ὄρει Ἄθῳ ἱερᾶς καὶ σεβασμίας Μεγίστης Μονῆς τοῦ Βατοπεδίου (St. Petersburg, 1898), no. 5; Oikonomidès, Docheiariou, no. 27; and the documents in notes 43 and 44 below.

42. Guillou, Prodrome, no. 16. Laiou, "Aristocracy," 145.

Further, as late as 1378 hereditary rights sometimes were granted with the stipulation that the grant could be transmitted to the recipient's sons as long as they rendered "the corresponding service" or "the service owed," though whether this was of a military or administrative nature cannot be determined.[43] Other documents lack such a phrase, though it is unlikely this meant that service was no longer required. It seems that hereditary grants with a continuing service obligation, while never automatic, became common, particularly since they cost the state little. On the other hand, hereditary grants without service, whether or not such a grant could still be called a pronoia at all, could never have become common for soldiers, because every such grant diminished the army by one military pronoiar. Lastly, we note that the posotes or land granted in hereditary tenure was often described as "from the oikonomia" of the pronoiar, or, more specifically, "inside the value of his oikonomia" which, in my view, meant that the practice was to grant hereditary rights over fractions of the oikonomia. Indeed in the cases of Demetrios Deblitzenos and Michael Monomachos, hereditary rights were granted respectively over twenty-five and fifty percent of their oikonomiai.[44]

Although the institution of pronoia was an indigenous development in Byzantium, not influenced to any significant degree by its neighboring civilizations, it had certain similarities to some Western and Islamic institutions. Most commonly the pronoia is compared to the Western fief. George Ostrogorsky went so far as to claim that "there was no essential difference between the Byzantine pronoia and the Western fief."[45] Acceptance of this statement depends on what one regards as the "essences" of pronoia and fief. There are undeniable similarities. Both pronoia and fief were used to raise soldiers; both were originally grants for life that could not be sold or otherwise alienated, though both in time became hereditary; the recipients of both derived the bulk or all of their livelihoods from the toil of specific members of the rural population, largely peasants; the recipients of both did not "own" the properties granted.

43. Lemerle et al., *Lavra*, III, no. 149. Dölger, *Schatzkammer*, no. 11. Even later there is the case of Gemistos Plethon and his sons: see Ostrogorsky, *Féodalité*, 181–86. It should be noted that there is some evidence that the word "service" in these contexts had nothing to do with the personal services of the recipient of a grant, but was actually an archaic reference to the labor services, now commuted for a cash payment, that the paroikoi of the property owed the fisc. See Petit and Korablev, *Chilandar*, no. 14.

44. Oikonomidès, *Docheiariou*, no. 26. Regel et al., *Zographou*, no. 29.

45. Ostrogorsky, "Observations," 17.

On the other hand, there were substantial differences. Unlike fiefs, pronoiai were granted only by the emperor, and so they played no role in producing the subinfeudation and the hierarchical social and political structure characteristic of Western feudalism. Pronoia was a fiscal and administrative institution; the fief territorial and personal. The grant of a pronoia was primarily a grant of revenue expressed as a monetary sum (the posotes), not in terms of a quantity of property. The paroikos paid his pronoiar the taxes and fulfilled the corvée obligations that were ordinarily due the state; the serf paid a rent. Unlike serfs, paroikoi were fundamentally free men. They could move from their village, buy and sell property and, at least under the aegis of their village community, sue in the courts. The pronoiar's obligation was to the state; the holder of a fief to his lord. The personal relation between lord and vassal was entirely lacking in the pronoiar's relation to the state or to the emperor. Because of this both the pronoiar and the constituent elements of his pronoia (including the peasants) were fungible.

Several characteristics of the pronoia still cannot be determined precisely, and here lies the last remaining hope for those scholars who wish to see an equivalence between pronoia and fief. For example, the extent of the pronoiar's jurisdiction over his paroikoi has still not been resolved. In particular, did the pronoiar have the right to judge his peasants? Although it is quite likely that this may have been the case with regard to certain large pronoiars who held entire villages, in my view it does not seem to have been an essential component of the pronoia grant. For some pronoiars it would have been simply inconvenient or impossible to attempt to exercise judicial authority over their paroikoi. The soldier Nicholas Maroules held seventeen paroikos households in two villages, and the soldier Michael Sabentzes held eight paroikos households in four villages. Neither of these pronoiars dominated the villages in which their paroikoi resided, and the notion that Sabentzes could have been the master of his paroikoi is absurd.

Perhaps the greatest and most significant difference between pronoia and fief is their position and frequency of appearance in their corresponding societies. Unlike the fief in Western European sources, one really has to scour the sources for much evidence about pronoia. Pronoia was hardly the most common form of remuneration for the army; there were probably more smallholding soldiers and certainly more mercenaries than pronoia soldiers. Nor was pronoia the dominant form of land tenure in late Byzantium, unless one wishes to regard the estates of monasteries and great patrimonial landowners as forms of pronoia, as some scholars do, thereby diluting the definition of pronoia into meaninglessness. On the whole, scholars who equate the pronoia with the Western fief, place pronoiars on a level with feudal lords, and refer to the incomes of pronoiars as "feudal rent" create a misleading image of late Byzantine society.

Pronoia had much more in common with two institutions of Islamic civilization: *iqta* and *timar*. The origins of iqta are obscure but the institution seems to have been created not long after the great period of conquests in the seventh century, and while it evolved over the years and experienced regional variations, it lasted through the thirteenth century. In its classical form an iqta, literally "reduction" (of state revenues), was a grant of a defined quantity of state revenues over a defined set of properties in return for state service, at first generally only civil but by the tenth century for military service as well. The holder of the iqta (called a *muqta*) neither lived on nor held property rights on the land that furnished the income. From a very early date the iqta included a hereditary component. While in the thirteenth-century Seljuk sultanate of Rum there is evidence that some soldiers held grants of iqta in the form of revenues from land, it is unclear how prevalent these grants were. By this time the institution seems to have been in decline. As in the case of pronoia, some scholars argue that the grant of iqta, in its final stages, included the cession of rights of governmental administration over the properties held.[46]

The word *timar* is of Persian origin and it passed into the Turkish language with the meaning "care, solicitude, administration." It is in fact synonymous with the word *pronoia*. The institution probably predates the Ottoman state itself although its origins, like those of the iqta, the pronoia and, for that matter, the fief, are rather obscure. In any event, by the second half of the fourteenth century a timar was a grant of state revenues made by the sultan, expressed as a monetary sum and derived from a defined territory and from a defined group of peasants. In return for the grant the timariot performed state service and furnished the fisc with the head tax collected from the peasants within his timar. These maintained possession of their properties and paid the timariot their state taxes and charges, sometimes in cash, sometimes in kind, and also furnished corvées. In addition to the taxes of peasants, the timariot usually also held land owned by the state, a "timarial reserve," which he worked through his peasants' corvée obligations or leased to other peasants. Periodic fiscal surveys reassigned and reconstituted timars.

46. C. Cahen, "L'évolution de l'iqtâᶜ du IXe au XIIIe siècle," *Annales* 8 (1953), 25–52; idem, *La féodalité et les institutions politiques de l'Orient latin* (Rome, 1956); and A. Bombaci, "The Army of the Saljuqs of Rūm," *Istituto orientale di Napoli, Annali*, n.s. 38 (1978), 350–52.

Timars were held by a wide range of people, from infantry to cavalry, from simple civil officials to provincial governors, though by far most were held by mounted soldiers, who by the fifteenth century were called *sipahis*, some of whom were Christian. Depending on his income, the sipahi was required to furnish one or more other soldiers financed from his own resources. He also collected the head tax of the population registered within his timar. In principle the timar was not hereditary; at the death of the timariot it devolved to the state. The principle of nonhereditability seems to have been maintained until the second half of the fifteenth century, although in exceptional cases, even in the second half of the fourteenth century, hereditary rights were granted.

The similarity between timar and pronoia is striking. The fiscal nature of the grant, its military and nonmilitary use, even its documentation, have strong parallels to pronoia. Since the Ottomans, a less sophisticated civilization, established their land tenure system within erstwhile Byzantine territory and even allowed many Byzantine landowners to keep their property, it is hardly surprising that they should have adopted and adapted Byzantine fiscal practices and land tenure concepts. Numerous scholars have suggested that the timar, on the whole or at least in its developed form, was an institution appropriated from Byzantium. The main difference between the two institutions seems to be that the timariot had closer ties to the central government than the pronoiar, that he was more of a tax collector than his Byzantine counterpart and that the timar played a more fundamental role in Ottoman society. All of these differences are related to the fact that the timar was part of a young, dynamic, growing society with a highly centralized government and administration, while the pronoia was part of a declining, decentralized society. A more thorough comparison of pronoia, timar and iqta awaits further research and a greater consensus among scholars regarding their fundamental characteristics.[47]

In summary, the remuneration of soldiers in late Byzantium took three forms: money, land (including tax exemption on land), and pronoia. Mercenaries received direct cash payments. Smallholding soldiers generally lived in communities located in strategic locations, and with few or no paroikoi, most farmed their own lands which were generally smaller than

47. Among the numerous works on the timar, see N. Beldiceanu, *Le timar dans l'État ottoman* (Wiesbaden, 1980), and "Le timar dans l'État ottoman (XIVe–XVe siècles)," in *Structures féodales et féodalisme dans l'occident méditerranéen* (Rome, 1980), 743–53; V. Mutaf-čieva, "Sur le caractère du *tīmār* ottoman," *Acta orientalia Academiae scientarium Hungaricae* 9 (1959), 55–61; and, for a different point of view, F. Babinger, *Mehmed the Conqueror and His Time* (Princeton, N.J., 1978), 444–47.

the holdings from which pronoiars derived their incomes. Pronoiars, on the contrary, with their larger holdings generally did not farm, but on an individual basis acted as landlords and tax collectors, frequently in out-of-the-way places. Moreover, it may be noted that the remuneration of all soldiers was supplemented with booty.

Within these categories there were further distinctions due to other variables such as frequency of service, function, and the authorities who hired the soldiers. Mercenaries served as both campaign and garrison troops, and their service was continuous. All of the known mercenaries were hired by the central government but it is possible that some were employed by local authorities (kephalai). Given the unreliability of disbursements of mercenary pay from Constantinople to the provinces and the need of every kephale to have at least some reliable and professional troops at his personal command (at least a bodyguard), such soldiers probably existed. Smallholding soldiers generally were employed by the central government to serve on an irregular basis as campaign troops. All pronoia soldiers were employed by the central government. Most were campaign troops who served when needed. Some collective pronoiars were garrison troops.

None of this suggests that there was a late Byzantine military system. There was no system, or rather, there were many systems, most inherited from the past and adapted to the moment, a few improvised more or less ex nihil. The Empire always needed more soldiers than were available and more service from those soldiers it did have, and this allowed veterans to renegotiate their contracts and new soldiers to bargain for satisfactory terms. Consequently, since the greatest variable was pay and type of pay, there was a blurring of categories to such an extent that few soldiers or groups of soldiers fit absolutely into one discrete category. Consider Michael VIII's Tzakones who received "yearly pay" as well as modest land allotments and thus were both mercenaries and smallholding soldiers. Moreover, the transformation of an imperial mercenary into a pronoiar was a phenomenon that may have occurred at times through very small increments. A mercenary/pronoiar was a liminal figure, yet his situation may have been much more common than we have been able to determine. It seems that this mixing of forms of remuneration was a characteristic of the Palaiologan military.[48]

Even more problematic is the apparent similarity between collective

48. This phenomenon was noted by Mutafčiev, "Vojniški zemi," 527.

pronoia soldiers and smallholding soldiers. The intrinsic similarity between pronoia and land as forms of remuneration often makes it difficult to distinguish grants of land to smallholding soldiers from grants of revenues from land to pronoia soldiers. In one instance Gregoras reports that during 1341 Kantakouzenos refurbished the military by distributing "properties" (*ktemata*) to the whole soldiery. While this may sound like a land distribution, Gregoras in fact was speaking of Kantakouzenos' reassessment (*exisosis*) of pronoiai, which according to Kantakouzenos involved "incomes" (*prosodoi*) rather than "properties." In another instance a praktikon from 1338 for the possessions around Verria of the Athonite monastery of Vatopedi mentions "the rights of the soldiers, that is, of the village of Kritzista" and later refers to Kritzista as "the village of the soldiers." Were the soldiers of Kritzista smallholders, collective pronoiars, or three or four holders of moderate grants of individually granted pronoiai?[49]

Although the individualized, personal nature of many pronoia grants distinguishes them adequately from grants of small holdings, the recipients of collective pronoiai in many ways could be practically identical to the recipients of small holdings. We may imagine two groups of soldiers. One, a group of smallholding soldiers, held parcels of land for cultivation, along with tax exemption. Rather than actually farming the lands themselves, they leased it to paroikoi who, twice a year, paid them a rent. Another group of soldiers, collective pronoiars, held a block of tax revenues from a particular village which they collected and divided among themselves twice a year. Aside from the different documentation used for each type of grant, both groups of soldiers, from an economic, fiscal, and social point of view, easily could have been indistinguishable.

Since there are some circumstances that fit our limited knowledge of the characteristics of both types of soldier, the question is whether this blurring of the distinction between smallholding soldiers and collective pronoia soldiers is simply due to our lack of adequate knowledge of each institution, or whether there was a real tendency for the evolving institution of pronoia to embrace forms of remuneration that in previous periods had been distinct. The latter possibility might explain why the historians so rarely distinguish pronoia from other kinds of noncash grants. Indeed, from what we know of military policies during the fourteenth century, it is quite possible, as Nicolas Oikonomidès has suggested, that the institution

49. Gregoras, II, 595; cf. Kantakouzenos, II, 58–63. G. Theocharides, *Μία διαθήκη καὶ μία δίκη Βυζαντινή* (Thessaloniki, 1962), no. 3.

of collective pronoia was supplanting that of the smallholding soldier.[50] Moreover, the parallel between the joint pronoia of collective pronoiars and the communal settlement of smallholding soldiers may have led to the eventual classification of both types of grants as "pronoia" regardless of their origin.

In late Byzantium the military pronoiar characterized the military institution of his age. This is not to say that he was the most numerous kind of soldier or that he was the most important soldier militarily but, rather, he best represents the era. Modern historians have long recognized that to understand the military pronoiar is to understand late Byzantine social and economic relations. For contemporary Byzantines as well, the military pronoiar represented, if not the typical soldier, then the "ideal" soldier. In Kantakouzenos' memoirs, for example, the stereotypical pronoia soldier was a well-equipped and well-trained native horseman, the most aristocratic of soldiers, who derived his livelihood not from vulgar pay, but from incomes from land.

In the middle Byzantine era, the soldier who best represented his age was the thematic soldier, ethnically Byzantine, living in the provinces, a reserve soldier whose remuneration was connected to land. The pronoia soldier, too, was generally a native reserve soldier who campaigned and whose remuneration was tied to land, though in a different way. There were also fundamental differences. The "employer" of the military pronoiar, in the sense of the authority that hired him and assigned his pay, was the central government, not the local thematic administration of the middle period. Thus, the military pronoiar was not a "provincial" soldier at all but a soldier commanded directly by the central government. His presence in the provinces was necessary only because that was where he found his pay. Further, the pronoia soldier's form of remuneration was created through a personal act of the emperor, not so in regard to the old thematic soldiers. Last, the emperor conferred upon the pronoiar rights that belonged to the state, interposing the pronoiar between the peasantry and the state. This meant that the pronoiar's remuneration was fundamentally bound to the state's fiscal apparatus, the reason in fact that we know as much as we do about pronoia. The thematic soldier's remuneration was essentially detached from the fisc. Either he received in-kind profit from the lands he or his family directly cultivated or a peasant or group of peasants provided his remuneration through an informal arrangement. Modern scholars disagree

50. Oikonomidès, "A propos des armées," 357.

as to which of these was the case for the very reason that the thematic soldier's remuneration was not as intimately connected to the fiscal system as was the pronoia soldier's.

Indeed this lack of knowledge regarding how the old thematic soldier derived his remuneration parallels the difficulties in defining the situation of the late Byzantine smallholding soldier. Since neither soldier's remuneration was the product of a personal imperial benefaction, and neither soldier's remuneration was so closely tied to the fiscal system as was the pronoiar's, the actual mechanism of remuneration for both remains nebulous. If the thematic soldier had a strong, palpable connection to the land providing his remuneration, then he was evidently very similar to the late Byzantine smallholding soldier. But even if there was a distinction between the thematic soldier and the men who actually farmed the land that provided his remuneration, he might still be similar to the smallholding soldier, depending on whether or not the late Byzantine smallholding soldier often arranged for family members or others to cultivate his lands. Aside from the fact that a land grant formed the basis of a military obligation, we know as little about how this worked for smallholding soldiers of the late period as for thematic soldiers of the middle period.

However, the imperial smallholding soldier differed from the old thematic soldier in two important and related ways. First, he was settled by the central government and, second, when he is encountered in late Byzantium, he is always settled with other similar soldiers in a group. In fact, there is no evidence from the Palaiologan period of the existence of any smallholding soldiers settled or living on an individual basis. This is because it was easier for the central government to administer soldiers living in groups. And the reason why the central government was administering these soldiers at all relates back to the nature of the reconquest of Europe. The area involved was small enough to keep the military administration centralized, and the manner of the reconquest only slowly lost the character of a military occupation. In essence the restored "themes" encountered in the second half of the thirteenth and early fourteenth centuries were not "provincial" administrative organs at all, but in reality were much more extensions of the central government.

The real "provincial" soldiers of the Palaiologan period (and here we exclude the Nicaean era as transitional) were the mercenaries hired, administered, and commanded by local kephalai. The middle Byzantine theme and its strategos were replaced by the katepanikion and its kephale, a man who held similar powers but over a much smaller area. The local troops under the kephale represented the first line of defence for the katepanikion, and their importance outside the katepanikion was negligible. Consequently, when dealing with the late Byzantine period, the old distinction between provincial and central troops, between the Themata and the Tagmata, between soldiers in the provinces and those in the capital, is no longer very useful and certainly misleading. Much more valid is a distinction based on the military function of the soldier, whether he was concerned primarily with defensive activities or offensive expeditions.

9. Professional Soldiers, Military Units, Recruitment

Within the late Byzantine army there were many kinds of soldiers. The previous chapters distinguished them by form of remuneration (cash, booty, land, tax exemption, revenues), but they can also be differentiated through other variables: ethnicity (native or foreign), domicile (resident or nonresident of the Empire), employment status (temporary or permanent), frequency of service (constant, regular, irregular), type of military obligation (temporary, lifetime, hereditary), primary type of service (guard/garrison or campaign), employer (imperial government or local governors), mode of combat (horse or foot), and military division. Further, there were men who, though not soldiers themselves, were closely associated with military or paramilitary activities: the nonprofessional supplemental infantry recruited for specific enterprises, the retainers and the servants who accompanied the campaign army, and urban and rural guards.

Not enough is known about the late Byzantine army to construct a neat schematic diagram of its organization. This chapter can only survey the varieties of professional soldiers and discuss their organization and recruitment, with a focus on campaign troops. Starting with military obligation as the first variable, we can offer a rough approximation of the range of soldier types found within the campaign army in outline form:

Campaign soldiers with a continuing military obligation

pronoiars (native and foreign)
smallholding soldiers (native and foreign)
imperial mercenaries (usually foreign)

Campaign soldiers without a continuing military obligation

supplemental mercenaries (foreign)
allied troops, or auxiliaries (foreign)

retainers (usually native)
supplemental infantry (native)

Nonsoldiers on campaign

servants (native and foreign)

The campaign soldiers with a standing, or permanent, military obligation were always residents of the Empire, as was the supplemental infantry, which was composed of nonprofessional soldiers, and some of the servants accompanying the soldiery. Other servants, the supplemental mercenaries, and allied troops were nonresidents contracted for a specific campaign, who naturally had no permanent military obligation. In this chapter we consider the first five types of soldiers in the list, and examine them by ethnicity. The next chapter will deal with the supplemental infantry, servants, and retainers, and after that we turn to the palace guard, garrisons, and urban and rural guards.

Ethnically "Byzantine" soldiers, or "Romans" (*Rhomaioi*) as they called themselves, were those soldiers accepted by other Byzantines as "of the same race" (*homophyloi*). In other words they spoke Greek, embraced Orthodox Christianity, followed Byzantine customs and dress, and therefore were culturally indistinguishable from other Byzantines. Some ethnically Byzantine soldiers were pronoiars employed on an individual basis (such as the Palaiologan highlanders, and those listed in the Appendix, nos. 17, 18, 31–32, 40, 44, 45, 48, 50, 55); others were employed on a group (collective) basis (such as the Klazomenitai soldiers of Serres). While individual pronoia soldiers seem to have been campaign soldiers, collective pronoiars were at least in one instance assigned to garrison service. Native Byzantines could also be smallholding soldiers, such as the Thelematarioi and the Prosalentai. The only natives known to have served as mercenaries were palace guard troops, the Gasmouloi, the Cretans transplanted to Asia Minor by Andronikos II, and the marine Tzakones. Inasmuch as the three latter groups were either half-breeds, Greek refugees from areas no longer held by Byzantium, or members of a distinct ethnic group within the Empire, they might better be called "semi-Byzantine."

Native soldiers were organized into a number of military groups or divisions. Groups such as the Thelematarioi, the Prosalentai, the Gasmouloi, and the Tzakones have figured most prominently up to this point.

Aside from these, from the later thirteenth through the first quarter of the fourteenth century, about one-third of the soldiers whom we know by name were associated with military divisions called imperial *allagia* (Appendix, nos. 29, 30) or *megala* ("grand") *allagia* (Appendix, nos. 36, 47, 49, 52–54, 56–58, 61). These may have been the largest divisions of ethnically Byzantine soldiers, and they included at least two kinds of soldiers: pronoia soldiers and frontier guards. These soldiers were "provincial" troops in the sense that they lived in the provinces, but their orders and their remuneration were issued by authorities in Constantinople. If they were mercenaries, their gold came from the emperor; if pronoiars, the revenues they received were granted by imperial command; and if smallholding soldiers, they farmed land distributed by the emperor.

Allagion is a general word meaning a division of troops, a "squadron" or "tactical unity," synonymous with the word *tagma* of literary sources. When modified it acquired special meanings. For example, an emperor's allagion was, reasonably enough, his military escort. Pachymeres mentions "soldiers of imperial allagia who suddenly fled from the east because of the onslaught of the Persians," and the implication is that these soldiers were stationed and settled in the provinces of Anatolia.[1] Once Asia Minor was lost these "imperial allagia" disappeared, never found in references to the European army. Instead, during the reign of Andronikos II the megala allagia first appeared, but only in Europe. Three are known by name: the Thessalonian ("Thessalonikaion") Mega Allagion, the Serriotikon Mega Allagion, and the Vizyeteikon Mega Allagion, named after the towns (Thessaloniki, Serres, Vizye) or homonymous themes in which they operated.

Some soldiers of megala allagia (or *megaloallagitai*, as they are called in the Pseudo-Kodinos treatise) were frontier guards, including archers, who manned frontier fortifications. Other megaloallagitai were cavalry soldiers who, as middle-level pronoiars, served on campaigns. The administrative machinery of the Palaiologan theme was especially important to the megaloallagites who was a pronoiar. Thematic officials wrote the praktikon for his pronoia and made periodic fiscal surveys to ensure his income did not far exceed or fall below the praktikon's bounds. It would seem that it was only the provincial administration, not the central administration in Constantinople, that knew the current status of each pronoiar and precisely

---

1. E. Stein, "Untersuchungen zur spätbyzantinischen Verfassungs- und Wirtschaftsgeschichte," *Mitteilungen zur osmanischen Geschichte* 2 (1923–26), 44. Akropolites, 122–23. Pachymeres, Bonn ed., II, 407.

where his landholdings were. A similar situation would also have existed if smallholding soldiers belonged to the megala allagia.

During the later thirteenth century a military official called the *tzaousios* made his appearance in connection with the provincial organization of the army and the megala allagia. The word itself is Turkish (from *çauş*) and seems to have been used by the Byzantines as a title perhaps as early as the late eleventh century. The tzaousios, who had only military duties, was the kephale's assistant in charge of the soldiers of a fortified town (*kastron*) and, according to the text of a formula of appointment, he was "obligated to tend to these and to urge them to be eager and tireless in the watch of the kastron there and the rest of the services of my majesty."[2] We know of only two tzaousioi from all of Thrace and Macedonia: Manuel Deblitzenos, "*pansevastos sevastos* [literally, 'all-august august'] tzaousios of the Thessalonian Mega Allagion," linked with the theme of Thessaloniki in a document from 1301, and Theodore Lykopoulos, "*sevastos* tzaousios of the ruler's mega allagion," who witnessed a private act in Thessaloniki in 1328.[3] In both cases the tzaousios was associated with a mega allagion and bore the title sevastos, placing him among the lower aristocracy. Evidently he commanded megaloallagitai, though his precise duties are unknown. All the other tzaousioi to whom we can firmly assign a function lived in Lakonia (around Mistra) where they played a very important role in the Byzantine Morea, apparently as military commanders if not also civil governors. Since the sources speak so rarely of tzaousioi in Thrace and Macedonia, however, it is very likely that in these areas they served strictly as military leaders without significant political or administrative responsibilities.[4]

Thessaloniki, Serres, and Vizye were the administrative centers of the three known megala allagia. The geographical compass of the megala allagia themselves embraced the entire theme that bore the name of its capital city, and it was through the theme that the mega allagion was administered. The Thessalonian Mega Allagion included soldiers found within the theme of Thessaloniki, an area bordered on the west by the Vardar River and on the east by the Strymon River and including the

2. K. Sathas, *Μεσαιωνικὴ Βιβλιοθήκη* (Venice, 1894; repr. Athens, 1972), VI, 647. The sources distinguish *tzaousioi* from *megaloi tzaousioi*. The latter title, as an honor found in the lists of precedence, did not necessarily imply a function. On this, see M. Bartusis, "The Megala Allagia and the Tzaousios," *REB* 47 (1989), 198–200.

3. F. Dölger, *Sechs byzantinische Praktika des 14. Jahrhunderts für das Athoskloster Iberon* (Munich, 1949), A 452–53. L. Petit and B. Korablev, *Actes de Chilandar, I. Actes grecs*, *VizVrem* 17 (1911), suppl. 1, no. 117, lines 157–58.

4. Bartusis, "Megala Allagia," 200–202.

Chalkidike peninsula. The Serríotikon Mega Allagion paralleled the theme of Serres and the Strymon, that is, the region adjacent to the theme of Thessaloniki from the Strymon to the Nestos rivers. Geographically, the Vizyeteikon Mega Allagion included Vizye in Thrace and the Black Sea littoral north to Mesembria and then west inland in the direction of Sliven, and probably eastern Thrace up to the suburbs of Constantinople and as far west as Arkadiopolis. This would be the area of the as yet unknown Palaiologan "theme of Thrace," or perhaps, "theme of Vizye and Thrace." There is no reason to suspect that these were the only megala allagia. Additional megala allagia may have been found in the area of the Rhodope mountains between the Nestos and Marica rivers, or in western Macedonia, in Albania, and in the Vardar and Strymon valleys between Melnik and Prosek. Nevertheless, little is known of the administration of these areas, and the fragility of Byzantine control over them may have led to other military arrangements.

The megala allagia are attested in the sources for a period of seventy years, from 1286 to 1355.[5] Because the 1286 terminus is determined by a reference to a deceased megaloallagites, there can be little doubt that megala allagia existed during Michael VIII's reign. Since there is no evidence that there were ever megala allagia in Anatolia, the origin of the institution can be dated to sometime after the beginning of the Nicaean state's reconquest of Europe. This means the first of the megala allagia—and they each could well have had different histories—was created by John Vatatzes, Theodore II Laskaris, or Michael VIII. On the basis of Michael VIII's military policies, it is likely that he created the first mega allagion, but it is just as easy to imagine either of the earlier emperors fashioning the megala allagia, and Michael expanding and institutionalizing them.

After 1355 there are no further known references to the megala allagia. Either the institution declined or later documents that mentioned them have not been preserved or yet come to light. While it is unlikely the Serriotikon Mega Allagion could have existed after Stefan Dušan's conquest of Serres in 1345, it is indeed possible that some remnant of the Thessalonian Mega Allagion survived even until 1387 when Thessaloniki fell to the Turks. The Vizyeteikon could have lasted until the early 1360s, until the final loss of Thrace.

The megala allagia indicate that with the reconquest of Europe there was an effort to reconstitute a provincial administrative apparatus com-

5. Ibid., 206.

posed of "thematic" regions for military as well as the usual fiscal purposes. This is significant because it shows that this aspect of the Palaiologan military system was a centralizing element in society, linking soldiers in the provinces with a provincial administrative center and, in turn, to the capital at a time when civil administration was becoming increasingly localized as more and more responsibilities fell upon the shoulders of the kephalai of individual towns.

The military significance of the megala allagia is more difficult to judge. This is because we do not know what percentage of the army in the provinces was included within them. Nor do we know what kind of troops, or even *whether* any particular kind of troops, was necessarily found within the megala allagia. At one extreme the megala allagia were the central element in the late Byzantine army; every soldier who lived in the provinces and who had a military obligation toward the state or the emperor was a megaloallagites. This would include all types of pronoiars, mercenaries, and smallholding soldiers, individuals and groups, both foreign and native. The administrative apparatus of the megala allagia might have been used even in the recruitment of foot troops for campaigns. The only soldiers who must be excluded from the megala allagia were the imperial bodyguard and retinue, and any soldiers kephalai themselves might have employed for local military service. At the other extreme the megala allagia were just another set of troop divisions in a mosaic of military organization; they existed in only certain European provinces, and they were composed only of individual soldiers (pronoiars, mercenaries, smallholding soldiers) who were not part of any other "group" of soldiers. Foreigners, perhaps even Latin kavallarioi, might have been excluded. At present it is not possible to say which of these scenarios is more accurate.

A substantial portion of the army was composed of foreigners, men who were not "Romans" and whose mother tongue was not Greek. Most were either Latins of various sorts (primarily Italians, Germans, Catalans, Frenchmen, and Spaniards), Turkic peoples (Turks, Alans, and Cumans), or Slavs (Serbs, Bulgarians, and other southern Slavs), but a variety of other ethnic groups, such as Vlachs, Albanians, Mongols, and Georgians, also appear within the army.[6] Mere residence in the Empire never made one a

6. For Georgians, see below. For Zychoi: *Chronicle of the Morea*, ed. J. Schmitt (London, 1904), vv. 1213–15. For Armenians(?): A. Heisenberg, *Neue Quellen zur Geschichte des lateinischen Kaisertums und der Kirchenunion*, in Heisenberg, *Quellen und Studien zur spätbyzantinischen Geschichte* (London, 1973), no. II (iii), 9. For Albanians: Kantakouzenos, I, 453; II, 322; Zakythinos, *Despotat*, II, 134–35; and L. Branouses, «'Αλβανοὶ πολεμισταὶ στὴν ὑπηρε-

"Roman." Only acculturation, with the adoption of the Orthodox faith, the Greek language, and Byzantine dress and manners, could do this. Many foreigners, especially Latins, made the transition after a generation or two.

In the last centuries attitudes toward foreigners were mixed. One might think that the Fourth Crusade and the steady encroachment of the Seljuks and later the Ottomans would have created a distrust and fear of foreigners, particularly of foreign soldiers, at all levels of society. Among the general population (*hoi polloi*) this attitude seems to have been widespread, but among the elite there were different points of view. While there was little affection from any quarter for the Italian merchants who frequented Constantinople, the elite of late Byzantium had a natural affinity with the military elite of foreign societies, whether Turk, Latin, or Slav. The late Byzantine elite was fundamentally a military aristocracy, and its members respected military ability whatever its origin.

The only late Byzantine emperor who displayed a marked hostility toward a foreign presence in the army was Theodore II Laskaris, and he had good reason. The preference shown by the Latin mercenaries at court for the upstart Michael Palaiologos was personally dangerous for Theodore. It is not at all surprising that he dreamed of recruiting an all-Greek army. In contrast are Michael VIII and John VI Kantakouzenos, the latter a Turcophile equally at home with emirs, his Latin soldiers, or the Serbian emperor Stefan Dušan.[7] Even Andronikos II Palaiologos, the historian Gregoras writes, "suspected all the Romans" and "dreamt day and night of foreign alliances."[8] Divisions within the aristocracy, resulting especially from the civil wars and from the perennial controversies over the union of the Greek and Latin Churches made emperors more reliant on individual foreigners and foreign armies. Emperors surrounded themselves with foreigners, and foreign soldiers were an element basic to every late Byzantine army.[9]

σία τῶν Δεσποτῶν τῆς Πελοποννήσου», paper read at the Α' Διεθνὲς Συνοδρίας Πελοπον-νησιακῶν Σπουδῶν, Sparta, 7–14 Sept. 1975 (abstract). For Spaniards: Pero Tafur, *Travels and Adventures, 1435–1439,* trans. M. Letts (New York and London, 1926), 123. The *Chronicle of the Morea* (vv. 3576–77, 3594–97, 3696ff., 3707) also mentions the presence at Pelagonia of 1,500 allied cavalry troops sent by the king of Hungary (but see D. Geanakoplos, "Greco-Latin Relations on the Eve of the Byzantine Restoration," *DOP* 7 [1953], 124 note 116, 125). For an overview of the ethnic groups in late Byzantium, see C. Asdracha, *La région des Rhodopes aux XIIIe et XIVe siècles* (Athens, 1976), 50–90.

7. *Theodori Ducae Lascari Epistulae CCXVII,* ed. N. Festa (Florence, 1898), 58. Geana-koplos, *Emperor Michael,* 35–36. Mutafčiev, "Vojniški zemi," 607. On Kantakouzenos' affection for Turks and distrust of Rhomaioi, see Gregoras, III, 151, 177.

8. Laiou, *Constantinople,* 84, citing Gregoras, I, 205.

9. E.g., Kantakouzenos, II, 415; Gregoras, I, 441–42; *The Letters of Manuel II Palaeologus,* ed. G. Dennis (Washington, D.C., 1977), 116–17, no. 44.

Both resident and nonresident foreigners campaigned for Byzantium. The former were permanent residents of the Empire and whose service was more or less ongoing. Among the Latins in this category were the kavallarioi, most of whom seem to have been pronoiars (Appendix, nos. 15, 39, 51, 69), and mercenaries who served the emperor on an individual basis. The presence of Latins in the East was a result of the Crusades and erstwhile Crusaders found themselves in the employ of the Seljuk sultanate of Rum as well.[10] Other resident foreigners, such as the Cumans settled by John Vatatzes, were smallholding soldiers. The Tourkopouloi employed by Michael VIII were either mercenaries or smallholding soldiers, though it is possible that some held pronoia as well (Appendix, nos. 37–38).

Nonresident foreign soldiers were those who served the Empire only temporarily for the sake of a specific enterprise and who, before and after the enterprise, had no obligation to serve the Empire. They may be divided into two main types: supplemental mercenaries and supplemental allied troops, or auxiliaries. The distinguishing characteristic between the two types was that a foreign prince invested some resources and effort in the expeditions of allied troops, while supplemental mercenaries campaigned without the assistance of any foreign ruler.

These categories become clearer if a few examples are cited. No foreign prince, through his financial backing or personal presence, was responsible for the Catalan campaigns. Therefore, the Catalans were supplemental mercenaries, as were the Alans who came to Byzantium in 1301, and the "few Acharnanian mercenaries" whom Manuel Kantakouzenos hired upon arriving in the Morea in 1349.[11] On the other hand, the Turks of Umur Pasha fought for Kantakouzenos only because Umur was interested in the plan and was willing to finance the transportation of his troops, frequently supplying his personal leadership. Similarly, the force which came to Constantinople with Marshall Boucicaut in 1399 were financed by Charles VI of France, and the few troops sent to Constantinople by the king of Georgia in the early fourteenth century were ready to serve "without pay and for only horses and expenses," indicating their king had made some investment in the enterprise.[12] Thus all of these soldiers were allied troops.

The advantage of allied troops over supplemental mercenaries was that

10. A. Bombaci, "The Army of the Saljuqs of Rūm," *Istituto orientale di Napoli, Annali*, n.s. 38 (1978), 357–61, 367.

11. Kantakouzenos, III, 88.

12. J. Barker, *Manuel II Palaeologus (1391–1425): A Study in Late Byzantine Statesmanship* (New Brunswick, N.J., 1969), 162–63, 200, 238 note 69. Pachymeres, ed. Bonn, II, 620; Laiou, *Constantinople*, 175 and note 65.

the foreign prince, by buying into the enterprise (for whatever motives), lessened the financial burden on the Byzantine side. Although the best allied troops, politically speaking, were those provided by a distant sovereign, these were also the most expensive for the allied prince to finance and consequently the most difficult to obtain. Manuel II Palaiologos' premature excitement when he thought Henry IV of England would be providing him with military assistance, "soldiers, archers, and money and ships to transport the army where it is needed," had echoes throughout the late period.[13] Yet, while allied troops required little direct expenditure from the imperial government, they often involved themselves in plunder and their ultimate disposition was up to their own leaders.

From the beginning of the fourteenth century both native and foreign troops were organized with increasing frequency into companies (*syntrophiai*) of soldiers. A soldier company was a kind of partnership in which the members proportionally shared profits and responsibilities. These companies generally were composed of small groups of foreigners or refugees from other parts of the Empire, and the soldiers within them were frequently commanded and paid not by imperial officials but by their own leaders. For their services they received cash, pronoia, land, or combinations of these, always as a group. Most companies probably began as mercenary bands, but with time it seems that some were gradually transformed into companies of pronoiars through modest grants of "collective pronoia," the form of pronoia shared by more than one person. Collective pronoia was an especially appropriate means of financing soldier companies because, like all pronoiai, it created a tie between the soldier and the land, and gave him a stake in the future of the Empire, and unlike individual grants of pronoia, it made the military and fiscal administration of such soldiers easier by treating them as a corporation under a single commander. Although these soldier companies did not change the fortunes of the Empire, the institution became in aggregate a significant component of the military.[14]

The Catalan Grand Company hired as a group through their leader, Roger de Flor, is certainly the most famous soldier company in Byzantine history. The Catalans evolved only gradually into a soldier company from

13. *Letters of Manuel II Palaeologus*, ed. Dennis, no. 38, lines 41–42 (trans. by ed.). Also, see John V's request to Innocent VI: A. Theiner and F. Miklosich, *Monumenta spectantia ad unionem ecclesiarum Graecae et Romanae* (Vienna, 1872), 29–33, no. VIII.

14. Oikonomidès, "A propos des armées," esp. 369–71.

the time of their recruitment in 1281 by Peter III of Aragon (1276–85) for his North African and later Sicilian campaigns. Roger de Flor was appointed admiral by Frederick II of Sicily (1296–1337) for a war against the Angevins and soon became the Catalans' leader. By the time of the peace of Caltabelotta in 1302, the Catalan Company, which had been engaged in warfare constantly during the preceding twenty years, had developed its own internal organization.

While in Andronikos II's employ, it was Roger de Flor who negotiated the rate of pay for the individual soldiers of the Company, who received this pay from the emperor, and who distributed it to the soldiers. In the *Chronicle of the Morea* the Catalans are called the *Megale Syntrophia* or *Megale Koumpania* ("Grand Company"). The adjective *grand* is appropriate because the word *syntrophia* is most commonly employed in this chronicle to mean a small detachment of troops. Indeed the Catalan Company was the largest soldier company ever found in Byzantium, and presumably because their employment proved to be so disastrous for the Empire, the Byzantines learned to keep soldier companies small. In fact, the typical company probably involved only a leader and a few dozen men, "a knight errant with his company," a phrase that indeed appears in one mid-fourteenth-century document and is reminiscent of the condottieri of Renaissance Italy.[15]

The Catalan Company was an anomaly, even by contemporary Western European standards. While mercenary soldier companies existed in late thirteenth-century Italy, they were normally not hired as companies but were organized into small companies, generally of fifty men, by the employing governments themselves. Prior to this, throughout most of the thirteenth century, mercenaries in Italy were recruited and served as individuals. During the fourteenth century, just as in Byzantium, though some mercenaries were still hired individually, the phenomenon of soldier companies became more and more common.[16]

The organization of mercenaries into companies in the West grew out of the preference for mercenaries and it paralleled the decline of the communal militias. Both of these developments had similar origins. The growing wealth of the towns led to greater rivalries and to more efficient means of raising armies. Political aggressiveness, mainly in the form of territorial expansion, increased the duration and burden of wars. Factionalism within the towns reduced the morale of the militias, increased the need for body-

15. Pachymeres, Bonn ed., II, 424. *Chronicle of the Morea*, v. 7273, etc., and cf. v. 5208. Oikonomidès, "A propos des armées," 370. MM, V, 261, apparatus.
16. M. Mallett, *Mercenaries and Their Masters* (London, 1974), 13–14, 43–44.

guards, and produced political exiles seeking employment. The general use of the crossbow in the thirteenth century as an infantry weapon led to the development of heavier and more expensive armor, a growing specialization in the ranks with the employment of troops such as shieldbearers, and the development of the cavalry lance formation (one or two knights with attendants). The need for large numbers of specialized, professional troops was met by the increased availability of soldiers due to the decline of the crusades and the presence of foreign troops in Italy, especially in the south as a result of the wars over the kingdom of Sicily.[17]

As mercenaries became semi-permanent they organized themselves into companies. Now, rather than appearing individually, companies of mercenaries arrived as pre-organized societies, a development not resisted by the employing governments who found the greater efficiency and availability of such troops to their liking. Like the Catalan Company these early fourteenth-century pre-organized companies were characterized by a relatively democratic organization, including a sharing of spoils. The captains and leading men of each company received and distributed the monthly pay for the lower ranks. However, in contrast to the Catalan Company, around the year 1300 in the West it was still uncommon to hire mercenaries in groups of more than twenty-five, and 200 is the largest attested figure. During the early fourteenth century there was a gradual increase in the sizes of pre-organized companies. For example, the Company of St. George, formed in 1339 and one of the first very large companies, consisted of 2,500 cavalry and one thousand infantry. The next thirty or so years was the age of the large company with as many as 10,000 soldiers.[18]

In Byzantium soldier companies always remained small. One, called the Varvarenoi, was a group of collective pronoia soldiers who held a grant of pronoia from around 1327 through the late 1340s on the Chalkidike peninsula in Macedonia. They were closely associated with a certain official, the megas adnoumiastes George Katzaras, who was evidently either their commander or the official liaison between the emperor and the company.[19] Another soldier company is known from a document from 1377 in which the emperor ordered an official to return some land to the monastery of

---

17. Ibid., 16–20. C. Bayley, *War and Society in Renaissance Florence: The* De Militia *of Leonardo Bruni* (Toronto, 1961), 3.

18. Mallett, *Mercenaries*, 14, 21, 29–35, 107. Bayley, *War and Society*, 52. Also, see N. Housley, "The Mercenary Companies, the Papacy and the Crusades, 1356–1378," *Traditio* 38 (1982), 253–80, and D. Waley, "Condotte and Condottieri in the Thirteenth Century," *Proceedings of the British Academy* 61 (1975), 337–71.

19. Oikonomidès, "A propos des armées," 360–63.

Vatopedi. The land had once belonged to Vatopedi but at some point it was transferred to soldiers from a company under the "jurisdiction" of the judge of the army Sgouros. Evidently the monastery had lost the land sometime after 1329, since a document issued in that year still listed it among its possessions.[20]

The parallel between the Varvarenoi and the company of Sgouros is striking. The ease with which the property was transferred to Vatopedi and the terminology of the document indicates that the soldiers had received the land in pronoia, not as smallholdings. Similar terminology was used in regard to the Varvarenoi. The soldiers of the company of Sgouros, like the Varvarenoi, were a company (syntrophia), and while the Varvarenoi were associated with the megas adnoumiastes Katzaras, these soldiers had a special relation to a certain judge of the army named Sgouros. Sgouros was the commander or administrator of these soldiers, as was the case with Katzaras and the Varvarenoi. If Sgouros and Katzaras were liaisons between state and soldier company, they perhaps paralleled the government representatives of northern Italian cities called *provveditori*, who were appointed to accompany soldier companies into the field.[21]

Although the Catalans, the Varvarenoi, and the soldiers under Sgouros were the only military units within Byzantine employ specifically denoted as "companies" (syntrophiai), there were other groups of soldiers with similar characteristics. One of these were the Klazomenitai soldiers, collective pronoiars who formed part of the garrison of Serres in 1342. Through them we can see a connection between the fall of Asia Minor to the Turks and the creation of soldier companies. Their name suggests that they had come from Anatolia, from the town of Klazomenai west of Smyrna, famous for its pirates.[22] It is likely that because of the Turkish danger they had fled their homes either during the second half of Andronikos II's reign or during Andronikos III's reign. The flight of soldiers and others from Anatolia during this period is well-attested by Pachymeres, Gregoras, and other writers, as well as by the documentary sources. Whether the Klazomenitai were soldiers in Anatolia is unknown, but once they arrived in Europe they were settled in Serres as a group, given a pronoia, and organized as a

20. *Regesten*, no. 3084. I wish to thank the Centre d'histoire et civilisation du monde byzantin of the Collège de France for providing me with access to a photograph of the prostagma and its accompanying *paradotikon gramma*.

21. Mallett, *Mercenaries*, 88.

22. E.g., Klazomenai pirates are mentioned in a letter of Maximos Planoudes from 1295: M. Planoudes, *Maximi monachi Planudis epistulae*, ed. M. Treu (Breslau, 1886–90; repr. Amsterdam, 1960), no. 86.

garrison. This was a practical and orderly method of dealing with refugees from the eastern provinces and at the same time it benefited western defenses. It was probably a common practice. Indeed the art of population transfer, a venerable tradition used throughout the centuries to forestall internal unrest and to raise soldiers, was not lost in late Byzantium.[23]

Another example is the Achyraïtai. In 1341, while on campaign with Kantakouzenos, the protokynegos John Vatatzes deserted to Constantinople "leading the *taxis* ['unit, or band'] called 'of Achyraïtai.'" Achyraous (modern Balikesir) was a major fortified town about sixty miles south of Kyzikos in Anatolia. It is last mentioned as a Byzantine possession in 1304 when the Catalans passed through it. The date of the town's fall to the Turks is not known but probably was not long afterward. There is some evidence of people from Achyraous settling in Europe: a minor official of the metropolitan of Kaisaropolis in the Strymon valley in 1320 was named Demetrios Acheraous, and the kastrophylax of nearby Zichna in 1321 was one Constantine Achyraïtes.[24] It seems very likely that the "taxis of Achyraïtai" was a soldier company made up of refugees from Achyraous who had been settled in Europe. If so, we can conclude also that there was a tendency for service in these companies to become hereditary. Since the Achyraïtai of 1341 were some thirty-five years distant from the fall of their hometown, most must have been the sons of those who had fled Anatolia. On the other hand, Smyrna, the principal city near Klazomenai, fell to the Turks in 1318,[25] and so it is possible that the Klazomenitai of 1342 still included some of their number who had fled Asia at least twenty-four years earlier. However, since the Klazomenitai in 1342 were granted the right to transmit at least part of their pronoia to their children on the condition that the children perform "the service owed," the hereditability of their military obligation is clearly implied.

In all of these cases it is difficult to say which of the companies were composed of individual soldiers organized by the authorities and which were pre-organized companies who presented themselves for employment

---

23. See H. Ahrweiler, "L'histoire et la géographie de la région de Smyrne entre les deux occupations turques," in Ahrweiler, *Byzance: les pays et les territoires* (London, 1976), no. IV, 28 note 147, 48–51, 61. A number of paroikoi named Klazomenites are found in documents from Mount Athos: P. Lemerle et al., *Actes de Lavra* (Paris, 1970–82), II, no. 73, line 65; no. 74, line 47; no. 77, line 74 (all 1284); no. 99, line 87 (1304); no. 109, line 118 (1321); and P. Lemerle, *Actes de Kutlumus*, rev. ed. (Paris, 1988), no. 21, line 12 (1348).

24. Kantakouzenos, II, 180. Pachymeres, Bonn ed., II, 423. Petit and Korablev, *Chilandar*, no. 53, lines 78–80; no. 69, line 92; and A. Guillou, *Les archives de Saint-Jean-Prodrome* (Paris, 1955), no. 28, lines 11–12.

25. P. Lemerle, *L'émirat d'Aydin, Byzance et l'Occident* (Paris, 1957), 50.

as a group. We do not know the manner in which the Varvarenoi and the company of Sgouros were created. The Varvarenoi may have been foreigners ("Berbers," as Nicolas Oikonomidès has suggested), while the ethnicity of the company of Sgouros is unknown. The Klazomenitai and the Achyraïtai, to the extent that they were refugees, were probably not pre-organized groups. Rather, if they had been soldiers before their flight from Asia, they were reorganized by imperial authorities in Europe; if they had not been soldiers previously, they were recruited upon their arrival in the west.

The hereditary element is strong not only in many soldier companies but also in many other military units. Service in the Thelematarioi, the Prosalentai, and the palace guard division of the Vardariotai, among others, seems to have had a hereditary aspect. In one of the more curious passages from his treatise Pseudo-Kodinos (p. 251) writes, "If one of the mercenary soldiers should die childless, his war horse and arms are to be returned to the megas domestikos." Hereditary service was one way to keep manpower levels relatively constant as well as creating a stronger bond between the state and the soldier via the soldier's father. We see all three economic groups of soldiers—pronoiars, smallholding soldiers, and mercenaries—assuming the hereditary obligation and benefits of military service. The agnatic continuity of military service was an aspect of late Byzantine military policy that was beneficial to both state and soldier.

When reviewing the various new groups of soldiers that appeared during the late thirteenth and fourteenth centuries, it is not always an easy matter to determine which were actually soldier companies and which were simply distinct divisions of the army. For example, it is possible that the Cretan cavalry which Andronikos II settled in Asia Minor was a group set apart from the rest of the army and commanded by its own leader, in other words, a soldier company. Similarly, a 1351 chrysobull of John VI Kantakouzenos speaks of certain "Digenatoi soldiers" who had been holding land, evidently in pronoia.[26] The peculiar name "Digenatoi" is otherwise unattested in the sources and we may speculate that it was not a family name, but a descriptive term (from *dis*, "twice," and *genatos*, the verbal adjective of *geno*, "to be born") along the lines and meaning of "Gasmoulos," and that the Digenatoi, like the Klazomenitai and the Varvarenoi, were a company of pronoiars.

A number of individuals are known from the literary sources who seem

26. Oikonomidès, "A propos des armées," 365. F. Dölger, *Byzantinische Diplomatik* (Ettal, 1956), 179, lines 31–33.

to have served Byzantium while commanding their own companies of soldiers. For example, there was Andrea Morisco, a Genoese pirate employed by Andronikos II in 1304 to harass the Venetians. Later we find a certain impetuous Sebastopoulos at the battle of Pelekanos in 1329, "one of those arranged [in battle-order] under the emperor, a Bulgarian by race, leading 300 soldiers not very well armed nor using good horses but holding last position in the army. Seizing as many as were his own [*tous idious*] and making companions [*prosetairisamenos*] of some infantry, he abandoned the rest of the army and hastily advanced against the Persians."[27] Still later we read of a pirate named Alexios from the town of Belikome in Bithynia who had been hired by Alexios Apokaukos during the civil wars. After Apokaukos' death in 1345 Alexios seized Anaktoropolis, from which he harassed Kavalla, Thasos, and Lemnos.[28]

After the 1370s there are no more references to soldier companies in Byzantium. This was the period in Italy when the growth of a more organized political structure and an emphasis on permanent defense brought the era of the roving independent companies to an end. As companies were gradually attached more and more closely to the state, we see the emergence of the individual captain, the condottiere hired as a recruiting general to provide a fixed number of troops at fixed rates.[29] There are no known parallels to this in Byzantium, partly because our knowledge of military developments declines dramatically during this period and partly, perhaps primarily, because the poverty of the Empire and the rapid Ottoman advance made it increasingly difficult to organize defenses. Since the references to identifiable soldier companies span a period from 1302 to the 1370s, we might attribute their appearance in Byzantium to Andronikos II and the Catalan Company. The memory of the Catalan debacle and the poverty of the Empire kept them small. Soldier companies in Byzantium never comprised more than a fraction of the military forces, unlike in Italian cities where for a time they were the dominant or at least the characteristic form of military organization.

Methods of recruiting soldiers varied according to whether the potential soldiers were Byzantine or foreign. At the highest levels of society, some

27. Oikonomidès, "A propos des armées," 364. Kantakouzenos, I, 354.

28. Kantakouzenos, III, 114–15. *PLP*, no. 624.

29. Mallett, *Mercenaries*, 43, 51. Bayley, *War and Society*, 51–52. The fifteenth-century condottiere company is discussed in great detail in M. Mallett and J. Hale, *The Military Organization of a Renaissance State: Venice c.1400 to 1617* (Cambridge, 1984), 20–210.

young men were recruited and trained to become individual pronoia soldiers and probably officers as well through admission into a group of imperial servants called the *archontopouloi* (or *archontopoula*), literally "sons of archons." The term is first encountered during the reign of Alexios I Komnenos (1081–1118), who created an elite troop contingent with this name from the sons of fallen soldiers.[30] However, late Byzantine archontopouloi had no connection to this elite troop (which did not survive Alexios' reign), nor does it seem that late Byzantine archontopouloi were a distinct military formation. Rather, the word was applied to two groups of men, one of which had no direct connection to the military. In documents where the word *archontopouloi* is found alongside *archons*, it appears to be a kind of diminutive form denoting a gradation within the aristocracy, "lesser archons" (for example, "kindred archons . . . and the other archons and archontopouloi").[31] On the other hand, the word *archontopouloi* was also applied to an informal group of young men who spent their early careers at the imperial court as aristocrats in training. Pseudo-Kodinos writes that archontopouloi "related to the emperor" appeared in court ceremony as attendants and took part in the ritual acclamation of the emperor. Thus, they can probably be identified with "the hundred well-born youth, well-armed and unarmed" who, Kantakouzenos reports, followed Andronikos III at his coronation.[32]

As adults these archontopouloi entered various types of imperial service and at least some retained the designation "archontopoulos." Some archontopouloi were pronoiars or the recipients of other imperial favors. Some appear in the sources performing the duties of fiscal officials or other imperial agents. Others appear as landholders. It is impossible to know whether such men were called "archontopouloi" because they spent their youths at the palace or because they were merely lesser aristocrats. Possibly no such distinction even existed. The designation, while imperially bestowed, was informal enough to adapt to the emperor's needs. There was probably a great deal of overlap in the two "groups" of archontopouloi.[33]

30. A. Hohlweg, *Beiträge zur Verwaltungsgeschichte des oströmischen Reiches unter den Komnenen* (Munich, 1965), 52.

31. MM, V, 168. A. Solovjev and V. Mošin, *Grčke povelje srpskih vladara* (Belgrade, 1936; repr. London, 1974), no. 9 (1346), and p. 403. Guillou, *Prodrome*, no. 44. Kantakouzenos, I, 236. Pseudo-Kodinos, 271.

32. Pseudo-Kodinos, 202, 212. Kantakouzenos, I, 200. Cf. Oikonomidès, "A propos des armées," 355, who suggests they were a military formation.

33. M. Nystazopoulou-Pelekidou, *Βυζαντινὰ ἔγγραφα τῆς μονῆς Πάτμου*, II (Athens, 1980), no. 66 (1261); Kantakouzenos, I, 236. Lemerle et al., *Lavra*, II, no. 106 (1319); MM, II, 382 (1400). N. Oikonomidès, *Actes de Docheiariou* (Paris, 1984), no. 29 (1355); Lemerle,

Similar to the archontopouloi were people called the emperor's, or imperial, *paidopouloi* (or *paidopoula*), literally "sons of children." Pseudo-Kodinos frequently mentions their role as attendants in palace ceremonies, and he states that the official called the parakoimomenos (literally, "he who sleeps near") of the imperial bedchamber was "the chief of the paidopouloi in the bedchamber." Michael Angold has translated the word, appropriately I think, as "pages," and suggests they may have been the emperor's childhood companions and were usually not drawn from aristocratic families. Though adult paidopouloi are encountered very infrequently (one appears as a fiscal agent, another as a landowner), they too entered imperial service. Like the archontopouloi, I do not see them as a discrete military division but rather as a courtly group from which soldiers and other imperial servants were recruited.[34]

The aristocracy of late Byzantium was in large measure a military aristocracy. Its members and those who aspired to join it learned the art of war at an early age. Manuel II Palaiologos once wrote of "activities suited to young men . . . such as exercises in arms, hunting, and contests which strengthen men in training." In a theological essay, Manuel alludes to his own military training which took place before he "had left childhood behind and before reaching manhood":

> As a child I was not allowed to frequent only the school of liberal arts and to devote myself entirely to this with the aim of surpassing all the learned. . . . But, according to a decision of the council, other studies followed one upon the other and I was compelled to alternate between many teachers each day who taught a number of different subjects; how to handle the bow and the spear and how to ride a horse.

On the basis of the chronology of Manuel's life, this training occurred prior to his sixteenth year.[35]

Military training continued through life and as in Western Europe

---

Kutlumus, no. 21 (1348). Other references to non-Byzantine or post-Byzantine archontopouloi: G. Schirò, ed., *Cronaca dei Tocco di Cefalonia di Anonimo* (Rome, 1975), vv. 2320, 2539; MM, III, 134, 260; *Chronicle of the Morea*, vv. 1639–50, 5457–65; and Oikonomidès, "A propos des armées," 355.

34. Oikonomidès, "A propos des armées," 355. Pseudo-Kodinos, 176 and index. Angold, *Byzantine Government*, 76, 176–77, 181. But cf. K. Amantos in Ἑλληνικά 6 (1933), 326, who thought *paidopoulos* meant a certain kind of soldier. Lemerle et al., *Lavra*, III, no. 132 (1351); Petit and Korablev, *Chilandar*, no. 115 (1327).

35. Manuel II Palaiologos, *Manuel II Palaeologus, Funeral Oration on His Brother Theodore*, ed. J. Chrysostomides (Thessaloniki, 1985), 104–105. Barker, *Manuel*, 529, lines 42–47; trans. in G. Dennis, *The Reign of Manuel II Palaeologus in Thessalonica* (Rome, 1960), 14.

often took the form of entertainment. Andronikos III, we are told, staged Western-style tournaments in which he himself jousted. While visiting Constantinople in 1432 the Frenchman Bertrandon de la Brocquière witnessed "a tournament after the manner of the country" which took place following the marriage of one of the emperor's relatives:

> In the middle of a square they had planted, like a quintain, a large pole, to which was fastened a plank three feet wide and five feet long. Forty cavaliers advanced to the spot, without any arms or armor whatever but a short stick. They at first amused themselves by running after each other, which lasted for about half an hour; then from sixty to fourscore rods of elder were brought, of the thickness and length of those we use for thatching. The bridegroom first took one, and set off full gallop towards the plank, to break it; as it shook in his hand, he broke it with ease, when shouts of joy resounded, and the musical instruments, namely, nacaires [cavalry kettledrums], like those of the Turks, began to play. Each of the other cavaliers broke their wands in the same manner. Then the bridegroom tied two of them together, which in truth were not too strong, and broke them without being wounded. Thus ended the feast, and everyone returned home safe and sound.[36]

No doubt lesser aristocrats, as well as soldiers of more modest station, like their counterparts East and West, spent some of their time off campaign engaged in similar activities, keeping their military skills sharp.

Since so little is known of native mercenary soldiers, aside from a few references to their presence among the palace guard divisions, little can be said about how they were recruited. Smallholding soldiers, whether native or foreign, were initially recruited as opportunity presented itself. John Vatatzes' settlement of the conquered Cumans in Asia Minor reflected a very old recruitment technique, the recruitment of prisoners of war, examples of which can be found throughout Byzantine history. The Prosalentai and Gasmouloi were recruited to satisfy the special needs Michael VIII faced following the reconquest of Constantinople, and the enlistment of the marine Tzakones was the result of Michael VIII's diplomatic efforts during his first Morean campaign. There is no evidence that later emperors made any continuing effort to recruit Prosalentai, Gasmouloi, and marine Tzakones to replace or refortify the existing contingents.[37]

36. Nicol, *Last Centuries*, 172. Bertrandon de la Brocquière, in *Early Travels in Palestine*, trans. T. Wright (London, 1848), 341–42.

37. It should be noted that the military taxes encountered from the later eleventh through the early fourteenth century (the *exelaseis*, or *ekbolai*, of *kontaratoi*, *pezoi*, *ploïmoi*, *toxotai*, etc.), despite the opinion of some scholars (e.g., P. Charanis, "On the Social Structure and Economic Organization of the Byzantine Empire in the Thirteenth Century and Later," in

The recruitment of foreign allied troops was a function of diplomacy. Through his agents the emperor petitioned and negotiated with allied rulers for help. On the other hand, the imperial government made little effort to recruit either groups of men or individuals to become supplemental mercenaries, resident foreign mercenaries, or pronoiars. Larger groups of soldiers, such as the Catalan Company and the Alans who entered the Empire in 1301, contacted the emperor and made application. Foreign prisoners of war were recruited occasionally as well. In 1329 when the Genoese Martino Zaccaria surrendered Chios to Andronikos III, his 800 Italian soldiers were given the choice of leaving or "taking the mercenary pay to serve the emperor." Most chose to become mercenaries and either stayed on Chios or "numbered themselves among the servants of the emperor."[38]

Individual mercenaries simply arrived on the scene and petitioned authorities. The scholar Demetrios Kydones provides a case in point. In a very interesting letter from around 1380 addressed to his close friend Manuel II, he recommends for employment a soldier originally from northern France:

> The soldier carrying this letter to you is of the race of Picardy of those of the West and of the Kelts beyond the Pillars [of Hercules, i.e., Gibraltar]. Following the custom of his fatherland he spent time far from his family wandering about and helping those in need with his own aid. And just now he has finished receiving pay from the governor [*hyparchos*] of Ainos [the semi-independent Genoese ruler Nicolo Gattilusio]. Earlier on Lesbos alongside [Nicolo's] brother [Francesco I Gattilusio, another semi-independent ruler] he used arms, and he lived with good order and righteousness, keeping his post, so that no one reproached him for the things of which nearly all soldiers are accused. . . . Everything went well in his service as a soldier except for one thing that he found distressing. Although he was quite accustomed to having well-born and well-ordered men as companions in war, there he was forced by the one distributing pay to be reckoned among some miserable foot and light-armed troops as well as certain unpaid men to whom fishing baskets and nets were a greater concern than arms. This indeed was a disgrace for him to bear. Trained in warfare he wanted to exchange this mass of fishermen for a regiment of the well-born, and even more strongly he wished to serve the emperor rather than to draw up battle array and to march out against invaders with a

---

Charanis, *Social, Economic and Political Life in the Byzantine Empire* [London, 1973], no. IV, 130), played no role in recruitment after 1204, if in fact they ever did (see herein, pp. 145–46.

38. Kantakouzenos, I, 376, 378–79.

host of farmers and plowmen. For it seems something of an honor to face danger in the midst of the best [*aristoi,* "aristocrats"]. I know him because he has come to the great city [Constantinople] and has begged me to recommend him to you, believing that through me he might meet you. Lead him to your father and emperor [John V] before whom it shall be possible to see kindness displayed amid virtue. Receive the man and give the emperor a ready soldier who will use his hands against enemies for his sake. The zealousness of the body and the love of honor shall certainly make him a livelihood however moderate.[39]

What is striking about this letter is the personal element. In his anonymity we may conclude that this soldier was no notable personage. Even if it would be precipitous to conclude that all foreign mercenaries were hired in this manner, the fact that the co-emperor was involved in the process points to the personalization and deterioration of administrative practices at the time.

Why did men become soldiers? Since the sources provide no direct information, discussion of this subject must assume a speculative air. First, it is reasonable to conclude that most if not all of the foreigners who came to Byzantium and were hired as soldiers wanted primarily to make a living, with adventure in some cases serving as a secondary motivation. For these men nothing else need or can be said. Moreover, inasmuch as foreign allied troops were soldiers before they arrived in Byzantium, the special case they present is of little importance to us. Consequently, the question narrows down to why native Byzantines chose to become soldiers.

Certainly motives for enlistment varied from soldier to soldier and were affected by social position, individual temperament, and numerous external factors. The most basic reason for enlistment, literal survival, was by definition not a factor for any of the soldiers I am dealing with in this chapter. The immediate defense of homeland, town, village, family, or one's own life was not a motive for the native Byzantine soldier who had enlisted prior to an imminent invasion or campaign or who from an early age had expected to become a professional soldier. The only troops who ever enlisted for reasons of self-preservation were some of the supplemental infantry recruited for specific campaigns or emergencies. These are such a special and troublesome case that they must be dealt with separately in the next chapter.

As for the professional native soldier we may assume that most en-

39. Demetrios Kydones, *Démétrius Cydonès correspondance,* ed. R. Loenertz, 2 vols. (Vatican, 1956, 1960), no. 231.

listed, like the majority of foreigners, to earn a livelihood and raise their station in life. The pay, pronoia, land or tax exemption received, plus the possibility of booty, may have been sufficient inducement to enlist. For refugees from Asia Minor military service may have been one of the few practical alternatives for starting a new life. For smallholding soldiers such as the Prosalentai and the Thelematarioi, a family tradition of service merged with the hereditary aspects and legal obligations of service that followed them or their landholdings. Pronoiars who had inherited their pronoiai from their fathers, such as the second generation of Klazomenitai, became soldiers to maintain their patrimony. At the upper levels of society, it is likely that social obligation played some role in the decision to become a soldier, one aspect of which was probably family tradition, applicable indeed to all social levels. Among the aristocracy substantial inducement could probably be found also in the social pressure to distinguish oneself and, at the highest level, in the desire to please the emperor.

Beyond this there is little sense of a general, normative societal obligation by which all subjects were expected to defend the Empire. War was the constitutional responsibility of the emperor, and the instrument through which the emperor made war was the army. Only as an emergency means of local defense, and even then only in the most dire of circumstances, was a civilian expected to make any effort at defense. Once he became a soldier this changed. His role was now to defend the Christian Empire.

As religious a world as Byzantium was, it would not be surprising if religion played a role in the decision to join the army. In the medieval West at all levels of society the idea that war could earn spiritual merit for its participants was not uncommon. On the whole the Byzantines rejected this idea. Evidently they first encountered it through contact with the Arabs, and it is frequently ridiculed in polemical writings against Islam. Only rarely did anyone argue that warfare could be spiritually meritorious.

The idea was proposed for the first time by the emperor Nikephoros II Phokas (963–69), a general of great genius and, in the opinion of many scholars, a religious fanatic. He is, for instance, the only emperor known to have forced defeated Muslims to convert. Nikephoros once suggested that soldiers who fell in war against the Arabs be granted the palm of martyrdom, a notion borrowed either from Islam or from the West. Immediately he faced vehement opposition from the patriarch and a synod of bishops, who invoked the advice of St. Basil the Great that soldiers who had killed in the course of war be deprived of the sacrament for three years. One should not think that Basil's suggestion was ever actually observed; reasons of state dictated otherwise. Rather, the patriarch and bishops were simply making the point that it was foolish to think that warfare could be an avenue to personal salvation.[40]

The only other appearance of the idea in a Byzantine context occurred in the first half of the thirteenth century. Emperors of Nicaea, in the midst of their struggles against the Latins, suggested that there be a remission of sins for soldiers falling in battle.[41] This was clearly an artificial attempt to adopt a Western form, and it too met with little success. These two examples, separated by three hundred years, show that the Byzantines could not accept the idea that warfare conferred personal spiritual merit. So while we may admit that certain individuals enlisted under the personal belief or through misleading intimations that serving in the army helped them get into heaven, the idea was repudiated by the official Church.

This does not mean that there were not religious reasons sanctioned by society that motivated men to enlist. The profession of arms did not have to be spiritually beneficial for the individual soldier in order to be considered a religious undertaking. While warfare may not have brought eternal salvation to the individual warrior, in the Byzantine worldview it could provide earthly salvation to God's Chosen People, the community of Christians, the Byzantines. God wanted His people preserved *in this world*, and the soldier could view himself as God's agent for that purpose.

While the soldier may not have earned spiritual merit by fighting on behalf of the Christian Empire, he did acquire what ancient Greek and Roman warriors earned: glory. We see this in a tenth-century oration written by Emperor Constantine VII and intended to be read before the troops in order to motivate them. "You should know," the emperor tells the host, "how good it is to fight for Christians, and how much he who does this acquires glory for himself."[42] The remarkable thing about this passage is that it would have been quite easy for Constantine to have added "and divine merit," especially since he was talking about saving Christians. But Constantine knew that even though the soldier fought for the true faith, his reward could be only earthly glory.

---

40. P. Lemerle, "Byzance et la croisade," in Lemerle, *Le monde de Byzance: histoire et institutions* (London, 1978), no. VIII, 618 and note 1. H. Ahrweiler, *L'idéologie politique de l'empire byzantin* (Paris, 1975), 80. M. Canard, "La guerre sainte dans le monde islamique et dans le monde chrétien," *Revue Africaine* 79 (1936), 612–13, 618–19. G. Schlumberger, *Un empereur byzantin au dixième siècle, Nicéphore Phocas*, nouv. éd. (Paris, 1923), 318–19, 441.

41. Ahrweiler, *Idéologie*, 112.

42. Constantine VII Porphyrogenitus, in H. Ahrweiler, ed., "Un discours inédit de Constantin VII Porphyrogénète," *TM* 2 (1967), 399, lines 67–69.

10. Peasants, Retainers, Servants

A significant portion of the participants in late Byzantine campaign armies were not employed by the imperial government as mercenaries, smallholding soldiers, or pronoia soldiers. In this category we find the supplemental infantry and those men who accompanied the army not to serve the emperor but to serve an individual soldier.

The temporary, nonprofessional foot troops that supplemented and often outnumbered the regular army of mercenaries, smallholding soldiers, and pronoiars were poorly trained, badly equipped, and ill-disciplined troops often described as farmers or townspeople. Frequently they engaged in local emergency campaigns to thwart an invasion or raiding party. In 1309 Michael IX assembled an army to fight Halil's Turks in Thrace which included "those who lived off the field and the pitchfork," and in 1328 Andronikos III threatened to order farmers to fight Michael Šišman's invading army. In 1334 while Andronikos III was on his way to Thessaloniki to quash Syrgiannes' rebellion, news reached the emperor that Turkish pirates had landed on the southern shores of the Chalkidike peninsula. Since there was some doubt whether Andronikos' army was strong enough to combat the Turks, the emperor ordered John Kantakouzenos to "call together another [army] from the neighboring villages sufficient for the deed," which then proceeded to repulse the enemy.[1]

This particular incident has been cited as evidence that peasants were under an obligation to render military service when summoned, but this is unlikely. In Byzantium there was never a general "citizens' duty" to fight for the state. In fact the very notion that a subject had an obligation to defend the state was foreign to the Byzantine mind and antithetical to both Roman and Byzantine ideology that identified the emperor, through his army, as the Defender of the Empire. In the case cited, since there was an immediate danger to the peasants' own lands, it could not have been very difficult to

---

1. Gregoras, I, 256. Kantakouzenos, I, 298, 455–56. Mutafčiev, "Vojniški zemi," 619. Other examples of emergency local defense by the population: Kantakouzenos, II, 403; III, 63; Pachymeres, Bonn ed., II, 629, 630.

motivate them to arms. On the other hand, amateur soldiers regularly took part in distant campaigns in which self-defense played little role. The 2,000 regular soldiers who crossed into Asia Minor in 1329 to fight the Ottoman emir Orhan represented far less than half of the entire campaign force; rather, most of the army was composed of inferior troops, "farmers," according to the historian Gregoras, "vulgar and common, and sure to debase the combat." Later that year an expedition to Chios included what Kantakouzenos describes as a large mob (*homilos*). Then again we have Akropolites' description of part of Manuel Laskaris' army against Epiros as a "thrown-together army and throng."[2] Troops like this were infantry. Contemporary historians frequently mention the scarcity of horses, and the praktika indicate that few peasants owned even draft horses, let alone destriers.

No doubt some individuals who heard of a campaign in the making approached the camp and found employment, but the historians naturally tend not to mention such trivial matters. In an interesting passage the historian Doukas writes that in 1453 Sultan Mehmet II "dispatched criers and heralds to all the provinces summoning everyone to join the campaign against the city [Constantinople]. The registered troops who served for pay came in large numbers. Who can say how many myriads were unregistered?"[3] Although the Muslim had more of an obligation than the Byzantine to fight for faith and ruler when called, the passage does illustrate the idea of the campaign as an "event" that drew people whether or not they were legally obligated.

Nevertheless, the state had to develop means of recruiting and raising supplemental campaign troops from the general population. Active measures were limited. There is no evidence of pronoiar or magnate playing any visible intermediary role in the raising of supplemental infantry. On occasion captives could be recruited into the army. This was done by the Catalans, as well as by Andronikos III and Kantakouzenos during the civil wars. For example, after Andronikos III captured the town of Apros from his grandfather in 1322, "all the foot except for a few chose to serve the emperor," and "to these he assigned the yearly pay."[4] Perhaps more common was the practice of imperial officials simply going to cities, towns, or

2. Gregoras, I, 433. Kantakouzenos, I, 375, and cf. II, 557. Akropolites, 146. Cf. Pachymeres, ed. Failler, I, 293 (Bonn ed., I, 222). Mutafčiev, "Vojniški zemi," 550, 619.

3. Doukas, 325; trans. H. Magoulias, *Doukas. Decline and Fall of Byzantium to the Ottoman Turks* (Detroit, 1975), 209.

4. Kantakouzenos, I, 142, and cf. II, 355, 392; III, 127; and Gregoras, I, 252.

villages, and recruiting people.[5] Since the overwhelming majority of the population worked on the land in more or less modest circumstances, and since the poor would be no less willing to join a campaign than the wealthy, the majority of those civilians who volunteered for campaign service must have been peasants and the urban poor with only fractional representation from the middle class, which was very small, and the upper class, most of whose members already had an obligation, whether customary (based on their social rank) or legal (as military pronoiars), to perform military service.

Further, the unsettled conditions in the Empire during most of the late period, characterized by substantial movement and displacement of the peasant population due to invasions, pestilence, piracy, famines, and other calamities, sometimes from one estate to another, sometimes between countryside and town, sometimes temporarily, sometimes permanently, doubtlessly led to a certain mixing of the peasantry and the urban poor.[6] Therefore, although there probably were some middle and upper class men who volunteered to be supplemental campaign soldiers, our subject is really the lower classes, the peasantry, and the urban poor. The towns with their unemployed day laborers and displaced peasants were certainly productive locales for recruiters. Gregoras (I, 302) notes that Syrgiannes and Kantakouzenos, while provincial governors in Thrace around 1320, "assembled forces, prepared arms and levied soldiers, some newcomers and as many as there were who lived life idly and uselessly through lack of necessities. And they made the most kindred and faithful of them guards of their cities."

There was never an effort to recruit settled dependent peasants (paroikoi). Monasteries rarely requested immunity from the importunities of official recruiters, and when they did, it was only to release their paroikoi from any obligation for local guard service.[7] Nor were the paroikoi of lay landowners a source of recruits, because if they had been, the monasteries would have sought explicit immunity for their own paroikoi. In addition, it

---

5. See Gregoras, I, III, 302; and Kantakouzenos, I, 456; II, 197. The verbs used in these passages, *stratologeo*, "to levy," and *syllego*, "to collect," can mean either to recruit men (who are not soldiers) to become soldiers or, less commonly, to muster a military force from among men who are already soldiers. Nowhere do we read that imperial agents "hired" peasants or townspeople.

6. A. Laiou-Thomadakis, *Peasant Society in the Late Byzantine Empire* (Princeton, N.J., 1977), 261. Lj. Maksimović, "Charakter der sozial-wirtschaftlichen Struktur der spätbyzantinischen Stadt," *Akten des XVI. internationalen Byzantinistenkongresses* (Vienna, 1981), I/1 = *JÖB* 31/1 (1981), 187 and notes 216–17.

7. E.g., W. Regel et al., *Actes de Zographou, I. Actes grecs, VizVrem* 13 (1907), suppl. I, no. 33.

would have been counterproductive for the government to lure state paroikoi or the paroikoi of pronoiars from their lands. The ideal recruit was a stable, free peasant who could accept both his tax burden and temporary military service, but in the late period there were very few such men. Consequently, it seems that the state tended to rely on rural and urban people outside the state's fiscal apparatus. Their employment as supplemental troops brought no loss to either production or revenues. Such were the displaced, the landless, and pastoral peoples.

The pastoral peoples of Thrace and Macedonia, commonly called Vlachs, were frequently associated with military activities. No doubt the army of the Bulgarian border lord Momčilo was composed in large measure of pastoral people from the area he ruled in the Rhodope mountains north of Xanthi. Byzantine leaders occasionally attempted to utilize the peasant forces gathered by peasant leaders. In 1322 the Vlach leader Syrbanos' light-armed shepherds assisted Andronikos III's troops in defeating a partisan of the older Andronikos in the Rhodope highlands.[8] And in 1294 Andronikos II sent the so-called Pseudo-Lachanas to Asia Minor where the latter managed to raise an army of peasants. "They knew nothing more than agricultural work, the spade and how to goad cattle. Shepherds of flocks and rustics, they left their own country and their farms and appeared unbidden with sticks and staffs alone, like soldiers and hoplites without arms and regiments without order." The emperor found he had no way to control such an army, and soon the Pseudo-Lachanas was recalled to Constantinople and his army dispersed.[9]

Supplemental native campaign troops may be characterized as soldiers who were not professionals, had no military obligation and probably little training. They were civilians who were voluntarily recruited or appeared unbidden for a particular campaign. At times they were offered pay, but more usually they fought with the hope of acquiring plunder.[10] One may

8. M. Bartusis, "Chrelja and Momčilo," *Byzantinoslavica* 41 (1981), 207. Kantakouzenos, I, 146–47. Also, Pachymeres, Bonn ed., II, 106, 549; Gregoras, I, 229–30; K. Sathas, Μνημεῖα Ἑλληνικῆς Ἱστορίας. Documents inédits relatifs à l'histoire de la Grèce au moyen âge (Paris, 1880–90), I, 146, lines 28–31; Laiou, *Constantinople*, 121–22; and Mutafčiev, "Vojniški zemi," 610, 620. On the Vlachs in general, see C. Asdracha, *La région des Rhodopes aux XIIIe et XIVe siècles* (Athens, 1976), 69–72, 182. On the settlement of Vlachs within the Empire, see the analysis of a letter of Chomatenos in A. Jameson, "The Responsa and Letters of Demetrios Chomatianos, Archbishop of Achrida and Bulgaria," diss., Harvard Univ. 1957, 256–65.

9. Pachymeres, Bonn ed., II, 191, and cf. 442–45. Laiou, *Constantinople*, 79–80 and cf. 191–92.

10. See Mutafčiev, "Vojniški zemi," 619, citing Pachymeres, Bonn ed., II, 414; and Oikonomidès, "A propos des armées," 357 and note 35.

hypothesize a cycle in which the authorities, responding to invasions, banditry, or the factional strife of the civil wars, sent representatives to the towns to raise foot troops. These new troops, composed of the urban poor and peasants who had sought refuge from earlier acts of violence, were thrown into the field and, lacking discipline and proper pay, ravaged the countryside, depriving still more agricultural workers of their livelihoods. While a supplemental infantry consisting of temporary soldiers recruited from among the peasantry and urban poor provided massive quantities of manpower at little direct cost to the state, such troops proved to be poor fighters and unmanageable. It was precisely the desire to avoid employing this kind of soldier that led to alternative practices, in particular, the hiring of foreign mercenaries such as the Catalans, and the creation of permanent military groups such as the resident soldier companies.

In connection with the role of peasants in late Byzantine armies it is useful to turn to the writings of the scholar George Gemistos Plethon. Several times in his substantial corpus Gemistos discussed the problems of the Byzantine Morea and offered solutions he hoped the despots and emperors would implement. In his *Address to Manuel II on Affairs in the Peloponnesos*, probably written in 1417 or 1418, he describes the contemporary military organization of the Morea and its shortcomings:

> The first thing to notice is that most of the Peloponnesians are at present engaged partly in farming or in pasturing flocks, and in providing thereby for the needs of their own livelihood and the payment of taxes to the fisc, and partly, at the same time, in doing military service. While the taxes paid are indeed small, they are numerous, they are collected by a number of agents, and the collection is mostly in money and not in kind. Whenever the order is given for a campaign, few come and most of these are unarmed. In camp they do not very much wish to stay when their work at home calls, for either at home or in camp it is necessary to meet expenses and still pay taxes. . . . How can the same person do military service and at the same time maintain himself and others? It is not even always possible for the army to carry off booty because, while there might be some profit from this to those serving in the army, most expenses have to be met from their own means and the fisc must receive its share of the booty.

Gemistos points out that not even the Hexamilion could be garrisoned under current practices, and that the idea of raising taxes to hire foreign mercenaries for the defense of the Isthmus of Corinth was no solution because taxes were already so high that no conceivable tax increase could possibly produce enough mercenaries to man it. "If danger should come, these foreigners will not in any way be sufficient for the defense; we shall still need to resort to our own troops, who are unarmed and untrained."[11]

Gemistos' solution was to divide the population into two groups based on natural ability. One would perform the military service and would pay no taxes. The other would work on the land and would be responsible for all the taxes, which would be paid all at once and in kind. Agricultural produce would be divided into three parts.

> The fruits of the labor of all . . . should be enjoyed so that one part goes to the laborer himself, one part to the stock [i.e., re-invested in the farm], and the third to the public treasury. . . . Those who pay this tax may be called helots because they are exempt from military service and are assigned to the taxpaying; they should be regarded as the foster-fathers of the community and should be subject to no further duty; nothing should be demanded from them other than or in addition to this tax; no one should be allowed to use them for forced labor, and especially they should not be treated in any way unjustly.
>
> The soldiers being organized on this basis [as a regular permanent body], I think that one helot should be assigned to each infantryman and two to cavalry, so that each soldier, while enjoying the produce of his own labor to the extent that there is no hindrance to his military service, will enjoy a share of the produce of his helot . . . and will be able to serve in the army with equipment and to remain where he is assigned. Where it is possible to divide the whole population into soldiers and helots (because all are not fit to be soldiers), this is the system that should be adopted. But where most of the population appear fit to be soldiers, they should be divided into pairs, each couple compelled to work their commonly-held farm, and each in turn working the common property of both while the other does military service.

Gemistos suggests that military leaders ("archons") and the elite (*logades*) of the soldiers should receive perhaps three helots, and from these each should furnish one cavalryman combining the functions of servant and soldier. The emperor, he adds, remembering his audience, should have as many helots as he needed. The well-trained troops raised by this plan would, he claims, be sufficient to defend the Isthmus through a system of rotation.[12]

Gemistos' fixation on the Isthmus and the Hexamilion was limitless. In a letter to Manuel II, written slightly earlier, probably in 1415 or 1416, he

11. S. Lampros, Παλαιολόγεια καὶ Πελοποννησιακά (Athens, 1912–30), III, 251–53 (hereafter Lampros, *P&P*). Trans. partially based on E. Barker, *Social and Political Thought in Byzantium* (Oxford, 1957), 199–200. C. Woodhouse, *George Gemistos Plethon, The Last of the Hellenes* (Oxford, 1986), 103. Zakythinos, *Despotat*, II, 138–39.

12. Lampros, *P&P*, III, 253–57, 260–61. Trans. partially based on Barker, *Social and Political Thought*, 201–203. Woodhouse, *George Gemistos Plethon*, 103–105.

raised for the first time the idea of separating the army from the taxpaying community. He writes that while *it had made sense in the past* for the population both to serve in the army and to pay taxes because campaigns were short, not very dangerous, and booty was plentiful, now due to the nature of campaigns and the heavy burden of taxation it was impossible to provide both. "So the soldiers must be set apart from the taxpayers, the best chosen from all, who instead of taxes provide a garrison for the Isthmus."

He argues that this would not result in a great loss of public revenue and, carried away by enthusiasm, he volunteers to carry out the project himself. This is curious, inasmuch as there is no evidence that Gemistos had any military experience or training whatsoever. "For I offer myself to put together this army without spending more for all those recruited than all the taxes bearing on each hearth even now for the garrison of the Isthmus, and to use this revenue to provide a body of around 6,000 native soldiers, so that one thousand in rotation always could be performing garrison duty," and all could be mobilized for emergencies. This plan, he concludes, would ensure that soldiers would be better equipped, would be more efficient because of greater specialization and would have higher morale since they would feel they were defending their own freedom, not serving as helots.[13]

Gemistos turned to this theme for the last time in his *Address to the Despot Theodore II on the Peloponnesos*, written sometime after his advice to Manuel II. His plan now became more complicated. The population still would be divided into soldiers and taxpayers (helots), but he modifies this slightly, suggesting that agricultural workers be grouped in pairs, each alternating military service and labor and functioning as reserve troops. As in his advice to Manuel, Theodore could have as many helots as he desired, some of which he would distribute to his officials and senior officers. Each of these would support an equivalent number of military clients (*stratiotikoi pelatai*) so the despot would not have to support them himself. Most of the army should be made up of citizens, since foreign mercenaries were unreliable. Finally, there should be no attempt to have a navy as well as an army, since that would only weaken both.[14]

Gemistos' views are echoed in a letter written around 1444 to the despot Constantine by one of his students, Cardinal Bessarion. Bessarion complains that while some Peloponnesians were courageous, others lacked

13. Lampros, *P&P*, III, 310–12. Woodhouse, *George Gemistos Plethon*, 100–101.
14. Lampros, *P&P*, IV, 121–22, 131–33. Woodhouse, *George Gemistos Plethon*, 92, 94, 97. Commentary by Zakythinos, *Despotat*, I, 176–80.

arms and training because of heavy taxes and "the cruelty of the rapacious overseers." Like Gemistos he argues that the military should be separated from the peasantry, and that only by releasing it from economic obligations could morale be restored.[15]

None of these proposals had much practical value. They would have required a reordering of society on a scale that has been attempted only in the present century. Nor is there anything very original in Gemistos' plans. The idea of separating the warrior class from the rest of the population is found and developed in the writings of Plato (*Republic*.ii.374A) and Aristotle (*Politics*.vii.9–10). The notion of helots supporting both themselves and their soldiers while the soldier defended himself and his helots, as well as the use of the term *helot*, recalls ancient Sparta, only a few miles from Mistra, the main town of the Byzantine Morea. Casting aspersions on foreign mercenaries was commonplace, as were complaints about high taxes.

The most interesting aspect of Gemistos' writing is what it suggests about contemporary military organization in the Byzantine Morea, a subject about which we know very little. Both Gemistos and Bessarion imply that the bulk of the army in the fifteenth-century Morea was composed of peasants. Indeed in Byzantium proper, at least during the first half of the fourteenth century, a significant portion of the army was made up of peasants recruited on a campaign-by-campaign basis. Further, there is no suggestion from Gemistos that Morean peasants received any compensation for their military service aside from the possibility of booty. This too was not unlike the situation in the rest of Byzantium. Yet, implicit in Gemistos' writing are several curious ideas: (1) that almost all of the Morean army was made up of peasants, (2) that there was a general customary obligation on the population to serve in the army, and (3) that this was no new policy but the traditional way of doing things which, under the current circumstances, was no longer adequate. Beyond this he laments (4) that the troops of the Morea tended to be unarmed and untrained. Aside from the last point, no other authors make such claims implicitly or otherwise.

There are two possibilities. Either the army in the Morea was organized in a manner different from the rest of Byzantium or Gemistos was altering the facts to fit his explanation of the Morea's ills. If the former was the case, we might first seek to attribute any idiosyncracies in the Byzantine

---

15. Lampros, *P&P*, IV, 35–36. Zakythinos, *Despotat*, II, 143. A. Vacalopoulos, *Origins of the Greek Nation* (New Brunswick, N.J., 1970), 172–78.

Morea to Western influence, as a product of the half century or more of Western domination and of its close proximity to the Principality of Achaia, Venetian Methone and Korone, and the Duchy of Athens. However, the employment of peasants was hardly characteristic of Western medieval armies. If it was customary for peasants in the Byzantine Morea to serve in the army, it was not something borrowed from the crusaders.

It seems most likely that Gemistos fabricated a straw-man "existing" system in order to present a classical Greek solution. In fact his "existing" system bears greater similarity to Periclean Athens than to fifteenth-century Byzantium. The best light we can put on Gemistos' description of the prevailing state of affairs in the Morea is to say that he did not create it entirely out of whole cloth. In Byzantium proper peasants did fight, they were recruited in emergencies, they joined armies, occasionally they formed their own rag-tag armies. It is reasonable to think the same thing occurred in the Morea. Perhaps the despots of the Morea, so in need of soldiers, sought them everywhere, even undertaking the active recruitment of untrained peasants, always a stopgap measure that could hardly have been effective. Observing such uses of peasants, Gemistos invented a bad "institution" which he felt had to be abandoned. Small wonder that the leaders to whom he addressed his advice paid no attention to him.

Numerous participants in the campaign army neither bore a military obligation toward the state nor even were employed or recruited by the state. These men, called *oikeioi* and *oiketai*, were both soldiers and noncombatants and were distinguished by their personal obligation toward an individual leader or soldier.[16] The words *oikeios* and *oiketes* did not so much define the function of an individual as they defined his relationship toward the man he accompanied. Although neither word had a rigid technical significance, *oikeioi* is most accurately rendered as "kith and kin," in other words, a man's companions and relatives, people of social rank similar to that of the leader or soldier with whom they were associated. Generally there was no great sense of subordination. A man in the presence of his oikeioi was more or less "first among equals," and in this sense the concept of "oikeioi" paralleled the protofeudal Germanic notion of the *Gefolgschaft*, a personal following based on loyalty.

Oikeioi were not "employees" of the soldier or leader. If he provided

---

16. On the term *oikeios*, see J. Verpeaux, "Les Oikeioi," *REB* 23 (1965), 89–99. On *oiketes*, see G. Weiss, *Joannes Kantakuzenos—Aristokrat, Staatsmann, Kaiser und Mönch—in der Gesellschaftsentwicklung von Byzanz im 14. Jahrhundert* (Wiesbaden, 1969), 143–45.

for them, it was out of familial or social obligation, though often they possessed their own financial resources. Oiketai, however, were servants distinctly subordinate to the soldier or leader. Generally he provided for them and they served him as either military retainers or domestic servants. Their livelihoods were in his hands. If the leader was a great man, the oikeioi and oiketai together constituted his retinue or entourage, and the position and duties of each oikeios and oiketes were probably well defined. Lesser soldiers had proportionately smaller followings that would not merit the label "retinue." If such a soldier campaigned with oikeioi, they were few in number and his oiketai had less well-defined functions.

The distinction between oikeioi and oiketai is illustrated in Kantakouzenos' description of the rebel Syrgiannes' following. As governor of Thessaloniki in the late 1320s and early 1330s, Syrgiannes gathered a force (*dynamis*) around him of many friends (*philoi*) and servants (*oiketai*). In Kantakouzenos' memoirs "friend" means "ally." Ostensibly Syrgiannes' allies were the wealthy landlords from that area of Macedonia. In peacetime they were scattered among the towns, but in war they gathered around their chief, Syrgiannes. The oiketai were Syrgiannes' military retainers and possibly his domestic servants, although Kantakouzenos' use of the word *dynamis*, with its military connotation, may exclude domestic servants from this particular group of followers. Thus, part of Syrgiannes' following were "companions"; the rest were retainers. Another passages illustrates this distinction even more clearly. Syrgiannes rode to his death in 1334 accompanied by "six of his oikeioi . . . and thirty of his oiketai." The former were his allies, the men close to him; the latter were subordinate military retainers.[17]

The emperor had the greatest number of oikeioi and oiketai. Together they formed his entourage at court and in the field. On campaign his oikeioi included relatives, many of whom were military leaders in their own right, and companions, who were military men generally of distinguished pedigree as well as nonmilitary aristocrats serving as advisors. Thus Kantakouzenos describes the civil wars as a contest between emperors "along with their oikeioi." To be an oikeios of the emperor was obviously desirable. The one hundred supporters of Andronikos III whom Kantakouzenos quickly mustered in Constantinople in 1321, "all brave and trained in battle," were men who were already or wanted to become companions of

17. Kantakouzenos, I, 436, 456. The term *friend* is applied to both Hrelja (Kantakouzenos, II, 193, 275) and Umur (II, 397–98).

the young emperor. Later, once hostilities had broken out, Kantakouzenos guessed that a little less than 5,000 cavalry were in Andronikos III's army, "for it was not possible to know the number precisely, since many of those not enrolled in the army campaigned along to please the emperor." These were undoubtedly men ready for battle who hoped to become "companions" or to establish even closer links to the emperor. The oikeioi of an emperor, perhaps excluding his close relatives, can be termed a *Gefolgschaft* properly speaking, since they were usually aristocrats in their own right, dependent on the emperor only for a small part of the status they enjoyed.[18]

The oiketai of the emperor were "servants," but since even the lowliest such position in imperial service conveyed a degree of prestige, imperial servants can be regarded as a breed apart. They were quite numerous. During a visit to the Serbian ruler Stefan Dušan, Andronikos III took along a few of the "illustrious" and 300 "of his own" (*ton idion*). Some imperial oiketai were military retainers. When some foot troops surrendered to Andronikos III in 1322, many chose to serve the emperor, and so "he assigned these the yearly pay and enrolled [them] among the oiketai." Later, after the fall of Chios, many of the surrendering Latin garrison troops similarly "numbered themselves among the oiketai of the emperor." The sense of these passages is that these men did not become simply imperial soldiers, but personal soldiers of the emperor and, at least in the first case, hired soldiers. What distinguished these men from other soldiers was their personal attachment to the emperor, and what distinguished them from oikeioi was their distinct subservience to the emperor, the fact that they owed their new position in life entirely to imperial kindness.[19] On campaign these retainers plus the military men among the oikeioi probably formed what was called the "imperial *taxis*" or "imperial allagion."

Imperial oiketai performed a broad range of functions. No doubt the emperor had a great number of simple domestic servants and military retainers, but some oiketai had responsibilities that far exceeded what we usually classify among a servant's duties. Kantakouzenos describes Hierax, the archon of Černomen, as having been "one of the oiketai of the emperor Andronikos" III. Of the large number of men he identifies "from the oiketai" of one or another emperor, or even of an empress, some had a

18. Kantakouzenos, III, 34; I, 64, 108. For early and middle Byzantine imperial retinues, see H.-G. Beck, *Byzantinische Gefolgschaftswesen* (Munich, 1965). Weiss, *Kantakuzenos*, treats at length the various circles surrounding this particular emperor.

19. Kantakouzenos, I, 475, 142, 378–79. In fact Kantakouzenos (II, 194) once distinguishes the mercenaries (*misthophorikon*) of the army from the emperor's (military) oiketai.

military function while others performed significant diplomatic tasks. Their names, such as Lantzaretos, Katabolenos, Broula, Zeianos, Kyparissiotes, and Gabras, indicate that they were usually not from aristocratic families ("Gabras" the only celebrated surname in the group).[20]

While the emperor had the most visible entourage with its oikeioi and oiketai, both military and domestic, more relevant to our concerns are the retinues of other men, particularly the oikeioi and oiketai who accompanied a soldier or military leader on campaign. The evidence suggests that indeed private retinues existed and that some members of these retinues fought with the man they accompanied. Great men on campaign, that is, aristocratic military commanders, had both oikeioi and oiketai. We know empirically that great men throughout history have had retainers, and in fact one may define a "great man," like the Jeffersonian "natural aristocrat," by his ability to attract a following. Kantakouzenos writes that the "especially illustrious" had "expended money, oikeioi and themselves" during the civil wars, and in 1342 we encounter the eparch Michael Monomachos marching along "with his oikeioi."[21] In these passages *oikeios* means "kith and kin," the relatives and close friends of the great man. It is likely that soldiers who were not great men marched at times with friends and relatives as well, but these were of less interest to contemporary writers. Yet the relatively infrequent mention of the oikeioi of military leaders and soldiers suggests that such oikeioi were not very numerous, a logical conclusion since we should expect many of the aristocratic friends and relatives of a great man to have had their own military obligations and their own retinues, and lowlier soldiers could not afford the upkeep of nonessential followers.

The oikeioi of private men were outnumbered by their oiketai. When Kantakouzenos left Didymoteichon in 1342, Gregoras states that he was accompanied by at least 2,000 cavalry in addition to "kinsmen and otherwise well-born men with as many of their retinues as there were," who raised the number by nearly 500.[22] Certainly relatives and aristocrats could account for only a fraction of this 500; the rest were oikeioi and oiketai. The oiketai were personal servants of great men, accompanying their masters in military or domestic capacities. While some oiketai, particularly those at-

20. Kantakouzenos, II, 526; II, 341, 382. Weiss, *Joannes Kantakuzenos*, 146–47. Oikonomidès, "A propos des armées," 353–54.

21. Kantakouzenos, III, 10; II, 236. For private retinues prior to 1204, see G. Ostrogorsky, "Observations on the Aristocracy in Byzantium," *DOP* 25 (1971), 12–16.

22. Gregoras, II, 628. Ostrogorsky, *Féodalité*, 178. Ostrogorsky, "Observations," 27. Mutafčiev, "Vojniški zemi," 583.

tached to less wealthy soldiers, performed both military and domestic duties, the sources tend to distinguish the occasions when oiketai performed each type of duty. While bearing in mind that the duties of some, perhaps most, oiketai were very broad, it is possible to differentiate "military retainers" who fought with their masters from "domestic servants" who did not.

Military retainers, as men dependent on great men for their livelihoods and status, were by definition subordinate to their master. As in the case of Syrgiannes cited above these retainers could be numerous; he had at least thirty. It is not difficult to imagine from what strata of society the bulk of these men usually came. Adventurers, both foreign and native, and displaced peasants were the likely candidates, with perhaps unemployed mercenaries leading the list. The latter is exemplified by the Gasmouloi who were dismissed from imperial service in 1285. Some, in the words of Gregoras (I, 175), "became hirelings to those renowned Romans distinguished by wealth." Presumably they were assigned tasks that made use of their military skills.

While great men and even lesser soldiers certainly had military retainers, the question is really one of their significance, whether a man's retainers formed a "private army," the kind of army that would indicate the breakdown of state authority in the late centuries. Syrgiannes had a private army, as did the Bulgarian border lord Momčilo, the Serbian renegade general Hrelja, and any other territorial lord who wished to establish himself as an independent power. But the independence and the private armies of these men did not last long: Syrgiannes was assassinated, Momčilo died in battle, and Hrelja was forced to return to his original master, Stefan Dušan.[23]

More enduring was the regime of the brothers Alexios and John who established an independent principality around Kavalla during the second half of the fourteenth century. The will of the megas primmikerios John commended a small group of men whom he calls "mine" (*ton kat' emauton*) or his children (*paidia*) to the monastery of Pantokrator so as to provide for them after his death. The will states that these men "labored greatly. They came to our aid and cooperated with us in every way they could and showed themselves most loyal and benevolent in their dealings with us, frequently exposing their very lives to all kinds of peril." They were to serve the monastery not "out of any dependent or servile obligation" but out of free

---

23. See Bartusis, "Chrelja and Momčilo."

choice. If they wished they could leave. George Ostrogorsky wrote that John "is referring to his retinue, the trusty followers who accompanied a feudal seigneur on his campaigns." Indeed these men were undeniably part of John's retinue. They were landless, dependent on John for their maintenance, and, therefore, oiketai. Their status was low, though they were not paroikoi, and they seem to have participated in some kind of military operations.

However, it is not quite accurate to characterize the megas primmikerios John as a "feudal seigneur" and his retainers as "the trusty followers who accompanied" a feudal seigneur on campaign. First of all, John was not a feudal seigneur; he owned extensive patrimonial estates (even through by 1384, when he wrote his will, the advance of the Ottomans would have effectively limited his landholdings to those on the isle of Thasos). But more than this, he and his brother were independent political rulers in their own right, and they commanded an army. Consequently, the will of the megas primmikerios only confirms what fact and common sense dictate, that he commanded soldiers and that some of these soldiers were dear to him.[24]

On the other hand, there is no evidence that great men who did not intend to rebel against the emperor or otherwise establish an independent territorial domain had private armies which accompanied them on campaigns and which formed part of the larger Byzantine campaign army. One passage often cited as evidence that wealthy Byzantines tended to have private armies is found in Demetrios Kydones' *Monody on the Fallen in Thessaloniki* (1346) in which he laments the tribulations endured by great men: "Those who were able to feed an army from their own means were suddenly brought down like a thunderbolt." Another passage, from the chronicle of the Catalan Muntaner, speaks of "a baron in the kingdom of Salonica, called Sir Cristovol Jordi" (George of Christoupolis?) who marched against the Catalans with "his company which consisted of about eighty horsemen." Such evidence is weak and unconvincing.[25]

The simple fact is that the historians never speak of great numbers of soldiers accompanying great men on campaign. At the most we read, as

24. V. Kravari, *Actes du Pantocrator* (Paris, 1991, no. 10, lines 36–37, and cf. no. 11; trans. by Ostrogorsky, "Observations," 26–27. On the brothers Alexios and John, see Kravari, *Pantocrator*, 7–12. I. Ševčenko, "On the Preface to a Praktikon by Alyates," in Ševčenko, *Society and Intellectual Life in Late Byzantium* (London, 1981), no. XIII, 67 note 9. Cf. Ostrogorsky, *Féodalité*, 176–77.

25. Migne, *PG*, 109, col. 645D. R. Muntaner, *Cronicà*, ed. E.B. (Barcelona, 1927–52), ch. 224; trans. Lady Goodenough, *The Chronicle of Muntaner* (London, 1920–21), II, 530.

cited above, that Kantakouzenos' kinsmen and well-born with their reti-nues amounted to 500 men. Now, if we assume that merely one hundred of these 500 were domestic servants, and that at the bare minimum, say, five kinsmen and fifteen "well-born" were present, then each of these great men could have had no more than an average of twenty soldiers accompanying him. Do twenty men constitute a private army? This of course depends on how one wishes to define the expression. I am inclined to view the one or two dozen soldiers who marched with a great man merely as retainers who were, as Ostrogorsky wrote, the "trusty followers" who accompanied a great man on his campaigns.

Another way to approach the question of private armies is to ask the question, Why would a great man, if he did not intend to rebel against the emperor, have a private army? Perhaps he felt he needed one or perhaps he was obligated by the state to provide for one. The first possibility, given the various threats to landed possessions posed by bandits and other invaders, cannot be dismissed. One may assume that all landowners who had the means, whether laymen or monasteries, had guards to protect their lands (see Chapter 13). By the same token, it would be unrealistic to suppose that any sizeable number of guards campaigned with their landowner, thereby leaving his lands underprotected. Therefore we should not expect the guards of a great man's estate to have campaigned with him.

Perhaps a great man thought he needed to campaign with a private army as a matter of prestige. For some men this would not have been a negligible concern. A private army is certainly an outward sign of status. However, the problem with this hypothesis is that the narrative sources do not give any impression that large numbers of soldiers accompanied the campaigning aristocrat. If any great man proudly marched along with one hundred horsemen financed from his own purse, the effect was entirely lost on contemporary historians who say nothing of such phenomena.

A second possibility why a great man may have campaigned with a private army has been raised in connection with the recruitment of foot troops for the campaign army. The underlying premise is that there was a legal obligation on patrimonial landlords or pronoiars, or both, to provide the state with a certain number of foot troops presumably drawn from the paroikoi on their estates. The hypothesis has two aspects. One suggests that the paroikoi-soldiers thus raised were not commanded by the patrimonial landowner or pronoiar himself but were incorporated into the general field divisions of the infantry. Since these troops would not have been under the personal control of the landowner or pronoiar, they could not be considered a private army or even a group of retainers, but supplemental infantry, a topic that has already been discussed.

The second aspect of the hypothesis has been treated most thoroughly by Ostrogorsky, who maintained that the pronoiar, as part of his customary "service" toward the emperor in return for his pronoia, was required to present not only himself personally for military duty but also his paroikoi. According to Ostrogorsky these paroikoi accompanied the pronoiar on campaign and formed his retinue. While Ostrogorsky is not clear on whether these paroikoi were actually commanded in the field by the pronoiar, his treatment of the evidence seems to point in this direction. The evidence consists of the testimony of three documents. First, the previously cited will of the megas primmikerios John speaks of his "children," who were, as I have suggested, retainers. Although it is possible that these men were paroikoi before entering John's personal service, they do not seem to have been paroikoi while serving John, and were clearly not to be paroikoi after John's death.

In any event John was not a pronoiar, but a patrimonial landowner and, for all practical purposes, an independent ruler. Recognizing this difficulty, Ostrogorsky wrote that "we may imagine that pronoiars, too, had similar retinues," because "it is difficult to conceive that owners of patrimonial estates should have had retinues, and pronoiars not."[26] This reasoning is moot. Certainly a military pronoiar who had the means to finance a retinue would no doubt appear on campaign with retainers. But the question is whether the pronoiar was under such an obligation. Since no one obligated the megas primmikerios in his role as a private landowner or as an independent ruler to have a retinue, this evidence cannot be used to support the contention that pronoiars were required to provide themselves with retinues, paroikoi-infantry, or anything of the sort.

Second, there is the praktikon for the eparch Michael Monomachos which Ostrogorsky once analyzed to demonstrate that Monomachos' paroikoi in 1333 in the theme of Serres and the Strymon were assessed at a lower tax rate than certain paroikoi belonging to the monastery of Zographou in 1320 in the theme of Thessaloniki, the conclusion being that the paroikoi of a pronoiar were subject to lower tax rates because they were obligated to accompany their master on campaign. However, Jacques Lefort's study of fourteenth-century tax rates indicates that tax rates varied across time and space, even for monastic paroikoi. Thus, Ostrogorsky's comparison, as well

---

26. Ostrogorsky, *Féodalité*, 120, 352, 355, and "Observations," 14.

as other similar analyses that ignore chronology and geography, is method-
ologically unsound. The relation between the tax rates of monastic paroikoi
and lay paroikoi remains unknown, but even if it were to be proved that lay
paroikoi paid less taxes, one would still need to establish a link between a
lower tax rate and military service.[27]

Another piece of evidence in support of the idea that pronoiars were
required to present themselves for military service at the head of a certain
number of men was cited by Peter Charanis. During the 1270s Michael VIII
granted the Italian adventurer Licario the island of Negroponte (Euboea)
on condition that he serve the emperor with 200 knights. This evidence
cannot be summarily dismissed, but it is far from conclusive. Licario was no
ordinary pronoiar. His pronoia, if we should so consider it, as Charanis did,
was similar to the kind of nearly independent appanage that emperors often
granted younger sons or other relatives. As was characteristic of appanages,
Licario was the ruler of an area far from Constantinople, he possessed both
an army and a navy which were responsible to him alone, and he conducted
an independent foreign policy.[28] Michael's cession of the island may have
been an anomalous expedient aimed at dealing with a possibly troublesome
foreigner and with a Byzantine outpost difficult to defend from the capital.
I do not think this, or any other evidence, allows us to conclude that
pronoiars or other landholders were required personally to lead paroikoi or
any other kind of retainers into battle.

Up to this point the discussion has centered around "great men":
wealthy patrimonial landowners, wealthy pronoiars, and perhaps even
some distinguished mercenaries. But what of the soldiers who were not
great men, such as the pronoia soldier with much more modest holdings
and the typically poorly paid mercenary? Did these have military retainers
who campaigned with them? There is no evidence nor has it ever been
suggested that foot troops or any but the wealthiest mercenaries had
retainers. But it has been suggested by Ostrogorsky that pronoia soldiers
generally had retainers. The single piece of evidence cited in this regard is a
formula for a preface (prooimion) to a document, dated to the second half of
the thirteenth century, and edited by Robert Browning and later by Ihor

27. Ostrogorsky, Féodalité, 112–22, 347–56, comparing Regel et al., Zographou, no. 29 to
no. 17. J. Lefort, "Fiscalité médiévale et informatique: recherches sur les barèmes pour
l'imposition des paysans byzantins du XIVe siècle," Revue Historique 512 (1974), 315–56.
28. P. Charanis, "On the Social Structure and Economic Organization of the Byzantine
Empire in the Thirteenth Century and Later," in Charanis, Social, Economic and Political Life in
the Byzantine Empire (London, 1973), no. IV, 131 note 173. For the concept of appanage in
Byzantine studies, see the ODB, s.v. "appanage."

Ševčenko, which from its title, "[Preface] of Alyates for a Praktikon" (*Tou Alyatou eis praktikon*), was intended to preface a praktikon bestowing some benefaction on someone. The text is poorly preserved and grammatically difficult, but one passage appears to speak of the bravery the soldier (*stratiotes*) will show in battle *ek tou peri auton polyarithmou synaspismou*, "because of the numerous support which surrounds him" (in R. Browning's translation) or "on account of the large numbers in the Knight's (?) retinue" (in I. Ševčenko's; the question mark is his). Ostrogorsky leaped upon Ševčenko's translation of the passage and, throwing the latter's judicious "(?)" to the wind, declared that the passage proved that it was general practice not only for wealthy pronoiars to march with retainers, but also for the much more numerous holders of more modest military pronoiai.[29]

A few objections can be raised against this reading. First, such a reading does not fit the theme of the preface, the invincibility of brotherly unity in a military context: Just as a wall can be impregnable only if one stone is placed next to another, just as a rope cannot be unbreakable unless individual strands are braided together harmoniously, so a line of battle will remain unbroken only if fit soldiers work together. As Alexander Kazhdan has pointed out, there is nothing in the preface that points to pronoia or any land or vassalage relationship. Indeed, the ideas expressed were as applicable in the third as in the thirteenth century. In particular, the use of the word *knight*, with its Western connotations, to translate *stratiotes* is unwarranted and generally should be avoided.

Second, Ševčenko's interrogative ("?") cannot be so easily discarded. In the key phrase *ek tou peri auton polyarithmou synaspismou*, the pronoun *autos* logically can refer either to the "soldier" or to the subject of that particular sentence, the general (*stratarches*). Kazhdan preferred to conclude that it referred to the general; Ševčenko, though opting for "soldier," had his doubts and wrote, "It is not sure that the retinue is the knight's rather than the Ruler's [sic]." Last, there is no need to render *synaspismos* as "retinue." In ancient Greek the word literally means a group of men putting their shields together, hence, "comrades-in-arms." In Pachymeres, it is "comradery." Today it means a "coalition" or "alliance," which is how

---

29. R. Browning, *Notes on Byzantine Prooimia* (Vienna, 1966), 30–31. Ševčenko, "Preface," 70–72: οὐκ ἂν καὶ στρατεία ἐκ πολυχειρίας κραταιωθήσεται, καὶ στρατιώτης γενικῇ πολυανδρίᾳ συστρατηγούμενος εἰς μείζονα καὶ θαρραλεωτέραν συγκροτηθῇ τὴν βελτίωσιν, καὶ οὕτω καὶ αὐτὸς ἐπὶ πλέον θρασύνται ὀχυρούμενος; ἀλλὰ καὶ ὁ στρατάρχης καὶ τοῦ παντὸς κατεξουσιάζων θαρρεῖν ἐπ' ἐκείνῳ σχοίη τὴν ἀδιάρρηκτον συμβολὴν ἐκ τοῦ περὶ αὐτὸν πολυαρίθμου συνασπισμοῦ. Ostrogorsky, "Observations," 14.

Akropolites used the word. I do not find any necessary sense of subordination in the word as, for example, would be clearly suggested by *hypaspistes*, which in the middle Byzantine period was indeed used to mean retainer.[30]

It is not difficult to offer a translation that involves no suggestion of retinues:

> And will not a military expedition be strengthened by many hands, and a soldier, being commanded together with a multitude of the same stock, be all the better disciplined and, thus strengthened, show more courage? In addition, the general exercising authority over all will have confidence in him, and the line of battle will not be broken on account of the large number of comrades fighting around him.

Nevertheless, the ambiguity of the passage allows much room for differences of opinion. It is possible that it does refer to some kind of "feudal retainers," as Ostrogorsky thought, but this interpretation is far from sure. Consequently, the preface cannot be used as evidence, much less as proof, that pronoiars campaigned with retainers.

Nevertheless, there is good evidence that many lesser soldiers employed oiketai in their more domestic capacities while on campaign. Domestic servants, often called *hyperetai* or the *hyperetikon*, words that clearly distinguish them from military retainers, performed the basic support functions essential to every field army throughout history: supply and transport. Thus servants were normally found with the baggage which, at least for well-to-do soldiers and leaders, was carried by horses. These servants were also responsible for gathering fodder.[31]

Occasionally the servants accompanying the army took part in more bellicose activities. Akropolites reports that John Vatatzes "gathered those serving the soldiers for pay, whom the vulgar tongue calls Tzouloukones, and he stirred [them] to conquer" the lower, unwalled part of the town of Serres. During Syrgiannes' siege of the fort of Sakkoi near Selymbria in 1322, the insults of the farmers defending the place so enraged "the oiketi-

---

30. A. Kazhdan, "The Fate of the Intellectual in Byzantium à propos of *Society and Intellectual Life in Late Byzantium*, by Ihor Ševčenko," *Greek Orthodox Theological Review* 27/1 (1982), 88–89, in fact has even questioned whether it is necessary to regard the recipient of an act prefaced by such a prooimion as a soldier. Ševčenko, "Preface," 72 note "f." Pachymeres, Bonn ed., II, 308. Akropolites, 49. For *hypaspistes*, see Ostrogorsky, "Observations," 13–14, citing passages from Attaleiates and Skylitzes.

31. After a skirmish between the forces of Andronikos II and Andronikos III, the latter's troops "seized the military baggage, oiketai, and horses not able to follow the [fleeing] army" (Kantakouzenos, I, 151). Kantakouzenos, I, 279, speaks of those "from the baggage of the well-born"; I, 267: a lack of horses prevented further transport of the soldiers' baggage; and I, 351.

kon of the soldiers" that they asked and received permission to seize the fort themselves.[32] Both of these examples, distant from one another in time, show that occasionally the servants in the army could be given light military tasks (capturing the unfortified part of a city or a fort manned by peasants) and that they formed a group distinct from the regular military forces. Moreover, since servants are never mentioned as participants in field battles, they should be distinguished from the infantry divisions, regular or irregular, that made up a large portion of the campaign army. Indeed the two episodes cited above were noted by our historians for the very reason that such military participation by servants was extraordinary.

The passage from Akropolites notes that the servants with Vatatzes' army were paid "by the soldiers." Servants did not so much follow the army as they followed the particular soldier who paid them. Since the soldiery varied greatly in their economic and social positions, some soldiers could afford more servants than others. Servants were not only a visible status symbol but were needed by their master to transport and supply the quantity and quality of food, arms, horses, wardrobe, and housing corresponding to his station. Naturally, the servants of those whom Kantakouzenos calls the "illustrious" and the "well-born" were the most numerous and highly visible, but Kantakouzenos' tendency to speak of "those serving the soldiers" suggests that servants were not the exclusive monopoly of the aristocracy.[33]

One can only guess the number of oiketai that accompanied a soldier or leader on campaign, but in a labor-intensive economy, that is, one in which labor is cheap, one should not think the numbers small. Wealthy aristocrats may have had dozens; well-paid mercenaries and pronoia soldiers like Maroules, Sabentzes, and Berilas, with their pronoiai of 70 to 80 hyperpyra, probably one or more. Poorer mercenaries and marginal pronoia soldiers had perhaps one, probably none. The bulk of the infantry

32. Akropolites, 75. Quite a few etymologies have been offered for the rare word *Tzouloukon*: Heisenberg in Akropolites, 307 (from the Slavic *sluga*); Mutafčiev, "Vojniški zemi," 625 (from *tzakon*); and Ch. Symeonides, Οἱ Τσάκωνες καὶ ἡ Τσακωνιά (Thessaloniki, 1972), 84–85 (from the Turkish *çoluk*). Cf. the modern Greek *tsoulochia*, "riff-raff." For a few other derivations, see S. Caratzas, *Les Tzacones* (Berlin, 1976), 131 note 1. The word is also found, with a figurative usage, in a letter of the metropolitan of Naupaktos John Apokaukos: J. Apokaukos, ed. S. Pétridès, in *Izvestija Russkogo arheologičeskago instituta v Konstantinopole* 14 (1909), 15, line 9. The grandfather of a paroikos is designated ca.1300 as "Tzouloukon" (a name or an occupation?): P. Lemerle et al., *Actes de Lavra* (Paris, 1970–82), II, no. 91, iii, lines 83–85; and cf. no. 109, lines 756–58. Further, the word is used in a pejorative sense in an anonymous demotic poem: W. Wagner, *Carmina Graeca medii aevi* (Leipzig, 1879), 293, 294, cited by Caratzas, *Les Tzacones*. Kantakouzenos, I, 144.

33. Akropolites, 122. Kantakouzenos, I, 279, 362, 475.

certainly had none. No doubt soldiers with only one or two oiketai had relationships with them much different from those the wealthier soldiers had with their more numerous servants. The sole oiketes of a single soldier had to perform a wide variety of tasks that could have been divided among the servants of a wealthier soldier. Naturally such a servant enjoyed a closer relationship with his master, perhaps commonly doubling as both military retainer and domestic servant.

Among the mass of soldiers I do not think there was a great distinction between those oiketai who were military retainers and those who were domestic servants. Further, even though there is absolutely no evidence for it, it is possible that most pronoia soldiers customarily had servants who campaigned as military retainers. One always needs to keep in mind both the type of soldier the typical pronoia soldier was—heavily armed cavalry—and the status of a man given an imperial writ providing him an income. A horse soldier with an official income of around 70 hyperpyra per year easily could have afforded to maintain one or two military assistants, as well as one or two domestic servants, assuming he paid them, directly or indirectly, 1/2 to 1 hyperpyron per month for the six months or so he might be called to campaign. These men would have been useful to him and would have confirmed his status. During the off-season such oiketai might have fulfilled other functions in the soldier's household or had other occupations.

It is not difficult to imagine the precariousness of the position of some of these oiketai. The oiketes who followed his master from home was the most secure. Even if his master was killed, he could probably return home. But the man who had sought out the army in search of employment as a domestic servant or military retainer was in a different position. He might not find work and, even if he did, it would disappear should his newly acquired master be slain or captured. Victories and defeats directly influenced the well-being of oiketai. The former meant booty requiring the transport services of additional servants; the latter meant lost masters, captured servants, and other servants scrambling to find new masters. The man unsuccessful in acquiring a new master had few options. He could quit the campaign; he could continue to tag along with the army, hoping employment would materialize and, in the meantime, sustaining himself by whatever opportunity for plunder presented itself; or, particularly if he had been a military retainer, he might join the light infantry (it is in this sense that one can think of a relation between the oiketai and the foot troops). None of these alternatives was without its risks.

In summary, a great man on campaign was accompanied by oiketai—military retainers and domestic servants—whom he personally maintained. The number of these oiketai probably did not exceed a few dozen, and this only in the case of the wealthiest of men. Middle-level military pronoiars probably had a few. The poorest soldiers, that is, foot troops and lesser mercenaries, smallholding soldiers, and companies of pronoiars, in all likelihood had none. Moreover, there appears to have been no obligation on any military person to campaign with military retainers. The system of military retainers was informal, based on custom and the perceived needs, wealth, and status of the possessor of retainers. Finally, there is insufficient evidence to conclude that anyone campaigned with and commanded anything that could reasonably be considered a private army.

11. The Campaign

There were two kinds of campaigns, those that could be carefully planned and those that could not. The planned campaign was a major enterprise usually months in the making and designed to expel an enemy from an entrenched position. The other kind, the emergency campaign, was undertaken as a rapid response to an enemy incursion. Naturally, the planned campaign was preferred because it afforded the benefits of an offensive posture, allowed the full preparation of the campaign army, and permitted one to choose the moment. The traditional season for planned campaigns began in March and extended through autumn and into December. The winter months were avoided because of the difficulty in traveling and in providing the army shelter from the elements. So risky were winter campaigns that it was stock praise to commend a general for awaiting neither spring nor summer to fight.[1]

Normally campaigns were not begun in the fall. When they were, the size of the campaign army was limited. In September 1341, announcing his plans for a fall campaign against Epiros, Kantakouzenos told his lieutenants, "I shall take the mercenaries of the army and the strongest of those holding incomes from villages, so that when the western army joins [us], I shall march to the west in the winter, permitting the others to spend time home and to prepare themselves for the campaign which shall take place in the spring" in the Morea. Thus, this campaign army was to be composed only of mercenaries and the most financially solvent pronoiars. The majority of pronoiars remained behind, where "cleansing their arms, they reequipped themselves and procured horses more and better than those before." In March, after they received their semi-annual payments from their paroikoi, these pronoiars would have been ready to campaign.[2]

---

1. References to the campaign season: *Chronicle of the Morea*, ed. J. Schmitt (London, 1904), vv. 4961–5006, 5043; Kantakouzenos, I, 136; II, 82, 185, 193; Gregoras, I, 561; II, 663; Akropolites, 46; N. Gregoras, *Correspondance de Nicéphore Grégoras*, ed. R. Guilland (Paris, 1927), 84.

2. Kantakouzenos, II, 81, 64, and cf. I, 488, 493. Mutafčiev, "Vojniški zemi," 548.

Since most of the army lived in the provinces, a certain amount of time was needed to muster a campaign army. For emergencies one had to trade size for rapidity of deployment. For example, Andronikos III was unable to assemble all his soldiers to counter a Mongol invasion in 1324 "for they were disbanded to the cities and each guarded his own" city. In 1329 Andronikos decided to fight the Ottoman emir Orhan in Anatolia, but he was able only to "assemble the army together from Byzantium [Constantinople], Didymoteichon, and Adrianople—for it was not possible to call the [army] from Macedonia and the rest of the west." According to Gregoras most of this expeditionary force consisted of peasants. Moreover, in 1334 we encounter "the emperor leading part of the Roman army through Macedonia—for most was still in preparation because the campaign had come up quickly."[3]

Presumably the amount of time required to muster all or part of the army varied considerably depending on the efficiency of provincial administrators, the morale of soldiers in the provinces, and the weather. In one particular case, Kantakouzenos (I, 136) notes that the time needed to muster the army from the area of Thrace and at least eastern Macedonia was about two weeks: "Just now spring began, about the beginning of the month of March, and letters were sent by the young emperor toward the provinces under him, ordering the army to appear in Didymoteichon by the fifteenth of" the month.

The sources provide very little information regarding the actual process of mustering. Kantakouzenos (II, 58) writes that in 1341 he "ordered the soldiers by city through letters to prepare themselves should it be necessary to wage war against the Bulgarians." Since letters could not have been sent to each individual soldier, the commander-in-chief had to rely on the provincial administration. Generally speaking, there were two levels of provincial administration, the theme and the katepanikion. The latter with its local kephale was probably not the direct recipient of an order to muster because every indication is that the necessary records, at least in regard to pronoiars, were kept in the main town of each theme. Hence the letters must have gone first to the administrative centers where the records were located, thus illustrating one of the areas in which the thematic administrative system was still useful. Doubtless the letters contained instructions for local officials that specified, depending on the kind of campaign the em-

3. Kantakouzenos, I, 136, 189, 342, 455. Gregoras, I, 433. And see Kantakouzenos, I, 179. Oikonomidès, "A propos des armées," 355. U. Bosch, *Kaiser Andronikos III. Palaiologos* (Amsterdam, 1965), 152–53.

peror had in mind, whether they should try to recruit new soldiers or simply muster all or part of those with a military obligation.

Evidently, then, when the emperor wished to gather the troops living in the provinces, he sent messengers to the major towns in each province (for example, Thessaloniki, Serres, Vizye, and a few others), ordering the troops to assemble at a particular place and time. Local officials in these towns then checked their records and notified the soldiers. On whom the responsibility lay at the provincial level and the actual mechanism of the mustering process are not very clear. Presumably the kephalai of major towns (Thessaloniki, Serres, Vizye, and so on) were involved, but it is uncertain whether the kephalai of lesser towns played any part at all. In the Morea the process seems to have been similar. George Sphrantzes once recounts how he fulfilled Despot Constantine Palaiologos' order to muster the Morean army in 1429: "We issued orders to all those in the region of Androusa to come on March 15 of the same year with their weapons and most of their men of the jurisdiction [*arche*] of each of them." The Ottomans seem to have adopted a similar system, perhaps through Byzantine influence. Administratively the Ottoman Empire was divided into *sancaks* or "banners": in the mid-fifteenth century there were twenty in Anatolia and twenty-eight in Europe. Orders transmitted to the governor of each sancak were then relayed to each of the local *timar* holders.[4]

Probably not all of the soldiers with an obligation to perform military service (*stratiotike douleia*) campaigned at any one time. For example, some imperial mercenaries certainly remained to garrison Constantinople, and lower-level pronoiars who were garrison soldiers normally did not campaign. Certainly there had to be some kind of arrangement that made clear who was supposed to muster. While there are no extant documents that hold any particular man liable for campaign service or that inform civic or state officials that a particular man was supposed to serve, there obviously had to be some kind of listing with the names of those who owed military service, one copy held by the emperor, another by local officials of a theme or of a town (in the case of semi-independent towns such as Ioannina).

In fact the literary sources do mention something called the "military roll" (*stratiotikos katalogos*), an expression with a long history. In ancient Athens the "military roll" was the list of men fit for military service (Thucydides 6.43 and 7.16). In the middle Byzantine period the expression could be

4. G. Sphrantzes, *Georgios Sphrantzes, Memorii 1401–1477*, ed. V. Grecu (Bucharest, 1966), 28. F. Babinger, *Mehmed the Conqueror and His Time* (Princeton, N.J., 1978), 444.

used figuratively to denote the army in general, but the expression also had a literal sense. There actually was a written list in which were inscribed the names of the smallholders who personally or whose properties bore a military obligation in regard to the thematic armies. A soldier's name was probably found on two lists, one held by authorities in the soldier's theme and one master list kept in Constantinople by the *logothesion tou stratiotikou* (literally, "military bureau").[5]

In the late period it is not clear that any such "list" really existed. Pseudo-Kodinos says that the official who ostensibly should have been in charge of it, the logothetes *tou stratiotikou*, had no function in the fourteenth century. The phrase "those of the military roll(s)," applied to both pronoia soldiers and soldiers in general, was most commonly used simply to distinguish soldiers from the "best," the "well-born," and the "senate."[6] Since the phrase only appears in literary sources, one may doubt whether there actually was such a list for all soldiers or for pronoia soldiers in particular.[7]

In fact the late Byzantine fiscal process speaks against there being such a master list of soldiers. By the tenth century holders of military lands in the themes had their lands registered in "military ledgers" (*stratiotikoi kodikes*).[8] A single set of lists were then used to keep track both of those who owed military service and of the disposition and tax burdens of a significant portion of the arable land within the Empire. One copy of these lists, or cadasters, was kept for military lands and another for "public" lands (those on which there was no military obligation burdening the owners). However, beginning even as early as the ninth century and rapidly gaining momentum in the tenth and eleventh centuries, there was a tendency for the holders of military lands to commute their military obligation for a monetary payment and for the lands of small landowners in general to gravitate toward larger landowners. In the long run this led, on the one

5. H. Glykatzi-Ahrweiler, "Recherches sur l'administration de l'empire byzantin au IXe–XIe siècles," in Ahrweiler, *Études sur les structures administratives et sociales de Byzance* (London, 1971), no. VIII, 7, 10. J. Haldon, *Recruitment and Conscription in the Byzantine Army c. 550–950* (Vienna, 1979), 44, 46, 50, 60, 63–64.

6. Pseudo-Kodinos, 184 and cf. 322. Skoutariotes in Akropolites, 286; Gregoras, I, 205; Kantakouzenos, II, 58, 84; III, 260. Cf. Gregory II, of Cyprus, in S. Eustratiades, ed., «Τοῦ σοφωτάτου καὶ λογιωτάτου καὶ οἰκουμενικοῦ πατριάρχου κύρου Γρηγορίου τοῦ Κυπρίου Ἐπιστολαί», Ἐκκλησιαστικὸς Φάρος 4 (1909), 119, no. 159. Mutafčiev, "Vojniški zemi," 532 note 53.

7. But see Kantakouzenos, I, 287–88, and Mutafčiev, "Vojniški zemi," 530.

8. A. Toynbee, *Constantine Porphyrogenitus and His World* (London, 1973), 135, and Haldon, *Recruitment and Conscription*, 33, 42, 49–50, 63–64.

hand, to the emasculation of the old thematic armies and, on the other, to the transformation of the Byzantine free peasant into a semi-dependent peasant who generally farmed both his own small holding and the domain land of a large landowner.

By the thirteenth century this transformation was more or less complete. The commuted military obligation burdening the properties of certain peasants had simply become another type of tax with no relation to military service. For the purposes of taxation the regional lists of property holdings (*kodikes*) were supplanted by the praktika, individual inventories of the holdings of large landowners. Each landowner, or landholder, held a praktikon listing the lands he owned, or held, the taxes on these lands, and the dependent peasants (*paroikoi*) who worked his domain lands along with their movable and landed property and the taxes owed the state on these. There were at least two copies of a praktikon. One was held by the individual landowner as proof of his possessions, and another was held by thematic officials as a record of the tax burden on the landowner and his paroikoi.

Stratiotika ("military") praktika were the praktika held by stratiotai, that is, military pronoiars. Since the holders of military praktika owed military service, a possible way to muster military pronoiars was to consult provincial tax records. Once provincial officials received word to muster military pronoiars, they may have gone to a file marked "Military Praktika," and contacted everyone holding such a praktikon. In this way there would have been no need for a military list distinct from the praktika. However, none of the extant military praktika mentions any military obligation or any service obligation whatsoever. This indicates that there had to be either some other general law that stated the military obligations of military pronoiars, or a specific document directed toward each military pronoiar stating his personal service obligation, or, less likely, a firmly established customary set of military obligations for military pronoiars that made it possible to do without any written statement.[9]

In favor of the first possibility we have a chrysobull for Ioannina from 1319 stating that the only people owing military service outside the town were those stratiotai "reckoned in the ranks of the allagia and holding an oikonomia."[10] Such a passage in conjunction with a military praktikon might have gone a long way toward ensuring that a particular military pronoiar living in Ioannina campaigned when summoned. For the second

---

9. Cf. N. Oikonomidès, "Contribution à l'étude de la pronoia au XIIIe siècle," in Oikonomidès, *Documents et études sur les institutions de Byzance* (London, 1976), no. VI, 173.

10. MM, V, 81, lines 19–20.

possibility we have a number of imperial acts directed toward individuals which say that the sons of a particular pronoiar may inherit the grant as long as they render "the service [*douleia*] owed by them" or "the service appropriate" to the contents of the grant.[11] When the recipient of the act was a soldier, the "service" was evidently military service. In others, such as acts that appointed someone kephale, the "service" involved was not merely personal military service, but the service of a civil governor and military commander.[12] Further, other documents do mention "state service" (*demosiake douleia*) which is what kephalai and tax collectors performed.[13] Thus, since *douleia* meant any state service—civil, military, and perhaps even the labor services peasants traditionally owed the state—it could not in itself have ensured "military" service.

Of course, military pronoiars and also smallholding soldiers knew who they were and knew at least roughly what their military obligations were. Yet one might think that in a society sufficiently concerned with legal form to state explicitly, in the praktika, the obligations of paroikoi to their lord (kind, amount, number, and date of payments), there was some statement somewhere of the precise obligations of each type of soldier. The obvious issue is number of days of required service, and for this there is no evidence.

In any event, letters were sent and those with a military obligation assembled at the determined place. Other men without a military obligation came too. Some, who served as retainers and servants, accompanied the soldiers or arrived independently. Others, primarily light-armed infantry, were recruited specifically for the campaign from among the peasantry and urban poor or appeared unbidden. A campaign was an event, and the number of people who finally arrived at the point of assembly probably exceeded by many times the number of pronoia soldiers, smallholding soldiers, and mercenaries.

After the army began its march, others joined it, particularly if the

---

11. F. Dölger, "Ein Chrysobull des Kaisers Andronikos II. für Theodoros Nomikopulos aus dem Jahre 1288," in Dölger, Παρασπορά (Ettal, 1961), 191–93. P. Lemerle, *Actes de Kutlumus*, rev. ed. (Paris, 1988), no. 20. N. Oikonomidès, *Actes de Docheiariou* (Paris, 1984), no. 27. P. Lemerle et al., *Actes de Lavra* (Paris, 1970–82), III, no. 149. F. Dölger, *Aus den Schatzkammern des Heiligen Berges* (Munich, 1948), no. 11. Ostrogorsky, *Féodalité*, 124–30.

12. Mutafčiev, "Vojniški zemi," 569. Ostrogorsky, *Féodalité*, 180–86. P. Magdalino, "An Unpublished Pronoia Grant of the Second Half of the Fourteenth Century," *ZRVI* 18 (1978), 157, line 8. S. Lampros, Παλαιολόγεια καὶ Πελοποννησιακά (Athens, 1912–30), IV, 108. MM, III, 173, 174–76, 227 (= Lampros, Παλαιολόγεια, IV, 105; III, 331–33; IV, 194). S. Kougeas in Ἑλληνικά 1 (1928), 373–75 = Lampros, Παλαιολόγεια, IV, 21.

13. MM, IV, 261, lines 3–5. E. Branouse, Βυζαντινὰ ἔγγραφα τῆς μονῆς Πάτμου, I (Athens, 1980), no. 12, line 13. A. Guillou, *Les archives de Saint-Jean-Prodrome* (Paris, 1955), no. 19, lines 15–16. Lj. Maksimović, *The Byzantine Provincial Administration under the Palaiologoi* (Amsterdam, 1988), 121, 231.

campaign proceeded successfully. This occurred most commonly during the civil wars. For example, in 1343 the citizens of Verria "welcomed [Kantakouzenos' army] and they readily opened the gates and presented themselves for military service most eager for honor and without expenses." Other cities followed suit and "in a short time the emperor assembled an army not small from the submitting cities" of Thessaly. John Angelos, appointed governor of Thessaly by Kantakouzenos, "led the Thessalian cavalry."[14]

The emperor led the army whenever he himself chose to campaign. Some, such as John Vatatzes, Andronikos III, and John VI Kantakouzenos, spent much of their time in the field, personally participating in most of their expeditions. Others such as Michael VIII and Andronikos II rarely or never took the field, preferring to delegate the authority. In the Morea the despots themselves usually led their armies, unless the emperor was visiting. In theory, when the emperor was not present, the campaign army was commanded by the megas domestikos (grand domestic), a title that under the Komnenoi originally signified the commander-in-chief of the army. According to Pseudo-Kodinos, the megas domestikos ordered the trumpet signal that began the march and assembled the troops for review by the emperor. Even when the emperor was with the army, the megas domestikos was permitted to deploy his own banner first.[15]

Nicaean and Palaiologan megaloi domestikoi did tend to be military leaders: Andronikos Palaiologos (Michael VIII's father), John Palaiologos (Michael VIII's brother), Alexios Philes, Michael Tarchaneiotes, Alexios Strategopoulos, and of course John Kantakouzenos. Nevertheless, as was the case with nearly all late Byzantine titulature, the correspondence between title and function was far from complete. There were famous generals who led major campaigns but were not megaloi domestikoi (for example, the pinkernes Alexios Philanthropenos), as well as megaloi domestikoi who never led armies (Andronikos and George Mouzalon, and Andronikos Palaiologos Kantakouzenos). Generally, there is truth in L.-P. Raybaud's observation that "the *basileus* [the emperor] and the megas domestikos affirmed more the theoretical than the real unity of the Byzantine high command."[16]

14. Kantakouzenos, II, 355. Cf. Gregoras, II, 657, and Kantakouzenos, II, 392; III, 127.

15. Zakythinos, *Despotat*, II, 140. A. Hohlweg, *Beiträge zur Verwaltungsgeschichte des östromischen Reiches unter den Komnenen* (Munich, 1965), 93–108. Angold, *Byzantine Government*, 183–85. R. Guilland, *Recherches sur les institutions byzantines* (Berlin and Amsterdam, 1967), I, 405–17. Pseudo-Kodinos, 248.

16. Angold, *Byzantine Government*, 184–85. D. Nicol, *The Byzantine Family of Kantakouzenos (Cantacuzenus) ca.1100–1460* (Washington, D.C., 1968), no. 68. L.-P. Raybaud, *Le*

Of all the men in the officer corps, far and away most is known about those at the highest level, the commanders of armies. The overwhelming majority of military commanders were drawn from the relatively small number of families that made up the late Byzantine aristocracy. Thus, the names Angelos, Aprenos, Asen, Glabas, Kantakouzenos, Kavallarios, Makrenos, Monomachos, Mouzalon, Palaiologos, Philanthropenos, Philes, Raoul, Strategopoulos, Synadenos, Syrgiannes, and Tarchaneiotes account for nearly all the military commanders. They also account for most of the aristocrats. Some families produced a disproportionate number of military leaders. Of the thirty-odd commanders mentioned in Part I of this study, the families of Asen, Palaiologos, Raoul, and Tarchaneiotes account for about half. Conversely, there were relatively few distinguished families without members who were military leaders. The families of Tornikes, Metochites, Choumnos, and Tzamplakon were not known for their military exploits, though indeed some of their members held military-sounding titles.

Those who held positions of command usually had a close relation to the emperor, a result of the personalization of late Byzantine government. The megas domestikos, then sevastokrator, then despot John Palaiologos and the sevastokrator Constantine Palaiologos were brothers of Michael VIII. The father of the great general Alexios Philanthropenos was a nephew of Michael VIII. The military commanders Michael and John Tarchaneiotes were Andronikos II's first cousins. The pinkernes John Angelos was John VI Kantakouzenos' cousin, and Kantakouzenos himself, as well as Theodore Synadenos, was a close friend of Andronikos III.

The families of military commanders were closely intertwined with the emperor's family and those of other military commanders. There is the case of the military commander Alexios Raoul, a son-in-law of a brother of John Vatatzes. He had a son, John, who married a niece of Michael VIII, and a grandson, the megas domestikos Alexios Raoul; both were commanders. Another member of the family, Demetrios Palaiologos Raoul, was a general in the Morea under Despot Theodore I. Then there was the military commander Andronikos Palaiologos Asen, a son of John Asen III of Bulgaria, Andronikos II's nephew, and John VI's father-in-law. He was the father of two military commanders: the megas primmikerios, then sevastokrator, then despot Manuel Komnenos Raoul Asen, and the sevastokrator, then despot John Asen, both brothers-in-law of John VI Kantakouzenos.[17]

Since military and civilian leaders tended to be drawn from the same pool of men and were bound not only through class affinities but through familial relations, one does not find the kind of distrust between military leaders and government authorities characteristic of other societies or even of Byzantium in its earlier centuries. Rather, rifts within the aristocracy occurred along family lines through tensions between the most distinguished families and between the most distinguished families and parvenus.

The commanders of armies had titles that corresponded to their exalted status but not necessarily to their military responsibilities. This can be seen by listing in order of precedence the most distinguished titles held by the military commanders mentioned in Part I: despot, sevastokrator, caesar, protovestiarios, megas domestikos, protostrator, megas stratopedarches, megas primmikerios, megas konostaulos, pinkernes, parakoimomenos, protovestiarites, megas hetaireiarches, tatas of the court.[18] From despot to megas konostaulos, these represent nine of the top twelve titles after that of emperor, but only about five of these titles (megas domestikos, protostrator, megas stratopedarches, megas konostaulos, and perhaps megas hetaireiarches) corresponded to a military function by origin.

Certainly not all military commanders were highborn. We know nothing of the family of the eunuch Andronikos Eonopolites, who, though a military commander, had the relatively low (and obscure) title of tatas of the court. Yet Eonopolites' case is a relative rarity. To identify men of truly modest status one must move on to officers at the second tier, those who commanded parts of armies. These men are not well documented in the sources, but it seems that their abilities rather than their family connections determined their rise or fall. A man named Hierax played a significant role in the civil wars between Kantakouzenos and John V as he shifted from one side to the other. At one point he was appointed governor of the town of Černomen yet his career began as an oiketes (servant or retainer) of Andronikos III. An even better example is Tagaris, a man, we are told, of low

---

17. S. Fassoulakis, *The Byzantine Family of Raoul-Ral(l)es* (Athens, 1973), nos. 5, 6, 13, 46. *PLP*, nos. 1489, 1506, 1499.

18. I have added the title of protovestiarites held by a man named Aprenos who died in battle while reportedly commanding 5,000 men against Bulgaria in 1279: Pachymeres, ed. Failler, I, 589; *PLP*, no. 1206.

origin but who, because of his military prowess, became a megas stratope-darches and married a niece of Andronikos II.[19]

We know little of the selection process or the type of men who held positions at the lowest levels of the officer corps, at what today we would call the company and platoon levels. Common sense would suggest that because ethnically Byzantine troops were often organized in units accord-ing to their region of origin, lower-level officers probably had some geo-graphical affinity with their troops, at times rising through the ranks like Constantine Margarites (Appendix, no. 6) who "achieved top rank in the theme of Neokastra." Indeed ethnic troops seem to have been commanded generally by men of their own ethnic group. Thus the Christianized Turk Nikephoros Rimpsas commanded the Turkish forces during the Thessalian campaign of 1273; the leader of the Cretan mercenaries who fought under Alexios Philanthropenos at the end of the thirteenth century was a Cretan named Chortatzes; in 1302 the Alans who had abandoned the Catalans and the Tourkopouloi were led by the Bulgarian Vojisil and "their own com-manders"; and in the Morea, the Albanian troops serving the despots were commanded by leaders of their own race.[20]

According to Pseudo-Kodinos there were a number of officers subor-dinate to the megas domestikos. The titles of three of them, the protostra-tor, the megas droungarios of the watch, and the judge of the army, existed for a long time prior to 1204. Four more, the megas konostaulos, the megas adnoumiastes, the megas stratopedarches, and the *epi tou stratou*, all seem to have been created during the second half of the thirteenth century. How-ever, even a cursory examination of the individuals who held these titles shows that any correspondence between title and function was at best very erratic and often merely coincidental. There were two reasons for this. First, given the fluid nature of the late Byzantine central administration, officeholders, drawn from a rather limited pool of aristocrats, tended to move from position to position as needs dictated, without concern for the literal meaning of the titles they held.

Second, by the thirteenth century the old distinction between office and court rank had almost completely disappeared and a single hierarchy of precedence arose. Consequently, the hierarchical value of a title was more

---

19. *PLP*, nos. 6713, 8108. A. Laiou, "The Byzantine Aristocracy in the Palaeologan Period," *Viator* 4 (1973), 139.

20. Pachymeres, ed. Failler, I, 425; Bonn ed., II, 221, 223, 523. Zakythinos, *Despotat*, II, 139.

important than the function the title literally implied. A man who served the emperor well enjoyed several promotions during his career, each accompanied by a title higher than the preceding one. Perhaps it was possible at times to grant him a title that suggested his function, but this was not the purpose of court titles. They were intended primarily to signify symbolically the emperor's estimation of a man's value in relation to others. A title was less indicative of a man's duties than of the importance of his duties, the quality of his performance, the availability of particular titles (each title could be held only by a very limited number of men, if not by only one), and the emperor's judgment of his worth, always taking into consideration the egos of other titleholders.

Therefore, Pseudo-Kodinos' descriptions of the duties of military officers tells us neither the real titles of campaign officers nor the real duties of those who held these titles. Nevertheless, Pseudo-Kodinos is useful for the *functions* he describes, because these confirm a commonsensical appraisal of campaign needs and, although a particular function had little relation to any formal title, the functions indeed were performed by one or more men on campaign.

We begin with the megas konostaulos ("grand constable") who Pseudo-Kodinos writes was "chief of the Frankish mercenaries." It seems this was true only in regard to the first megas konostaulos, Michael Palaiologos, for whom the title was evidently created in the last years of John Vatatzes' reign, borrowed perhaps from the Normans of Sicily.[21] Apparently the creation of this office was one more recognition of the great importance of Latins in the Nicaean army. Later megaloi konostauloi, such as Andronikos Tarchaneiotes who was given this title simultaneously with his appointment as governor of the region of Adrianople in the early 1270s, had little to do with leading Latins. The title also became an appropriate honor to bestow upon minor foreign leaders with whom the emperor was allied.[22]

21. Pseudo-Kodinos, 175. Angold, *Byzantine Government*, 187–88. Geanakoplos, *Emperor Michael*, 26. D. Polemis, *The Doukai* (London, 1968), 157. Guilland, *Recherches*, I, 471–74. Raybaud, *Gouvernement*, 241–42. Pachymeres, ed. Failler, I, 37, 79 (Bonn ed., I, 21, 54). See also P. Karlin-Hayter, "Notes sur le ΛΑΤΙΝΙΚΟΝ dans l'armée et les historiens de Nicée," *Byzantinische Forschungen* 4 (1972), 142–50. On the Seljuk title of *kundistabl*, see A. Bombaci, "The Army of the Saljuqs of Rūm," *Istituto orientale di Napoli, Annali*, n.s. 38 (1978), 363.

22. Pachymeres, ed. Failler, I, 417–19 (Bonn ed., I, 322). A. Papadopulos, *Versuch einer Genealogie der Palaiologen, 1259–1453* (Speyer, 1938), no. 23. Guilland, *Recherches*, I, 472. See Nicol, *Byzantine Family*, 64, 76, and no. 12; and Zakythinos, *Despotat*, II, 61 note 2. Latins with the title: Pachymeres, ed. Failler, I, 413 (Bonn ed., I, 413); Geanakoplos, *Emperor Michael*, 236f., 295–300; *PLP*, no. 8154; Kantakouzenos, I, 517; A. Solovjev and V. Mošin, *Grčke povelje srpskih vladara* (Belgrade, 1936; repr. London, 1974), no. 32, lines 3–6.

"The megas adnoumiastes of the army," again quoting Pseudo-Kodinos, "conducts roll call in the presence of the megas domestikos. If any of those [soldiers] should lack horses or arms, he inventories the things lacking and tends to their replacement." The title itself may be derived from the Latin *ad nomen*, "by name." It first appears in 1290, and the known megaloi adnoumiastai were frequently provincial fiscal officials.[23] The megas adnoumiastes George Katzaras was in charge of the Varvarenoi soldier company, and it is possible that there was a connection between the title and Katzaras' function.[24]

Whether this process of replacing arms actually took place during campaign is unknown. As a matter of fact, given the paucity of horses during the late period, a commander generally would have been able to do precious little for a soldier who lost his mount. A cavalryman without a horse probably became an infantryman.[25] It would then be left to his own initiative and resourcefulness to figure out how to rejoin his mounted comrades.

Whereas very little is known about the replacement of arms and horses during campaign, a bit more can be said about the issuance and return of arms and horses at the beginning and end of a soldier's employ. Here we recall Pseudo-Kodinos' statement that if a mercenary should die childless, his arms and war horse were to be returned to the megas domestikos. Aside from the implication that mercenary service was hereditary, Pseudo-Kodinos was suggesting that the equipment of mercenaries was the property of the army, or of the state, and that it was held by the soldier only conditionally. This information receives support from one important example. When the several thousand Alan warriors entered the Empire in 1301 and asked to join the army, Andronikos II hastily sent out tax collectors to Thrace and Macedonia to gather funds, weapons, and horses for the recruits. Supplied with this equipment they marched eastward with Michael IX, whom they soon abandoned. They returned to Constantinople and, after some negotiation, agreed to return the arms and horses to the emperor.

23. Pseudo-Kodinos, 250. W. Regel et al., *Actes de Zographou, I. Actes grecs, VizVrem* 13 (1907), suppl. 1, no. 12, line 18; L. Petit and B. Korablev, *Actes de Chilandar, I. Actes grecs, VizVrem* 17 (1911), suppl. 1, nos. 103, 104; Arkadios Vatopedinos, «Ἁγιορειτικὰ ἀνάλεκτα ἐκ τοῦ ἀρχείου τῆς μονῆς Βατοπεδίου», *Γρηγόριος ὁ Παλαμᾶς* 3 (1919), no. 24; Dölger, *Schatzkammer*, no. 37, among other references. See Guilland, *Recherches*, I, 594–96; Raybaud, *Gouvernement*, 240; E. Stein, "Untersuchungen zur spätbyzantinischen Verfassungs- und Wirtschaftsgeschichte," *Mitteilungen zur osmanischen Geschichte* 2 (1923–26), 53; and Hohlweg, *Beiträge*, 110–11.

24. Oikonomidès, "A propos des armées," 361 note 51.

25. As Mutafčiev, "Vojniški zemi," 613, 617–18, suggested.

Some Alans remained and these received "three nomismata per month in addition to the horses given to them which was ordained by the agreement."[26] Thus, the Alans were hired with the understanding that they were to receive horses and arms along with their regular pay, and it was at least the emperor's contention that they should return them if they left imperial service.

Although some mercenaries did receive their equipment from the emperor as Pseudo-Kodinos maintains, the practice was hardly universal. The unfortunate French mercenary who received a letter of introduction from Demetrios Kydones owned his equipment. When his pay fell in arrears, he sold his horse and was intending to sell his arms.[27] Moreover, there is no record that the Catalans received any kind of military equipment from the emperor. Evidently practices varied.

A parallel concern was the provisioning of victuals. According to Pseudo-Kodinos, "the megas stratopedarches is overseer of the necessities of the army, namely, food, drink and everything necessary." Since this title was created in 1255 for George Mouzalon, a man who never saw battle, it is fairly certain that the megas stratopedarches (literally, "grand camp leader") never had any such function, though indeed several known megaloi stratopedarchai were military leaders.[28] Yet soldiers on campaign must have been provided with some rations if strategic integrity and discipline were to be maintained. A commander could not expect each of his men to carry his own supplies or to possess the foresight, or the means, to set out from home with enough gold to keep himself fed. Thus, commanders had to depart with sufficient supplies or have secure methods of obtaining supplies while on campaign.

In the early Byzantine period mercenary soldiers (that is, most soldiers) received, in addition to their regular pay (*stipendium*) and irregular gifts (*donativa*), a maintenance allowance in kind (*annona*) as well as feed for their animals (*capitum*). In the eleventh century soldiers also had their pay supplemented by monthly rations (*siteresia*), fodder (*chortasmata*), and gifts (*dorea*).[29] In the late period some soldiers did receive rations to

26. Pseudo-Kodinos, 251. Pachymeres, Bonn ed., II, 307–308, 319–22, 420. Gregoras, I, 205. Laiou, *Constantinople*, 90.

27. D. Kydones, *Démétrius Cydonès correspondance*, ed. R. Loenertz (Vatican, 1956–60), II, no. 238.

28. Pseudo-Kodinos, 174. Angold, *Byzantine Government*, 184–86. Guilland, *Recherches*, I, 502–13. Stein, "Untersuchungen," 54. Raybaud, *Gouvernement*, 241.

29. G. Ostrogorsky, "Löhne und Preise in Byzanz," *BZ* 32 (1932), 303. Glykatzi-Ahrweiler, "Recherches," 7 note 2, 25 note 5, and see the source references on pp. 8 note 2, 12 note 3, and 24, as well as in Ahrweiler's study, *Byzance et la mer* (Paris, 1966), 149 note 2, 151 note 3.

supplement their other incomes, but since there were more categories of soldiers as well as a greater diversity in their economic and social circumstances, the situation was more complicated than in preceding centuries. The Alans, as mercenaries, received provisions and, as a kind of exception that proves the rule, the Catalans began their plundering on the pretext that "daily expenses" (that is, food) were not included in their contract. From this it may be concluded that it was not uncommon for mercenaries to receive daily rations, at any event lest they plunder.[30] As for pronoiars and smallholding soldiers, there is no evidence that these received rations, even though logic would suggest that some did, depending on their relative economic means. Soldiers wealthy enough to have entourages of servants accompanying them naturally provided their own provisions.

There were centrally located stores of provisions located in the fortified towns (*kastra*).[31] It seems that provincial governors (kephalai) were responsible for maintaining reserves of provisions to be used by locally stationed troops and by campaign armies passing through the particular territory. The kephalai were assisted in this task by means of an obligation called *mitaton*, a burden on the local population requiring them to sell provisions to officials and troops at a price below the prevailing market price.[32] In the late Byzantine period there were two kinds of mitaton—one for the kephalai themselves and one for the army—representing respectively the right of requisition for civil and military officials. Mitaton was an active burden in the thirteenth and fourteenth centuries, though it seems to have been imposed only intermittently. In the fifteenth century nothing is heard of it; instead a number of documents mention new levies in kind for the navy.[33] These were not mitata, that is, forced sales, but simple demands in kind newly created to provision the remains of the navy.

Normal remuneration and possible maintenance allowances were supplemented by plunder. The promise of booty could move wary troops against an imposing or unknown enemy, and the acquisition of booty could make mercenaries forget their pay was in arrears. Plunder was also a source

30. Gregoras, I, 222; III, 511. Pachymeres, ed. Failler, I, 635 (Bonn ed., I, 503); Bonn ed., II, 307.

31. See M. Nystazopoulou-Pelekidou, Βυζαντινὰ ἔγγραφα τῆς μονῆς Πάτμου, II (Athens, 1980), 242, line 15, and Angold, *Byzantine Government*, 193. Kantakouzenos, II, 243.

32. Maksimović, *Byzantine Provincial Administration*, 157–59, and M. Bartusis, "State Demands for the Billeting of Soldiers in Late Byzantium," *ZRVI* 26 (1987), 115–20.

33. Bartusis, "Billeting," 120–21. Ostrogorsky, *Féodalité*, 114–16, 359–60. N. Oikonomidès, "Le haradj dans l'empire byzantin du XVe siècle," in Oikonomidès, *Documents et études*, no. XIX, 685–86. Dölger, *Schatzkammer*, 89.

of pay for mercenaries. In 1344 after the town of Gratianoupolis had surrendered to him, Kantakouzenos was able to pay the 3,100 Turks who had joined his employ after coming to Europe to plunder. The art of plunder was a fundamental institution of Byzantine warfare from which all soldiers could profit. Pseudo-Kodinos writes that, "First, the fifth part of the booty by calculation is given to the emperor; second, [another fifth is given] by calculation to the megas domestikos of the whole army; and third, [the rest is given] by calculation to the lesser captains for the part [of the army] each commands." Pseudo-Kodinos was envisioning an orderly process in which the booty of a vanquished enemy was assembled and divided fairly with each soldier receiving his proper share. He even names the official he thought was responsible for settling disputes over plunder, the judge of the army.[34]

Kantakouzenos confirms Pseudo-Kodinos' testimony, while admitting that the division of booty was not always so organized. After Andronikos III's allies, the Turks of Umur Pasha, defeated and enslaved an army of Albanians in 1337, a great deal of booty in sheep, cattle, and horses was left behind for the Byzantine troops present. Kantakouzenos (I, 498) remarks that "earlier [in his experience] it had been the custom for the army, whenever it won more or less booty, that the best fifth was granted to the emperor, and after this an equal part to the megas domestikos as leader of the whole army; but this time they did not do the customary things." The men simply took what they wished, their actions undoubtedly beyond the control of their commanders. One could hardly expect late Byzantine troops, notorious for their lack of discipline, to remain aloof from the spoils when their fellow fighters the Turks were carrying off human plunder.

The late Byzantine army itself does not seem ever to have made slaves of prisoners. At one point Kantakouzenos notes that "it was the custom among neither the Bulgarians nor the Romans for one to enslave the other in raids." This evidence may be safely extrapolated to include Serbs as well as those captured in the civil wars and, from the evidence of the passage mentioned above, less-cultured races such as fourteenth-century Albanians. Byzantine defeats in Asia Minor afforded little opportunity to enslave Turks who, for their part, regularly employed captured Christian slaves as soldiers. Thus plunder generally was restricted to the horses, arms, and apparel

34. Kantakouzenos, II, 425–26. Pseudo-Kodinos, 184, 251. For the earlier period, see A. Dain, "Le partage du butin de guerre d'après les traités juridiques et militaires," *Actes du VIe Congrès international d'études byzantines, Paris 1948*, I (Paris, 1950), 347–54.

of the defeated enemy, as well as whatever baggage was left behind in the enemy camp, which might include grain, draft animals, and sometimes precious items.[35]

There were essentially two kinds of military plundering: the scavenging of battlefields as already described, and the pillaging of hostile countryside. The latter was clearly the more profitable and, as a military enterprise, always much less hazardous. Pseudo-Kodinos writes about this aspect of plunder when he offers his opinion about another high court title:

> The protostrator is defender of the plundering [corps]. Since these have neither rank-order nor banners of their own but are simply sent off irregularly, the protostrator, being behind them, defends them if they should find war. The protostrator receives his name because of this, because he himself is in advance of the whole army. It is customary for the protostrator to take from the animals plundered all the various things [evidently harness gear, goods, etc.] that are called *phytilia* [an otherwise unknown word].

The *Chronicle of the Morea* indicates that it was standard procedure to send out such "plunderers" (*koursatoroi*) ahead of the rest of the army. *Koursatoros* comes from the medieval Latin *cursarius*, from which the word *corsair* also is derived.[36]

However, there are problems with linking the protostrator to this procedure. First, the only officer who ever performed a function even remotely similar to "defending the plunderers" was an *epi tou stratou* mentioned in a passage from Pachymeres' history.[37] Moreover, the protostrator, first mentioned in the eighth century, was so-named not because he was "in advance of the army" (*proegeisthai . . . tou stratou*) as Pseudo-Kodinos claims, but because he was originally chief (*protos*, literally "first") of the *stratores*, a guard division attached to the imperial stables.[38] Thus it seems

---

35. Kantakouzenos, I, 171, 190; II, 256, 302. And see Bombaci, "The Army of the Saljuqs," 343–69.

36. Pseudo-Kodinos, 168, 173. *Chronicle of the Morea*, vv. 3670, 6652. For *koursoroi, chosarioi* ("hussars"), and similar terms for spies, scouts, and plunderers in the earlier centuries, see *Le traité sur la guérilla (De velitatione) de l'empereur Nicéphore Phocas*, ed. G. Dagron and H. Mihaescu (Paris, 1986), 251–54; and *Three Byzantine Military Treatises*, ed. G. Dennis (Washington, D.C., 1985), 153, 293, 303.

37. Pachymeres, Bonn ed., II, 624, 627. Laiou, *Constantinople*, 169. Other examples of such "guerrilla tactics": Pachymeres, Bonn ed., II, 271–72; Gregoras, I, 538.

38. Angold, *Byzantine Government*, 183. Raybaud, *Gouvernement*, 241. A. Heisenberg, *Aus der Geschichte und Literatur der Palaiologenzeit*, in Heisenberg, *Quellen und Studien zur spätbyzantinischen Geschichte* (London, 1973), no. I, 58. Stein, "Untersuchungen," 53–54. Hohlweg, *Beiträge*, 111–17. Guilland, *Recherches*, I, 478–90.

that in his desire to associate a concrete function with each of the titles he lists, Pseudo-Kodinos resorted to an erroneous etymology.

Nevertheless, the known protostratores did indeed tend to be military leaders, but this is probably because the protostrator occupied a very high position in the hierarchy of courtly ranks, eighth from the top in Pseudo-Kodinos' list. Of the seven higher ranks, four were reserved for close relatives of the emperor, and the other three, the megas domestikos, the protovestiarios, and the megas doux, were also held frequently by military leaders. This simply shows that military leaders received high honors.

Plundering hostile territory had two purposes. First, it harmed the enemy by wreaking havoc upon the tax base of his countryside and at the same time forced him to divert military resources in order to limit the scope of the plundering. Second, plundering the enemy's land was an effective means of supplementing the pay of troops, and when gold was in short supply, plunder often served as the primary source of pay. While many or most examples of military plunder during the late Byzantine period had some tactical value, all served as important sources of pay.

This is particularly evident in the instances of plundering during the civil wars, which, given the nature of the sources, provide most of the information about military plundering. In these cases, whenever the forces of Andronikos II or Andronikos III, of Kantakouzenos or Alexios Apokaukos, overran technically hostile but nevertheless Byzantine territory, the military advantages of plunder were completely outweighed by long- and shorter-term economic and political disadvantages.[39] It can hardly be denied that these leaders and their subordinates were aware of the repercussions of looting their own territory. Indeed Kantakouzenos (I, 134) writes that Andronikos III purposely disbanded his army at the end of 1321 so that it would not plunder the surrounding countryside. Nevertheless, some exigencies transcended political and fiscal considerations, and one of these was the need to satisfy the troops.

In some instances military plundering took place against the will of the commanders involved, but this cannot account for all or even most of the plundering of Byzantine territory. An army can scarcely remain a functional unit if it violates continually its commanders' orders. The late Byzantine army, despite all else, was always something more than a rabble. Perhaps it would be accurate to say that commanders frequently acquiesced to plun-

39. E.g., Kantakouzenos, I, 136–37, 140–41; II, 292, 381, 484.

der during the civil wars. Yet given the circumstances, there was not much difference between this and positive orders for plunder. Sometimes this method of "pay"—consisting of animals, grain, firewood, and military materials[40]—represented nothing less than the sole means of maintenance for the troops, plunder alone separating them from starvation. For example, lacking supplies and besieged by hostile forces, Kantakouzenos' garrison in Didymoteichon in 1342 was forced to plunder the countryside, refusing even to accept the surrender of neighboring towns.[41]

It seems that there were limits to acceptable plunder. While the Byzantine sources say nothing of this (except perhaps when they occasionally speak with disapproval of Turkish allied troops enslaving their captives), the Serbian Law Code of Stefan Dušan does address the issue, if only briefly and in regard to one specific case: "Whoever overturns a church on campaign, let him be slain or hanged."[42]

Few late Byzantine soldiers became rich through plunder. It was an incentive, a reward, a type of pay accepted at least temporarily in lieu of salary, or a means of subsistence, but it seems never to have changed the social position of its recipients. Soldiers remained soldiers, although with stomachs quieted and morale improved.

Once the campaign army was supplied with arms, horses, and food, the next requirement was a place to sleep each night. The choice of billeting had two aspects. One involved military considerations. The historian Akropolites, for example, writes that when Michael Palaiologos made camp he sought level ground with adequate pasturage. The other involved the rights of the owner of the land chosen for the campsite. If the army was in hostile territory, this concern was moot, but campaign armies usually had to cross friendly territory as well. Military necessity dictated that imperial armies camp in the most convenient and strategic sites, whether or not the particular landowner objected. Consequently, as early as the eleventh century privileged landowners, usually monasteries, in order to protect themselves, sought and often received exemption from *aplekton* ("camps," from the Latin *applicatum*) on their lands.[43]

---

40. Kantakouzenos, I, 137; II, 288, 305.

41. Kantakouzenos, II, 302–303, 349. For this and other examples of military plundering, see M. Bartusis, "Brigandage in the Late Byzantine Empire," *Byz* 51 (1981), 386–409. Also, see Gregoras, III, 511.

42. *Zakonik cara Stefana Dušana, 1349 i 1354*, ed. N. Radojčić (Belgrade, 1960), art. 130, pp. 67, 124.

43. Akropolites, 146. Bartusis, "Billeting," 121. For the middle Byzantine period, see Toynbee, *Constantine Porphyrogenitus*, 304–11.

In the late Byzantine period privileged monasteries and lay land-owners were exempted from aplekton in a half-dozen documents, dating from 1259 to 1310. During the second quarter of the fourteenth century the term nearly disappears and was replaced by *pezeuma* (from *pezos*, "on foot," and ultimately from *pedon*, "ground"), *pesimon* (from *pesein*, "to fall"), and similar terms, all of which meant "camp" or "camping." Like aplekton, they appear so infrequently that the burden must have been either rarely de-manded or rarely exempted. The latter was more likely the case since, by its nature, it would have been difficult to commute the burden for a cash payment and even more difficult to exempt it on a widespread basis. Since an army on the march had to camp on someone's land, a generally com-muted or exempted aplekton/pesimon is unthinkable. Logically, aple-kton/pesimon must have been an active burden for at least a significant number of landowners. In other words, the commander of a campaign army had the right to make camp on whatever land he pleased, unless a specific exemption had been granted on this land by the emperor.[44]

Pseudo-Kodinos writes that the *epi tou stratou* (literally, "in charge of the encamped army") picked the campsite. This title first appears in the early years of the fourteenth century and most of the men who held the title were military leaders, though their responsibilities far surpassed choosing a campsite.[45] After the site was selected, the wise commander immediately posted watch. As Pseudo-Kodinos writes, "Before leaving the army when it encamps the megas droungarios of the watch appoints that which is called the day-guard [*hemeroviglion*] as ordered by the megas domestikos," and he adds that it was customary to choose light-armed archers for this task. No evidence from the late period corroborates this information, and in fact only infrequently are any megaloi droungarioi of the watch (*tes vigles*) identifiable as military men at all.[46]

If the opposing army was nearby, this was the time to employ strat-agems to mislead and confuse the enemy. While encamped prior to the battle of Pelagonia in 1259, Michael VIII's commander the sevastokrator John Palaiologos ordered local peasants to light fires each evening and to ride their animals up the mountains to give the impression of cavalry.

---

44. Bartusis, "Billeting," 121–23.

45. Pseudo-Kodinos, 248–49. Guilland, *Recherches*, I, 527–28; Raybaud, *Gouvernement*, 240, 242; Stein, "Untersuchungen," 53. The title could be held by foreigners, e.g., Jean de Giblet: Kantakouzenos, I, 195; *PLP*, no. 6589; Laiou, *Constantinople*, 303 and note 79.

46. Pseudo-Kodinos, 249. Cf. Kantakouzenos, II, 559; Raybaud, *Gouvernement*, 239; Guilland, *Recherches*, I, 563–87; and Hohlweg, *Beiträge*, 59.

Everyone was instructed to raise a clamor, and some men were sent to the enemy camp to spread disinformation.[47]

Finally, there was a need for someone to adjudicate disagreements between soldiers. While the Byzantine sources say little of such matters, the Law Code of Stefan Dušan contains the following article: "On campaign no one should quarrel, [but] if two quarrel, let them fight, and no other soldiers should help them; if someone comes and helps the one calling out, let him be slain." Dušan recognized that while disputes between soldiers could not be prevented, the loss of discipline resulting from other soldiers joining the fray was intolerable. The situation was probably similar in Byzantium, although Pseudo-Kodinos claims that matters were a bit more organized. As usual he associates a particular officer with this concern: "When the emperor is with the army, the judge of the army [*krites tou phossatou*] arranges and straightens out the incidental affairs of soldiers relating to horses, arms, booty and the like." This title first appeared in the eleventh century, but it does not seem that late Byzantine judges of the army had any such function. In one of his epitaphs the poet Manuel Philes mentions a certain "slayer of barbarians" named Gabras Komnenos, "whom the most noble king [that is, the emperor] honored out of kindness with [the title] judge of the army." Philes viewed the title as an honor, as should we.[48]

Nevertheless, someone with the *function* of the judge of the army was needed during campaigns to settle disputes between soldiers and also to deal with endemic indiscipline. The teacher Theodore Hyrtakenos once complained to a high official about the drinking, gambling, and general indiscipline within the army: "Nothing is common to Hermes and Ares, an adage says. But it's worse when Hermes is subject to Dionysos." Criminal activity by soldiers was not uncommon. Soldiers in Constantinople were always available for factional struggles, and Kantakouzenos frequently speaks of the "disorder of the army" which, he says, had made reconciliation impossible between Andronikos II and Andronikos III. One episode, in which the emperor himself dealt with indiscipline, occurred after Kantakouzenos personally had managed to convince a number of marauding Turks to surrender. Just as they were laying down their arms, some of his troops, including Kantakouzenos' son-in-law and "other well-born

---

47. *Chronicle of the Morea*, vv. 3712–31.
48. *Zakonik cara Stefana Dušana*, ed. Radojčić, art. 131, pp. 68, 125. Pseudo-Kodinos, 184. Cf. Zakythinos, *Despotat*, II, 134 note 3, and O. Tafrali, *Thessalonique au quatorzième siècle* (Paris, 1913), 58. On the title, Guilland, *Recherches*, I, 528–29. M. Philes, *Manuelis Philae Carmina*, ed. E. Miller (Paris, 1855–57), I, 293, no. 106, lines 37–41.

youths," started to attack the disarmed Turks. "The emperor in anger separated his son-in-law and soldiers from the Persians, and he imposed punishment for the disorder."[49]

One of the most serious discipline problems was desertion. Sometimes soldiers felt they had served too long or too far from home. Other times they were exhausted, out of money, or they felt their commanders were not supplying their daily needs. Sometimes the factionalism of the civil wars led soldiers to abandon their commanders.[50] And of course individual soldiers had personal reasons for desertion. Generally, the greatest enemy of the campaign army was time. Pronoiars, who were expected to maintain themselves during campaign, could not stay with the army indefinitely.[51] Supplemental mercenaries, hired for the campaign, often abandoned the army at the end of their contractual period of service if more gold was not forthcoming (see Chapter 7). Those who farmed—smallholding soldiers and perhaps supplemental infantry—eventually had to return to their fields.

In order to minimize desertions, commanders employed a number of strategies. Preferably no artifice would be required: victory would come quickly and the army sent home. But such was not the character of fourteenth-century campaigns. On the contrary, they tended to be prolonged and, for the Byzantines, indecisive at best. So commanders turned to a panoply of incentives to maintain morale: the bestowal of honors, gifts, rewards, pay raises, and of course the promise of pay raises. Pronoiars might be given some pay to maintain themselves. Other methods included promising a fixed period or a limited area of service, or improving morale by granting soldiers adequate periods for rest and relaxation.[52] In Kantakouzenos' 1342 chrysobull for his nephew John Angelos, appointing the latter governor of Thessaly for life, Angelos' military obligations were "that in all the western lands, where my majesty should need them, he himself should serve with the whole army of Romans and Albanians. If my majesty should need [them] beyond Christoupolis [Kavalla], he himself should

49. T. Hyrtakenos, in F. La Porte-du Theil, ed., "Les opuscules et lettres anecdotes de Théodore l'Hyrtacènien," *Notices et extraits des manuscrits de la Bibliothèque Nationale* 5 (1798), 740, no. 22. Bartusis, "Brigandage," 396–99. Kantakouzenos, I, 96, 97, 149, and also, II, 84–87, and Gregoras, II, 586. Kantakouzenos, III, 66.

50. General desertion: Gregoras, I, 229; Kantakouzenos, I, 105; II, 241, 243, 246–47, 287, 293–94, 296, 331. Desertion after excessively long service: Kantakouzenos, II, 294, 331. Desertion due to factionalism: Kantakouzenos, II, 246–47.

51. Kantakouzenos, II, 365–66, 367. Oikonomidès, "A propos des armées," 354.

52. Pachymeres, Bonn ed., II, 483. Kantakouzenos, I, 88. Oikonomidès, "A propos des armées," 354–55.

serve with as much of the army as possible." While there can be little doubt that limiting the service of the Thessalians to the area west of Kavalla was an extraordinary concession granted in return for the allegiance and aid of the individualistic people of this region, the passage illustrates the problems a commander faced.[53]

Once all of these matters were attended to, the campaign army could make war. Before combat, troops were arranged in battle-order. In the *Chronicle of the Morea* this is expressed as "separating the allagia (or *syntaxeis*)." The number of allagia varied, once as high as twenty-seven, and it seems that the main purpose of the procedure was to divide the army into combat units differentiated by ethnic group and by mode of combat (horse and foot). This "separating" is also mentioned by Kantakouzenos and Gregoras but in their case the army was separated usually into three *taxeis* (or *syntaxeis* or *lochoi*).[54] At the battle of Peritheorion in 1345 in which Kantakouzenos defeated the rebel Momčilo there were three tagmata: John Asen took the left flank with the Byzantine heavy cavalry (*kataphraktoi*), Umur Pasha led the right flank with his Turkish archers, and Kantakouzenos himself held the center with "picked" (*logades*) Byzantine and Turkish troops. At the battle of Apros in 1305 there were five syntaxeis, differentiated by ethnicity: the Alans and Tourkopouloi in the van, followed by the Macedonians, the Anatolians, the Vlach infantry, and the Thelematarioi (who served as a rearguard), and the imperial taxis.[55] While *tagma* was an all-purpose word, it sometimes meant a very small group of soldiers, as in "selecting sixteen tagmata from the [army] present."[56] Kantakouzenos employs *phalanx* synonymously. In the *Chronicle of the Morea* the smallest group of soldiers is called a *syntrophia*, "company," but this sense of the word is not encountered in the Byzantine historians.[57]

The tactical divisions of the late Byzantine army, as well as the armies of its allies and adversaries, can be categorized as either horse or foot troops. Kantakouzenos most often describes a campaign army as "the foot and horse army" or "force" (*he peze kai hippike stratia* or *dynamis*).[58] This

53. Kantakouzenos, II, 322. On this chrysobull, see H. Hunger, "Urkunden- und Memoirentext: Der Chrysobullos Logos der Johannes Kantakuzenos für Johannes Angelos," *JÖB* 27 (1978), 107–25.

54. *Chronicle of the Morea*, vv. 644, 1137–38, 3665, 3700, 3710–11, 4015, 4657–63 (3 allagia = 1,000 kavallarioi), 6651. Gregoras, I, 485; II, 836–37. Kantakouzenos, II, 430.

55. Kantakouzenos, II, 532. Pachymeres, Bonn ed., II, 549–50.

56. Kantakouzenos, I, 97, 134, 261; II, 175, 246; III, 128.

57. Kantakouzenos, I, 465. Cf. Gregoras, II, 836. *Chronicle of the Morea*, vv. 5168, 5208.

58. E.g., Kantakouzenos, II, 301, 333, 381, 518; III, 135, 196, 228, 320. Cf. Kantakouzenos, II, 123, 334, 360; Akropolites, 116; and A. Makrembolites in A. Papadopoulos-Kerameus, Ἀνάλεκτα Ἱεροσολυμιτικῆς Σταχυολογίας (St. Petersburg, 1891), I, 153.

distinction between horse and foot was less an absolute classification of soldiers by training and competence than a simple recognition that because of the cost and accessibility of horses some soldiers would have them and some would not.[59] There is no reason to doubt that a soldier who lost his horse or horses in battle would serve on foot until he could buy or steal a replacement. Similarly it is unlikely that a foot soldier would shun any opportunity to acquire an animal, at least for transport. Further, the distinction corresponds to the method of fighting in that horse and foot fought in separate bodies. The "separation of the allagia" that took place before battles separated horse from foot and soldiers from noncombatants and also provided a rare opportunity for the commander to estimate the numerical breakdown of his forces.

As in most European armies during this period, cavalry (*hippeis*) was the most important component of Byzantine forces. Kantakouzenos usually describes the sizes of armies simply in terms of numbers of horse troops, even when foot troops were participating as well.[60] Likewise the sizes of Turkish, Serbian, and Bulgarian allied armies often are cited through numbers of cavalry alone. In regard to the army of the Latin Empire of Constantinople in the early thirteenth century, Benjamin Hendrickx has written that "the actual strength of the army was based on the number and quality of the cavalry and the mounted sergeants, while the others [crossbowmen, archers, etc.] were of less importance."[61] There were also times when a force contained only horse troops, particularly when speed of movement was required.[62] It is surprising, in light of the variety of terms Kantakouzenos employs when speaking of foot soldiers, that he rarely distinguishes horse troops by armament or quality. When he does, they are always "heavily armed" (*kataphraktoi*).[63] This contrasts with the cavalry contingents of foreign troops (the Cumans, the Alans, the Tour-

59. As Kantakouzenos, II, 392, 394, notes.

60. Kantakouzenos, II, 437.

61. Kantakouzenos, I, 295; II, 530; III, 111, 246, 248. B. Hendrickx, «Οἱ πολιτικοὶ καὶ στρατιωτικοὶ θεσμοὶ τῆς Λατινικῆς Αὐτοκρατορίας τῆς Κωνσταντινουπόλεως κατὰ τοὺς πρώτους χρόνους τῆς ὑπαρχεώς της», diss., Thessaloniki 1970, 148. Similarly, M. Mallett and J. Hale, *The Military Organization of a Renaissance State: Venice c.1400 to 1617* (Cambridge, Eng., 1984), 74–75, write that in the fourteenth century the Venetian infantry primarily served, in time of war, as a subordinate complement to cavalry.

62. Kantakouzenos, I, 277; III, 211.

63. Kantakouzenos, I, 108, 429; II, 356, 532; III, 64. Cf. Akropolites, 126. While Kantakouzenos usually regards the term *kavallarios* as an honor given to Latins, rather than a specific function (e.g., Kantakouzenos, II, 166, and cf. I, 204), the *Chronicle of the Morea* uses the term to denote the horse soldier (e.g., vv. 3696ff.) and frequently makes the distinction between kavallarioi and *elaphroi* (e.g., vv. 3586–607).

kopouloi and other Turks) which consisted of highly mobile light-armed archers.

The foot troops or infantry (*pezoi*) were divided into two groups, heavily and light-armed, for which Kantakouzenos and other authors use the classical terms *hoplitai* (or *to hoplitikon*) and *psiloi* (or *to psilon*).[64] *Hoplitai*, "hoplites," were usually present when an army was being transported by ship or was fighting aboard ship.[65] Occasionally hoplites formed part of a land army or a garrison, but their presence on land in at least one case was due to a lack of horses.[66] This suggests that "hoplites" could be either cavalry who lacked horses or were temporarily fighting without their horses, or well-equipped troops who usually fought on foot. From the number of references to "light-armed archers" (*psiloi toxotai*), it seems proper to classify native Byzantine archers as light-armed foot troops.[67]

Kantakouzenos occasionally qualifies troops, both foot and horse, Byzantine and foreign, with terms denoting high quality: *logades* and *epilektoi*, both of which are usually translated as "picked" or "select."[68] Often the words are applied to assemblies of troops whose consent was sought for some policy: "He gathered all the *logades* of the army and those in command."[69] *Epilektoi* and *logades* also could be applied to rather large forces numbering in the thousands.[70] Neither word seems to have had any technical significance.

It is not an easy task to estimate the sizes of late Byzantine campaign armies. There is simply not enough reliable data with which to work, though not for lack of figures. The sources, both Byzantine and non-Byzantine, offer many figures but often they are suspect. The data derived from narrative histories and chronicles are subject to several distorting

---

64. Pachymeres, Bonn ed., II, 624: *psilika tagmata*.

65. Kantakouzenos, III, 174. Cf. Makrembolites in Papadopoulos-Kerameus, I, 153. Other similar passages: Kantakouzenos, I, 373, 375; II, 253, 358; III, 283; and much later, Manuel II Palaiologos, *The Letters of Manuel II Palaeologus*, ed. G. Dennis (Washington, D.C., 1977), 102–103, no. 38. *Epibatai* is also used in this sense: Kantakouzenos, II, 345.

66. Land army: Kantakouzenos, I, 326; II, 253, 436. Garrison: Kantakouzenos, I, 140; II, 187, 129; III, 213. Lack of horses: Kantakouzenos, III, 120, 122–23, 128.

67. Gregoras, I, 319. Kantakouzenos, I, 326; II, 187, 253, 418. Also cf. Pseudo-Kodinos, 249; Pachymeres, ed. Failler, I, 223 (Bonn ed., I, 164); Kantakouzenos, I, 146, 173, 496; II, 282; Gregoras, III, 49; and Akropolites, 115, 120.

68. Kantakouzenos, I, 173, 255, 270, 301; II, 346; III, 88. *Epilektos* is Gregoras' favorite of the two: Gregoras, I, 221, 230, 257; II, 773, 851; III, 47. And cf. Makrembolites in Papadopoulos-Kerameus, I, 157. The *Chronicle of the Morea* prefers *eklechtoi* (e.g., vv. 3586ff., 4549ff.).

69. Kantakouzenos, I, 142, 110, 154. Cf. Akropolites, 42.

70. Kantakouzenos, II, 394, 430, 563, 584; III, 63.

influences. First, even if a figure was based on eyewitness testimony, modern problems in estimating crowd sizes show that even fair-minded observers can arrive at vastly different estimates. Second, partisan motives may have led authors to alter the perceived figure. For example, Kantakouzenos might have exaggerated the size of his forces to impress posterity with the grand forces under his command. Alternatively, he may have exaggerated even more grossly the size of enemy hosts to explain defeat or to prove, in victory, the courage of his troops or his ability as a general. Even when two sources offer similar figures, there is every reason to be skeptical. While the stated sizes of the Catalan army correspond in both the Byzantine and non-Byzantine sources (Pachymeres: 8,000; Muntaner: 7,000), both historians for reasons not difficult to discern had motives for exaggeration, if indeed there was not a common source for both figures. Further, literary style also comes into play. It is not reassuring that almost all the figures provided by Byzantine authors are round numbers and that almost all large figures are multiples of one thousand.

It seems that commanders did not have any official records at their disposal or, if they did, they were not of much use. At almost every moment in his career Kantakouzenos ought to have been the best informed authority on such matters, but in fact on two occasions he reports his uncertainty about troop strength. In 1334 during the campaign against Syrgiannes, some Turks attacked the Chalkidike peninsula. Andronikos III, "summoning the megas domestikos [Kantakouzenos], asked about the army encamped there, whether it seemed sufficient for combat with the barbarians. He answered that he did not know the number exactly." In a second example, at the outbreak of the civil war in 1321, Andronikos III "set out with a little less than 5,000 cavalry, as it was guessed, for it was not possible to know the number exactly, since many of those not enrolled in the army marched along to please the emperor." In this case even accurate official records would have been useless for estimating troop strength.[71]

Nevertheless, it is possible to provide some sense of the size of late Byzantine campaign armies by seeking simply an order of magnitude. To do this, we assemble a few lists of figures pulled from the histories of Kantakouzenos and Gregoras (Table C). The lists are not necessarily complete, but they do provide a range of figures. The data have been divided into serviceable categories (and are not intended to be absolute judgments

71. Kantakouzenos, I, 108, 455. In the second example, the text reads "50,000," but this cannot be accepted, as the editor, who suggested "5,000," pointed out.

TABLE C. Comparative troop strengths compiled from the histories of Kantakouzenos and Gregoras

Kantakouzenos			Gregoras
Byzantine Forces			
I	108	5,000	
		3,000	I 485
II	563	3,000	
		3,000	I 255
II	253	2,000	
		2,000	II 628
		2,000	I 433
I	255	1,300	
		1,000 + 60	III 177
II	605	1,000	
II	404	1,000	
		1,000	II 839
I	301–302	500 + 200 + 100 / 800	I 422
II	296	500	
III	228	300 / 500	III 151
		300	I 353
I	475	300	
I	270	300	
III	88	300	
II	232	300	
I	277	200	
		20 + 40 + 60	I 540
II	188	60	
II	429	60	
Allied Forces			
		10,000	I 204
		4,000	I 149
I	177	3,000	
I	259	2,000	
I	35	2,000	
		2,000	I 268
Turkish Forces—Allied or Enemy			
II	344	29,000	
III	148	24,000	
II	530	20,000	
III	111	20,000	
III	248	10,000 / 12,000	III 181

III	32	10,000	
		8,000	I 434
		8,000	I 548
II	394	6,000 + 200 / 6,000	II 676
III	324	5,000 / 4,000–5,000	III 564
II	426	3,100	
		2,000	I 545
III	63	2,000 / 1,200	II 836
I	427	1,500	I 427
II	416	1,000	II 416
		1,000	I 229

Other Allied or Enemy Forces

I	189	120,000	
		10,000	I 430
		10,000	I 485
III	246	7,000 / 4,000	III 181
II	437	4,000	
I	295	3,000 / 3,000	I 418
II	532	1,500	
II	430	1,000	
II	584	1,000	
I	108	300	

about the troops involved): Byzantine troops, including whole armies and fractions of armies (it is often impossible to distinguish the two); foreign troops temporarily allied with Byzantium; allied or enemy Turkish troops (usually fighting on one side or another during the civil wars); and other allied or enemy troops (also on one side or another during the civil wars). Where Kantakouzenos and Gregoras offer parallel figures for the same troops, the two figures appear separated by a slash. References to each of the texts are provided to the left and right of each list.

In these lists 71 figures appear utilizing 27 discrete numerals. Since the six numerals that appear more than three times account for 38 (54 percent) of the figures, Kantakouzenos and Gregoras clearly preferred particular numerals. These are 10,000 (five times), 4,000 (four), 3,000 (six), 2,000 (eight), 1,000 (eight), and 300 (seven).[72] This is not surprising. Nor is it

72. The two historians had similar preferences. Calculated individually, of the seventeen numerals Gregoras employs, the five most frequently occurring (10,000, 4,000, 3,000, 2,000, 1,000) account for 16 (55 percent) of his twenty-nine figures.

surprising that the largest forces reported by Kantakouzenos and Gregoras were Turkish, and that the sizes of other non-Byzantine forces on the whole fell between those of Turkish and Byzantine forces. However, it is interesting that the sixteen highest figures (from 6,000 to 120,000) were all non-Byzantine forces. The highest Byzantine force strength cited is 5,000, and this involved the case where Kantakouzenos admitted it was only a guess. After this the commonly occurring sizes for a large Byzantine campaign force are 3,000, 2,000, and 1,000. This allows us to conclude that the largest campaign armies the late Byzantines fielded, in the fourteenth century at least, numbered no more than a few thousand men.

Other fourteenth-century figures also point to the small size of campaign armies. In a letter John V Palaiologos once asked Pope Innocent VI for 500 cavalry and 1,000 infantry, and Kantakouzenos notes that a relatively major expedition to Chios in 1329 brought along 300 mounts for the cavalry. One source that offers quite interesting figures for troop sizes is the *Chronicle of the Tocco*, in which hostile Turkish forces number in the tens of thousands, allied Turks and hostile Greeks in the high hundreds, and local forces in the low hundreds. Some encounters in fact involved mere dozens of men.[73]

We have no sources as detailed as Kantakouzenos and Gregoras with which to make a satisfactory estimate of the size of thirteenth-century Byzantine armies. Very few figures are available from the Nicaean era. Nevertheless, early Nicaean armies must have been quite small, for Villehardouin, the chronicler of the Fourth Crusade, asserts that at the battle of Poimanenon in 1204, the army of Theodore I Laskaris was defeated by a force of 140 knights plus an unknown number of mounted sergeants. Indeed, according to Hendrickx, the entire cavalry force of these knights' lord, the Latin emperor of Constantinople Baldwin of Flanders, numbered only in the hundreds, something between 500 and 1,000. The only reliable figure for the size of a Nicaean army is furnished in regard to the battle of Antioch in 1211: 2,000 including 800 Latin mercenaries. Otherwise the main historian for the period, Akropolites, like Kantakouzenos and Gregoras, displays an affinity for the numerals 300 and 500 when describing smaller units.[74]

73. A. Theiner, F. Miklosich, *Monumenta spectantia ad unionem* (Vienna, 1872), 30. Kantakouzenos, I, 375. G. Schirò, ed., *Cronaca dei Tocco di Cefalonia* (Rome, 1975), vv. 435, 3189 (hostile Turks); v. 743 (allied Turks); v. 3908 (hostile Greeks); vv. 2419, 3553, 3889 (locals), and cf. vv. 2767, 2786, 2800.

74. Villehardouin, *La conquête de Constantinople*, ed. E. Faral, 2 vols. (Paris, 1938–39), 319–20. B. Hendrickx, "A propos du nombre des troupes de la quatrième croisade et de

The battle of Antioch was a Seljuk defeat, resulting in the death of the sultan, yet the principal source for the history of the Seljuks of Rum, the late thirteenth-century history of Ibn Bibi, provides a wide range of figures for the sizes of Seljuk armies, all of which are dramatically larger than 2,000: 5,000 soldiers, 14,000 cavalry, 50,000 cavalry, 60,000 soldiers, 70,000 cavalry, and 100,000 soldiers. Evidently these are wild exaggerations. Similarly a feeble Georgian source claims a total of 800,000 troops in the Seljuk army, and the Western traveler Simon de Saint-Quentin offers the figure 11,000.[75] It is the fundamental impossibility of establishing acceptable estimates of the numbers of troops during battles that precludes satisfactory discussion of the effectiveness of late Byzantine armies.

With the reign of Michael VIII the reported sizes of Byzantine armies become substantially larger, and scholars have occasionally drawn the reasonable though incorrect conclusion that Michael assembled armies that dwarfed those of his immediate predecessors and even his successors. This misleading impression is due to the nature of the sources for his military activities, primary among which are the *Chronicle of the Morea* and the history of Pachymeres. The *Chronicle*, written from a Latin perspective, speaks of the size of Byzantine forces the way Kantakouzenos and Gregoras speak of the size of Turkish armies. For example, when recounting the battle of Prinitza in 1262, the *Chronicle* states (in three passages) that the Byzantine army, composed of 15,000, 18,000, or 20,000 troops, was set to flight by a mere 300 or 312 Franks.[76] The sizes offered for the Byzantine force are worthless but the figure of 300 Franks is notable. If it had any basis in reality, the Byzantine forces could not possibly have numbered more than a few thousand or they would have walked over the Franks. In fact, prior to the battle the *Chronicle* (vv. 4618–34) reports that the Byzantine leader, the parakoimomenos Makrenos, sent word to Michael VIII that with more men the entire Morea could be conquered. In reply Michael authorized him to hire a *thousand* more soldiers. If this figure is no exaggeration, then the *Chronicle* missed an opportunity to overstate the vastness of the Byzantine forces in the Morea.

Most of Pachymeres' figures are suspect, especially when he had no

l'empereur Baudoin I," Βυζαντινά 3 (1971), 29–41. Akropolites, 16. Gregoras, I, 18–19. Angold, *Byzantine Government*, 182, 191.

75. Bombaci, "The Army of the Saljuqs," 345–46, 349, 353, 359, 362. Simon de Saint-Quentin. *Histoire des Tartares*, ed. J. Richard (Paris, 1965), 64.

76. *Chronicle of the Morea*, vv. 4700, 4897, 5011, 5501. For the general view of the sizes of Michael's armies, see, e.g., Angold, *Byzantine Government*, 192.

firsthand knowledge of the relevant operation. Sometimes this can be demonstrated. Prior to the battle of Pelagonia, King Manfred of Sicily sent Michael of Epiros some aid, which according to Akropolites and the Venetian chronicler Sanudo consisted of 400 German cavalry. Pachymeres, however, raises this figure to 3,000.[77] Another instance involves the army and fleet Michael VIII sent against Thessaly in 1273. According to Sanudo the army was composed of 30,000 cavalry; according to Pachymeres, the land and naval forces amounted to 40,000 troops. While the land army was laying siege to Neopatras, John I of Thessaly escaped from the town and quickly obtained some extra troops from John de la Roche, ruler of Athens and Thebes. With these troops, John I launched a surprise attack against the besieging Byzantine forces who abandoned the siege and dispersed. What casts both Sanudo's and Pachymeres' figures for the total size of the Byzantine force into doubt is the reported number of troops with which John I broke the siege. Pachymeres speaks of 300 troops, Gregoras of 500 cavalry. Even if we accept Gregoras' figure of 500 and estimate that there were but 20,000 troops besieging the town (the other 20,000 being with the fleet), John I's success in the face of a forty-to-one inferiority in troop strength would be nothing less than miraculous. But Pachymeres was no fool. His citation of unreasonably high figures for the Byzantine troop strength was deliberate. As is often the case in his history, he provides a moral for this incident: the powers of reason (the alleged cleverness of John I) will outdo brute force every time.[78]

Pachymeres' numbers cannot be accepted at face value. When he later speaks of 10,000 soldiers taking part in a campaign against Bulgaria in 1279, we are justified in being skeptical. Medieval armies were very small. Consider the reported number of troops (probably exaggerated as well) that participated in two major thirteenth-century battles in Italy. At Montaperti in 1260 the Florentine army was composed of about 1,600 cavalry and about 14,000 infantry, and at Campaldino in 1289 the Tuscan Guelf League led by Florence fielded 1,600 cavalry and about 10,000 infantry, while the Ghibelline army led by Arezzo was composed of 800 cavalry and 8,000 infantry. Further, it is beyond credulity that Michael VIII could have assembled 30,000 or 40,000 troops of any sort when the thirteenth-century kings of France could only raise some 700 cavalry.[79] We must also remember that

77. Akropolites, 168. M. Sanudo, *Istoria del regno di Romania*, ed. C. Hopf in *Chroniques gréco-romanes* (Berlin, 1873), 107. Pachymeres, ed. Failler, I, 117.

78. Sanudo, *Istoria*, 121. Pachymeres, ed. Failler, I, 421, 423–27. Gregoras, I, 114.

79. Pachymeres, ed. Failler, I, 589 (Bonn ed., I 466). M. Mallett, *Mercenaries and Their Masters* (London, 1974), 12, 14, 21, 116–20, for the sizes of some fifteenth-century Italian armies.

the highly centralized, expanding Ottoman state of Mehmet II, in area over twice the size of Michael VIII's dominion, assembled far less than 100,000 troops, perhaps as few as 60,000, for the singular occasion of the siege of Constantinople in 1453, and as many as half of these were irregular troops enticed by the thought of booty.

The lack of reliable figures for the sizes of Byzantine armies continues throughout the first half of Andronikos II's reign. The *Chronicle of the Morea*, the only source for the siege of Ioannina in 1292, claims that the Byzantine force consisted of 30,000 infantry and 14,000 cavalry. Since it also reports that news of the approach of the prince of Achaia Florent of Hainault with 400 or 500 men led to a disorganized withdrawal with Florent pursuing the Byzantines into southern Macedonia, we may disregard these high numbers.[80]

Gregoras writes that the Alans who entered the Empire in 1301 numbered more than 10,000; Pachymeres provides the figure 16,000, although he adds that only half were warriors. Such figures are ultimately no more worthy of credence than those of the anonymous Western author of the *Advice for an Overseas Passage* who claims that Michael IX had 14,000 cavalry plus a great deal of infantry at the battle of Apros in 1305, and 10,000 when he was defeated by the Turks of Halil in 1310. Most unbelievable is a chronicle entry from 1320 which claims that "the Morean army" (*to Moraïtikon phousato*) was composed of 36,000 men. We recall that at this same moment Andronikos II was briefly entertaining plans to hire another 3,000 mercenary cavalry through vigorous efforts at raising taxes. In sum, though Michael VIII's armies, amassed at a time when the fortunes of the Empire were temporarily in the ascendant, were indeed probably larger than anything the Byzantines could field in the early fourteenth century, we still must think only of thousands and not tens of thousands.[81]

The 1320 chronicle entry for the size of the Morean army is characteristic of the reported sizes of the armies in that distant province. None can be accepted for the simple reason that there is no evidence that any emperor ever received or even requested transfers of Morean troops to other parts of the Empire. An Italian source claims that Theodore I's army at the siege of

---

C. Bayley, *War and Society in Renaissance Florence: The* De Militia *of Leonardo Bruni* (Toronto, 1961), 3. C. Gaier, "Analysis of Military Forces in the Principality of Liège and the County of Looz from the Twelfth to the Fifteenth Century," *Studies in Medieval and Renaissance History* 2 (1965), 221–24, 228.

80. *Chronicle of the Morea*, vv. 8791–93, 9086.

81. Gregoras, I, 204. Pachymeres, Bonn ed., II, 307–08. *Directorium ad faciendum passagium transmarinum*, ed. C. Beazley in *American Historical Review* 13 (1907–1908), 80. P. Schreiner, *Die byzantinischen Kleinchroniken* (Vienna, 1975–79), I, 242. Gregoras, I, 317–18.

Corinth in 1395 consisted of nearly 20,000 troops. Another Italian source asserts that John VIII and Theodore II in 1417 marched against Centurione Zaccaria of Achaia with 10,000 cavalry and 5,000 archers. An anonymous memoir of the Council of Basel from 1437 reports that the Morea had thirty large cities, 200 strong fortresses, and 4,000 towns, and was governed by three brothers of the emperor who together could furnish 50,000 cavalry, not counting infantry. In 1439 the Western writer Jean Torzelo in his *Advis* to Philip the Fair of Burgundy claimed that there were 15,000 men under the emperor in the Morea. And finally, we have the historian Doukas' report that 60,000 Albanians and Greeks were defending the Hexamilion at the Isthmus of Corinth in 1446. The absurdity of this figure can be demonstrated by noting that if this many men were to stand shoulder-to-shoulder, they could form a phalanx six miles long (the length of the Hexamilion) and four men deep.[82]

There are a few ways to obtain some idea of the size of the army without relying on the figures provided directly by the sources. One is to calculate the maximum number of troops the Empire could support based on imperial finances. To determine the maximum possible number of mercenaries, one divides the state military budget by average mercenary pay. As shown earlier in Chapter 7, with the Venetian ducat as the standard, infantry pay ranged from 1.9 to 5.2 ducats per month, or an average of around 3.6 ducats per month. For the yearly outlay for a permanent mercenary, we might multiply this figure by ten (since governments usually tried to underpay mercenaries), arriving at 36 ducats per year. If mercenary cavalry received four times average mercenary infantry pay, then the average pay rates for mercenary cavalry and infantry were respectively 144 and 36 ducats per year. Earlier I also calculated the military budget of the Empire in the 1320s as between 100,000 and 150,000 hyperpyra per year. Using the higher figure this would be about 100,000 ducats per year.[83] On a permanent basis this sum could finance, for example, 1,111 mercenaries, half horse and half foot, or 347 mercenary cavalry and 1,389 mercenary infantry. If fewer per-

82. L. LeGrand, "Relation du Pèlerinage à Jérusalem de Nicolas de Martonia, notaire Italien (1394–1395)," *Revue de l'Orient latin* 3 (1895), 657. Zakythinos, *Despotat*, I, 181, citing a passage from the *Cronica Dolfina* in N. Iorga, *Notes et extraits pour servir à l'histoire des Croisades au XVe siècle* (Paris and Bucharest, 1899–1915), I, 267 note 3. S. Lampros, «Ὑπόμνημα περὶ τῶν ἑλληνικῶν χωρῶν καὶ ἐκκλησιῶν κατὰ τὸν δέκατον πέμπτον αἰῶνα», *Νέος Ἑλληνομνήμων* 7 (1910), 364. Baron de Reiffenberg, *Monuments pour servir à l'histoire des provinces de Namur, de Hainaut et du Luxembourg*, V (Brussels, 1848), 542, inaccessible to me, cited, as all the other references in this note, by Zakythinos, *Despotat*, II, 136–37. Doukas, 279.

83. Using the exchange rates in T. Bertelé, "Moneta veneziana e moneta bizantina," *Venezi e il Levante fino ad secolo XV* (Florence, 1973), I, pt. 1, 41–42.

manent mercenaries were hired, correspondingly more temporary troops would be available for campaigns. Considering that many of these troops would have served in garrisons, one or two thousand soldiers is not an unreasonable estimate for the size of the mercenary element within the campaign army.

To approximate the size of the pronoiar contingent within the army, one would divide the state revenues set aside for financing military pronoiars by the value of a typical military pronoia grant. But since we have no idea how much state revenue was reserved for pronoiars, this calculation is impossible. Nevertheless, there is a way to get some idea of how expensive pronoia soldiers were. Nicolas Svoronos has calculated that in the early fourteenth century the yearly income of Lavra, the wealthiest monastery on Mount Athos, and possibly the largest single landowner in Macedonia (other than the state), was about 12,000 hyperpyra.[84] Let us imagine an audacious Andronikos II, contemplating the utter confiscation of all of Lavra's holdings for the sake of increasing the pronoiar contingent of the army. How many new pronoia soldiers could have been financed? If we use 200 hyperpyra as an average true value of a pronoia, we divide and see that through the dissolution of the largest monastery of Athos, Andronikos could have financed another sixty soldiers. This suggests that there could never have been more than several hundred pronoia soldiers in late Byzantium at any one time. If we add these several hundred pronoiars to the couple of thousand mercenaries, and include even a couple of thousand smallholding soldiers, the figure obtained for the number of imperial soldiers (excluding paramilitary guards and local soldiers) residing in the Empire during the first half of the fourteenth century could have been no larger than 5,000. Since only a portion of these campaigned together at any one time, this figure is consistent with the numerical evidence of the literary sources.

Another way to estimate the army's size is to examine casualty reports. At times casualty figures are ridiculous. Gregoras reports that Andronikos III with three unarmed triremes and Kantakouzenos with seventy cavalry once attacked a large group of marauding Turks, seizing fourteen enemy ships, killing 1,000 Turks and capturing 300, all without losing a man. Gregoras was not an eyewitness to this battle, nor was Kantakouzenos with Umur Pasha's troops in 1342 when he reports that 500 died of exposure during a single night. Still, Umur's army was quite large, and it is more than

84. Lemerle et al., *Lavra*, IV, 171.

likely that as in most armies throughout history the majority of campaign casualties did not result from battle. Indeed, Kantakouzenos once notes that 1,500 of his soldiers died from a single episode of food poisoning.[85]

When Kantakouzenos was actually on the scene, the figures for casualties from hostile action are quite low. The following list presents the casualty figures offered by Kantakouzenos (and in one case by Gregoras) of killed (k) and wounded (w) in several military encounters (NA = no report):

siege of Apros, 1322 (Kantakouzenos, I, 140)

Andronikos III's	vs.	Andronikos II's partisans
NA		1 k, many w

siege of Philippopolis, 1323 (Kant., I, 175)

Byzantines	vs.	Bulgarians
3 k, many w		none k, many w

battle of Mauropotamos, 1328 (Gregoras, I, 415)

Andronikos II	vs.	Andronikos III
	10 k, in all	

preliminary skirmishing and battle of Pelekanos, 1329 (Kant., I, 347–62)

Byzantines	vs.	Turks
none k or w		40 k
none k or w		30 k
1 k, a few w		50 k
none k or w		150 k
1 k		more than 400 k
45 k		NA

85. Gregoras, I, 540–41. Kantakouzenos, II, 347–48; II, 293.

35 k   NA
47 k   NA

encounter with Mongols, 1331 (Kant., I, 467)

Byzantines   vs.   Mongols
  37 + 65 k or captured   NA

capture of Verria, 1350 (Kant., III, 126)

Byzantines   vs.   Serbs
  1 k   none k or w

capture of Vodena, 1350 (Kant., III, 129)

Byzantines   vs.   Serbs
               none k or w

Except for the battle of Pelekanos and the encounter with the Mongols, the casualty figures make the episodes appear to be minor events, certainly not struggles to the death. The figures Kantakouzenos offers for the Byzantine casualties at Pelekanos and at the Mongol encounter are precise enough to suggest some degree of accuracy. Both encounters were major Byzantine defeats. Therefore, if a couple of hundred dead constituted a serious defeat, the total force could not have numbered more than a couple of thousand. One may conclude that some planned campaigns might have numbered a few thousand, but most planned campaigns and all emergency campaigns probably involved hundreds rather than thousands of troops.

At the conclusion of a campaign, whether successful or unsuccessful, the soldiers were sent home. Disbanding the army was as important a concern as the initial assembly and campaign itself. As Kantakouzenos explains, Andronikos III disbanded his army at Didymoteichon prior to the winter of 1321–22 because he did not want them plundering the surrounding countryside that was under his control. An army was a volatile creature, at best with a large appetite, at worst without a conscience, and unless there was an enemy against which to direct it, the wise commander scattered it. On the other hand, the decision to disband an army had to be well thought out because once the order to disband was given, a repetition of the entire mustering process was required in order to reassemble it. The only soldiers who remained behind were the imperial mercenaries. Sometimes when a future campaign was already in the planning stage, the emperor ordered the troops to return on a particular day, thereby making the mustering process more orderly.[86]

The soldier returning home might discover that his financial and personal affairs had gone awry during his absence. The respite from campaigning was a time to reorganize these and settle disputes that had arisen while he was away. The Serbian Law Code of Stefan Dušan contains an article that attempted to make the soldier's homecoming less stressful: "When a lord or someone who was a soldier arrives home from the army, if someone summons him to court, let him remain home three weeks, then go to court."[87]

Like Agamemnon, the soldier who spent much time on campaign might find that family relationships were difficult to maintain. In a few thirteenth-century legal cases involving adultery the husbands claiming injury can be identified as soldiers (Appendix, nos. 11–13), and in one case we are told the alleged incident of infidelity occurred while the husband "was away from home at camp." Another case, decided by the metropolitan of Naupaktos John Apokaukos, involved the "*megalodoxotatos* most obedient *kyr* Manuel Monomachos," who claimed his wife had committed adultery with a servant. Apokaukos reacted with repugnance at Monomachos' demand that the wife undergo the ordeal by hot iron, and his comments provide us with one ecclesiastic's opinion of the soldierly temperament: "For the soul of a soldier who knows nothing of law and who, as everyone knows, is bold by profession and deems his own will law, is generally difficult to change in such matters, and even when it listens it is mulish and hard to persuade."[88]

---

86. Kantakouzenos, I, 134, 146, 329; III, 20, 63–64, 116.
87. *Zakonik cara Stefana Dušana*, ed. Radojčić, art. 61, pp. 54, 106.
88. J. Apokaukos, in A. Papadopoulos-Kerameus, ed., «Συνοδικὰ γράμματα Ἰωάννου τοῦ Ἀποκαύκου, μητροπολίτου Ναυπάκτου», Βυζαντίς 1 (1909), 27–28.

12. Palace Guard, Garrisons, Borders

Not all soldiers campaigned, or rather, the primary function of some soldiers was not campaign service. Many soldiers on a more or less fulltime basis guarded the palace and person of the emperor, the governmental centers of towns, or the frontiers of the Empire. Even though at times they did accompany the emperor on campaign, march outside the walls of their town to face an invader, or leave the frontier to serve elsewhere in the Empire, their organization, financing, and duties justify treating them separately from campaign troops.

The history of the palace guard is a convoluted tale characterized by a continuous evolution in the names and functions of guard divisions. Throughout the centuries guard divisions were created and disappeared; some grew in importance, others declined. Often the functions of guard divisions were modified, either as their duties within the realm of guard service were extended or as field troops were transferred to palace service. The resulting institutional structures and distinctions became quite complex.

During the tenth and early eleventh centuries the emperor, the palace, and Constantinople itself were guarded by the Tagmata, the so-called household troops, assisted by various other divisions of imperial bodyguards and palace guards. By the reign of Alexios I Komnenos (1081–1118), most of these divisions had disappeared or faded into obscurity. The only two still attested at the time (called the Exkoubitoi and the Athanatoi) were supplemented by a couple of new guard divisions (the Vestiaritai and the Varangians), both organized as palace guard troops in the first half of Alexios' reign. After his death all these divisions disappear from the sources except for the Varangians, who, along with a new division called the Vardariotai, first securely attested during the latter part of the reign of Manuel Komnenos (1143–80), formed the palace guard of the later Komnenoi.[1]

1. N. Oikonomidès, *Les listes de préséance byzantines des IXe et Xe siècles* (Paris, 1972), 327–33. H. Glykatzi-Ahrweiler, "Recherches sur l'administration de l'empire byzantin aux IXe–XIe siècles," in Ahrweiler, *Études sur les structures administratives et sociales de Byzance* (London,

This relatively rapid evolution in the structure and composition of the palace guard has been noted by Armin Hohlweg.[2] He advanced three reasons for why guard divisions had a tendency to appear and to disappear: first, it was sometimes difficult for a guard division to adapt to a new ruler, and a new ruler might have decided it best to disband groups of questionable loyalty; second, there might have been difficulties recruiting guards for particular divisions (especially, perhaps, when a division had an ethnic basis); and third, a new emperor might have wished to create his own personal guard division. I would add a fourth reason: that there were not always sufficient financial resources to maintain all the existing guard divisions, a factor that has particular relevance for the men who guarded the persons and the palaces of the emperors after 1204.

Because of their proximity to the emperor, much more is known about the palace guards than the garrison troops of Constantinople or of any other urban centers of the Empire. Nevertheless, while several divisions of palace guards can be identified and differentiated by ethnicity, weaponry, type of service (foot or mounted), location of service post within the palace, and title of commanding officer, we cannot be sure of the relative importance of each palace guard division, their specific functions, or even their overall importance during the late Byzantine period. We have no information on the size of any palace guard division at any time during the thirteenth, fourteenth, and fifteenth centuries. At some moments, as in May 1328, when Andronikos II and his friend Theodore Metochites spent the night alone in the Blachernai palace with only a few servants, palace guards were entirely absent.[3]

In his treatise on the offices of the Empire, Pseudo-Kodinos speaks of five distinct groups of palace guards: the Varangians, the Paramonai, the Mourtatoi, the Tzakones, and the Vardariotai. From the numerous references to the Varangians in Palaiologan sources, these seem to have constituted the most visible, if not the largest division of palace guards. Russian and Scandinavian mercenaries had appeared in the army from the time of the first contacts between Russia and Byzantium in the ninth century, and the conversion of the Kievan state in 988 marked the beginning of the great

1971), no. VIII, 24–31. A. Toynbee, *Constantine Porphyrogenitus and His World* (London, 1973), 285–86. A. Hohlweg, *Beiträge zur Verwaltungsgeschichte des oströmischen Reiches unter den Komnenen* (Munich, 1965), 45–63.

2. Hohlweg, *Beiträge*, 61.

3. U. Bosch, *Kaiser Andronikos III. Palaiologos* (Amsterdam, 1965), 51. Laiou, *Constantinople*, 297.

age of the Varangians in Byzantium. By the early eleventh century regiments of Varangians were firmly established as an important part of the campaign army. Soon afterward they began to appear as palace guards with the task of guarding the person of the emperor. Gradually, beginning in the second half of the eleventh century, the Varangian guard lost its Scandinavian character as more and more Anglo-Saxons joined the regiment following the battle of Hastings. Perhaps by the end of the twelfth century, certainly by the thirteenth, the Varangian guard was more or less entirely English in composition. According to Pseudo-Kodinos, they voiced their acclamations of the emperor in English. Thus, by the thirteenth century, references to "Keltic bodyguards," "Keltic garrisons," and probably even "Kelts," should be regarded as allusions to the Varangians. Their weapon was always the famous two-edged axe (*pelekys*) carried on the right shoulder. Since they were the only troops who ordinarily carried axes, the sources often refer to them obliquely as "the imperial axe-bearers [*pelekyphoroi*]," "the imperial axe-bearing regiment," or "the Keltic axe-bearers."[4]

The function of late Byzantine Varangians changed somewhat from their earlier role in the Byzantine military. After the twelfth century they no longer took part in battle and their activities were restricted to guard functions proper, of which there were three. The first, of course, was as a group of imperial bodyguards. To this end, as Pseudo-Kodinos writes, "the Varangians are found serving at the doors of the bedchamber [*kellion*] of the emperor and in the reception hall [*triklinos*]." Gregoras reports that because of his firm faith in God, Andronikos III "spent his time unguarded for the most part, without the imperial axe-bearers" who nevertheless were present at his deathbed in 1341. In a letter from around 1360, Demetrios Kydones complained that Varangians in his day elicited bribes from those wishing to enter the palace: "a Varangian terrifies and demands payment for entry which is not owed for this." A function related to guarding the emperor is

4. Pseudo-Kodinos, 209–10, and also 342 note 5. Pachymeres, ed. Failler, I, 101, 145, 485, 615 (Bonn ed., I, 71, 103, 378, 486). Pachymeres, Bonn ed., II, 77. Gregoras, I, 303, 398, 566. R. Guilland, *Recherches sur les institutions byzantines* (Berlin and Amsterdam, 1967), I, 522. R. Dawkins, "The Later History of the Varangian Guard," *Journal of Roman Studies* 37 (1947), 43. The literature on the Varangians during the eleventh and twelfth centuries is extensive. See, e.g., A. Vasiliev, "The Opening Stages of the Anglo-Saxon Immigration to Byzantium in the Eleventh Century," *Seminarium Kondakovianum* 9 (1937), 39–70; J. Shepard, "The English and Byzantium: A Study of Their Role in the Byzantine Army in the Later XIth Century," *Traditio* 29 (1973), 53–92; Hohlweg, *Beiträge*, 46–50; and K. Ciggaar, "L'émigration anglaise à Byzance après 1066," *REB* 32 (1974), 301f. On the axe as a weapon, see T. Kolias, *Byzantinische Waffen: ein Beitrag zur byzantinischen Waffenkunde von den Anfängen bis zur lateinischen Eroberung* (Vienna, 1988), 162–72, esp. 165, 171.

mentioned by Kantakouzenos. In 1329, after the Genoese surrendered the city of Nea Phokaia to Andronikos III, the emperor ordered "the Varangians having the axes to carry the keys of the city—for it was the custom that these hold the keys of the cities wherever the emperor stayed." I have found no other evidence for such a custom, but apparently it was based on their role as bodyguards who stood at the door of the imperial bedchamber with authority to regulate admission.[5]

In at least one instance the Varangians also guarded imperial treasure. In the first clear reference to a reconstituted Varangian guard in the Nicaean era, "the axe-bearing Keltikon" guarded an imperial treasury at Magnesia in 1258. In that year Michael Palaiologos, as regent for John IV Laskaris and with the new title of megas doux, was given charge of this treasury, which he set about to appropriate for his own political ambitions. Evidently the guards felt they had substantial discretionary control over the treasury, for Michael had to persuade them to release the sums he wanted.[6]

If the Varangians of the late period had any one specialty it was prison guarding, at least during the reign of Michael VIII and the early portion of Andronikos II's rule, along with the related job of torturing individuals according to imperial order. A number of distinguished figures from the second half of the thirteenth century, including the patriarchs Arsenios and John Bekkos, wrote firsthand accounts of their mistreatment at the hands of Varangians. Pachymeres reports that in 1299 the "chief [*epistates*] of the rest of the guards who had many in his hands" in the palace prison in Constantinople was one "Erres ex Engklinon," that is, "Harry from the English," probably a Varangian.[7]

The commanding officers of the Varangians were called primmikerioi and there appear to have been a number of these, each commanding his own contingent of Varangians. For example, Theodore Diabatenos, an inhabitant of Ioannina around 1220, was "primmikerios of the Varangians

5. Gregoras, I, 566. Kantakouzenos, I, 560. D. Kydones, *Démétrius Cydonès correspondance*, ed. R.-J. Loenertz (Vatican, 1956–60), I, no. 46; German trans. in F. Tinnefeld, *Demetrios Kydones Briefe*, I, pt. 1 (Stuttgart, 1981), no. 44, and see p. 273 note 8. Kantakouzenos, I, 389.

6. Pachymeres, ed. Failler, I, 101, 97 (Bonn ed., I, 71, 68). Angold, *Byzantine Government*, 187. Geanakoplos, *Emperor Michael*, 43–44.

7. Migne, *PG*, 140, col. 956B. Pachymeres, ed. Failler, I, 485, 615 (Bonn ed., I, 378, 486). Pachymeres, Bonn ed., II, 103. A. Mai, *Novae patrum bibliothecae*, vol. 10 (Rome, 1905), 325, col. 2. Gregory II, of Cyprus, ed. S. Eustratiades, in Ἐκκλησιαστικὸς Φάρος 4 (1909), 110–13. Also, *Chronicle of the Morea*, ed. J. Schmitt (London, 1904), v. 4319; English trans. in E. Lurier, *Crusaders as Conquerors* (New York, 1964), 197, with a note; and Geanakoplos, *Emperor Michael*, 43 note 57, 65 note 79. On Harry: Pachymeres, Bonn ed., II, 73–74.

in Ioannina." At least in this instance, the primmikerios of the Varangians need not have been a foreign, first-generation Varangian himself. There is also a lead seal from the late period of a certain Michael, "grand interpreter of the Varangians," the only known appearance of this title. If it was not merely an honorific, it would support the notion that late Byzantine Varangians, like their middle Byzantine predecessors, were not Greek speakers.[8]

The last references to the Varangians come from around the turn of the fifteenth century. In 1395 a "universal judge" (*katholikos krites*) named Adam "from the Varangians" was visited at his home in Constantinople by a colleague who had come in search of a law book. This suggests that the close proximity of the Varangians to the imperial office had permitted some of their number to depart from their customary occupation. Further, a pair of documents from 1400 or a little later speak of a certain *kyrios* Simon "from the most faithful Varangians," whose deceased daughter had been married to a doctor in Constantinople. While the adjective "most faithful" certainly implies that the Varangians were still a coherent group of imperial servants, the reference tells us nothing of their duties at this late date.[9]

Finally, a Western European source may contain the last reference to the Varangians of Byzantium. In the chronicle of the Englishman Adam of Usk we read that in 1404, while visiting Rome, Adam had the opportunity to speak with some Byzantine ambassadors who had come to meet with Pope Boniface IX. "From these Greeks I learned that the princes of Greece were fully descended from the said Constantine [the Great] and his three uncles, Trehern, Llewellyn, and Meric, and from another 30,000 Britons who were carried thither from Britain with him; and that such men of British race, in token of their blood and lordship, bear axes in their country, which others do not."[10]

That such an incident actually occurred in Rome in 1404, and that imperial ambassadors were really involved cannot be confirmed independently. Yet, despite whatever else Adam says in the passage, the mention of axes (*secures*) gives the story some credibility. It does seem reasonable to

---

8. Pseudo-Kodinos, 216. J. Apokaukos, in N. Bees, ed., "Unedierte Schriftstücke aus der Kanzlei des Johannes Apokaukos," *Byzantinisch-Neugriechische Jahrbücher* 21 (1971–74), 60, and E. Bee-Sepherle in loc. cit., 170–71. G. Schlumberger, *Sigillographie de l'empire byzantin* (Paris, 1884), 350–51.

9. M. Fögen, "Zeugnisse byzantinischer Rechtspraxis im 14. Jahrhundert," *Fontes Minores* 5 (1982), 223, 225. MM, II, 476, 485.

10. *Chronicon Adae de Usk, A.D. 1377–1421*, ed. and trans. by E. Thompson, 2nd ed. (London, 1904; repr. New York, 1980), 96–97; trans. adapted from that of the editor, 272.

think that the reply of the ambassadors was a likely response to one of the first questions we should expect Adam to have put to exotic foreigners: "Are there any English where you come from?" In any event, that an Englishman living at the turn of the fifteenth century should claim that there were axe-bearing warriors from Britain living in Constantinople does indeed suggest that, even at this very late date, the Varangians had maintained their ethnic identity, their military role, and their reputation.

Much less is known about the four other groups of palace guards mentioned by Pseudo-Kodinos. The Paramonai (from the verb *parameno*, "to stand near someone or something") are an obscure division of palace guards, not in evidence before the second half of the thirteenth century, appearing altogether in only a half-dozen passages from the sources. According to Pseudo-Kodinos, "in the court of the palace [there are] soldiers called Paramonai, having horses, over whom [as commander, is] an allagator. And after these, [there are] others, Paramonai as well, except without horses, having an allagator also, all bearing swords in their hands." In Michael VIII's 1272 prostagma for his son Andronikos, the earliest securely dated reference to the Paramonai, and in the paraphrase of Niketas Choniates' history, they appear side by side with the Varangians.[11] But unlike the Varangians, the Paramonai were native troops. The archdeacon George Metochites, who spent most of his life in prison because of his religious views, wrote of "the two tagmata in the palace, of which the name of those from our race was Paramonai, while those from a foreign and alien one were called Varangians."[12] Whether there actually were two divisions of Paramonai, one mounted and one on foot with swords, each commanded by an officer called an allagator, cannot be confirmed. The last known reference to an allagator outside of Pseudo-Kodinos is from 1247, and nothing connects him to the Paramonai. The Paramonai are last mentioned in 1315 when a synodal letter notes that some "imperial Paramonai" were sent to apprehend a fugitive from justice.[13]

Without any doubt the Mourtatoi are the most obscure palace guard division that Pseudo-Kodinos mentions. Pseudo-Kodinos asserts that they

---

11. Pseudo-Kodinos, 180, 226. A. Heisenberg, *Aus der Geschichte und Literatur der Palaiologenzeit*, in Heisenberg, *Quellen und Studien zur spätbyzantinischen Geschichte* (London, 1973), no. I, 39, and commentary, 61–62. N. Choniates, *Nicetae Choniatae Historia*, ed. I. Bekker (Bonn, 1835), 224, 239, 447, 756 (hereafter Choniates, Bonn ed.). Regarding this late Byzantine paraphrase, see J. van Dieten, "Bemerkungen zur Sprache der sog. vulgärgriechischen Niketasparaphrase," *Byzantinische Forschungen* 6 (1979), 37–77.

12. Mai, *Novae patrum bibliothecae*, vol. 8 (Rome, 1871), 122.

13. H. Ahrweiler, *Byzance: les pays et les territoires* (London, 1976), no. IV, 141. MM, I, 12.

fought on foot as archers and were commanded by the stratopedarches of the Mourtatoi, this last detail not corroborated by any other source, except for the other late Byzantine lists of precedence which merely mention this stratopedarches.[14] The word *mourtatoi* itself ought to derive from the Arabo-Turkish word *murtedd, murtat* meaning "apostate" or "renegade," and it has generally been thought that the Mourtatoi were therefore Christianized Turks.[15] However, a passage in the *Advice for an Overseas Passage* makes a slight revision of this view necessary.

The Mourtatoi ("Murtati" in the Latin) are described by the anonymous Western author as follows:

> They are descendants of Turks by one parent and of Greeks by the other. As bad as the circumstance of their birth make them, they are all the worse from the union of two bad bloods, that is, Greek and Turkish, so one can say of their origin that on one side they are of Satan and on the other of the Devil. Although they are called Christians, they are quite foreign to Christian worship and works, and without exception given to the exercise of arms, for they have no other occupation. They apply themselves assiduously to the vice and sin to which that manner of men is fully accustomed. No exercise of arms that requires a faithful, vigorous and steady warrior includes them, but rather theft, plunder, destruction and rapine.[16]

These Mourtatoi were not merely Christianized Turks, but products of mixed marriage between Greeks and Turks. The author does not consider them a Byzantine palace guard unit, nor even soldiers who served Byzantium specifically. Rather, "Mourtatos" was an ethnic and religious designator, paralleling "Gasmoulos" (someone part Greek and part Latin) and similar, though not identical, to "Tourkopoulos" (applied by Pachymeres and Gregoras to certain Christianized Turks). Like those other ethnic groups the Mourtatoi were employed as soldiers by both the Byzantines and the crusader states of the eastern Mediterranean. Some support for Pseudo-Kodinos' assertion that the Mourtatoi fought on foot as archers is provided by a passage from the *Chronicon Tarvisinum*. It speaks of "all the crossbowmen and archers of Candia [Chandax] who are called Mortati"

14. Pseudo-Kodinos, 180, 139, 165, 187.

15. G. Moravcsik, *Byzantinoturcica*, 2nd ed. (Berlin, 1958), II, 197. E. Stein, "Untersuchungen zur spätbyzantinischen Verfassungs- und Wirtschaftsgeschichte," *Mitteilungen zur osmanischen Geschichte* 2 (1923–26), 55.

16. *Directorium ad faciendum passagium transmarinum*, ed. C. Beazley in *American Historical Review* 13 (1907–1908), 102; also in *Recueil des historiens des croisades. Documents Arméniens*, II (Paris, 1906), 492–93, and cf. 375–76. On this work, see herein, pp. 44–45.

(balisterios omnes atque arcerios de Candia quos Mortatos appellabant), fighting in Italy on behalf of Venice during a war with Padua in 1372–73.[17]

Thus, if the Mourtatoi were palace guards as Pseudo-Kodinos asserts, they nevertheless were not exclusively palace guards. This observation helps make sense of what to my knowledge is the first appearance of the word. In a 1259 chrysobull Michael VIII exempted the monastery of Lavra on Mount Athos from a number of relatively common taxes and burdens. However, one of the items exempted is called simply "mourtatoi." Since the chrysobull offers no clue regarding the meaning of the term, and since the only other source to mention this particular tax or burden is an unauthentic version of a 1329 chrysobull that used the 1250 chrysobull for some interpolated phrases, we can say for sure only that "mourtatoi" was levied on someone at some time prior to 1259. Nonetheless, through analogy with other military taxes also listed in the 1259 chrysobull, such as the *kontaratikion* ("charge for lances"), the *exelasis ploïmon* ("extraction of sailors"), and the *dosis toxarion* ("giving of bows"), as well as with the even closer parallel of the *euresis basmoulon* ("finding of Gasmouloi") found in a fifteenth-century document, we may at least hypothesize that "mourtatoi" was a charge for hiring a specific type of soldier, some of whom might have served in the imperial palace.[18]

The only evidence outside of Pseudo-Kodinos and the other lists of precedence that the Mourtatoi were a division of guard troops is found in a letter of Nikephoros Choumnos written to Patriarch Niphon I (1310–14) which speaks of "the Mourtatoi of the patriarch from Herakleion" in unflattering terms. Evidently they originated from Herakleion, a region (*chora*) somewhere along the coast of northwestern Asia Minor where the Constantinopolitan patriarchate held numerous property possessions.[19] Moreover, "patriarchal" Mourtatoi could not have been guards in the imperial palace, though the very fact that Choumnos specifies that these were Mourtatoi "of the patriarch" might suggest that there were other, *imperial* Mourtatoi. In any event, we cannot confirm Pseudo-Kodinos' testimony that the Mourtatoi were palace guards.

17. L. Muratori, *Rerum Italicarum Scriptores*, vol. 19 (Milan, 1731), cols. 748D, 749D. Moreover, a document from 1565 speaks of "Mortati" in the service of the Venetian authorities on Tinos: C. Sathas, Μνημεῖα ʽΕλληνικῆς ʽΙστορίας. *Documents inédits relatifs à l'histoire de la Grèce au moyen âge*, IV (Paris, 1882), 287. As a proper name the word appears as Mourtatos, Mortatos, and Mourtatopoulos in Greek sources, Murtat in Serbian documents, and Mortato or Murtato in Venetian documents from Crete.

18. P. Lemerle et al., *Actes de Lavra* (Paris, 1970–82), II, no. 71, and III, App. XI. Arkadios Vatopedinos, in Γρηγόριος ὁ Παλαμᾶς 3 (1919), 335, no. 34. See herein, pp. 145–46.

19. J. Boissonade, *Anecdota Graeca* (Paris, 1829–33), V, 275. For Herakleion: J. and P. Zepos, *Jus graecoromanum* (Athens, 1931), I, 661, 663.

Yet another palace guard division, according to Pseudo-Kodinos, were the Tzakones who served as bodyguards, were armed with clubs or cudgels (*apelatikia*), and wore distinctive breastplates adorned with white lions. As discussed in Chapter 2, the word *Tzakon* was applied to the light-armed troops recruited by Michael VIII to defend his restored capital and to serve aboard his new fleet. Some of these soldiers came from among the Gasmouloi, others came from the Peloponnesos, at first perhaps only Monemvasia, and later from other parts of the Morea (these being *ethnic* Tzakones); still others came from unknown areas outside Constantinople. Michael VIII's Tzakones performed a number of tasks: guarding the walls of Constantinople, manning the fleet, and, evidently, serving as palace guards. What made matters confusing was that some but not all of these Tzakones were ethnic Tzakones, that is, native inhabitants of the southeastern corner of the Morea.

Like the Tzakones who served as marines, the Tzakones of the palace guard probably received mercenary pay as well as small properties near Constantinople. Outside of Pseudo-Kodinos, only the archdeacon George Metochites refers to the Tzakones as an imperial guard. In a theological tract he notes that, probably in the early 1280s, crossbowmen who had been assigned to the prison of the Grand Palace were transferred to the regular army and replaced by "Lakones" (as Pachymeres notes, another name for Tzakones).[20] Since nothing is heard of the Tzakones in Constantinople after the 1280s, it is possible that they disappeared pursuant to Andronikos II's budget-cutting reduction of the navy.

Finally, the Vardariotai were a group of imperial servants found in the palace or entourage of the emperor whose duty, as Pseudo-Kodinos notes, was "to keep the people orderly" during state ceremonies. To this end "whips, which they call *manglabia*, hang from each of their belts," and they also bore staffs or batons (*dikanikia*) which were not merely ceremonial accoutrements.[21] Although the Vardariotai were frequently associated with palace guards such as the Varangians and the Paramonai,[22] they had more of a policing than a military function, and their "weapons" were not in the same class as the Varangian's axe and the sword of the Paramones. In fact

---

20. Pseudo-Kodinos, 180. S. Caratzas, *Les Tzacones* (Berlin, 1976), 335. The Grand Palace began its decline under the early Komnenoi with the cost of upkeep, the Komnenian preference for the Blachernai Palace, and, finally, the Latin Conquest all playing a role. In 1345 a prison within the Grand Palace was still in use: Kantakouzenos, II, 542–43.

21. Akropolites, 131. Pachymeres, ed. Failler, I, 417 (Bonn ed., I, 321). Pseudo-Kodinos, 181–82. On the word *manglabia*, more commonly thought to be a club or cudgel, see the *ODB*, s.v. "manglabites."

22. Heisenberg, *Palaiologenzeit*, 39. Paraphrase of Choniates: Choniates, Bonn ed., 447.

Pseudo-Kodinos lists them not with the regular palace guards but with the *kortinarioi*, unarmed palace servants. They were commanded by the primmikerios of the Vardariotai, a title first attested in 1166. Akropolites writes that in 1256 the Vardariotai and their primmikerios were encamped in Thrace with Theodore II. For unknown reasons they were not in the immediate vicinity of the emperor, as a bodyguard, but were encamped separately at a distance of what appears to have been a short horseback ride.[23]

The origin and ethnicity of the Vardariotai have been much discussed. Pseudo-Kodinos' assertions that a certain, unnamed emperor "transplanted them, who are of old Persians by race, from there to the Vardar River, for which reason they are called Vardariotai," and that they voiced their imperial acclamation "in Persian," are certainly not to be taken literally. By "Persian" he means "Turk," but neither Seljuk nor Ottoman. Rather, he appears to be referring to a resettlement of Hungarians (whom the Byzantines called "Turks" in the tenth and eleventh centuries) in Macedonia along the Vardar valley during the tenth century. By the late tenth century, these "Turks" had been Christianized, and probably not much later emperors drew on their manpower for military needs. By the twelfth century, if not earlier, they were formed into a palace guard division. The centuries between the first transplanting and the Palaiologan era probably ensured that late Byzantine Vardariotai had a mixed ethnicity, regardless of the language in which they ceremonially acclaimed the emperor.[24]

A letter of Patriarch Germanos II (1223–40) tells us something about the recruitment of Vardariotai and the unattractiveness of service as a Vardariotes. A man named George Pissas came before the patriarch with a problem. He wished to be married but the archbishop of Lopadion had forbidden it. Pissas explained to the patriarch "that some time ago he was being forced to enroll permanently in the ranks [*taxis*] of the Vardariotai who endure work in imperial service and duties, and since he preferred to die rather than enter such service, he knew enough to flee by donning monastic garb." A few days later he doffed the habit and went on his way. The stratagem worked and he eluded his pursuers, but since the archbishop and others still regarded him as a monk, he was denied the right to marry. Germanos took pity on Pissas and happily it was decided that he should be allowed to take a wife as a layman. While it is clear that Pissas considered

23. Cf. Pseudo-Kodinos, 181–82 to 179–80. Migne, *PG*, 140, cols. 237A, 253D; and L. Petit, "Documents inédits sur le concile de 1166," *VizVrem* 11 (1904), 479, 491. Cf. MM, VI, 130 (from 1195). Akropolites, 131–32.

24. Pseudo-Kodinos, 182, 210. N. Oikonomidès, "Vardariotes," *Südost-Forschungen* 32 (1973), 1–8.

service as a Vardariotes quite onerous, offering us a rare glimpse of the underside of imperial employment, the most provocative element in the story is lacking. What kind of hold did these people have on Pissas? I think it most likely that Pissas had a hereditary obligation to be a Vardariotes, that he either held land encumbered by such an obligation or was the son of a Vardariotes. This would have given his pursuers a reason for tracking him down.[25]

Since the palace guard divisions tended, by their nature and function, to be near the person of the emperor, they played a visible role in whatever court ceremony took place during the late period. A late fourteenth-century writer describes such a scene: "the emperor himself being present, sitting quite imperially and loftily on the throne, and the bodyguard around him, the senate and the *taxeis* present as customary." Pseudo-Kodinos writes that at the entrance to the coronation mass "the Varangians, all axe-bearing, and about one hundred young nobles accompany him [the emperor] on both sides," and Kantakouzenos confirms this by observing that "those having axes called Varangians" took part in Andronikos III's coronation procession in 1325. The Russian traveler Ignatius of Smolensk has left us a description of Manuel II's coronation in 1392. On entering the church of Hagia Sophia, "on either side of the emperor [walked] twelve men-at-arms, completely [covered in] iron from head to foot, and in front of them walked two black-haired standard-bearers with red staffs, clothing and hats. Heralds with silver-covered staffs walked before the two standard-bearers."[26]

The presence of the palace guard certainly had a practical as well as a ceremonial significance. Aside from the standing necessity of guarding the person of the emperor, the particular circumstances of a coronation could mandate the active participation of guards. For example, the attitude of "the axe-bearing Keltikon," present at Michael VIII's coronation at Nicaea in 1259, silenced opposition to Michael's refusal to grant a real crown to the child John Laskaris. Pachymeres notes grimly that they were "ready to guard as well as to attack should they be ordered by those in power."[27]

According to Pseudo-Kodinos, the Varangians accompanied the emperor during a number of religious ceremonies involving travel through

25. A Makrembolites, in A. Papadopoulos-Kerameus, Ἀνάλεκτα Ἱεροσολυμιτικῆς Σταχυολογίας (St. Petersburg, 1891–98), I, 466, lines 15–19.

26. Migne, PG, 151, col. 570B. Pseudo-Kodinos, 264. Kantakouzenos, I, 200. Ignatius of Smolensk, in Russian Travelers to Constantinople in the Fourteenth and Fifteenth Centuries, ed. G. Majeska (Washington, D.C., 1984), 106–109.

27. Pachymeres, ed. Failler, I, 145 (Bonn ed., I, 103). Geanakoplos, Emperor Michael, 46. S. Blöndal, The Varangians of Byzantium (Cambridge, 1978), 171.

Constantinople. On February 2, the feast of the Purification, the emperor visited

> the church of the Blachernai, accompanied by the Varangians. They always accompany the emperor when he is on horseback, carrying their axes on their shoulders and going as far as [the place called] Hypsela. But for this feast they accompany him as far as the church, although not for the return; by custom they are found waiting for the emperor at the gate of the Hypsela, and accompany him as far as the place for dismounting.

Similarly, they escorted him to a monastery for the feasts of the Birth (June 24) and Decapitation (August 29) of John the Baptist, as well as to a church for the feast of the Deposition of the Veil of the Virgin (August 31).

On Christmas Eve and Christmas Day a whole series of ceremonies were observed, some with a clear religious emphasis, others of a more secular nature. According to Pseudo-Kodinos most involved the palace guard. On Christmas Eve, during the ceremony of Prokypsis, "the Varangians [then come], and they stand in the court near the columns of the *prokypsis* [a ceremonial wooden platform], carrying their axes in their hands. When the emperor appears from on high on the *prokypsis*, they raise them to their shoulders as is the custom." The next day, a procession of officials entered the court and ceremonially acclaimed the emperor. "Then the Varangians come and wish the emperor 'many years' in their native language, that is, English, striking their axes together with a clash. After that all those of the palace wish the emperor 'many years' according to their rank, up to the Vardariotai (in their old native language, that is, Persian)." Later, during the ceremonial Christmas banquet, again according to Pseudo-Kodinos, an old ritual took place whereby the emperor distributed gifts to the members of his court. The megas domestikos (evidently as the formal commander of the army)

> calls all the archons by name, up to all those wearing the red *skaranikon* [a type of head-covering denoting rank]. And as they all receive a plate, not one leaves, but all stand in their places out of reverence for the megas domestikos. Then following the protonotarios come the primmikerioi of the Varangians and all the Varangians with them, and they receive plates. And after them soldiers and Paramonai and many others.[28]

On Palm Sunday, there was a ceremonial procession (called the Pe-

28. Pseudo-Kodinos, 243–46, 197, 209–10, 216. On the *prokypsis* and its ceremony: Pseudo-Kodinos, 171 note 1; and Heisenberg, *Palaiologenzeit*, 85–97.

ripatos) from the imperial palace to a nearby church along a corridor decorated with myrtle, laurel, and olive branches, which according to Pseudo-Kodinos involved the Varangians and the Paramonai. "After the emperor as well as the patriarch and the priests have performed the Peripatos, a young servant [*paidopoulos*] of the emperor comes out and seizes a branch, showing that the imperial command is to plunder the walkway, and immediately this happens. It is despoiled by the Varangians, the Paramonai, and by the other units [*taxeis*] found in the court."[29]

Other ceremonies involving the palace guard seem to have had a purely secular basis. Michael VIII's 1272 prostagma for his son Andronikos, which laid out the rights and responsibilities of Andronikos as co-emperor, specified that when Andronikos performed the ritual of receiving petitions, he should be accompanied by Varangians and Paramonai with Vardariotai leading the way. Further, during joint ceremonial horseback rides at court, "the Anglo-Varangians [*Engklinobarangoi*] of both [emperors] accompany [them] in common and the Vardariotai go in front."[30]

The Varangians and the Vardariotai are the only divisions securely attested before 1204. The Varangians last appear in the very early years of the fifteenth century; the Vardariotai are last mentioned, as a palace guard, by Pachymeres when speaking of developments in 1272 involving Michael VIII's brother John. The Paramonai are first referred to in Michael VIII's prostagma of 1272 and last encountered in the synodal letter of 1315 cited above. The "patriarchal" Mourtatoi are only found in Nikephoros Choumnos' letter from the period 1310–14. And the Tzakones, in their role as palace guards, are mentioned for the first time by Pachymeres regarding events around 1262, and for the last time by George Metochites regarding his tribulations around 1285. Thus, aside from Pseudo-Kodinos, there is no direct evidence that the Vardariotai or the Tzakones were palace guards in the fourteenth century, or that any of these guard divisions, except for the Varangians, survived beyond the reign of Andronikos II.

No information is available regarding the size of any palace guard division. Overall it seems that the Varangians were the most important, certainly the most visible, guard division, followed by the Paramonai. Nor do we have much information regarding how palace guards were remunerated. The Tzakones received pay and small land parcels which served at least for habitation. The other guards either had similar arrangements or were

---

29. Pseudo-Kodinos, 226. On the Peripatos, which also took place on Christmas and Epiphany, see Heisenberg, *Palaiologenzeit*, 82–85.

30. Heisenberg, *Palaiologenzeit*, 39, and commentary, 60–63.

simple mercenaries. Service with the Tzakones and probably with the Vardariotai seems to have had a hereditary component. Given the tendency for the custom or obligation of hereditary service to follow an ethnic identity, we should expect a hereditary component in service with the Varangians and the Mourtatoi as well.

There were guards at court who cannot be placed into any of the divisions Pseudo-Kodinos' mentions. Gregoras writes that in 1352 some Catalan (or Aragonese) sailors chose to remain in Constantinople after the Venetian-Genoese war: "The emperor Kantakouzenos gathered about 500 of the Catalans . . . light-armed and beggars going about the city in every direction, and he armed them and fed them to be a bodyguard . . . since the Romans of his own race were distrusted and arranged on the side of the enemy" John V.[31] Nothing suggests that these Catalans joined one of the palace guard divisions Pseudo-Kodinos mentions. Rather, there was an opportunity to recruit a personal guard, and the emperor took advantage of it.

Although there is no clear evidence that this new group of guards survived Kantakouzenos' abdication in 1354, Elizabeth Zachariadou, in order to explain a puzzling reference to a group of imperial guards in Sylvester Syropoulos' account of the Council of Ferrara-Florence, hypothesized that this Catalan guard division may have remained in existence well into the fifteenth century.[32] According to Syropoulos, before John VIII Palaiologos and Patriarch Joseph II departed Constantinople in 1437, the latter complained that the stipend which the emperor had granted him was inadequate to fund a proper entourage for his appearances at the council. Through intermediaries he explained to John VIII that since "You yourself haven't given up the *ianitzaroi*, why shouldn't I travel with my entourage?"

In Ferrara, as the business of the council dragged on, "the emperor found a monastery six miles from Ferrara and stayed in it with a few archons and soldiers [*stratiotai*] and *gianitzaroi*, leaving the majority in Ferrara." Some time later, in Florence, in order to pressure the Byzantine mission into accepting the church union proposals, the Latins suspended their living allowance for over three months, and "while all suffered from want, the *gianitzaroi* of the emperor more than others since they were the neediest and poorest." They asked the megas protosynkellos to intervene with the

31. Gregoras, III, 151. Cf. Kantakouzenos, III, 228. For further references to these Catalans: Kantakouzenos, III, 243 (cf. Gregoras, III, 177), 286.
32. On the following, E. Zachariadou, "Les 'janissaires' de l'empereur byzantin," in Zachariadou, *Romania and the Turks* (London, 1985), no. XI, 591–97.

emperor on their behalf, but in the end this church official could do little but give them some of his vestments that they might sell them for food. Several days later they returned to the megas protosynkellos and explained that no one wanted to buy the vestments, that their indigence had worsened, and that "one of them had sold his arms, another pawned his uniform." The megas protosynkellos suggested they visit two other high churchmen, the bishop of Ephesus and the megas sakellarios, and ask them why they opposed the union of the Churches. "More than twenty" of them confronted the megas sakellarios and asked, "Why don't you allow the union to take place? Do you want us to die here? Is it good that we perish from famine?" Though "fearful and trembling," the megas sakellarios managed to quiet them and promised to take their complaint to the patriarch.[33]

As Zachariadou has noted, these "Ianitzaroi" were with the emperor in Constantinople; more than twenty of them were part of his immediate entourage while in Italy; and as the lowliest members of the imperial entourage, they were distinguished from "archons" and "soldiers." In addition, we observe that they were armed and played a minor political role in the church union negotiations. Thus, they seem to have been a light-armed imperial guard. Zachariadou has proposed that their name is the Greek transliteration of *genetari, giannetario, janizzeri,* and so on, a military term derived from the name of a Berber tribe renowned as light cavalry. Since the end of the thirteenth century the term had been applied in Western Europe to denote light-armed cavalry generally. She suggests that the Byzantines may have picked the word up from the Catalans, whose troops included light-armed cavalry which in Spanish sources are referred to as *cavallers genets* or *ianets*. Her hypothesis that the origin of the Ianitzaroi lay in the 500 Catalans who became Kantakouzenos' personal guard in 1352 is certainly possible. So too is her suggestion that the famous Ottoman corps of Janissaries (*yeniçari*) received their name from the Western term, via the Byzantines.

Aside from Syropoulos' "Janissaries," only one new division of guards makes its appearance, briefly to be sure, after the time of the Pseudo-Kodinos treatise. In 1422 a man named Theologos Korax, blamed for the failure of an embassy to Murad II, was arrested, tortured by Cretan guards, blinded, and then died.[34] Nothing else is known of these "Cretan guards."

33. Sylvester Syropoulos, *Les "Mémoires" du Grand Ecclésiarque de l'Église de Constantinople Sylvestre Syropoulos sur le concile de Florence (1438–1439)*, ed. V. Laurent (Rome, 1971), 192, 296, 404.

34. Doukas, 231–35. J. Barker, *Manuel II Palaeologus (1391–1425): A Study in Late Byzantine Statesmanship* (New Brunswick, N.J., 1969), 361–63 and note 111.

While there must have been a few palace guards present in Constantinople in 1453, no source, as far as I can tell, notes their existence.

The fortified towns called *kastra* (from the Latin *castrum*, "fortress, castle") remain one of the preeminent symbols of late Byzantium. No other monuments evoke more vividly the nature and tone of provincial life during these centuries. As a center of administration and economic and social life, the kastron performed a variety of functions, one of which was defense. Behind its walls townspeople aided by garrisons defended their homes, and peasants and their animals sought refuge from enemy incursions. Within its walls government officials administered the local soldiery and the supplies needed to provision campaign armies in transit. The typical kastron was a walled hill crowned with a fortified acropolis. There one found the garrison's barracks, stables, administrative offices, occasionally jails, and if need be, a last refuge from invaders who had breached the curtain walls of the town below. The acropolis, or citadel, was also a symbol of authority separating the governmental and military aristocracy from the other urban inhabitants, and as a consequence its walls often served to protect its privileged inhabitants from insurrections mounted by the less-privileged population below.[35]

The serious archaeological study of late Byzantine kastra is still in its infancy. The relatively meager on-site work that has been done is primarily descriptive and is, as yet, of little value to historians. Overall, Byzantine archaeology has always taken a backseat to its ancient cousin, and within the Byzantine field the study of churches has always had precedence over the study of fortifications and other secular structures. Consequently, most of what we know about kastra is derived from written sources.[36]

---

35. As a refuge: Kantakouzenos, I, 179; II, 79. As a supply depot: Kantakouzenos, II, 243, 257–58; and cf. I, 267. On jails: Gregoras, III, 566.

36. In general, see the relevant chapters of C. Foss and D. Winfield, *Byzantine Fortification: An Introduction* (Pretoria, 1986), and the nonscholarly but interesting books of A. Paradissis, *Fortresses and Castles of Greece*, 3 vols. (Athens and Thessaloniki, 1972–82). Numerous studies that include histories and description (occasionally with plans) have been made of particular kastra. Among the more useful, if not necessarily the most accessible, are O. Tafrali, *Topographie de Thessalonique* (Paris, 1913); A. Woodward, "The Byzantine Castle of Avret-Hissar," *Annual of the British School at Athens* 23 (1918–19), 98–103 (on Gynaikokastron); A. Xyngopoulos, Ἔρευναι εἰς τὰ βυζαντινὰ μνημεῖα τῶν Σερρῶν (Thessaloniki, 1965) (on Serres); A. Dunn, "The Survey of Khrysoupolis, and Byzantine Fortifications in the Lower Strymon Valley," *JÖB* 32/4 (1982), 605–14 (a report on an archeological survey of the Chrysopolis region in Macedonia); K. Andrews, *Castles of the Morea* (repr. Amsterdam, 1978) (a fine overview of Byzantine and Frankish fortifications); K. Tsoures, «Ἡ βυζαντικὴ ὀχύρωση τῶν Ἰωαννίνων», Ἠπειρωτικὰ Χρονικά 25 (1983), 133–57 (Ioannina); C. Foss, "Late Byzantine

Building, repairing, and maintaining fortifications both within kastra and in the countryside was an ongoing concern, and there is evidence of extensive construction activity during the reigns of most of the late Byzantine emperors. For example, according to Kantakouzenos, Andronikos III rebuilt and resettled Arkadiopolis (modern Lüleburgaz), walled Gynaikokastron and rebuilt a tower there, built Siderokastron, walled and colonized Chrysopolis (at the mouth of the Strymon), partially rebuilt Peritheorion, and rebuilt Dipotamon (somewhere in western Thrace). Further, Kantakouzenos says that he himself, evidently during Andronikos II's reign, built the fort of Pythion near Didymoteichon "from its foundations," and walled the fort of Teristasin (somewhere in Thrace) "with his own money." Such accounts are often subject to hyperbole. For example, the contrast between the well-fitting elegant ashlar masonry of the foundation and lower levels of Pythion and its rough brick and rubble middle and upper courses belies Kantakouzenos' claim that he built the fort "from its foundations."[37]

One of the methods by which the state built and maintained fortifications was through an obligation on landowners called *kastroktisia* (literally, "castle-building"). The burden first appears in the late tenth century and originally it was a corvée that required the subjects of the Empire to perform building services. Within the first sixty years of the Palaiologan era most monasteries seem to have been exempted from kastroktisia for all or most of their lands. From the time of Stefan Dušan's conquest of Macedonia until the end of Byzantium only rarely does any document mention

Fortifications in Lydia," *JÖB* 28 (1979), 297–320 (on numerous sites in Asia Minor including Magnesia and Nymphaion, with general comments on the problems and the state of late Byzantine archaeology); A. Deroko, *Srednjovekovni gradovi u Srbiji, Crnoj Gori i Makedoniji* (Belgrade, 1950) (southern Yugoslavia); idem, "Srednjovekovni grad Skoplje," *Spomenik SANU* 120, odeljenje društvenih nauka, nova serija 22 (Belgrade, 1971), 1–16 (Skopje); and I. Zdravković, *Srednjovekovni gradovi i dvorci na Kosovu* (Belgrade, 1975).

37. Kantakouzenos, I, 541–42; II, 195, 475. For the building activity of Theodore I Laskaris, see Angold, *Byzantine Government*, 98–99. For John Vatatzes, see Foss, "Late Byzantine Fortifications." For Michael VIII, see the inscription from Adrianople: Z. Taşliklioğlu, *Traky'da epigrafya araştirmalari* (Istanbul, 1961–71), II, 42; and from Thessaloniki (1278/9?): J.-M. Speiser, "Inventaires en vue d'un recueil des inscriptions historiques de Byzance," *TM* 5 (1973), 167, no. 18. For Andronikos II, Gregoras (I, 484) reports that the emperor built or rebuilt "more than fifteen forts" in the Haimos range of Thrace. See also the inscription from Thessaloniki of 1283/4: M. Demitsas, Ἡ Μακεδονία ἐν λίθοις φθεγγομένοις καὶ μνημείοις σωζομένοις . . . Μακεδονικῶν (Athens, 1896), I, 524, no. 594; and of 1315/6: Speiser, "Inventaires," 170, no. 23. Sometime before 1341 Alexios Apokaukos built the fort of Epibatai on the Sea of Marmara: Nicol, *Last Centuries*, 193. On Stefan Dušan's refortification of Verria in 1350: Kantakouzenos, III, 120. For John V's rebuilding of parts of the walls of Thessaloniki in 1355/6, see the inscription in Speiser, "Inventaires," 175–76, no. 28.

kastroktisia. Evidently this was because Dušan granted a blanket exemption of all state burdens to all the monasteries of Mount Athos in 1345. After this only new additions to monastic possessions required specific exemption of kastroktisia. It is apparent that Dušan's tendency to grant wholesale exemption of various taxes to all sorts of monasteries rendered kastroktisia, along with a number of other charges, defunct, at least for monasteries.[38]

Although the overwhelming majority of Greek documents that mention kastroktisia during the late period exempt monasteries (never a private landowner) from this specific obligation, it occasionally appears as a real burden. For example, Andronikos II's 1319 chrysobull for Ioannina specifies that the inhabitants of the town owed kastroktisia only for their own kastron: "There shall be no demand of kastroktisia from them [the inhabitants of Ioannina] for the sake of another kastron, since only for their own kastron are they obligated to struggle, as possible, for its care and maintenance and rebuilding." While it is not clear from the document whether kastroktisia took the form of a corvée or a cash payment, there is no hard evidence that it was ever levied as a corvée during the late period. Rather, for those landowners required to provide kastroktisia, it seems to have been commuted for a cash payment. From a fragmentary praktikon from the late thirteenth century, we may calculate the rate of commuted kastroktisia: 1.5 hyperpyra per twenty-two paroikos households, or about 1/15 of a hyperpyron per household.[39]

When kastroktisia was exempted for the citizens of a particular town, the funds and labor for the necessary work had to come from elsewhere, from the countryside or from other civic taxes. Such was the case in regard to Monemvasia. In 1442 the despot of the Morea Theodore II Palaiologos established that income from the *abiotikion* (the appropriation by the state of the property of those who died without heirs) be applied "to the rebuilding and strengthening and security of the kastron of Monemvasia," and that neither his treasury nor the kephale of the city, nor anyone else, should assume any part of this income. Eight years later Despot Demetrios Palaiologos granted the inhabitants of the town the abiotikion and the *kommerkion* (the main tax on trade) along with "the other rights which they hold there designated for the sake of the building of the walls of their

---

38. M. Bartusis, "State Demands for the Building and Repairing of Fortifications in Late Byzantium and Medieval Serbia," *Byzantinoslavica* 49 (1988), 209–10. On the early kastroktisia, see S. Trojanos, «Καστροκτισία», *Βυζαντινά* 1 (1969), 39–57.

39. MM, V, 82. J. Lefort, *Actes d'Esphigménou* (Paris, 1973), no. 7, lines 8–13, and p. 64.

kastron." He specified that these taxes were still to be levied, once again not for the personal benefit of the collectors or the kephalai, but "carefully and justly" for the stated purposes only. It seems that the proceeds from the abiotikion were insufficient for the proper fortification of the city, so Demetrios decided it was practical to assign the kommerkion as well to this end. Since the proceeds from the kommerkion and the abiotikion were usually enjoyed by the ruler and the kephalai, both documents stress the despot's selfless intentions in maintaining these taxes.[40]

Neither document speaks of kastroktisia. This is because a false imperial chrysobull, bearing the date 1316 and created sometime during the fourteenth century, exempted Monemvasia from this burden.[41] Even if the inhabitants had received no genuine exemption of kastroktisia, undoubtedly they were using the false chrysobull in the fifteenth century to prove exemption from it. Since the despots could not easily reimpose an exempted tax, they had to find new ways to fund the vital function of fortification maintenance.

A similar situation existed in regard to the *phloriatikon*, a tax created apparently for the upkeep—mercenary pay and maintenance—of the Hexamilion that Manuel II rebuilt and refortified in 1415–16 across the Isthmus of Corinth. Unlike the abiotikion, the phloriatikon (its name connected with the Italian coin the florin) was a new tax. It appears in a document from 1436 or 1451 in which the despot of the Morea Thomas Palaiologos exempted a group of sixteen ethnic Albanian soldiers in his service from the burden since "they are obligated to serve my majesty with their horses and arms where they are ordered."[42] It is found also in a group of documents dating from 1427 to 1450 which granted the kastron of Phanarion and the village of Brysis to the scholar George Gemistos Plethon and his sons. In 1427 Gemistos received Phanarion with all its revenue and taxes except for the phloriatikon; at around the same time he was also given Brysis with all its rights "except for the assigned and ordained taxes [*kephalaia*] for the Hexamilion." In 1433, when Theodore Palaiologos transferred these same localities to the sons of Gemistos, it was still stipulated, for both Phanarion

---

40. MM, V, 175, 170–71. Bartusis, "State Demands for the Building," 206. On the abiotikion, which first appears at the end of the thirteenth century, see the *ODB*, s.v. "abiotikion."

41. MM, V, 166.

42. Zakythinos, *Despotat*, II, 237–38, 351. Trojanos, «Καστροκτισία», 53–54. L. Branouses, «Ἀλβανοὶ πολεμισταὶ στὴν ὑπηρεσία τῶν Δεσποτῶν τῆς Πελοποννήσου», a paper read at Τὸ Α΄ Διεθνὲς Συνοδρίας Πελοποννησιακῶν Σπουδῶν, Sparta, 7–14 Sept. 1975.

and Brysis, that the phloriatikon was still owed the state. Finally, in 1449 Constantine XI granted the sons of Gemistos even the phloriatikon.[43]

When this series of documents is compared with what is known of the actual history of the Hexamilion, there is a remarkable lack of correspondence. Four years prior to the issuance of the first extant document demanding the phloriatikon, the Hexamilion was destroyed by the Turks. During the twenty years it lay in ruins, the phloriatikon was demanded of Gemistos and his sons. In 1443 the fortification was rebuilt and again destroyed by the Turks in 1446. Three years later the emperor in Constantinople exempted Gemistos' sons of the charge. We should conclude that the phloriatikon was not used exclusively for the fortification of the Isthmus, although when it was collected, it no doubt did finance mercenaries or the building of fortifications in general. Indeed the last reference to a charge "for the Hexamilion" occurs in 1428; after that, only the phloriatikon appears.[44]

Generally it seems that forced or conscripted labor was not used to build or repair fortifications. Rather, the standard practice seems to have been to hire workers funded through taxes. An anonymous eulogy for John VIII specifically points out that a rebuilding program for the walls of Constantinople was carried out using hired labor, and in Stephen Sgouropoulos' eulogy for Alexios II Komnenos of Trebizond (1297–1330) we read that the emperor similarly employed hired workers (*misthophoreuontes*) to build a fort (*phrourion*) in his capital.[45]

In medieval Serbia the obligation to build and repair fortifications seems to have retained the character of a corvée. From the early 1340s the obligation that paralleled kastroktisia was most commonly called *gradozidanije*, literally "fortress-building." Since both the Greek word *kastron* and the Serbian word *grad* had the dual meanings of "town" and "fortress" (inasmuch as most late medieval Balkan towns were fortified), "gradozidanije" was the precise translation of "kastroktisia." Through Byzantine influence and the impact of Stefan Dušan's legal system on later Serbia, *gradozidanije* became the regular term for the construction corvée, and it

43. MM, III, 173, 174–76 = S. Lampros, Παλαιολόγεια καὶ Πελοποννησιακά (Athens, 1912–30), III, 331–33. S. Kougeas, «Χρυσόβουλλον Κωνσταντίνου τοῦ Παλαιολόγου πρωτό-γραφον καὶ ἀνέκδοτον», Ἑλληνικά 1 (1928), 373–75 = Lampros, Παλαιολόγεια, IV, 106–109.

44. Zakythinos, *Despotat*, II, 140–42. MM, III, 174, 175.

45. Lampros, Παλαιολόγεια, III, 298. Papadopoulos-Kerameus, Ἀνάλεκτα Ἱεροσο-λυμιτικῆς Σταχυολογίας, I, 433.

appears in a score of documents through 1417.[46] While terminology became more or less formalized under Dušan, prior to his reign the obligation was probably understood to be included within the general phrases freeing monasteries of urban corvées, for example, "let them not do work in a fortress" (da ne rabotaju s' gradom),[47] or within other irregular terminology specifically referring to building activity, e.g., "not to build fortresses" (grada ne zidati), phrases which in fact continued to appear occasionally throughout the fourteenth and into the fifteenth century.[48]

The Law Code of Stefan Dušan explains the obligation of gradozidanije: "For the building of a fortress [grad] where a fortress or a fort [kula] is ruined, let the citizens of that fortress, and of the district [župa] of that fortress, repair it." Significantly, those who lived in the vicinity of towns, as well as town inhabitants, fell under the obligation. In contemporary Byzantium kastroktisia likewise touched landowners whose property laid outside urban areas, but unlike in Byzantium, the obligation of gradozidanije seems to have always remained a corvée. In Kantakouzenos' description of Dušan's refortification of Verria in 1350 the sense of a corvée is clear: "Encamped outside the walls were another crowd of laborers, more than 10,000 so they said, led from all the land under the king [Dušan] for the rebuilding of the acropolis" of the town. A number of documents confirm this, such as Milutin's foundation charter for the monastery of St. Stephen in Banjska which obligated certain dependent peasants of the monastery to perform building corvées: "And as all reap hay [for the monastery], so shall they build fortifications." Thus, in Serbia the obligation paralleling kastroktisia remained a corvée and one from which even monasteries were never completely exempted.[49]

The defence of kastra was undertaken by two types of men: garrison soldiers and paramilitary guards. Due to the nature of the sources we know much more about the latter than the former. Documents, for their part,

46. See Bartusis, "State Demands for the Building," 211 note 34.

47. S. Novaković, *Zakonski spomenici srpskih država srednjega veka* (Belgrade, 1912), 388 x (1276–81).

48. See, e.g., Novaković, *Zakonski spomenici*, 580 v = A. Solovjev, *Odabrani spomenici srpskog prava (od XII do kraja XV veka)* (Belgrade, 1926), no. 43 v (ca.1296); V. Mošin et al., *Spomenici za srednovekovnata i ponovata istorija na Makedonija*, I (Skopje, 1975), 211, 223 (1299/1300) = Novaković, *Zakonski spomenici*, 609 iii, 614 xxxii = Solovjev, *Odabrani spomenici*, no. 44; and Novaković, *Zakonski spomenici*, 486 viii (ca.1331), 466 viii (1411).

49. *Zakonik cara Stefana Dušana: 1349 i 1354*, ed. N. Radojčić (Belgrade, 1960), art. 127. Kantakouzenos, III, 124. Novaković, *Zakonski spomenici*, 625 xlix = Solovjev, *Odabrani spomenici*, 93, no. 51. Bartusis, "State Demands for the Building," 211.

provide a fair amount of information about paramilitary guards but almost nothing about garrison soldiers. This is because garrisoning a town was a function not directly related to the holding or administering of land. While the documents make frequent reference to soldiers, usually those somehow connected to the agrarian economy, they had little reason to identify such soldiers as garrison troops, and consequently there is no direct way to determine which soldiers encountered in the documents were garrison troops. Paramilitary guards, on the other hand, can often be identified because most derived their livelihoods from the land, and even those who were paid money, unlike imperial garrison troops, were still financed by the local economy.

The narrative histories routinely speak of garrisons (*phroura*) but usually only during times of war. A town occupied by a conquering army or a town preparing for an enemy attack naturally had a garrison enlarged by soldiers who were normally not garrison soldiers but campaign troops, paramilitary guards, or perhaps even ordinary citizens. For example, Kantakouzenos (II, 162) writes that, on the eve of his acclamation as emperor in 1341, he sought the support of "all the cities of Macedonia and Thrace," and he sent "garrisons of hoplites and light archers to those cities that he knew to be easily held by garrisons." In fact some towns garrisoned during particularly difficult moments, such as during the civil wars, may not otherwise have had imperial garrisons at all.

Thus, the frequent passages that note some military leader "placing a garrison" in a particular town or some town possessing a garrison tell us very little at all about garrison troops. A few examples illustrate this. In 1307 during the Catalan crisis, Gregoras writes that Andronikos II sent generals to enroll troops "who were to be fit guards of the cities in Macedonia." Once the danger had passed, these men, no doubt a sorry lot, probably returned to the plough, the wheel, or the road. In other cases towns were garrisoned by soldiers who were more of an occupation force. In Vodena in 1350 "there was an army of Serbs settled in the city for a garrison," and the fortress of Gynaikokastron "had a settled army of Serbs and confederate Romans."[50]

Sometimes the difficulties are caused by literary conventions. Kantakouzenos, who of all the historians speaks most frequently of garrisons, had the unfortunate tendency to view the countryside as merely a collection

---

50. Gregoras, I, 246; other examples: Kantakouzenos, I, 177; II, 253. Kantakouzenos, III, 127, 136.

of towns, so that when he mentions soldiers in a particular town, there is often some confusion about what he means. For example, one might conclude that the phrase "the large population in Adrianople and the army installed there" indicates a standing garrison. But did he have garrisons in mind when he wrote of "whatever military forces were established in the small Thracian towns"? Since a small town (*kome*) was not ordinarily fortified, it is not easy to view these soldiers as garrison troops.[51]

Despite all this it is still possible to make some general observations about garrisons. First, garrisons had a twofold function: to form the core of a town's defenses against external threats, and to defend members of the state apparatus and of the aristocracy from the *demos* "the common people," that is, the "few" (*hoi oligoi*) from the "many" (*hoi polloi*). Disharmony between the classes was not a negligible concern, particularly during the civil wars when factions tended to draw their support along class lines. A garrison in an acropolis was an easy symbol with which to stir the demos, and consequently garrisons frequently found themselves under siege from the town below.[52] While hostile attitudes toward a garrison were most common when it was composed of foreigners or other troops from outside the town, locals were not always reliable. The attempt of Alexios Apokaukos' son John to hand Thessaloniki over to Kantakouzenos in 1345 failed because his garrison soldiers, friends and relatives of the Zealots, opposed the move. When the Zealots attacked the acropolis, the garrison put up no resistance.[53]

Sometimes friction between demos and garrison was caused not so much by factionalism and xenophobia as by disagreements over the proper response to external threats. In 1307 the Catalans attacked the town of Vizye. The temporary garrison, 200 cavalry commanded by the megas tzaousios Houmbertopoulos, had intended to remain inside the town and avoid a confrontation in the field, but "the mob of Vizye was seized by a martial spirit" and demanded an offensive sally against the Catalans. Reluctantly Houmbertopoulos led his cavalry and many townspeople out of Vizye only to be crushed by the Catalans. In another example, when some Mongols invaded the Empire in 1342 and set up camp near Skopelos in Thrace, "the demos in Skopelos, learning that the plundering Mongols had

---

51. Kantakouzenos, I, 39, 101.
52. Kantakouzenos, II, 277; III, 188; and Gregoras, III, 178, among numerous examples. On this subject, see also MM, V, 80, lines 6–7; 261, lines 2–4.
53. Kantakouzenos, I, 272; II, 578. Gregoras, II, 634–35. O. Tafrali, *Thessalonique au quatorzième siècle* (Paris, 1913), 58.

not returned home, were stirred recklessly by their customary stupidity, and each grabbed whatever arms he had. They forced Michael the governor of the town to take hold of the soldiers, as many as were among them, and to engage the nearby barbarians." Michael refused and was imprisoned. The leaders of the demos then threatened the soldiers, saying that "if it should be necessary, it would be preferable to die fighting the barbarians than to be destroyed household and all by fellow citizens." The soldiers, convinced by this logic, accompanied the common people as they advanced against the Mongols. In the subsequent battle the only survivors from Skopelos were those mounted soldiers able to flee the debacle.[54]

The garrison of Constantinople was composed of those standing troops, excluding palace guards, who were ready at a moment's notice to defend the city from within its walls or to march or ride outside the city to respond to nearby crises. On the whole, very little is known about the garrison of the capital. There is no evidence that divisions of garrison troops had any special names or that garrison soldiers were distinguishable from any of the mercenaries, aside from the palace guards, who lived in the city. For the most part the sources speak of soldiers inside Constantinople only when it was threatened, such as during the civil wars and Turkish sieges. At those times soldiers were found wherever possible, creating a misleading impression of the nature and certainly the size of the city's garrison troops.

The best example of a garrison in Constantinople is the group of Catalans holding the Golden Gate fort for Kantakouzenos in 1352. Because we are told that their commander Juan de Peralta had known Kantakouzenos since their days in Serbia years earlier, these mercenaries can probably be identified as the group of "Latin" or "German" mercenaries who had deserted Stefan Dušan's employ in 1343.[55] Dušan, it seems, frequently employed Catalan (or Aragonese) mercenaries.[56] The function of this garrison of Catalans was not only to defend the city if attacked by John V's forces but to maintain Kantakouzenos' control over the city. Gregoras

---

54. Pachymeres, Bonn ed., II, 629–30. Laiou, *Constantinople*, 169. Kantakouzenos, II, 303–05.

55. Kantakouzenos, II, 354–55; III, 292, 301–303; and also, III, 30. D. Nicol, *The Byzantine Family of Kantakouzenos (Cantacuzenus)* (Washington, D.C., 1968), 84–85. John VI Kantakouzenos, "The History of John Cantacuzenus (book 4): Text, Translation and Commentary," ed. T. Miller, diss., Catholic Univ. 1975, 275.

56. Kantakouzenos, I, 429; III, 124. Gregoras, I, 455. Bosch, *Andronikos*, 74 and note 4. On the question of ethnicity, see M. Dinić, "Španski najamnici u srpskoj službi," *ZRVI* 6 (1960), 15–28.

reports that the emperor threatened the people of Constantinople that if they surrendered to John V during his absence, they would face both the Turkish allies of Kantakouzenos and the garrison of the city.[57]

Kantakouzenos should provide the most reliable information about the sizes of garrisons since he had firsthand knowledge of the fall of many kastra. Yet references to their size are rare from the start and difficulties are compounded by the fact that garrison strengths are reported only when the possession of a kastron was being contested. Therefore the figures we have for garrison sizes do not necessarily represent the ordinary standing body of troops guarding a kastron (which during those infrequent periods of peace may have been quite small), but the forces positioned or assembled to counter the external threat of a besieging army or the internal threat of a hostile populace. For instance, after the Bulgarian George Terter conquered Philippopolis in 1322 he installed a garrison of "one thousand picked cavalry of Alans and Bulgarians and twice as many foot shieldbearers" led by three archons and a general. Clearly this was an army of occupation which, quite rightly, expected a Byzantine attempt to retake the city.[58]

That same year when Apros was besieged by Andronikos III, we learn from Kantakouzenos' account that the town had been specially reinforced by 220 cavalry, 200 archers, and thirty crossbowmen from Constantinople. The local forces amounted to one hundred cavalry, "not a few archers and slingers," "a great number" of those living around Apros (*perioikoi*: paroikoi?) "who came together because of the war," and a large light-armed force. Therefore the local soldiery assigned to Apros included at most one hundred cavalry and an undisclosed number of archers and "slingers." Doubtless some of the archers and most if not all of the so-called light-armed were the paramilitary guards of Apros and the inhabitants of the town and the surrounding area who had armed themselves for the siege. In his lively account of the siege of Constantinople in 1422, John Kananos similarly speaks of how the numbers of defenders swelled at the time of an attack:

> And with help of the All-Holy [Mother of God] they were strengthened in courage and hastened with sword in hand and with stones against the impious

57. Gregoras, III, 180; and cf. II, 727. *Regesten*, no. 2996. Other references to garrisons and garrison soldiers: Gregoras, I, 419; and Kantakouzenos, I, 300, 302; II, 343.

58. Kantakouzenos, I, 173. The use of the word "shieldbearers" (*peltastai*) here is imprecise and can probably be attributed to archaizing. In the medieval world, shieldbearers were used as defensive troops for bowmen and slingers, without whom a corps of shieldbearers had no function.

ones . . . each with the arms possible, some without arms, others with swords and spears. Others who were not well-off tied on drums made from barrels from where they ate mess and carried these instead of shields. Some not from among those [in the city] came to the war and with stones alone fought courageously and bravely as if they were heavily armed.[59]

The few figures Kantakouzenos offers for the size of a force "sufficient for the garrison of a [small] city" in time of war are fairly credible.[60] When Rhentina surrendered to him in 1342 he installed a garrison of 200 stratiotai. Similarly, after he seized Vodena in 1350 he again placed a force of 200 hoplites and light-armed troops (psiloi), and when the town was retaken by Dušan in 1351, these 200 troops were still stationed there.[61] In late 1341 when Kantakouzenos ordered out on campaign a force of one thousand stratiotai and one hundred hoplites and archers which had been encamped at Pamphilon, he left behind 300 cavalry to guard the town. Pachymeres lends support to the magnitude of Kantakouzenos' figures when he states that Houmbertopoulos defended Vizye against the Catalans in 1307 with about 200 cavalry. According to Muntaner the Catalans garrisoned Gallipoli with one hundred Almugavars and fifty cavalry plus their sailors. Later he says there were 200 foot and twenty horse, and that this was further reduced through desertion to 132 foot (sailors and Almugavars) and seven horse.[62]
     Villehardouin's figures for the Frankish garrisons of Thrace following the Fourth Crusade are similar: Adrianople had forty cavalry and one hundred mounted sergeants; Tzouroullos, eighty cavalry; Rhousion, 140 cavalry and many mounted sergeants; Vizye, 120 cavalry and many mounted sergeants; and Selymbria, fifty cavalry. According to Kritoboulos, Mehmet II's garrisons at Corinth, Mistra, and Mytilene each had 400 men, as did the Byzantine fortress of Kastrion north of Mistra. On the other hand, the desperate situation faced by the Byzantines in 1453 is brought home by the figures he provides for the garrisons of the forts near Constantinople seized by Mehmet II just prior to the city's fall. The forts of Therapeion, of Stoudion, and the fort on Prinkipo island contained respectively forty, thirty-six, and thirty armed defenders at the time of their surrender.[63]

59. Kantakouzenos, I, 140. Giovanni Cananos, *L'assedio di Costantinopoli*, ed. E. Pinto (Messina, 1977), lines 421–32 (see under Kananos in Bibliography).
     60. The phrase is from Kantakouzenos (II, 232).
     61. Kantakouzenos, II, 236, 277; III, 129, 161.
     62. Kantakouzenos, II, 187. Pachymeres, Bonn ed., II, 629. Laiou, *Constantinople*, 169. R. Muntaner, *Cronicà*, ed. E.B. (Barcelona, 1927–52), II, chs. 222, 225; English trans. Lady Goodenough, *The Chronicle of Muntaner* (London, 1920–21), II, 527, 533–34.
     63. B. Hendrickx, «Οἱ πολιτικοὶ καὶ στρατιωτικοὶ θεσμοὶ τῆς Λατινικῆς Αὐτο-κρατορίας τῆς Κωνσταντινουπόλεως κατὰ τοὺς πρώτους χρόνους τῆς ὑπαρχεώς της»,

In all of these cases the number of garrison troops was provided at a time when a state of war existed. In peacetime the permanent garrisons of these towns certainly would have been much smaller. For purposes of comparison, we may note that in English castles during the late eleventh and twelfth centuries, the variance in sizes between standing, permanent, peacetime garrisons and wartime garrisons was dramatic. Since knights generally owed forty days of garrison service per year, peacetime garrisons had one-ninth the number of troops that owed garrison service in time of war. Thus, for one group of castles for which there is sufficient evidence to make such calculations, peacetime garrisons ranged from two to fifty knights (or an equivalent, and larger, number of sergeants), whereas the number of knights on call in time of war for these same castles was nine times higher, from eighteen to 450, with an average of 180. These latter figures are more in line with the testimony of the Byzantine sources.[64]

Naturally some cities required more troops. When Kantakouzenos left Didymoteichon in 1342, he says that he provided it with one thousand cavalry under four archons and 8,000 archers under eight archons. These "archers" were part of the demos that staged an abortive uprising against the "powerful" (*dynatoi*) in the acropolis later that year. Hence, the figure of 8,000 foot archers probably represented the number of inhabitants of Didymoteichon capable of bearing arms plus whatever irregular foot troops had come to Didymoteichon from the surrounding countryside. Hence the effective garrison of Didymoteichon was really the thousand-man cavalry. Later, during the winter of 1342–43, after most of the horses were lost through famine and another 400 troops left the town to plunder the suburbs, only 200 of the remainder still had mounts.[65]

Kantakouzenos tends to give higher figures for enemy garrisons. For example, Martino Zaccaria commanded 800 Genoese mercenaries on Chios in 1329; in 1350 the Serb garrison of Verria—an occupation force—consisted of thirty nobles with their families, 1,500 soldiers, and a contingent of Western mercenaries; and Gregory Preljub's Serb garrison in Servia in 1350

---

diss., Thessaloniki 1970, 156–57. Villehardouin, *La conquête de Constantinople*, ed. E. Faral, 2 vols. (Paris, 1938–39), 273, 343, 402, 403, 411; English trans. M. Shaw, in *Joinville and Villehardouin, Chronicles of the Crusades* (Baltimore, Md., 1963), 100, 117, 133, 135–36. Kritoboulos, *Critobuli Imbriotae historiae*, ed. D. Reinsch (Berlin and New York, 1983), 127, 144, 190, 145, 47–48. Cf. Doukas, 307: the sultan assigned a garrison of 400 men to Rumeli Hisar.

64. S. Painter, "Castle-Guard," *American Historical Review* 40 (1934–35), 451–54.

65. Kantakouzenos, II, 195, 282. Gregoras (II, 627) says he left behind "more than 500 armed stratiotai and cavalry." Kantakouzenos, II, 287–88, 348. On this episode, see C. Asdracha, "Formes de brigandage pendant la deuxième guerre civile byzantine au XIVe s.," *Études Balkaniques* 7 (1971), 118–20.

numbered more than 500 men.[66] Compared with Kantakouzenos' other figures, these could well be slight exaggerations. Yet the tally of forces at the siege of Apros mentioned above demonstrates the difficulty in assessing the number of troops. Does one count everyone, down to the last octogenarian with cudgel? As difficult as it is for the historian to determine garrison sizes, it was also difficult, and much more critical, for those actually conducting war.

Venetian sources provide some useful information on garrison sizes, and at times they also show this tendency to exaggerate the size of enemy forces. In 1425 the chronicle of Morosini reports that while the Venetian adventurer Fantin Michiel conquered Kavalla by defeating a force of about 400 Turks, he installed a garrison there of only eighty men.[67] Venice's own garrisons in the Aegean area could be very small. In 1387 the fortress of Butrinto across from Kerkyra (Corfu) had fifteen crossbowmen, and in 1394 Argos had a garrison of eight crossbowmen and six sergeants.[68]

On the other hand, an important city facing an immediate threat required a larger garrison. In 1423 at the beginning of Venice's possession of Thessaloniki, the Senate agreed to ask the government of Crete for 500 crossbowmen (*ballistarii*) for the city and also allowed the governors of Thessaloniki to hire "one hundred mercenary stratiotai" (*soldandi Stratiotos centum*). In addition, the governors were given a sum of money, 2,200 ducats of which was to be used for infantry troops (*pedites*) and other matters. Thus the garrison of Thessaloniki in 1423 had well over 600 men. Two years later the Senate supplemented this force with one hundred infantry. An entry from the chronicle of Morosini confirms that during a siege in 1426 there were 700 crossbowmen defending Thessaloniki. Nevertheless, while lamenting the fall of the city in 1430, the historian Doukas asks rhetorically, "What could five hundred or one thousand or two thousand men accomplish in such a large city? There was barely one crossbowman to cover ten turrets."[69]

The evidence cited above indicates that crossbowmen were the back-

66. Kantakouzenos, I, 376, 378; III, 124, 131.

67. K. Mertzios, Μνημεῖα Μακεδονικῆς Ἱστορίας (Thessaloniki, 1947), 26–27. The chronicle of Zancaruola says he left 130 (idem, 28).

68. F. Thiriet, *Régestes des délibérations du Sénat de Venise concernant la Romanie* (Paris, 1958–61), I, nos. 730, 861.

69. Sathas, Μνημεῖα, I, 146, lines 21–31, and 150, lines 17–25 (Thiriet, *Régestes*, II, no. 1898). Mertzios, Μνημεῖα, 62–63 (*Régestes*, II, no. 2004), 64. Doukas, 249; English trans. H. Magoulias, *Doukas. Decline and Fall of Byzantium to the Ottoman Turks* (Detroit, 1975), 171.

bone of garrison forces. Crossbowmen served on foot and, at least in the Greek sources, always fought within fortifications, never on campaign service. The Byzantines were slow to adopt the crossbow, and this is seen in the absence of a consistent spelling for the word for crossbowmen (*tzangratores* or *tzangratoroi*). The early thirteenth-century historian Niketas Choniates speaks of them as *tzangratoxotai* (literally, "crossbow-archers"), and the late thirteenth- or fourteenth-century paraphrase of Choniates' history, written in a simplified and more current Greek, substitutes for this the words *tzagratores* or *zangkratores*. *Tzagratoroi* are frequently encountered in the *Chronicle of the Morea*, and the fifteenth-century *Chronicle of the Tocco* offers many examples of *tzakratoroi* in the garrisons of kastra, distinguishing them from regular "stratiotai." Also in the fifteenth century, the historian Doukas differentiates between the tzagratoroi and the simple archers (*toxotai*) present in Constantinople in 1453. According to Pseudo-Kodinos, who is evidently speaking only of the crossbowmen in the garrison of Constantinople, they were commanded by a stratopedarches of the Tzangratores, an office found in all the late Byzantine lists of precedence. Pachymeres mentions someone with this title named Siouros, who was a military figure at the beginning of the fourteenth century.[70]

As for the social status of garrison troops, there is little evidence with which to work. This in itself suggests that these soldiers enjoyed a relatively modest social and economic status. Beyond this, an act from 1288 of the inhabitants of Kos, both lay and religious, contains the signs of three crossbowmen (tzangratores) toward the end of a long list of laymen (Appendix, nos. 33–35). Given that the other signatories to the act included the kastrophylax of Pelion, and several individuals (or families) well known through other preserved documents, we can be sure that these crossbowmen, though perhaps of modest status, were not the lowliest inhabitants of Kos. Perhaps we can see a parallel in the brotherhoods of marksmen in thirteenth- and fourteenth-century Belgium. These were guilds of bowmen

---

70. *Nicetae Choniatae Historia*, ed. J. van Dieten (Berlin, 1975), 539; and for the paraphrase, ed. I. Bekker (Bonn, 1835), 104, 714, and ed. van Dieten, 78 apparatus. *Chronicle of the Morea*, ed. Schmitt, index. In Lurier's translation (*Crusaders as Conquerors* [New York, 1964], 218 note 7), the word is incorrectly rendered as "siege machines." G. Schirò, ed., *Cronaca dei Tocco di Cefalonia di Anonimo* (Rome, 1975), index, and v. 597. Doukas, 355. *Pseudo-Kodinos*, 139, 187, and index. Two versions of a mid-fifteenth-century or later list of precedence (probably from Trebizond) say (mistakenly) they were led by a protallagator: *Pseudo-Kodinos*, 345, 348. Pachymeres, Bonn ed., II, 414. See also, L.-P. Raybaud, *Le gouvernement et l'administration centrale de l'empire byzantin sous les premiers Paléologues* (Paris, 1968), 243, and Stein, "Untersuchungen," 55.

funded by the towns, the only permanent urban armed forces before standing mercenaries appeared in the late fifteenth century.[71]

By far the most common method of financing garrison soldiers was with cash. Mercenary garrison soldiers, like all mercenaries, were expensive to maintain, and even a moderately sized town facing any external threat at all required scores if not hundreds of men to defend it. Kantakouzenos says that at least one thousand mercenaries were needed to garrison Mytilene and Phokaia when under siege, and in 1350 Stefan Dušan's army of occupation in Verria consisted of some 1,500 soldiers.[72] Yet the Byzantine state did not have the resources and probably lacked the manpower to supply each town with a proper standing garrison. At best, in times of need, the state allocated its soldiers, both standing and reserve, where they were most needed.[73] Otherwise it could attempt to hire additional soldiers temporarily, as when Andronikos II sent generals to Macedonia to recruit an army to defend its towns from the Catalans.[74]

Kantakouzenos (I, 87–88) writes that when he was appointed governor of Thessaly in 1321, he delayed his departure with the excuse that he could not go "before the money was given to him that was to be used for the mercenaries of the army and for the garrisons of the towns of Thessaly." The sum was 50,000 hyperpyra, and its magnitude, even allowing for exaggeration, indicates that Kantakouzenos' activities were to constitute a major step in consolidating Byzantine control over the area. How many soldiers could it have financed? If mercenary infantry pay ranged from the equivalent of 1.9 to 5.2 ducats per month, or an average of about 3.6 ducats per month (see Chapter 7), we can use the figure of 36 ducats as the approximate yearly cost of a permanent mercenary. In 1321 50,000 hyperpyra were equivalent to about 25,000 ducats. Dividing (and ignoring administrative expenses), we see that the sum might have hired some 694 mercenaries. Assuming that a few hundred campaign mercenaries were involved there would have been enough money remaining to finance perhaps 500 garrison soldiers for all the towns held in Thessaly, and most of

---

71. M. Nystazopoulou-Pelekidou, Βυζαντινὰ ἔγγραφα τῆς μονῆς Πάτμου, II (Athens, 1980), no. 75: the act is entitled "Written request of the inhabitants of the island of Kos, priest, soldiers, and common people, servants and slaves of your mighty and holy majesty." C. Gaier, "Analysis of Military Forces in the Principality of Liège and the County of Looz from the Twelfth to the Fifteenth Century," *Studies in Medieval and Renaissance History* 2 (1965), 251f.

72. Kantakouzenos, I, 490 (cf. Gregoras, I, 535); III, 124.

73. See Pachymeres, ed. Failler, I, 153 (Bonn ed., I, 107); Kantakouzenos, I, 136; and Gregoras, II, 596.

74. Gregoras, I, 246.

these soldiers would have been lesser-paid archers, not crossbowmen. This was all the imperial government could do, and it was quite little considering the importance of Thessaly. Consequently, alternatives had to be found to finance garrison troops without resorting to cash.

One method is illustrated by the Klazomenitai soldier company, the group of collective pronoiars who in 1342 received a chrysobull in the name of John V granting each of them the right to transmit to their sons a posotes—for some of them 12 hyperpyra, for others 10—from the pronoia they held jointly. Since the document speaks of them explicitly as "the Klazomenitai soldiers living in the God-preserved city of Serres" (very rare information in such a document), and since other sources speak of a gate called *tou Klazomenou* in Serres at that very moment, it is reasonable to conclude that they formed part of the garrison of Serres. This conclusion conveniently provides us with the reason for the document's issuance. The Klazomenitai were being rewarded for loyal (and successful) service during a period of civil war, immediately after a failed attempt of Kantakouzenos to capture the town.[75]

There is only one other reference that possibly links garrison troops to land. A document from 1355 identifies a particular property on Lemnos as located "near the land of the tzangratores."[76] While it is certainly possible that, in this case, "Tzangrator" could be an otherwise unattested family name, it is more likely that this document is referring to land held by a group of crossbowmen, though there is no evidence connecting this land to their military service. It is conceivable, though hardly certain, that these crossbowmen were collective pronoiars or smallholding soldiers who were receiving at least part of their remuneration from land.

What is known of the method of remunerating the Klazomenitai is discernible only because land was involved. No doubt other innovative ways to finance garrison soldiers without relying on the imperial treasury existed, but no knowledge of these has survived because they involved undocumented payments in gold or in kind. In particular one may think of purely local, informal arrangements between kephale and garrison soldier, something paralleling the great man and the retainers who accompanied him on campaign. The kephale was a great man, usually *ex persona* as well as

75. P. Lemerle, *Actes de Kutlumus*, rev. ed. (Paris, 1988), no. 20. A. Guillou, *Les archives de Saint-Jean-Prodrome* (Paris, 1955), 28–29, 29 note 1. Oikonomidès, "A propos des armées," 368–69.

76. W. Regel, E. Kurtz, and B. Korablev, *Actes de Philothée*, VizVrem 20 (1913), suppl. 1, no. 10, lines 62–63.

ex officio, and given the vicissitudes of urban life, troops personally loyal to and dependent on the kephale may have been both a luxury he could afford and a necessity he could not live without.

Finally, we turn to the guarding of borders. In the pre-modern world there were basically two military methods for guarding a frontier: with a wall or a line of forts or fortified towns garrisoned by standing troops, or with reserve troops that held lands personally at the border. In Byzantium the former method was represented by the Hexamilion in the Morea and Anastasios' Long Walls outside Constantinople, though indeed the best-known examples are the Great Wall of China and the Roman walls of Britain and along the Rhine. For the latter method we have the middle Byzantine border soldiers settled along the Empire's eastern frontier. Parallels are seen in the Carolingian marches and in the late Roman *limitanei* and *foederati*. The preferred frontier defense has always been a wall manned by a standing garrison. Naturally this is the most expensive program of all, requiring the greatest initial investment as well as the greatest outlays for maintenance and salaries. The failure of the Hexamilion across the Isthmus of Corinth was not the result of faulty tactics but of flawed strategic and logistical considerations: Manuel II was unable to win sufficient political support for his wall among the aristocrats of the Morea, and whatever plan he devised for keeping it manned proved ineffectual. But if a wall can be properly financed, it is not only the most secure system militarily, but the dependence of the frontier troops on the governmental center makes it also an effective tool for maintaining political control over the frontiers and the troops guarding them.

In the interest of economy or while a wall is being completed, a string of forts, incorporating or supplementing existing town fortifications, can be erected, though with a corresponding reduction in overall security. In the Roman Empire of the first and early second centuries this was the policy that was followed, particularly along the *limes* of Germania Superior and Raetia. However, by the mid-second century the strain on the Empire's resources produced by this grand program was seen in the growing tendency to employ native auxiliaries to supplement regular legionnaires on the frontier. During the early third century the degeneration of the Empire's frontier policy continued as local troops (limitanei) were given land and settled along the frontier in return for military service. Finally, in the late fourth and fifth centuries, for financial and other reasons, the northern frontiers were abandoned to the foederati, Germans settled in groups along the frontiers and charged with their defense. Each of these successive steps created a frontier force that was less reliable and that at the same time lessened the central government's control over the frontier until it disappeared entirely.

In Byzantium frontier walls were rarely ever constructed. The reasons for this were military, political, economic, and ideological.[77] It is quite possible that in the long run ideological reasons predominated, that the mission of the Empire was reconquest, and that the Empire's spiritual power radiating from Constantinople could not be circumscribed by walls. Be that as it may, the de facto borders of the Empire, in the Balkans and especially in the East, were throughout most of its existence lines of natural fortification, that is, mountains broken by passes (*kleisourai*) where forts were constructed. Even had individual emperors or commanders wished to construct walls, an endemic lack of resources deterred them. Further, the geography of Asia Minor and the Balkans is inappropriate for wall construction. Mountains with forts placed at their passes are a thoroughly adequate barrier to invading armies. Hills, which only at great expense can be fortified with walls, also provide an adequate natural defense against enemy cavalry and, if they are forested, even against infantry. Any invading army that succeeded in entering the Empire did so through the natural breaks in the highland chains, through defiles or river valleys.

Given the frequent success of invading armies, notably Slav and Arab, in penetrating Byzantine frontier defenses and the usual Byzantine response, it must be emphasized that frontier defenses in the middle Byzantine period were only part of a larger defensive system based upon the themes. The evolution of the theme system from the seventh through the tenth century displayed, as each new theme was created, a concentric extension of military control from Constantinople toward both east and west. With Byzantine conquest, as a theme was transformed from being the furthermost to the penultimate outpost of imperial power, its military defensive organization underwent no abrupt change. Indeed its institutionalized and localized provincial, or thematic, army remained essentially the same numerically because, with a shift of fortune, today's heartland could become tomorrow's march. Consequently, if the kleisourai were violated, the invader faced but another defensive zone in the adjoining theme, and then another, until he was obliged to withdraw. In this sense the

77. In general see H. Ahrweiler, "La frontière et les frontières de Byzance en Orient," in Ahrweiler, *Byzance: les pays et les territoires*, no. III, 209–30.

thematic system made the entire Empire a series of concentric defensive zones and made all thematic soldiers frontier soldiers.

Since the strength of imperial control diminished as one moved further from the capital, the soldiers of the kleisourai were the least regimented and the most indulgent of their own priorities and those of the local aristocracies. These were the soldiers called *akritai*, "borderers," of the middle Byzantine period, semi-independent native warriors, whose activities were celebrated in the epic poem *Digenes Akrites*. Although the middle Byzantine akritai were soldiers who at regular intervals did garrison the frontier forts and participate in campaigns outside the Empire, their real usefulness lay in their domiciliary deployment. Even though the fortified kleisourai and mountain chains deterred the invasion of enemy armies, these could not prevent the incursions of smaller bands of soldiers and bandits who found ways to circumvent the artificial or natural fortifications. While they posed no threat to the Empire as a whole, they were a particular vexation to frontier officials and magnates in their endeavors to stabilize the area politically and economically. On the frontiers the akritai could be mobilized to respond quickly and eagerly to such threats against their lands. This bond between the akrites and his land served well the interests of the state.

As discussed earlier (Chapters 1 and 2), the security of the Anatolian frontier during the Nicaean period was maintained against the incursion of Turkoman and splinter Seljuk bands by settlers granted tax exemption and other privileges in return for occupying the frontier zone. Their usefulness lay too in their strong attachment to their land. But while it is possible that they may have acted at times in concert with the central Nicaean army, they were not really part of the army, but rather a quasi-military, independently acting force only nominally under Nicaean control. They were not soldiers, nor do the sources ever call them "akritai." Only during Michael VIII's reign were they converted from a local independent militia into campaign troops, that is, into real Byzantine soldiers, and this had negative consequences for the eastern frontier. Demoralization, caused by the chronic lateness of their pay, and increased Turkish pressure forced numbers of them to make separate peace with the Turks. In this way more and more land fell out of Byzantine control. Some of the settlers fled to Europe or took up brigandage. Only a few retreated to the shrinking Anatolian frontier where they are last encountered in the 1290s.

For the frontiers in the west information is very scarce, and for the thirteenth century it is practically nonexistent. Presumably the reconquest of Macedonia and Thrace, along with the slow reorganization of the European provinces which lasted well into Michael VIII's reign, relying as heavily as it did on military governors, placed great emphasis on military border guards. Little more can be said. In the fourteenth century military border guards are often in evidence. Andronikos III learned of a Mongol invasion in 1331 from "look-outs" (*skopoi*) who "were assigned" to the passages into Byzantium; through such look-outs Kantakouzenos heard of a Serbian invasion; and during the civil wars of the 1320s there was "a guard of the borders of the realm apportioned to [Andronikos III] which faced toward Constantinople."[78] Still there was nothing in the west like the Nicaean highlanders.

In comparison, Dušan's Law Code explains that Serbian border lords (*vlastela krajišnici*) were obligated to prevent anyone from crossing their land and were financially liable for damages to other people's lands. If an army crossed the border lord's land and plundered the Serbian ruler's land, the border lord made good the loss. If, however, bandits were able to cross his land and then plundered anyone else's land, the border lord paid seven times the loss. King Dragutin's chrysobull for the monastery of Chilandar notes that its dependency at Prizren, at that time near the border with the Empire, had been maintaining a guard against Byzantium.[79] In such case, a monastic or lay landowner naturally preferred that his dependent peasants undertake this responsibility, but it is also possible that more effective professionals might be hired to perform the necessary guard service. In Byzantium there is no evidence for any general or specific obligation on the part of landowners to guard the state's borders.

78. Kantakouzenos, I, 456; and Gregoras, III, 181; I, 355. Also, Gregoras, I, 229, 266, 499, 500.

79. *Zakonik cara Stefana Dušana*, ed. Radojčić, arts. 49, 143. B. Korablev and L. Petit, *Actes de Chilandar, II. Actes slaves, VizVrem* 19 (1915), suppl. 1, no. 6 = Novaković, *Zakonski spomenici*, 387 iii.

13. Guard Service: Kastron, Countryside

The number of garrison soldiers needed in a kastron was minimized by employing paramilitary guards for the duties not requiring the services of a trained soldier. Thus there was a distinction between the military service performed by garrison troops and the paramilitary guard service performed by men who were not soldiers but guards, watchmen, and police. Depending on a town's size, location, and level of social organization, this guard service was undertaken either by members of the entire population or by a more or less professional group of men who regularly carried out the requisite duties.

Paramilitary guards had much less status than garrison troops. One of the best illustrations of this is found in a 1342 act of Michael Gabrielopoulos, a semi-independent governor in Thessaly, which granted certain privileges to the inhabitants of the kastron of Phanarion. Predominant among these privileges was Gabrielopoulos' promise that, while the soldiers (*stratiotai*) of Phanarion were still obligated to perform military service (*stratiotike douleia*), they were exempted specifically from something called *tzakonike phylaxis*. This phrase, which literally means "tzakonian guard," refers to an institution with a very long history in Byzantium. People called "tzakones" are first mentioned in the tenth century by Constantine VII Porphyrogennetos as certain troop divisions assigned to the Empire's forts and composed of impoverished soldiers who were no longer able to maintain themselves properly.[1] As we have already seen, the name was later applied to the light-armed marines and palace guards that Michael VIII transplanted from the Morea and other areas and settled in Constantinople in the early 1260s. As an institution, the guards about whom the Porphyrogennetos spoke continued to exist into the late period, and as in the tenth century they possessed no special ethnic or geographic character.

1. MM, V, 260, lines 20–22. Constantine VII Porphyrogenitus, *De cerimoniis aulae byzantinae*, ed. I. Reiske (Bonn, 1829–30), I, 696. M. Bartusis, "Urban Guard Service in Late Byzantium: The Terminology and the Institution," *Macedonian Studies* 5, n.s. 2 (1988), 53–54, 61.

Michael Gabrielopoulos' act distinguishes between tzakonike and stratiotike service, that is, between guard duty and military service. Other
sources confirm this distinction. The founder of one of the monasteries of
Meteora is described as "one of those called tzakones or guards [*phylakes*]."
At the fall of Constantinople, the historian Doukas speaks of stratiotai and
viglai (literally, "watchers"), and a Neapolitan source of 1301/2 divides
Greek mercenaries in Epiros into "zacconos et stratiotas."[2] This indicates
that mercenaries could be either tzakones or stratiotai (more properly that
they could perform either tzakonike or stratiotike service).

Tzakonike service meant sentinel duty at the gates, night-watch and
process serving, the watch over the kastron, particularly at night and for the
control of fire, and the enforcement of the orders of civil magistrates. These
were the daily, tedious yet necessary, paramilitary burdens that did not
require the skills of a trained soldier and as such would be the duties from
which stratiotai, as an elite segment of the population, would endeavor to
disassociate themselves. The onerous tzakonike phylaxis mentioned in Michael Gabrielopoulos' act was not service "befitting a stratiotes" and yet its
superficial similarity to stratiotike douleia compelled the soldiers of Phanarion to demand the explicit pronouncement that it was not part of their
duties. As a result, these duties—which we often associate with police,
sheriff, or militia—fell upon other inhabitants of the town.

Kantakouzenos (III, 123) speaks of such nonmilitary guards in regard
to his surprise seizure of Verria in 1350. At night he sent some troops over
the town's wall: "Those soldiers who were inside first met some guards,
seized them and ordered them to be quiet or die. Then they went to the gate
called Opsikkiane and met other citizen guards [*phylakes politai*] and ordered them to help them break the bolts." There is no indication here that
either of these two groups of guards was armed. In fact their easy capture
without struggle suggests they were unarmed or insubstantially armed.
They may have been militiamen mustered for the present crisis, but they
clearly were not soldiers. As such they were the lowliest element in the
defensive structure.

In moments of crisis an entire town was mobilized, the army joined by
the citizenry. John Kananos describes how the siege of Constantinople in
1422 brought out the best in the city's inhabitants:

2. N. Bees, «Συμβολὴ εἰς τὴν ἱστορίαν τῶν μονῶν τῶν Μετεώρων», Βυζαντίς 1
(1909), 274. Doukas, 345. C. Hopf, *Geschichte Griechenlands vom Beginn des Mittelalters bis auf
unsere Zeit*, in H. Brockhaus, *Griechenland*, vol. 6: *B. Griechenland im Mittelalter und in der
Neuzeit* (Leipzig, 1870), 354.

And the many women turned into brave men at that most chilling hour of war, neither hiding nor being afraid like women, but rather going to the outer fortifications at the hour of war and carrying stones to the walls for the Roman warriors, drawing water for them, and pushing them on to battle and war. Others took hold of furs and rags and tended to the wounded or gave water and wine to those scorched by thirst from fighting, or followed behind their brothers and sons and husbands, not descending from the walls of the fortifications.[3]

It seems, however, that only direct threats motivated most townspeople to take up arms. In the early fourteenth century Thomas Magistros wrote a treatise called *On the Relation of Citizens to the State (Peri politeias)* in which he suggested that all the subjects of a well-ordered state should be trained in arms and be ready to supplement the state's army:

In order that those who practice crafts not be held in high repute for this alone and be [only] half as useful to the State, performing for their citizenship only works of peace, they should also have in their minds a spirit and a readiness for combat. Since it is not in the least necessary for us to divide life into peace and war . . . I urge each of these to possess arms of every sort. While they eagerly devote their time to and carefully do not neglect their usual works, whenever they enjoy leisure they should practice the use of arms and train for battle. Thus when enemies attack and lay siege, with such preparation they can stoutly oppose and completely withstand [them]. . . . In addition to the armies the State has, these [militiamen] should also be held in high repute and defend [the State] physically. And indeed, I should think that those of the soldiers not magnificent in wealth, having a different lot, [while] not abandoning their arms, should be skilled in crafts, lest they lack necessary things on campaign, or . . . sell their arms for the sake of these [things they need], or if they are captured by the enemy [these skills may serve them in captivity].[4]

Since Thomas had observed the depredations of the Catalan Company and the inability of the imperial army to curb them, it is understandable that he regarded the civilian population as an untapped reservoir of manpower. Certainly he implies that there was a firm division between soldiers and civilians, that soldiers generally knew only arms and civilians generally knew nothing of warfare. In other words, the military was a profession.

His advice that every subject should be trained in arms to supplement the state's army underscores the fact that the state did not foster the development of urban militias. While the inhabitants of towns defended

3. Giovanni Cananos, *L'assedio di Costantinopoli*, ed. E. Pinto (Messina, 1977), lines 471–83 (see under Kananos in Bibliography).
4. Migne, *PG*, 145, col. 509. Also in A. Mai, *Scriptorum veterum nova collectio* (Rome, 1825–38), III, 180.

their homes and occasionally even the surrounding countryside, there is no evidence that they had any formal training or that they were ever asked to campaign outside their walls. In the medieval West the situation was rather different. For example, in the towns of thirteenth-century northern Italy, mass levies of urban and later rural militias were the central component of the armies of the city-states. Exhibiting a high degree of organization, the militias were paid in cash for their services and furnished their own arms and, if cavalry, horses. And even though the role of the militias was primarily defensive, they received sufficient training to fight pitched battles now and then. Similarly, during the thirteenth century in the low countries of northern Europe there were urban infantry militias, which by the fourteenth century were organized as corporations, as well as rural militias and communal cavalry.[5]

In Western Europe these urban militias arose out of very specific historical conditions. Relative prosperity and the need for each town to see to its own defense fostered the creation of urban militias. Rural militias developed much later, in the fourteenth century, and depended on the extension of social bonds from the towns to the countryside and on the emergence of a well-organized, prosperous peasantry with the leisure for military training. The decline of the northern Italian communal militias in the fourteenth century and the growing reliance on mercenaries were the results of the increasing frequency of wars and the need to project control farther and farther beyond the walls of towns.[6]

Since independence and isolation were characteristics increasingly applicable to the towns of late Byzantium, particularly in areas such as Thessaly, Epiros, and Asia Minor, it is quite possible that rudimentary urban militias did emerge. We know nothing of them because the conditions of isolation that spawned their development have also hidden them from contemporary historians. On the other hand, in areas still under central control, the imperial government had no interest in creating alternative military units which had no role in a coordinated defensive system and which could possibly present political difficulties to an already too decentralized state. For these reasons Thomas' advice was not a very practical solution to the problems of the Empire. Practicality, it has been often noted, was not the strong suit of Byzantine intellectuals.

Despite the fact that the towns of late Byzantium did not develop

---

5. M. Mallett, *Mercenaries and Their Masters* (London, 1974), 10–13. C. Gaier, "Analysis of Military Forces in the Principality of Liège and the County of Looz from the Twelfth to the Fifteenth Century," *Studies in Medieval and Renaissance History* 2 (1965), 233ff.

6. Mallett, *Mercenaries*, 43–44.

urban militias capable of replacing a trained soldiery, a regulated town guard was necessary because individual professional soldiers walking the walls were at once both too skilled for the requirements of guard service and too isolated to perform the duty for which they were best suited, coordinated point defense. Thus the method of defense that emerged was a traditional one: paramilitary guards, armed or otherwise, patrolled the walls while soldiers garrisoned in forts awaited the alarm that would draw them in force to the spot where they were needed.

In the 1319 chrysobull for the town of Ioannina, Andronikos II specified who was obligated to perform guard duty: "Those who have been assigned to it earlier according to earlier practice should again be in the *apoviglisis* [literally, 'watching'] of the kastron, and the local people should not be compelled into such *apoviglisis* of the kastron without a certain necessity and violence temporarily constraining them to this." The "local people" (*topikoi*)—as distinct from those called "kastron inhabitants" (*kastrinoi*), "citizens" (*politai*), and "inhabitants" (*epoikoi*) found elsewhere in the document—denotes all the inhabitants of the area of Ioannina, both inside and outside the kastron, and this suggests that it was not at all outlandish to expect the inhabitants of surrounding villages to share responsibility for the guard of the kastron of Ioannina. Further, since everyone except "those earlier assigned" to the apoviglisis were exempted from this type of service, Ioannina had evidently developed a municipal organization whereby some of the inhabitants undertook guard duty as an occupation. While there is no need to regard such guard duty as a fulltime job, there is good evidence that by 1314 the night-watch in distant Trebizond was indeed organized into a kind of corporation.[7]

Our knowledge of the municipal institutions of the late Byzantine era suggests that the forms and details of guard duty varied widely and evolved relatively independently from area to area. While the organization of the guard service in any particular town is difficult to reconstruct, there were two basic variations. In areas where the division of labor was less articulated, in the smaller Byzantine towns remote from the major centers, and possibly in Serbia, guard service was an obligation on most of the population, probably performed on a rotating basis. To the extent to which the inhabitants of the surrounding territory were dependent on the protection of the kastron, they too were obliged to bear part of the burden.

7. MM, V, 83. See H. Grégoire, "Les veilleurs de nuit à Trébizonde," *BZ* 18 (1909), 492, and commentary, 493–95.

In more prosperous and populous kastra with a higher degree of social organization, part-time obligatory guard service gave way to the creation of a professional class of guards with its own special status and identity. The traditional civic responsibility of guard service was discharged through payment of a tax. In Byzantium this tax, representing the commutation of the obligation of tzakonike phylaxis was called the *vigliatikon* (from *vigla*, "watch"). Such tax revenues, in addition to more creative ways of financing guard service, were used to hire professional tzakones who performed guard service on a fulltime or part-time but nonetheless permanent basis.[8]

Professional tzakones seem to have spanned a broad socioeconomic spectrum. For example, in 1268 the despot John Palaiologos instructed an official to return possession of a village in Thessaly with a yearly income of 50 hyperpyra to the monastery of Makrinitissa, and to "give to the tzakones holding it [at that moment], that is, to Christopher and Papanikolopoulos, [something] of equal value to this elsewhere." A year and a half later Despot John issued another act denying the request of Christopher that he maintain possession of the village and again ordering the transfer be made. Since the two men were to be compensated with other land of equal value, they were not holding the property illegally. The village itself with its 50-hyperpyra income was a substantial holding even for two men. There can be no question that the two did not work the village themselves; rather, they were its landlords as the monastery of Makrinitissa had been before them. Although we cannot conclude that there was any relation between the village and their service as tzakones, it is clear that Christopher and Papanikolopoulos were not peasants but co-pronoiars of a somewhat modest status.[9]

A few documents do confirm a link between landholding and tzakonike service. For example, an imperial prostagma from 1342 granted a certain Margarites hereditary and tax-free possession of arable land and vineyards he had acquired "in the villages of Kato Ouska and Rachoba from both *tzakonikai* and state *hypostaseis*." The term *hypostaseis* denotes properties, usually modest and usually associated with peasants. Because state hypostaseis are properties that belonged to the state, tzakonikai hypostaseis analogously must have been properties that belonged to tzakones. Margarites had initially paid the fisc 9 hyperpyra annually for these lands; therefore, the purpose of the document was to grant him a tax exemption

8. Bartusis, "Urban Guard Service," 60–61.
9. MM, IV, 389. Bartusis, "Urban Guard Service," 62.

(*exkousseia*) and to confirm his full ownership of them (hence the phrase granting him hereditary rights).[10]

The most likely connection between "state" and "tzakonian" hypostaseis is that there was a state obligation attached to the latter. This document, among other things, released the land from this obligation. It is reasonable then to suppose that the previous possessors of these tzakonikai hypostaseis were tzakones whose service was somehow tied to these hypostaseis. Since the multiple pieces of "land and vineyards" involved bore a tax of only 9 hyperpyra, we are dealing with small landowners, and thus the relation between tzakonike service and tzakonike land corresponded to one of two situations. Either the tzakones received or inherited their hypostaseis on condition of tzakonike service and on which there may or may not have been some tax obligation as well (a situation resembling that of the Prosalentai who received land from Michael VIII), or they received or inherited a tax exemption for the hypostaseis they had already been holding, perhaps accompanied by some cash, but only on condition of tzakonike service (this situation resembling that of fifteenth-century Gasmouloi). In either case, the tzakones involved must be viewed as peasants who worked their own lands and served part-time but nonetheless regularly as professional tzakones.

Both types of tzakonikon holding—conditional tenure based on service, and a conditional tax exemption, possibly with supplemental pay— probably existed, perhaps even side by side. However, the latter situation was probably more common because, unlike the case of the Prosalentai, no evidence exists of any major policy directed toward settling tzakones, and so it would seem that tzakonike service usually fell to people who already owned land in a particular area and who inherited or received tax exemption in return for their part-time guard duties.[11] Thus, while some tzakones, like Christopher and Papanikolopoulos, might have been pronoiars, others, certainly the majority, were little or not at all different from paroikoi.

"The stratopedarches of the Tzakones," writes Pseudo-Kodinos, "is in charge of the guards [*phylakes*] found in the kastra who are called tzakones." Although this statement may seem unequivocal, the title "stratopedarches of the Tzakones" appears only in Pseudo-Kodinos' treatise and other late

10. A. Guillou, *Les archives de Saint-Jean-Prodrome* (Paris, 1955), no. 36, lines 4–5. Bartusis, "Urban Guard Service," 62–63. Another example of tzakonikon land: P. Lemerle et al., *Actes de Lavra* (Paris, 1970–82), III, no. 146, line 35.

11. Cf. Oikonomidès, "A propos des armées," 357.

Byzantine lists of precedence, and so, like much of Pseudo-Kodinos' testimony, it cannot be corroborated. Rather, guard service appears to have been organized by the kastrophylax, the local official who was the kephale's assistant in maintaining the defensive integrity of the kastron. His personal charge was the maintenance and defense of the walls of the kastron: "to look after and tend to the rebuilding, maintenance, and watch and all else of the security and fortification with God's help by every means in the imminent service of my majesty." For example, in 1355/6 a kastrophylax named John Chamaetos rebuilt one of the city gates of Thessaloniki.[12]

In addition to fortification upkeep, the kastrophylax was also responsible for sentinel duty. Pachymeres describes a miracle which apparently occurred in the early years of the fourteenth century in Magnesia: "As the town was entrusted to a kastrophylax, awake at watch late in the night he often observed a kindled torch going around the town. When this happened two or three times, it led the kastrophylax to think. Consulting with his superiors according to custom, he threw them into like consternation."[13] Evidently Pachymeres believed a kastrophylax's duty was to keep watch and report suspicious occurrences to his superiors. According to Pachymeres' story, these superiors then sent out men to investigate (who fell upon the ghost of Emperor John Vatatzes). Presumably these men were armed and constituted what might be called the town's police force. Thus, at least in this instance, the kastrophylax commanded no soldiers. Evidently there were a number of sentinels responsible to a single kastrophylax who in turn was responsible to superiors who decided whether irregularities required police action.

The only other real evidence for the role of the kastrophylax in the kastron dates to 1232 when Demetrios Chomatenos wrote of "the kastrophylax with the tzakones of the castle [*kastellion*]" of Thessaloniki, who delivered a legal summons in regard to a property dispute. These tzakones were performing a function entirely appropriate to their nature as paramilitary guards. And a kastrophylax acting with such tzakones, possibly even commanding them, was not far out of line from his charge to look after the security of the kastron. Nevertheless, the Nicaean kastrophylax had a larger official role than did his Palaiologan counterpart, since the administration

12. Pseudo-Kodinos, 187, and other lists of precedence: 139, 165, 301, 305, 308, 309, 322, 337, and cf. 345, 348. K. Sathas, Μεσαιωνική Βιβλιοθήκη (1872–94; repr. Athens, 1972), VI, 644 (hereafter, Sathas, *MB*). Inscription: J.-M. Speiser, "Inventaires en vue d'un recueil des inscriptions historiques de Byzance: I," *TM* 5 (1973), 175–76, no. 28.

13. Pachymeres, Bonn ed., II, 400–401.

of the kastron was handled alone by him and the civil official called the prokathemenos, the office of kephale only slowly gaining currency in the thirteenth century. On the other hand there is no evidence at all to suggest that either the Nicaean or Palaiologan kastrophylax commanded actual soldiers, though it is entirely possible that certain abnormalities of circumstances required him to do so, just as a certain Iatropoulos, prokathemenos of Philadelphia, was apparently once required in the mid-thirteenth century to assume military command of his city.[14]

In Constantinople, guard service was organized by neighborhood under a *demarchos*. This official's responsibility, paralleling that of the Roman tribune, was to safeguard the rights and well-being of the people within his neighborhood and to ensure their honesty and compliance with the law. While the demarchos commanded no soldiers, he was obligated "to look after and tend to the rebuilding and maintenance and watch and all else" of his neighborhood.[15] The watch that he organized was as much, if not primarily, a watch against fires and crime as against outside invaders. The men who performed this watch, however they were organized, were not under the direct authority of the emperor, like the palace guard and the city garrison, but like the paramilitary guards of other urban centers they were administered entirely by imperial functionaries.

The substantial number of towers (*pyrgoi*) erected in Thrace and Macedonia during the last centuries of Byzantium, many of which still stand, is eloquent testimony to the guarding of localities outside major population centers. Unlike the kastra associated with towns, the towers found in villages, in monasteries, and alone in the countryside functioned as refuges and look-out posts and were never intended to be bases from which to project control.[16] They were not manned by soldiers but by peasants who

---

14. J. Pitra, *Analecta sacra et classica spicilegio solesmensi parata* (Paris, 1876–91; repr. Farnborough, Eng., 1967), VI, col. 452. Lj. Maksimović, *The Byzantine Provincial Administration under the Palaiologoi* (Amsterdam, 1988), 171–76, 265. *Theodori Ducae Lascari Epistulae CCXVII*, ed. N. Festa (Florence, 1898), 197, no. 140.

15. Sathas, *MB*, VI, 643–44.

16. On monastic towers, with emphasis on those of Chilandar, see M. Živojinović, *Svetogorske kelije i pirgovi u srednjem veku* (Belgrade, 1972), 103–28. For monastic fortifications on Mount Athos, see P. Theocharidis, "The Byzantine Fortified Enclosure of the Monastery of Chelandariou," *Hilandarski Zbornik* 7 (1989), 59–70; and A. Deroko and S. Nenadović, "Konaci manastira Hilandara," *Spomenik SANU* 120, odeljenje društvenih nauka, nova serija 22 (Belgrade, 1971), 17–39. For the tower of the Rila monastery in southern Bulgaria, see L. Praškov, *Hrel'ovata kula* (Sofia, 1973). On towers as refuges, see the *Life* of St. Romylos (d.1389): trans. M. Bartusis, K. Ben Nasser, A. Laiou, "Days and Deed of a Hesychast Saint," *Byzantine Studies/Études byzantines* 9, pt. 1 (1982), 36.

were simple watchmen. The clearest example of this appears in a chrysobull from 1364 of Alexios III Komnenos of Trebizond. Even though the institutions of the Empire of Trebizond had been evolving along different lines, this document describes rural guard service in such a straightforward way that its testimony is worth citing. In it the emperor granted the monastery of Soumela various privileges, properties, and paroikoi. In regard to the defense of the monastery the emperor decreed,

> Since the kastron at the hallowed mountain and cave of Melas [i.e., a fortification at the monastery itself] requires a sufficient guard because of the hostile disposition of the Hagarenes [sc., Turks] toward us, my majesty orders the present and future abbot and hermits to set apart from the said paroikoi those who are very brave and expert, that through these [men] the guard and maintenance of the kastron should be most watchful and attentive.[17]

The necessary guards were to be recruited from the forty or so paroikoi (actually heads of households) listed earlier in the document who were held by the monastery and lived in several villages. The monastery received all the taxes and burdens these paroikoi owed the state except for one called the *kapalion*, which all the paroikoi had been paying to the treasury. However, the emperor ordered that the monastery should receive back 300 aspra of this tax for the "guard of the kastron." Thus, the paroikoi of the monastery provided not only the manpower but also indirectly a continuous source of funds for financing the guard service. The amount of money involved, equivalent to around 10 Byzantine hyperpyra,[18] shows that the fortification, though it was called a "kastron," was small, employing only a handful of men. And these men, whose selection was left to the monks themselves, were not soldiers.

The utilization of monastic paroikoi to man monastic fortifications was not restricted to Trebizond. In Serbia monasteries could demand that their paroikoi perform guard service for the monastery and its possessions.[19] Though direct evidence is lacking, we may assume that the practice

---

17. MM, V, 280, lines 9–14; 278, lines 10–11. S. Trojanos, «Καστροκτισία», Βυζαντινά I (1969), 49–50 and note 46, cited this passage as evidence that "the obligation of peasants to work at building fortifications themselves appears to have survived the fourteenth century." But the passage is clearly more concerned with the guard of the fortification than with its construction. To term this guard service an "obligation of peasants" is not quite accurate, because only certain paroikoi were to be chosen for this and, further, they were paid.

18. See E. Schilbach, *Byzantinische Metrologie* (Munich, 1970), 125.

19. V. Mošin et al., *Spomenici za srednovekovnata i ponovata istorija na Makedonija*, III (Skopje, 1980), 395 = A. Solovjev, *Odabrani spomenici srpskog prava* (Belgrade, 1926), 138 = S. Novaković, *Zakonski spomenici srpskih država srednjega veka* (Belgrade, 1912), 697.

was also current in Byzantium, where occasionally a concern was expressed that the peasants manning a particular public or private fortification *not* be paroikoi of another landlord. It seems the practice was to man a private fortification either with the paroikoi of the fortification's owner or with free peasants, and to man a public (state) fortification with state paroikoi or free peasants.

Certain aspects of these distinctions are illustrated by a document from 1325. After imperial intervention, the monks of Iviron acceded to the desire of the Protaton (the group of monks who governed Mount Athos) that a tower be built on some of Iviron's land in the village of Komitissa at the entrance to the peninsula of Athos "for the sake of the guard and maintenance of the place due to the attacks and harm caused them by enemies." The monks agreed to give up 200 *orgyiai* (less than one modios, a square about thirty yards on a side) of rocky, useless land for the tower as well as "fifty modioi of land for the sake of the future people to be settled outside this" tower. Lest Iviron be totally deprived of the benefits of these fifty modioi (less than twelve acres or five hectares), it was ordered that the "men" (*anthropoi*) and "people" (*laos*) settling outside the tower pay their *kephalaion* (which is to say their *telos*, or land tax) to the monks of Iviron. However, the future "inhabitants" (*epoikoi*) who would man the tower would pay nothing, from which it may be inferred that they were not to be Iviron's or any other monastery's paroikoi but free peasants.[20]

Further, since the document nowhere speaks of these settlers as soldiers or military personnel in any sense, and since the actual procurement of these settlers seems to have been the responsibility of the Protaton alone, these settlers may be regarded as private guards who in no way could be considered Byzantine soldiers. Moreover, a handful of soldiers in a lone tower would have had little defensive or offensive value. Bandits, the anticipated enemy, would simply bypass the tower and those within the tower would not dare leave the fortification. Rather, the settlers were to be watchmen who from their vantage at Komitissa warned neighboring peasants of the approach of enemies by land or sea. Once alerted, peasants and their animals found refuge in the tower and waited. If directly attacked, the

20. F. Dölger, *Aus den Schatzkammern des Heiligen Berges* (Munich, 1948), no. 93, lines 2–3 and 16; and also see no. 88. For the story of this tower, see G. Ostrogorski, "Komitisa i svetogorski manastiri," *ZRVI* 13 (1971), 227–28, 233–34; J. Darrouzès, *Les regestes des actes du patriarcat de Constantinople*, I, fasc. 5 (Paris, 1977), no. 2129; and cf. Dölger, *Schatzkammer*, 249. On the *orgyia*, see Lemerle et al., *Lavra*, III, 138.

peasants defended themselves from inside their tower as best they could with their limited means.[21]

Since "adulterine" fortresses were one "feudalizing" tendency that the Byzantine state could tolerate no more than the Norman kings of England, the right to build any kind of fortification remained an imperial prerogative and required a license. As in the case of the 1325 Komitissa document, the government frequently stipulated that the fortification be manned by people who were *xenoi* and *eleutheroi* ("strangers and free," technical designations of landless peasants) and not by dependent peasants.[22] Given these guidelines, the owner of the tower apparently had great latitude in staffing his fortification.

The sources provide numerous examples of towers constructed by monasteries or by private individuals for the benefit of monasteries. On Lemnos in 1362, the emperor granted George Synadenos Astras permission to build a tower and to donate it to a monastery of Athos "for the sake of his soul," and in 1366/7 a tower a few miles north of the mouth of the Strymon was built for a monastery by its founders, the brothers Alexios and John.[23]

In a couple of instances the emperor granted property to monasteries on condition that they construct a tower on it. In 1313 the monastery of Alypiou received some land on Mount Athos with the proviso that the monks restore a tower there that had been destroyed by Turkish pirates. Similarly, the monastery of Dionysiou was granted a property on the Kassandreia peninsula in 1408 on condition that a tower be built. When the monastery proved unable to do this, the despot Andronikos Palaiologos, governing Thessaloniki at the time, undertook the project himself sometime between 1418 and 1420.[24]

21. There is one good example of peasants defending a tower: Kantakouzenos, I, 144–45.

22. *Regesten*, nos. 2750–51 (1329), and Lemerle et al., *Lavra*, III, no. 141 (1362). G. Ferrari, "Formulari notarili inediti dell'età bizantina," *Bullettino dell' Istituto Storico Italiano* 33 (1913), 55–56, no. 18. Cf. Angold, *Byzantine Government*, 194; and Živojinović, *Kelije*, 115–16. For earlier fortification building, see N. Oikonomidès, "The Donation of Castles in the Last Quarter of the Eleventh Century," in Oikonomidès, *Documents et études sur les institutions de Byzance* (London, 1976), no. XIV, 413–17. On the terms *xenoi* and *eleutheroi*, see the *ODB*, s.v. "eleutheros."

23. Lemerle et al., *Lavra*, III, no. 141. M. Demitsas, Ἡ Μακεδονία ἐν λίθοις φθεγγομένοις καὶ μνημείοις σωζομένοις . . . Μακεδονικῶν (Athens, 1896), II, 708–709, no. 872. And see P. Lemerle, *Actes de Kutlumus*, rev. ed. (Paris, 1988), nos. 26, 29, 30, for the construction of the towers and walls ("kastron") of the monastery of Kutlumus on Mount Athos which cost more than 1,000 hyperpyra and was eventually paid for by the prince of Wallachia John Vladislav (1364–74).

24. Lemerle, *Kutlumus*, no. 9. N. Oikonomidès, *Actes de Dionysiou* (Paris, 1968), nos. 10, 13, 18, and p. 83, as well as p. 90 for other references to the building of towers.

The defense of the Kassandreia peninsula was of particular interest to the rulers of Thessaloniki in the early fifteenth century. Their activities in the area show that while the guard of state domain lands and of state lands held by state paroikoi naturally was organized by the state, the state also played a direct role in the building and maintenance of fortifications benefiting private landowners when an area was particularly vulnerable to attack and when these fortifications formed a coordinated defense system. For example, in the early years of the fifteenth century John VII Palaiologos, at the time he was governing Thessaloniki, built a wall to protect the peninsula and rebuilt a number of older towers. At about the same time he granted the monastery of Saint Paul a village on Kassandreia along with its fifteen peasant families with the stipulation that these families "give annually the thirtieth part from the income of their produce for the sake of the guard of the castle [*kastellion*] and the rest of the towers, and in time of the peninsula's need, they come together and help in every possible way with the security and guard of the castle and of the peninsula, as the times and necessity dictate."[25] Either dependent peasants or their landlords could be required to finance guard service, and the money raised hired professional guards who fulfilled this function on a more or less fulltime basis.

Rural guards are encountered very infrequently in the sources. A ruling of the metropolitan of Naupaktos John Apokaukos from 1228 mentions a group of men who had been entrusted with the guard of an oak coppice in the vicinity of Vonitza in southern Epiros. Evidently the property was owned by the state, because it produced acorns for certain "imperial" animals (probably pigs). The men, armed only with staffs, were in fact guarding acorns, a task not requiring the services of soldiers.[26]

With respect to rural guards no less than town guards, we can distinguish two basic types: the professionals who received money and were fulltime guards, such as those indicated by the Saint Paul document above, and those who served only part-time, though regularly, remaining primarily farmers, such as those who would man the tower at Komitissa. Such a distinction, however, given the paucity of data, can hardly be considered

25. J. Bompaire, *Actes de Xéropotamou* (Paris, 1964), no. 28 (1407). Dölger, *Schatzkammer*, no. 45–46 II, lines 13–16; no. 45–46 I, lines 15–16. In 1425, the Venetian Senate directed Venetian authorities in Thessaloniki to hire twenty-five men for this fort at Kassandreia and another twenty-five for two other towers there: K. Mertzios, Μνημεῖα Μακεδονικῆς Ἱστορίας (Thessaloniki, 1947), 62–63. For another example of peasants financing guard service organized by the state: A. Sigalas, «Ὁρισμὸς Δημητρίου Δεσπότου τοῦ Παλαιολόγου (Ἰούλιος 1462)», Ἑλληνικά 3 (1930), 344–45.

26. J. Apokaukos, in N. Bees, ed., "Unedierte Schriftstücke aus der Kanzlei des Johannes Apokaukos," *Byzantinisch-neugriechische Jahrbücher* 21 (1971–74), 78–79, no. 18, lines 5–8.

absolute. If anything it seems there was a large measure of creativity involved in the organization of guard service.

Nevertheless, this basic distinction, though crude, is useful for the purpose of examining the institution. For example, in a pair of false chrysobulls with the date 1342 for the monastery of Zographou (almost certainly created in the third quarter of the fourteenth century), the emperor decreed "that no one have permission to dare extract anyone from the villages of this monastery, either as foot or mounted watch [*vigla*]."[27] This would indicate that at the time these documents were made, state officials (probably kephalai) were attempting to conscript Zographou's peasants into guard service. And the reference to mounted guard service suggests service outside of any fortified position. Certainly these peasants were not professional guards, and it is unlikely their services would have been demanded for any extended period. The officials involved were simply seeking an inexpensive source of manpower. This expedient was intolerable to the monks of Zographou, and so they created a document in which the emperor agreed with them.

Monasteries themselves had to make sure their lands were guarded. An act of the Protos of Mount Athos from 1287, turning a ruined monastery over to the monks of Kutlumus, remarks that the new owners were required "according to custom" to perform guard service commensurate with their new possession.[28] In the *Life* of Patriarch Niphon (1310–14) we read that novice monks were assigned this task. As a young monk, Niphon had come to the monastery of Dionysiou "in which there was, as they said, a custom ordered by the founder of the monastery that whoever came to the monastery to be a monk had to agree to be a muleteer or carry wood or do other services ordered by the head monk." At one point Niphon was assigned guard duty

> on a high place facing the monastery because of pirates who suddenly came at that time to the Holy Mountain and enslaved many and seized whatever they could catch. Therefore, in the middle of the night, when the saint was standing in prayer there as he guarded, several virtuous monks that kept watch all around at that place saw a flame rising from the ground to the sky, and one brother, on guard with the saint and awake at that hour, saw the saint all

27. W. Regel et al., *Actes de Zographou, I. Actes grecs*, *VizVrem* 13 (1907), suppl. 1, no. 33, lines 72–74. In the other chrysobull this appears twice in nearly the same form: Regel et al., *Zographou*, no. 34, lines 78–80 and 83–85. On the subject of their authenticity, see *Regesten*, nos. 2874–75.

28. Lemerle, *Kutlumus*, no. 3, line 16. Živojinović, *Kelije*, 63.

aflame, and becoming frightened fled that place and went into the monastery and told all the frightful wonder he had seen.[29]

The mixture of sacred and profane in this passage illuminates the ritual connotations of the word "vigil."

On the other hand there were also lay guards on Mount Athos. King Dragutin of Serbia (1276–82) ordered that Chilandar's small dependency in Prizren "give a man to the Holy Mountain, to maintain a guard on the sea at the harbor." This probably refers to a dock belonging to Chilandar which at the time seems not yet to have had a tower erected near it. The man involved presumably formed part of a group of professional fulltime guards. Later, Andronikos II's 1324 chrysobull for Chilandar's tower at Chryseia on Athos speaks of "monks and laymen [kosmikoi] found in the said tower," which may be a reference to these lay guards.[30]

Roads were also guarded, sometimes by men who were given this duty by the emperor,[31] and sometimes by those who were not. The latter case is encountered extremely infrequently, though it was undoubtedly quite common. On his embassy to Serbia in 1327, while still in Byzantine Macedonia, the historian Nikephoros Gregoras and party met a group of "Bulgarian settlers" who "were to be guards of the roads and should scare off anyone that wanted to enter the neighboring land secretly to plunder," but who, apparently through lack of supervision and sufficient pay, had turned to banditry. Although nothing is known of the person who engaged these men, whether a local kephale or a large landowner, or how they were to be rewarded, whether with salary or with tax exemption, it is clear they were not Byzantine soldiers.[32]

Stefan Dušan's Law Code speaks of guards who performed a similar function. In regions where lands were held by a mixture of religious and lay landowners and the state, the ruler's local governor (in Serbian kefalija, from the Greek kephale) was responsible for maintaining road guards against bandits. The implication is that the kefalija had this responsibility

29. Nikodemos Hagioreites, Νέον Ἐκλόγιον (Venice, 1803; Constantinople, 1863; repr. Athens, 1974), 341–42. Nikodemos' text is a modern Greek metaphrase. V. Grecu's edition, Viaţa sfântului Nifon (Bucharest, 1944), is inaccessible to me.

30. Novaković, Zakonski spomenici, 387 = B. Korablev and L. Petit, Actes de Chilandar, II. Actes slaves, VizVrem 19 (1915), suppl. 1, no. 6. Živojinović, Kelije, 116–17. L. Petit and B. Korablev, Actes de Chilandar, I. Actes grecs, VizVrem 17 (1911), suppl. 1, no. 101, lines 25–26. See also Oikonomidès, Dionysiou, no. 8, line 28 and p. 75.

31. Kantakouzenos, I, 210. Gregoras, I, 353, 395; II, 616.

32. Gregoras, I, 378. M. Bartusis, "Brigandage in the Late Byzantine Empire," Byz 51 (1981), 394–96.

only because state lands were involved. In areas where there were no state lands, guard service evidently was not coordinated by state officials, and lay and religious landowners arranged their own guard service.[33] A similar situation must have existed in Byzantium, and this explains why there are so few references to guard service in the sources. Every document dealing with guard service outside urban centers arose because of state intervention in the guarding of private lands.

33. *Zakonik cara Stefana Dušana: 1349 i 1354*, ed. N. Radojčić (Belgrade, 1960), art. 157, and cf. arts. 158, 160; English trans. M. Burr, "The Code of Stephan Dušan," *Slavonic and East European Review* 28 (1949–50), 198–217, 516–39. For a private arrangement: P. Ivić and M. Grković, *Dečanske hrisovulje* (Novi Sad, 1976), 263, lines 10–12.

14. Weapons and Equipment

Medieval armor and weapons are studied through archaeology, pictorial art, and written material. Although archaeology should provide the best information on the arms and armor of late Byzantine soldiers, almost nothing that can be dated to the thirteenth through fifteenth century has been identified securely as Byzantine. One reason for this is that since the Empire was at war almost constantly in its last centuries and was ultimately conquered and subsumed within a foreign civilization, no contemporaries or near-contemporaries had the opportunity, means, and inclination to collect specimens of military artifacts, as did, for example, the noble families of England. Another is that Byzantium's close contact during its last centuries with numerous other societies, including its extensive use of foreign soldiers, resulted in reciprocal influences in military fashions and technology which have led researchers all too frequently to emphasize the non-Byzantine characteristics of weapons and armor, and to see non-Byzantine origins in whatever military accoutrements have been found in areas within the Byzantine sphere. Thus objects that may in fact be Byzantine are identified as "Norman" or "Catalan" or "Turkish."

Pictorial art presents its own problems. Soldiers appear in all the major media—wall paintings, mosaics, icons, manuscript illuminations, lead seals, and coins. However, the intention was almost never to depict contemporary soldiers but rather the timeless soldiers of the Bible (Pilate's guard, Herod's slaughterers of the Innocents) or the saints who were or were thought to have been soldiers (George, Demetrios, the two Theodores, and others). The strict religious and political ideology motivating most Byzantine art produced a high degree of stylization and archaism. As a result, there was a strong, even overwhelming tendency to base depictions of arms and armor on Hellenistic and Roman models long after these fell out of use. And so the historian is forced to adopt a general methodology that accepts as current equipment only those items that appear in art as novelties.[1]

1. The sources for the study of Byzantine arms and armor, and the difficulties they pose, are discussed by T. Kolias, *Byzantinische Waffen: ein Beitrag zur byzantinischen Waffenkunde von*

To a great extent it is true that for the late period one no longer can speak of "Byzantine weapons" in the sense of mass production and a discrete style.[2] The mixing of Norman, Italian, Turkish, and nomadic influences with indigenous developments produced a cosmopolitan style. But rather than viewing this as an obstacle to understanding the arms of late Byzantium, we can use the opportunity this presents to go further afield and make greater use of comparative material.

A description of the equipment of an early fourteenth-century cavalryman is contained in the *Instructions* of Theodore Palaiologos, marquis of Montferrat, written in 1326. Although Theodore was thoroughly Westernized and his treatise generally reflects Western practices, this particular passage has some relevance for Byzantine affairs. He writes that the ordinary mounted man-at-arms should have

> two small horses in the manner of the Greeks or the Turks—that is, geldings—or two mares in hand. And according to the strength of the horses or mares he should furnish arms, that is, a *pourpoint*, *hauberjon* and *gorgeré*, the *cuiriee* and some *gambison*, chapel-de-fer, sword or *glaive* at the side, greaves, *cuisses*, with the lance and shield. And if large horses are desired—that is, destriers—in the manner of the Latins, he should be armed with arms heavy and sufficient for that.[3]

Theodore indicates that he is not describing the true "Latin" style of armor but the kind of hybrid outfit, mixing Byzantine, Western, and Eastern fashions, that one might have found all over the southern Mediterranean area in the early fourteenth century. We can use Theodore's list as a kind of template for discussing what little we know of late Byzantine armor and weapons.

Theodore begins with the clothing and armor covering the trunk, evidently proceeding from the outermost to the innermost garments. The first is the *pourpoint*, a general term for quilted or padded soft armor. In this context, it probably refers to a padded surcoat, something Western Europeans picked up during their experiences in the Middle East. In the cathe-

---

den *Anfängen bis zur lateinischen Eroberung* (Vienna, 1988), 30–35. See also the comments of P. Underwood, *The Kariye Djami* (New York, 1966), I, 252–58. But cf. E. Manova, "Les armes défensives au Moyen Age d'après les peintures murales de la Bulgarie du sud-ouest au XIIIe, XIVe et XVe s.," *Byzantino-Bulgarica* 3 (1969), 223, who concludes that in the Slavic areas of the southern Balkans arms and armor were painted realistically.

2. Kolias, *Byzantinische Waffen*, 29.

3. T. Palaiologos, *Les Enseignements de Théodore Paléologue*, ed. C. Knowles (London, 1983), 58.

dral of Salerno in southern Italy there is a carved funerary effigy wearing such a garment.[4] Under the surcoat was the *hauberjon*, a smaller mail hauberk, or coat of mail, of the style without an attached mail head covering. Late Byzantine soldiers wore a variety of chain mail hauberks. Some were short-sleeved (figure 1), others were long-sleeved (the rightmost archer in figure 2) and worn sometimes with either attached or separate mittens. Some hauberks extended only slightly below the waist while others fell almost to the knees. In figure 4 the soldier wears what appears to be a fabric-covered mail shirt or hauberk that suggests Islamic influence. According to the historian Doukas, the Serbs who fought on the Ottoman side at the battle of Ankara were impervious to arrows because they were covered in "black iron," that is, chain mail, and he says that the lead balls shot from devices at the 1440 siege of Belgrade could pierce someone "wearing iron armor" (*siderophoroi kai enoploi*).[5]

Some late Byzantine warriors wore cuirasses on top of or instead of mail hauberks. These cuirasses were not the archaic, stylized type so often depicted in Byzantine art; the old Roman-style cuirass of metallic scale or lamellar, or of forged iron or bronze, was no longer in use, except perhaps for ceremonial armor. Rather, the common late Byzantine style was a metallic or hardened leather lamellar cuirass of a distinctive Oriental (Turco-Mongol) form (frontispiece and figure 1). There is also evidence from art of the use of metal or leather lamellar horse armor, also of an Oriental design (figure 2).[6]

Theodore Palaiologos' *gorgeré* (from the French *gorge*, "neck") was some kind of neck guard, of either mail or plate. Byzantine art from the late thirteenth through the early fifteenth century depicts various kinds of rigid or semi-rigid lamellar neck guards of iron plate or hardened leather. These seem to have been a late medieval Balkan fashion. Alternatively the soldier wore a more Western-style mail coif or hood (figure 1).[7] The *cuiriee*, a leather garment worn under the hauberk, is not mentioned or seen in the

---

4. D. Nicolle, *Arms and Armour of the Crusading Era, 1050–1350* (White Plains, N.Y., 1988), p. 525, fig. 1431 (ca.1325).

5. Manova, "Les armes défensives," 189, 222. Nicolle, *Arms*, p. 49, fig. 130; 51, fig. 136N; 48, fig. 127A. Doukas, 97, 265.

6. Nicolle, *Arms*, p. 98, figs. 249D and E (Bulgarian?), and p. 51. Cf. Manova, "Les armes défensives," 208.

7. Nicolle, *Arms*, p. 48, fig. 127; 49, fig. 131C; 51; 97–98, fig. 247C (Serbian); 496; and 50, fig. 132A–C.

Byzantine sources. The *gambison* was a padded cloth garment worn under the hauberk and corresponded to the tunic worn by Greeks since antiquity.[8]

Perhaps the most common, even standard, late Byzantine helmet was the type called the "war-hat," or chapel-de-fer (literally, "iron hat"). It was conical, sometimes onion-shaped or even roundish, relatively tall, with a brim that was either flat and usually wide, or narrow and sloping downward, and was made either in one piece, with a single seam, or in two segments riveted to a central comb. Sometimes it had attached mail aventails or was worn over a mail hood (figure 1). It is common in Byzantine art of the thirteenth and fourteenth centuries and is seen frequently in Balkan and Russian sources as well. Similar brimmed helmets were used throughout Europe at this time, especially in Spain, Italy, and Germany.[9]

Conical helmets without brims, constructed from one or two pieces of iron, also appear. In the frontispiece some of these have decorative attachments on the front reminiscent of certain helmets in late thirteenth- and early fourteenth-century Spanish art, which might suggest influence from the Catalan Company.[10] There were also simpler round helmets. In one particular wall painting, two round helmets have reinforced rims, and in another, the round helmet is framed by reinforcing strips and is worn over a mail hood (coif) in the Western fashion.[11] One unusual style is a rounded, often tall, helmet usually with a decorative finial on top (figure 3). The helmet itself appears to extend far down the wearer's back. These are depicted as well in Serbian and Bulgarian art and may have had an Islamic or Russian origin.[12] Nose-guards (nasals) rarely ever appear on any type of helmet.

For leg and foot protection Byzantine as well as Western art emphasizes mail stockings (called *chausses* in the West), which are worn by the hooded rider in figure 1. The Russian traveler Ignatius of Smolensk, who was present in Constantinople in 1392 to witness the coronation of Manuel II,

8. The editor of the *Instructions*, p. 130, translates *cuiriee* as "cuirass," but the *cuiriee* was a garment distinct from the cuirass (Nicolle, *Arms*, 595). The position of the item in Theodore's description suggests it was worn under the hauberk and over the *gambison*. Manova, "Les armes défensives," 189, 222.

9. Nicolle, *Arms*, 45, 48, 50–51, 82, 96, 99, and figs. 127A, 135; 207 and 229G (Russian); 243C and 253 (Serbian). Cf., idem, figs. 561K (Egypt); 656 and 661 (Spanish); 772M (French); 1057 (Scandinavian); 1193 (German); 1274C (Bohemian); 1313 and 1373A (Italian).

10. Nicolle, *Arms*, p. 51, and figs. 136D and L; cf. figs. 656O and P.

11. Manova, "Les armes défensives," 219. Nicolle, *Arms*, p. 50, fig. 134B (early fourteenth century); also, 48, fig. 127C.

12. Nicolle, *Arms*, p. 51, figs. 136G and N, and cf. figs. 245C, 249D, 257, 259.

Figure 1. Above, Alexander the Great reviews his troops. Below, Alexander receives gifts outside Thessaloniki. Miniature painting from the *Alexander Romance*, early or mid-fourteenth century. Library of S. Giorgio di Greci, Venice, fol. 36v (photo: Istituto Ellenico di Studi Bizantini e Postbizantini di Venezia).

Figure 2. Siege of Athens by Alexander the Great. Miniature painting from the *Alexander Romance*, early or mid-fourteenth century. Library of S. Giorgio di Greci, Venice, fol. 39r, upper half (photo: Istituto Ellenico di Studi Bizantini e Postbizantini di Venezia).

Figure 3. Siege of Tyre by Alexander the Great. Miniature painting from the *Alexander Romance*, early or mid-fourteenth century. Library of S. Giorgio di Greci, Venice, fol. 53v, upper half (photo: Istituto Ellenico di Studi Bizantini e Postbizantini di Venezia).

Figure 4. St. Theodore Tiro. Wall-painting, church of the Chora
(Kariye Djami), Constantinople, ca.1315–21 (photo: Byzantine
Visual Resources, copyright 1992, Dumbarton Oaks, Wash-
ington, D.C.).

Figure 5. St. Demetrios. Icon, fourteenth century. Muzej primenjene umetnosti, Belgrade (photo: Vojislav Djurić).

Figure 6. SS. Arethas, Niketas, and Nestor. Wall-painting, Resava monastery, Serbia, Yugoslavia, 1407–18 (photo: Zavod za zaštitu spomenika, Belgrade).

notes that upon entering the Church of Hagia Sophia, "On either side of the emperor [walked] twelve men-at-arms, completely [covered in] iron from head to foot."[13] These soldiers, probably foreign mercenaries and perhaps members of the Varangian guard, were evidently not wearing any surcoat to obscure this profusion of chain mail, which would have included chausses. Theodore Palaiologos does not mention these, either overlooking them or regarding them as a standard part of the hauberk. Instead he speaks of the equipment that was worn over the chausses: greaves and *cuisses* (padded thigh and knee armor). I have not seen evidence for either of these anywhere in late medieval Balkan art. Nevertheless, hardened-leather greaves, often decoratively tooled, and padded cuisses were quite common in Italy in the late thirteenth and early fourteenth centuries, and they certainly would have been encountered in Byzantium, even if they were not the prevailing fashion.[14]

Representational art does show various other pieces of clothing soldiers may have worn, such as capes and trousers and boots, but it is difficult to know where archaism ends and current styles begin.[15] As for the dress of infantry, we know practically nothing. Heavy infantry, including crossbowmen, probably wore the kind of padded tunics reaching to the knees, along with a few pieces of mail, seen in Italian and Spanish art.[16] Light infantry, armed with bows, slings, and perhaps spears, probably dressed like the peasants they were.

The last defensive piece of equipment Theodore mentions is the shield. The standard late Byzantine shield seems to have been of an elongated triangular design, three to five feet high, with a pronounced curve or bow along its width (figures 4 and 5). Its sides were either straight, creating a true triangular silhouette, or slightly convex. The narrow bottom point of the shield protected the rider's left leg, and the broad, flat top curved around the left arm and upper body. When not in use, it was carried on the soldier's back, sometimes upside down.[17] This type of shield appeared around the middle of the twelfth century in Western Europe,[18] and perhaps

13. Also, Nicolle, *Arms*, p. 50, fig. 132A. Ignatius of Smolensk, in *Russian Travelers to Constantinople in the Fourteenth and Fifteenth Centuries*, ed. G. Majeska (Washington, D.C., 1984), 106–107.
14. Cf., e.g., Nicolle, *Arms*, p. 483, fig. 1322; 486, fig. 1335C; 525, fig. 1431.
15. Manova, "Les armes défensives," 189, 222–23.
16. E.g., Nicolle, *Arms*, fig. 695.
17. Kolias, *Byzantinische Waffen*, 121–22.
18. E.g., Nicolle, *Arms*, figs. 729A–H (southern French). Kolias, *Byzantinische Waffen*, 114–17, argues that Manuel I introduced the triangular shield for cavalry.

at around the same time in Byzantium. Whereas the Western Europeans gradually adopted a much smaller flat-topped shield with a less prominent or no horizontal bow and with a more pronounced curve to the shield's sides,[19] the bowed, long triangular shield, in its straight or slightly curved form, remained the most important type for the late Byzantine army.[20] This shield developed from the large almond-shaped shield that was popular in the eleventh and early twelfth centuries in Byzantium and throughout Europe. Since the most notable examples of this type of shield can be seen in the Bayeux tapestry, it is often called the "Norman" shield.[21] Both this almond-shaped shield, with its rounded top and pointed bottom, and the triangular shield, with its flat top and pointed bottom, are often called, because of their bow, "kite-shaped," though they are never in fact four-sided like the standard North American image of a kite.

Other shield types probably existed but little is known for certain about them. In art, very large, very concave, round shields appear, but these would seem to be archaisms. On the other hand, smaller round shields (about two feet across) may have been a common shield style for infantry in the Balkans and Asia Minor as well as in fourteenth-century Italy.[22]

Shields were constructed of wood, animal hide, and iron. The large triangular shields were almost certainly not iron-plated. Their weight would have made them unwieldy to say the least, and since the Byzantines did not adopt iron-plate body armor, it seems unlikely that they would have adopted iron shields. In fact, references to iron shields in the twelfth and earlier centuries are usually in a naval context, suggesting that iron shields, or even iron-covered wooden shields, were preferred only when fire was a danger and great mobility was not essential. Rather, it seems that the large triangular cavalry shields were framed with wood or iron and covered with hardened leather. The late-thirteenth-century writer Maximos Planoudes once complained to a friend about the quality of writing parchment, facetiously declaring that it was better suited for covering shields or drums. Such construction made the shields lightweight. An early fourteenth-century painting from a church in southern Yugoslavia portrays a mounted

---

19. E.g., Nicolle, *Arms*, fig. 1371 (Italian).

20. Kolias, *Byzantinische Waffen*, 118. Nicolle, *Arms*, 44. Slightly curved sides: Nicolle, *Arms*, p. 48, fig. 126; figs. 245A and 258B (Serbian); straight sides: p. 51, figs. 137A, C, and G; 96, fig. 243A (Serbian); 100, fig. 256 (Serbian).

21. Nicolle, *Arms*, fig. 870. Kolias, *Byzantinische Waffen*, fig. 23.2.

22. Kolias, *Byzantinische Waffen*, 111. Cf. Manova, "Les armes défensives," 214. See Nicolle, *Arms*, p. 100, fig. 254 (Serbian); 191, fig. 502A (Seljuk). P. Strässle, "Ein spätbyzantinisches Holzrelief militär- und kunsthistorisch beurteilt," *Byz* 60 (1990), 389.

soldier in a moderate walk. His large triangular shield, tethered by a long strap across his chest, appears to be flying behind him at a forty-five-degree angle, like a kite.[23]

Theodore's list of offensive weapons begins with the sword. The swords of the late Byzantine army were generally either long straight swords, sometimes with a slight taper toward the tip (frontispiece and figures 3, 4, and 5), or curved sabers (frontispiece and figures 3 and 6). The straight swords and their sheaths were very similar to what was used in Western Europe at the time, especially in Italy. One particular decorated straight sword found in Belgrade, which is probably Byzantine, has a slightly tapering blade 1.65 inches (4.2 cm) at its widest point.[24] The influence of Turkish cavalry on Byzantine weapons in the thirteenth century is seen in the adoption of the curved saber as well as in the occasional appearance of nonsymmetrical handguards (quillons), even on straight swords.[25] Most sabers were sharply curved with a regular taper.[26] However, in one case, from a Serbian painting, a slightly curved, heavy, shorter saber is depicted of the kind frequently seen in fourteenth-century Mamluk art in Egypt.[27] There is also some evidence that daggers were in use.[28]

Ornamented swords were used in combat, as we learn from a judgment of a patriarchal synod. Sometime before 1361 a certain Kontostephanos fell in battle, and his sword, richly decorated in gold and silver, was seized by the enemy. Later the sword turned up in Didymoteichon and ultimately came into the possession of his widow. However, the synod reports that the actual owner of the sword was a relative of Kontostephanos, the *epitrapezaina kyra* Anna Laskarina, who had unsuccessfully been seeking its return from his widow. In or slightly before 1365 the patriarchal synod ordered the widow to compensate Laskarina with something of equal value. While it is interesting that Kontostephanos carried this precious sword into battle, it is even more interesting that it was recovered after having fallen into enemy hands. This indicates that Kontostephanos lost his life during civil war, probably during the final period of hostilities

23. Kolias, *Byzantinische Waffen*, 97, 92–93. But cf. Manova, "Les armes défensives," 214. Nicolle, *Arms*, fig. 256.

24. Nicolle, *Arms*, p. 48, figs. 127A and B; 49, figs. 131B and F; 50, figs. 133A–E; 51, figs. 136A, B, K, M, and N. Kolias, *Byzantinische Waffen*, 145, 147.

25. Nicolle, *Arms*, pp. 50–51, fig. 135.

26. Kolias, *Byzantinische Waffen*, 145. Nicolle, *Arms*, p. 48, fig. 127A; 51, figs. 136K and N; 101, fig. 258A (Serbian).

27. Nicolle, *Arms*, p. 100, fig. 255 (Serbian), and cf. figs. 555D, 556A, 569B. Strässle, "Ein spätbyzantinisches Holzrelief," 389.

28. Nicolle, *Arms*, p. 49, fig. 131D; 97, fig. 245D (Serbian); p. 483.

between the Palaiologoi and the Kantakouzenoi. Moreover, Laskarina's title, indicating that her husband had held the relatively high court title of *epi tes trapezes* (literally, "in charge of the table"), and the use of a patriarchal synod to settle this quarrel suggests there was much more to this dispute than a simple disagreement over a sword.[29]

The weapon called the *glaive* which, according to Theodore Palaiologos, could be worn at the soldier's side as a substitute for the sword (*espee*) is somewhat mysterious. Ordinarily the word signified a spear or lance blade mounted on a bamboo haft and used in tournaments; in other words, not a real weapon of war at all. A long-bladed weapon on a short haft does appear in Byzantine art but it seems to have been an infantry weapon, as were similar weapons depicted in twelfth- and thirteenth-century French art.[30] The editor of Theodore's *Instructions* thought *glaive* referred to a kind of sword, one of the meanings it does have in modern French. Another possibility is that he was speaking of the mace, which Theodore in his own Latin translation of his *Instructions* may have rendered as *clava* and which, in turn, the fourteenth-century French translator of the work may have mistranslated as *glaive*. Illustrations of maces are indeed found in late Byzantine sources (figure 5).[31]

The lance or spear was always a part of the Byzantine arsenal for both foot and mounted warriors. East or West, it was not a very complicated device, basically a long wooden shaft with an iron tip (figures 5 and 6). In the tenth century, the thrown spear became the primary weapon of the Byzantine heavy cavalry. Due to Western influence, the couched lance, held high under the arm, was adopted during the reign of Alexios I Komnenos (1081–1118). As Byzantine equipment increasingly mirrored that of the West in the twelfth century, Manuel I (1143–80) emphasized heavy cavalry armed with a large shield and the couched lance. Although usually made of hardwood, from a very early date the Byzantines adopted the Arab technique of making spears and lances from bamboo or cane.[32]

29. I. Sakkelion, «Συνοδικαὶ διαγνώσεις τῆς ΙΔ΄ ἑκατονταετηρίδος», Δελτίον τῆς Ἱστορικῆς καὶ Ἐθνολογικῆς Ἑταιρείας τῆς Ἑλλάδος 3 (1890), 274. J. Darrouzès, *Les regestes des actes du patriarcat de Constantinople*, I, fasc. 5 (Paris, 1977), no. 2500. The date of the document is uncertain.

30. E.g., Nicolle, *Arms*, pp. 48–49, fig. 128E, and cf. figs. 707G, 744, 772.

31. Palaiologos, *Enseignements*, 121 note 116. Nicolle, *Arms*, pp. 46–47, figs. 120 and 121; and cf. figs. 245C and 252B (Serbian). On the axe as weapon, see the discussion of the Varangian guard herein, pp. 273–76.

32. Kolias, *Byzantinische Waffen*, 114–17, 204–208; and on the spear and lance in general, 185–213. Nicolle, *Arms*, 29. Strässle, "Ein spätbyzantinisches Holzrelief," 389–90. Held couched-style: Nicolle, *Arms*, figs. 109C, 111A; 249D (Bulgarian?). Made of bamboo or cane: Nicolle, p. 36, fig. 79C (tenth century); fig. 243A (Serbian).

Theodore does not mention the bow as a weapon. In a Western European context this makes perfect sense because the Western horse soldier did not use this weapon. Native Byzantine cavalry as well employed the sword and lance almost exclusively, though they were certainly familiar with horse archery. A scene described by Bertrandon de la Brocquière, a Frenchman who visited Constantinople in 1432, suggests that the aristocracy was fascinated by horse archery even if they never turned to it in combat. Bertrandon writes that, in the old Hippodrome,

> I saw the brother of the emperor, the despot of the Morea, exercising himself there, with a score of horsemen. Each had a bow, and they galloped along the enclosure, throwing their hats before them, which, when they had passed, they shot at; and he who with his arrow pierced his hat, or was nearest to it, was esteemed the most expert. This exercise they had adopted from the Turks, and it was one of which they were endeavoring to make themselves masters.

On the other hand, in the Empire of Trebizond, closer contact with the Seljuk and Ottoman Turks seems to have led to the adoption of horse archery as a standard form of warfare. In the early fifteenth century, the Spanish traveler Clavijo remarked that the Greeks of Trebizond "arm themselves with bows and swords, like the Turks, and ride the very same way." The last phrase means that they rode nomad-style with short stirrups, almost in a crouch, which allowed the greater mobility in the saddle required of horse archery.[33]

In the Byzantine army horse archery, beginning in the twelfth century, was in the hands of foreign mercenaries, especially Turks. The various nomadic people the Byzantines encountered in the last centuries were often utilized as light cavalry: Tourkopouloi, Cumans, Alans, as well as auxiliary troops such as those of Umur Pasha. The only indigenous Byzantines to use the bow were the light infantry troops (figure 2), of which we know very little. The bow in use was of the short recurved composite style, often called the "Scythian" bow, usually with bone or horn tips, which with its short draw and small size was ideally suited to cavalry use.[34]

On horse or foot, a quiver hung at the archer's side. These were of two types. By far the most commonly depicted is long and box-like, usually with

33. Bertrandon de la Brocquière, in *Early Travels in Palestine*, trans. T. Wright (London, 1848), 339. Clavijo, *Embajada a Tamorlán*, ed. F. López Estrada (Madrid, 1943), 778.

34. Nicolle, *Arms*, p. 51; 100–101, figs. 257, 258B, and 260D (Serbian); 98, fig. 249A (Bulgarian?). On the bow before the thirteenth century, see Kolias, *Byzantinische Waffen*, 214–38.

a laced door-like flap or cover, the arrows inside carried with their points up (figure 5). This quiver was developed by the mounted nomadic Turco-Mongol peoples of the steppes of central Asia.[35] Less commonly seen in art is the smaller, Middle Eastern Mamluk form of quiver whose arrows were exposed for rapid extraction. In figure 2 the arrows of the rightmost archer have their points up, whereas the feathers of the other archers' arrows protrude from their quivers in the traditional manner for this type of quiver. Nothing is known of how arrows were supplied, though in his account of the siege of Constantinople in 1422 John Kananos reports that every household under Turkish control in Europe and Asia was required to provide from ten to twenty arrows for the besiegers.[36]

The numerous descriptions of the crossbow (*tzangra* or *tzagra*) in Byzantine sources show that this weapon was used infrequently, and then almost exclusively in sieges and sea battles. The twelfth-century historian Anna Komnene presents this nasty device as a novelty brought to Byzantium by the Latins of the First Crusade:

> The crossbow is a barbarian bow, completely unknown to the Greeks. It is stretched not by the right hand pulling the string while the left pushes the bow away from the body, but he who stretches this far-shooting instrument of war must lie almost on his back, each foot pressed against the semicircles of the bow, while the two hands draw the string most forcibly. At the middle of the string is a semi-cylindrical groove cut away by the string itself. It is about the length of a good-sized arrow, extending from the string itself to the center of the bow. Along this groove arrows of all kinds are fired. While the arrows are very short, they are very thick with a heavy iron tip. When fired the string exerts tremendous violence and force, so that whatever the darts strike, they do not rebound but bore through a shield, cut through a heavy iron breastplate and continue out the other side, so irresistible and violent is the discharge. Such an arrow has been known to pass right through a bronze statue, and when fired at the wall of a great city its point either protrudes from the inner side or buries itself in the wall and disappears altogether. Such is the crossbow, a truly diabolical machine. Its blow is so great that whoever is struck by it is most unfortunate; he dies without feeling or knowing what hit him.[37]

A century later the churchman Nicholas Mesarites shortly after a brief

35. Nicolle, *Arms*, p. 51, fig. 136C; 98, fig. 249A (Bulgarian?); 100–101, figs. 257, 258B, and 260D (Serbian); and cf. figs. 9, 57C, and 64.

36. Cf. Nicolle, *Arms*, fig. 447A. Giovanni Cananos, *L'assedio di Costantinopoli*, ed. E. Pinto (Messina, 1977), lines 184–87 (see under Kananos in Bibliography).

37. A. Komnene, *Anne Comnène. Alexiade*, ed. B. Leib (Paris, 1937–45), II, 217–18, and 217 note 1; trans. adapted from E. Sewter, *The Alexiad of Anna Comnena* (Baltimore, Md., 1969), 316 note 36. And cf. Kolias, *Byzantinische Waffen*, 247, 250.

sea voyage in 1208 notes that the bows of the pirates (of unspecified ethnicity) who raided his ship were not of the normal variety

> but the kind that a barbarous and murderous spirit contrived. They are made of strong wood without bone and sinew, which is relaxed when not directed at a target. It [the wood] is stretched with feet and hands, and the bow string is not stretched sinew but tightly twisted linen stretched around the attached bone to another wooden support on which hangs an iron bar which is operated after aiming at a target. It does deadly things once he who aims it casts the undeflectable spike of death.[38]

And even after the passage of another century, Constantine Hermoniakos, from Epiros, in his demotic adaptation of the *Iliad*, thought the crossbow was worth a description. He writes that the bow and center support formed a T. Where they came together there was a ring like a stirrup. A semicircular iron ring hung on a wide belt around the hips of the shooter. The bow was strung by pressing the "stirrup" to the ground with the foot while the right hand with the help of the spanning hook pulled the string, and while the left hand pressed the bow to the ground. Then the string was fastened to a nut by which the device was fired.[39]

Anna Komnene was not the only author to associate the crossbow with Westerners. A late thirteenth-century theological treatise speaks of "the bows that the race of Latins is accustomed to using," and Kantakouzenos refers to it as "the Latin bow." The Greek word *tzangra* or *tzagra*, which first appears perhaps as far back as the 1020s, is derived from the Latin *cancer* ("crab") via the medieval French *cancre* or *chancre* (because of the weapon's shape) or perhaps from the Persian *charkh*, a type of crossbow. While there is a possibility that the Byzantines had some kind of handheld crossbow weapon in earlier centuries (from which the Western crossbow in fact may have evolved), no such weapon was in common use in the eleventh century. In any event medieval man was uncomfortable with the crossbow. In the West the Second Lateran Council (1139) forbade its use against Christians, and in the East the Arabs forbade its use against Muslims.[40]

38. A. Heisenberg, *Neue Quellen zur Geschichte des lateinischen Kaisertums und der Kirchenunion, II: Die Unionsverhandlungen vom 30. August 1206*, in Heisenberg, *Quellen und Studien zur spätbyzantinischen Geschichte* (London, 1973), no. II (ii), 37. Kolias, *Byzantinische Waffen*, 248.

39. *La guerre de Troie. Poème du XIVe siècle en vers octosyllabes par Constantin Hermoniacos*, in *Bibliothèque grecque vulgaire*, ed. É. Legrand, V (Paris, 1890), pp. 86–90, cited by Kolias, *Byzantinische Waffen*, 252–53.

40. S. Caratzas, *Les Tzacones* (Berlin, 1976), 335. Kantakouzenos, I, 174. D. Nishimura, "Crossbows, Arrow-Guides, and the *Solenarion*," *Byz* 58 (1988), 431–34. G. Dennis, "Flies,

We know nothing about the cost of weapons and practically nothing about where weapons were obtained. One reason for this is that there is little evidence that the Byzantine government supplied soldiers with weapons or other equipment. As discussed in Chapter 11, Pseudo-Kodinos indicates that the government did supply some soldiers with equipment, evidence supported only by the example of the several thousand Alans who entered the Empire in 1301 and received horses and arms which they returned when they quit the emperor's employ. On the other side of the question, the Catalans provided their own horses and arms, and the French mercenary from Picardy whom Demetrios Kydones recommended to Manuel II seems to have owned his own equipment. Like so much in late Byzantium, practices probably varied to fit the situation.

We also know very little about Byzantine mining operations, the first step in the production of most arms. There were traditional sources of various ores available in Asia Minor, Thrace, Macedonia, and Greece, but the extent to which they were exploited in the late period is unknown. Some iron was being mined in the thirteenth century on Mount Sipylos southwest of Magnesia, and as late as 1301 Andronikos II tried to increase government revenues by raising the duties on the internal trade in salt and iron. Nevertheless, because the treaty of Nymphaion (1261) contained a clause permitting the exportation of weapons from Genoa to Byzantium, perhaps one can conclude that the Empire imported a significant portion of its weapons.[41]

With horses our lack of knowledge is similar. The passage cited above from Pseudo-Kodinos and the episode involving the Alans indicate that horses were provided on occasion to mercenary troops. Further, Pachymeres tells us that the allied troops sent to Constantinople by the king of Georgia in the early fourteenth century were ready to serve "without pay and for only horses and expenses." Generally, however, there was a shortage of horses, and it seems that most soldiers provided their own mounts. Presumably the more distinguished the warrior, the more horses he cam-

---

Mice, and the Byzantine Crossbow," *Byzantine and Modern Greek Studies* 7 (1981), 1–5. Nikephoros II Phokas, *Le traité sur la guérilla (De velitatione) de l'empereur Nicéphore Phocas*, ed. G. Dagron and H. Mihaescu (Paris, 1986), 143 note 10. J. Haldon, "ΣΩΛΗΝΑΡΙΟΝ—The Byzantine Crossbow?," *University of Birmingham Historical Journal* 12 (1970), 155–57. Cf. Kolias, *Byzantinische Waffen*, 245, 248–50. For a mid-fourteenth-century Serbian crossbow, see Nicolle, *Arms*, p. 102, fig. 261C.

41. MM, IV, 105, cited by Angold, *Byzantine Government*, 102. Laiou, *Constantinople*, 188. Geanakoplos, *Emperor Michael*, 81–90. See S. Vryonis, "The Question of the Byzantine Mines," *Speculum* 37 (1962), 1–17. Nicolle, *Arms*, 26.

paigned with, but the Byzantine sources offer absolutely no figures. Theodore Palaiologos writes that an ordinary man-at-arms should have "a good
and sufficient [horse] with a good jade," and "the vassals and the honorable
men should have three horses, that is, a destrier, a big palfrey, and a good,
large jade to carry their proper things," while a baron should have five. But
since Theodore tends to reflect Western practices, I hesitate to draw conclusions regarding Byzantium from this evidence.[42]

Byzantium was rather slow to utilize firearms. The wartime use of
firearms in Western Europe had begun in the second quarter of the fourteenth century, and by the middle of the century firearms were found in the
cities of the Adriatic coast and in Hungary. By 1378 Dubrovnik (Ragusa)
was engaged in making cannon, and in that same year we have the first
recorded use of firearms in the Balkans, when the Adriatic city of Kotor
used cannon to defend itself from a Venetian attack. Evidently the military
advances of the Ottomans spurred the spread of firearm technology and
manufacture. Firearms could be found in Serbia by 1386 and by the end of
the fourteenth or early fifteenth century in most of the cities of the eastern
Adriatic all the way down to the Venetian possessions in the Morea.[43]

The first firearms to appear were medium-sized bombards, a meter in
length with a caliber as high as 20 cm. The bombard, light and easy to
transport, was made in two parts of cast or forged copper or bronze, the
back part shaped like a tube and the front part like a horn. These were
followed by the large cannon bombard, first mentioned in the Balkans at
Dubrovnik in 1393. Finally, in the early decades of the fifteenth century the
arquebus made its debut.[44]

Although the use of firearms in the long run revolutionized warfare by
prompting the development of new fortification designs and by necessitating longer campaigns, longer sieges, larger armies, and more expensive
wars, the late Byzantine army itself was affected by little of this. The advent
of firearms in the Balkans coincided with the virtual disappearance of the

---

42. Pachymeres, Bonn ed., II, 620. Palaiologos, *Enseignements*, 58.

43. D. Petrović, "Fire-arms in the Balkans on the Eve of and After the Ottoman
Conquest of the Fourteenth and Fifteenth Centuries," in *War, Technology and Society in the
Middle East*, ed. V. Parry and M. Yapp (London, 1975), 165, 169–71. And cf. M. Dinić, "Prilozi
za istoriju vatrenog oružja u Dubrovniku i susednim zemljama," *Glas Srpske kraljevske akademije* 161 (drugi razred 83) (1934), 55–97. For a rare Greek description of mid-fifteenth-century
cannon making, see Kritoboulos, *Critobuli Imbriotae historiae*, ed. D. Reinsch (Berlin and New
York, 1983), 43–46.

44. Petrović, "Fire-arms in the Balkans," 173, 176.

army and the ultimate impoverishment of Byzantium. The few firearms the Byzantines possessed were small and made little impact on the course of events. Nevertheless, it was indeed firearms that brought the Empire to an end in 1453.[45]

On the whole, however, it was not until the sixteenth century that firearms began to have a major impact on the outcome of battles. In the field the noise and smoke of early firearms produced more terror and confusion than casualties. Typical are the accounts of their use by the Serbs at the battle of Kosovo in 1389. According to a Serbian monk, "There were the cries of men and the din of arms. Flying arrows concealed the sun. Gunfire boomed and the earth groaned. The air resounded with thunder and was filled with murky smoke." An Ottoman chronicler reports that the Serbs had devices "which sounded like lightning causing a thunderclap."[46] Rather, early firearms were used most effectively in siege warfare on the side of the besieged. Even in fifteenth-century Italy, the ineffectiveness of small guns and the difficulty of transporting large guns limited the use of firearms by besiegers.[47]

The earliest possible reference to the use of firearms in Byzantium involves John VII's siege of the Golden Gate fortress where his grandfather John V had taken refuge in 1390 after a coup. The Russian traveler Ignatius of Smolensk reports, in one modern translation: "All summer long he shelled the castle of the old emperor with firearms, but he was unable to vanquish him."[48] The word translated as "shelled" comes from the Russian verb *bit'*, which literally means "to beat or strike." The word translated as "firearms" is *puška*, which today means one or another kind of firearms in a variety of Slavic languages. The word is derived from the verb *pustati*, the original meaning of which was simply "to emit, discharge, or release." Indeed, in an early fifteenth-century Bulgarian chronicle, *puške* seems to mean nothing more than siege weapons in general.[49] Further, Ignatius mentions no other siege machinery except for these puške. One might think that if firearms had really been in use during these events, Ignatius would

---

45. J. Hale, *War and Society in Renaissance Europe, 1450–1620* (Baltimore, 1985), 46–47.

46. Petrović, "Fire-arms in the Balkans," 172.

47. M. Mallett, *Mercenaries and Their Masters* (London, 1974), 160, 163.

48. Ignatius of Smolensk, in *Russian Travelers*, ed. Majeska, 102–103. G. Kolias, «Ἡ ἀνταρσία Ἰωάννου Ζ΄ Παλαιολόγου ἐναντίον Ἰωάννου Ε΄ Παλαιολόγου (1390)», Ἑλληνικά 12 (1952), 49 note 1. D. Hadjopoulos, "Le premier siège de Constantinople par les Ottomans (1394–1402)," diss., Université de Montréal 1980, 107 note 212.

49. Ed. J. Bogdan, "Ein Beitrag zur bulgarischen und serbischen Geschichtschreibung," *Archiv für slavische Philologie* 13 (1891), 533, 542.

have found them a bit more remarkable. I think it is unlikely that the 1390 siege involved firearms.

During Bayezid's 1396–97 siege of Constantinople the Turks still did not have firearms. The sources speak only of conventional siege machinery (*helepoleis*, "city-destroyers"), especially stone-throwing trebuchets which were not able to inflict much damage to the walls. On the other hand, the defenders did possess some firearms. The fifteenth-century Bulgarian chronicle mentioned above notes that these were in the hands of the "Franks" of Galata, and that their military effectiveness was due chiefly to their sound and smoke: "The sound of much clamor like thunder was released through the air, but nothing was achieved by these terrors, to wit, the shooting of slings, of other stratagems, of crossbows [*cagri*] and of bombards [*lubardi*]. . . . But the Franks did not stop, boldly they shot crossbows and catapults along with bombards, and because of the anguish of the fire and smoke produced [the Turks] in a while withdrew."[50] It seems that the bombards referred to were some of the more than sixty acquired by the Genoese of Galata in 1392. As such, they were not under Byzantine control.[51]

Terminology is always a problem in identifying early uses of firearms. Byzantine authors needed to find new words to describe such devices. For example, we have Kritoboulos' description of cannon: "No ancient name is found for this contrivance [*mechane*], unless someone may speak of it as the 'city-destroyer' [*helepolis*] or the 'thrower' [*apheterion*]. But everyone living today calls it by the common name 'apparatus' [*skeue*]." Aside from *skeue*, other terms for cannon included *boumbardos* (bombard), *telebolos* ("far-thrower"), and *chonos* ("funnel, horn"). "City-destroyer" (*helepolis*), the general term for any siege weapon, at times included firearms. Thus when the Greek satirist Mazaris wrote that Manuel II had put down a rebellion on Thasos in 1414 with "stone-throwing machines" (*petrobola mechane-mata*), it is not absolutely clear what was meant, firearms or mechanical trebuchets and catapults. A half-century later Kritoboulos used this expression to denote firearms.[52]

50. Hadjopoulos, "Le premier siège," 106–107, 220. Ed. P. Gautier, "Un récit inédit du siège de Constantinople par les Turcs," *REB* 23 (1965), 106, 109. Bogdan, "Ein Beitrag," 533, 541–42.

51. L. Belgrano, "Prima serie di documenti riguardanti la colonia di Pera," *Atti della Società ligure di storia patria* 13 (1877–84), 174. I owe this reference to Prof. Stephen Reinert.

52. Kritoboulos, ed. Reinsch, 46. S. Lampros, «Τὰ ὀνόματα τοῦ πυροβόλου, τοῦ τυφεκίου καὶ τῆς πυρίτιδος παρὰ τοῖς Βυζαντίνοις», *Νέος Ἑλληνομνήμων* 5 (1908), 401–403, 405–408. For gunpowder, the Greek sources speak of "fodder" (*botane*, cf. "cannon-fodder"), or less commonly "powder" (*konis*): Lampros, «Τὰ ὀνόματα», 402–404, 406. Mazaris, ed. A. Ellissen, *Analekten der mittel- und neugriechischen Litteratur*, IV (Leipzig,

The first Ottoman use of firearms seems to have occurred in 1422 during Murad II's siege of Constantinople. Chalkokondyles' statement that Murad was accompanied by cannoneers from "Germany" supports the reasonable notion that the Ottomans acquired the technology from the West.[53] The main source of information for this siege, the account of John Kananos, provides an uncommon wealth of detail about firearms, other weapons, and the general nature of sieges. He writes that the Turks had "crossbows [tzagra] and bows and great apparatuses [skeuai] and countless small ones." The cannon and other siege machinery seem to have been constructed at the site. They

> made falcons [a short, fat cannon] and tortoises [a wheeled wooden hut covered with hides and used for mining] and great bears [some type of siege device named after the constellation] and many other wooden and most ingenious works, and fashioned city-destroyers and ingenious arms with small wheels, and constructed great and middling shelters beyond number, and against the gates of the city they moved great monsters; they made enormous wooden towers with iron-covered wheels.

He continues:

> and with all kinds of weapons and great equipment [paraskeuai] and most ingenious devices they attacked savagely by division. And while some carried ladders, all kinds of ladders, great and small, others chocks, and others beams, and others fire with mazalades [a handled sling?], others handguns [sclopi], others bore iron battle weapons with long blades called falci [scythe-shaped weapons], others solid and large shields, all with iron, others ploquets [small shields], and others pavesi [large rectangular infantry shields], others grappling hooks, and they carried in hand every other war device. And all were heavily armed with strong iron armor and great helmets. . . . And those with ladders, grappling hooks and falci climbed up the walls. Others pierced the towers with beams, other loosened the walls with chocks, others bent the gates of the outside wall.[54]

Among the besiegers there was a festive atmosphere. Present were "not only those skilled in pillage and war, but those unskilled and traders, that is merchants, profiteers, perfumers and shoemakers," buying and selling prisoners and plunder. The defenders had some firearms themselves, and this

1860), 242, cited by J. Barker, *Manuel II Palaeologus (1391–1425): A Study in Late Byzantine Statesmanship* (New Brunswick, N.J., 1969), 299, 300 note 11.

53. Chalkokondyles, *Laonici Chalcocondylae Atheniensis Historiarum libri decem*, ed. I. Bekker (Bonn, 1843), 231–33: *teleboloi*. Barker, *Manuel*, 364 and note 113. Petrović, "Fire-arms in the Balkans," 177, 190.

54. Kananos, ed. Pinto, lines 90–91, 126–34, 305–17, 404–408.

forced the Turks to build barricades "in order to receive the arrows of the bows and of the crossbows of the Romans, and the stones of the bombards."[55]

At the final siege of Constantinople in 1453 cannon played the most fundamental of roles. Medieval walls were not constructed to withstand the trauma of bombardment by firearms. The manpower shortage was felt most dramatically when the defenders quickly tried to restore and rebuild the walls so as to soften the impact of the stone projectiles. Nor were the walls of the city adequate to serve as emplacements for firearms. Leonard of Chios remarks that "the largest cannon had to remain silent for fear of damage to our own walls by vibration." And Chalkokondyles: "At first the Greeks also set their cannon on the walls, and fired shot weighing a talent and a half [ca.75 pounds] at the sultan's cannon. But this shook the walls and did more damage to them than to the enemy."[56]

Nicolò Barbaro writes that at one point "a plan was made to plant two fairly large cannon by one of the water gates near the cannon of the fleet in the basin." The Turks planted their cannon directly across from them on the other side of the Golden Horn and "this cannon fire on both sides lasted about ten days both day and night continuously." He points out, however, that the cannon fire had little effect on either side since the balls had to carry half a mile, an indication of the effective range of such devices.[57]

It is quite likely that without cannon Mehmet would not have been able to take the city. If the story is true about the defection of the Western engineer Urban, it shows the poverty of the Byzantine Empire and Mehmet II's openness to technological innovation. The Turkish eyewitness Tursun Beg emphasizes throughout all his accounts of Mehmet's campaigns the role of cannon.[58]

The Turks also had arquebuses or other varieties of handguns as well as traditional artillery at the fall. Leonard of Chios writes that "with handguns [*sclopi*], *spingardi* [large frame-mounted crossbows], crossbows [? *zarbathani*], slings and arrows, they attacked our walls day and night and killed our men." The arquebus probably came into common use during the 1420s and was introduced into the Ottoman army by the early 1440s. For small arms, especially the musket, the Byzantine sources use the term "lead-

55. Ibid., lines 168–75, 83–85.

56. Kritoboulos, 49. Leonard of Chios, in Migne, *PG*, vol. 159, col. 928; trans. J. Melville Jones, *The Siege of Constantinople 1453* (Amsterdam, 1972), 16. Chalkokondyles, Bonn ed., 389; trans. Jones, *Siege*, 46.

57. N. Barbaro, *Diary of the Siege of Constantinople*, trans. J. Jones (New York, 1969), 43.

58. Tursun Beg, *The History of Mehmed the Conqueror by Tursun Beg*, ed. with summary trans. by H. Inalcik and R. Murphey (Minneapolis and Chicago, 1978), passim.

thrower" (*molybdobolon*) or transliterations of the Italian *sclopo*, *schioppo* (from the verb "to strike") or *touphax*, from the Turkish *tufenk*, an early word for pipe-shaped fire weapons.[59]

The defenders had firearms also, along with a range of more conventional weapons including the usual bows and swords. Most of the larger weapons seem to have been in the hands of the Italians, but this may be attributable to the fact that the most detailed eyewitness accounts were written by Westerners. While nationalism certainly was a factor, so too was the simple fact that the authors were serving beside Italians. Thus the Venetian Barbaro writes that his countrymen had cannon and crossbows, that the 200 men who arrived with Isidore of Kiev included "gunners and crossbowmen," that the 300 foreigners at the Gate of St. Romanos "had with them some good cannon and good guns and a large number of crossbows and other equipment," and that there were guns mounted on the defenders' ships. Leonard of Chios adds that the Venetian Bochiardi brothers fought with large frame-mounted crossbows (*spingardis horrendis et balistis torneis*).[60]

Cannon balls made of stone were used until the middle of the fifteenth century, though lead shot was introduced earlier in smaller devices. Doukas claims such a weapon was used by the defenders of Constantinople. They fought, he says,

> from the ramparts of the walls, some by discharging quarrels from crossbows and others by shooting plain arrows. Some, however, shot lead balls [*molybdobolon*] which were propelled by powder [*botane*], five and ten at a time, and as small as Pontic walnuts [i.e., filberts]. These had tremendous perforating power and, if one ball happened to penetrate an armorclad [*siderophoroi*] soldier, it would transpierce both shield and body, passing through and striking the next person standing in the way. Passing through the second individual, it would strike a third until the force of the powder was dissipated. Thus, with one shot it was possible to kill two or three soldiers. The Turks learned of these weapons and not only employed them but had even better ones.

This is not the most reliable information because Doukas was not an eyewit-

---

59. Leonard of Chios, col. 928. Petrović, "Fire-arms in the Balkans," 186, 191. Lampros, «Τὰ ὀνόματα», 410–12. Other references to handguns: A. Pertusi, "The Anconitan Colony in Constantinople and the Report of Its Consul, Benvenuto, on the Fall of the City," in *Charanis Studies*, ed. A. Laiou-Thomadakis (New Brunswick, N.J., 1980), 207. Kritoboulos, 64, 66–68. Tursun Beg, *History of Mehmed the Conqueror*, 34.

60. Barbaro, *Diary*, 32, 63, 11, 50, 51. And cf. Doukas, 335. Oddly, Kritoboulos, though he speaks of other weapons, makes no mention whatsoever of firearms among the defenders. Leonard of Chios, col. 934.

ness and, moreover, he uses this same description earlier in his history when recounting Murad II's unsuccessful six-month siege of Belgrade in 1440: the defenders "shot lead balls as large as a Pontic walnut from a bronze apparatus whose tube held the balls in rows of five or ten." Nevertheless, it does indicate that Doukas regarded such weapons as novelties.[61]

The only evidence from an eyewitness that some firearms were under Byzantine control is provided by Leonard of Chios. He writes that at one point during the siege Giustiniani had "asked the megas doux Loukas Notaras for the public bombards of the city" (*communes urbis bombardas*) for his section of the defenses, but Notaras refused.[62]

The most exotic weapon in the traditional Byzantine arsenal was Greek fire or, as they themselves called it, "liquid fire." From the seventh through the twelfth century, it was commonly used aboard ships and traditionally projected from tubes. Its formula—some combination of pitch, naphtha, resin, sulfur, and other ingredients—was a closely guarded secret not known for certain even today.[63] So celebrated was its destructive potential that similar concoctions were developed by neighboring peoples. In the late period there are numerous scattered references to various peoples using what is called "Greek fire." For example, in the thirteenth century there is evidence that both the Seljuk Turks and the Mongols employed something called "Greek fire." Writing of the latter people, the papal ambassador Friar John of Pian Carpino offers a grisly reference to the substance: "They throw Greek fire and the lard of the men they kill and throw this same liquid on houses, and wherever fire comes upon that grease, it burns and cannot be extinguished. However, pouring wine or beer over can extinguish it, and if it falls upon the skin, it is extinguished by rubbing with the hand."[64]

61. Doukas, 331, 263–65; trans. H. Magoulias, *Doukas. Decline and Fall of Byzantium to the Ottoman Turks* (Detroit, 1975), 178. Petrović, "Fire-arms in the Balkans," 181.

62. Leonard of Chios, col. 936. Cf. Pseudo-Phrantzes, in *Georgios Sphrantzes, Memorii 1401–1477*, ed. V. Grecu (Bucharest, 1966), 406.

63. J. Haldon and M. Byrne, "A Possible Solution to the Problem of Greek Fire," *BZ* 70 (1977), 91–99. For a few translated references to Greek fire, see Michael Psellus, *Fourteen Byzantine Rulers*, trans. E. Sewter (Baltimore, 1966), 201–02; *The Alexiad of Anna Comnena*, trans. E. Sewter (Baltimore, Md., 1969), 360–62, 402; John Kinnamos, *Deeds of John and Manuel Comnenus*, trans. C. Brand (New York, 1976), 157, 212; and D. Geanakoplos, *Byzantium: Church, Society, and Civilization Seen Through Contemporary Eyes* (Chicago, 1984), 112–13, 121. Cf. p. 291 in the latter, where a passage from Pachymeres (ed. Failler, I, 539) is mistranslated. For Geanakoplos' "in order to withstand the Greek fire," read instead "so that the ship might adequately withstand fire and everything thrown." There is no need to think the anticipated fire would have been produced by anything more exotic than flaming arrows.

64. In Simon de Saint-Quentin, *Histoire des Tartares*, ed. J. Richard (Paris, 1965), 44. See A. Bombaci, "The Army of the Saljuqs of Rūm," *Istituto orientale di Napoli, Annali*, n.s. 38 (1978), 368.

The only evidence of its use by the Byzantines in the late period is furnished by accounts of the fall. In Makarios Melissourgos' unreliable rewriting of Sphrantzes' memoirs it is claimed that both sides used "liquid fire," especially in countermining measures. The only eyewitness to maintain that Greek fire was used by the defenders is the Ottoman official and author Tursun Beg. Moreover, Barbaro reports that, in the attempt to burn Turkish ships, a ship was loaded with "pitch and brushwood and gunpowder." One wonders whether the legendary nature and effects of Greek fire led to its confusion with firearms or with less exotic mixtures of pitch, sulfur, and saltpeter.[65]

The failure of the Byzantines to make extensive use of firearms can be attributed largely to economic factors. One had to either buy the finished product or build one's own firearms. The latter required raw materials and the necessary technical knowledge. Both options required money, and Byzantium by the year 1400, indeed by the middle of the fourteenth century, was in penury. Although there were Westerners willing for a price to provide Byzantium with the technology, such as the cannon-maker Urban at the time of the fall, the price could not be met. In contrast Byzantium's Balkan neighbors, the Serbs, the Bosnians, the Adriatic cities, and the Venetians, had accepted and enthusiastically developed this new technology at an early date. By the early fifteenth century Stefan Lazarević of Serbia had large-caliber cannon and mortars similar to those in the West, and their manufacture began soon afterward. Even in relatively backward Bosnia cannon were being manufactured by 1444.[66] The fact that there is no evidence that the Byzantine despots in the Morea ever utilized firearms points out again the incongruity between their military successes, the reported sizes of their armies, and reality.

Yet money was not the only factor, or else the Turks would have acquired and employed firearms long before the 1420s. Of the numerous reasons why the sultans adopted firearms as late as they did—a lack of raw materials and technical knowledge (at least until they firmly controlled Serbia), the refusal of Western Europeans to sell them firearms, a mind-set that did not regard firearms as useful—some may have applied equally well to Byzantium.

65. E.g., Pseudo-Phrantzes, 424. Tursun Beg, *History of Mehmed the Conqueror*, 36. Barbaro, *Diary*, 40.

66. Petrović, "Fire-arms in the Balkans," 183–85.

Conclusion: Soldiers, Army, Society

O Stranger,
Not only was this noble man an unconquerable hoplite
in close combat with the enemy,
but, as is fitting, he had an affable manner
when the moment did not lead him to war.
But Time the Destroyer enshrouded him
in close combat falling amid the arms.
Yet his image is painted not in red, but in white
and this Ares' sweat cannot wash away
although he sleeps the sleep of death.
                                    —Manuel Philes, "Epitaph to Romanos,
                                        Locked in Combat and Slain"[1]

The late Byzantine period was not the bloodiest of ages, but it was the one period in Byzantine history in which no part of the Empire escaped first-hand contact with carnage and destruction. It was a violent age. Except for the Anatolian provinces of the Nicaean state which knew relative security and prosperity for a time (from about 1215 to about 1260), no area in the Aegean basin was immune to sudden and frequent attack by any of a host of enemies. Far from being restricted to the frontiers and beyond, most war took place within the Empire itself. It affected everyone. One either fought, was besieged, or saw his crops burnt. The social transformations of late Byzantium, the economic dislocations, the civil unrest, perhaps even the direction of religious currents, were directly influenced, if not at times determined, by military developments. Consider the major crises after the reconquest of Constantinople: the loss of the East and the flight of the population, the Catalan-Alan episodes, the civil wars, the Serbian invasion, and the Ottoman conquest. Pepper this with minor revolts and frequent incursions by Serbs, Mongols, Bulgarians, and piratical Turks, add a common incidence of small-scale banditry and lawlessness, and the result is a

1. *Manuelis Philae Carmina Inedita*, ed. E. Martini (Naples, 1900), no. 37.

society ever on the alert, ever mobilized and, to use V. Smetanin's character-ization of Byzantium after 1282, in a state of "permanent war."[2]

Under these circumstances the army was a highly visible institution. This study has attempted to show what the late Byzantine army did, how it was organized and administered, and how military and economic institu-tions were related. Further, in an effort to capture the flavor of daily life as closely as possible without departing from the central topic, considerable attention has been paid to guard service, a ubiquitous defensive institution in accord with the spirit of the age, which, while usually not employing professional soldiers, directly touched the lives of every inhabitant of the Empire. If the picture that emerges of the organizational structure of the army seems fragmented, if somehow the interrelation of the various divi-sions and the types of soldiers seems not quite as orderly as we might wish, this may be less attributable to the inadequacy of the sources than to the nature of the Empire's military forces. Whatever kind of system existed was very flexible, loosely structured, and curiously appropriate to an Empire that itself was highly fragmented.

L.-P. Raybaud has written that the two basic characteristics of the army during the thirteenth and fourteenth centuries were a growing nu-merical weakness and a growing heterogeneity of composition.[3] This is a good point of departure for a general consideration of the effectiveness of the late Byzantine military. Heterogeneity of composition is not in itself a negative trait. Each of the major types of soldiers—pronoiars, mercenaries, smallholding—had its own strengths which in aggregate compensated for the intrinsic weakness of each other type of soldier. Thus, pronoia soldiers, unlike smallholding soldiers, were usually heavy cavalry and were less expensive than mercenaries because they were paid "at the source" and could be given properties in pronoia that the state otherwise might have found difficult to administer. Pronoia soldiers, however, often held their pronoiai in out of the way places and this made them difficult to muster, and their dependence on these revenues hindered their participation in long or distant campaigns.

Mercenaries campaigned as long as their salaries were paid, but they were the most expensive troops, and the state frequently found itself short

2. V. Smetanin, "O specifike permanentnoj vojny v Vizantii v 1282–1453 gg.," *Antičnaja drevnost' i srednie veka* 9 (1973), 89–101, and "O tendencijah ideologičeskoj i social'noj dinamiki pozdnevizantijskogo obščestva v period permanentnoj vojny," *Antičnaja drevnost' i srednie veka* 11 (1975), 99–109.

3. L.-P. Raybaud, *Le gouvernement et l'administration centrale de l'empire byzantin sous les premiers Paléologues* (Paris, 1968), 243.

of the ready cash to pay them. Smallholding soldiers were the best bargain, and their attachment to the land upon which they lived made them better suited to hold frontier positions than either pronoia soldiers or mercenaries. But, as far as we can tell, smallholding soldiers were at best light cavalry, and since they were frequently backward, clannish foreigners, they were not the most reliable or disciplined troops. Therefore, it would not be a great simplification to say that the army could not have been composed exclusively of mercenaries because there was not enough cash, nor exclusively of pronoia soldiers or smallholding soldiers because some troops were needed who could campaign at a moment's notice and for long periods. Neither pronoiars nor smallholding soldiers alone could supplement mercenaries, because both heavy cavalry and soldiers attached to specific lands were in demand.

Scholars have wondered whether pronoia was effective as a means of defending the Empire. George Ostrogorsky concluded that it was indeed effective during the time of the Komnenoi, despite the Empire's continuing reliance on mercenaries, but that its effectiveness declined by Andronikos II's reign, when Gregoras writes that the army had become a laughingstock. Ostrogorsky adds that pronoia never furnished the firm economic and social base that the small proprietor did, and that "one may certainly doubt that pronoia was sufficiently efficacious in consolidating the armed forces of the Empire." Speros Vryonis as well has written that while pronoia was effective under the Komnenoi and the Laskarides when western Asia Minor was retrieved from the Seljuks, it collapsed as a functioning military institution "due to territorial loss to the enemy and to increasing alienation of pronoia land by the magnates." As a result the army was transformed "into agglomerates of foreign mercenaries seeking temporary employment and of ethnic enclaves settled in Byzantium."[4]

In truth there is no real evidence that pronoia was ever, in any period, an especially productive means of raising soldiers or that pronoia soldiers ever were especially competent in combat. There is not a single battle or campaign in which the historians single out the decisive role played by pronoia soldiers. At the battle of Antioch in 1211, we are told only of the valor of the Latin mercenaries. Indeed the major conquests of John Vatatzes occurred in the 1240s, just after the Cumans were settled as smallholding

4. Gregoras, I, 223. Ostrogorsky, *Féodalité*, 174–75, 179. S. Vryonis, "Byzantine and Turkish Societies and Their Sources of Manpower," in *War, Technology and Society in the Middle East*, ed. V. Parry and M. Yapp (London, 1975), 128.

soldiers. In this light, Andronikos II's plan to use the tax revenues he raised around 1320 to finance 3,000 mercenary cavalry is less indicative of the decline of pronoia as a military institution than a confirmation that even contemporaries did not view pronoia as a means toward an effective defensive force. Mercenaries were the soldiers of choice but there were not many of them around, they were expensive, and most were foreigners. The money needed to train, equip, and finance native mercenaries was unavailable. The economy had been in decline since the eleventh century, a result of competition from the young Italian city-states and the declining economic and social status of the peasantry. Consequently pronoia was turned to as a means of creating an army without relying on foreign mercenaries or outlays of large sums of cash.

The heterogeneity of the army was less the product of a coherent policy than of a series of responses to dangers and opportunities. Most of the major administrative and organizational decisions affecting the army in the last centuries resulted from the pressure of unforeseen and unforeseeable developments. Sometimes the hand of an emperor was forced when new men appeared on the horizon, as in the case of the Cumans settled by Vatatzes, the Turks of Izz al-Din, the Cretans settled in Anatolia, and the Alans. If by "policy" we mean a consistent method of dealing with problems, no policy existed for dealing with these foreigners. The story of each group is quite different, as were the results.

In Andronikos II we have the clearest example of an emperor with very little military policy. He spent his reign extemporizing. Immediately after his accession, the Mongol allied force called by his father appeared, and he ineptly directed it toward Serbia. Then at the end of the century he pondered the idea of establishing soldiers in Anatolia, but found it unworkable. Next the Alans appeared and after them the Catalans. Finally, around 1320 he considered financing new permanent mercenary forces and a navy to defend the Empire, but again to no avail. The only consistent policies during his reign were related to his practice of settling groups of refugees from Anatolia in Europe (the Klazomenitai and perhaps the Achyraïtai) and possibly the practice of importing small, integrated groups of soldiers from abroad (like the Varvarenoi soldier company). Institutionally it appears to have been during Andronikos' reign that soldier companies and collective pronoia had their origins in Byzantium.

The Laskarides' policy in regard to the highlanders of Asia Minor was successful and consonant with the circumstances of the age. And John

Kantakouzenos had a consistent, if simple, military policy. When there was trouble, he called in the Turks. But the real master of late Byzantine military organization and deployment was Michael VIII. His methodical resettlement of Constantinople, reconstitution of a Byzantine navy, and creation of numerous divisions of soldiers (Gasmouloi, Thelematarioi, Prosalentai, marine Tzakones) long outlasted his reign. More significant was his policy, motivated by political as well as military considerations, of employing Anatolian troops for his European campaigns and then settling these troops in the newly established European provinces. In the long run this policy had disastrous consequences for the East, but at the time it was highly successful.

Institutionally, while Michael may have been responsible for the creation of the megala allagia, he was certainly the first emperor to grant hereditary rights over pronoia on a widespread basis. Generally, throughout the late period, there was a tendency for all military service to acquire a hereditary character but, at least in the case of pronoia, there is no evidence that hereditary rights were ever granted automatically. Rather, even in the second half of the fourteenth century they were granted ad hoc and always required special imperial approval. In fact it does seem that one of the major reasons for the heterogeneity of the army was that there was little consistent policy. Emperors tended to deal with problems as they arose, and although adapting institutions to particular needs sometimes produced successful results, the army became a variegated collection of little groups of soldiers. Hybrid phenomena such as collective pronoiars and mercenaries with small pronoiai do not seem to have been so much well thought-out policies as momentary expedients taking their place on the shelf of half-tested elixirs for an enfeebled army.

Certainly the sources give the impression that the army's quality was not very high. But was it any worse than those of its adversaries? To estimate its combat effectiveness man for man and unit for unit, one needs a series of battles for which the outcomes and the approximate numbers of troops on each side are known. When comparable forces clash, the more effective one prevails (excluding the rare case where genius or simple luck decides the outcome). Unfortunately there is not a single battle from the period under consideration for which we can make a meaningful comparison of the sizes of opposing armies. All of our data are derived from narrative histories whose figures are subject to exaggeration or are incomplete (for example, only figures for one side in a contest are provided). As a result, relative force sizes cannot be determined, and so it is not possible to make any objective conclusion regarding whether the Byzantine army, man for man, was better or worse than the armies of its enemies.[5]

We really can only look at the larger issue, whether the army won battles or deterred aggressors, in other words, the extent to which it was effective in ensuring the survival of Byzantium. Here we are not concerned about the relation between the army's size and the quality of its troops, only whether it did the job. Since the deterrent effect of the army cannot be determined, we focus on battles and campaigns.

In addition to heterogeneity of composition, Raybaud also pointed to the growing numerical weakness as one of the basic characteristics of the late Byzantine army. Numerical weakness is not an independent variable but is linked to the strengths of opposing armies and to the political climate. We may define a numerically adequate army as one that is impressive enough and strong enough to deter or repel an enemy. This in turn is dependent on the strength and determination of the enemy, as well as the desirability of invading or conquering the territory the army is charged with defending. According to this definition, the army of the Nicaean period was numerically adequate. The eastern frontier, though always subject to the raids of plundering bands of Turks, successfully deterred Seljuk adventurism. Nor was the western border with the weak Latin Empire the object of much concern. From their firm base in Anatolia, the Laskarides could push on into Europe.

Whereas Vatatzes and Theodore II had been content with reconquering Thrace and Macedonia, Michael VIII's ambitions in Thessaly, Epiros, and the Morea led to a situation in which he found himself facing increasingly large alliances of Balkan and Western rulers. One could argue that his campaigns against Thessaly and Epiros were necessary to secure his Macedonian frontier, but since the Latins in the Morea were no real threat to his Empire, his costly Morean expeditions merely robbed Peter to pay Paul. To gain the west, he lost the east. Michael stepped up the process of sending soldiers from the politically unreliable east to Europe with the result that during the 1260s, in combination with the breakdown of the Seljuk sultanate in Anatolia, the eastern frontier began to fall. At this point, although Michael was probably fielding armies larger than any of his recent predecessors, the army became numerically inadequate.

Andronikos II and his successors inherited an Empire vulnerable on all

5. On the general topic of military effectiveness, see J. Lynn, *The Bayonets of the Republic: Motivation and Tactics in the Army of Revolutionary France, 1791–94* (Urbana, Ill., 1984), 21–40.

sides: to the east, the Turks; to the northeast, the Bulgarians; to the northwest, the Serbs; to the west and southwest, the petty Thessalian principalities, Epiros, and the Albanians; and by the end of Andronikos' reign, to the south on the Aegean littoral, Turkish marauders. Yet, with the exception of the loss of Anatolia, the Empire struggled on through the first half of the fourteenth century with relatively little loss of territory. Military policy and the army itself could not take the credit for this. Rather, it was diplomacy, the natural enmity of Byzantium's neighbors toward one another, their own domestic difficulties, and plain good luck, that prevented the Balkan rulers from anything more than nibbling at Byzantium's frontiers, even during the civil wars of the 1320s. The military response of the emperors to crises usually meant employing more foreign mercenaries (the Catalans) or foreign allied troops (the Turks of Umur Pasha), or as a last resort, coopting the energies of peasants. The few military successes enjoyed by the Byzantines against foreign enemies during this period were followed by disasters (the Philanthropenos revolt, the Catalan episode).

The rough balance between Byzantium and its Balkan neighbors during the first half of the fourteenth century came to an end with Stefan Dušan's conquest of Macedonia and Thessaly. Within the next twenty years Thrace fell to the Ottomans, leaving only two cities, their hinterlands, and the Morea as the remainder of the Byzantine Empire. The illusory strength of the Morea suggested by its cultural brilliance and the exaggerated Western accounts of the size of its army should not overshadow the fact that the rulers of the Morea, from the 1380s sons or brothers of the emperor, never provided military or financial aid to the Empire proper.

Even though the army was ultimately unsuccessful in maintaining the state, it was nonetheless effective against a number of its enemies. It prevailed over the Latins in the Morea and on the Aegean islands, as well as those from the West (such as Charles of Anjou) who made occasional war against the Empire, and it at least held its ground against the Bulgarians throughout the late period, the Turks of Asia Minor through the 1290s, and the Serbs until the era of Stefan Dušan (the 1340s). Through military operations, diplomacy, and the exploitation of the internal problems of these enemies, leaders such as Theodore I Laskaris of Nicaea, Theodore Doukas of Epiros, John Vatatzes, Michael VIII, and Andronikos II were able to deal with the threats they posed.

On the other hand, the army was not effective against the Turks in Asia from the early fourteenth century, the Mongols, the Catalans, the Serbs under Dušan, and the Turks once they entered Europe during the 1350s. Yet the assaults of most of these enemies were short-lived and with patience were overcome. Even though the Byzantines could not prevent the brief, infrequent plundering expeditions of the Mongols, the army was at least part of the reason why the Mongols did not establish permanent possession of Byzantine territory. The success of the Catalans was due to the special circumstances of their presence within the Empire. When a foreign allied army turns on its host, the blame can be laid at the feet of the political leadership. Moreover, in the long run the Catalans were unable to sustain their drive against Byzantium. Although imperial forces could not defeat them in the field, they were able to make their stay in Thrace and Macedonia sufficiently unpleasant to induce their departure from the Empire. The Catalan conquest of the Duchy of Athens shows that the Byzantine army and state were not the weakest in the Balkans. The successes of Dušan's Serbs were similarly ephemeral and were a direct result of the civil wars of the 1340s. Since Kantakouzenos, without great difficulty, was able to retake towns seized by the Serbs, a united Byzantium could have probably drive him out of Greece. So too the victories of the Turks in Europe, beginning in the 1350s, were a result of the civil wars.

In fact, despite the enervating effects of the civil wars of the first half of the fourteenth century, if the only enemies Byzantium faced had been Bulgarians, Serbs, the Latins of the Morea and the Aegean, the Catalans, and the Mongols, the Empire might well not have fallen. By the 1350s, despite over thirty years of intermittent civil war, no Balkan state had been able to take permanent advantage of the Empire's weaknesses. Rather it was the Turks who first in Asia Minor and later in the Balkans capitalized on Byzantium's frailties.

The Turks proved to be the implacable enemy. Though the situation in Asia had begun to worsen in the 1260s, Michael VIII did not take it seriously, preoccupied as he was with western affairs. The window of opportunity for crushing the Turks closed once the various Turkish groups that appeared in the wake of the collapse of the Seljuk state of Rum were brought, usually forcibly, within Ottoman control. By the time Andronikos II came to the throne the moment had passed. The last Byzantine successes against the Turks of Asia Minor came with the Catalan campaign of 1304, and prior to that, with Alexios Philanthropenos' victories in 1294 and 1295. But it would have taken much more than a few isolated efforts to curb the Turkish spirit of conquest, and for political reasons these successes could not be sustained. Vryonis has pointed out that as the various Turkish groups advanced into Byzantine territory in Asia Minor, they were joined by disaffected Greek magnates. This provided the manpower for the rapid conquest and decreased the manpower reserves of the shrinking Byzantine Empire.[6]

If the army was numerically inadequate from the 1260s on, and the Byzantines knew it, why, we ask ingenuously, did they not do something about it? Of course they tried, but at best were only partially successful. They hired mercenaries, singly and in groups, of almost every ethnicity, they employed pronoia in various permutations to maintain a small, well-equipped campaign force, and they created smallholding soldiers, some native, some foreign, and tried to create still more. But they could not do more than break even. The reasons for this go to the very heart of late Byzantine society and beyond the bounds of this study. Put simply, the economy was not healthy enough, nor was the state's fiscal apparatus efficient enough, to produce sufficient resources to finance enough mercenaries. In regard to pronoiars and smallholding soldiers, the weakness of the state's administrative apparatus could not guarantee the service obligations of these soldiers would be met. Without adequate supervision smallholding soldiers disappeared into the landscape and pronoia soldiers discarded their arms and adopted the pretensions of petty aristocrats. Further, the piecemeal approach to strengthening the army placed a heavy reliance on foreigners, and the resultant ethnic antagonisms between soldiers (for example, Catalans and Alans) and between soldiers and the population at large,[7] together with the disjunctive effects of the civil wars, weakened morale and discipline among soldiers, and morale within society as a whole.

Throughout history warfare has often been a unifying force in society. During the period of Ottoman expansion, during the reign of Justinian, no less than during the Napoleonic era, offensive war improved morale and assuaged social discontent through the redirection of hostility outward toward a foreign foe. Defensive war as well, with its inherent legitimacy as defense of the homeland, can unite a people and partially offset the misery of war, so long as an end to the conflict is in sight and the defenders, through their actions, can maintain the moral high-ground. With few exceptions Byzantine emperors went to war for only two reasons: either

6. S. Vryonis, *The Decline of Medieval Hellenism in Asia Minor and the Process of Islamization from the Eleventh Through the Fifteenth Century* (Berkeley, Calif., 1971), 468.

7. On this, see Kantakouzenos, I, 301, and Doukas, 61.

they felt their Empire was or would soon be under direct attack, or they wished, in their role as the legitimate heirs of the Roman Empire, to restore to the Empire territory that had once been Byzantine. In the late period all of the offensive wars launched by Byzantium can be placed under the rubric of reconquest: those of the Nicaean emperors in Asia Minor, Thrace, and Macedonia; Michael VIII's campaigns in western and southern Greece; Andronikos II's expeditions into Asia Minor and Greece; Andronikos III's campaigns against the Turks and the Latins of the Aegean. Thus the desire for glory and territory could be legitimized. So too the civil wars, while advancing personal ambitions, were framed as the avenging of wrongs.

The Byzantines were well-equipped for warfare with a thousand-year panoply of ideological defenses and weapons. Supplementing, or even transcending, the Roman imperial tradition was the religious concept of the Byzantines as the Chosen People of God. Although religion, even broadly conceived, played an insignificant role in the decision to make war, the connection between war and religion, the Army and the Church, was quite strong. Throughout Byzantine history we can see this in countless manifestations. In the early seventh century, prior to Emperor Herakleios' campaign against the great Persian Empire, the coins minted to pay the army bore the Cross and the words that Constantine the Great reportedly once saw in the sky: "In this sign, conquer" (*en touto nika*). In the tenth century Emperor Constantine VII Porphyrogennetos sent holy water and relics of the Passion to his army on campaign. Another tenth-century emperor ordered that a huge cross be carried into battle at the head of his army, and pictorial representations of battle flags consistently show the cross as the most common motif. In tenth-century Constantinople, only the closest inspection of a procession of young men dressed in white, singing psalms and hymns, carrying an enormous cross, and crying rhythmically, "Christ the Conqueror! Christ the Conqueror! " would reveal that these were soldiers on parade.

In the tenth century, we see the first military saints on icons: George, Demetrios, the two Theodores. In the next century they began to appear on lead seals and by the late eleventh century on the coinage. And certainly whenever a city came under attack, one could expect to find on the battlements not only soldiers but also icons of the city's patron saint and holy banners: St. Demetrios in military dress for Thessaloniki and the Mother of God for the Queen of Cities, Constantinople. In 626 when Constantinople was surrounded by Avars and Arabs, the image of the Virgin was paraded atop the city's walls. And 800 years later, in 1453, she was there again defending Constantinople, though this time not as successfully.[8]

If viewed from a purely secular perspective, every Byzantine war was motivated by political necessity, preserving or restoring the territory of the Roman Empire. But, by the same token, if viewed from a religious perspective, as was natural for the Byzantines, every war, whether offensive, defensive, or preventive, was fought by and for the people of Christ. The Byzantines appropriated the ancient Jewish concept of a Chosen People doing God's will, and they employed it time and again throughout their history. They regarded themselves as a sacred people who had a special relationship to God, who had both the privilege of being protected by God and the obligation to be the instrument of God's earthly justice. This concept had been embraced and developed by imperial authorities no later than the seventh and eighth centuries during the struggle with the Arabs, and it portrayed Byzantium as the New Israel, Constantinople the New Jerusalem, and the Byzantines themselves as the new Chosen People. Once developed, this concept could be applied to every war conducted from the imperial throne. For example, Pachymeres reports that after the reconquest of Constantinople in 1261 Michael VIII addressed the Byzantine people with the following words:

> Sometime ago, when God was angered He made use of the Italians as an impetuous wind to punish the Romans [i.e., the Byzantines], and our fathers were driven from their country and their rule was limited to a narrow area. . . . But if we have just retaken Constantinople in spite of the resistance of those who defended it, and if we are going to maintain ourselves there despite the efforts of the Franks . . . to strip our conquest from our hands, it is the result of the Divine Power. . . . If we have undergone so much fatigue trying to take Constantinople without securing any result, although we were greater in number than those who defended it, it is because God wished us to recognize that the possession of the City is a grace that depends only on His bounty. . . . He will revenge our injuries; He will crush the pride of our enemies. He has seen fit to show us this great compassion that He refused to our fathers, and He has bestowed it upon us through His inscrutable divine will. . . . Formerly,

8. Constantine VII Porphyrogenitus, in R. Vári, ed., "Zum historischen Exzerpten-werke des Konstantinos Porphyrogennetos," *BZ* 17 (1908), 83, and in H. Ahrweiler, ed., "Un discours inédit de Constantin VII Porphrogénète," *TM* 2 (1967), 397. For the general use of holy banners in medieval warfare, see C. Erdmann, *The Origin of the Idea of Crusade* (Princeton, N.J., 1977), 35–56. R. Guerdan, *Byzantium, Its Triumphs and Tragedy* (New York, 1957), 17. Pseudo-Phrantzes, III.8, trans. in M. Philippides, *The Fall of the Byzantine Empire: A Chronicle by George Sphrantzes, 1401–1477* (Amherst, Mass., 1980), 120 (see under Makarios Melissourgos in the Bibliography).

He promised the Israelites an abundant land and all kinds of possessions. Yet, when they left Egypt, they died in the desert and were interred in a foreign land. The promise He had made to the nation in the person of Abraham was fulfilled only after a long period. That is how He dispenses His favors, with a weightiness and a full measure of justice.[9]

Because the Byzantines had a special relation to God, their actions, including war, were sanctioned by and manifestations of divine will. If they suffered, it was because of their sins; if they prospered, it was God's will to help His people. Calamities had no independent connection to what foreign peoples wanted or did; God simply allowed them to harm His people. History, then, was the story of God's relationship to His people, previously the Jews, now the Byzantines, and thus all war in Byzantium was legitimized because the army, representing God's Chosen People of the New Israel and the New Christian Rome which was Byzantium, performed actions that served God's will.

There can be little doubt that these two powerful ideological tools made no small contribution to the longevity of the Empire. And yet, as much as these themes could be used for the benefit of the Empire, they were also limiting. The Roman imperial tradition dictated that war was the constitutional responsibility of the emperor and that the instrument through which the emperor made war was the army. This can explain why only as an emergency means of local defense and, even then, only in the most dire of circumstances, did the imperial authorities make popular appeals to anti-Muslim or anti-Latin feelings, or even to a general desire to preserve the fatherland. Generally they preferred not to encourage, let alone create such popular enthusiasm. When it did appear, they found it unmanageable and counterproductive, reinforcing the ideological position that defense was purely the job of the army.

This explains the hesitancy of the Byzantines to capitalize on the popular antipathy toward the Latins fanned by the Fourth Crusade. Rather, the emperors of Nicaea only exploited the idea within governmental and military circles, and later emperors who dabbled with the idea of the union of the Eastern and Western Churches reverted to the idea of a pan-Christian defense against the Turks. For example, in 1275 at the Council of Lyons, the Byzantine ambassador, George Metochites, meeting with Pope Gregory X

9. Pachymeres, ed. Failler, I, 209–13 (Bonn ed., I, 153–55); trans. adapted from D. Geanakoplos, *Byzantium: Church, Society, and Civilization Seen Through Contemporary Eyes* (Chicago, 1984), 36–37.

on behalf of Michael VIII, spoke enthusiastically of a Greco-Latin action against the Turks "for the extermination of Infidels" and "for the triumph of the true religion."[10]

Within Byzantine religious ideology there was also a strong measure of fatalism. So long as the Empire prospered it was possible to maintain the conceit that God was on their side, but whenever the tide turned against the Empire, the Byzantines tended to conclude that God was punishing them for their iniquities. After the reign of Michael VIII, once the long final decline began, this idea became common, and by the end of Andronikos II's reign, it had become a commonplace. By the middle of the fourteenth century many Byzantines, and certainly most intellectuals, had resigned themselves to the inability of their civilization to recover.

The military situation of the Empire and the nature of the wars of the last centuries contributed to these attitudes. On the one hand, warfare was localized within the Empire or in areas that had recently been part of the Empire and, on the other, the inability of the state to acquire enough trained soldiers from the native population led to the employment of troops that had no affinity with or responsibility toward the Empire's indigenous residents. The defensive aspect of late Byzantine warfare, the circumstances which tended to keep warfare inside the shrinking borders of the Empire, was the more decisive of the two. If warfare could have been taken beyond the Empire's borders, if most of the Empire's territory could have been kept free from the devastation of warring troops, the social and economic costs of war could have been reduced dramatically. But this was impossible. The rulers of late Byzantium had inherited an international situation which left them with hostile neighbors on all sides, neighbors who were fully aware of the internal weaknesses of Byzantium, and who were, due to the social dynamics within their own societies, driven to foreign conquest.[11] Byzantium had to accept, as a fact of life, that any attempt to revitalize the Empire's security would have to begin with successful warfare within its borders.

Warfare and defense had two effects on society. First, there was the direct human cost paid by any society that goes to war or must defend itself. Whether victorious or defeated, there will be the dead, the maimed, the

10. H. Ahrweiler, *L'idéologie politique de l'empire byzantine* (Paris, 1975), 103. V. Laurent, "L'idée de guerre sainte et la tradition byzantine," *Revue historique du Sud-Est européen* 23 (1946), 83, 89–90.

11. See, e.g., G. Ostrogorsky, "Étienne Dušan et la noblesse serbe dans la lutte contre Byzance," *Byz* 22 (1952), 157.

wounded, the prisoners, and, in the pre-modern era, the enslaved. The soldiers who fought for Byzantium or for a faction in one of the civil wars faced danger not only from the enemy, whoever that may have been, but from the elements and from hunger, as well as from the population itself. At times civilians were enslaved as a result of imperial policy decisions—one thinks of John Kantakouzenos' employment of Umur's Turks—and occasionally civilians died at the hands of the enemy, a tragedy usually resulting from their refusal to stand clear of conflict. But the cost of warfare in terms of the direct loss of human lives was relatively low. Casualties of more than a hundred for any single battle were rare.

The economic effects of warfare fall into two categories: decreased production due to the ravages of war, and decreased production due to the diversion of resources—men, animals, and land—to military ends. The first is illustrated by a passage from Kantakouzenos' memoirs (I, 136–37) which deals with the effects of the civil war between the Andronikoi in 1322. We are told that Andronikos III was

> at a loss for the money by which [he] could provide for the mercenaries. For the public taxes [*demosia*] had not been exacted because of the disorder from the war and because the farmers from whom especially the taxes are exacted left their own villages because the soldiers of the older emperor plundered, and because those of the young [emperor] who were sent out as garrisons led away and carried off the property [of the peasants] because of military greed and behaved no better than the enemy.

Thus, because of war, taxes were not collected, peasants fled, and soldiers plundered, resulting in decreased production overall.

Much more significant are the social costs which contribute to the erosion or disintegration of the social bonds which hold society together, the interpersonal ties of dependence between men and the social ties between men and institutions. Without them civilization is impossible, and as they are eroded, civilization itself disintegrates. Warfare was not the only factor that played a role in the social transformations of late Byzantium, but it did have several characteristics which undermined a variety of societal bonds, all of which proceeded from the two fundamental facts of late Byzantine warfare. First, the scene of warfare was always territory either held or recently held by Byzantium, and second, it was impossible for the state to acquire an adequate number of professional soldiers from the native population. Very few areas escaped the march of warring troops. And since the number of trained, professional troops was small, it was necessary not only to supplement the size of the army but to alter tactics as well. The value of each professional soldier was raised to the point where pitched battles were avoided, military commanders preferring less hazardous tactics such as skirmishing, pillaging, and treachery to accomplish what could not be done through overt force or through attrition.

The presence of the military in Byzantine territory and the nature of its activities while there had numerous detrimental effects. Since the pay of mercenaries was frequently late or simply unpaid, and since plunder was an important supplement to the official remuneration of all soldiers, there was much pillage, both officially sanctioned and at the soldiers' own initiative. The act of laying waste hostile territory was the most effective, time-honored means of punishing towns that refused to surrender. Yet, it is during attempts to recover lost territory that the propriety of military plundering becomes most questionable. For example, Gregoras (III, 564) reports that in 1355 troops under the command of John Kantakouzenos' son Matthew plundered the environs of Philippi, an area that had been held by the Serbs only since 1345. In this instance, as in many others, it is not known whether the commander actually ordered his troops to plunder or whether his troops, probably being no more disciplined than other late Byzantine forces, decided to pillage on their own. Yet either scenario makes plundering a cost of warfare; in the first, the commander, wishing to harm the economic base of the occupied territory or wishing to improve the morale of his troops or seeking a way to pay his troops, orders pillage. In the other, the cost of employing ill-disciplined troops manifests itself in unauthorized plunder. In this case the cost was borne by those Byzantine peasants living in the land occupied by the Serbs.

The pillage by unpaid or poorly disciplined soldiers was often duplicated by the irregular bands of peasant or urban troops that often supplemented the regular campaign armies. At times the state actively recruited such supplemental forces, while at other times such "peasant armies" appeared unbidden but were nevertheless employed reluctantly to make up for a shortage of trained manpower. In one notable case, that of the peasant army led by the pigherd Choiroboskos, the irregular force of farmers quickly degenerated into a pillaging expedition in the vicinity of Thessaloniki. It is quite likely that the example of soldiers and quasi-soldiers, acting quite literally like bandits, fostered an atmosphere of lawlessness within the Empire, contributing to the endemic brigandage of the era and to a general disregard of the basic rules of civilized life. In addition, it would seem that the actions of soldiers created an antipathy toward the military most clearly seen in the enmity between garrison and urban population and between natives and foreigners but extending as well to hostility toward the state itself.

The pillaging by soldiers and those who followed their example served to uproot a substantial fraction of the population, creating a refugee population which sought shelter in the fortified towns of the Empire. As the populations of towns were increased by this influx of peasants, new enmities arose which exacerbated the tensions between rich and poor, garrison and people, and the authorities and the populace.

The geographical structure of the late Byzantine Empire, lacking defined and defensible borders, brought warfare to all areas and required the provincial urban centers to deal with crises on their own. This, along with the state's inability to respond adequately to crises, furthered the process of political fragmentation, dramatically manifesting itself in the appearance of independent borderlords on the fringes of the Empire. In this way the cost of warfare involved a continuing erosion of the bonds between man and man, man and state, man and the local community, and between the local community and the state.

Since political fragmentation in the Middle Ages is closely connected to the Western institution of feudalism, scholars have often applied Western medieval terminology to the Byzantine scene. Often this creates impressions that are either inaccurate or deceptive. Of many examples, one may suffice. In the 1380s, by suppressing an uprising of unruly Byzantine magnates, Despot Theodore I, in the words of Dionysios Zakythinos, humbled his "barons" who then "submitted and agreed to pay taxes and furnish military service." Along similar lines, Raymond Loenertz spoke of these "grand Greek seigneurs" as "vassals of Theodore." The only source for these events is Manuel II Palaiologos' funeral oration for Theodore. While Manuel notes that certain "enemies" (*dysmenees* or *echthroi*) of Theodore did in fact submit to him, nowhere is there any mention of their agreement to "furnish military service," and nowhere are they referred to by any Greek word that can be rendered as "seigneur," "baron," or "vassal." Manuel is actually rather vague about the identity of these men. Only his statements that a member of the Kantakouzenos family was at the center of the revolt and that these enemies of Theodore had sided with the Turks and Latins permit us to identify them as Byzantine magnates. The uninitiated can easily be misled.[12]

12. Zakythinos, *Despotat*, II, 135, citing S. Lampros, Παλαιολόγεια καὶ Πελοπον-νησιακά (Athens, 1912–30), III, 42–44 = *Manuel II Palaeologus, Funeral Oration on His Brother Theodore*, ed. and trans. J. Chrysostomides (Thessaloniki, 1985), 123–27, specifically 123. R.-J. Loenertz, "Pour l'histoire du Péloponèse au XIVe siècle (1382–1404)," *Études byzantines* I

To what degree was the late Byzantine army a "feudal" institution, and to what degree did it contribute to what some scholars refer to as the "feudalization" of late Byzantium? Numerous scholars use the word "feudal" when discussing certain late Byzantine institutions, practices, and even the society itself. These scholars, the majority of whom adopt the Marxist view of feudalism as a stage in historical development immediately and inevitably following an age of slavery, must construct a definition of feudalism which is broad enough to include Byzantium, or at least late Byzantium, and which equates late Byzantine and Western feudal society, at least socioeconomically. Thus, they may characterize feudalism as "the presence of the seigneurial estate peopled by dependent peasants" or "the exercise of public authority by private persons," or as a social system marked by "the territorial aspect of political relations and the political aspect of territorial relations."[13] The first of these characterizations can apply to late Byzantium depending on how the words "seigneurial" and "dependent" are defined, and the second can at least be debated, while the third, though quite elegant, is comprehensible perhaps to few but the most devoted Marxists.

Most other scholars, the "bourgeois historians" in the vocabulary of Marxism, prefer to view feudalism as primarily a system of hierarchical relationships among members of the ruling class, and since the Western feudal concepts of fealty, homage, the benefice, and vassalage found little or no expression in Byzantium, they consider it misleading to apply the term *feudalism* to Byzantium at all, as laden as it is with autochthonous Western European connotations. Nevertheless, nearly all scholars see certain parallels or analogies between Western medieval and late Byzantine institutions, and while there is a hesitancy to employ the word *feudalism*, one often encounters reference to "feudalizing tendencies" or the "feudalization" of Byzantium. Along these lines what is most noticeable in late Byzantium was the decentralization of political authority and the devolution of public (state) power into private hands through the granting of privileges—fiscal, administrative, and, in the opinion of some scholars, judicial—to large landowners and even to towns.[14]

(1943), 174. Similar misconceptions have arisen when scholars have tried to use the *Chronicle of the Morea*, a work written within a Western European feudal milieu, to illuminate Byzantine practices.

13. For the first two views, see the comments of D. Jacoby, "The Encounter of Two Societies: Western Conquerors and Byzantines in the Peloponnesus after the Fourth Crusade," in Jacoby, *Recherches sur la Méditerranée orientale du XIIe au XVe siècle* (London, 1979), no. II, 879 and note 15. For the third, A. Vasiliev, "On the Question of Byzantine Feudalism," *Byz* 8 (1933), 585.

14. On the Byzantine feudalism debate, see K. Watanabe, "Problèmes de la 'féodalité'

This is not the place to conduct an extended discussion on whether or not late Byzantium was a "feudal" society. Rather, we are interested merely in whether the army included elements that could be considered "feudal." We first consider what made Western European armies feudal: the *remuneration* of the majority of soldiers was derived from the fief; the *recruitment* and the *military obligation* of the majority of soldiers was based on vassalage; the process of *mustering* the host and its *internal organization* were based on the feudal hierarchy; and the *command structure* of the host was closely related to the ranks within the feudal hierarchy.

The concept of vassalage and the hierarchy it produced was foreign to Byzantium.[15] Although oaths of loyalty did exist in which a subject pledged that he would serve faithfully and be "a friend of the friends and an enemy of the enemies" of the emperor, these had only the most superficial similarity to feudal vassalage because the element of reciprocality was completely absent. No specific obligation was placed upon the emperor. Nor, for that matter, was there anything especially military about these oaths, which had precedents in earlier oaths of loyalty to the sovereign taken by government officials and high clergymen. Further, since such oaths were normally only made with the emperor, no hierarchy of relations was possible.

Exceptions did occur, as when the officer Kotertzes around 1308 established an emergency defense in Asia Minor and drew a following of men who, according to Pachymeres, were "as enemies of his enemies and friends of his friends." While it is likely that these followers swore oaths to him, there was no hierarchy of relations. The episode really shows only that a

byzantine: une mise au point sur les diverses discussions," *Hitotsubashi Journal of Arts and Sciences* 5 (1965), 32–40; 6 (1965), 8–24; and A. Kazhdan and G. Constable, *People and Power in Byzantium* (Washington, D.C., 1982), 6–7, 118–21. For the traditional Soviet/Marxist point of view, see K.-P. Matschke, "Die Entwicklung der Konzeption eines byzantinischen Feudalismus durch die sowjetische marxistische Byzantinistik 1930–1966," *Zeitschrift für Geschichtswissenschaft* 15 (1967), 1065–86; I. Sorlin, "Bulletin des publications en langues slaves. I. Les recherches soviétiques sur l'histoire byzantine de 1945 à 1962," *TM* 2 (1967), 494–500; *Le féodalisme à Byzance: problèmes du mode de production de l'empire byzantin* (Paris, 1974); Vasiliev, "On the Question of Byzantine Feudalism," 584–604, essentially reprinted in his *History of the Byzantine Empire*, 2nd English ed., rev. (Madison, Wisc., 1952), II, 563–79; and D. Zakythinos, "Processus de féodalisation," in Zakythinos, *Byzance: état—société—économie* (London, 1973), no. XIII, 499–534. For the rebuttal to the Soviet/Marxist view, see M. Mladenović, "Zur Frage der Pronoia und des Feudalismus im byzantinischen Reiche," *Südost-Forschungen* 15 (1956), 123–40; and Jacoby, "Encounter of Two Societies," 878–81.

15. Cf. Zakythinos, *Despotat*, II, 137, who wrote that in the Morea "except perhaps for several corps attached immediately to the person of the prince, the recruitment of troops was based essentially on the principle of 'military vassalage.'" As evidence he cited several passages from the *Chronicle of the Morea* which, however, has a tendency to describe Byzantine institutions from a Western feudal perspective.

complete disintegration of government authority leads to a variety of makeshift expedients. Certainly, too, oaths of loyalty may perhaps be found in the "familiars" and retainers (*oikeioi* and *oiketai*) of great men, but the element of reciprocality did not exist with regard to retainers, and the bond between a great man and his oikeioi was, unlike fealty and homage, informal and as much social, political, and familial as personal.[16]

The Byzantines did appropriate the Western feudal concept of liege-homage. During the twelfth and thirteenth centuries the term *lizios*, from "liege," was applied to certain Western Europeans with whom the emperor wished to establish a political and personal bond. Like Western homage, it was always characterized, at least formally, by the free consent of both parties. At first the term was only applied in the emperors' relations with distinguished Westerners (such as between Alexios I and the Norman prince Bohemund in 1108, and between Manuel I and King Ladislas of Bohemia in 1147), but by the second half of the twelfth century, as liege-homage lost its special character in the West, so the term *lizios* was extended in application to lesser personages in imperial service who received a grant (probably of a pronoia) from the emperor.[17]

After 1204 the term was applied in only two instances. In documents from 1231 to 1251 the distinguished Latin pronoiar Syrgares (Appendix, no. 15) is called "lizios kavallarios of the emperor," or some similar variant. Syrgares, the first man to have the title *kavallarios* attached to his name, was the only kavallarios associated with the term *lizios*. In fact he was the only specific individual linked to the term after 1204. The term is last encountered in Pachymeres' history. In 1273, in order to ensure the fidelity of the Genoese of Galata, Michael VIII "by kindnesses made them his own men [*idious*]—'lieges [*lizioi*]' as one of them might say." These "kindnesses" (*eumeneiai*) probably included grants of pronoiai.[18]

Since Byzantium knew neither vassalage nor the kind of vertical hierarchy of relations created by private vassalage, it would seem that there was little that could be considered feudal about the late Byzantine army. The

16. K. Sathas, Μεσαιωνικὴ Βιβλιοθήκη (Venice, 1872–94; repr. Athens, 1972), VI, 652–53. N. Svoronos, "Le serment de fidélité à l'empereur byzantin et sa signification constitutionelle," *Actes du VIe Congrès international d'études byzantines, Paris 1948* (Paris, 1950–51), I, 191–97. Angold, *Byzantine Government*, 65–66. Pachymeres, Bonn ed., II, 407–408.

17. J. Ferluga, "La ligesse dans l'empire byzantin," *ZRVI* 7 (1961), 97–123.

18. P. Charanis, "On the Social Structure and Economic Organization of the Byzantine Empire in the Thirteenth Century and Later," in Charanis, *Social, Economic and Political Life in the Byzantine Empire* (London, 1973), no. IV, 97–99. M. Bartusis, "The *Kavallarioi* of Byzantium," *Speculum* 63 (1988), 346. Pachymeres, ed. Failler, I, 471 (Bonn ed., I, 366). Geanakoplos, *Emperor Michael*, 209 note 71, 323 note 72.

remuneration, recruitment, and military obligation of mercenaries were based on the cash nexus. The remuneration of the smallholding soldier was based on a simple land grant; their recruitment and military obligation were based on administrative acts and heredity. For all soldiers the process of mustering always retained its administrative character. Internal organization was based on factors such as ethnicity, regionalism, and mode of combat (horse or foot). The command structure was based on military rank and rank in the courtly hierarchy of titles. Solely at the highest levels, where commanders of entire armies usually were related to the emperor through blood or marriage, can one regard this decentralization, "de-bureaucratization," and "personalization" of late Byzantine administration as the reflection of a "feudalizing tendency."

Only in the institution of pronoia do even the most doctrinaire scholars see any truly feudal aspects of the army. If pronoia and fief were equivalent institutions, then an important part of the late Byzantine army was based on a feudal institution. But the two were not equivalent since pronoia was fundamentally a fiscal institution, a grant of the taxes of paroikoi and a grant, not of land, but of the right to the income derived from land. But what aspects of pronoia were feudal? Certainly pronoia had nothing in common with the conception of feudalism that calls to mind fealty, homage, and vassalage. But then there is the broader view of feudalism for which we recall two of the characterizations of feudalism cited earlier: "the presence of the seigneurial estate peopled by dependent peasants" and "the exercise of public authority by private persons." There is little evidence that pronoiars generally lived on or even near the properties whose incomes they held in pronoia. Given the disparate elements that made up the pronoia grants of the soldiers Sabentzes, Maroules, and Berilas, it would be difficult to consider their pronoiai "estates" or "manors." Moreover, the element of self-sufficiency characteristic of the Western manor was lacking, as well as the reliance on the natural economy.

But did the pronoiar enjoy rights of sovereignty? In other words, was he master of the peasants inscribed in his praktikon? Socially some pronoiars may have exercised such power, but formally no such power was granted. Pronoiars who held the taxes of handfuls of peasants in two or more villages could not have had such power. Further, paroikoi were not dependent peasants in the Western sense. The obligations of a paroikos to his pronoiar were limited: he furnished taxes to the pronoiar, performed corvée services for the pronoiar, and furnished the pronoiar with certain agricultural produce in kind. The sources do not specify any other control the pronoiar had over him. The pronoiar enjoyed such rights not in his capacity as landlord, but as a holder of state rights. Most if not all of the power that the pronoiar had over his paroikoi derived from state obligations.

Even when a pronoiar received hereditary rights to his pronoia (with or without the continuance of a service obligation), there is still no evidence that he assumed any measure of political control over his pronoia. Though some scholars argue that pronoiars enjoyed immunity from the entry of state officials onto their properties, this opinion is not supported by the evidence. Those relatively rare individuals and monasteries that are known to have received this privilege from the emperor were not pronoiars, but the recipients of simple grants via chrysobull (whom the sources call *chrysoboullatoi*). Indeed if one wishes to find feudal lords in late Byzantium, this is where one should look. It seems that the pronoiar approximated the Western feudal lord far less than the large landowner who owned land unconditionally as patrimony or through imperial grant.

In sum, the late Byzantine army was no feudal army. Moreover, it contributed little to the "feudalization" of Byzantine society. Pronoia reflected the decentralization of the fiscal authority of the state and was a logical response to the state's inability to collect its own taxes. To the extent that the part of the army composed of pronoiars reflected the "feudalizing tendencies" of late Byzantium, pronoia had a deleterious effect on the Empire's ability to defend itself. But it was hardly the principal factor in undermining the strength of the Empire.

Finally, we turn to the soldiers themselves, a motley group of men. Direct information about soldiers when they were not at war is quite meager. Their daily lives were of little interest to the historians of the time, and the soldiers themselves, most probably semi-literate at best, were unable or disinclined to tell their own story. Consequently, what little we can say about the personal lives of particular soldiers must be sought in scattered references found in legal decisions, letters, and documents. For those soldiers who held no landed property—mercenaries, mostly foreigners—we know very little.

There was certainly no "typical" late Byzantine soldier, no more than there was any "typical" clergyman. The group of professional soldiers spanned a broad section of the social and economic spectrum. At the upper end were men like the pronoia soldier Demetrios Deblitzenos (Appendix, no. 44) with patrimonial estates and a pronoia of 400 hyperpyra who, with the title *sevastos*, had nearly broken into the aristocracy of courtly hierarchical rank. In the documents, these men appear as landowners, pronoiars, and witnesses to transactions. We see them buying, selling, bequeathing, piously donating, and quarreling over land and other property, as well as receiving and losing imperial privileges.[19] Such activities show that they were fully integrated members of society, behaving not unlike any Byzantine subject of middling or high status and position.

Many soldiers, as patrimonial landowners, pronoiars, or both, owned or held substantial assets in the form of property or paroikoi and, like other Byzantines, they expressed their piety by contributing materially to the Church through donations, either while they were alive or posthumously as bequests. Most frequently the religious recipient was a monastery, not surprising since most surviving documents, the chief sources for such information, were issued by or on behalf of monasteries and were preserved in monastic archives, primarily those of Mount Athos. Thus, in the early fourteenth century two soldiers from northern Macedonia each donated a chapel to the monastery of Iviron, and a third donated a paroikos family to another monastery (Appendix, nos. 41, 42, 46). Another soldier, Euthymios Philommates (Appendix, no. 45), identified as one of a number of otherwise unnamed "soldier archons," donated six escheated peasant properties (*exaleimmatika stasia*) to the monastery of Docheiariou at about the same time.

Sometimes death intervened before a soldier could make his donation. John Sarantenos of Verria, for example, had wanted to found a monastery in his town but, as his brother Theodore explains, he died in battle before the plan could be realized.[20] Untimely death could lead to other problems. In 1266 *sevastos* George Petritzes donated some land to the monastery of the Lemviotissa outside Smyrna. In this act of donation, he swore to uphold the agreement, and if not, "I am no longer worthy to serve militarily our mighty and holy lord and emperor." A year and a half later he was dead and the monastery was claiming another parcel of land that it said Petritzes had intended to transfer to it as compensation for the 10 hyperpyra the monastery had given Petritzes "to outfit himself for military service." Here we have a cash-poor warrior who died prematurely before settling a loan with a monastery.[21]

Side by side with the wealthiest of pronoiars, or perhaps a bit lower,

19. E.g., N. Oikonomidès, *Actes de Docheiariou* (Paris, 1984), nos. 15, 22, 34–36, 38.
20. Appendix, no. 59. John was killed while "in the imperial service of Klepision," an odd phrase that the editor of the relevant documents suggests was the name of a battle that would have taken place long before 1325.
21. Appendix, no. 22. MM, IV, 161, lines 23–24; 160, lines 9–11.

were the most distinguished Latin mercenaries, cavalry certainly, and then lesser pronoia soldiers into which category collective pronoia soldiers (for example, the Klazomenitai of Serres) probably fit. Toward the lower end of the spectrum were mercenary infantry, garrison troops, and marines (Gasmouloi and Tzakones), and the smallholding soldiers (for example, Prosalentai and Cumans). Most of these soldiers lived within the social milieu of the peasantry, spending their time and marrying among them. While the majority of soldiers found themselves at the lower end of the spectrum, there is no need for any sharp division between, say, lesser pronoia soldiers and wealthier smallholding soldiers.

On the basis of a reading of Kantakouzenos and other late Byzantine sources, Ihor Ševčenko once concluded that the men called *stratiotai* in late Byzantium were members of the upper class and that, especially in Kantakouzenos, stratiotai were "a special group within the armed forces and are generally associated with the 'best citizens,' nobles and 'senators,'" adding that "the 'soldiers' and the 'army' of these and other passages were not common soldiery or mere army 'officers,'" but knights on horseback who held pronoiai. Ševčenko was making the case that pronoia soldiers were a group apart from other soldiers, that they were both elite warriors and aristocrats.[22]

In general Ševčenko is indeed correct. Kantakouzenos does not usually refer to large numbers of soldiers as "stratiotai" (he prefers words like *logades*, "picked," and *hippeis*, "cavalry"), and stratiotai were not part of the "mob" (*ochlos*), the "many" (*polloi*), or the "people" (*demos*).[23] But although they were identified at times with the "best" (*aristoi*), the "illustrious" (*epiphaneis*), or the "well-born" (*eugeneis*),[24] they were frequently clearly distinguished from the "powerful" (*dynatoi*), the "best," the senate, the "higher-born" (*eugenesteroi*), the "well-born," and the "magnates" (*megistanes*).[25] What this suggests is that while Kantakouzenos' image of a stratiotes was a soldier having more in common with aristocrats than with the mass of the population, the stratiotes' position was not so elevated that

22. I. Ševčenko, "An Important Contribution to the Social History of Late Byzantium," *Annals of the Ukrainian Academy of Arts and Sciences in the U.S.* 2 (1952), 454–56.

23. Kantakouzenos, III, 120, 130; II, 297–98. There are of course exceptions. For example, there were "noble" soldiers who were not pronoiars; such were the "well-born" (*eupatrides*) from among the Latin mercenaries faithful to Andronikos III (Kantakouzenos, I, 98). Further, there is no possibility that the 3,000 "picked" (*epilektoi*) stratiotai Kantakouzenos once campaigned with were all pronoia soldiers (Kantakouzenos, II, 563).

24. Kantakouzenos, II, 371, 506; III, 10, 65–66.

25. Kantakouzenos, II, 162, 233, 506, 573; III, 120, 130, 286. Skoutariotes in Akropolites, 286. Cf. Pachymeres, Bonn ed., II, 195.

he could not be excluded from the aristocracy and placed in a class by himself. I think we can say that Kantakouzenos' stratiotes was a pronoia soldier and a lesser aristocrat.

The documentary evidence supports such a characterization. For example, in 1340 a group of inhabitants of the town of Trikkala "from the archons . . . from the stratiotai of Trikkala and many chrysoboullatoi" witnessed an act of the metropolitan of Larissa. Although it is difficult to know exactly what the status of these stratiotai was, the fact that they were included among archons and the recipients of chrysobulls indicates that they were clearly among the best citizens of the town. Another act, from 1280, was witnessed by "the local people, both stratiotai and private landowners (*oikodespotai*)" of a particular village.[26] While these stratiotai may not have been the most distinguished individuals, they were clearly the village's leading inhabitants.

Did such men form the heart of the army, and did they form what could be called a military class? What we know of pronoia soldiers does indicate that many, but not all, held an elevated position in society. We note that the 1319 chrysobull for Ioannina contained a preemption clause that forbade local landowners from selling their property to either a local archon or a stratiotes unless he was a member of the community.[27] Nevertheless, "stratiotes" did not have to imply a pronoia soldier, and collective pronoia soldiers certainly held a less distinguished position. Whether pronoia soldiers formed the heart of the army depends on one's perspective. Generals like Kantakouzenos naturally surrounded themselves with such troops. They were perhaps the best-equipped soldiers and perhaps the most reliable, but hardly the most numerous. They were a minority within any campaign force, and so to make them a military class (with a societal breakdown such as "aristocrats, clergy, stratiotai, other soldiers, peasants") would be to regard them as more than they were. Most pronoia soldiers (stratiotai) were not military leaders but soldiers. And while they were landlords, they were not particularly great landlords.

Given the broad range of social and economic levels held by soldiers, it cannot be said that soldiers as a group formed a distinct class in Byzantine society. It is only within particular social and economic strata that we see a sense of group identity. This could manifest itself in marriage bonds. For

---

26. N. Bees, «Σερβικὰ καὶ Βυζαντιακὰ γράμματα Μετεώρου», *Βυζαντίς* 2 (1911–12), pp. 62–72, no. 18, lines 15–16 (1340). Cited by B. Ferjančić, *Tesalija u XIII i XIV veku* (Belgrade, 1974), 184 note 403. MM, IV, 128, lines 14–19 (1280).

27. MM V, 83, lines 18–21.

example, the soldier Alexander Neokastrites had been planning to marry the daughter of Basos, another soldier (Appendix, nos. 7, 9), but there was a question whether such a union could be sanctioned by the Church, since Neokastrites and Basos' brother Hydros (Appendix, no. 8) had symbolically become brothers through the custom of *adelphopoiïa* (literally, "brother-making"). Happily the archbishop of Ohrid Demetrios Chomatenos ruled that this should be no obstacle to the proposed marriage. Such bonds between men could strengthen both the personal and the social relationships between soldiers. By the same token the tradition of military service within families, such as the Deblitzenoi (Appendix, nos. 44, 77), furthered the group identity of soldiers at a particular socioeconomic level.

In addition to professional soldiers, there were nonprofessional soldiers and there were guards. The nonprofessionals were the peasants and townspeople who accompanied a campaign army, perhaps only once, or who followed a peasant leader such as a Choiroboskos, a Pseudo-Lachanas, or a Syrbanos. Such men, ill-equipped and ill-disciplined, were at the lowest end of the socioeconomic spectrum. Guards, like soldiers, were divided into a professional group (tzakones) and a nonprofessional group. The status of professional tzakones varied greatly. Some, like Papanikolopoulos and Christopher from the area of Demetrias, were pronoiars. This in itself elevated them above smallholding soldiers and lowlier mercenaries. At the other extreme were the peasants hired for a pittance by the Soumela monastery near Trebizond to guard the monastery's fortification. Nonprofessional tzakones or, rather, people who performed tzakonike service on a part-time basis, were evidently either peasants who carried out this duty in return for partial tax exemption or townspeople who did it as part of a civic obligation.

Most guard service was organized by private landowners and by towns. A fair number of professional soldiers as well were not imperial employees but personal retainers of private individuals. In other words, a significant portion of the defensive structure was not organized by the central government but by private individuals and local communities. Beyond this, it is apparent that the Empire utilized the services of a great number of people from all levels of society from the lesser aristocracy on down. Naturally, if we include military leaders, then all levels and ranks of society had their warriors or guards.

The military represented one of the few ways a man could improve his status in society. There were soldiers at every level of society, and there were opportunities for anyone to become a soldier. We see this in the examples of

Constantine Margarites, born a peasant, who worked his way through the ranks to become a military leader in the mid-thirteenth century, and in the Bulgarian Momčilo, a bandit who through acquaintance with Andronikos III and Kantakouzenos became a petty commander and ruler in his own right.[28] In the turbulent era of late Byzantium, one avenue for those willing to pursue a new life was the army.

28. Appendix, no. 6. M. Bartusis, "Chrelja and Momčilo," *Byzantinoslavica* 41 (1980), 201–21.

Appendix: A List of Soldiers

The following is a list, more or less chronological, of men from the thirteenth, fourteenth, and early fifteenth centuries who appear to have been soldiers. They are identified as such by an epithet (*stratiotes* or *kavallarios*), through membership in a known military division, or through a direct reference to their military activities. Of these eighty men, at least twenty-two were pronoiars; another seven were probably pronoiars. Only one (no. 71) can be identified more or less securely as a smallholding soldier and another (no. 5) as a mercenary. Men whose numbers are preceded by an asterisk (*) have been identified as soldiers solely through references to their military deeds. It is possible that some of these may have held hierarchical imperial titles and thereby enjoyed a status much higher than the other men in the list.

A few men called "stratiotai" have been omitted from the list. For example, the stratiotes George Kinnamos, according to a judgment of the archbishop of Ohrid Demetrios Chomatenos, was the governor (*epitropos*) by imperial appointment of the region of Drama in the early thirteenth century. To call such a man a "soldier" would be a profound understatement of his position.[1] There is a parallel for Chomatenos' use of the word *stratiotes* in the *Chronicle of the Morea* which, in one of its infrequent uses of the word, calls Leon Sgouros, ruler of Corinth at the time of the Fourth Crusade, a "stratiotes."[2]

Men whose numbers are preceded by a plus sign (+) are mentioned elsewhere in the text (see the Index). Those who flourished in or after 1259 are also listed in the *PLP*.

1. J. Pitra, *Analecta sacra et classica spicilegio solesmensi parata* (Paris, 1876–91), VI, col. 413. A. Jameson, "The Responsa and Letters of Demetrios Chomatianos, Archbishop of Achrida and Bulgaria," diss., Harvard Univ. 1957, 268–70. D. Angelov, "Prinos kŭm narodnostnite i pozemelni otnošenija v Makedonija," *Izvestija na Kamarata na narodnata kultura* IV/3 (1947), 31–32, 36. Ostrogorsky, *Féodalité*, 88.

2. Ed. J. Schmitt (London, 1904). Although situations in the Empire of Trebizond are generally outside the scope of this study, one can add to this list a number of soldiers who appear as witnesses to documents there: see F. Uspenskij and V. Beneševič, *Actes de Vazélon* (Leningrad, 1927), nos. 12, 16, 23, 48, 82.

1 and 2. stratiotes kyr George Mangaphas, and stratiotes kyr Teires (sc., Thierry) Alexios, all syntrophoi of the megalodoxotatos Andronikos Mauropous (fl.1216) ·

Witnesses to an act of Mauropous. The appellation *syntrophos*, "comrade," was an unofficial title that appears in documents several times during the early Nicaean period. While it suggests a special relationship between these soldiers and Mauropous, we can only guess its social and legal aspects (M. Nystazopoulou-Pelekidou, Βυζαντινὰ ἔγγραφα τῆς μονῆς Πάτμου, II [Athens, 1980], no. 61 [hereafter Nystazopoulou, *Patmos*]. For other examples of the use of *syntrophos*, see MM, IV, 147; VI, 154; Nystazopoulou, *Patmos*, no. 72; and also, Oikonomidès, "A propos des armées," 360–63, 369–71).

3. stratiotes kyr Theodore Gylielmos (sc., Guillaume), syntrophos of the megalodoxotatos Andronikos Mauropous (fl.1209–16)

Another witness to the act of Mauropous. In 1209 he was holding paroikoi, perhaps as a pronoiar, in the region of Miletos in Asia Minor. From their names he and Thierry Alexios above were evidently either Latins or recent descendants of Latins (Nystazopoulou, *Patmos*, no. 61; MM, VI, 154, lines 16–17 [1209]).

4. stratiotes kyr Nikephoros Limniotes, syntrophos of the megalodoxotatos Andronikos Mauropous (fl.1214–16)

Another witness to the act of Mauropous. In 1214 he and his cousin Basil, with whom he lived, owned a property in the region of Miletos (Nystazopoulou, *Patmos*, no. 61; MM, VI, 170).

+5. George Pissas (fl. second quarter thirteenth century)

A Vardariotes (A. Papadopoulos-Kerameus, Ἀνάλεκτα Ἱεροσολυμιτικῆς Σταχυολογίας [St. Petersburg, 1891], I, 466).

+6. Constantine Margarites (fl. second quarter thirteenth century to 1250s)

According to Akropolites, Margarites, "so the story went, was a rustic born of rustics, raised on barley bread and corn husks, and only knowing how to howl. He hailed from Neokastra and achieved top rank in the army of this theme, thereupon becoming tzaousios. Since the report was presented to the emperor John [Vatatzes] that he was sufficiently skillful to serve at court, he removed him from there and made him tzaousios of his *taxis*, and thereupon the [titular adjective] 'megas' was added by him. The emperor Theodore [II Laskaris] named him archon of his *taxis*—not up to that time had such [a title] gone to anyone. And he [Theodore] annexed 'megas' to his name." Rising through the ranks of the thematic army of Neokastra Margarites became tzaousios. Later, as megas tzaousios, he was commander of Vatatzes' retinue, and then, as megas archon, at least in theory, he performed the same function in Theodore II's retinue. In 1255, as megas archon, he defended Didymoteichon along with the emperor's uncle Manuel Laskaris (Akropolites, 123–26).

The following soldiers are spoken of in the judgments of the archbishop of Ohrid Demetrios Chomatenos (1216/7 to ca.1236) and of the metropolitan of Naupaktos John Apokaukos (1199/1200 to 1232). Most of them fought for the rulers of Epiros. Unless otherwise noted all flourished sometime during the first third of the thirteenth century.

+7 and +8. stratiotes Basos and stratiotes Hydros
Brothers (Pitra, *Analecta sacra*, VI, no. 5, col. 31; Angelov, "Prinos," 31–32).

+9. andrikotatos stratiotes Alexander Neokastrites
Son-in-law of Basos above (Pitra, *Analecta sacra*, VI, no. 5, col. 31).

*10. Theodore Demnites
According to Demetrios Chomatenos, Demnites "hailed from the eastern region but now resides in the theme of Acheloos" in Epiros. During an altercation he killed a tax collector who repeatedly had been harassing "certain men subject to him [Demnites] for service through life from a grant of the despot." Appearing before the archiepiscopal court at Ohrid, Demnites was assigned appropriate penance for involuntary manslaughter.

Demnites is not called a soldier directly, yet Chomatenos makes a couple of references to his "military labors." Ostensibly he was a soldier who came to Epiros from the east and was assigned men who had to "serve" him for life. Since tax collectors were bothering these men, it seems that they were not domestic servants but farmers, and that Demnites' original complaint was that the officials were unjustly demanding money or produce that they did not owe or else owed only to Demnites. Evidently Demnites was a pronoia soldier who had received a grant of paroikoi (*dorea paroikon*) from the ruler of Epiros. The connection between his pronoia and his military service is speculative but likely (Pitra, *Analecta sacra*, VI, no. 118, cols. 504–506).

11. stratiotes Rados
Lived in Mokros near Ohrid and was in the army of Theodore Doukas (1215–30). His wife committed adultery while he was away at camp (Pitra, *Analecta sacra*, VI, no. 139, col. 547).

12. stratiotes Rados (son?) of Motzilos (*tou Motzilou*)
Inhabitant of Prespa in Epiros. His wife committed adultery too (Pitra, *Analecta sacra*, VI, no. 142, col. 555).

13. stratiotes Stephen Mauromanikos
Inhabitant of Naupaktos (John Apokaukos, ed. S. Pétridès, in *Izvestija Russkogo arheologičeskago instituta v Konstantinopole* 14/2–3 [1909], 20).

+*14. megalodoxotatos kyr Manuel Monomachos
(A. Papadopoulos-Kerameus in Βυζαντίς 1 [1909], 27–28).

The following thirteenth-century soldiers are mentioned in documents of the cartulary of the Lemviotissa monastery near Smyrna.

+15. andrikotatos and pistotatos lizios kavallarios Syrgares (fl.1231–37)
Pronoiar (MM, IV, 36, 39–41, 61, 81, 135).

16. stratiotes Monomachos (fl.1239)
Landholder (MM, IV, 157; H. Ahrweiler, "L'histoire et la géographie de la région de Smyrne," in Ahrweiler, *Byzance: les pays et les territoires* [London, 1976], no. IV, 156).

17. stratiotes Michael Petritzes (fl.1257–76 or 1257–83)
Landowner and pronoiar (MM, IV, 69, 88, 130, 173; the last page number cited refers to a Michael, brother of George Petritzes, who may or may not be the same individual. Ahrweiler, "Smyrne," 174; Angold, *Byzantine Government*, 125 note 18; Ostrogorsky, *Féodalité*, 80; Mutafčiev, "Vojniški zemi," 574).

+18. stratiotes Michael Angelos (fl.1259)
Pronoiar (MM, IV, 169, 241; Ahrweiler, "Smyrne," 142; Ostrogorsky, *Féodalité*, 83–84).

19. andrikotatos stratiotes kyr Nikephoros Pharissaios (fl. 1259–83)
Brother-in-law of Michael Barycheir below (MM, IV, 153, 128, 101, and cf. 166–68; Ahrweiler, "Smyrne," 168; N. Oikonomidès, "Contribution à l'étude de la pronoia au XIIIe siècle," in Oikonomidès, *Documents et études sur les institutions de Byzance* [London, 1976], no. VI, 166–67).

20. stratiotes Michael Barycheir (fl.1259–93)
Landholder (MM, IV, 25, 153, 180; Ahrweiler, "Smyrne," 147, 168).

21. kavallarios syr Nicholas Adam (fl.1260)
Probably a pronoiar (MM, IV, 79, 91, 104; *PLP*, no. 287).

+*22. sevastos George Petritzes (d. soon before 1268)
Landholder (MM, IV, 160–61; Ostrogorsky, *Féodalité*, 81; Angold, *Byzantine Government*, 131).

23. stratiotes Constantine Planites (fl.1268)
Landowner and probably a pronoiar (MM, IV, 73, 89; C. Zuckerman, "The Dishonest Soldier Constantine Planites and His Neighbours," *Byz* 56 [1986], 314–31).

24. stratiotes kyr George Petritzes (fl.1274–93)
Landowner and probably a pronoiar (M. Bartusis, "On the Status of Stratiotai During the Late Byzantine Period," *ZRVI* 21 [1982], 53–54; Oikonomidès, "Contribution," 166–67; Ahrweiler, "Smyrne," 174).

*25. kyr Leon (fl.1280)
Probably a pronoiar and probably being called a "stratiotes" in a document (MM, IV, 128; Ahrweiler, "Smyrne," 172; Oikonomidès, "Contribution," 166–67; Bartusis, "Status," 58 note 36).

26. stratiotes Constantine Abalantes (fl.1280)
Witness to an act (MM, IV, 94; Ahrweiler, "Smyrne," 115–16).

27. andrikotatos kavallarios Syraliates (fl.1280)
Witness to an act (MM, IV, 94).

28. stratiotes Michael Angelos Koumpariotes (fl.1291)
Landholder (MM, IV, 140).

29 and 30. kyr Manuel Kaloeidas and kyr Constantine Phrangopoulos, both stratiotai from the imperial allagia (fl.1293)
Assisted the judge of the army Constantine Cheilas in settling a property dispute (MM, IV, 179).

There is one known military family from northwest Anatolia.

+31 and +32. stratiotes Chrysokompas and son (fl.1280s)
Lived in the area of Skammandros; pronoiars (Gregory II, of Cyprus, ed. S. Eustratiades, in Ἐκκλησιαστικὸς Φάρος 3 [1909], 295–96, no. 129).

The following are the only garrison troops known by name.

+33, +34, and +35. George Matzones, Nicholas Kritzes, and George Likardites (all fl.1288)
Crossbowmen (tzangratores) on the island of Kos (Nystazopoulou, *Patmos*, no. 75).

All of the remaining soldiers lived in Europe (almost exclusively in Thrace and Macedonia).

36. Gazes from the Thessalonian Mega Allagion (d. before 1286)
Landowner and pronoiar (W. Regel et al., *Actes de Zographou, I. Actes grecs, VizVrem* 13 [1907], suppl. 1, no. 10).

37 and 38. Andronikos and brother (fl.1280s)
Sometime between 1283 and 1289 Patriarch Gregory II wrote a letter to the megas logothetes Theodore Mouzalon requesting him to intercede on behalf of Andronikos and his brother, the sons of Peter, a Turk who had been known as Fahr al-Din before he was baptized. The affair which prompted the sons to approach Gregory for help is not at all clear, but it seems they were in the process of being forcibly transplanted. In his letter to Mouzalon, the patriarch writes that he had explained the situation to the sons with the words, "You shall be, or you might already be, deprived of the pronoia, and you shall be moved to the region around Thrace and Macedonia, where you shall enroll yourself, by your wish, in the Turkish military lists [*Persikoi stratiotikoi katalogoi*], and provisions [*siteresia*] shall be given and arable land [*ge arosimos*] as well."

Ostensibly there was a forcible exchange of something called "pronoia" for "provisions" (*siteresion* is a problematic word) and arable land somewhere in Thrace or Macedonia. Andronikos and his brother were Christianized and more or less Hellenized (for Gregory notes their eloquence in speaking). Their audience with the patriarch suggests that at that moment they lived in or near Constantinople, and that they were men (or sons of a man) of some importance. If we consider chronology, it would be appropriate for their father to have come to Constantinople with Sultan Izz al-Din in the early 1260s.

The nature of the "pronoia" involved cannot be determined. We can only say that it was something granted to the sons—and probably to the father—providing them a livelihood. It is not possible even to say that the sons had been Byzantine soldiers. Nevertheless a plausible reconstruction of their situation is that father Fahr al-Din came to Byzantium as a distinguished member of Izz al-Din's retinue or army. Michael VIII took him in his service and granted him a pronoia of some sort. The father was baptized, became Peter, and had two sons, one of whom was named after Michael VIII's young son. Then either Peter died and his sons claimed the pronoia but were not granted it, or his sons were given their own "pronoia" in or around Constantinople but later fell out of favor. In any event they were not allowed to maintain possession of the pronoia and were ordered westward to become reserve soldiers—without doubt light cavalry—enrolled in the Turkish contingent of the army and settled on their own land which they apparently were to farm.

It is difficult to say whether the line "provisions shall be given and arable land as well" means that Andronikos and his brother were to become pronoiars after they moved. My inclination is to think not, that they were to be some kind of smallholding soldiers, living in a colony, like the Cumans or Prosalentai (Gregory II, ed. Eustratiades, in Ἐκκλησιαστικὸς Φάρος 4 [1909], 119, no. 159; V. Laurent, *Les regestes des actes du patriarcat de Constantinople*, I, fasc. 4 [Paris, 1971], no. 1536; M. Bibikov, "Svedenija o pronii v pis'mah Grigorija Kiprskogo i 'Istorii' Georgija Pahimera," *ZRVI* 17 [1976], 95, 97–98).

39. kavallarios syr Peros Martinos (fl. before 1300)
Pronoiar with holdings on the Longos peninsula of the Chalkidike (D. Papachryssanthou, *Actes de Xénophon* [Paris, 1986], nos. 4, 5).

+40. imperial stratiotes Demetrios Harmenopoulos (fl.1299/1300)
Pronoiar with holdings on the Longos peninsula of the Chalkidike (Papachryssanthou, *Xénophon*, no. 6).

Harmenopoulos is the first of four known imperial (*basilikoi*) stratiotai (the others are nos. 41, 42, and 58 below). Since the four appearances of this expression are all in private acts, the designation "imperial stratiotes" was most likely not part of official terminology, that is, not a title bestowed by the emperor or a term denoting a precise legal status. It was probably a popular designation for a pronoia soldier (see N. Oikonomidès, "The Properties of the Deblitzenoi in the Fourteenth and Fifteenth Centuries," in *Charanis Studies*, ed. A. Laiou-Thomadakis [New Brunswick, N.J., 1980], 177).

41. stratiotes Knenstopoulos (fl. before 1310)
From Strumica; donated a chapel to the monastery of Iviron (F. Dölger, *Aus den Schatzkammern des Heiligen Berges* [Munich, 1948], no. 37).

42. stratiotes Kalameas (fl. before 1310)
Donated a chapel to the monastery of Iviron (Dölger, *Schatzkammer*, no. 37).

43. imperial stratiotes kyr Manuel Doukas Hadrianos (fl.1311)
Witness to an act (N. Oikonomidès, *Actes de Docheiariou* [Paris, 1984], no. 11).

+44. imperial stratiotes kyr Demetrios Deblitzenos (fl.1311–49)
Probably a son of Manuel Deblitzenos, tzaousios of the Thessalonian Mega Allagion; in 1311 witness to an act, in 1321 a landowner on the Chalkidike, and in 1349 an *oikeios* of the emperor and a pronoiar (Oikonomidès, *Docheiariou*, nos. 11, 26; P. Lemerle et al., *Actes de Lavra* [Paris, 1970–82], II, no. 108; Oikonomidès, "Deblitzenoi," 177–79, 192 note 7).

+45. stratiotes archon kyr Euthymios Philommates (fl. before 1315–16)
Pronoiar (Oikonomidès, *Docheiariou*, nos. 15, 22, and p. 112; Lemerle et al., *Lavra*, II, nos. 90, 108).

46. stratiotes Hekatides (fl. before 1316)
From Melnik; donated a paroikos family to a monastery (Lemerle et al., *Lavra*, II, app. VIII).

47. kyr Michael Chamaidrakon from the Thessalonian Mega Allagion (fl.1314–22)
Witness to acts in 1314 and 1322 (L. Petit and B. Korablev, *Actes de Chilandar, I, VizVrem* 17 [1911], suppl. 1, nos. 28, 29, 84).

+48. stratiotes, later sevastos, Nikephoros Martinos (fl.1317–27)
Pronoiar in the region of Serres (A. Guillou, *Les archives de Saint-Jean-Prodrome* [Paris, 1955], nos. 7, 16, 17, 22; Ostrogorsky, *Féodalité*, 147–49; Bartusis, "Status," 59).

49. kyr Manuel Garianos from the Serriotikon Mega Allagion (fl.1318)
Landowner and pronoiar (Dölger, *Schatzkammer*, no. 50).

50. (?) stratiotes Sarabares (d. before 1320)
A document from 1320 remarks that the monastery of Zographou had been granted 650 modioi of land in Hierissos on the Chalkidike "which was taken away from Sarabares." Another act from around the same time refers to this property as *"exaleimmatike* land . . . called 'of Sarabares.'" Half a century later the bishop of Hierissos disputed the ownership of the property, and it required an act of the autonomous Serbian despot Uglješa in

1369 to confirm Zographou's right to the land "that the stratiotes Sarabares held in his pronoia."

Ostensibly then, sometime before 1320 the soldier Sarabares held land in pronoia and subsequently lost it. My reservations about this conclusion are based on two points: (1) the first and only mention of Sarabares as a soldier and pronoiar occurred in 1369, and (2) there was a small monastery on Mt. Athos named Sarabares. Thus, it is possible that no "stratiotes named Sarabares" ever existed. (Regel et al., *Zographou*, no. 17, lines 82–83 [1320]; no. 18, lines 11–14 [after May 1325]; cf. no. 54, lines 115ff. [1320–21]. A. Solovjev and V. Mošin, *Grčke povelje srpskih vladara* [1936; repr. London, 1974], no. 36, lines 76–77, 104 [1369]; *Zographou*, no. 44, lines 4, 43, 65–66 [1369]. On the monastery, Th. Papazotos, «Ἡ μονὴ τοῦ Σαράβαρη στὸ Ἅγιον Ὄρος», *Κληρονομία* 12 [1980], 89–90.)

51. kavallarios Serpes (d. before 1321)
Pronoiar on the Longos peninsula on the Chalkidike (Papachryssanthou, *Xénophon*, no. 15).

52. Alexander Eurippiotes from the Thessalonian Mega Allagion (d. before 1321)
Patrimonial landowner (Petit and Korablev, *Chilandar*, no. 67).

+53. kyr Michael Sabentzes from the Thessalonian Mega Allagion (fl.1321)
Pronoiar on the Longos peninsula of the Chalkidike (Papachryssanthou, *Xénophon*, no. 15).

+54. kyr Nicholas Maroules from the Thessalonian Mega Allagion (fl.1321)
Pronoiar on the Longos peninsula of the Chalkidike (Papachryssanthou, *Xénophon*, no. 16).

+55. stratiotes Neokastrites (fl.1321–37)
Pronoiar on the Chalkidike (Lemerle et al., *Lavra*, II, no. 108; Oikonomidès, *Docheiariou*, nos. 18, 21, 23.)

56. sevastos Euthymios Kardames from the Thessalonian Mega Allagion (d. before 1322/3)
Landholder on the Chalkidike (Papachryssanthou, *Xénophon*, no. 19).

57. kyr Demetrios Isauros from the Thessalonian Mega Allagion (fl. 1322/3)

Erstwhile landholder on the Chalkidike (Papachryssanthou, *Xénophon*, no. 19, and cf. no. 16), probably a landholder on the Longos peninsula of the Chalkidike (see J. Bompaire, *Actes de Xéropotamou* [Paris, 1964], no. 22).

+58. kyr Basil Berilas from the Thessalonian Mega Allagion (fl.1323)
Pronoiar in the katepanikion of Rhentina on the Chalkidike (P. Schreiner, "Zwei unedierte Praktika," *JÖB* 19 [1970], 37–39; N. Oikonomidès, "Notes sur un praktikon de pronoiaire," in Oikonomidès, *Documents et études*, no. XXIII).

+*59. kyr John Sarantenos (d. before 1325)
(G. Theocharides, *Μία διαθήκη καὶ μία δίκη Βυζαντινή* [Thessaloniki, 1962], no. 2, and pp. 17, 54–55).

60. imperial stratiotes kyr John Radenos (fl.1324)
Witness to an act (Petit and Korablev, *Chilandar*, no. 97).

61. kyr Stephen Soumanes from the Mega Allagion of the Thessalonian stratiotai (fl.1327)
Witness to an act (Regel et al., *Zographou*, no. 25).

+62. Katakalon from the Thelematarioi stratiotai (fl.1328–49)
Probably a pronoiar (Arkadios Vatopedinos in *Byzantinisch-Neugriechische Jahrbücher* 13 [1937], 308, no. 3).

63. andrikotatos Chalkiopoulos (fl.1329)
Witness to an act. The adjectival epithet *andrikotatos* attached to his name and to Kromodares' below should identify these men as soldiers (Petit and Korablev, *Chilandar*, no. 118).

64. andrikotatos Kromodares (fl.1329)
Witness to an act (Petit and Korablev, *Chilandar*, no. 118).

65. kavallarios Nicholas Apsaras (fl.ca.1330)
In Epiros (Nicol, *Epiros II*, 222, 244).

66 and 67. stratiotes Makros and stratiotes Jacob (fl.1334)
Landholders in Thrace, a dozen or so miles west of Constantinople (Lemerle et al., *Lavra*, III, no. 122).

68. kavallarios syr Alexios (fl.1340)
From around Larissa (N. Bees in *Βυζαντίς* 2 [1911–12], 62–72).

+69. andrikotatos and pistotatos kavallarios Syrmanuel Mesopotamites (fl.1343)

Pronoiar in a place called Drachoba in Macedonia (Petit and Korablev, *Chilandar*, no. 132).

70. kavallarios Mouzakios (d. before 1352)
Probably a pronoiar on the Chalkidike (Papachryssanthou, *Xénophon*, no. 29).

71. prosalentes Eustratios Chiotes (fl.bef.1355)
Landholder on Lemnos (Lemerle et al., *Lavra*, III, no. 136).

72. Theodore Mouzalon, from the Thessalonian Mega Allagion (d. before 1355)
Pronoiar on the Chalkidike (Oikonomidès, *Docheiariou*, no. 29; J. Lefort, *Villages de Macédoine* [Paris, 1982], 140; *PLP*, no. 19438).

73. kavallarios Staneses (d. before 1360)
From around Serres (Petit and Korablev, *Chilandar*, no. 151).

+*74. Kontostephanos (d. before 1365)
From Thrace (I. Sakkelion in Δελτίον τῆς Ἱστορικῆς καὶ Ἐθνολογικῆς Ἑταιρίας τῆς Ἑλλάδος 3 [1890], 274; J. Darrouzès, *Les regestes des actes du patriarcat de Constantinople*, I, fasc. 5 [Paris, 1977], no. 2500).

75. kavallarios kyr Demetrios Trikanas (fl.1361–66)
Involved in a dispute with the monastery of Docheiariou over possession of the estate of a deceased relative (Oikonomidès, *Docheiariou*, nos. 34–36, 38).

76. kavallarios Myrsioannes Amirales (fl.1367–69)
In Epiros (*PLP*, no. 19884; Nicol, *Epiros II*, 144, 222).

+*77. kyr Manuel Deblitzenos (d.1384)
Son of the soldier Demetrios Deblitzenos (no. 44); pronoiar and patrimonial landowner, resident of Thessaloniki; died in battle (Oikonomidès, *Docheiariou*, nos. 47–51, 53, 58).

78. kavallarios John Koutroules (fl.1394)
Inhabitant of Methone (MM, II, 210–11).

79. stratiotes Kaspax (fl.1401)
Owned a house in Constantinople a long time before 1401 that he permitted to have torn down; sold the land to the *exkoubitor* George (MM, II, 554–56; *PLP*, no. 11367); perhaps identical to the Kaspax (MM, II, 391; *PLP*, no. 11366) who owned land near Constantinople in 1391.

80. (?) stratiotes David (fl. before 1415[?])

Landholder on Lemnos mentioned in a false act probably created around the middle of the fifteenth century (Lemerle et al., *Lavra*, III, app. XVIII).

Glossary

andrikotatos—"most brave," an unofficial epithet sometimes applied to soldiers.

archon—a general term for a member of the ruling class broadly conceived, including the leading citizens of a town.

chrysobull—the most formal imperial document, so named because of the gold seal (*chryse boulla*) attached to it.

despot (*despotes*)—a title second in precedence only to that of emperor, usually held by sons or brothers of the emperor; also held by the semi-independent rulers of the Byzantine Morea and applied to other rulers in the southern Balkans. For most of the late period, with slight variations over time, the first twelve court titles after that of emperor were despot, sevastokrator, caesar, panhypersevastos, protovestiarios, megas doux, megas domestikos, protostrator, megas logothetes, megas stratopedarches, megas primmikerios, and megas konostaulos.

eparch—a court title with no fixed function.

hyperpyron—the name for the basic late Byzantine gold coin, equivalent to the *nomisma*. As with the Roman *solidus* there were seventy-two to the pound, though, due to frequent debasement, its value steadily declined.

judge of the army—a court title with no fixed function, originally the official who settled disputes involving soldiers.

kastron—the most common designation for a fortified town. The word could also be applied to almost any fortification including the walls of Constantinople.

kastrophylax—"castle-guard," the official responsible for the upkeep of a town's fortifications and for organizing the watch.

katepanikion—a provincial unit usually consisting of a kastron and its environs.

kavallarios—from the Latin *caballarius*, "knight," a semi-official title applied to certain Western Europeans in imperial service, to certain native Byzantine warriors, and also, from the late fourteenth century, to certain high-ranking Byzantine assistants to the emperor.

kephale—literally, "head," the military and civil governor of a katepanikion.

konostaulos, kontostaulos—"constable," a title encountered in the Morea with unknown responsibilities. See megas konostaulos.

kyr, kyrios, kyris—an unofficial title of respect corresponding to "Mister" (for women, *kyra* or *kyria*).

lizios—"liege," the Byzantine appropriation of the concept of liege-homage; in the twelfth century applied by the emperor to certain high-ranking Western Europeans. It is encountered only rarely after 1204.

megalodoxotatos—"exceedingly most glorious," an unofficial epithet.

megas adnoumiastes—a court title with no fixed function, originally connected with the muster lists of the army.

megas archon—a court title created in the mid-thirteenth century to designate the highest-ranking officer within the emperor's personal entourage. In the fourteenth century its bearer had no fixed function.

megas domestikos—"grand domestic," a high-ranking court title, often held by the commander-in-chief of the army.

megas doux—"grand duke," a high-ranking court title, often with no fixed function, originally held by the commander of the navy, frequently granted as an honorary title to important foreigners.

megas hetaireiarches—a court title with no fixed function, originally connected with the imperial bodyguard (*hetaireia*).

megas konostaulos—"grand constable," a high-ranking court title originally designating the officer in charge of the Latin mercenaries.

megas logothetes—a high-ranking court title usually held by the first minister of the Empire, often responsible for directing both domestic and foreign affairs.

megas primmikerios (or *primikerios*)—a high-ranking title with no fixed function, originally the master of ceremonies in the imperial palace.

megas stratopedarches—a high-ranking title with no fixed function, originally in charge of the military camp (*stratopedon*).

megas tzaousios—a court title with no fixed function.

modios—the standard Byzantine unit of area, equivalent to about one-quarter of an acre or 1,000 m^2; also a unit of capacity.

nomisma—the earlier name for the hyperpyron.

oikeios—"familiar, kin," an appellation indicating a personal relationship to someone, especially the emperor. An individual who signed a document as "*doulos* (slave) of the emperor" was usually addressed by the emperor as "oikeios of my Majesty."

oikonomia—in fiscal terminology, the economic and fiscal resources comprising an imperial grant; often used to designate a pronoia.

pansevastos—literally, "all-august," an honorary epithet.

paroikos—literally, "one who dwells around," the term for the semi-dependent peasant. By the fourteenth century almost all peasants were paroikoi.

pistotatos—literally, "most faithful," an honorary epithet.

posotes (pl. *posotetes*)—"quantity," a fiscal term denoting a sum of money which represented the total annual fiscal revenue produced by a property or collection of properties; used as a means of denoting the size of imperial grants, including pronoiai.

praktikon—the primary form of tax records in late Byzantium, an inventory listing the taxes, property, and paroikos households held by an individual or religious institution.

prokathemenos—in the thirteenth century, the top civil official in a kastron; in the fourteenth, the immediate subordinate of the kephale in civil matters.

pronoiar—holder of a pronoia, a modern term derived from the relatively rare Byzantine term *pronoiarios*.

prostagma—a type of imperial document usually issuing a command.

protokynegos—literally "first huntsman," a court title with no fixed function, originally the official who managed the emperor's hounds.

protostrator—a high-ranking court title with no fixed function, originally the head of the imperial guard called the *stratores*.

senate (*synkletos*)—a general term for the aristocracy, especially in Constantinople.

sevastokrator—a very high title subordinate in precedence only to that of despot and emperor, held by close relatives of the emperor and also by the rulers of Thessaly.

sevastos—"august," an honorary epithet.

stratiotes—"soldier," often with the added sense of "pronoia soldier."

syr—the Greek transliteration of "Sir," occasionally found preceding or attached to the names of certain Western Europeans in Byzantine service.

tagma—a military unit of no precise size, generally corresponding to the battalion or company.

taxis—a military unit of no precise size, often used synonymously with *tagma*; also applied to the imperial entourage.

telos—"tax," the basic tax on agricultural land and property.

theme—the technical term for a large provincial administrative unit.

tzaousios—a military officer associated with the megala allagia; in the Morea, an official with unknown responsibilities.

Lists of Rulers

Rulers not mentioned in the text are omitted.

Byzantine Emperors

1204–22	Theodore I Laskaris
1222–54	John III Doukas Vatatzes
1254–58	Theodore II Laskaris
1258–61	John IV Laskaris
1259–82	Michael VIII Palaiologos
1282–1328	Andronikos II Palaiologos
1294–1320	Michael IX Palaiologos (co-emperor)
1328–41	Andronikos III Palaiologos
1341–91	John V Palaiologos
1347–54	John VI Kantakouzenos
1353–57	Matthew Kantakouzenos (co-emperor)
1376–79	Andronikos IV Palaiologos
1390	John VII Palaiologos
1391–1425	Manuel II Palaiologos
1425–48	John VIII Palaiologos
1448–53	Constantine XI Palaiologos

Rulers in Epiros

1204–15	Michael I Doukas
1215–30	Theodore Doukas, emperor in Thessaloniki from 1224
ca.1230–67/8	Michael II Doukas, despot from ca.1249
1267/8–96	Nikephoros I Doukas, despot
1296–1318	Thomas, despot
1323–36/7	John II Orsini, despot

Rulers in Thessaloniki

1224–30	Theodore Doukas, emperor
1244–46	Demetrios, despot

Sevastokratores in Thessaly

1271–ca.1289	John I Doukas (the Bastard)
ca.1303–18	John II Doukas

Despots in the Morea

1349–80	Manuel Kantakouzenos
1380–83	Matthew Kantakouzenos
1383	Demetrios Kantakouzenos
1383–1407	Theodore I Palaiologos
1407–43	Theodore II Palaiologos
1428–49	Constantine Palaiologos
1428–60	Thomas Palaiologos
1449–60	Demetrios Palaiologos

Latin Emperors of Constantinople

1204–05	Baldwin I of Flanders
1206–16	Henry of Flanders
1228–61	Baldwin II

Rulers of Serbia

1243–76	Stefan Uroš I
1276–82	Stefan Dragutin
1282–1321	Stefan Uroš II Milutin
1321–31	Stefan Uroš III Dečanski
1331–55	Stefan Dušan, emperor from 1345

(1365–71   King Vukašin)
1371–89   Prince Lazar
1389–1427   Stefan Lazarević, despot from 1402
1427–56   George Branković, despot from 1429

Tsars of Bulgaria

1197–1207   Kalojan
1218–41   John Asen II
1241–46   Koloman Asen
1257–77   Constantine Tich
1279–80   John Asen III
1300–22   Theodore Svetoslav
1322–23   George II Terter
1323–30   Michael Šišman
1330–31   John Stephen
1331–71   John Alexander
1360–96   John Stracimir, ruler at Vidin

Ottoman Turkish Rulers

1288–1326   Osman
1326–62   Orhan
1362–89   Murad I
1389–1402   Bayezid I
1402–21   Mehmet I
1402–10   Sulayman
1411–13   Musa
1421–51   Murad II
1451–81   Mehmet II the Conqueror

Bibliography of Works Cited

REGISTERS

Darrouzès, Jean. *Les regestes des actes du patriarcat de Constantinople*, I: *Les actes des patriarches*, fasc. 5: *Les regestes de 1310 à 1376*. Paris: Institut français d'études byzantines, 1977. Fasc. 6: *Les regestes de 1377 à 1410*. Paris: Institut français d'études byzantines, 1979.

Dölger, Franz. *Regesten der Kaiserurkunden des oströmischen Reiches*, Corpus der griechischen Urkunden des Mittelalters und der neueren Zeit, Reihe A, Abt. I, 5 pts. Munich and Berlin: Oldenbourg, 1924–32. Munich: C.H. Beck, 1960–65.

Dölger, Franz, and Peter Wirth. *Regesten der Kaiserurkunden des oströmischen Reiches von 565–1453*, Teil 3: *Regesten von 1204–1282*. Munich: C.H. Beck, 1977.

Laurent, Vitalien. *Les regestes des actes du patriarcat de Constantinople*, I: *Les actes des patriarches*, fasc. 4: *Les regestes de 1208 à 1309*. Paris: Institut français d'études byzantines, 1971.

Thiriet, Freddy. *Délibérations des assemblées vénitiennes concernant la Romanie*, 2 vols. Paris: Mouton, 1966–71.

———. *Régestes des délibérations du Senat de Venice concernant la Romanie*, 3 vols. Paris: Mouton, 1958–61.

Trapp, Erich, Rainer Walther, Hans-Veit Beyer. *Prosopographisches Lexikon der Palaiologenzeit*. Vienna: Österreichische Akademie der Wissenschaften, 1976ff.

SOURCES

A. GREEK DOCUMENTARY SOURCES

Arkadios Vatopedinos. «Γράμματα τῆς ἐν Κωνσταντινουπόλει μονῆς τῆς Θεοτόκου τῆς Ψυχοσωστρίας». *Byzantinisch-Neugriechische Jahrbücher* 13 (1937), 308 γ´ –ιγ´.

———. «Ἁγιορειτικὰ ἀνάλεκτα ἐκ τοῦ ἀρχείου τῆς μονῆς Βατοπεδίου». *Γρηγόριος ὁ Παλαμᾶς* 2 (1918), 449–52; 3 (1919), 209–23, 326–39, 429–41.

Bees, Nikos. «Σερβικὰ καὶ Βυζαντιακὰ γράμματα Μετεώρου». *Βυζαντίς* 2 (1911–12), 1–100.

Bompaire, Jacques. *Actes de Xéropotamou*, Archives de l'Athos III. Paris: P. Lethielleux, 1964.

Branouse, Era. *Βυζαντινὰ ἔγγραφα τῆς μονῆς Πάτμου*, vol. 1: Αὐτοκρατορικά. Athens: Ethnika Idryma Ereunon, 1980.

Branouses, L. «Ἀλβανοὶ πολεμισταὶ στὴν ὑπηρεσία τῶν Δεσποτῶν τῆς Πελοποννήσου. Ἀνέκδοτος ὁρισμὸς (τοῦ 1436 ἢ 1451) γιὰ τὶς φορολογικές τους ἀπαλλαγὲς καὶ τὶς στρατιωτικές τους ὑποχρεώσεις—Ἀναγραφὴ ὀνομάτων». Paper read at the Α´ Διεθνὲς Συνοδρίας Πελοποννησιακῶν Σπουδῶν, Sparta, 7–14 Sept. 1975, one-page abstract.

Demitsas, M. *Ἡ Μακεδονία ἐν λίθοις φθεγγομένοις καὶ μνημείοις σωζομένοις . . . Μακεδονικῶν*, 3 vols. Athens, 1896.

Dmitrievskij, A. *Opisanie liturgičeskih rukopisej . . . Tom I.* Τυπικά. Kiev, 1895; repr. Hildesheim: G. Olms, 1965.

Dölger, Franz. *Aus den Schatzkammern des Heiligen Berges. 115 Urkunden und 50 Urkundensiegel aus 10 Jahrhunderten*, 2 vols.: Textband, Tafelband. Munich: Münchener Verlag, 1948.

———. *Byzantinische Diplomatik: 20 Aufsätze zum Urkundenwesen der Byzantiner.* Ettal: Buch-Kunstverlag, 1956.

———. "Ein Chrysobull des Kaisers Andronikos II. für Theodoros Nomikopulos aus dem Jahre 1288," in *Miscellanea Georg Hofmann S.J.* = *Orientalia Christiana Periodica* 21 (1955), 58–62; repr. in Dölger, *Παρασπορά*: 30 Aufsätze zur Geschichte, Kultur und Sprache des byzantinischen Reiches, 189–93. Ettal: Buch-Kunstverlag, 1961.

———. *Sechs byzantinische Praktika des 14. Jahrhunderts für das Athoskloster Iberon. Mit diplomatischen, sprachlichen, verwaltungs- und sozialgeschichtliche Bemerkungen*, Abhandlungen der Bayerischen Akademie der Wissenschaften, phil.-hist. Kl., N.F. 28. Munich, 1949.

Ferrari dalle Spade, G. "Formulari notarili inediti dell' età bizantina." *Bullettino dell'Istituto Storico Italiano* 33 (1913), 41–128.

———. "Registro Vaticano di atti bizantini di diritto privato." *Studi Bizantini e Neoellenici* 4 (1935), 248–67.

Fögen, Maria T. "Zeugnisse byzantinischer Rechtspraxis im 14. Jahrhundert." *Fontes Minores* 5 (1982), 215–80.

Grégoire, Henri. "Les veilleurs de nuit à Trébizonde (XIVe siècle)." *BZ* 18 (1909), 490–99.

Guillou, André. *Les archives de Saint-Jean-Prodrome sur le mont Ménécée.* Paris: Presses Universitaires de France, 1955.

Heisenberg, August. *Aus der Geschichte und Literatur der Palaiologenzeit*, Sitzungsberichte der Bayerischen Akademie der Wissenschaften, Philos.-philol. und hist. Kl., Abh. 10 (Munich, 1920); repr. in Heisenberg, *Quellen und Studien zur spätbyzantinischen Geschichte*, no. I. London: Variorum Reprints, 1973.

Kougeas, Sokrates. «Χρυσόβουλλον Κωνσταντίνου τοῦ Παλαιολόγου πρωτόγραφον καὶ ἀνέκδοτον, δι᾽ οὗ ἐπικυροῦντα δωρεαὶ εἰς τοὺς υἱοὺς τοῦ Γεμιστοῦ (1449)». Ἑλληνικά 1 (1928), 371–400.

Kravari, Vassiliki. *Actes du Pantocrator*, Archives de l'Athos XVII. Paris: Centre National de la Recherche Scientifique and P. Lethielleux, 1991.

Lampros, Spyridon P. *Παλαιολόγεια καὶ Πελοποννησιακά*, 4 vols. Athens, 1912–30; repr. Athens: V. Gregoriades, 1972.

Lefort, Jacques. *Actes d'Esphigménou*, Archives de l'Athos VI. Paris: P. Lethielleux, 1973.

Lemerle, Paul. *Actes de Kutlumus*, Archives de l'Athos II, rev. ed. Paris: P. Lethielleux, 1988.

———. "Un praktikon inédit des archives de Karakala (janvier 1342) et la situation en Macédoine orientale au moment de l'usurpation de Cantacuzène," in Χαριστήριον εἰς Ἀναστάσιον Κ. Ὀρλάνδον, 4 vols. (Athens, 1965–68), I, 278–98; repr. in Lemerle, *Le monde de Byzance: histoire et institutions*, no. XVIII. London: Variorum Reprints, 1978.

Lemerle, Paul, André Guillou, Nicolas Svoronos, Denise Papachryssanthou, and Sima Ćirković. *Actes de Lavra*, 4 vols., Archives de l'Athos V, VIII, X, XI. Paris: P. Lethielleux, 1970–82.

Magdalino, Paul. "An Unpublished Pronoia Grant of the Second Half of the Fourteenth Century." *ZRVI* 18 (1978), 155–63.

Miklosich, Franz, and J. Müller. *Acta et diplomata Graeca medii aevi sacra et profana*, 6 vols. Vienna, 1860–90.

Nystazopoulou-Pelekidou, Maria. Βυζαντινὰ ἔγγραφα τῆς μονῆς Πάτμου, vol. 2: Δημοσίων λειτουργιῶν. Athens: Ethnika Idryma Ereunon, 1980.

Oikonomidès, Nicolas. *Actes de Dionysiou*, Archives de l'Athos IV. Paris: P. Lethielleux, 1968.

———. *Actes de Docheiariou*, Archives de l'Athos XIII. Paris: P. Lethielleux, 1984.

Papachryssanthou, Denise. *Actes de Xénophon*, Archives de l'Athos XV. Paris: P. Lethielleux, 1986.

Petit, Louis. "Documents inédits sur le concile de 1166." *VizVrem* 11 (1904).

Petit, Louis, and B. Korablev. *Actes de Chilandar, I. Actes grecs. VizVrem* 17 (1911), suppl. 1; repr. Amsterdam: Hakkert, 1975.

Regel, W. Χρυσόβουλλα καὶ γράμματα τῆς ἐν τῷ Ἁγίῳ Ὄρει Ἄθω ἱερᾶς καὶ σεβασμίας Μεγίστης Μονῆς τοῦ Βατοπεδίου. Saint Petersburg, 1898.

Regel, W., E. Kurtz, and B. Korablev. *Actes de Philothée. VizVrem* 20 (1913), suppl. 1.

———. *Actes de Zographou, I. Actes grecs. VizVrem* 13 (1907), suppl. 1; repr. Amsterdam: Hakkert, 1969.

Sakkelion, I. «Συνοδικαὶ διαγνώσεις τῆς ΙΔ´ ἑκατονταετηρίδος». Δελτίον τῆς Ἱστορικῆς καὶ Ἐθνολογικῆς Ἑταιρίας τῆς Ἑλλάδος 3 (1890), 273–74; 4 (1891), 413–27.

Sathas, K. Μεσαιωνικὴ Βιβλιοθήκη, 6 vols. Venice, 1872–94; repr. Athens, 1972.

Schlumberger, Gustave. *Sigillographie de l'empire byzantine*. Paris, 1884.

Schreiner, Peter. "Zwei unedierte Praktika aus der zweiten Hälfte des 14. Jahrhunderts." *JÖB* 19 (1970), 33–49.

Sigalas, A. «Ὁρισμὸς Δημητρίου Δεσπότου τοῦ Παλαιολόγου (Ἰούλιος 1462)». Ἑλληνικά 3 (1930), 341–45.

Solovjev, Aleksandar, and Vladimir Mošin. *Grčke povelje srpskih vladara, izdanje tekstova, prevod i komentar*, Srpska Kraljevska Akademija, Zbornik za istoriju, jezik i književnost srpskog naroda, treće odeljenje, knjiga 7. Belgrade, 1936; repr. London: Variorum Reprints, 1974.

Speiser, J.-M. "Inventaires en vue d'un recueil des inscriptions historiques de Byzance: I. Les inscriptions de Thessalonique." *TM* 5 (1973), 145–80.

Taşliklioğlu, Zafer. *Traky'da epigrafya araştirmalari*, 2 vols. Istanbul, 1961–71.

Theocharides, G. Μία διαθήκη καὶ μία δίκη Βυζαντινή, 'Ανέκδοτα Βατοπεδινὰ ἔγγραφα. Thessaloniki: Hetaireia Makedonikon Spoudon, 1962.

Uspenskij, Fedor, and V. Beneševič. *Actes de Vazélon (Vazelonskie akty), Matériaux pour servir à l'histoire de la propriété rurale et monastique à Byzance aux XIII–XV siècles.* Leningrad: Gosudarstvennaja Publičnaja Biblioteka, 1927.

Vatopedi no. III, 8; E.-A.-N. 30 (*Regesten*, no. 3084): unpublished *prostagma* of John V Palaiologos and *paradotikon gramma* of Demetrios Phakrases (June 1377).

Zepos, J., and P. Zepos. *Jus graecoromanum*, 8 vols. Athens: G. Fexis, 1931; repr. Aalen: Scientia, 1962.

B. GREEK NARRATIVE AND LITERARY SOURCES

Akropolites, George. *Georgii Acropolitae Opera*, ed. A. Heisenberg, vol. 1. Leipzig: Teubner, 1903; repr. Stuttgart: Teubner, 1978.

Apokaukos, John, metropolitan of Naupaktos. Ed. A. Papadopoulos-Kerameus, «Συνοδικὰ γράμματα Ἰωάννου τοῦ Ἀποκαύκου, μητροπολίτου Ναυπάκτου». *Βυζαντίς* 1 (1909), 3–30.

———. Ed. Nikos Bees, "Unedierte Schriftstücke aus der Kanzlei des Johannes Apokaukos des Metropoliten von Naupaktos (in Aetolien)." *Byzantinisch-Neugriechische Jahrbücher* 21 (1971–74), 55–160. E. Bee-Sepherle, «Προσθῆκαι καὶ παρατηρήσεις». *Byzantinisch-Neugriechische Jahrbücher* 21 (1971–74), 161–243.

———. Ed. Sophrone Pétridès, "Jean Apokaukos, lettres et autres documents inédits." *Izvestija Russkogo arheologičeskago instituta v Konstantinopole* 14 (1909), 1–32.

Athanasios I, Patriarch. *The Correspondence of Athanasius I Patriarch of Constantinople, Letters to the Emperor Andronicus II, Members of the Imperial Family, and Officials*, ed. and trans. Alice-Mary Maffry Talbot, Dumbarton Oaks Texts 3, CFHB 7. Washington, D.C.: Dumbarton Oaks Center for Byzantine Studies, 1975.

Barker, Ernest. *Social and Political Thought in Byzantium from Justinian to the Last Palaeologus: Passages from Byzantine Writers and Documents*. Oxford: Clarendon Press, 1957.

Bartusis, Mark, Khalifa Ben Nasser, and Angeliki Laiou. "Days and Deeds of a Hesychast Saint: A Translation of the Greek Life of St. Romylos." *Byzantine Studies/Études byzantines* 9 (1982), 24–47.

Bees, Nikos. «Συμβολὴ εἰς τὴν ἱστορίαν τῶν μονῶν τῶν Μετεώρων». *Βυζαντίς* 1 (1909), 191–319.

Bessarion, John, Cardinal. Letter to Despot Constantine (ca.1444): Βησσαρίων καρδινάλιος Κωνσταντίνῳ Δεσπότῃ τῷ Παλαιολόγῳ χαίρειν, in Lampros, Παλαιολόγεια καὶ Πελοποννησιακά, IV, 32–45.

Boissonade, J. *Anecdota Graeca*, 5 vols. Paris, 1829–33.

Browning, Robert. *Notes on Byzantine Prooimia*, Wiener Byzantinische Studien 1: Supplement. Vienna, 1966.

Chalkokondyles. *Laonici Chalcocondylae Atheniensis Historiarum libri decem*, ed. I. Bekker, CSHB. Bonn, 1843. *Laonici Chalcocandylae Historiarum Demonstrationes*, ed. E. Darkò, 2 vols. Budapest, 1922–23. Trans. sections on the fall of Constantinople in Jones, *The Siege of Constantinople*, 42–55.

Choniates, Michael. Μιχαὴλ Ἀκομινάτου τοῦ Χωνιάτου τὰ σωζόμενα, ed. S. Lampros, 2 vols. Athens, 1879–80.

Choniates, Niketas. *Nicetae Choniatae Historia*, ed. I. Bekker, CSHB. Bonn, 1835. Ed. Jan L. van Dieten, CFHB. Berlin: W. de Gruyter, 1975. English trans. Harry J. Magoulias, *O City of Byzantium: Annals of Niketas Choniates*. Detroit: Wayne State University Press, 1984.

Chronicle of the Morea, ed. John Schmitt. London: Methuen, 1904; repr. Groningen: Bouma's Bockhuis, 1967. English trans. Harold E. Lurier, *Crusaders as Conquerors: The Chronicle of the Morea*. New York: Columbia University Press, 1964.

Constantine VII Porphyrogenitus. *De cerimoniis aulae byzantinae*, ed. I. Reiske, 2 vols., CSHB. Bonn, 1829–30.

———. Ed. Hélène Ahrweiler, "Un discours inédit de Constantin VII Porphyrogénète." *TM* 2 (1967), 393–404.

———. Ed. R. Vári, "Zum historischen Exzerptenwerke des Konstantinos Porphyrogennetos." *BZ* 17 (1908), 75–85.

Doukas. *Ducas. Istoria Turco-Bizantina (1341–1462)*, ed. Vasile Grecu. Bucharest, 1958. English trans. Harry J. Magoulias, *Doukas. Decline and Fall of Byzantium to the Ottoman Turks: An Annotated Translation of "Historia Turco-Bizantina."* Detroit: Wayne State University Press, 1975. Sections on fall of Constantinople in Jones, *The Siege of Constantinople*, 56–116.

Gautier, Paul, ed. "Un récit inédit du siège de Constantinople par les Turcs (1394–1402)." *REB* 23 (1965), 100–17.

Geanakoplos, Deno. *Byzantium: Church, Society, and Civilization Seen through Contemporary Eyes*. Chicago: University of Chicago Press, 1984.

Gemistos Plethon, George. Address to Manuel II: Εἰς Μανουὴλ Παλαιολόγον περὶ τῶν ἐν Πελοποννήσῳ πραγμάτων, ed. Lampros, Παλαιολόγεια καὶ Πελοποννησιακά, III, 246–65. Ed. Migne, *PG*, 160.

———. Advice to Despot Theodore II: Πλήθωνος συμβουλευτικὸς πρὸς τὸν δεσπότην Θεόδωρον περὶ τῆς Πελοποννήσου, ed. Lampros, Παλαιολόγεια καὶ Πελοποννησιακά, IV, 113–35. Ed. Migne, *PG*, 160.

———. Letter to Manuel II on the Isthmus, ed. Lampros, Παλαιολόγεια καὶ Πελοποννησιακά, III, 309–12.

———. Προθεωρία εἰς τὸν Ἐπιτάφιον Μανουὴλ Παλαιολόγου εἰς τὸν ἀδελφὸν Θεόδωρον, ed. J. Chrysostomides in *Manuel II Palaeologus, Funeral Oration on His Brother Theodore*, CFHB 26. Thessaloniki: Association for Byzantine Research, 1985. Ed. Lampros, Παλαιολόγεια καὶ Πελοποννησιακά, III, 3–7.

Grecu, Vasile, ed. *Viaţa sfântului Nifon. O redacţie grecească inedită*. Bucharest, 1944.

Gregoras, Nikephoros. *Correspondance de Nicéphore Grégoras*, ed. R. Guilland. Paris: Société d'édition "Les Belles Lettres," 1927.

————. *Nicephori Gregorae Byzantina Historia*, ed. L. Schopen, 3 vols., CSHB. Bonn, 1829, 1830, 1855.

Gregory II (George), of Cyprus, Patriarch of Constantinople. Ed. Sophronios Eustratiades, «Τοῦ σοφωτάτου καὶ λογιωτάτου καὶ οἰκουμενικοῦ πατριάρχου κύρου Γρηγορίου τοῦ Κυπρίου Ἐπιστολαί». *Ἐκκλησιαστικὸς Φάρος* 1 (1908), 77–108, 409–39; 2 (1908), 195–211; 3 (1909), 5–48, 281–96; 4 (1909), 5–29, 97–128; 5 (1910), 213–26, 339–52, 444–52, 489–500. Repr. in *Γρηγορίου τοῦ Κυπρίου οἰκουμενικοῦ πατριάρχου Ἐπιστολαὶ καὶ Μῦθοι*, ed. S. Eustratiades. Alexandria, 1910.

La guerre de Troie. Poème du XIVe siècle en vers octosyllabes par Constantin Hermoniacos, in *Bibliothèque grecque vulgaire*, ed. É. Legrand, vol. V. Paris, 1890.

Harmenopoulos, Constantine. *Πρόχειρον Νόμων ἢ Ἑξάβιβλος*, ed. K.G. Pitsakis. Athens: Dodone, 1971.

Heisenberg, August. *Neue Quellen zur Geschichte des lateinischen Kaisertums und der Kirchenunion, I: Der Epitaphios des Nikolaos Mesarites auf seinen Bruder Johannes; II: Die Unionsverhandlungen vom 30. August 1206; III: Der Bericht des Nikolaos Mesarites über die politischen und kirchlichen Ereignisse des Jahres 1214*, Sitzungsberichte der Bayerischen Akademie der Wissenschaften, Philos.-philol. und hist. Kl. Munich, 1922: Abh. 5, and 1923: Abh. 2–3. Repr. in Heisenberg, *Quellen und Studien zur spätbyzantinischen Geschichte*, no. II. London: Variorum Reprints, 1973.

Hyrtakenos, Theodore. Ed. F.J.G. La Porte-du Theil, "Notices et extraits d'un volume de la Bibliothèque Nationale, coté MCCIX parmi les manuscrits grecs, et contenant les opuscules et lettres anecdotes de Théodôre l'Hyrtacènien." *Notices et extraits des manuscrits de la Bibliothèque Nationale* 5 (1798), 709–44; 6 (1800), 1–48.

John VI Kantakouzenos. "The History of John Cantacuzenus (book 4): Text, Translation and Commentary," ed. Timothy Miller. Diss., Catholic Univ. Ann Arbor, Mich.: University Microfilms, 1975.

————. *Ioannis Cantacuzeni eximperatoris historiarum libri IV*, 3 vols., vol. 1, ed. L. Schopen; vols. 2–3, ed. B. Niebuhr, CSHB. Bonn, 1828, 1831, 1832.

Jones, J.R. Melville, trans. *The Siege of Constantinople 1453: Seven Contemporary Accounts*. Amsterdam: Hakkert, 1972.

Kananos, John. *Διήγησις περὶ τοῦ ἐν Κωνσταντινουπόλει γεγονότις πολέμου.* Giovanni Cananos, *L'assedio di Costantinopoli*, ed. and Italian trans. Emilio Pinto. Messina: Edas, 1977.

Kinnamos, John. *Ioannis Cinnami epitome*, ed. A. Meineke, CSHB. Bonn, 1836. English trans. Charles W. Brand, *Deeds of John and Manuel Comnenus*. New York: Columbia University Press, 1976.

Komnene, Anna. *Anne Comnène, Alexiade. Règne de l'empereur Alexis I Comnène 1081–1118*, ed. Bernard Leib, 3 vols. Paris: Société d'édition "Les Belles Lettres," 1937–45. English trans. E.R.A. Sewter, *The Alexiad of Anna Comnena*. Baltimore: Penguin, 1969.

Kritoboulos. *Critobuli Imbriotae historiae*, ed. Diether R. Reinsch, CFHB 22. Berlin and New York: W. de Gruyter, 1983. English trans. Charles T. Riggs, *History of Mehmed the Conqueror by Kritovoulos*. Princeton, N.J.: Princeton University Press, 1954.

Kydones, Demetrios. *Démétrius Cydonès correspondance*, ed. R.-J. Loenertz, 2 vols., Studi e Testi 186, 208. Vatican: Biblioteca apostolica vaticana, 1956, 1960.

———. *Demetrios Kydones Briefe*, German trans. F. Tinnefeld, I, pt. 1. Stuttgart: Hiersmann, 1981.

Mai, Angelo, ed. *Novae patrum bibliothecae*, 10 vols. Rome, 1852–1905.

———. *Scriptorum veterum nova collectio*, 10 vols. Rome, 1825–38.

Makarios Melissourgos (Pseudo-Phrantzes). Ed. Vasile Grecu in *Georgios Sphrantzes, Memorii 1401–1477, în anexâ Pseudo-Phrantzes: Macarie Melissenos Cronica 1258–1481*. Bucharest, 1966. Section on the fall of Constantinople trans. Marios Philippides in *The Fall of the Byzantine Empire: A Chronicle by George Sphrantzes, 1401–1477*. Amherst: University of Massachusetts Press, 1980.

Makrembolites, Alexios. *Λόγος ἱστορικός*. In A. Papadopoulos-Kerameus, Ἀνάλεκτα Ἱεροσολυμιτικῆς Σταχυολογίας, I, 144–58. St. Petersburg, 1891.

Manuel II Palaiologos. *The Letters of Manuel II Palaeologus*, text, trans., and notes by George T. Dennis, Dumbarton Oaks Texts 4, CFHB 8. Washington, D.C.: Dumbarton Oaks Center for Byzantine Studies, 1977.

———. *Manuel II Palaeologus, Funeral Oration on His Brother Theodore*, intro., text, trans., and notes by Juliana Chrysostomides, CFHB 26. Thessaloniki: Association for Byzantine Research, 1985.

Mazaris. In A. Ellissen, ed., *Analekten der mittel- und neugriechischen Litteratur*, IV, 187–250. Leipzig, 1860.

Nikephoros II Phokas. *Le traité sur la guérilla (De velitatione) de l'empereur Nicéphore Phocas*, ed. G. Dagron and H. Mihaescu. Paris: Centre National de la Recherche Scientifique, 1986.

Nikodemos Hagioreites. *Νέον Ἐκλόγιον*. Venice, 1803; Constantinople, 1863; repr. Athens: Aster, 1974.

Pachymeres, George. *Georges Pachymérès. Relations historiques*, ed. Albert Failler, French trans. Vitalien Laurent, vol. 1, 2 pts., CFHB 24. Paris: Société d'édition "Les Belles Lettres," 1984.

———. *Georgii Pachymeris de Michaele et Andronico Palaeologis*, ed. I. Bekker, 2 vols., CSHB. Bonn, 1835.

Palaiologos, Theodore (1291–1338), marquis de Montferrat. *Les Enseignements de Théodore Paléologue*, ed. Christine Knowles, Texts and Dissertations 19. London: Modern Humanities Research Association, 1983. Modern French summary by Julia Bastin, "Le traité de Théodore Paléologue dans la traduction de Jean de Vignai." *Études romanes dédiées à Mario Roques*, 77–88. Paris: Droz, 1946.

Papadopoulos-Kerameus, A. Ἀνάλεκτα Ἱεροσολυμιτικῆς Σταχυολογίας, 5 vols. St. Petersburg, 1891–98.

———. «Ἰωάννης Ἀπόκαυκος καὶ Νικήτας Χωνιάτης», in Τεσσαρακονταετηρὶς τῆς καθηγεσίας Κ.Σ. Κόντου, 373–82. Athens, 1909.

Philes, Manuel. Ed. E. Martini, "A proposito d'una poesia inedita di Manuel File." *Reale Istituto Lombardo di Scienze e Lettere, Rendiconti*, serie II, 29, (Milan, 1896), 460–71.

———. *Manuelis Philae Carmina*, ed. E. Miller, 2 vols. Paris, 1855–57.

———. *Manuelis Philae Carmina Inedita*, ed. E. Martini. Naples, 1900.

Pitra, Jean. *Analecta sacra et classica spicilegio solesmensi parata*, 6 vols. Paris, 1876–91; repr. Farnborough, Hant., England: Gregg, 1967.

Planoudes, Maximos. *Maximi monachi Planudis epistulae*, ed. Maximilian Treu. Breslau, 1886–90; repr. Amsterdam: Hakkert, 1960.

Psellos, Michael. Michael Psellus, *Fourteen Byzantine Rulers*, trans. E.R.A. Sewter. Baltimore : Penguin: 1966.

Pseudo-Kodinos. *Traité des offices*, ed. and French trans. Jean Verpeaux. Paris: Centre National de la Recherche Scientifique, 1966. *Codini curopalatae de officialibus palatii Cpolitani et de officiis magnae ecclesiae liber*, ed. I. Bekker, CSHB. Bonn, 1839.

Pseudo-Phrantzes: see Makarios Melissourgos.

Schirò, Giuseppe, ed. and trans. *Cronaca dei Tocco di Cefalonia di Anonimo*, CFHB 10. Rome: Accademia nazionale dei Lincei, 1975.

Schreiner, Peter. *Die byzantinischen Kleinchroniken*, 3 vols., CFHB 12. Vienna: Österreichische Akademie der Wissenschaften, 1975–79.

Sphrantzes, George. *Georgios Sphrantzes, Memorii 1401–1477, în anexâ Pseudo-Phrantzes: Macarie Melissenos Cronica 1258–1481*, ed. Vasile Grecu. Bucharest, 1966. Trans. Marios Philippides, *The Fall of the Byzantine Empire: A Chronicle by George Sphrantzes, 1401–1477*. Amherst: University of Massachusetts Press, 1980.

Syropoulos, Sylvester. *Les "Mémoires" du Grand Ecclésiarque de l'Église de Constantinople Sylvestre Syropoulos sur le concile de Florence (1438–1439)*, ed. and trans. Vitalien Laurent. Rome: Pontificium institutum orientalium studiorum, 1971.

Theodori Ducae Lascari Epistulae CCXVII, ed. N. Festa, Pubblicazioni del Reale Istituto di studi superiori pratici de di perfezionamento in Firenze, Sezione di filosofia e lettere, no. 29. Florence, 1898.

Thomas Magistros. Λόγος περὶ πολιτείας, ed. Migne, *PG*, 145, cols. 495–548. Ed. A. Mai, *Scriptorum veterum nova collectio*, III. Rome, 1825–38.

Three Byzantine Military Treatises, text, trans., and notes by George T. Dennis, Dumbarton Oaks Texts 9. CFHB 25. Washington, D.C.: Dumbarton Oaks Research Library and Collection, 1985.

Wagner, Wilhelm. *Carmina Graeca medii aevi*. Leipzig, 1879.

C. WESTERN SOURCES

Barbaro, Nicolò. *Giornale dell'Assedio di Constantinopoli 1453*, ed. Enrico Cornet. Vienna, 1856. English trans. J.R. Jones, *Diary of the Siege of Constantinople, 1453*. New York: Exposition Press, 1969.

Belgrano, L.T. "Prima serie di documenti riguardanti la colonia di Pera." *Atti della Società ligure di storia patria* 13 (1877–84), 97–336.

Bertrandon de la Brocquière. English trans. Thomas Wright, *Early Travels in Palestine*, 283–382. London, 1848.

Carbone, Salvatore, ed. *Pietro Pizolo, notario in Candia*, vol. 1: *1300*. Venice: Comitato per la pubblicazione delle fonti relativa alla storia di Venezia, 1978.

Chronicon Adae de Usk, A.D. 1377–1421, ed. and trans. E.M. Thompson, 2nd ed. London, 1904; repr. New York: AMS Press, 1980.

Clavijo, Ruy González de. *Embajada a Tamorlán*, ed. Francisco López Estrada. Madrid: Instituto Nicolas Antonio, 1943. English trans. Guy Le Strange, *Clavijo, Embassy to Tamerlane, 1403–1406*. London: G. Routledge, 1928.

Directorium ad faciendum passagium transmarinum, ed. C. Raymond Beazley in *American Historical Review* 12 (1906–1907), 810–57; 13 (1907–1908), 66–115, with English summary. Also in *Recueil des historiens des croisades. Documents arméniens*, II, with French trans. from 1455 by Jean Miélot. Paris: Academie des inscriptions et belles-lettres, 1906.

Dolfin, Zorzi. *Cronaca*. Sections on fall of Constantinople, English trans. in Jones, *The Siege of Constantinople*, 125–30.

Iorga, N. *Notes et extraits pour servir à l'histoire des Croisades au XVe siècle*, 4 vols. Paris and Bucharest, 1899–1915.

Jones, J.R. Melville, trans. *The Siege of Constantinople 1453: Seven Contemporary Accounts*. Amsterdam: Hakkert, 1972.

Lampros, Spyridon, ed. «Ὑπόμνημα περὶ τῶν ἑλληνικῶν χωρῶν καὶ ἐκκλησιῶν κατὰ τὸν δέκατον πέμπτον αἰῶνα». *Νέος Ἑλληνομνήμων* 7 (1910), 360–71.

LeGrand, L. "Relation du Pèlerinage à Jérusalem de Nicolas de Martonia, notaire Italien (1394–1395)." *Revue de l'Orient latin* 3 (1895), 566–669.

Leonard of Chios. *Historia Cpolitanae urbis a Mahumete II captae per modum epistolae die 15 Augusti anno 1453 ad Nicolaum V Rom. Pont.*, in Migne, *PG*, vol. 159, cols. 923–44. English trans. in Jones, *The Siege of Constantinople*, 11–41.

Livre de la Conqueste de la princée de l'Amorée. Chronique de Morée (1204–1305), ed. Jean Longnon. Paris: Librairie Renouard, 1911. The French version of the *Chronicle of the Morea*.

Le livre des faicts du bon messire Jean le Maingre, dit Boucicaut, Maréschal de France et Gouverneur de Jennes, in J. de Froissart, *Les Chroniques*, ed. J.A.C. Buchon, vol. 3 (Paris, 1838), 563–695. Ed. M. Petitot, in *Collection complète des mémoires relatifs à l'histoire de France*, vols. 6–7. Paris, 1819–25.

Loenertz, Raymond-J. "Fragment d'une lettre de Jean V Paléologue à la commune de Gênes, 1387–1391." *BZ* 51 (1958), 37–40.

Mertzios, K. *Μνημεῖα Μακεδονικῆς Ἱστορίας*. Thessaloniki: Hetaireia Makedonikon Spoudon, 1947.

Moncada, Francisco de. *The Catalan Chronicle of Francisco de Moncada*, English trans. Frances Hernández. El Paso: Texas Western Press, 1975.

Muntaner, Ramon. *Cronicà*, ed. E.B., 9 vols. in 2. Barcelona, 1927–52. English trans. Lady Goodenough, *The Chronicle of Muntaner*, 2 vols. London: Hakluyt Society, 1920–21; repr. Nendeln, Liechtenstein: Kraus Reprint, 1967.

Muratori, L.A. *Rerum Italicarum Scriptores*, 28 vols. Milan, 1723–51.

Pertusi, Agostino. "The Anconitan Colony in Constantinople and the Report of Its Consul, Benvenuto, on the Fall of the City," in *Charanis Studies: Essays in Honor of Peter Charanis*, ed. A. Laiou-Thomadakis, 199–218. New Brunswick, N.J.: Rutgers University Press, 1980.

Raymond d'Aguilers. *Historia Francorum qui ceperunt Iherusalem*, ed. and trans. John H. Hill and L.L. Hill. Philadelphia: American Philosophical Society, 1968.

Reiffenberg, Baron de, ed. *Monuments pour servir à l'histoire des provinces de Namur, de Hainaut et du Luxembourg*, 8 vols. Brussels, 1844–74.

Sanudo, Marino (Torsello). *Istoria del regno di Romania*, ed. C. Hopf, in *Chroniques gréco-romanes* (Berlin, 1873), 99–170.

Sathas, K. Μνημεῖα Ἑλληνικῆς Ἱστορίας. *Documents inédits relatifs à l'histoire de la Grèce au moyen âge*, 9 vols. Paris, 1880–90.

Simon de Saint-Quentin. *Histoire des Tartares*, ed. Jean Richard, Documents relatifs à l'histoire des Croisades VIII. Paris: P. Geuthner, 1965.

Tafur, Pero. *Travels and Adventures, 1435–1439*, trans. Malcolm Letts. New York and London: Harper and Bros., 1926.

Tedaldi, Giacomo. English trans. in Jones, *The Siege of Constantinople*, 3–10.

Theiner, A., and F. Miklosich. *Monumenta spectantia ad unionem ecclesiarum Graecae et Romanae*. Vienna, 1872.

Thomas, G.M. *Diplomatarium Veneto-Levantinum*, 2 vols. Venice, 1880–99.

Villehardouin. *La conquête de Constantinople*, ed. Edmond Faral, 2 vols. Paris: Société d'édition "Les Belles Lettres," 1938–39; repr. 1972–73. English trans. Margaret R.B. Shaw, in *Joinville and Villehardouin, Chronicles of the Crusades*. Baltimore: Penguin, 1963.

Zerlentis, P. «Γράμματα Φράγκων δουκῶν τοῦ Αἰγαίου πελάγους (1433–1564)». *BZ* 13 (1904), 136–57.

D. SLAVIC AND ORIENTAL SOURCES

Balaščev, G. Ὁ αὐτοκράτωρ Μιχαὴλ Η΄ ὁ Παλαιολόγος καὶ τὸ ἱδρυθὲν τῇ συνδρομῇ αὐτοῦ κράτος τῶν Ὀγούζων παρὰ τὴν δυτικὴν ἀκτὴν τοῦ Εὐξείνου. Sofia, 1930. 26 pp.

Benjamin of Tudela. *The Itinerary of Benjamin of Tudela*, ed. and trans. Marcus Adler. London: Henry Frowde, 1907.

Bogdan, Joan, ed. "Ein Beitrag zur bulgarischen und serbischen Geschichtschreibung." *Archiv für slavische Philologie* 13 (1891), 481–543.

Ignatius of Smolensk. *Journey to Constantinople*, ed. and trans. George P. Majeska, in *Russian Travelers to Constantinople in the Fourteenth and Fifteenth Centuries*, Dumbarton Oaks Studies 19 (Washington, D.C.: Dumbarton Oaks Research Library and Collection, 1984), 48–113.

Ivić, Pavle, and M. Grković. *Dečanske hrisovulje*. Novi Sad, 1976.

Korablev, B., and Louis Petit. *Actes de Chilandar, II. Actes slaves*. *VizVrem* 19 (1915), suppl. 1; repr. Amsterdam: Hakkert, 1975.

Mihailović, Konstantin. *Memoirs of a Janissary*, trans. and ed. Benjamin Stolz, commentary and notes by Svat Soucek. Ann Arbor: Univerity of Michigan Press, 1975.

Mošin, Vladimir. "Akti iz svetogorskih arhiva." *Spomenik Srpske kraljevske akademije nauka* 91 (1939), 155–260.

Mošin, Vladimir, Lidija Slaveva, et al. *Spomenici za srednovekovnata i ponovata istorija na Makedonija*, I–III. Skopje: Arhiv na Makedonija, 1975–80. Vol. IV. Skopje: Institut za istražuvanje na staroslovenskata kultura, 1981. Vol. V. Prilep: Institut za istražuvanje na staroslovenskata kultura, 1988.

Novaković, Stojan. *Zakonski spomenici srpskih država srednjega veka*. Belgrade: Srpska Kraljevska Akademija, 1912.

Solovjev, Aleksandar. *Odabrani spomenici srpskog prava (od XII do kraja XV veka)*. Belgrade: Gece Kona, 1926.

Tursun Beg. *The History of Mehmed the Conqueror by Tursun Beg*, text published in facsimile with English trans. (summary) by Halil Inalcik and Rhoads Murphey, American Research Institute in Turkey, Monograph Series 1. Minneapolis and Chicago: Bibliotheca Islamica, 1978.

Wittek, Paul. "Yazijioghlu 'Ali on the Christian Turks of the Dobruja." *Bulletin of the School of Oriental and African Studies* (London University) 14 (1952), 639–68.

Zakonik cara Stefana Dušana: 1349 i 1354, ed. N. Radojčić. Belgrade: SANU, 1960. English trans. M. Burr, "The Code of Stephan Dušan." *Slavonic and East European Review* 28 (1949–50), 198–217, 516–39.

Secondary Works

Ahrweiler: see also Glykatzi-Ahrweiler.

Ahrweiler, Hélène. *Byzance: les pays et les territoires*. London: Variorum Reprints, 1976.

———. *Byzance et la mer; la marine de guerre, la politique et les institutions maritimes de Byzance aux VIIe–XVe siècles*. Paris: Presses Universitaires de France, 1966.

———. *Études sur les structures administratives et sociales de Byzance*. London: Variorum Reprints, 1971.

———. "Les fortresses construites en Asie Mineure face à l'invasion seldjoucide." *Akten des XI. internationalen Byzantinistenkongresses*, Munich 1958 (Munich: Beck, 1960), 182–89; repr. in Ahrweiler, *Études sur les structures*, no. XVII.

———. "La frontière et les frontières de Byzance en Orient." *Actes du XIVe Congrès international des études byzantines, Bucarest 1971*, I (Bucharest: Academiei Republicii Socialiste Romania, 1974), 209–30; repr. in Ahrweiler, *Byzance: les pays et les territoires*, no. III.

———. "L'histoire et la géographie de la région de Smyrne entre les deux occupations turques (1081–1317) particulièrement au XIIIe siècle." *TM* 1 (1965), 1–204; repr. in Ahrweiler, *Byzance: les pays et les territoires*, no. IV.

———. *L'idéologie politique de l'empire byzantin*. Paris: Presses Universitaires de France, 1975.

———. "La 'pronoia' à Byzance," in *Structures féodales et féodalisme dans l'occident méditerranéen (Xe–XIIIe s.)*, Collection de l'école française de Rome 44, 681–89. Rome: École française de Rome, 1980.

Amantos, K. «Τουρκόπωλοι» ["Tourkopouloi"]. *Ἑλληνικά* 6 (1933), 325–26.

Andrews, Kevin. *Castles of the Morea*, Gennadeion Monographs 1. Princeton, N.J.: American School of Classical Studies at Athens, 1953; repr. Amsterdam: Hakkert, 1978.

Angelov, D. "Prinos kŭm narodnostnite i pozemelni otnošenija v Makedonija (Epirskija despotat) prez pŭrvata četvurt na XIII vek. (glavno spored doku-

menti na Ohridskata arhiepiskopija)" ["Contribution to the Ethnography and
Agrarian Relations in Macedonia (Despotate of Epiros) during the First
Quarter of the Thirteenth Century (Based Mainly on the Documents of the
Archiepiscopate of Ohrid)"]. *Izvestija na Kamarata na narodnota kultura*
(Serija: Humanitarni nauki) IV/3 (1947), 1–46.

Angold, Michael. *The Byzantine Empire 1025–1204: A Political History*. London:
Longman, 1984.

———. *A Byzantine Government in Exile: Government and Society Under the Laska-
rids of Nicaea (1204–1261)*. London: Oxford University Press, 1975.

Antoniadis-Bibicou, Hélène. *Études d'histoire maritime de Byzance à propos du "thème
de Caravisiens."* Paris: S.E.V.P.E.N., 1966.

Arnakis, G.G. "Byzantium's Anatolian Provinces during the Reign of Michael
Palaeologus." *Actes du XIIe Congrès international d'études byzantines, Ohrid 1961*
(Belgrade, 1953–64), II, 37–44.

Asdracha, Catherine. "Formes de brigandage pendant la deuxième guerre civile
byzantine au XIVe s." *Études Balkaniques* 7 (1971), 118–20.

———. *La région des Rhodopes aux XIIIe et XIVe siècles: étude de géographie historique*,
Texte und Forschungen zur Byzantinisch-Neugriechischen Philologie 49.
Athens: Byzantinisch-Neugriechische Jahrbücher, 1976.

Babinger, Franz. *Mehmed the Conqueror and His Time*, trans. Ralph Manheim, ed.
William C. Hickman, Bollingen Series XCVI. Princeton, N.J.: Princeton
University Press, 1978.

Barker, John. *Manuel II Palaeologus (1391–1425): A Study in Late Byzantine Statesmanship*. New Brunswick, N.J.: Rutgers University Press, 1969.

Bartusis, Mark. "Brigandage in the Late Byzantine Empire." *Byz* 51 (1981), 386–409.

———. "Chrelja and Momčilo: Occasional Servants of Byzantium in Fourteenth
Century Macedonia." *Byzantinoslavica* 41 (1980), 201–21.

———. "The Cost of Late Byzantine Warfare and Defense." *Byzantinische Forschungen* 16 (1990), 75–89.

———. "Exaleimma: Escheat in Byzantium." *DOP* 40 (1986), 55–81.

———. "The *Kavallarioi* of Byzantium." *Speculum* 63 (1988), 343–50.

———. "The Megala Allagia and the Tzaousios: Aspects of Provincial Military
Organization in Late Byzantium." *REB* 47 (1989), 183–207.

———. "A Note on Michael VIII's 1272 Prostagma for His Son Andronikos." *BZ* 81
(1988), 268–71.

———. "On the Problem of Smallholding Soldiers in Late Byzantium." *DOP* 44
(1990), 1–26.

———. "On the Status of Stratiotai during the Late Byzantine Period." *ZRVI* 21
(1982), 53–59.

———. "State Demands for the Billeting of Soldiers in Late Byzantium." *ZRVI* 26
(1987), 115–23.

———. "State Demands for the Building and Repairing of Fortifications in Late
Byzantium and Medieval Serbia." *Byzantinoslavica* 49 (1988), 205–12.

———. "Urban Guard Service in Late Byzantium: The Terminology and the
Institution." *Macedonian Studies* 5, n.s. 2 (1988), 52–77.

Bayley, Charles C. *War and Society in Renaissance Florence: The* De Militia *of Leonardo Bruni.* Toronto: University of Toronto Press, 1961.

Beck, Hans-Georg. *Byzantinisches Gefolgschaftswesen*, Sitzungsberichte der Bayerischen Akademie der Wissenschaften, philos.-hist. Klasse. Munich, 1965.

Beldiceanu, Nicoară. "Le timar dans l'État ottoman (XIVe–XVe siècles)," in *Structures féodales et féodalisme dans l'occident méditerranéen (Xe–XIIIe s.)*, Collection de l'école française de Rome 44, 743–53. Rome: École française de Rome, 1980.

———. *Le timar dans l'État ottoman (début XIVe-début XVIe siècle)*. Wiesbaden: O. Harrassowitz, 1980.

Bertelé, Tommaso. "Lineamenti principali della numismatica bizantina." *Rivista Italiana di Numismatica* 12, serie quinta, 66 (1964), 31–118.

———. "Moneta veneziana e moneta bizantina," in *Venezi e il Levante fino ad secolo XV*, Convegno internazionale di storia della civiltà veneziana, no. 1, Venice, 1968, I, pt. 1, pp. 3–146. Florence: L.S. Olschki, 1973. Also published separately. Florence: L.S. Olschki, 1973.

Bibikov, M.V. "Svedenija o pronii v pis'mah Grigorija Kiprskogo i 'Istorii' Georgija Pahimera" ["Information Regarding Pronoia in the Letters of Gregory of Cyprus and the *History* of George Pachymeres"]. *ZRVI* 17 (1976), 93–99.

Blöndal, Sigfus. *The Varangians of Byzantium: An Aspect of Byzantine Military History*, trans., rev., and rewritten by Benedikt S. Benedikz. Cambridge: Cambridge University Press, 1978.

Bombaci, Alessio. "The Army of the Saljuqs of Rūm." *Istituto orientale di Napoli, Annali*, n.s. 38 (1978), 343–69.

Bosch, Ursula V. *Kaiser Andronikos III. Palaiologos. Versuch einer Darstellung der byzantinischen Geschichte in den Jahren 1321–1341*. Amsterdam: Hakkert, 1965.

Bowman, Steven B. *The Jews of Byzantium, 1204–1453*. University: University of Alabama Press, 1985.

Browning, Robert. "A Note on the Capture of Constantinople in 1453." *Byz* 22 (1952), 379–87.

Cahen, Claude. "L'évolution de l'iqtâᶜ du IXe au XIIIe siècle, contribution à une histoire comparée des sociétés médiévales." *Annales, économies—sociétés—civilisations* 8 (1953), 25–52.

———. *La féodalité et les institutions politiques de l'Orient latin*. Rome: Accademia nazionale dei Lincei, 1956. 26 pp.

———. *Pre-Ottoman Turkey: A General Survey of the Material and Spiritual Culture and History c.1071–1330*, trans. J. Jones-Williams. New York: Taplinger, 1968.

Canard, M. "La guerre sainte dans le monde islamique et dans le monde chrétien." *Revue Africaine* 79 (1936), 605–23.

Caratzas, Stamatis. *Les Tzacones*, Supplementa Byzantina 4. Berlin and New York: W. de Gruyter, 1976.

Carrère, C. "Aux origines des compagnies: la compagnie catalane de 1302," in *Recruitement, mentalités, sociétés: Colloque international d'histoire militaire, Septembre 1974*, 1–7. Montpellier: Université Paul-Valery, 1974.

Charanis, Peter. "The Monastic Properties and the State in the Byzantine Empire."

DOP 4 (1948), 51–119; repr. in Charanis, *Social, Economic and Political Life in the Byzantine Empire*, no. I.

―――. "On the Social Structure and Economic Organization of the Byzantine Empire in the Thirteenth Century and Later." *Byzantinoslavica* 12 (1951), 94–153; repr. in Charanis, *Social, Economic and Political Life in the Byzantine Empire*, no. IV.

―――. "Piracy in the Aegean during the Reign of Michael VIII Palaeologus." *Mélanges Henri Grégoire*, II (Brussels, 1950) = *Annuaire de l'Institut de philologie et d'histoire orientales et slaves* 10 (1950), 127–36; repr. in Charanis, *Social, Economic and Political Life in the Byzantine Empire*, no. XII.

―――. *Social, Economic and Political Life in the Byzantine Empire: Collected Studies*. London: Variorum Reprints, 1973.

Ciggaar, K.N. "L'émigration anglaise à Byzance après 1066." *REB* 32 (1974), 301f.

Colloque international sur la paléographie grecque et byzantine. *La paléographie grecque et byzantine*. Paris: Centre National de la Recherche Scientifique, 1977.

Dain, A. "Le partage du butin de guerre d'après les traités juridiques et militaires." *Actes du VIe Congrès international d'études byzantines, Paris 1948*, I (Paris: École des hautes études, 1950), 347–54.

Dawkins, R. "The Later History of the Varangian Guard." *Journal of Roman Studies* 37 (1947), 39–46.

Dennis, George T. "The Capture of Thebes by the Navarrese (6 March 1378) and Other Chronological Notes in Two Paris Manuscripts." *Orientalia Christiana Periodica* 26 (1960), 42–50; repr. in Dennis, *Byzantium and the Franks, 1350–1420*, no. XV. London: Variorum Reprints, 1982.

―――. "Flies, Mice, and the Byzantine Crossbow." *Byzantine and Modern Greek Studies* 7 (1981), 1–5.

―――. *The Reign of Manuel II Palaeologus in Thessalonica, 1382–1387*, Orientalia Christiana Analecta 159. Rome: Pontificium institutum orientalium studiorum, 1960.

Deroko, A. "Srednjovekovni grad Skoplje" ["The Medieval Fortress of Skopje"]. *Spomenik SANU* 120, odeljenje društvenih nauka, nova serija 22 (Belgrade, 1971), 1–16.

―――. *Srednjovekovni gradovi u Srbiji, Crnoj Gori i Makedoniji* [Medieval Fortresses in Serbia, Montenegro, and Macedonia]. Belgrade, 1950.

Deroko, A., and S. Nenadović. "Konaci manastira Hilandara" ["The Buildings of the Monastery of Chilandar"]. *Spomenik SANU* 120, odeljenje društvenih nauka, nova serija 22 (Belgrade, 1971), 17–39.

Diehl, Charles. *Études byzantines*. Paris, 1905; repr. New York: Burt Franklin, n.d.

Dieten, Jan L. van. "Bemerkungen zur Sprache der sog. vulgärgriechischen Niketasparaphrase." *Byzantinische Forschungen* 6 (1979), 37–77.

Dinić, Mihailo J. "Prilozi za istoriju vatrenog oružja u Dubrovniku i susednim zemljama" ["Contributions to the History of Firearms in Dubrovnik and Neighboring Areas"]. *Glas Srpske kraljevske akademije* 161 (drugi razred 83) (1934), 55–97.

―――. "Španski najamnici u srpskoj službi" ["Spanish Mercenaries in Serbian Service"]. *ZRVI* 6 (1960), 15–28.

Dölger, Franz. *Beiträge zur Geschichte des byzantinischen Finanzverwaltung, besonders des 10. und 11. Jahrhunderts*, Byzantinisches Archiv 9. Leipzig and Berlin: Teubner, 1927; repr. Hildesheim: G. Olms, 1960.

———. Review of *Vojniški zemi i vojnici v Vizantija prez XIII–XIV v.* by P. Mutafčiev. *BZ* 26 (1926), 102–13.

Dunn, Archie. "The Survey of Khrysoupolis, and Byzantine Fortifications in the Lower Strymon Valley." *JÖB* 32/4 (1982), 605–14.

The Encyclopaedia of Islam, new ed. Leiden: Brill, 1960ff.

Erdmann, Carl. *The Origin of the Idea of Crusade*. Princeton, N.J.: Princeton University Press, 1977.

Failler, Albert. "Chronologie et composition dans l'histoire de Georges Pachymère." *REB* 38 (1980), 5–103; 39 (1981), 145–249.

Fassoulakis, S. *The Byzantine Family of Raoul-Ral(l)es*. Athens: S. Fassoulakis, 1973.

Le féodalisme à Byzance: problèmes du mode de production de l'empire byzantin. Paris: Éditions de "La Nouvelle Critique," 1974.

Ferjančić, Božidar. "Quelques significations du mot stratiote dans les chartes de basse Byzance." *ZRVI* 21 (1982), 95–102.

———. *Tesalija u XIII i XIV veku* [Thessaly in the Thirteenth and Fourteenth Centuries], Posebna izdanja, knjiga 15. Belgrade: Vizantološki institut SANU, 1974.

Ferluga, Jadran. "La ligesse dans l'empire byzantin." *ZRVI* 7 (1961), 97–123.

Fisher, Elizabeth. "A Note on Pachymeres' 'De Andronico Palaeologo.'" *Byz* 40 (1970), 230–35.

Foss, Clive. "Late Byzantine Fortifications in Lydia." *JÖB* 28 (1979), 297–320.

Foss, Clive, and D. Winfield. *Byzantine Fortification: An Introduction*. Pretoria: University of South Africa, 1986.

Gaier, Claude. "Analysis of Military Forces in the Principality of Liège and the County of Looz from the Twelfth to the Fifteenth Century." *Studies in Medieval and Renaissance History* 2 (1965), 205–61.

Geanakoplos, Deno J. *The Emperor Michael Palaeologus and the West, 1258–1282: A Study in Byzantino-Latin Relations*. Cambridge, Mass.: Harvard University Press, 1959.

———. "Greco-Latin Relations on the Eve of the Byzantine Restoration: The Battle of Pelagonia, 1259." *DOP* 7 (1953), 99–141.

Georgiadis-Arnakis, G. Οἱ πρῶτοι Ὀθωμανοί, Συμβολὴ εἰς τὸ πρόβλημα τῆς πτώσεως τοῦ Ἑλληνισμοῦ τῆς Μικρᾶς Ἀσίας (1282–1337) [The First Ottomans, Contribution to the Problem of the Fall of the Greeks of Asia Minor]. Athens, 1947.

Glykatzi-Ahrweiler: see also Ahrweiler.

Glykatzi-Ahrweiler, Hélène. "La concession des droits incorporels, donations conditionelles." *Actes du XIIe Congrès international d'études byzantines, Ohrid 1961* (Belgrade, 1963–64), II, 103–14; repr. in Ahrweiler, *Études sur les structures*, no. I.

———. "Recherches sur l'administration de l'empire byzantin aux IXe–XIe siècles." *Bulletin de Correspondance Hellénique* 84 (1960), 1–109; repr. in Ahrweiler, *Études sur les structures*, no. VIII.

Guerdan, René. *Byzantium, Its Triumphs and Tragedy*, trans. D.L.B. Hartley. New York: Capricorn, 1957.

Guilland, Rodolphe. *Recherches sur les institutions byzantines*, 2 vols. Berlin and Amsterdam: Hakkert, 1967.

Hadjopoulos, Dionysios. "Le premier siège de Constantinople par les Ottomans (1394–1402)." Diss., Université de Montréal, 1980. 318 pp.

Haldon, John F. *Recruitment and Conscription in the Byzantine Army c. 550–950. A Study of the Origins of the Stratiotika Ktemata*, Sitzungsberichte der Österreichischen Akademie der Wissenschaften, Philos.-hist. Kl., vol. 357. Vienna, 1979.

———. "ΣΩΛΗΝΑΡΙΟΝ—The Byzantine Crossbow?" *University of Birmingham Historical Journal* 12 (1970), 155–57.

Haldon, John, and M. Byrne. "A Possible Solution to the Problem of Greek Fire." *BZ* 70 (1977), 91–99.

Hale, John R. *War and Society in Renaissance Europe, 1450–1620*. Baltimore, Md.: St. Martin's Press, 1985.

Hendrickx, Benjamin. "A propos du nombre des troupes de la quatrième croisade et de l'empereur Baudoin I." *Βυζαντινά* 3 (1971), 29–41.

———. «Οἱ πολιτικοὶ καὶ στρατιωτικοὶ θεσμοὶ τῆς Λατινικῆς Αὐτοκρατορίας τῆς Κωνσταντινουπόλεως κατὰ τοὺς πρώτους χρόνους τῆς ὑπαρχεώς της» ["The Political and Military Institutions of the Latin Empire of Constantinople during the First Years of Its Existence"]. Diss., Thessaloniki 1970.

Hendy, Michael. *Studies in the Byzantine Monetary Economy c.300–1450*. Cambridge: Cambridge University Press, 1985.

Hohlweg, Armin. *Beiträge zur Verwaltungsgeschichte des oströmischen Reiches unter den Komnenen*, Miscellanea Byzantina Monacensia, Heft 1. Munich: Institut für Byzantinistik und Neugriechische Philologie der Universität, 1965.

———. "Zur Frage der Pronoia in Byzanz." *BZ* 60 (1967), 288–308.

Hopf, Carl. *Geschichte Griechenlands vom Beginn des Mittelalters bis auf unsere Zeit*, in H. Brockhaus, *Griechenland*, vol. 6: *B. Griechenland im Mittelalter und in der Neuzeit*. Leipzig, 1870.

Housley, N.J. "The Mercenary Companies, the Papacy and the Crusades, 1356–1378." *Traditio* 38 (1982), 253–80.

Hunger, Herbert. *Die hochsprachliche profane Literatur der Byzantiner*, 2 vols. Munich: Beck, 1978.

———. "Urkunden- und Memoirentext: Der Chrysobullos Logos der Johannes Kantakuzenos für Johannes Angelos." *JÖB* 27 (1978), 107–25.

Hvostova, Ksenija V. *Osobennosti agrarnopravovyh ostnošenij v pozdnej Vizantii XIV–XV vv.* [Peculiarities of Agrarian Relations in Late Byzantium, Fourteenth to Fifteenth Centuries]. Moscow: Akademija nauk, 1968.

Jacoby, David. "The Encounter of Two Societies: Western Conquerors and Byzantines in the Peloponnesus after the Fourth Crusade." *American Historical Review* 78 (1973), 873–906; repr. in Jacoby, *Recherches*, no. II.

———. "Les états latins en Romanie: phénomènes sociaux et économiques (1204–1350 environ)." *XVe Congrès international d'études byzantines, Athens 1976*, Rapports et co-rapports, I. Histoire: 3 (Athens, 1976), 1–51; repr. in Jacoby, *Recherches*, no. I.

——. "Quelques considérations sur les versions de la 'Chronique de Morée.'" *Journal des Savants* (1968), 133–89; repr. in Jacoby, *Société et démographie à Byzance et en Romanie latine*, no. VII. London: Variorum Reprints, 1975.

——. *Recherches sur la Méditerranée orientale du XIIe au XVe siècle: Peuples, sociétés, économies*. London: Variorum Reprints, 1979.

——. "Les Vénitiens naturalisés dans l'empire byzantin: un aspect de l'expansion de Venise en Romanie du XIIIe au milieu du XVe siècle." *TM* 8 (1981), 217–35; repr. in Jacoby, *Studies on the Crusader States and on Venetian Expansion*, no. IX. London: Variorum Reprints, 1989.

Jameson, A. "The Responsa and Letters of Demetrios Chomatianos, Archbishop of Achrida and Bulgaria: A Study in Byzantine Legal and Economic History of the Thirteenth Century." Diss., Harvard Univ. 1957.

Jeffreys, Michael. "The Chronicle of the Morea: Priority of the Greek Version." *BZ* 68 (1975), 304–50.

Karlin-Hayter, Patricia. "Notes sur le ΛΑΤΙΝΙΚΟΝ dans l'armée et les historiens de Nicée." *Byzantinische Forschungen* 4 (1972), 142–50.

——. "Preparing the Data from Mount Athos for Use with Modern Demographic Techniques." *Byz* 48 (1978), 501–18.

Katele, Irene B. "Piracy and the Venetian State: The Dilemma of Maritime Defense in the Fourteenth Century." *Speculum* 63 (1988), 865–89.

Kazhdan, A.P. *Agrarnye otnošenija v Vizantii XIII–XIV vv.* [Agrarian Relations in Byzantium, Thirteenth to Fourteenth Centuries]. Moscow: Akademija nauk, 1952.

——. "The Fate of the Intellectual in Byzantium à propos of *Society and Intellectual Life in Late Byzantium*, by Ihor Ševčenko." *Greek Orthodox Theological Review* 27/1 (1982), 83–97.

Kazhdan, A.P., and Giles Constable. *People and Power in Byzantium: An Introduction to Modern Byzantine Studies*. Washington, D.C.: Dumbarton Oaks Center for Byzantine Studies, 1982.

Klopf, Margaret. "The Army in Constantinople at the Accession of Constantine XI." *Byz* 40 (1970), 385–92. Unreliable.

Kolias, Georgios. «Ἡ ἀνταρσία Ἰωάννου Ζ΄ Παλαιολόγου ἐναντίον Ἰωάννου Ε΄ Παλαιολόγου (1390)» ["The Rebellion of John VII Palaiologos against John V Palaiologos"]. Ἑλληνικά 12 (1952), 34–64.

Kolias, Taxiarchis G. *Byzantinische Waffen: ein Beitrag zur byzantinischen Waffenkunde von den Anfängen bis zur lateinischen Eroberung*, Byzantina Vindobonensia 17. Vienna: Österreichische Akademie der Wissenschaften, 1988.

Kravari, Vassiliki. *Villes et villages de Macédoine orientale*, Réalités Byzantines. Paris: P. Lethielleux, 1989.

Kuhn, Hans-Joachim. *Die byzantinische Armee im 10. und 11. Jahrhundert: Studien zur Organisation der Tagmata*. Vienna: Verlag Fassbänder, 1991.

Laiou, Angeliki. "The Byzantine Aristocracy in the Palaeologan Period: A Story of Arrested Development." *Viator* 4 (1973), 131–51.

————. *Constantinople and the Latins: The Foreign Policy of Andronicus II, 1282–1328.* Cambridge, Mass.: Harvard University Press, 1972.

————. "Some Observations on Alexios Philanthropenos and Maximos Planoudes." *Byzantine and Modern Greek Studies* 4 (1978), 89–99.

Laiou-Thomadakis, A. *Peasant Society in the Late Byzantine Empire: A Social and Demographic Study.* Princeton, N.J.: Princeton University Press, 1977.

Lampros, Spyridon. «Τὰ ὀνόματα τοῦ πυροβόλου, τοῦ τυφεκίου καὶ τῆς πυρίτιδος παρὰ τοῖς Βυζαντίνοις» ["The Byzantine Names for Cannon, Musket, and Gunpowder"]. *Νέος Ἑλληνομνήμων* 5 (1908), 400–413.

Langdon, John. "John III Ducas Vatatzes' Byzantine Imperium in Anatolian Exile, 1222–54: The Legacy of His Diplomatic, Military and Internal Program for the Restitutio Orbis." Diss., Univ. of California. Ann Arbor, Mich.: University Microfilms, 1979.

Laurent, Vitalien. "Une famille turque au service de Byzance: les Mélikès." *BZ* 49 (1956), 349–68.

————. "L'idée de guerre sainte et la tradition byzantine." *Revue historique du Sud-Est européen* 23 (1946), 71–98.

Lefort, Jacques. "Fiscalité médiévale et informatique: recherches sur les barèmes pour l'imposition des paysans byzantins du XIVe siècle." *Revue Historique* 512 (1974), 315–56.

————. *Villages de Macédoine. Notices historiques et topographiques sur la Macédoine orientale au Moyen Âge. 1. La Chalcidique occidentale.* Paris: Diffusion de Boccard, 1982.

Lemerle, Paul. *The Agrarian History of Byzantium from the Origins to the Twelfth Century: The Sources and Problems.* Galway: Galway University Press, 1979.

————. "Byzance et la croisade." *Relazioni del X Congresso Internazionale di Scienze Storiche*, Rome 1955, vol. III: *Storia del medioevo* (Florence, 1955), 595–620; repr. in Lemerle, *Le monde de Byzance*, no. VIII.

————. "Un chrysobulle d'Andronic II Paléologue pour le monastère de Karakala." *Bulletin de Correspondence Hellénique* 60 (1936), 428–46; repr. in Lemerle, *Le monde de Byzance*, no. XVII.

————. *Cinq études sur le XIe siècle byzantin.* Paris: Centre National de la Recherche Scientifique, 1977.

————. *L'émirat d'Aydin, Byzance et l'Occident: recherches sur "La Geste d'Umur Pacha."* Paris: Presses Universitaires de France, 1957.

————. *Le monde de Byzance: histoire et institutions.* London: Variorum Reprints, 1978.

Loenertz, Raymond-J. "Pour l'histoire du Péloponèse au XIVe siècle (1382–1404)." *Études byzantines* 1 (1943), 152–96; repr. in Loenertz, *Byzantina et Franco-Graeca*, I, 227–65. Rome: Edizioni di storia e letteratura, 1970.

Lowry, Heath. "Changes in Fifteenth Century Ottoman Peasant Taxation: The Case Study of Radilofo," in *Continuity and Change in Late Byzantine and Early Ottoman Society*, ed. Anthony Bryer and H. Lowry, 23–37. Birmingham, Eng., and Washington, D.C.: University of Birmingham Centre for Byzantine Studies and Dumbarton Oaks Research Library and Collection, 1986.

Lynn, John A. *The Bayonets of the Republic: Motivation and Tactics in the Army of*

Revolutionary France, 1791–94. Urbana and Chicago: University of Illinois Press, 1984.

Majeska, George P., ed. *Russian Travelers to Constantinople in the Fourteenth and Fifteenth Centuries,* Dumbarton Oaks Studies 19. Washington, D.C.: Dumbarton Oaks Research Library and Collection, 1984.

Maksimović, Ljubomir. *The Byzantine Provincial Administration under the Palaiologoi.* Amsterdam: Hakkert, 1988. Trans. of *Vizantijska provincijska uprava u doba Paleologa.* Belgrade: Vizantološki institut SANU, 1972.

———. "Charakter der sozial-wirtschaftlichen Struktur der spätbyzantinischen Stadt (13.–15. Jh.)." *Akten des XVI. internationalen Byzantinistenkongresses* (Vienna: Österreichische Akademie der Wissenschaften, 1981), I, pt. 1 = *JÖB* (1981) 31/1, 150–88.

Mallett, Michael E. *Mercenaries and Their Masters: Warfare in Renaissance Italy.* London: Bodley Head, 1974.

Mallett, Michael E. and J.R. Hale. *The Military Organization of a Renaissance State: Venice c.1400 to 1617.* Cambridge: Cambridge University Press, 1984.

Manova, E. "Les armes défensives au Moyen Âge d'après les peintures murales de la Bulgarie du sud-ouest au XIIIe, XIVe et XVe s." *Byzantino-Bulgarica* 3 (1969), 187–223.

Matschke, Klaus-Peter. "Die Entwicklung der Konzeption eines byzantinischen Feudalismus durch die sowjetische marxistische Byzantinistik 1930–1966." *Zeitschrift für Geschichtswissenschaft* 15 (1967), 1065–86.

———. "Johannes Kantakuzenos, Alexios Apokaukos und die byzantinische Flotte in der Burgerkriegsperiode, 1340–1355." *Actes du XIVe Congrès international des études byzantines, Bucarest 1971,* II (Bucharest: Academiei Republicii Socialiste Romania, 1975), 193–205.

Mavromatis, Leonidas. *La fondation de l'empire serbe: le kralj Milutin.* Thessaloniki: Kentron Vyzantinon Ereunon, 1978.

Mayer, Hans E. *The Crusades,* trans. John Gillingham. Oxford: Oxford University Press, 1972.

Mijatovich, Chedomil. *Constantine, the Last Emperor of the Greeks, or the Conquest of Constantinople by the Turks.* London, 1892. Repr. as *Constantine Palaeologus, the Last Emperor of the Greeks, 1448–1453, or the Conquest of Constantinople by the Turks.* Chicago: Argonaut, 1968.

Mladenović, Miloš. "Zur Frage der Pronoia und des Feudalismus im byzantinischen Reiche." *Südost-Forschungen* 15 (1956), 123–40.

Moravcsik, Gyula. *Byzantinoturcica,* 2nd ed., Berliner byzantinische Arbeiten 10–11, 2 vols. Berlin: Akademie-Verlag, 1958.

Mutafčiev, Petur. *Dobrudža, sbornik ot studii* [The Dobrudja: Collected Studies]. Sofia, 1947.

———. "Vojniški zemi i vojnici v Vizantija prez XIII–XIV v." ["Military Lands and Soldiers in Byzantium during the Thirteenth and Fourteenth Centuries"]. *Spisanie na Bulgarskata Akademija na naukite,* Kniga 27, Klon istoriko-filologičen i filosofsko obščestven 15 (Sofia, 1923), 1–113; repr. in Mutafčiev, *Izbrani proizvedenija,* I (Sofia, 1973), 518–652. All of the page numbers cited refer to the reprint.

Mutafčieva, Vera P. "Sur le caractère du *tīmār* ottoman." *Acta orientalia Academiae scientarium Hungaricae* 9 (1959), 55–61.

Nicol, Donald M. *The Byzantine Family of Kantakouzenos (Cantacuzenus) ca.1100–1460: A Genealogical and Prosopographical Study*, Dumbarton Oaks Studies XI. Washington, D.C.: Dumbarton Oaks Center for Byzantine Studies, 1968.

———. *The Despotate of Epiros*. Oxford: Blackwell, 1957.

———. *The Despotate of Epiros, 1267–1479: A Contribution to the History of Greece in the Middle Ages*. Cambridge: Cambridge University Press, 1984.

———. *The Last Centuries of Byzantium, 1261–1453*. London: Hart-Davis, 1972.

Nicolle, David C. *Arms and Armour of the Crusading Era, 1050–1350*, 2 vols. with continuous pagination. White Plains, N.Y.: Kraus International, 1988.

Nishinura, David. "Crossbows, Arrow-Guides, and the *Solenarion*." *Byz* 58 (1988), 422–35.

Oikonomidès, Nicolas. "A propos des armées des premiers Paléologues et des compagnies de soldats." *TM* 8 (1981), 353–71.

———. "Contribution à l'étude de la pronoia au XIIIe siècle." *REB* 22 (1964), 158–75; repr. in Oikonomidès, *Documents et études*, no. VI.

———. *Documents et études sur les institutions de Byzance (VIIe–XVe s.)*. London: Variorum Reprints, 1976.

———. "The Donation of Castles in the Last Quarter of the Eleventh Century (Dölger, *Regesten*, no. 1012)," in *Polychronion, Festschrift Franz Dölger zum 75. Geburtstag*, ed. Peter Wirth (Heidelberg: C. Winter, 1966), 413–17; repr. in Oikonomidès, *Documents et études*, no. XIV.

———. "Le haradj dans l'empire byzantin du XVe siècle." *Actes du premier Congrès international des études balkaniques*, III (Sofia, 1969), 681–88; repr. in Oikonomidès, *Documents et études*, no. XIX.

———. *Les listes de préséance byzantines des IXe et Xe siècles*. Paris: Centre National de la Recherche Scientifique, 1972.

———. "Notes sur un praktikon de pronoiaire (juin 1323)." *TM* 5 (1973), 335–46; repr. in Oikonomidès, *Documents et études*, no. XXIII.

———. "The Properties of the Deblitzenoi in the Fourteenth and Fifteenth Centuries," in *Charanis Studies: Essays in Honor of Peter Charanis*, ed. A. Laiou-Thomadakis, 176–98. New Brunswick, N.J.: Rutgers University Press, 1980.

Ostrogorski, Georgije. "Još jednom o proniarima Kumanima" ["Once Again on the Cuman Pronoiars"], in *Zbornik Vladimira Mošina*, ed. Dimitrije Bogdanović, B. Jovanović-Štipčević, Dj. Trifunović, 63–74. Belgrade: Savez bibliotečkih radnika Srbije, 1977.

———. "Komitisa i svetogorski manastiri" ["Komitissa and the Monasteries of Mount Athos"]. *ZRVI* 13 (1971), 221–56.

Ostrogorskij, Georges. *Pour l'histoire de la féodalité byzantine*. Brussels: Institut de philologie et d'histoire orientales et slaves, 1954. Includes a trans. of G. Ostrogorski, *Pronija, Prilog istoriju feudalizma u Vizantiji i u južnoslovenskim zemljama*. Belgrade: Vizantološki institut SAN, 1951.

Ostrogorsky, George. "Étienne Dušan et la noblesse serbe dans la lutte contre Byzance." *Byz* 22 (1952), 151–59.

———. *History of the Byzantine State*, rev. ed., trans. Joan Hussey. New Brunswick, N.J.: Rutgers University Press, 1969.

———. "Löhne und Preise in Byzanz." *BZ* 32 (1932), 293–333.

———. "Observations on the Aristocracy in Byzantium." *DOP* 25 (1971), 1–32.

The Oxford Dictionary of Byzantium, ed. A.P. Kazhdan et al., 3 vols. New York: Oxford University Press, 1991.

Painter, Sidney. "Castle-Guard." *American Historical Review* 40 (1934–35), 450–59.

Papadopulos, A. *Versuch einer Genealogie der Palaiologen, 1259–1453*, diss., Munich. Speyer, 1938; repr. Amsterdam: Hakkert, 1962.

Papazotos, Thanazes. «Ἡ μονὴ τοῦ Σαράβαρη στὸ Ἅγιον Ὄρος, Ἱστορικὲς καὶ Ἀρχαιολογικὲς Μαρτυρίες» ["The Monastery of Sarabares on Mt. Athos: Historical and Archaeological Evidence"]. *Κληρονομία* 12 (1980), 85–94.

Paradissis, A. *Fortresses and Castles of Greece*, 3 vols. Athens and Thessaloniki: Efstathiadis Bros., 1972–82.

Pascot, J. *Les Almugavares: mercenaires Catalans du Moyen Age (1302–1388)*. Brussels, 1971.

Petrović, Djurdjica. "Fire-arms in the Balkans on the Eve of and After the Ottoman Conquest of the Fourteenth and Fifteenth Centuries," in *War, Technology and Society in the Middle East*, ed. V.J. Parry and M.E. Yapp, 164–94. London: Oxford University Press, 1975.

Polemis, Demetrios I. *The Doukai: A Contribution to Byzantine Prosopography*. London: Athlone, 1968.

Praškov, L. *Hrel'ovata kula* [Hrelja's Tower]. Sofia, 1973.

Raybaud, L.-P. *Le gouvernement et l'administration centrale de l'empire byzantin sous les premiers Paléologues*. Paris, 1968.

Riley-Smith, Jonathan. *The Feudal Nobility and the Kingdom of Jerusalem, 1174–1277*. London: Macmillan, 1973.

Runciman, Steven. *Byzantine Civilization*. New York: New American Library, 1956.

———. *The Fall of Constantinople, 1453*. Cambridge: Cambridge University Press, 1965.

———. *The Sicilian Vespers*. Cambridge: Cambridge University Press, 1958.

Schilbach, Ernst. *Byzantinische Metrologie*. Munich: C.H. Beck, 1970.

Schlumberger, Gustave. *Un empereur byzantin au dixième siècle, Nicéphore Phocas*, nouv. éd. Paris: Boccard, 1923.

Setton, Kenneth. *A History of the Crusades*, vol. 3: *The Fourteenth and Fifteenth Centuries*, ed. Harry Hazard. Madison: University of Wisconsin Press, 1975.

Ševčenko, Ihor. "An Important Contribution to the Social History of Late Byzantium." *Annals of the Ukrainian Academy of Arts and Sciences in the U.S.* 2, pt. 4 (1952), 448–59.

———. "Nicolas Cabasilas' 'Anti-Zealot' Discourse: A Reinterpretation." *DOP* 11 (1957), 79–171; repr. in Ševčenko, *Society and Intellectual Life in Late Byzantium*, no. IV. London: Variorum Reprints, 1981.

———. "On the Preface to a Praktikon by Alyates." *JÖBG* 17 (1968), 65–72; repr. in Ševčenko, *Society and Intellectual Life in Late Byzantium*, no. XIII. London: Variorum Reprints, 1981.

Shepard, J. "The English and Byzantium: A Study of Their Role in the Byzantine Army in the Later XIth Century." *Traditio* 29 (1973), 53–92.

Sjuzjumov, M.Ja. "Suvernitet, nalog i zemel'naja renta v Vizantii" ["Sovereignty, Tax and Income from Land in Byzantium"]. *Antičnaja drevnost' i srednie veka* 9 (1973), 57–65.

Smail, R.C. *Crusading Warfare (1097–1193)*. Cambridge: Cambridge University Press, 1956, repr. 1967.

Smetanin, V. "O specifike permanentnoj vojny v Vizantii v 1282–1453 gg." ["On the Specifics of Permanent War in Byzantium, 1282–1453"]. *Antičnaja drevnost' i srednie veka* 9 (1973), 89–101.

———. "O tendecijah ideologičeskoj i social'noj dinamiki pozdnevizantijskogo obščestva v period permanentnoj vojny" ["On the Ideological Tendencies and Social Dynamics of Late Byzantine Society during the Period of Permanent War"]. *Antičnaja drevnost' i srednie veka* 11 (1975), 99–109.

Sorlin, Irène. "Bulletin des publications en langues slaves. I. Les recherches soviétiques sur l'histoire byzantine de 1945 à 1962." *TM* 2 (1967), 489–564.

Soulis, George C. *The Serbs and Byzantium during the Reign of Tsar Stephen Dušan (1331–1355) and His Successors*. Washington, D.C.: Dumbarton Oaks Library and Collection, 1984.

Stadtmüller, G. *Michael Choniates, Metropolit von Athen (ca.1138–ca.1222)*, Orientalia Christiana Analecta 91, vol. 33, 2. Rome: Pontificium institutum orientalium studiorum, 1934.

Stein, Ernst. "Untersuchungen zur spätbyzantinischen Verfassungs- und Wirtschaftsgeschichte." *Mitteilungen zur osmanischen Geschichte* 2 (1923–26), 1–62.

Strässle, Paul M. "Ein spätbyzantinisches Holzrelief militär- und kunsthistorisch beurteilt." *Byz* 60 (1990), 382–400.

Svoronos, Nicolas. "Le serment de fidélité à l'empereur byzantin et sa signification constitutionelle." *Actes du VIe Congrès international d'études byzantines, Paris 1948*, 2 vols. (Paris: École des hautes études, 1950–51), I, 191–97.

Symeonides, Charalambos. *Οἱ Τσάκωνες καὶ ἡ Τσακωνιά* [The Tzakones and Tzakonia], Βυζαντινὰ Κείμενα καὶ Μελέται 5. Thessaloniki: Kentron Vyzantinon Ereunon, 1972.

Tafrali, Oreste. *Thessalonique au quatorzième siècle*. Paris, 1913.

———. *Topographie de Thessalonique*. Paris, 1913.

Theocharidis, P. "The Byzantine Fortified Enclosure of the Monastery of Chelandariou: A Preliminary Report." *Hilandarski Zbornik* 7 (1989), 59–70.

Toynbee, Arnold. *Constantine Porphyrogenitus and His World*. London: Oxford University Press, 1973.

Trojanos, S. «Καστροκτισία» ["Kastroktisia"]. *Βυζαντινά* 1 (1969), 39–57. Article in German.

Tsangadas, Bryon C.P. *The Fortifications and Defense of Constantinople*. Boulder, Col.: East European Monographs; New York: distributed by Columbia University Press, 1980.

Tsoures, K. «Ἡ βυζαντικὴ ὀχύρωση τῶν Ἰωαννίνων» ["The Byzantine Fortifications of Ioannina"]. *Ἠπειρωτικὰ Χρονικά* 25 (1983), 133–57.

Underwood, Paul A. *The Kariye Djami*, 3 vols., Bollingen Series 70. New York: Pantheon, 1966.

Uspenskij, Fedor I. "K istorii krest'janskogo zemlevladenija v Vizantii" ["On the History of Peasant Land Ownership in Byzantium"]. *Žurnal Ministerstva narodnogo prosveščenija* 225 (Jan. 1883), 30–87; (Feb. 1883), 301–60.

Vacalopoulos, Apostopolos E. *Origins of the Greek Nation: The Byzantine Period, 1204–1461.* New Brunswick, N.J.: Rutgers University Press, 1970.

Vasiliev, A.A. "On the Question of Byzantine Feudalism." *Byz* 8 (1933), 584–604. Essentially repr. in his *History of the Byzantine Empire*, 2nd English ed., revised, II, 563–79. Madison: University of Wisconsin Press, 1952.

———. "The Opening Stages of the Anglo-Saxon Immigration to Byzantium in the Eleventh Century." *Seminarium Kondakovianum* 9 (1937), 39–70.

Vernadsky, G. "Zametki o vizantijskih kupčih gramatah XIII veka" ["Remarks on Thirteenth-Century Byzantine Purchase Deeds"], in *Sbornik v čest' na Vasil N. Zlatarski.* Sofia, 1925.

Verpeaux, Jean. "Les Oikeioi: notes d'histoire institutionelle et sociale." *REB* 23 (1965), 89–99.

Vryonis, Speros, Jr. "Byzantine and Turkish Societies and Their Sources of Manpower," in *War, Technology and Society in the Middle East*, ed. V.J. Parry and M.E. Yapp, 125–52. London: Oxford University Press, 1975.

———. *The Decline of Medieval Hellenism in Asia Minor and the Process of Islamization from the Eleventh Through the Fifteenth Century.* Berkeley: University of California Press, 1971.

———. "The Question of the Byzantine Mines." *Speculum* 37 (1962), 1–17; repr. in Vryonis, *Byzantium: Its Internal History and Relations with the Muslim World,* no. VI. London: Variorum Reprints, 1971.

Waley, D.P. "Condotte and Condottieri in the Thirteenth Century." *Proceedings of the British Academy* 61 (1975), 337–71.

Watanabe, Kin-ichi. "Problèmes de la 'féodalité' byzantine: une mise au point sur les diverses discussions." *Hitotsubashi Journal of Arts and Sciences* 5 (1965), 32–40; 6 (1965), 8–24.

Weiss, Günter. *Joannes Kantakuzenos—Aristokrat, Staatsmann, Kaiser und Mönch—in der Gesellschaftsentwicklung von Byzanz im 14. Jahrhundert.* Wiesbaden: O. Harrassowitz, 1969.

Werner, E. *Die Geburt einer Grossmacht—Die Osmanen (1300–1481): Ein Beitrag zur Genesis des türkischen Feudalismus.* Weimar: H. Bohlaus Nachfolger, 1985.

Wifstrand, A. *Laonikos Chalkokondyles, der letzte Athener.* Lund, 1972.

Wittek, Paul. *Das Fürstentum Mentesche: Studien zur Geschichte Westkleinasiens im 13.–15. Jh..* Istanbul: Universum druckerei, 1934.

Woodhouse, C.M. *George Gemistos Plethon: The Last of the Hellenes.* Oxford: Clarendon Press, 1986.

Woodward, A. "The Byzantine Castle of Avret-Hissar." *Annual of the British School at Athens* 23 (1918–19), 98–103.

Xanalatos, Diogenes. *Beiträge zur Wirtschafts- und Sozialgeschichte Makedoniens im*

Mittelalter, hauptsächlich auf Grund der Briefe des Erzbischofs Theophylaktos von Achrida. Speyer, 1937.

Xyngopoulos, A. Ἔρευναι εἰς τὰ βυζαντινὰ μνημεῖα τῶν Σερρῶν [Researches on the Byzantine Monuments of Serres]. Thessaloniki, 1965.

Zachariadou, Elizabeth. «Cortazzi καὶ ὄχι Corsari» ["Cortazzi and Not Corsari"]. Θησαυρίσματα 15 (1978), 62–65.

———. "Les 'janissaires' de l'empereur byzantin." *Studia turcologica memoriae Alexii Bombaci dicata*, Istituto universitario orientale, seminario di studi asiatici, series minor 19 (Naples, 1982), 591–97; repr. in Zachariadou, *Romania and the Turks (c.1300–c.1500)*, no. XI. London: Variorum Reprints, 1985.

Zakythinos, Dionysios A. "Crise monétaire et crise économique à Byzance du XIIIe au XVe siècle." *L'hellénisme contemporain* 2 (Athens, 1948), 1–149; also published separately (Athens: L'hellénisme contemporain, 1948), and in Zakythinos, *Byzance: état—société—économie*, no. XI. London: Variorum Reprints, 1973.

———. *Le despotat grec de Morée*, 2 vols. Paris: Les Belles Lettres, 1932; Athens: L'hellénisme contemporain, 1953. Rev. ed. by Chryssa Maltezou. London: Variorum Reprints, 1975.

———. "Processus de féodalisation." *L'hellénisme contemporain* 2 (1948), 499–534; repr. in Zakythinos, *Byzance: état—société—économie*, no. XIII. London: Variorum Reprints, 1973.

Zdravković, I. *Srednjovekovni gradovi i dvorci na Kosovu* [Medieval Fortresses and Palaces in Kosovo]. Belgrade: Turistička Štampa, 1975.

Živojinović, Mirjana. *Svetogorske kelije i pirgovi u srednjem veku* [Kellia and Towers of Mount Athos in the Middle Ages], Posebna izdanja, Knjiga 13. Belgrade: Vizantološki institut SANU, 1972.

———. "Žitije arhiepiskopa Danila II kao izvor za ratovanja Katalanske Kompanije" ["The Hagiography of Archbishop Danilo II as a Source for the Warring of the Catalan Company"]. *ZRVI* 19 (1980), 251–73.

Zuckerman, Constantine. "The Dishonest Soldier Constantine Planites and His Neighbours." *Byz* 56 (1986), 314–31.

Index

University of Pennsylvania Press
MIDDLE AGES SERIES
Edward Peters, General Editor

F. R. P. Akehurst, trans. *The* Coutumes de Beauvaisis *of Philippe de Beaumanoir.* 1992

Peter Allen. *The Art of Love: Amatory Fiction from Ovid to the* Romance of the Rose. 1992

David Anderson. *Before the Knight's Tale: Imitation of Classical Epic in Boccaccio's* Teseida. 1988

Benjamin Arnold. *Count and Bishop in Medieval Germany: A Study of Regional Power, 1100–1350.* 1991

Mark C. Bartusis. *The Late Byzantine Army: Arms and Society, 1204–1453.* 1992

J. M. W. Bean. *From Lord to Patron: Lordship in Late Medieval England.* 1990

Uta-Renate Blumenthal. *The Investiture Controversy: Church and Monarchy from the Ninth to the Twelfth Century.* 1988

Daniel Bornstein, trans. *Dino Compagni's* Chronicle *of Florence.* 1986

Betsy Bowden. *Chaucer Aloud: The Varieties of Textual Interpretation.* 1987

James William Brodman. *Ransoming Captives in Crusader Spain: The Order of Merced on the Christian-Islamic Frontier.* 1986

Kevin Brownlee and Sylvia Huot. *Rethinking the* Romance of the Rose: *Text, Image, Reception.* 1992

Otto Brunner (Howard Kaminsky and James Van Horn Melton, eds. and trans.). Land *and Lordship: Structures of Governance in Medieval Austria.* 1992

Robert I. Burns, S.J., ed. *Emperor of Culture: Alfonso X the Learned of Castile and His Thirteenth-Century Renaissance.* 1990

David Burr. *Olivi and Franciscan Poverty: The Origins of the* Usus Pauper *Controversy.* 1989

Thomas Cable. *The English Alliterative Tradition.* 1991

Anthony K. Cassell and Victoria Kirkham, eds. and trans. *Diana's Hunt/Caccia di Diana: Boccaccio's First Fiction.* 1991

Brigitte Cazelles. *The Lady as Saint: A Collection of French Hagiographic Romances of the Thirteenth Century.* 1991

Anne L. Clark. *Elisabeth of Schönau: A Twelfth-Century Visionary.* 1992

Willene B. Clark and Meradith T. McMunn, eds. *Beasts and Birds of the Middle Ages: The Bestiary and Its Legacy.* 1989

Richard C. Dales. *The Scientific Achievement of the Middle Ages.* 1973

Charles T. Davis. *Dante's Italy and Other Essays.* 1984

Katherine Fischer Drew, trans. *The Burgundian Code.* 1972

Katherine Fischer Drew, trans. *The Laws of the Salian Franks.* 1991

Katherine Fischer Drew, trans. *The Lombard Laws.* 1973

Robert D. Fulk. *A History of Old English Meter.* 1992

Nancy Edwards. *The Archaeology of Early Medieval Ireland.* 1990

Margaret J. Ehrhart. *The Judgment of the Trojan Prince Paris in Medieval Literature.* 1987

Richard K. Emmerson and Ronald B. Herzman. *The Apocalyptic Imagination in Medieval Literature.* 1992

Felipe Fernández-Armesto. *Before Columbus: Exploration and Colonization from the Mediterranean to the Atlantic, 1229–1492.* 1987

Patrick J. Geary. *Aristocracy in Provence: The Rhône Basin at the Dawn of the Carolingian Age.* 1985

Peter Heath. *Allegory and Philosophy in Avicenna (Ibn Sînâ), with a Translation of the Book of the Prophet Muhammad's Ascent to Heaven.* 1992

J. N. Hillgarth, ed. *Christianity and Paganism, 350–750: The Conversion of Western Europe.* 1986

Richard C. Hoffmann. *Land, Liberties, and Lordship in a Late Medieval Countryside: Agrarian Structures and Change in the Duchy of Wrocław.* 1990

Robert Hollander. *Boccaccio's Last Fiction: Il Corbaccio.* 1988

Edward B. Irving, Jr. *Rereading* Beowulf. 1989

C. Stephen Jaeger. *The Origins of Courtliness: Civilizing Trends and the Formation of Courtly Ideals, 939–1210.* 1985

William Chester Jordan. *The French Monarchy and the Jews: From Philip Augustus to the Last Capetians.* 1989

William Chester Jordan. *From Servitude to Freedom: Manumission in the Sénonais in the Thirteenth Century.* 1986

Ellen E. Kittell. *From Ad Hoc to Routine: A Case Study in Medieval Bureaucracy.* 1991

Alan C. Kors and Edward Peters, eds. *Witchcraft in Europe, 1100–1700: A Documentary History.* 1972

Barbara M. Kreutz. *Before the Normans: Southern Italy in the Ninth and Tenth Centuries.* 1992

E. Ann Matter. *The Voice of My Beloved: The Song of Songs in Western Medieval Christianity.* 1990

María Rosa Menocal. *The Arabic Role in Medieval Literary History.* 1987

A. J. Minnis. *Medieval Theory of Authorship.* 1988

Lawrence Nees. *A Tainted Mantle: Hercules and the Classical Tradition at the Carolingian Court.* 1991

Lynn H. Nelson, trans. *The Chronicle of San Juan de la Peña: A Fourteenth-Century Official History of the Crown of Aragon.* 1991

Charlotte A. Newman. *The Anglo-Norman Nobility in the Reign of Henry I: The Second Generation.* 1988

Joseph F. O'Callaghan. *The Cortes of Castile-León, 1188–1350.* 1989

William D. Paden, ed. *The Voice of the Trobairitz: Perspectives on the Women Troubadours.* 1989

Edward Peters. *The Magician, the Witch, and the Law.* 1982

Edward Peters, ed. *Christian Society and the Crusades, 1198–1229: Sources in Translation, including* The Capture of Damietta *by Oliver of Paderborn.* 1971

Edward Peters, ed. *The First Crusade: The* Chronicle of Fulcher of Chartres *and Other Source Materials.* 1971

Edward Peters, ed. *Heresy and Authority in Medieval Europe.* 1980

James M. Powell. *Albertanus of Brescia: The Pursuit of Happiness in the Early Thirteenth Century.* 1992

James M. Powell. *Anatomy of a Crusade, 1213–1221.* 1986

Michael Resler, trans. Erec *by Hartmann von Aue.* 1987

Pierre Riché (Jo Ann McNamara, trans.). *Daily Life in the World of Charlemagne.* 1978

Jonathan Riley-Smith. *The First Crusade and the Idea of Crusading.* 1986

Joel T. Rosenthal. *Patriarchy and Families of Privilege in Fifteenth-Century England.* 1991

Steven D. Sargent, ed. and trans. *On the Threshold of Exact Science: Selected Writings of Anneliese Maier on Late Medieval Natural Philosophy.* 1982

Sarah Stanbury. *Seeing the* Gawain-Poet: *Description and the Act of Perception.* 1992

Thomas C. Stillinger. *The Song of Troilus: Lyric Authority in the Medieval Book.* 1992

Susan Mosher Stuard. *A State of Deference: Ragusa/Dubrovnik in the Medieval Centuries.* 1992

Susan Mosher Stuard, ed. *Women in Medieval History and Historiography.* 1987

Susan Mosher Stuard, ed. *Women in Medieval Society.* 1976

Jonathan Sumption. *The Hundred Years War: Trial by Battle.* 1992

Ronald E. Surtz. *The Guitar of God: Gender, Power, and Authority in the Visionary World of Mother Juana de la Cruz (1481–1534).* 1990

Patricia Terry, trans. *Poems of the Elder Edda.* 1990

Frank Tobin. *Meister Eckhart: Thought and Language.* 1986

Ralph V. Turner. *Men Raised from the Dust: Administrative Service and Upward Mobility in Angevin England.* 1988

Harry Turtledove, trans. *The* Chronicle *of Theophanes: An English Translation of* Anni Mundi *6095–6305 (A.D. 602–813).* 1982

Mary F. Wack. *Lovesickness in the Middle Ages: The* Viaticum *and Its Commentaries.* 1990

Benedicta Ward. *Miracles and the Medieval Mind: Theory, Record, and Event, 1000–1215.* 1982

Suzanne Fonay Wemple. *Women in Frankish Society: Marriage and the Cloister, 500–900.* 1981

This book has been set in Linotron Galliard. Galliard was designed for Mergenthaler in 1978 by Matthew Carter. Galliard retains many of the features of a sixteenth-century typeface cut by Robert Granjon but has some modifications that give it a more contemporary look.

Printed on acid-free paper.